The Wars of the Lord

The Wars of the Lord

*The Puritan Conquest of
America's First People*

MATTHEW J. TUININGA

OXFORD
UNIVERSITY PRESS

OXFORD
UNIVERSITY PRESS

Oxford University Press is a department of the University of Oxford.
It furthers the University's objective of excellence in research, scholarship,
and education by publishing worldwide. Oxford is a registered trade mark of
Oxford University Press in the UK and certain other countries.

Published in the United States of America by Oxford University Press
198 Madison Avenue, New York, NY 10016, United States of America.

© Oxford University Press 2025

CIP data is on file at the Library of Congress

ISBN 978–0–19–767176–4

DOI: 10.1093/oso/9780197671764.001.0001

Printed by Sheridan Books, Inc., United States of America

To Elizabeth,
the love of my life

Contents

PART III. WAR

Acknowledgments

When I began researching Puritan political theology, I thought I was going to write a journal article. I gradually became convinced that a much larger story needed to be told. I am grateful to George Marsden, James Bratt, Harry Stout, and others for encouraging me in this regard. My manuscript gradually evolved to the size and scope that my wife, Elizabeth, joked that I would have to write a trilogy. Thankfully, prospective publishers and agents persuaded me to reduce the story to a more manageable size, though, like any author, I can only lament the precious detail that was lost along the way. I am deeply grateful to Cynthia Read from Oxford University Press, who not only accepted my proposal on behalf of OUP but enthusiastically encouraged me, sure that I had an important story to tell.

Many people have assisted me along the way, beginning with several diligent research assistants at Calvin Theological Seminary. HyunKwan Kim and Ruan Bessa compiled secondary and primary sources for me. Charlie Wineman tracked down documents and spent countless painstaking hours poring over nearly illegible seventeenth-century handwriting to produce draft transcripts. Zachary Kime fulfilled numerous tasks and offered advice on the manuscript. Many librarians, archivists, and other library staff were generous with their assistance, especially Beth Steele of Hekman Library at Calvin University and Hannah Elder of the Massachusetts Historical Society. Much of this research was made possible by a generous grant from the Heritage Fund at Calvin Theological Seminary.

I am grateful to the excellent scholars who offered advice or provided feedback on chapter drafts, including David Silverman, John Turner, Daniel Mandell, Harry Stout, George Marsden, and Kristin Kobes Du Mez. John Turner and Jenny Pulsipher generously provided me with their own transcriptions of some difficult-to-read handwritten documents. Jason Van Horn from Calvin University spent many hours making the maps for this book and was enthusiastic in doing so. My Calvin Seminary colleagues Jul Medenblik and Yudha Thianto generously read the entire manuscript. Karin Maag and Lyle Bierma provided helpful feedback on individual chapters.

Others who read part or all of the manuscript include Peter Rockhold, Josef Disby, Kevin Zabihi, and the students in my Puritans and Colonialism seminars. I must thank several family members for reading some of the earliest—and worst—drafts: Calvin and Ellen Tuininga, Elyssa and Ehren Gaebler, and Eric Tuininga.

My editor, Theo Calderara, offered invaluable advice on many aspects of the book and made sure the manuscript read well. I am also grateful to Rachel Ruisard and other staff from Oxford University Press for making publication possible. I am thankful to Joshua Carter, executive director of the Pequot Museum, and his team for providing photos of their displays for publication in this book. I truly hope that this book honors their ancestors.

My wife and children have lived with this book for years. Joel, Katherine, and Sarah, ages nine to thirteen at the time, were profoundly inspired by their visit to the Pequot Museum, the highlight of many historic sites to which I dragged them. They listened as I read the narrative to them and let me know when the story didn't make sense. None of this would have been possible without the steadfast support of my wife and best friend, Elizabeth, who made it possible for me to spend countless hours researching and writing. She also read the earliest drafts and endured lengthy conversations about what the book might look like and how it could be better. Words cannot express how much I owe her. I dedicate this book to her.

Dramatis Personae

Ahawton, William. Massachusett praying Indian, minister at Punkapoag

Alexander. Also known as Wamsutta, Pokanoket sachem, high Wampanoag sachem, son of Ousamequin and brother of Philip, married to Weetamoo

Anthony. Natick praying Indian, missionary

Appleton, Samuel. Massachusetts military officer

Atherton, Humphrey. Massachusetts military officer, Indian superintendent, leader of the Atherton Company

Awashonks. Female Sakonnet sachem

Black James. Nipmuc praying Indian, constable of newer praying towns

Bradford, William. Separatist, early governor of Plymouth, United Colonies commissioner

Bradford, William, Jr. Plymouth military officer

Bradstreet, Simon. United Colonies commissioner for Massachusetts, Atherton Company shareholder

Brewster, Jonathan. Trader and agent from Plymouth, later Connecticut

Canonchet. Narragansett sachem, son of Miantonomo

Canonicus. Narragansett high sachem, uncle of Miantonomo and father of Mixanno

Cassacinamon, Robin. Pequot sachem

Chickataubut. Massachusett sachem

Church, Benjamin. Plymouth entrepreneur and military officer

Coddington, William. Exile from Massachusetts, later Rhode Island governor

Cojonoquant. Narragansett sachem, brother to Pessicus and father of Quinnapin

Corman. Narragansett counselor to Ninigret

Cotton, John. Prominent Puritan minister and theologian in England and later Boston

Cotton, John, Jr. Puritan minister and missionary to Wampanoags in Plymouth colony

Curtis, Ephraim. Massachusetts trader and agent

Cutshamekin. Massachusett sachem at Neponset, later praying Indian ruler at Natick

Danforth, Thomas. Massachusetts magistrate

Denison, Daniel. United Colonies commissioner for Massachusetts, Atherton Company shareholder, later general

Denison, George. Connecticut military officer

Dudley, Thomas. Governor and later deputy governor of Massachusetts

Easton, John. Quaker and deputy governor of Rhode Island

Eliot, John. Puritan minister at Roxbury, Massachusetts, and missionary to the Indians

Endecott, John. Governor of Massachusetts, later military officer, United Colonies commissioner

Fitch, James. Puritan minister at Norwich, Connecticut, missionary to Mohegans, son-in-law of John Mason

Gardener, Lion. Military commander at Fort Saybrook

Gookin, Daniel. Massachusetts magistrate, superintendent of praying Indians, military officer

Gorton, Samuel. Religious leader expelled from Plymouth, founder of Warwick, Rhode Island

Harris, William. Wealthy landholder and later Rhode Island magistrate

Henchman, Daniel. Massachusetts military officer

Hinckley, Thomas. Plymouth magistrate

Hoar, John. Supervisor of the Nashobah praying Indians at Concord, Massachusetts, father of Daniel Hoar

Hooker, Thomas. Prominent Puritan minister in England, Massachusetts, and later Connecticut

Hubbard, William. Puritan minister at Ipswich, Massachusetts, historian of King Philip's War

Hutchinson, Anne. Informal teacher in Boston, later exile to Rhode Island and New Netherland, mother of Edward Hutchinson

Hutchinson, Edward. Leader of Atherton Company, later Massachusetts agent, son of Anne Hutchinson

Jethro, Peter. Praying Indian teacher, son of Old Jethro

John, Sagamore. Pennacook sachem

John, Sagamore. Nipmuc sachem at praying town of Pakachoog

Kattenanit, Job. Nipmuc pastor at Magunkog, later spy and soldier for Massachusetts, brother of James Printer and Joseph Tuckawillipin

Leete, William. Deputy governor of Connecticut

Leverett, John. Governor of Massachusetts

Ludlow, Roger. Colonist in Massachusetts, Connecticut, and New Haven

Mason, John. Connecticut military officer, magistrate, patron to Uncas

Mather, Increase. Puritan minister in Boston, historian of King Philip's War, son-in-law of John Cotton

Mayhew, Thomas. Founder of colonies on Martha's Vineyard and Nantucket, lay missionary to island Wampanoags

Mayhew, Thomas, Jr. Minister on Martha's Vineyard and missionary to island Wampanoags

Miantonomo. Narragansett high sachem, nephew of Canonicus and father of Canonchet

Mixanno. Narragansett sachem, son of Canonicus and father of Scuttup, husband of Quaiapin

Monoco. Nipmuc leader from Nashaway

Mosely, Samuel. Massachusetts military officer

Muttaump. Nipmuc sachem at Quaboag

Newman, Noah. Minister at Rehoboth, Plymouth colony

Ninigret. Eastern Niantic sachem, later de facto Narragansett high sachem, nephew of Canonicus and cousin of Miantonomo and Pessicus

Numphow, Samuel. Pennacook praying Indian, teacher at Wamesit, son of Numphow

Oldham, John. Massachusetts trader

Oliver, James. Massachusetts magistrate and military officer

Ousamequin. Pokanoket sachem, high Wampanoag sachem, father of Alexander and Philip

Owaneco. Mohegan sachem, son of Uncas

Passaconaway. Pennacook sachem at Pawtucket, father of Wannalancet

Pessicus. High Narragansett sachem, nephew of Canonicus and brother of Miantonomo, cousin of Ninigret

Petavit, Joseph. Nipmuc praying Indian, teacher at Hassanamesit, brother of Sampson Petavit

Petavit, Sampson. Nipmuc praying Indian, teacher at Wabquisset, brother of Joseph Petavit

Philip. Also known as Metacom, Pokanoket sachem, Wampanoag high sachem, son of Ousamequin and brother of Alexander

Pomham. Shawomet sachem

Potuck. Narragansett counselor to Quaiapin

Prence, Thomas. Governor of Plymouth

Printer, James. Nipmuc praying Indian, assistant to John Eliot, minister at Waeuntug, brother of Job Kattenanit and Joseph Tuckawillipin

Pynchon, John. Wealthy trader, magistrate, and later military officer at Springfield, Massachusetts, son of William Pynchon

Quaiapin. Female Narragansett sachem, wife of Mixanno, and mother of Scuttup

Quanapohit, James. Nashaway praying Indian, spy and soldier for Massachusetts

Quinnapin. Narragansett sachem, cousin of Canonchet and later husband of Weetamoo

Rowlandson, Joseph. Puritan minister at Lancaster, Massachusetts

Rowlandson, Mary. Wife of Joseph Rowlandson

Russell, John. Puritan minister at Hadley, Massachusetts

Sassacus. High Pequot sachem

Sassamon, John. Praying Indian interpreter, missionary assistant to John Eliot, and later teacher to the Wampanoags, married to Philip's niece

Savage, Thomas. Massachusetts military officer, son-in-law of Anne Hutchinson

Scuttup. Narragansett sachem, son of Mixanno and Quaiapin

Shoshanim. Nipmuc sachem at Nashaway

Smith, Richard, Jr. Trader at Wickford, in Narragansett Country

Standish, Miles. Pilgrim leader, Plymouth military officer

Stanton, Thomas. Trader and interpreter at Fort Saybrook and later Connecticut

Stonewall John. Prominent Narragansett

Treat, Robert. Connecticut magistrate and military officer

Tuckawillipin, Joseph. Nipmuc praying Indian, teacher at Hassanamesit, brother of James Printer and Job Kattenanit

Turner, William. Baptist, Massachusetts military officer

Tuspaquin. Sachem at Nemasket, brother-in-law of Philip

Uncas. Mohegan sachem, brother-in-law of Sassacus

Underhill, John. Massachusetts military officer, later military officer for New Netherland

Vane, Henry, Jr. Governor of Massachusetts

Waban. Massachusett sachem at Nonantum, later praying Indian ruler at Natick

Waldron, Richard. Massachusetts trader and military officer

Walley, Thomas. Minister at Barnstable, Plymouth colony

Wampatuck, Josias. Massachusett sachem, nephew of Cutshamekin

Wamsutta. See Alexander

Wannalancet. Pennacook sachem at Pawtucket, son of Passaconaway

Weetamoo. Female Pocasset sachem, daughter of Corbitant, wife of Alexander, and sister-in-law of Philip, later wife of Quinnapin

Wequash. Pequot scout for the English

Willard, Simon. Massachusetts trader, magistrate, and military officer

Williams, Roger. Puritan then separatist minister, exile from Massachusetts, founder of Providence and of Rhode Island, trader, magistrate

Wilson, John. Puritan minister in Boston

Winslow, Edward. Pilgrim, governor of Plymouth, United Colonies commissioner, Massachusetts agent to England, father of Josiah Winslow

Winslow, Josiah. United Colonies commissioner for Plymouth, magistrate, governor, later general, son of Edward Winslow

Winthrop, John. Puritan lay leader in England, governor of Massachusetts, United Colonies commissioner

Winthrop, John, Jr. Explorer and entrepreneur, governor of Saybrook colony, founder of Nameag, later governor of Connecticut, United Colonies commissioner

Winthrop, Wait. Connecticut military officer, son of John Winthrop Jr.

Wuttasacomponom, Captain Tom. Nipmuc praying Indian, ruler of the newer praying towns

Wyandanch. Montauk sachem

Indian Communities

Wampanoags	Massachusetts	Pennacooks	Narragansetts	Nipmucs	Pequots	Mohegans	Connecticut valley Indians	Long Island Indians	Outside Lower New England
Cohannet	Natick	Nashobah	Aquidneck Island	Chabanakongkomun	Caussatuck	Shantok	Agawam	Montauks	Abenakis
Manomet	Neponset	Naumkeag	Cowesett	Hassanamesit	Mashantucket		Norwottucks	Shinnecocks	Caughnawaga
Mashpee	Nonantum	Pawtucket Falls	Eastern Niantics	Maanexit	Mystic		Peskeompscut Falls		Mi'kmaqs
Mattapoisett	Punkapoag	Wamesit	Manisses	Magunkog	Nameag		Pocumtuck		Mohawks
Monomoy Island	Wessagusset		Pawtuxet	Manchage	Noank		Podunks		Paquayag
Mount Hope			Pettaquamscut	Mount Wachusett	Weinshauks		Pyquag		Quinnipiac
Nantucket			Shawomet	Menameset	Western Niantics		Sokokis		Sasquas
Nausets			Niantic	Nashaway			Squakeag		Munnacommock Swamp
Nemasket				Okommakamesit			Wangunks		Wabanakis
Noepe (Martha's Vineyard)				Pakachoog					
Patuxets				Quaboag					
Pocassets				Quantisset					
Pokanokets				Quinebaug Valley					
Sakonnets				Quinsigamond Lake					
Sowams				Tantiusque					
Titicut				Wabquisset					
Wepoiset				Waeuntug					

English Towns

Plymouth	Massachusetts	Connecticut	Rhode Island
Barnstable	Andover	Hartford	Providence
Bridgewater	Billerica	Farmington	Newport
Dartmouth	Boston	New Haven*	Portsmouth
Middleborough	Braintree	New London	Warwick
Plymouth	Brookfield	Norwich	Westerly
Rehoboth	Cambridge	Saybrook*	
Sandwich	Chelmsford	Stonington	
Scituate	Concord	Wethersfield	
Swansea	Dedham	Wickford*	
Taunton	Deerfield	Windsor	
	Dorchester		
	Dover		
	Groton		
	Hadley		
	Hatfield		
	Hingham		
	Lancaster		
	Lynn		
	Marlborough		
	Medfield		
	Medford		
	Mendon		
	Northampton		
	Quinsigamond		
	Roxbury		
	Salem		
	Springfield		
	Squakeag		
	Sudbury		
	Watertown		
	Westfield		
	Weymouth		
	Woburn		

Note on Terms

I have used the term "Puritan" broadly in this book. While many colonists who came to New England during 1620–1676 were not Puritans, their leaders were, and Puritanism shaped their collective identity and ethos. New England gradually diversified, especially after 1660, but even during King Philip's War, in 1675–1676, a Puritan theological outlook shaped the rhetoric, policy, and public discourse of magistrates, ministers, and lay leaders. Indeed, it is difficult to find writings from the time that are not saturated with a religious perspective that can broadly be described as Puritan, even from those who were not themselves devout Puritans. Collectively, the colonies of Plymouth, Massachusetts, and Connecticut are appropriately described as Puritan.

To assist readers and avoid distractions, I have taken the liberty of updating spelling, punctuation, and capitalization to modern standards when quoting primary sources. Readers should also note that nearly all quotations of Indian sources come from the writings of colonists. Sometimes those colonists edited the precise words Indians used to reflect seventeenth-century English-speaking conventions.

Abbreviations

ACUC	*Acts of the Commissioners of the United Colonies of New England,* vols. 9 and 10 in *Records of the Colony of New Plymouth in New England,* ed. David Pulsifer (Boston, MA: William White, 1861; reprinted New York: AMS Press, 1968)
CA-War-I	Connecticut Archives, War, vol. 1, Hartford, CT
CHSC	*Connecticut Historical Society Collections*
CJCJ	*The Correspondence of John Cotton Junior,* vol. 79, *Publications of the Colonial Society of Massachusetts,* ed. John W. Tyler (Boston: The Colonial Society of Massachusetts)
CR	*The Public Records of the Colony of Connecticut,* ed. J. Hammond Trumbull (Hartford, CT: F. A. Brown, 1850–1890)
CRW	*Correspondence of Roger Williams,* 2 vols., ed. Glenn W. LaFantasie (Hanover, NH: Brown University Press, 1988)
CWRW	*The Complete Writings of Roger Williams,* 7 vols. (Eugene, OR: Wipf & Stock, 2007)
EAL	*Early American Literature*
ERTD	*The Early Records of the Town of Dedham, Massachusetts, 1659–1673,* vol. 4, ed. Don Gleason Hill (Dedham, MA, 1894)
ET	*The Eliot Tracts: With Letters from John Eliot to Thomas Thorowgood and Richard Baxter,* ed. Michael P. Clark (Westport, CT: Praeger, 2003)
MA	Massachusetts Archives, Boston, MA
MHS	Massachusetts Historical Society. Boston, MA
MHSC	*Collections of the Massachusetts Historical Society*
MHSP	*Massachusetts Historical Society Proceedings*
MR	*Records of the Governor and Company of the Massachusetts Bay in New England,* ed. Nathaniel B. Shurtleff (New York: AMS Press, 1968)
NEHGR	*New England Historical and Genealogical Register*
NEQ	*New England Quarterly*
NNRC	Native Northeast Research Collaborative, https://nativenortheastportal.com/.
NYCD	*Documents Relating to the Colonial History of the State of New-York,* ed. O'Callaghan, E. B. (Edmund Bailey), 1797–1880, Fernow, Berthold, 1837–1908, contrib. by Brodhead, John Romeyn, 1814–1873, 15 vols. (Albany: Weed, Parsons, and Co., 1853–1887)
OPP	*Of Plymouth Plantation, 1620–1647,* ed. Samuel Eliot Morison (New York: Knopf, 1952)

PP   *Pynchon Papers,* vols. 60 and 61, in *Publications of the Colonial Society of*
              Massachusetts, ed. with an Introduction by Carl Bridenbaugh, collected
              by Juliette Tomlinson (Boston: The Colonial Society of Massachusetts,
              1982)

PR   *Plymouth Records* in *Records of the Colony of New Plymouth in New*
              England, ed. David Pulsifer (Boston: William White, 1861; reprinted
              New York: AMS Press, 1968)

RCAMB   *Records of the Court of Assistants of the Colony of the Massachusetts Bay,*
              1630–1692, ed. John Noble, 1829–1909, John F. Cronin, 1872– (Boston,
              MA: The County of Suffolk, 1901)

RICR   *Rhode Island Colonial Records Bay, 1630–1692,* in *Records of the Colony*
              of Rhode Island and Providence Plantations in New England, vols. 1 and
              2, ed. John Russell Bartlett (Providence, 1857)

RIHSC   *Rhode Island Historical Society Collections*

WJ   *Winthrop's Journal* ed. James Kendall Hosmer, (New York: Charles
              Scribner's Sons, 1908)

WMQ   *William and Mary Quarterly*

WFP-II, MHS   Winslow Family Papers II, Ms. N-268, Massachusetts Historical Society,
              Boston, MA

WFP, MHS   Winthrop Family Papers, Massachusetts Historical Society, Boston, MA

WP, MHS   Unpublished Winthrop Papers, Massachusetts Historical Society,
              Boston, MA

WP   *Winthrop Papers,* 6 vols. (Boston: Massachusetts Historical Society,
              1929–1992)

YIP   Yale Indian Papers, Yale University, New Haven, CT

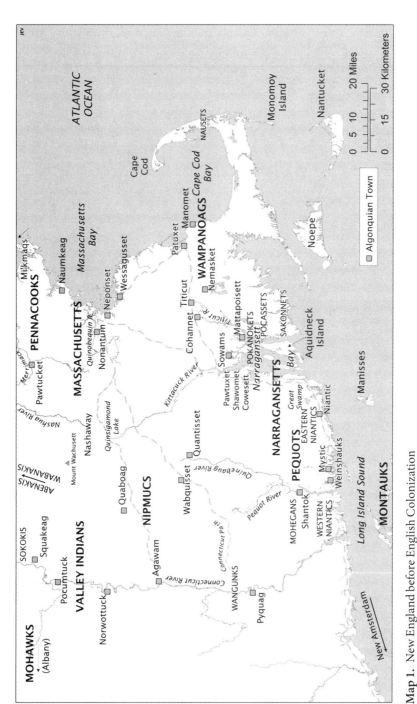

Map 1. New England before English Colonization

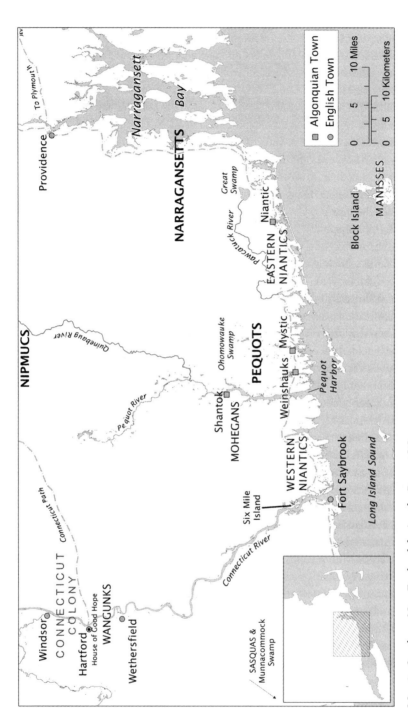

Map 2. Southern New England during the Pequot War

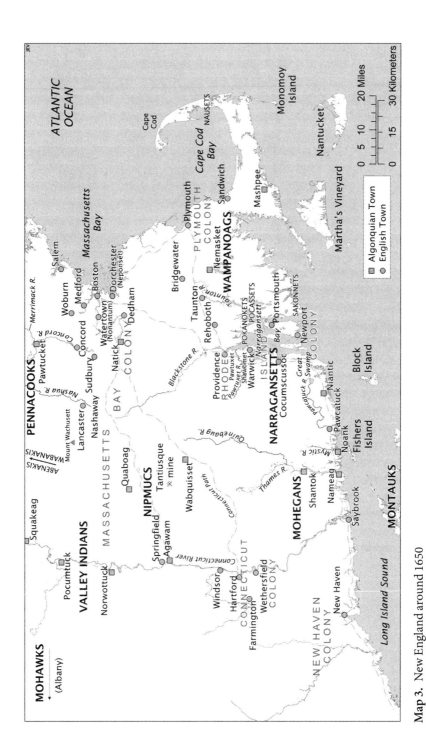

Map 3. New England around 1650

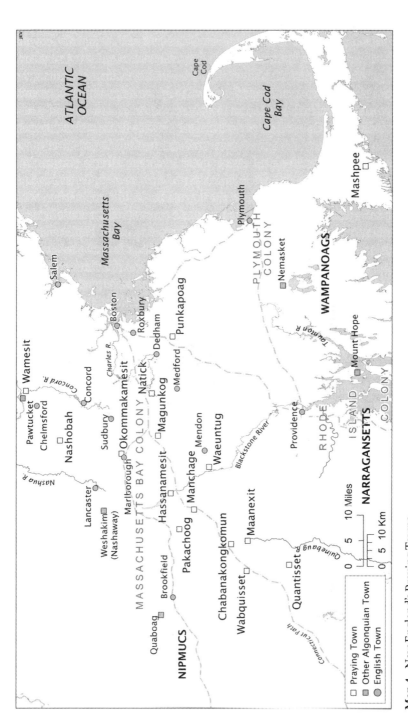

Map 4. New England's Praying Towns

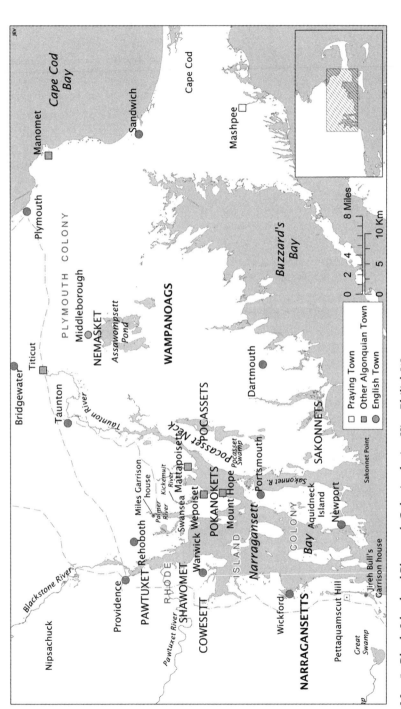

Map 5. Rhode Island and Plymouth Colonies during King Philip's War

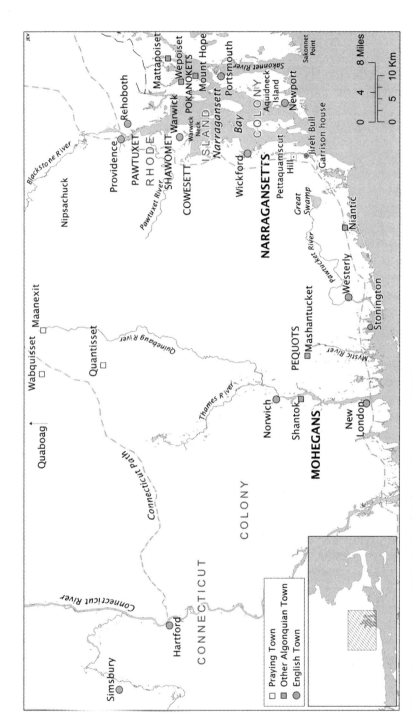

Map 6. Connecticut and Rhode Island Colonies during King Philip's War

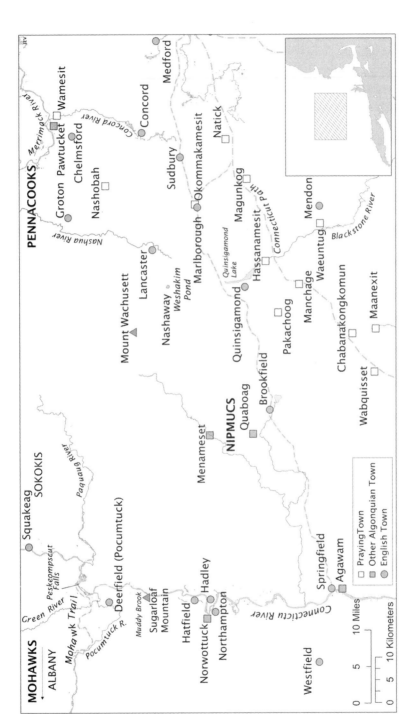

Map 7. Western Massachusetts during King Philip's War

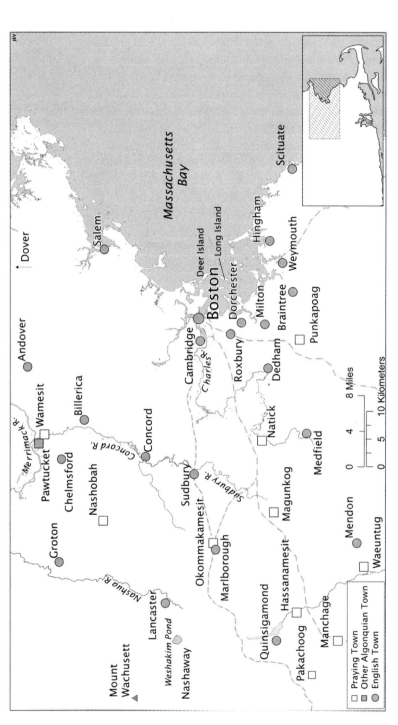

Map 8. Eastern Massachusetts during King Philip's War

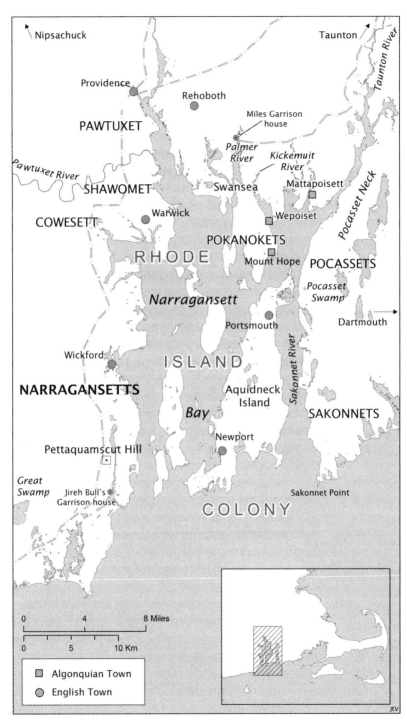

Map 9. Narragansett Bay Area during King Philip's War

Introduction: The First Encounter

1620

ON A COLD November day in 1620, sixteen heavily armored Englishmen stepped out of a rowboat and onto the beach of Cape Cod. Their ship, the *Mayflower*, lay at anchor just offshore. Wearing breastplates and helmets and carrying muskets, the men were prepared for a confrontation. But for four days they did not see a single human being.[1]

Finally, on November 15, they spotted some: five or six Natives walking with a dog. As soon as the Natives noticed the intruders, they took off into the woods. The Englishmen pursued, eager to make contact, but they could not catch up. The next day, they discovered some graves and an underground stockpile of corn. A few dug up the corn while the rest stood guard. After "much consultation," they decided to take as much corn as they could carry, planning to pay the Natives later. They were desperate for food and needed seed for spring planting. Was this not God's provision?[2]

A couple of weeks later, the English were back for more. They raided one of the Natives' stockpiles, taking more corn, two or three baskets of wheat, and a bag of beans.

The next day they went even further. The men happened upon a large grave and decided to dig it up. Inside were bowls, trays, dishes, bracelets, weapons, and other tools, typical of the Algonquian practice of burying valued possessions with the remains of prominent men. Opening a large bundle, they discovered a corpse whose "skull had fine yellow hair still on it" and a smaller bundle with "the bones and head of a little child." They stole some of the "prettiest things" and reburied the bodies.[3]

The Natives from whom they stole lived nearby in *wetus*, or *wigwams*, which the English soon located. They were "made with long young sapling trees bended, and both ends stuck into the ground," and covered with thick mats. Each had a door about three feet high and a large hole at the ceiling for smoke ventilation, with removable coverings. Pots hung over fireplaces, and along the walls were beds made of mats and furs. Finding the dwellings empty, the Englishmen stole what they considered valuable. They had intended to bring "some beads and other things" and leave them behind as a "sign of peace" and an invitation to trade, but did not have the time. Again they told themselves they would make amends later.[4]

The people who owned these homes were Nausets, part of a larger group later known as the Wampanoags, who like all New England Natives belonged to a language group called the Algonquians. But they would simply refer to themselves as "the people." The armored strangers plundering their possessions were not the first Europeans they had met; traders and explorers had been coming for two decades now, and many of them proved more than willing to steal, kill, and kidnap. Now these men were ransacking the graves of their dead, looting their homes, and plundering their precious food supply.[5]

At first the Nausets kept their distance. But soon they struck back. One night, a group of Englishmen lay sleeping on the beach behind a six-foot barricade of logs and pine boughs. Among them were William Bradford, his friend Edward Winslow, and their short military officer Miles Standish. Suddenly the sleeping men were jolted awake by a "hideous and great cry," followed by an alarm from the guard. They took up positions and fired their muskets into the darkness. Then all fell silent. Believing that they must have heard a wolf or fox, they returned to sleep.

The next morning they heard the cry again. Arrows began flying. Captain Standish and a few others had their muskets nearby, but others had moved their weapons closer to the water's edge. As they raced across the sand to retrieve them, they were terrified by the Nauset war cry, *Woach, woach, ha ha hach woach!* Standish fired his flintlock. Another man fired as well. Standish ordered them to take their time and aim carefully. They did not know what they were up against and needed to make every shot count.

Some of the men had taken refuge in their shallop, a small boat anchored just off shore, and needed to light the wicks of their matchlocks. A man grabbed a burning log and dashed bravely to their relief. A Nauset hiding behind a tree unleashed arrow after arrow, but each time the English were able to dodge the projectiles. Arrows from thirty or forty Nausets "came close by them and on every side," but the English kept the warriors at bay. Three times they fired in return, and three times they missed before a musket ball slammed into the tree, sending bark and splinters flying. The stunned warrior fled into the woods, followed by his companions. Standish's band pursued them for a quarter of a mile, but the Nausets escaped.

The Nausets were defending their home from pillaging Englishmen. But the English saw it differently. To Bradford the attack was proof that the Nausets were the enemies of God's people. Thankfully, in his view, God had fought for his people, and no English were harmed. As he later explained, "It pleased God to vanquish their enemies and give them deliverance, and by his special providence so to dispose that not any one of them were either hurt or hit."

The English named the clash "The First Encounter."[6]

THIS "FIRST ENCOUNTER" offered a glimpse of the tragedy to come. Over the next few decades, tens of thousands of devout English colonists known as Puritans came to America. They believed that bringing Christ's kingdom to the Natives would liberate them from darkness. But their understanding of Christianity also spurred them to dominate the Natives. A conquest they believed would be spiritual, peaceable, and benevolent devolved into a conquest that was virtually genocidal.

This book tells the story of how this happened. As much as possible, it does so from the perspective of those who lived it, both English and Indians. It shows the central role that Christianity played in the conquest of America's first people, and thus in the birth of America as we know it. Its central theme is that Puritan Christianity, including the impulse to establish the kingdom of God and evangelize Native Americans, shaped this conquest from beginning to end. It is not only that the people who did these things happened to be Christians. It is that Christianity was the framework they used to guide, interpret, and defend everything they did. They made sincere efforts to treat Indians according to Christian principles as they understood them, and their sustained missionary efforts, unparalleled among English colonies, demonstrate how serious some of them were about saving Native souls. Yet they appealed to Christianity just as confidently when they subjugated, enslaved, or killed Native people.

Christianity gave Puritans the conviction that they had far more to offer Indians than what Indians could give them in return, imbuing the Puritans with a sense of moral and cultural superiority that led them to dominate the Natives. How the Natives responded to Christianity, in turn, shaped the way they experienced colonization, whether they resisted it, accepted it, or something in between.

Puritans believed they were engaged in a war against the Devil for the soul of humanity. Their task was to advance, preserve, and defend Christ's kingdom, which required evangelizing non-Christian people. Massachusetts missionary superintendent Daniel Gookin referred to such efforts as a "War of the Lord" in which Christ was liberating souls from Satan's bondage. But that was only half the battle. Puritans believed God had chosen England to advance true Christianity in a hostile world. And so it was not enough to convert the Natives to Christianity; they had to be converted to Englishness. When Indians resisted such efforts, the Puritans believed, they were resisting Christ's kingdom. And when their resistance took the form of violence, it had to be crushed. Thus Boston minister Increase Mather referred to King Philip's War as a "War of the Lord" in which God was leading his people in triumph over their enemies.

The spiritual and military "wars of the Lord" were therefore inseparable. In both, Puritans identified victory with the cause of Christ's kingdom, and in both, they sought a conquest of America's first people. In the process, many Natives experienced the Puritan dream of liberation as a nightmare of domination.

IT IS ALL TOO easy to turn the story of colonialism into a simple morality tale. Earlier generations often thought of colonists as honest folk who fled tyranny in the old world to establish religious liberty and democracy in the new. They concluded that conflict with Native Americans was tragic yet inevitable, and ultimately essential for progress. America, in this myth, is and always has been the land of the Dream. More recently it has become common to go to the opposite extreme, offering a narrative in which greedy and racist Europeans intentionally used Christianity as a tool to justify the enslavement and genocide of innocent Native Americans. The American Dream, in this version, has always been a nightmare, especially for persons of color.

The reality is more complicated and disturbing. The Puritans did not separate the spiritual and the secular. When they thought about colonialism, land, trade, or war, they thought in religious terms. They believed their society had a covenant with God like that of Old Testament Israel. As long as they kept that covenant, God would bless them, but when they broke it, he would punish them. Their theology was not mere window dressing; it was the source of their most basic convictions. Christianity accounts for much of what was laudable and what was lamentable about the Puritans.

We often assume the Puritans came to America with racist attitudes toward Native Americans. But racism as we know it emerged over the course of the colonial period. Puritans were certainly prejudiced, but initially their prejudice was religious and cultural, not racial. They did not think in terms of white and red. They thought in terms of Christian and heathen, English and Indian.[7] They had complex motives, but they genuinely believed they had more to offer Native Americans than they took from them. Their ministers preached the need to treat Indians as human beings made in God's image, with love and justice. They imagined a future in which Indians and English lived side by side as civilized Christians. Their political leaders recognized that Christians had no right to steal Native territory and insisted that they occupy only land that was vacant or had been properly purchased. They denounced aggressive war and passed laws recognizing Indian rights to land, material resources, and equal treatment under the law. When colonists exploited Natives, missionaries often advocated on the Indians' behalf.

To a certain extent, the Puritans were successful. Initially, the colony expanded in a way that, for all its frustrations, most Algonquians found it possible to live with. Between 1620 and 1675, there were only two years of war. Time and again, crises were defused because Puritan or Algonquian leaders pursued diplomacy. Puritan Christianity had a lot to do with that.

At the same time, Puritan leaders could be unscrupulous, aggressively expansionist, and ruthlessly brutal. Christianity had a lot to do with that too. It was not that the Puritans were hypocrites who did not believe what they preached. By and large they did. Nor was it simply that they were flawed human beings, inclined to pursue their own interests. They were that, and thanks to their theology, they were the first to admit this. They did not hesitate to condemn covetousness or prejudice when they saw it, and there was more than enough to go around.

The problem was that some of their ideals, including the way they understood Christian theology, fostered prejudice, arrogance, greed, violence, and domination. Missionary efforts devolved into military conquest because Puritans conflated the spiritual and the political. Believing their society to be the embodiment of Christianity, they interpreted cultural differences as religious differences. They assumed that if Indians were to become Christian, they first had to be "civilized," which required living like the English and submitting to English government. They equated the advance of English law, justice, and political dominion with Christian progress, even when it happened violently. And that led them to justify behavior that was self-serving, manipulative, unscrupulous, and harmful. When Indians resisted, Puritan soldiers fought back, certain that they were defending the kingdom of God and that military service was as much God's work as missionary service. They justified Indian suffering on the grounds that Indians would be saved through the process.[8]

Such conflict proved the forge out of which the ideology of racism emerged. Prejudice rooted in a sense of Christian superiority evolved into white supremacy. Some leading Puritans resisted this shift, but with limited success.

Some Puritans recognized the contradiction between the gospel they professed and the imperious ways colonists often acted. They denounced the most egregious abuses and advocated for peace. But when war did break out, they remained loyal to their countrymen. It would have been surprising had they done anything else, for they believed everyone's ultimate interests depended on the flourishing of English society. A surprising number of Indians came to share that vision. New England was not simply a battlefield with Indians on one side and English on the other. If it had been, the Algonquians might have driven the English out long before they solidified their position in America.

But Native Americans did not view themselves as one people. They had kinship and linguistic and sometimes political ties, but each community had its own identity—Nausets, Pokanokets, Narragansetts, Pequots. Uniting against the English would have required setting aside their own conflicting interests. For a long time, most Algonquians viewed the English as one power among many that could be managed and manipulated. And the English had much they desired: high-quality tools, clothing, guns and ammunition, alcohol, and, yes, spiritual power and the promise of salvation. Natives welcomed them as trading partners and as potential allies against rival tribes. Many worked for the English, wore English clothes, and adopted English customs, although in other respects they maintained Algonquian ways. A substantial number accepted Christianity. Natives became preachers, teachers, and effective missionaries. Many decided their future lay with the English, even when the English did not treat them as equals. They had a stake in Puritan society they were willing to defend with their lives. Some even came to see the struggle for New England's future as a war of the Lord.

Others became convinced of the need to resist. They discerned that the colonial hunger for land was insatiable. They resented efforts to usurp their sovereignty. They despised Christianity because it demanded the rejection of traditional ways and submission to colonial authority. As colonists occupied nearly all the best land, subjected Natives to their government, and sought to erase Native culture, these Indians resisted with every tool at their disposal. Some advocated attacks against the English, but they were never able to persuade all their fellow Algonquians to support them. There were always plenty of Indians, not all Christian, who worked hard to maintain peace with the English or actively supported them, believing it in the best interests of their people.

ULTIMATELY, IT IS less important to judge the dead than to discern why they did what they did. Our noblest dreams and grandest projects are often inextricably intertwined with our darkest atrocities. Puritan New England was arguably the most democratic, educated, religious, and idealistic society in the seventeenth-century world. Yet it was also where Puritans dominated, conquered, and enslaved Native peoples in some of the most brutal episodes in American history, forging patterns of oppression that endure to this day. The story of that paradox is the story of this book.

PART I

SETTLEMENT

1

The Pilgrims

1620 to 1623

THE COLONISTS WHO met the Nausets in the First Encounter are known to history as the Pilgrims, but their contemporaries called them separatists because they had separated from the Church of England. They shared many convictions with a much larger group that remained in the Church of England and were derided as "puritans" because they sought to purify it of practices they considered superstitious and unbiblical. But the separatists thought the Church of England was beyond saving, so they left it.

All English Protestants viewed the Roman Catholic Church as a false church and its leader, the pope, as the Antichrist prophesied in scripture. They also believed that God stood in a covenant relationship with Christian nations much like the one he had established with his chosen people, Israel, long ago. The covenant stipulated that when they served God faithfully, he would bless them, but when they strayed from his will, he would punish them. When the Protestant Queen Elizabeth led England to victory over the powerful Catholic Spanish Armada in 1588, therefore, many interpreted it as a sign that God not only looked with favor on England but had great purposes for it.

The Spanish had been colonizing North and South America for decades. Their priests spread the Roman Catholic religion, while their soldiers and colonists treated Natives brutally, sending thousands to their deaths. Surely, Protestants reasoned, it was God's will for England to bring true Christianity to America. The English would treat the Natives justly, the Natives would welcome them gratefully, and the kingdom of Christ would be established in regions long ruled by the Devil, securing salvation for people who desperately needed it.

The Puritan movement emerged because many Protestants believed the Church of England needed to become more like Reformed churches in Europe that followed the teachings of John Calvin. Reformed churches preached, worshiped, and governed themselves strictly in accord with scripture, Puritans believed, untrammeled by superstitious human traditions or the tyranny of bishops. The Church of England, by contrast, maintained many ancient traditions derived from the Roman Catholic Church. It failed to teach the people adequately, leaving them ignorant and their faith impoverished. Many were Christians in name only, having never experienced the transforming power of God's grace.

Puritans found ways to advance their cause, preaching, teaching, and meeting in voluntary associations. But the situation deteriorated when James I became king in 1603. "I shall make [the Puritans] conform themselves," he declared, "or I will harry them out of the land." His policies, though poorly enforced, drove some Puritans to become separatists. Separatists formed illegal congregations, modeling them as closely as possible on the teachings of the Bible as they understood them. Viewed as extremists, they were harassed, fined, imprisoned, and occasionally executed.[1]

ONE OF THESE SEPARATISTS was William Bradford, who later found himself under fire from the Nausets on Cape Cod beach. A native of Yorkshire, by the time he was twelve Bradford had lost his parents, a sister, and the grandfather who raised him. Then he came down with a severe illness that left him incapable of physical labor. As a teenager, he poured his energy into studying the Bible. Troubled by the practices of his local church, he joined a congregation of separatists in Scrooby, Nottinghamshire.[2]

He later recalled that after James came to the throne separatists "were hunted and persecuted on every side, so as their former afflictions were as flea-bitings in comparison with these that now came upon them." Some were "taken and clapped up in prison, others had their houses beset and watched night and day and hardly escaped their hands." Many were forced to flee their homes and lost their livelihoods. In 1608 the Scrooby congregation fled to the Netherlands, which had just won a tenuous independence from Spain and which offered a greater degree of religious freedom. They eventually found their way to the city of Leiden.[3]

Bradford purchased a home, secured citizenship, married, and became a father. But other separatists struggled, working long hours for low wages in the cloth industry. Parents bemoaned their inability to provide their children with a quality English education. And they feared their children would be seduced by the country's "manifold temptations." To make matters worse, the Twelve Years' Truce between the Netherlands and Spain would expire in 1621; war seemed imminent, and the Spanish were notorious for their brutality.

John Robinson, the congregation's pastor, and William Brewster, its elder, proposed a novel solution. In 1607, English colonists had established a plantation at Jamestown in Virginia. Why should they not do the same? America was "fruitful and fit for habitation," they argued, "being devoid of all civil inhabitants." The only natives were "savage and brutish men which range up and down, little otherwise than the wild beasts."

The idea was not immediately embraced by the congregation. Colonization was expensive and involved "unconceivable perils and dangers." They would be "liable to famine and nakedness and the want . . . of all things. The change of air, diet and drinking of water would infect their bodies with sore sickness and grievous diseases." At Jamestown 70 of 108 settlers had died in the first year and 440 of 500 the following winter. Even if they survived, they would be in "continual danger of the savage people, who are cruel, barbarous, and most treacherous." They had heard tales of Natives flaying living captives and dismembering them, broiling their flesh and eating it before their eyes.

Others countered that while the risks were great, God would bless them because they had the noblest of purposes, including "laying some good foundation . . . for the propagating and advancing [of] the gospel of the kingdom of Christ in those remote parts of the world." Even if they lost their lives, it would be for an honorable cause.

After much prayer and fasting, the congregation reached the consensus that God was calling them to America. They petitioned King James, who had laid claim to the region by right of discovery, for permission to establish a colony where freedom of conscience would prevail and colonists would work for "the advancement of his Majesty's dominions and the enlargement of the gospel." The king was pleased, especially by their plan to secure profit by fishing. "So God have my soul, 'tis an honest trade, 'twas the apostles' own calling," he said.[4]

They obtained a patent from the Virginia Company and investments from "adventurers" sympathetic to separatism and willing to accompany them. For military leadership they hired Miles Standish, a thirty-six-year-old veteran of the Dutch War for Independence. Including servants and about fifty members of the congregation, there would be 102 passengers, plus the crew, when the *Mayflower* set sail in 1620.

Their beloved pastor, John Robinson, remained behind in hopes of following later. Many tears were shed when they bade farewell. Bradford and his wife, Dorothy, were especially sorrowful, having decided to leave their three-year-old son until they were established in America. All knew how much they were giving up, but as Bradford famously wrote, "they knew they were pilgrims, and looked not much on those things, but lift up their eyes to the heavens, their dearest country, and quieted their spirits."[5]

It was as the Pilgrims that they would be known to history.

They intended to settle near the Hudson River, but winds and currents forced them to Cape Cod, north of the bounds of their patent. Before heading ashore, forty-one leading men signed a covenant, since known as the Mayflower Compact. In it, they established a "civil body politic" to which they promised "due submission and obedience" and reaffirmed their several purposes: "the glory of God and advancement of the Christian faith and honor of our king and country."[6]

☙❧

THE ENGLISH VIEW OF Native Americans as "savage and brutish" predisposed them to fear Indians, raising the likelihood of conflict. But it bore no resemblance to reality. For all its foreignness to Europeans, Algonquian culture was civil, humane, and orderly. If the Nausets proved hostile when the Pilgrims arrived on Cape Cod, it was not because they were barbarians. It was because decades of experience taught them to view Europeans as barbarians.

Algonquians had been interacting with Europeans for nearly a century. In 1524, the explorer Giovanni da Verrazzano, working for France, arrived at Narragansett Bay in what is now Rhode Island. "This is the finest looking tribe, the handsomest in their costumes that we have found in our voyage," he wrote. "They exceed us in size, and they are of a very fair complexion; some of them incline more to a white, and others to a tawny color. Their faces are sharp, and their hair long and black, upon the adorning of which they bestow great pains. Their eyes are black and sharp, their expression mild and pleasant." Europeans did not yet think of themselves as "white" or Indians as "red."[7] Over the following decades, coastal Algonquians had many encounters with European explorers, fishermen, and traders. Information about the foreigners was passed along trade routes from village to village.

Each community was led by a sachem, typically a man but sometimes a woman, who was advised by counselors. Sachems were responsible for their people's material welfare and protection and the administration of justice. They had authority over the possession and use of land. They cared for widows, orphans, and the needy when their families could not, hosted guests and travelers, and conducted trade, diplomacy, and war. In return, their people paid them tribute. Lesser sachems, sometimes called sagamores, submitted and paid tribute to a greater sachem who ruled over a larger group or confederation. But groups were often in flux, for lesser sachems were known to shift their loyalties amid competition over land, trade, and influence.[8]

With a population of about forty thousand, the Narragansetts were New England's most powerful confederation. They inhabited the islands of Narragansett Bay and land to the west, which Verazzano claimed was "so fertile that any kind of seed would produce excellent crops." Led by a sachem named Canonicus, they included groups like the Eastern Niantics and Shawomets and received tribute from many others.[9]

The Wampanoags inhabited the region from Narragansett Bay to Cape Cod, including the islands of Nantucket and Noepe (which the English called Martha's Vineyard). Their population was at least twenty thousand, and many followed a sachem named Ousamequin, often known as Massasoit, whose people, the Pokanokets, lived on the northeast side of Narragansett Bay. Groups with at least some allegiance to Ousamequin included the Nausets, Pocassets, Sakonnets, Nemaskets, and Patuxets.

By the 1600s, Wampanoag encounters with Europeans had become an annual occurrence. Many ended violently. In 1602, an English trader clashed with Wampanoags on Noepe. A few years later, French traders battled them on Cape Cod and nearby Monomoy Island. By 1608, an Englishman named Captain Edward Harlow had kidnapped several Wampanoags, displaying a young man named Epenow before the fascinated English public. But Epenow persuaded Englishmen to take him to Noepe by regaling them with tales of gold. When the ship neared shore, he jumped overboard and escaped. His would be a leading voice urging resistance to the English.

In 1612, French traders clashed with Massachusett Indians living around Massachusetts Bay, whose population totaled more than twenty thousand. A French captive learned Algonquian and attempted to evangelize them, and when they mocked him, he warned that God might destroy them. A skeptical sachem gathered his people and asked if "his God had so many people and [was] able to kill all those." God "surely would," the Frenchman replied, and would "bring in strangers to possess their land." His prophecy would haunt Natives in years to come.[10]

Two years later, the Englishman Thomas Hunt kidnapped twenty-four Algonquians, carried them across the Atlantic, and sold them into slavery. One was a Wampanoag named Tisquantum, or Squanto, from Patuxet on Cape Cod Bay. Eventually freed by friars in Spain, he found his way to England, where in 1619 he joined an expedition led by Captain Thomas Dermer and headed for home. At the time of Squanto's capture, Patuxet had been a flourishing community of two thousand inhabitants, with "many little houses, scattered over the fields," and "a great many cabins and gardens."[11] But when he returned, it had been abandoned and was overgrown and littered with bones. Disease, unintentionally carried by European traders, had swept through the area in the ensuing years, killing Natives by the thousands, in some places wiping out as much as 90 percent of the population. Years later, colonists commented on still unburied "bones and skulls" that made one forest seem like a "new found Golgotha." The Wampanoags were reduced to a few thousand and the Massachusetts to a few hundred. Land that had been farmed for generations was abandoned. A region that once pulsed with life seemed vacant.[12]

Like Christians, Algonquians believed such disasters were not mere accidents but were caused by spirits who needed to be honored and appeased. Sickness meant the spirits were angry. People sought help from shamans known as powwows, who were believed to have special access to the spirit world and skill in healing, among other powers. Powwows practiced various rituals—chanting, "bellowing and groaning," "antic and laborious gestures"—to induce a trance that would enable them to importune spirits. But they proved powerless against the epidemic. Traumatized survivors questioned the teachings of their elders, especially when they discovered that the English did not suffer from the disease.

Although coastal tribes were devastated, others, such as the Narragansetts, were spared. Some believed the Narragansetts were rewarded for their faithfulness to Kiehtan, the chief power and creator of the world, for they maintained a large temple where they regularly offered kettles, pelts, hatchets, beads, knives, and other valued possessions as sacrifices. Now they took advantage of their weakened rivals, seizing land north of Narragansett Bay from the Wampanoags and subjugating the Massachusetts.[13]

Meanwhile, Wampanoag hostility toward the English grew, especially following an ugly incident in which some English traders shot several Wampanoags on board their ship. When Captain Dermer returned to the region with Squanto in 1620, his ship was attacked by Wampanoags led by Epenow, the young man who had been displayed before the English public. They mortally wounded Dermer, killed most of his men, and captured Squanto, sending him to Ousamequin, the great Pokanoket sachem.

WHEN THE PILGRIMS arrived on Cape Cod, therefore, they were entering a war zone. By ransacking graves and stealing food, they confirmed their reputation for viciousness. The Nausets who attacked them were defending their homes. But the Pilgrims did not see it that way. They considered themselves God's people, which meant that those who attacked them were God's enemies. It followed that God would fight for them when they defended themselves.

They took it as a sign of God's blessing when they discovered abandoned Patuxet. Here was "a great deal of land" already cleared and planted with corn just "three or four years ago." Its woods had been cleared of underbrush to facilitate hunting, and a high hill commanded the area, ideal for a fort. A "very sweet brook" ran below, and there were "many delicate springs of as good water as can be drunk." On December 23, 1620, a work party began chopping down trees and assembling lumber to begin building the town they would call Plymouth.

Twice over the next few days men sounded the alarm that Indians were near, but no one actually spotted any. The leading Wampanoag sachem, Ousamequin, whose home was forty miles west at Sowams, was biding his time. Some Wampanoags, recalling the Frenchman's prophecy, wanted to destroy the fledgling settlement. But others counseled patience. They feared the colonists' guns, which some suspected the English used to spread disease. They also realized these foreigners were different from the violent men who had come before, for they included women and children and evidently planned to stay. Ousamequin considered them potential allies against the domineering Narragansetts.[14]

The Pilgrims barely survived these first months. Bradford's wife, Dorothy, suffered the first blow when she fell off the *Mayflower* and drowned. Then a spate of illnesses began striking down colonists; the first victim was just seven years old. At one point, two or three people were dying each day, and the sick lay side by side, wall to wall, in the recently constructed common house. Six or seven who were healthy enough "spared no pains night nor day, but with abundance of toil and hazard of their own health, fetched them wood, made them fires, dressed them meat, made their beds, washed their loathsome clothes, clothed and unclothed them."[15]

In mid-February, some of their tools were stolen. The next day, Wampanoags on a far hill beckoned them, only to withdraw when the Pilgrims' military commander Miles Standish began to approach. Hearing "a great many" Indians, he braced the colony for an attack, but it never came. The alarm sounded again on March 16 when a tall Indian with long black hair boldly strolled into the settlement, "stark naked" except for "a leather about his waist with a fringe about a span long." Carrying a bow and two arrows, "the one headed and the other unheaded," he walked down the dirt street with its few crude houses and headed for the common building. Colonists blocked him. Then, much to their surprise, he greeted them in English: "Welcome."

His name was Samoset, and he was a visiting Wabanaki sachem from Maine. Having learned a smattering of English from some fishermen, he had agreed to initiate contact on Ousamequin's behalf. He told them what had happened to the people of Patuxet, which assured the Pilgrims that "there is none to hinder our possession, or to lay claim unto it." He explained that the Nausets were hostile—they had killed three Englishmen the year before—because of the kidnappings perpetrated by Captain Hunt. Ousamequin, however, was open to trade, and Samoset's arrows symbolized the choice he was offering: peace or war.[16]

The Pilgrims wisely offered him gifts, and he soon returned with warriors bearing pelts and the stolen tools. On March 22, he brought Squanto, the former English captive, who spoke better English, and Ousamequin appeared on the hill with sixty warriors. Colonist Edward Winslow gave Ousamequin and his brother knives, jewelry, biscuits with butter, and alcohol. He informed the sachem that "King James saluted him with words of love and peace, and did accept of him as his friend and ally." He added that John Carver, Plymouth's governor, wanted to trade and "confirm a peace." To prove their good intentions, Winslow would remain with the Pokanokets as a hostage while Ousamequin went to meet Carver.

Ousamequin descended the hill with twenty warriors. He was in the prime of life, and the English thought him "grave of countenance and spare of speech." He wore "a great chain of white bone beads about his neck" and carried a pouch of tobacco. His face was painted "a sad red," his head oiled and greasy. His warriors' faces were painted "in part or in whole . . . some black, some red, some yellow, and some white, some with crosses and other antic works." Some wore large skins. Others were partially "naked." All were strong and tall.

Standish and half a dozen men carrying muskets led the Pokanokets to an unfinished building, sparsely decorated with a green rug and some cushions. Governor Carver arrived to the beating of a drum and the blowing of trumpets. The two leaders kissed each other and sat down to eat and drink, Ousamequin taking "a great draft" of alcohol that "made him sweat all the while after." The English thought "he trembled for fear," but it may have been an effect of the alcohol, to which he was unaccustomed.[17]

The leaders proceeded to negotiate a treaty. The English drew up a written version, but given Squanto's limited English, some scholars question how well Ousamequin understood it. The fact that Ousamequin agreed that Wampanoags who harmed colonists would be turned over to Plymouth for punishment suggests that he might not have known what he was consenting to. But there is another possible interpretation: that the powerful Ousamequin was granting a favor to a vulnerable community unable to protect its own people. Aside from that provision, the treaty was eminently fair. Plymouth promised Ousamequin, "If any did unjustly war against him, we would aid him," and the Pokanokets promised the reverse. Plymouth declared that King James esteemed Ousamequin "his friend and ally."[18]

When Ousamequin departed, he left Squanto behind. Over the following months, Squanto showed the English how to plant, fertilize, and tend corn, catch fish during their spawning runs, and procure other necessary resources. To Bradford, he was "a special instrument sent of God for their good."[19] The Pilgrims had reason to be grateful. Although they had plundered, vandalized, and occupied land without permission, Ousamequin's generosity saved them from destruction. He was taking a tremendous risk, since many sachems staunchly opposed such accommodation and might turn against him. He had no idea how many English were coming, no grasp of how the tsunami of colonization would destroy his people's way of life. One day, Ousamequin's son would regret his father's favor toward Plymouth.[20]

BY SPRING, HALF THE colonists were dead, including Governor Carver. But warmer weather brought a merciful end to the misery. Much to the Pilgrims' delight, the region produced herbs, grapes, strawberries, gooseberries, raspberries, and plums. During summer, they caught cod, bass, lobsters, and later eels. They collected mussels and shellfish and purchased oysters from Wampanoags. Natives streamed to the bay to fish and catch seafood as they had done for generations. Many visited Plymouth, where colonists tried to be hospitable despite their tenuous food supply and their discomfort at seeing men and women walking about with "only a skin about their middles."[21]

Bradford, who succeeded Carver as governor, sent Edward Winslow, Stephen Hopkins, and Squanto to visit Ousamequin at Sowams. Among other things, he wanted Ousamequin's help making amends with the Nausets. They also needed corn seed for planting. The men set out on July 2, reaching Nemasket, about fifteen miles from Plymouth, that afternoon. Nemaskets hosted them generously, offering bread made from maize, boiled acorns, and herring eggs. Winslow and Hopkins thrilled them by shooting crows who had been devouring their corn.

From there the party pushed on about eight miles to Cohannet, on the Titicut (later Taunton) River, where hundreds of Wampanoags gathered each spring to fish. The next day they followed the river toward Sowams. Wampanoags offered to carry their belongings or hoist them on their backs when crossing streams. The colonists rewarded them with gifts. Winslow marveled at verdant forests watered by abundant springs and streams. "There is much good timber, both oak, walnut tree, fir, beech, and exceeding great chestnut trees," he observed. There was so little underbrush that a horseman could ride easily among the trees.

He marveled at signs of a once bustling civilization along the river. "Upon it are and have been many towns. . . . The ground is very good on both sides, it being for the most part cleared." But weeds taller than he betrayed the tragic reality. "Thousands of men have lived there, which died in a great plague not long since," he reflected, "and pity it was and is to see so many goodly fields, and so well seated, without men to dress and manure the same." Skulls and bones lay "where their houses and dwellings had been, a very sad spectacle to behold."[22]

Every once in a while they came upon a hole in the ground, about a foot deep and carefully maintained. Wampanoags explained that such holes marked places where notable events had occurred. When people passing by inquired about them, the stories were passed from person to person, ensuring that Wampanoags knew their land and history.[23]

At last they reached Sowams, where Ousamequin welcomed them into his wigwam. They gave him a coat and chain, which he donned, "not a little proud to behold himself, and his men also to see their king so bravely attired." After they discussed their concerns, Ousamequin addressed his men: "Was not he, Ousamequin, commander of the country about them? Was not such a town his, and the people of it? And should they not bring their skins unto us?" He called the names of at least thirty places, and each time the men applauded in agreement, promising to maintain peace and trade with Plymouth.

Turning to his guests, he declared that this "was King James's country, and he was also King James's man." Although he did not have any food, having just returned home, he gave them tobacco. That night, much to their chagrin, he invited them to share a bed with him and his wife, "they at the one end and we at the other." Two warriors slept alongside, singing themselves to sleep. Along with the lice and fleas infesting the wigwam and the mosquitoes outside, the "barbarous singing" kept the discomfited Englishmen wide awake. By morning they felt more "weary of our lodging than of our journey."

That day many sachems and their men arrived. They gambled for pelts and knives, and the English impressed them by riddling a target with hail-shot. The colonists returned to Plymouth the next day, leaving Ousamequin "grieved and ashamed" that he could not feed so many guests.[24]

OUSAMEQUIN PERSUADED MANY Wampanoag communities to welcome Plymouth into their network of friendship, but the Nausets were an exception. Plymouth had to send Winslow and ten men to Cape Cod to make amends with the Nauset sachem, Aspinet. On the way, they met an old woman who fell "weeping and crying excessively" whenever she saw them. All three of her sons had been kidnapped by Captain Hunt and sold into slavery seven years earlier. Winslow and his men offered her "some small trifles" and assured her they were sorry. All Englishmen condemned Hunt's actions, they claimed. Eventually they met Aspinet, who affirmed his friendship after they paid for the goods they had stolen.

While they were there, however, disgruntled Wampanoags, led by the Pocasset sachem Corbitant, rebelled against Ousamequin. The Narragansetts supported them, driving Ousamequin from Sowams, while Corbitant marched to Nemasket and seized Squanto, Plymouth's interpreter, and Hobbomock, an esteemed member of Ousamequin's council. Hobbomock escaped to Plymouth and reported what had happened.[25]

Plymouth realized that if it did not protect its Wampanoag allies, its treaties would be meaningless, so it dispatched Captain Standish with a dozen men to take Corbitant's head. Arriving at Nemasket during the night, Standish's men opened fire on a wigwam full of sleeping Indians. Boys cried out, *Neen squaes!* (I am woman!), in hopes their lives would be spared, while women desperately clung to Hobbomock. Three were wounded. Corbitant was not even there, but Squanto was found safe, so Standish offered a defensive apology and promised to treat the wounded. Clumsy as it was, the show of force helped persuade Ousamequin's opponents to cease their resistance. On September 13, 1621, Corbitant, Epenow, and several other sachems acknowledged themselves "royal subjects of King James." The Narragansetts withdrew, and Ousamequin returned to Sowams.[26]

Standish and Winslow also led an expedition to secure the allegiance of the Massachusett people. The islands of Massachusetts Bay had recently been "inhabited, some being cleared from end to end," Winslow observed, but now "the people are all dead or removed." They met a sachem who agreed to a treaty in exchange for protection from the Mi'kmaqs, feared Indians from the north. But other Massachusetts fled as the men approached. Time and again the colonists came across dismantled wigwams and abandoned stockpiles of corn, until they finally encountered a band of terrified women and a man "shaking and trembling with fear." Although the women offered them boiled cod and drink, Squanto urged the colonists to steal what they wanted, claiming "they are a bad people and have oft threatened you." The colonists warned the Massachusetts that if they proved treacherous, Plymouth would do "far worse" than Squanto desired. The women "sold their coats from their backs and tied boughs about them," Winslow reported, "with great shamefacedness, for indeed they are more modest than some of our English women."[27] Their people would not forget the insult.

BY THE TIME OF the 1621 harvest, Plymouth consisted of seven houses and four common buildings. Their pea crop failed, and their barley was "indifferent," but their corn flourished, fertilized with herring or alewives as the Natives had taught them. The colonists also shot deer, ducks, geese, and turkeys. Afterward, they hosted Ousamequin and ninety warriors for a three-day celebration, romanticized by history as the "first thanksgiving." "[By the] goodness of God," Winslow wrote a friend in England, "we are so far from want, that we often wish you partakers of our plenty."

The Pilgrims owed their survival to Ousamequin, but they credited God. "We have found the Indians very faithful in their covenant of peace with us, very loving, and ready to pleasure us," Winslow admitted. "Yea, it hath pleased God so to possess the Indians with a fear of us and love unto us, that ... all the princes and peoples round about us have either made suit unto us or been glad of any occasion to make peace." In fact, "there is now great peace amongst the Indians themselves, which was not formerly, neither would have been but for us," he claimed. "We entertain them familiarly in our houses, and they as friendly bestowing their venison on us. They are a people without any religion or knowledge of any God, yet very trusty, quick of apprehension, ripe-witted, just." The part about religion was false, but Winslow's point was that aspiring colonists need not fear Indians. America's nearly boundless land was theirs for the taking, and all they needed was to cross the Atlantic and claim it.[28]

Colonists believed Indians had everything to gain from colonization. That November, Robert Cushman, a respected member of the Leiden congregation, briefly visited the settlement, whose numbers had been bolstered by a second wave of migrants. He urged colonists to offer a good example to the "poor heathens, whose eyes are upon you," by bearing each other's burdens and sharing with the needy. Christian love would "preach louder to them than if you could cry in their barbarous language," he exhorted.[29]

Returning to England, Cushman urged supporters to send more colonists. He speculated that God was preparing to punish his English people. If so, might God be sending his people "amongst the heathens that so a light may rise up in the dark, and the kingdom of heaven be taken from them which now have it and given to a people that shall bring forth the fruit of it?" The Indians might become God's new chosen people.

The colonists' arrival had already improved the Natives' lives substantially, he argued. "They were wont to be the most cruel and treacherous people in all these parts, even like lions, but to us they have been like lambs, so kind, so submissive, so trusty, as a man may truly say, many Christians are not so kind nor sincere." This was partly because disease and war with the Narragansetts had left them dejected. Although they could have easily destroyed Plymouth, "such a fear was upon them as that they never offered us the least injury in word or deed."

The Pilgrims had treated them with "equity, justice, and compassion," Cushman maintained. "They have received much favor, help, and aid from us, but never the least injury or wrong." Colonists welcomed them into their homes, "eating and drinking and warming themselves." It was only a matter of time before they embraced Christianity and civilization.[30]

Cushman knew that some people questioned the morality of colonization, so he wrote a tract to set their minds at ease. God had not given America to the English the way he gave Canaan to Israel in Old Testament times, he admitted. God commanded Israel to conquer Canaan and destroy its people so that Canaan might become a "type" or symbol of "eternal rest in heaven." Now that Christ had come, "no land . . . can be said to be given of God to any nation, as was Canaan." But God wanted his people to go where they could do the most good for others. That was America, "where a drop of the knowledge of Christ is most precious." It was not enough to "pray for the conversion of the heathens." Christians had to take action. "To us they cannot come. Our land is full. To them we may go. Their land is empty."

What right did colonists have to occupy the land? Cushman had no doubt that "discoveries, contracts, and agreements" gave England full rights with respect to other Christian monarchs. As for the Natives, America was "spacious and void, and there are few [people], and [they] do but run over the grass, as do also the foxes and wild beasts. They are not industrious, neither have art, science, skill or faculty to use either the land or the commodities of it, but all spoils, rots, and is marred for want of manuring, gathering, [and] ordering." Colonists had every right to occupy unused land, just like the Old Testament patriarchs.

What about land that Indians did claim? Cushman claimed that Ousamequin loved the English so much that he not only acknowledged King James as "his master and commander," but permitted them to settle "in all his dominions, taking what place we will, and as much land as we will, and bringing as many people as we will."

Thus the English were eminently justified in coming to America, both to enlarge the king's dominion and to proclaim the gospel to "poor blind infidels." By contrast, to remain in England was to be consigned to religious conflict, suffocating economic competition, overcrowding, unemployment, and poverty. If Indians "had but a drop of that knowledge" of Christianity that "flieth about the streets" in England, he predicted, they "would be filled with exceeding great joy and gladness."[31] All they needed was godly men and women to bring it to them.

CUSHMAN'S ROSY RHETORIC bore little resemblance to reality. Wampanoag sachems did not believe they had surrendered their sovereignty or land. Rather, they considered the English to be trading partners, friends, and allies. Other sachems resented the English presence. Canonicus, the Narragansett sachem, was vexed at Plymouth for undermining his domination over the Pokanokets, and Indians talked openly of his preparations for war. In early 1622, Canonicus sent Plymouth a bundle of arrows wrapped in a rattlesnake skin. It was a symbolic assertion of his dominance, backed by the threat of attack.

The Pilgrims were in no position to fight the Narragansetts, but they were unwilling to kowtow to a Native sachem. So they returned the snakeskin with a symbol of their own: a bundle of powder and shot. It was a bluff, and a dangerous one at that. Edward Winslow admitted, "[If] God had let them loose, they might easily have swallowed us up, scarce being a handful in comparison of those forces they might have gathered together against us." Plymouth spent the next month building a fort, but Canonicus allegedly refused to accept the bundle of ammunition, resulting in an uneasy standoff.[32]

Later that year, Ousamequin's counselor Hobbomock warned that the Massachusetts and Narragansetts were conspiring against Plymouth and that Squanto, Plymouth's Wampanoag interpreter, was part of the plot. Then a member of Squanto's family reported that Ousamequin, the Pocasset sachem Corbitant, and many Narragansetts and Wampanoags were preparing to attack Plymouth. An investigation revealed that Squanto, who shared his name with an Indian god, was posturing himself as Ousamequin's rival. He was telling Wampanoags that the English "kept the plague buried in the ground and could send it amongst whom they would." Squanto promised to protect anyone who submitted to him.

An enraged Ousamequin demanded Squanto's death. Governor Bradford refused, declaring that Plymouth needed him. Relations quickly soured. When news arrived that Indians had massacred hundreds of colonists in Virginia, Wampanoags spoke of how easy it would be to destroy Plymouth. Nor did Plymouth benefit from Bradford's stubbornness. A few months later, Squanto developed a fever, bleeding profusely from his nose. Some thought he was poisoned. He asked Bradford to pray "that he might go to the Englishmen's God in heaven." Within days, he was dead.[33]

The situation worsened that winter. Thomas Weston, a leading merchant who had financed the Pilgrims' migration, had given up his interest in the colony and sent sixty men to establish a new colony at Wessagusset, more than twenty miles north, on Massachusetts Bay. Weston's men arrived too late to plant corn, though they did build a fort. By February they were on the brink of starvation. Some began working for the Massachusetts, "fetching them wood and water" in exchange for food. But others stole the Indians' corn, and Wessagusset's leaders sent Plymouth a letter suggesting they attack the Massachusetts to seize more food. Aghast, Plymouth protested that an unprovoked attack would alienate all Indians, violated "the law of God and nature," and would incite God's wrath.[34]

Around the same time, Plymouth learned that Ousamequin was dying. It was Algonquian custom to visit a prominent man when he was sick. If he died, his guests would perform "the most doleful" rites. If he recovered, he would host a great dance and shower them with gifts. Although Bradford was not on good terms with Ousamequin, he dutifully sent Winslow and Hobbomock to Sowams. A few miles from their destination, they were informed that Ousamequin had died. "My loving sachem, my loving sachem! Many have I known, but never any like thee!" Hobbomock lamented. He told Winslow that Ousamequin was an honest, reasonable, and loving sachem, "not bloody and cruel like other Indians." Now that he was dead, the Wampanoags would surely turn against Plymouth, which "had not a faithful friend left among the Indians."

They pushed on to Sowams, arriving well after dark. Much to their relief, it was a false report, but Ousamequin did appear to be dying. The town was full of Indians, and Ousamequin's wigwam was so crowded they could hardly get in. Powwows were "in the midst of their charms for him, making such a hellish noise as it distempered us that were well, and therefore unlike to ease him that was sick," Winslow observed. Women rubbed the sachem's arms and legs to keep him warm.

Ousamequin permitted Winslow to treat him. Winslow discovered that Ousamequin's tongue was "exceedingly furred" and so swollen he had not swallowed anything in two days. Winslow fed him some "comfortable conserves" on the tip of his knife, scraped an "abundance of corruption" from his tongue, and washed his mouth. That enabled Ousamequin to drink and swallow more conserves. Within half an hour his condition had improved noticeably. "Never did I see a man so low . . . recover in that measure in so short a time," Winslow marveled. The grateful sachem asked Winslow to clean the mouths of other Wampanoags too. Winslow humbly acquiesced, though he admitted that "it were much offensive to me, not being accustomed with such poisonous savors."

Winslow's medical diplomacy changed everything. Before he arrived, a sachem had been urging Ousamequin to attack the English. Now that Winslow had saved his life, "I see the English are my friends and love me," Ousamequin declared, sitting up in bed. "Whilst I live, I will never forget this kindness they have showed me."[35]

Among those who changed their minds was Corbitant, the Pocasset sachem, whom Winslow visited on his way back to Plymouth. Corbitant was "full of merry jests and squibs," Winslow recalled, "and never better pleased than when the like are returned again upon him." He asked if Winslow would care for him if he were sick. Winslow said he would. He asked how Winslow dared travel without an escort. Winslow replied that "where [there] was true love, there was no fear." If they loved Indians, Corbitant countered, why did they post men with muskets and cannons when Indians came to Plymouth? When Winslow explained that this was the honorable way to greet friends, Corbitant shook his head, declaring that "he liked not such salutations."

The conversation turned to religion. Corbitant asked why the English prayed before meals. Winslow recalled, "I took occasion to tell them of God's works of creation and preservation, of his laws and ordinances, especially of the Ten Commandments, all of which they hearkened unto with great attention and liked well." Since all good things came from God, he explained, it was important to thank him and ask for his continued blessing. The Pocassets affirmed that "they believed almost all the same things" about Kiehtan. However, they did not like the command against adultery, "thinking there were many inconveniences in it, that a man should be tied to one woman." They talked well into the night, and Winslow believed the conversation "no less delightful to them than comfortable to us."

The next day, Hobbomock revealed that Ousamequin had warned him that Massachusetts and Wampanoags from Cape Cod and Noepe were conspiring to attack Wessagusset, Thomas Weston's struggling colony on Massachusetts Bay. Ousamequin urged a preemptive strike, for if Wessagusset were destroyed, Algonquians would be emboldened against Plymouth. Why Hobbomock waited so long to relay this intelligence is unclear, but the men hastened to Plymouth.[36]

A Massachusett sachem had sent Plymouth a similar warning, so Plymouth ordered Captain Standish to take eight men to Wessagusset. His pretense would be trade, but his orders were to take the head of a Massachusett sachem named Wituwamat, thought to be the plot's ringleader. Before they set sail, Wessagusset colonist Phinehas Pratt arrived with a dire report. Wessagusset had executed a colonist for stealing from the Massachusetts, he explained, but the Massachusetts still refused to sell them food. Several colonists had died. Others wandered around looking for food. "The savages seemed to be good friends with us while they feared us," he later wrote, "but when they see famine prevail, they begun to insult us." Armed Natives lurked about the fort, and an attack seemed imminent. Wessagusset implored Plymouth's aid.[37]

When Standish arrived at Wessagusset, he was shocked to discover colonists gathering food on the shore. They told him "they feared not the Indians, but lived and suffered them to lodge with them, not having sword or gun, or needing the same." Baffled, he met the fort's leaders, who claimed the Massachusetts were hostile and urged Standish to attack. If the Massachusetts were planning an attack, their coming and going was surprisingly casual. Wituwamat boasted of having killed Europeans, while a warrior named Pecksuot mocked that though Standish "were a great captain, yet he was but a little man." But they were sufficiently trusting to meet Standish and his men in a room with the door "fast shut."

Suddenly Standish seized the knife hanging from Pecksuot's neck and began stabbing him repeatedly. Others attacked Wituwamat. "It is incredible how many wounds these two . . . received before they died," Winslow later wrote, "not making any fearful noise, but catching at their weapons and striving to the last." It was an assassination, plain and simple. Standish then ordered his men to kill every Massachusett man they could find. The soldiers returned to an enthusiastic welcome in Plymouth, leaving seven more dead Massachusetts in their wake. They hung Wituwamat's head on a pike, a fate reserved for rebels and traitors. The Massachusetts retaliated by killing three Wessagusset colonists who had been working for them.[38]

According to Winslow, Standish's "sudden and unexpected execution, together with the just judgment of God upon their guilty consciences," terrified the Massachusetts and Cape Cod Wampanoags. They abandoned their villages for swamps and forests, where many died of hunger and disease. It was said that one sachem, before he died, exclaimed that "the God of the English was offended with them and would destroy them." Ousamequin's pro-English policy would not be seriously challenged again during his lifetime. He was at the height of his power.[39]

Winslow admitted that the Massachusetts had been provoked by "seeming Christians" whose conduct "made Christ and Christianity stink in the nostrils of the poor infidels," but he never doubted that Standish's preemptive strike was justified or that God favored Plymouth's endeavors. "When I seriously consider," he wrote, "I cannot but think that God hath a purpose to give that land as an inheritance to our nation." Surely "every honest man" should support the colonial enterprise, he thought, "where religion and profit jump together (which is rare) in so honorable an action."[40]

THE PILGRIMS' PASTOR, JOHN Robinson, thought differently. "Oh, how happy a thing had it been, if you had converted some before you had killed any!" he wrote from Leiden. True, some Massachusetts deserved death, but had their plot not been provoked by "heathenish Christians"? And what right did Plymouth have to kill so many? The English were "no magistrates" with authority to judge Indians and should have considered "not what they deserved, but what you were by necessity constrained to inflict." Standish had gone far beyond that. He was a gifted soldier, but he lacked Christian "tenderness" toward human beings made in God's image. Men might think it glorious to terrorize "poor barbarous people," but God did not. Standish had set a terrible precedent.[41]

The Pilgrims had come to America with peaceful intentions and hopes that the Natives would embrace Christianity. They intended to fight a spiritual war whose weapons were truth and love, but ended up waging war with knives and muskets.

2

The Puritans

1629 to 1633

A WAVE OF Puritan migration hit New England a decade after the Pilgrims founded Plymouth. It engulfed the region around Massachusetts Bay, homeland of the Massachusett people and their northern neighbors, the Pennacooks. Devastated by disease, these Indians lacked the power to negotiate with the English, who dominated them from the beginning.

Puritan leaders defended colonialism on theological grounds, and they were emphatic that their goal was to convert the Natives to Christianity. But other concerns proved more urgent: settlement, agriculture, trade, government, church, and security. The experiences of other colonies demonstrated that the first years of a new settlement were crucial. Their chief priority was establishing Christ's kingdom in the form of a stable English commonwealth. The Natives would be converted in God's good time.

Puritan visionaries began exploring the possibility of a colony during the mid-1620s. John White, minister of the prosperous commercial town of Dorchester, England, organized a company known as the Dorchester Adventurers in 1623. Its goal was to establish agricultural communities that could serve fishermen working off New England's coast, evangelize Indians, and raise money for Puritan causes. The project failed, but about fifty hardworking colonists remained near Naumkeag, a Pennacook town on Massachusetts Bay.

In 1628, White and other investors formed the New England Company. They received a patent from the Council for New England to establish a colony extending from three miles south of the Charles (or Quinobequin) River to three miles north of the Merrimack River. They sent forty-year-old John Endecott and about fifty others to join the struggling community at Naumkeag, which would form the nucleus of the new colony. Colonists named the settlement Salem, the Hebrew word for "peace."[1]

Endecott was a zealous Puritan who would prove to be a force in colonial affairs for decades to come. He established ties with Plymouth, concluding that the Pilgrims and Puritans shared "one and the same heart, guided by one and the same spirit of truth." That winter, Salem suffered from conflict, cold, hunger, and sickness that claimed the life of Endecott's wife. Plymouth did its best to aid the new settlement.[2]

SALEM MIGHT HAVE remained insignificant had conditions for Puritans in England not deteriorated during the 1620s. King James appointed anti-Puritan bishops, refused to intervene on the Protestant side in the Thirty Years' War raging in Europe, and married his son Charles, heir to the throne, to Henrietta Maria, Catholic sister of Louis XIII of France. He also soured against the Reformed doctrine of predestination (which emphasized God's sovereign grace in choosing which sinners he would save), supporting an alternative view known as Arminianism.

After Charles became king in 1625, he appointed anti-Puritan bishops and advisors and attempted to raise revenue without Parliament's consent, a violation of ancient English liberties. Members of Parliament and other prominent resisters found themselves imprisoned. "God is departing from us," a Puritan clergyman warned Parliament. The House of Commons struck back, declaring that anyone who promoted Catholicism or Arminianism was "a capital enemy to this kingdom." The king's bishops, for their part, declared that the church's worship and government were of divine origin and essential to Christian obedience. Charles finally dissolved Parliament in 1629, resolved to rule without it, while his bishops harassed Puritan ministers and summoned them before ecclesiastical courts.[3]

Puritans began to consider seeking a better future in America. By 1629, so many had decided to emigrate that the New England Company was preparing an expedition of six ships to carry four hundred colonists and three ministers. These Puritans were emigrating to protect their form of Christianity, not to evangelize foreign peoples, but the company's governor, Matthew Cradock, reminded John Endecott in Salem that the colony's "main end" was "to bring the Indians to the knowledge of the gospel." They were to "demean themselves justly and courteous towards the Indians," feeling compassion for their "woeful state and condition," for only God's grace made the English better off. Once Indians discerned the superiority of English culture, they might be persuaded to let their children receive instruction from the colonists, and the mission would take off from there. Preserving the Puritan way of life and evangelizing Natives thus fulfilled the same basic mission: "the enlargement of the kingdom of Jesus Christ."

Time would show that these goals were less compatible than the Puritans imagined. Since preservation was their primary goal, security took priority over evangelism. Cradock warned Endecott not to "be too confident of the fidelity of the savages." After all, in 1622 Natives in Virginia—taking advantage of their freedom to come and go among English settlements—had massacred hundreds of colonists. Cradock admonished the settlers to be "innocent as doves" and "wise as serpents," as Jesus commanded his disciples.[4] The Puritans hoped for peace, but if violence proved to be unavoidable, they were determined to have the upper hand.

The company undertook numerous measures in order to avoid conflict. Colonists who sold guns and ammunition to Indians or harmed them "in the least kind" were to be punished severely. Since "familiarity" would multiply opportunities for conflict, Indians should be admitted to Salem only at specified times and places. The company implored Endecott to make sure colonists did not steal Native land. "If any of the savages pretend right of inheritance to all or any part of the lands granted in our patent, we pray you endeavor to purchase their title, that we may avoid the least scruple of intrusion."[5] They had no desire to conquer New England by force. They saw themselves as liberators. If they were loving and just, surely Indians would welcome them with open arms.

It was a hopeful vision, but it was tragically naïve.

BY THE SPRING OF 1629, Salem consisted of about ten houses, including "a fair house newly built for the governor." In his inaugural oath, Governor Endecott swore "to draw on the natives of this country, called New England, to the knowledge of the true God, and to conserve the planters and others coming hither, in the same knowledge and fear of God."[6]

About three hundred immigrants arrived that spring, some of whom founded Charlestown on the north bank of the Charles River, about fifteen miles southwest of Salem. Those in Salem organized the colony's first church. In the absence of bishops, they followed a procedure developed by separatists, which would have been scandalous in England but set a precedent for New England: they formed a congregation and elected and ordained ministers. Governor Bradford and a delegation from Plymouth attended the service. The new church disregarded the Church of England's *Book of Common Prayer*, and when two colonists hosted gatherings that involved readings from the prayer book, Endecott sent them back to England. This too was an important precedent.[7]

Colonists understood little about Native culture, and what they did not understand, they despised. Pastor Francis Higginson thought Indians had no concept of landownership. "The Indians are not able to make use of the one fourth part of the land, neither have they any settled places as towns to dwell in, nor any ground as they challenge for their own possession, but change their habitation from place to place," he wrote.

But Algonquians did have a strong sense of landownership, albeit one quite different from English conceptions of property rights. Sachems owned land on behalf of their people and assigned agricultural plots based on social status and need. Their way of life also required seasonal access to vast areas of woodland, streams, and, for some communities, the coast. They traveled to waterfalls to catch salmon, shad, and alewives during spring and to coastal areas to gather lobsters, clams, and oysters during summer. They burned forest underbrush to create ideal conditions for deer, bear, moose, fowl, and other game, and for wild berries and nuts, relocating to such areas to gather and hunt during fall and winter. Each community possessed such lands, for without them, their way of life was doomed. Communal ownership reflected a culture of hospitality, generosity, and reciprocity. The English ideal of acquiring, dividing, clearing, and developing as much land as possible to maximize economic productivity, regardless of the impact on its inhabitants, would provoke untold surprise and frustration.

Colonists despised Algonquian men for spending so much time hunting and fishing while leaving agriculture and other food-gathering activities to women. Since hunting and fishing were recreational activities in England and prosperous English women did not work in the fields, they concluded that Indian men were lazy and exploiting their women. This was unfair, for hunting and fishing in America required considerable skill and labor (as colonists would learn) and was essential to the Algonquian diet. Here, too, cultural misunderstanding bred prejudice.

Colonists assured themselves that the Indians wanted them there. The Natives "generally profess to like well of our coming and planting here, partly because there is abundance of ground that they cannot possess nor make use of, and partly because our being here will be a means both of relief to them when they want, and also a defense from their enemies," Pastor Higginson claimed. But he admitted that colonists did not trust them.[8]

In April 1630, a Pennacook sachem named Sagamore John warned that a coalition of Narragansett and Massachusett Indians was planning to attack English settlements. Terrified, Charlestown's residents got busy "digging and building" a palisade with flankers on the town hill. They breathed a sigh of relief when they were told that the Indians had been frightened off by a cannon shot at Salem.[9]

Clearly, colonists were more afraid than Higginson let on.

DESPITE THE KING'S hostility toward Puritanism, the New England Company somehow managed to obtain a royal charter for the colony, now known as Massachusetts Bay (or Massachusetts). The charter completely disregarded Indian sovereignty, presupposing that the king had authority over land in America by right of discovery. It declared that "the principal end" of the colony was to "win and incite the natives of [the] country to the knowledge and obedience of the only true God and Savior of mankind, and the Christian faith."[10]

The colony's seal revealed much about Puritan preconceptions of Native Americans. It exhibited an Indian imploring the English with words from scripture, "Come over and help us." He held a bow and arrow but stood vulnerably, in a posture of peace. It was pure fiction, but it reflected the English belief that colonization was an act of benevolence from which Indians had everything to gain.

Such idealized portrayals did not prepare colonists to engage the actual human beings they met in America. Unrealistic expectations were sure to breed disappointment, resentment, and anger.

To prevent the king from interfering with the colony's government, the company, renamed the Massachusetts Bay Company, voted to transfer its charter and seat of government to America. Worried that Governor Endecott's Puritan zeal might alienate the king, they elected one of their most energetic and conscientious members to replace him, a man whose name and family would tower over New England's history: John Winthrop.[11]

Born to an English gentry family in 1588, Winthrop grew up keenly aware of his disposition toward lewdness and "all kind of wickedness." When he was barely seventeen, he dropped out of Trinity College, Cambridge, and married Mary Forth, but their marriage was difficult. He lacked substantial career prospects and struggled through cycles of guilt, confession, assurance of forgiveness, and pride. "I desired no other happiness but to be embraced [by Christ]," he wrote. "I held nothing so dear that I was not willing to part with for him." Finally, he felt a sense of Jesus's love, "far exceeding the affection of the kindest husband."

His career prospects improved markedly when he acquired Groton Manor from his uncle and became a magistrate. Like most Christians, he believed magistrates were responsible for promoting true Christianity and punishing idolatry and blasphemy. He knew that rulers who took such tasks seriously were despised and reviled as "puritans," but he was determined to fulfill his calling rather than pursue worldly honor and pleasure.

Tragedy struck when Mary died, leaving him with four children. His second wife died too. He eventually married Margaret Tyndal, a well-educated, pious woman with whom he raised seven children.

They watched anxiously as Puritan fortunes deteriorated. John feared that God was about to judge England and discussed going to America, where God might provide a "shelter and a hiding place." Friends sought to dissuade him. "To adventure your whole family upon so many manifest uncertainties standeth not with your wisdom and long experience," one protested. Winthrop was well aware of the risks. His son Henry had gone to Barbados to plant tobacco in 1626, where he was one of "three score of Christians and forty slaves of Negroes and Indians." The enterprise failed miserably, and Henry was fortunate to have survived.[12]

Nevertheless, Winthrop decided to go. He drew up what he called "General Observations" to justify the colonial enterprise, which he shared with friends and prospective colonists and revised repeatedly based on their feedback. Like most migrants, he emphasized the spiritual and economic welfare of the English, but he considered Native American interests too. As long as Indians remained ignorant of the gospel, Christians believed, they were under Satan's domination and destined for hell. Nor was their fate improved by Jesuit missionaries who converted thousands to Catholicism, the religion of Antichrist. Winthrop argued that the English needed to "raise a bulwark" against the Jesuits, establishing Christ's kingdom, saving Native souls, and speeding "the coming of the fullness of the Gentiles" into Christianity.

There were many good reasons to leave England. Protestants across the English Channel were suffering war and persecution, and he feared "like judgment is coming upon us." Might God be preparing New England as "a refuge for many whom he meaneth to save in the general destruction?" Besides, England's future looked gloomy. It was overpopulated, land was scarce, and social competition spawned materialism and moral compromise. It was "almost impossible for a good, upright man to maintain his charge and to live comfortably in his profession." America, by contrast, contained vast lands that "lie waste without inhabitant." The earth belonged to God, and God had commanded human beings to be fruitful and multiply, filling the earth and subduing it. Colonizing the land was a religious duty.

Some Puritans accused colonists of abandoning England, making God's judgment upon it more likely. Winthrop replied that many godly people remained, and that in any case, God wanted the gospel preached to all nations. Others urged potential colonists to wait to see whether conditions in England improved. But Winthrop countered that complacency was foolhardy. Better to flee while they had the chance. True, they might face hunger, starvation, and war. Loved ones would die. But surely God would provide for his people, sustaining them until they reached heaven, their ultimate reward. They would be careful to avoid the mistakes of previous colonies, which "aimed chiefly at profit and not the propagation of religion," involved "a multitude of rude and misgoverned persons, the very scum of the land," and "did not establish a right form of government." Winthrop's colonists were people of the best quality. They would advance Christ's kingdom and foster good government.

What about the Natives? "What warrant have we to take the land which is and hath been so long time possessed by other sons of Adam?" Winthrop was confident in his answer, invoking the well-known legal doctrine of *vacuum domicilium*: God made the world for all human beings in common, and no one had the right to hoard land they were not using, especially when other regions were overcrowded. Property rights had to be respected, but "these savage people ramble over much land without title or property." There was "more than enough for them and us."

Over time he sharpened this argument into a refined legal case: "God hath given to the sons of men a double right to the earth. There is a natural right and a civil right. The first right was natural when men held the earth in common, every man sowing and feeding where he pleased. Then as men and their cattle increased, they appropriated certain parcels of ground by inclosing and peculiar manurance, and this in time gave them a civil right." The Indians had a natural right, but not a civil right: "They enclose no land, neither have any settled habitation, nor any tame cattle to improve the land by." It followed that "if we leave them sufficient [land] for their use, we may lawfully take the rest."

Winthrop believed God had already cleared space for his people by killing Indians: "God hath consumed these nations in a miraculous plague whereby a great part of their country is left void without inhabitants." Those who were left would offer little trouble. "We shall come in with good leave of these nations," he concluded. He was not concerned about preserving the Native way of life. He did not believe the English should conquer America's first people, but by attributing the death of thousands to God's miraculous intervention, he showed that Indian flourishing played no necessary role in his vision for America. He hoped God would save many Indians, but he was confident Christ's kingdom would advance even if most of them died.[13]

JOHN WHITE, THE Massachusetts Bay Company's visionary founder, offered an equally passionate defense of colonialism in a tract titled *The Planters Plea*. Like Winthrop, he drew on God's commands in Genesis 1:28 and 9:1 to fill the earth and subdue it. It was absurd to expect people in one part of the world to endure miserable, overcrowded conditions, while vast tracts elsewhere lay vacant and undeveloped.[14]

White connected this argument with the Christian imperative to spread the gospel. Certain people remained under the Devil's rule, but now Christ was using colonialism to claim them as his inheritance, in fulfillment of biblical prophecy. Just as the Romans had once conquered the barbarian Picts, ancestors of the English, eventually civilizing and evangelizing them, so now God was showing the same mercy to Native Americans. But the English had to hurry, for their efforts lagged far behind the Catholic Jesuits, who were busy advancing "the Devil's kingdom."[15]

The coastal Natives had everything to gain, he thought. Weakened by disease, they would welcome English protection from rivals like the Narragansetts and Mi'kmaqs. Then, once the colony was established, the English would lift them from poverty by teaching "providence and industry," commerce, discipline, and hard work. All this would "breed civility," and Puritan godliness would attract Natives to "love of the truth," securing for them the most precious gift of all: salvation. They would be conquered for Christ, not by sword or cannon but by love and good works.[16]

White viewed Indians as lazy and short-sighted, but his prejudice was religious and cultural, not racial. The two peoples were fundamentally equal, he insisted. There was only one reason Natives were "beasts" and the English were not: God's grace. "We are translated into the glorious liberty of the son of God. They are bond slaves of Satan. Who hath made us to differ? How long shall we scorn what we should commiserate? What if God should show mercy unto them, erect a church among them, recover them out of the power of the Devil? Could any conquest be so glorious?"[17]

White spoke of conquest, but he interpreted that conquest as a spiritual and benevolent struggle for liberation. He foresaw a future in Christ's kingdom that was glorious for English and Indian alike. But what if the Indians resisted? White did not say, but his reference to the Roman conquest of England implied the answer. Military conquest, if necessary, would be more than justified by the blessings Indians received from it.

WINTHROP'S EXPEDITION WAS scheduled for March 1630. He ordered provisions, worked out governing arrangements, enlisted clergy, and recruited colonists. Large portions of churches and communities decided to move together. A majority would travel as families, but there were also many servants. Most colonists were middle class and well educated, though servants were poorer. Emigration required months of preparation as colonists settled their affairs and stockpiled supplies. They had to bring food (enough to last a year), clothing and shoes, bedding, and kitchenware. They needed tools to clear land, build houses, and ply their trades, as well as guns, ammunition, and fishing implements. The cost for a family might exceed £25, about a year's rent for a family farm.[18]

People emigrated for many reasons. Some, especially servants, held little allegiance to Puritanism, but most understood what they were getting into. "Necessity may press some," White admitted, "novelty draw on others, hopes of gain in time to come may prevail with a third sort; but that the most, and most sincere and godly part, have the advancement of the gospel for their main scope, I am confident."[19] Their chief concerns were salvation and prosperity, not the welfare of Indians, but many hoped the Natives would eventually share in these blessings.

The plan, Winthrop informed his pregnant wife, was for eleven ships to carry 700 passengers, 240 cows, and about 60 horses. He had made the difficult decision to leave Margaret behind, but he brought twenty-two-year-old Henry, with his Barbados experience, and his preteen boys, Stephen and Adam. He would travel on the *Arbella*, a 350-ton ship rechristened in honor of Lady Arbella Johnson, daughter of the Earl of Lincoln, who was on board. A few days before departure, Winthrop dined with friends who would remain behind. "Breaking into a flood of tears himself, [he] set them all a weeping... while they thought of seeing the faces of each other no more in the land of the living."[20]

Before the first ships set sail, John Cotton, a prominent Puritan minister from Lincolnshire, preached a farewell sermon, assuring the departing colonists that God went with them. Widely respected for his wisdom and moderation, Cotton had survived ecclesiastical scrutiny thanks to the protection of a sympathetic bishop. His preaching was brilliant yet plain and pastoral, attracting thousands of listeners from his and other parishes. It would not be long before he too was forced to seek refuge in America.[21]

In typical Protestant fashion, he interpreted their endeavor in light of scripture's story of salvation. Just as the Israelites were exiled from their homeland because they broke God's covenant, so now God's people faced exile because England had broken its covenant. But that did not mean God had abandoned them. On the contrary, God would bless them as long as they pursued his promises. In 2 Samuel 7:10, Cotton's sermon text, God declared to King David, "I will appoint a place for my people Israel, and I will plant them, that they may dwell in a place of their own, and move no more." God's relationship with Israel was unique, Cotton admitted. Nevertheless, God's promise to David still applied to God's people. They would "plainly see a providence of God leading them from one country to another," making room for them to dwell.[22]

How could they know God was providing them a place in America? Cotton declared that if they sought God's presence through preaching, the sacraments, and church discipline   what Puritans called God's ordinances   God promised to give them the land they occupied. "Others take the land by his providence," he preached, "but God's people take the land by promise." The ordinances were the marks of Christ's kingdom, the heartbeat of Reformed Christianity, and the cause for which they were leaving England. By submitting to them, the colonists proved they were God's people, and if they were God's people, he would enable them to overcome all obstacles. "As soon as God's ordinances cease, your security ceaseth," Cotton warned, no doubt thinking of the Church of England. But "look into all the stories, whether divine or human, and you shall never find that God ever rooted out a people that had the ordinances planted amongst them, and themselves planted into the ordinances."[23]

But what about the Natives? Various propagandists argued that the English had the right to drive the Natives out of America just as Israel had purged Canaanites from the Promised Land. But Cotton, like most theologians, rejected this abuse of scripture. God had commanded Israel to slaughter the Canaanites and seize their land, but that was a "special commission" not given to any other nation.

There were other ways to procure land, however. God sometimes "gives a foreign people favor in the eyes of any native people to come and sit down with them," he said. This might happen by way of sale or a grant of friendship, as with the Old Testament patriarchs. Either way, they had to negotiate fairly. On the other hand, sometimes God gave his people land by making it, "though not altogether void of inhabitants, yet void in that place where they reside," as he had done in America by decimating coastal Natives with disease. "If, therefore, any son of Adam come and find a place empty, he hath liberty to come and fill and subdue the earth there." It was a natural law (the law of *vacuum domicilium*) confirmed in scripture: "That in a vacant soil, he that taketh possession of it and bestoweth culture and husbandry upon it, his right it is."

Did Cotton consider that the Natives might resist such claims? Was it this that led him to consider war as another means of gaining land? "Indeed," he went on, "no nation is to drive out another without special commission from heaven, such as the Israelites had, unless the natives do unjustly wrong them and will not recompense the wrongs done in peaceable sort, and then they may right themselves by lawful war and subdue the country unto themselves."[24] In other words, a just war would place the English in a position like that of Israel after all. If they were attacked, they had permission not only to defend themselves but to conquer. Cotton said nothing about limits or proportionality. He spoke of license. And the criteria he offered were the precise criteria Puritan leaders would later use to justify wars of conquest.

But Cotton urged them to aim for something better. "Offend not the poor natives," he exhorted, "but as you partake in their land, so make them partakers of your precious faith. As you reap their temporals, so feed them with your spirituals. Win them to the love of Christ, for whom Christ died." Here was an argument to assuage the conscience of those who recognized that Indians would suffer from colonialism, one that seemed to echo biblical exhortations to give material aid to those who preached the gospel. The Natives would give material wealth, but Cotton considered the gospel, which they would receive in return, a far superior treasure. Indians had as much right to God's love as the English, he said. "They never yet refused the gospel, and therefore more hope they will now receive it. Who knoweth whether God have reared this whole plantation for such an end?"[25]

The sermon suggested two sharply contrasting possibilities: one promised salvation for America's first people; the other threatened domination. The first was preferable, but either would suffice to advance Christ's kingdom. Puritans paid close attention to preaching, and here were all the arguments they needed for an aggressive pursuit of Native land alongside an aggressive pursuit of Native souls.

THE MODEL FOR THE society they hoped to establish was old, gleaned from the pages of scripture. Pastors would preach the word and congregations would guard the purity of God's ordinances, as in the New Testament church. The state would preserve justice and punish idolatry, false teaching, and immorality, as in Old Testament Israel. It would be a living testimony to the love, justice, and peace of Christ's kingdom.[26]

That is, if they actually loved one another. Knowing human nature, Winthrop, the new governor, feared they might not. He addressed the matter in a document titled "A Model of Christian Charity." In his "most holy and wise providence," Winthrop began, God disposed of human affairs such that some were rich and others poor, some had power and dignity, while others were their subjects. God did this because he wanted human beings to need one another, being knit together in the "bond of brotherly affection." All were obligated to use their gifts for the common good, practicing justice and mercy toward the weak and loving even their enemies "as the same flesh and image of God."[27]

Winthrop worried about how the colonists would treat each other amid the harsh realities of the American wilderness. Extraordinary circumstances required extraordinary generosity, even toward those who could not repay, but the bond of love among Christians—especially among those who had chosen to emigrate together—was stronger than any other. They needed to remember why they had come: "that ourselves and posterity may be the better preserved from the common corruptions of this evil world, to serve the Lord and work out our salvation under the power and purity of his holy ordinances." He said little about evangelizing Indians.[28]

They were entering a covenant with God, he reminded the colonists. They had promised that if God brought them safely to America, they would serve him faithfully. "Now if the Lord shall please to hear us and bring us in peace to the place we desire, then hath he ratified this covenant and sealed our commission." If so, God would "expect a strict performance of the articles contained in it," which placed them in a situation like that of Israel. If they acted justly, loved mercy, and walked humbly with God, "we shall find that the God of Israel is among us, when ten of us shall be able to resist a thousand of our enemies, when he shall make us a praise and glory, that men shall say of succeeding plantations: the Lord make it like that of New England."

But if they fell short, "we must consider that we shall be as a city upon a hill. The eyes of all people are upon us, so that if we shall deal falsely with our God in this work we have undertaken and so cause him to withdraw his present help from us, we shall be made a story and a byword throughout the world. We shall open the mouths of enemies to speak evil of the ways of God. . . . We shall shame the faces of many of God's worthy servants and cause their prayers to be turned into curses upon us, till we be consumed out of the good land whither we are going."

He quoted Moses's final words to Israel from Deuteronomy 30. If they obeyed God's commands and kept his ordinances, they would prosper, but if they served pleasure and profit, "we shall surely perish out of the good land whither we pass over this vast sea to possess it. Therefore let us choose life, that we and our seed may live by obeying his voice and cleaving to him, for he is our life and our prosperity."[29]

AFTER A TEN-WEEK voyage, the *Arbella* signaled its approach to Salem early on the morning of June 12, 1630, by firing two cannons. After they landed, John Endecott gave Winthrop a discouraging briefing. Eighty settlers had died over the winter, many were in poor health, and there was little food. Winthrop settled at Charlestown, where he and others formed a church pastored by John Wilson. Others established towns around the bay: Lynn, Medford, Watertown, Roxbury, and Dorchester. They established a General Court to govern. Its members, known as assistants or magistrates, were elected by the colony's freemen.

The death toll was staggering. On July 2, Winthrop's adult son, Henry, drowned while swimming across a river. "My son Henry, my son Henry, ah poor child!" Winthrop lamented in a letter to his wife. Scurvy and other diseases claimed more victims, including the Lady Arbella and Salem minister Francis Higginson. "We may not look at great things here," Winthrop conceded to his wife. "It is enough that we shall have heaven, though we should pass through hell to it. We here enjoy God and Jesus Christ, is not this enough?" It was not enough for the two hundred colonists who gave up and returned to England.

Charlestown lacked sufficient fresh water, so in September Winthrop and others resettled on a peninsula across the river connected to the mainland by a narrow neck. They named the settlement Boston. Conditions deteriorated during the winter. Many "poorer" colonists still lived in tents and struggled to keep warm. Provisions ran dangerously low, reducing them to eating "clams and muscles and ground-nuts and acorns." Practicing what he preached, Winthrop dressed humbly and labored alongside his servants. He was so generous with his provisions that, according to an early historian, on February 5 he "was distributing the last handful of the meal in the barrel unto a poor man" when they spotted a ship, "laden with provisions." By then another two hundred people were dead.[30]

Winthrop was encouraged to learn that Roger Williams, "a godly minister," was on board. About twenty-eight years old, Williams was winsome, ambitious, and incessantly thoughtful. But as Winthrop would learn, he was not one to compromise on religious matters. He would pursue his own understanding of Christianity, even when it led to radical conclusions that undermined the Puritan certainty that their colonial endeavors were blessed by God. He would play an outsized role in New England over the next half-century.[31]

Williams grew up in the bustling Smithfield neighborhood of London. Refugee and separatist groups met nearby, and when he was around eight, a heretic was burned at the stake within sight of his home. Later he recalled that as a boy God "touched my soul with a love to himself, to his only begotten, the true Lord Jesus, [and] to his holy scriptures." As a teenager, he caught the eye of Sir Edward Coke, chief justice of the King's Bench and a hero to opponents of royal absolutism, who selected Williams as an apprentice. Coke's instruction and devotion to liberty left a profound mark on Williams. He went on to study at Pembroke College, Cambridge, and was ordained as a minister. He married Mary Bernard, a Puritan pastor's daughter, and soon decided that the *Book of Common Prayer* violated his conscience. John Cotton, the popular Puritan preacher, suggested he select faithful prayers from the *Book of Common Prayer* while ignoring the rest, but Williams declared this too great a compromise.[32]

His reputation preceded him, so Boston's church voted unanimously to call him as a minister. Yet it bothered Williams that the congregation considered itself part of the Church of England. "I conscientiously refused," he later recalled, "because I durst not officiate to an unseparated people."[33] The people of Boston were irritated when he subsequently agreed to serve at Salem. But soon Williams moved on to join the separatist community at Plymouth. Plymouth governor William Bradford wrote that "his teaching was well approved, for the benefit of which I still bless God and am thankful to him, even for his sharpest admonitions and reproofs, so far as they agreed with the truth."[34]

Williams had no intention of settling as a minister. He longed to be a missionary.[35] He began trading with Wampanoags and Narragansetts and tried to learn their language. "God was pleased to give me a painful, patient spirit to lodge with them in their filthy, smoky hills," he later recalled. He gave gifts to Ousamequin, the Wampanoag sachem, and befriended Canonicus, the Narragansett sachem "most shy of all English." As he considered purchasing land for a trading post, he thought about colonization in a way few English did: from the Indians' perspective. He began to question the king's right to claim Native land.[36]

MASSACHUSETTS GOVERNOR WINTHROP could not have been happier about the Native response to English settlement. The Massachusetts and Pennacooks were too weak to oppose the English and viewed them as potential protectors against the Mi'kmaqs. On March 23, 1631, the wary Massachusett sachem Chickataubut, whose men Captain Standish's Plymouth forces had murdered eight years earlier, presented Winthrop with a hogshead of corn. Winthrop responded with a night of hospitality and dinner the next day. A few weeks later, Chickataubut traded two large beaver pelts for English clothes. Three days after that, the "handsome young" Pennacook Sagamore John and his brother

Sagamore James, who together had thirty or forty men, obtained Winthrop's aid in recovering beaver skins of which they had been cheated. By May, John and Chickataubut had promised to "make satisfaction" whenever their men wronged colonists.[37]

Larger, more distant tribes also reached out. On April 4, Sagamore John brought the sachem Wahginnacut from the distant Connecticut Valley. Wahginnacut's people had been defeated by the mighty Pequots, who lived in what is now southeastern Connecticut. Hoping an alliance might strengthen his hand, he described the fruitfulness of the valley and offered tribute if colonists settled there. But Winthrop declined, not wanting to see his godly society scattered. Three months later, Sagamore John brought Canonicus's son to see Winthrop. The Narragansett gave Winthrop a pelt, and Winthrop reciprocated with dinner and a pewter pot.[38]

Time and again Algonquians demonstrated goodwill: rescuing colonists who were shipwrecked and stranded, capturing a man wanted for bigamy. They welcomed travelers into their wigwams, fed them, and guided them through the woods. "These Indians are of affable, courteous, and well-disposed natures, ready to communicate the best of their wealth to the mutual good of one another," praised colonist William Wood. "They are as willing to part with their mite in poverty as treasure in plenty."

Even so, there was conflict from the start. Colonists did not confine their cattle, which were invasive to America, so wandering animals trampled and devoured Native crops, and Indians retaliated by harming the animals. The court attempted fair settlements, requiring each party to pay restitution, but instead of making colonists control their cattle, as in English law, it told sachems they had to fence their own fields.

The court punished colonists for theft and other crimes against Indians. When an Indian couple complained that a young colonist solicited the woman for sex, the court had him whipped. It tried to forestall conflict by limiting trade to specified times and locations and forbidding the sale of guns, and it forbade settlers from employing Natives without a license. Most important, it prohibited colonists from purchasing land directly from Indians or settling anywhere without court permission. All land transactions had to be processed by the court. This enabled the government to protect Indians from predatory colonists, but it also prevented competition, ensuring that land remained cheap.[39]

It was clear that when push came to shove, the English held the upper hand. Unlike Plymouth, which had to treat the Wampanoags as allies, the Massachusetts Bay colonists heavily outnumbered the Massachusetts and Pennacooks and treated them as subjects. Its court issued the final judgment in all disputes, holding sachems accountable for their people's behavior. While it tried to rule fairly, it was inevitably biased and followed English principles of justice, not

Algonquian. Given that they regarded the Natives as savages, colonists would not have had it any other way.

Many believed it was only a matter of time before Indians recognized the superiority of English culture and embraced Christianity. Sagamore John wanted to learn English, dress in English clothes, and learn about Christianity, because, he said, "Much good men, much good God." One man urged John Winthrop Jr., Governor Winthrop's son, to win over the sachem by giving him a scarlet coat. "The more love and respect you show to the sagamores and sachems, the more love and fear shall you gain from the common Natives," he argued. If gifts could "blind the wise," according to a proverb, "how much more them that are ignorant and simple, as I think all the Natives are."[40]

But although Sagamore John "did resolve and promise to leave the Indians and come live with us," a colonist reported, he could not overcome his fear of the "scoffs of the Indians."[41] Nor did other Natives flock to Christianity. This was disappointing, but Puritans had a ready explanation: saving Native souls meant driving the Devil from his kingdom, which he was sure to resist. Boston pastor John Wilson found a metaphor for the struggle in a story about a mouse that killed a snake. The snake represented the Devil, while the mouse represented the "poor contemptible people which God had brought hither, which should overcome Satan here and dispossess him of his kingdom."[42]

Puritans concluded that until Indians were converted, they remained servants of Satan who could not be trusted. This, in turn, bred fear of Indian attack. The smallest incident, such as a colonist firing his musket while searching for a lost calf, could send men scurrying for their guns. Algonquians remained far more likely to fight each other, however. In August 1631, Mi'kmaq warriors attacked a Pennacook village, killing seven men, wounding sagamores John and James, and capturing James's wife. Not wanting to be drawn into an Indian war, the colony ransomed the woman for wampum and pelts. Winthrop also refused to retaliate when Mi'kmaqs murdered a trader off the coast of Maine, noting the trader "was a wicked fellow and had much wronged the Indians."

Colonial authorities did respond when security demanded it. When Mi'kmaqs captured a ship and murdered five colonists, the authorities hanged the perpetrators. When they learned that warriors were gathering nearby, they sent militia to disperse them. In April 1632, Narragansetts attacked Ousamequin at Sowams with a "great army," forcing him to take refuge at a Plymouth trading post. Plymouth dispatched Captain Standish with soldiers and requested help from Massachusetts Bay. The Narragansetts withdrew, fearing an attack from the Pequots to the west, but two weeks later Winthrop learned that the Narragansetts and Pequots were making peace. This was distressing, for friendship between such "professed enemies" raised the specter of a pan-Algonquian alliance. For a while, tensions seemed to settle down. The Narragansett sachem Canonicus's nephew Miantonomo even attended church during a visit to Boston. But by September there were reports of large gatherings of Narragansetts and Pennacooks, an English trader was murdered in a Pennacook wigwam, and Massachusetts Bay mobilized its militia again.[43]

The dream of Indian conversion was fading in the face of tensions that threatened to burst into war at any moment.

HARASSMENT OF PURITANS in England intensified during the 1630s, leading thousands more to migrate to New England. By 1632 the population of Massachusetts had reached two thousand, dwarfing that of Plymouth. In 1634 it reached four thousand, and by 1637 it had doubled again, to eight thousand.[44] In 1633, John Cotton arrived along with his friend and fellow minister Thomas Hooker. It brought him immense "grief to be cast out into a wilderness," Cotton admitted, but his success in evading the authorities had come to an end. They had to disguise themselves to avoid inspectors at their port of embarkation. Now they became New England's leading clergy. Cotton was installed alongside Wilson as pastor in Boston. Hooker became a minister in Newtown, later renamed Cambridge.[45]

Puritans wanted Massachusetts to be a Christian commonwealth and developed a unique political system over the course of the 1630s. It was a creative reflection of Puritan ideals, combining an unprecedented measure of republican democracy with firm religious constraints. In 1631, the court extended voting rights to all male church members. (In England, only men with substantial property could vote.) In each new community, Puritans established covenants forming self-governing towns and churches. They tried to apportion land equitably, following a basic policy of equality while granting slightly larger tracts to men of higher social status. Based on the principle that people should not be taxed without their consent, the magistrates granted towns the right to send two deputies to meetings of the General Court. The government became bicameral, with a Court of Assistants (or magistrates) that met regularly and a House of Deputies that assembled less often. Though Puritans agreed that government's power came from God, not the people, Massachusetts was the most democratic society in Christendom. An unprecedented proportion of men, women, and children were literate, since Puritans wanted everyone to read the Bible and other religious material. Harvard College was founded in 1636. Three years later, Cambridge had a printing press.[46]

The churches also evolved in a democratic direction. Nearly all followed Salem's example, in which members established a covenant forming a church, electing pastors and elders while maintaining congregational control of worship and discipline. The General Court approved these arrangements, occasionally intervening to mediate conflicts and ensure that churches' teachings and practices remained within acceptable bounds. During the following years, however, churches tightened qualifications for membership. Since they aspired to be a body of true believers, congregations required that individuals seeking full membership, which allowed participation in the Lord's Supper, offer a compelling testimony of God's work in their lives.

Since only church members could vote, this development had political implications. Only men who could describe the Spirit's work in their lives to the satisfaction of their congregations could vote or hold political office. Massachusetts might be more democratic than any other society, but it was also determined to be governed by godly men. Furthermore, the General Court never adopted a significant policy without consulting the ministers. The clergy drafted "A Model of Church and Civil Power," articulating the distinct yet complementary responsibilities of church and state. They also endorsed the republican principle that "in a free state no magistrate hath power over the bodies, goods, lands, liberties of a free people, but by their free consent."[47]

Cotton wrote *An Abstract of the Laws of New England* as a draft for the General Court, following the premise that while Massachusetts did not have to adopt the laws of Moses, which were designed for Israel, it should conform to their basic principles. Massachusetts never enacted Cotton's laws, but it did follow his basic approach.[48] For example, while England stipulated the death penalty for certain types of theft, there was no warrant for this in scripture, so Massachusetts lightened the sentence. On the other hand, following the Old Testament, Massachusetts re-established the death penalty for adultery, which was not a capital crime in England (though only two people were ever executed for adultery in Massachusetts).

Puritan noblemen in England looked askance at these trends, which were both too democratic and too theocratic for their liking. When they lobbied for changes, Cotton responded. He conceded that democracy was illegitimate if it meant government by the people, for it was the people who needed to be governed. But he defended the people's right to elect their leaders, which had precedent in the Old Testament. Such a system was not properly identified as democracy, he insisted, because the government was "administered, not by the people, but by the governors." Rather, it was a *status popularis*, or popular constitution, designed according to three fundamental principles: "authority in magistrates, liberty in people, purity in the church."[49]

The Puritan dream was to establish a godly society, and Cotton was thrilled by what they had accomplished. According to a later source, he wrote a friend that "the order of the churches and the commonwealth was now so settled in New England, by common consent, that it brought into his mind the new heaven and the new earth, wherein dwells righteousness."[50]

In time, Puritans hoped, the Natives would embrace the gospel and civilization. The future had never seemed brighter.

3

The Lord Has Cleared Our Title

1633 to 1636

IT WAS ONLY a matter of time before colonists from Plymouth and Massachusetts cast their vision toward the Connecticut Valley. The valley's rich soil beckoned to colonists seeking available farmland. And the Connecticut River offered direct access to Native communities engaged in the lucrative fur trade. But the Dutch were already there, as were many Algonquian communities, and competition was turning the region into a powder keg.

Dutch traders had established a post on the Hudson River, near present-day Albany, six years before the Pilgrims landed, and by 1624 were building New Amsterdam on Manhattan Island. Trade took off when they discovered the Indian fascination with wampum. Algonquians along Long Island Sound and Narragansett Bay produced wampum by stringing together white and purple beads made from the shells of whelks and clams. Prestigious individuals wore it as jewelry and exchanged it during political and social rituals.

The Dutch began using wampum as currency, which was a boon for the powerful Pequots and Narragansetts. The Pequots, whose thirteen thousand people lived east of the Connecticut River, dominated wampum-producing communities on both sides of Long Island Sound as well as fur-trading communities in the lower valley. Through them, the Dutch obtained as many as ten thousand pelts a year. The Narragansetts, according to one colonist, emerged as New England's wealthiest and "most industrious [Natives]," trading wampum to both Indians and English. The Narragansetts and Pequots were rivals, but prosperity had produced a fragile peace.

In 1633, the Dutch built a trading post known as the House of Good Hope forty miles up the Connecticut River, enabling them to trade directly with Indians from the interior. The Pequots rightly saw this as a direct threat to their dominance of the fur trade, so they took action, attacking a party of Indians on their way to Good Hope. In retaliation, the Dutch seized the Pequot sachem Tatobem while he was trading aboard a Dutch vessel, demanding wampum for his release. After the Pequots paid it, the Dutch killed him anyway. The enraged Pequots sought revenge, as demanded by Algonquian justice. Soon they were at war with both the Dutch and the Narragansetts—and on a collision course with the English.[1]

When Plymouth proposed a joint trading venture in the valley, therefore, Massachusetts governor John Winthrop demurred, explaining that "the place was not fit for plantation, there being three or four thousand warlike Indians." So Plymouth acted on its own. It shrewdly undercut the Dutch, procuring land north of Good Hope from a sachem named Natawante in exchange for a promise to help him recover land taken from him by the Pequots. Plymouth built a fortified trading post on the newly acquired land.

Winthrop did send envoys to inform New Netherland that the valley belonged to Massachusetts by charter from the king. The Dutch governor countered that his government had granted it to the Dutch West India Company. He also sent seventy soldiers to demonstrate against Plymouth's post, but without success. That winter, Dutch traders traveled upriver to an Indian fort to dissuade its inhabitants from trading with the English. While they were there, a force beyond anyone's control shattered the region's balance of power: smallpox swept through the community, killing nearly all of its one thousand people. The stunned Dutchmen fled to Good Hope, "almost spent with hunger and cold."[2]

The disease decimated Native communities that had escaped the earlier epidemic. It claimed as many as 75 percent of the Pequots, reducing their population to around three thousand. Colonists reported that seven hundred Narragansetts died, but the actual toll was probably higher.[3] Plymouth governor William Bradford described horrific conditions among Connecticut Valley Indians: "For want of bedding and linen and other helps, they fall into a lamentable condition as they lie on their hard mats, the pox breaking and mattering and running one into another, their skin cleaving by reason thereof to the mats they lie on. When they turn them, a whole side will flay off at once, as it were, and they will be all of a gore blood, most fearful to behold." Desperate for warmth but unable to gather wood, Indians burned the possessions in their homes. Others crawled for water, only to die before they reached it. "Seeing their woeful and sad condition and hearing their pitiful cries and lamentations," compassionate Plymouth traders daily gathered wood and made them fires, brought food and water "while they lived, and buried them when they died." The Natives were grateful, according to Bradford, though few survived to express it.[4]

Smallpox also decimated the remaining Massachusetts and Pennacooks. At one point, colonists entered a wigwam full of dead Indians and found a "poor infant, which lay on the ground sucking the breast of its dead mother."[5] The Massachusett sachem Chickataubut, the Pennacook Sagamore James, and most of their people died. Indians observed that the plagues hardly touched the English. Some concluded that the Christian God was more powerful than their gods and vowed that "if they recovered, they would serve him."

The Pennacook Sagamore John battled hard, expressing his desire to "live with the English and serve their God," but eventually resigned himself to his fate.

"The God of the English is much angry with me and will destroy me," he declared from his bed. "Ah, I was afraid of the scoffs of these wicked Indians. Yet my child shall live with the English, and learn to know their God when I am dead. I'll give him to [Boston pastor] Mr. Wilson. He is a much good man, and much loved me." John died, according to a colonist, "in a persuasion that he should go to the Englishmen's God." His son was one of several Indian orphans who would be raised by colonists.[6]

Despite their sympathy toward suffering Natives, Puritans interpreted the plague as an act of God that would make way for Christ's kingdom in a land long ruled by the Devil. God used this "awful and admirable dispensation" to "make room for his people of the English nation," a colonist wrote. Without this "terrible stroke of God upon the Natives," immigrants would have had "much more difficulty" finding land, and it would have been much more expensive.[7] By killing Indians with small pox, Winthrop argued, "the Lord hath cleared our title to what we possess."[8] God sent the smallpox because Indians had begun "to quarrel with them about their bounds of land" even though colonists had purchased it fairly, one colonist believed. "Thus did the Lord allay their quarrelsome spirits and made room for the following part of his army."[9]

That "army" was not long in coming. The English wanted land, and Massachusett and Pennacook survivors had plenty to spare. They did not have to be forced to give it up. They were eager to acquire English tools, pots, clothing, and other products—and to forge alliances. Despite prices that now seem shocking, they often believed they were getting a fair deal, at least at first. But they did not grasp the full implications of the sales, let alone of colonization.

This was partly due to the relatively slow pace of settlement. Massachusetts and Plymouth typically granted colonists tracts of land on the condition that they purchase it from the Natives, and colonists often purchased land before they were able to settle much of it. Indians continued living on it, hunting and fishing as they had before. Even after settlers began clearing land and constructing towns, nearby Native villages maintained their traditional way of life. As a result, the consequences of the transactions did not seem particularly dire at first. Indians viewed them as treaties of friendship and hospitality permitting shared use, not acts of permanent dispossession. Sometimes they came to colonists expecting further gifts. When colonists did not respond in kind, they were surprised and offended. They had no idea how many thousands of English were coming, or how their way of life would become impossible to sustain.[10]

WHILE THE PURITANS believed God was clearing land for English settlement, the separatist minister Roger Williams was struggling with his conscience. Williams had become convinced that Massachusetts's charter was unjust because it presupposed that "Christian kings (so called) are invested with right by virtue of their Christianity to take and give away the lands and countries of other men." He shared a treatise outlining his arguments with the Plymouth magistrates. Contrary to King James's assertion, he pointed out, England was not the first Christian nation to discover America. Nor was England a genuinely Christian nation. Indeed, King Charles actively supported the cause of Antichrist! Yet even if Charles were a true Christian king, Christianity did not give him the right to take Indians' land without their consent.[11]

Plymouth's governor William Bradford wrote that Williams was "very unsettled in judgment" and began "to fall into some strange opinions, and from opinion to practice, which caused some controversy between the church and him." Williams eventually returned to Salem, where he continued teaching. Plymouth warned authorities in Massachusetts about his ideas.[12]

Governor Winthrop asked Williams for a copy of the treatise, and the magistrates in Boston met to discuss it. They did not like what they read. They showed it to the ministers, who "much condemned Mr. Williams's error and presumption." Massachusetts had a reputation—which it was working hard to dispel—as a refuge for radicals, and even now the king was considering revoking its charter. What would he do if he learned of Williams's treatise? "If it be not treason, yet I dare say it is strange boldness and beyond the limits of his calling," Winthrop wrote former governor John Endecott. If Williams had any love for New England, he would not "have provoked our king against us and put a sword into his hand to destroy us."

What frustrated Winthrop was how Williams caricatured the case for colonization. Massachusetts's right of possession did not depend on Christianity, he argued, nor on discovery, nor solely on the king's charter. It depended on the doctrine of *vacuum domicilium*, which allowed them to occupy unused land, and on their scrupulous care to pay for any land Indians claimed. Every tract they occupied was "by good liking of the Natives." And "if God were not pleased with our inheriting these parts," Winthrop continued, "why did he drive out the Natives before us? And why doth he still make room for us by diminishing them as we increase? Why hath he planted his churches here? Why doth he declare his favorable presence among us by making his ordinances effectual to the saving of many souls? [Even if] we had no right to this land, yet our God hath right to it, and if he be pleased to give it to us (taking it from a people who had so long usurped upon him and abused his creatures), who shall control him or his terms?" In short, God was conquering America; his people were simply accepting his blessings.

Whatever Williams thought of these arguments, he responded meekly. He assured Winthrop that he had never intended his treatise for public consumption and reaffirmed his loyalty. Boston ministers Cotton and Wilson then admitted that the treatise had been "written in very obscure and implicative phrases." Perhaps, they conceded, its arguments were not "so evil as at first they seemed."[13]

⟨≈⟩

THE SITUATION IN THE Connecticut Valley continued to deteriorate. The Pequots sought to avenge their murdered sachem, but fatefully it was on an Englishman, not the Dutch, that they unleashed their fury. In January 1634, word reached Boston that Pequots had killed a Virginia trader named John Stone near the mouth of the Connecticut River. Apparently three of Stone's men had been killed when they went ashore to hunt fowl. A sachem and his men then boarded Stone's vessel while he lay sleeping and "knocked him on the head." They killed his crew and left the boat in flames.[14]

The leaders of Massachusetts had little sympathy for Stone himself. Though he hailed from a prominent London family, Stone had alienated colonial authorities time and again. Once, in New Amsterdam, he tried to steal a vessel from Plymouth loaded with £500 of goods. He was accused of attempting to stab the governor of Plymouth with a dagger.[15] During a visit to Boston, he got drunk and was caught in bed with a married woman. From jail, he threatened to use his connections against Massachusetts. The court banished him, and he was on his way to Virginia when the Pequots killed him. "Thus did God destroy him that so proudly threatened to ruin us," wrote a colonist.[16]

Colonists had no reason to fear the Pequots. Colonist William Wood described them as "just and equal in their dealings, not treacherous either to their countrymen or English."[17] Although the killing of Stone and his crew was alarming, Governor Winthrop was no more inclined to seek revenge than he had been when other renegade colonists were murdered.[18] Few could have imagined that one day Stone's death would be cited as cause for war.

The Pequots were reeling from the epidemic and wars with the Dutch and Narragansetts, and they were desperate for allies and trading partners. In November they sent two ambassadors to Boston with a gift of wampum. According to Winthrop, they offered Massachusetts exclusive trading rights, "all their right to Connecticut," as well as "four hundred fathom of wampum and forty beaver and thirty otter skins" in exchange for trade and friendship. Massachusetts would have no military obligations.[19]

Although it was an incredible offer, the ministers persuaded the magistrates to add one condition: the Pequots had to surrender the men who killed John Stone and his crew. The Pequots demurred. They claimed their warriors had attacked Stone only because he had kidnapped two Pequots and forced them to guide him upstream. Besides, there were few men left to punish: the sachem who led the attack had since been killed by the Dutch, and all but two of his men had died from smallpox. Nevertheless, they agreed to communicate Massachusetts's demand to their sachems, who would decide if the men "were worthy of death." After conferring with the ministers and praying, the magistrates agreed to the treaty.

The next day, they were alarmed to hear that as many as three hundred Narragansetts were at Neponset, several miles from Boston, planning to kill the Pequot ambassadors. They raised a body of troops, but as usual the threat had been exaggerated. Twenty Narragansetts were simply hunting in the woods. The magistrates seized the opportunity to broker peace between the rival Native powers. The Pequots protested that it was dishonorable for them to give wampum to their traditional enemies, so Massachusetts paid it on their behalf. The Pequots then accepted the treaty.[20] It was a high point in Algonquian-English diplomacy and an incredible deal for Massachusetts. In one fell swoop, the colony had secured a claim to the Connecticut Valley, trade with the Pequots, and peace between the region's dominant Native groups.

Tragically, it would not endure. Massachusetts sent a trader named John Oldham to confirm the treaty and initiate trade in early 1635, but the Pequot sachems believed their ambassadors had offered too much wampum and were unwilling to surrender Stone's killers. In effect, they declined to ratify the treaty.[21]

But Massachusetts was unwilling to relinquish its newfound claim to the Connecticut Valley. The year before, the people of Newtown had complained that they lacked sufficient grazing land for cattle and asked to relocate to the valley. After days of heated debate, the magistrates rejected the petition. Massachusetts was a Christian community, Governor Winthrop explained, and colonists ought to remain united as one body. They did permit Oldham to establish a trading post at Pyquag, later renamed Wethersfield.[22]

Now, however, recognizing that smallpox had "cleared" the region of many inhabitants, Massachusetts authorized several towns to migrate to the valley on the condition that "they continue still under this government."[23] Former deputy governor Roger Ludlow led one group to Plymouth's trading post, to the chagrin of Plymouth agent Jonathan Brewster. "Massachusetts men are coming almost daily, some by water and some by land," Brewster complained. "I hope they will hear reason, as that we were here first and entered with much difficulty and danger, both in regard of the Dutch and Indians, and bought the land." But they did not "hear reason." Migrants occupied the meadows around the trading post, establishing what became the town of Windsor. Ignoring Brewster's protests, they claimed that since it was "the Lord's waste, and . . . altogether void of inhabitants," they had as much right to settle there as anyone.[24]

"These oppressors deserve no favor," complained Plymouth's Edward Winslow. It was shameful that "religion should be a cloak for such spirits."[25] But the migrants kept coming, sixty or more at a time: men, women, and children, along with pigs, horses, and cattle.[26] Five parties now had an interest in the same stretch of river: New Netherland, Plymouth, Massachusetts, valley Indians, and the Pequots.

As if it were not crowded enough, in 1635 another colony was established on the river. Rebuffed in their effort to make Massachusetts more aristocratic, several Puritan noblemen claimed a poorly defined tract of land extending from Narragansett Bay westward, based on a patent from the Earl of Warwick. (No certified copy of the Warwick Patent has ever been found, but it would serve as a basis of colonial claims for decades.)[27] They asked twenty-nine-year-old John Winthrop Jr. to initiate the enterprise.

The oldest son of the Massachusetts governor, Winthrop Jr. was an intelligent, ambitious entrepreneur. He was devout but not dogmatic and preferred diplomacy to conflict. As a student at London's prestigious Inner Temple, he had discovered the exciting world of alchemy, a branch of natural philosophy that had as much to do with science and experimentation as with magic or turning metal into gold. He had traveled as far as Constantinople, befriending scholars all over Europe. Like many of them, he believed advances in knowledge, technology, agriculture, and medicine were essential to the progress of humanity. He even brought glassware, chemicals, and books to America and built a research laboratory. While managing Massachusetts's fur trade and serving as a magistrate, he explored the region looking for metal and mineral deposits.[28]

The Warwick patentees instructed him to build a fort and "houses as may receive men of quality" at the mouth of the Connecticut River.[29] A lieutenant named Lion Gardener, former engineer of fortifications for the Dutch Prince of Orange, commenced the work on Winthrop's behalf. On a ten-foot rise near an abandoned Dutch trading post, he built a palisade from which his artillery commanded the river. He named it Saybrook, after two of the patentees, Lord Say and Sele and Lord Brook.[30]

As Saybrook's governor and a Massachusetts magistrate, Winthrop was in an awkward position, for both colonies claimed the Connecticut Valley. Characteristically, he chose to negotiate. In 1636 the settlers upriver recognized his authority as governor, while he recognized their right to the lands they had settled. But with Massachusetts's consent, the settlers established a General Court to govern themselves, the embryo of what would become the colony of Connecticut. Their numbers grew when the minister Thomas Hooker and most of his Newtown congregation purchased land from local sachems and founded Hartford. As historian Francis Jennings observed, Connecticut "presented the curious spectacle of a substantial colony upriver, pretending to have a governor, and a fortified governor downstream, pretending to have a colony."[31]

COLONISTS ALSO SETTLED on Narragansett Bay in 1636, but this colony would not be Puritan. In fact, it would prove an embarrassment to Puritan hopes and an obstacle to Puritan expansion. Its origins lay in the separatist Roger Williams's argument with Massachusetts. Williams had resumed preaching against the charter and, with support from leading colonists, drafted a letter to the king declaring that his "donation of land" was "evil." For months Cotton, Hooker, and other Puritan ministers reasoned with him in vain. They were baffled by his accusation that they claimed Native lands simply by virtue of the king's authority, as if by "murder of the Natives, or by robbery." On the contrary, their intent was "either to take possession of the void places of the country by the law of nature (for *vacuum domicilium*)" or "by way of purchase and free consent."

But Williams rejected their claim that America's forests were "void places." Not only did Indians depend on these forests for game, he pointed out, but they managed them by regularly burning underbrush, just as the nobility in England maintained forests for hunting, which "no man might lawfully invade." Puritan leaders countered that the nobility was entitled to such holdings because of its great "service to church and commonwealth." It also used its land for timber and agriculture. The Indians could hardly own "so vast a continent" simply because they burned it once in a while for "pastime." Anyway, colonists did not interfere with their hunting, and if they did, the General Court provided remedies.[32]

Puritan leaders failed to grasp that hunting was no mere "pastime" for Indians; it was essential to their survival. But their real disagreement with Williams was over jurisdiction. They believed the king held jurisdiction over land the Indians did not directly occupy and that even on land Indians *did* occupy, English law was supreme. Land purchases required the sachems' consent, but once that consent was given, the land no longer remained under Native jurisdiction, as it would in a conventional real estate transaction. It was, in the colonists' view, placed permanently under colonial control. While particular Indians might continue to occupy land their sachems sold, they did so at the colonists' discretion, not as a matter of legal right, whether or not they had personally received compensation. And all were ultimately subjects of the crown. Williams, by contrast, considered the Indians sovereign powers, even of land they did not occupy, over whom the king held no jurisdiction. Thus Indians sold land on their own terms, which colonists had to respect, regardless of English law. While Massachusetts sought to make Indians subjects, albeit by their consent, Williams attempted to treat them as equals.[33]

This was one of many disagreements between Williams and Massachusetts. The colony required residents to swear an oath of allegiance, but Williams had come to believe in religious liberty and viewed oaths as a form of worship the state had no right to impose. He also insisted that Salem cut its ties with Massachusetts's other churches, since they remained part of the Church of England. On October 9, 1635, with the agreement of all ministers present save one, the court banished Williams. Since he was ill and his wife was pregnant, however, the court permitted him to remain until spring, as long as he ceased promulgating his views.

In January the government learned that he was continuing to criticize the colony in meetings at his home. Just as troubling, he was planning a settlement on Narragansett Bay, from which, as Winthrop put it, "the infection would easily spread into these churches." They decided to send Williams back to England at once. Winthrop respected Williams, and he knew he would receive a much harsher sentence in England. He also hoped Williams might yet prove valuable to the colony. So when the government ordered Captain John Underhill to arrest Williams, Winthrop sent a warning. He urged Williams to flee to the wilderness, where he might serve "many high and heavenly and public ends," free from English patents and authorities.

To Williams, it was like a "voice from God." Amid a raging blizzard, he took off through the snow and headed south. Trudging through six-foot drifts in cold that pierced his very soul, he reached Wampanoag country. Edward Winslow "lovingly advised" him that, out of deference to Massachusetts, Plymouth could not let him stay there. He should go to Narragansett country, where he "might be as free as themselves, and we should be loving neighbors."[34]

Williams would never forget the kindness of Winthrop and Winslow, whom he regarded as "eminently wise and Christian governors," but Cotton, the Boston minister, was a different story. While Williams wandered "amongst the barbarians . . . destitute of food [and] of clothes" and "exposed to the mercy of a howling wilderness in frost and snow," Cotton castigated him for his sin. "Had you perished, your blood had been on your own head," the minister wrote.[35]

It was at this time that Williams's friendship with the Narragansett sachem Canonicus paid off. Canonicus and his nephew Miantonomo allowed Williams to settle west of the Seekonk River, a region of rolling, forested hills. Canonicus was unwilling "to sell his land to let in foreigners," Williams claimed, but he gave it to Williams in exchange for gifts. "It was not thousands nor ten thousands of money could have bought of him an English entrance into this bay," Williams insisted. It was friendship.[36]

This was not the whole truth, for Canonicus had recently conquered the land from the Pokanokets, and Ousamequin, the Pokanoket sachem, protested that it was not Canonicus's to give. The Pokanokets had defeated repeated Narragansett attempts to take it, he claimed, until "God . . . subdued me by a plague, which swept away my people and forced me to yield." Canonicus and Miantonomo retorted that Ousamequin had been their subject until his alliance with Plymouth enabled him to rebel against them.[37] Eventually Plymouth governor William Bradford intervened on Williams's behalf. Even if Ousamequin's claim was true, he declared, Williams would "not be molested and tossed up and down again while they had breath in their bodies."[38] Ousamequin must have found this verdict distressing. What did it suggest about Plymouth's commitment to protecting Wampanoag land?

None of this seems to have bothered Williams. Conscious of God's care, he named his settlement Providence and resolved to make it "a shelter for persons distressed for conscience." Joined by his family and a steady trickle of settlers, he granted land to all comers and drew up a compact giving landowners a voice in government. In one respect the compact was unprecedented. It made no mention of God. Williams was devout as any Puritan, but he had come to believe in a sharp separation of church and state.[39] To the Puritans of Massachusetts, the idea was abhorrent. They considered Williams's colony, which would become Rhode Island, a direct challenge to their mission to establish Christ's kingdom in America.

COLONIAL EXPANSION IN the Connecticut Valley and on Narragansett Bay made future conflict inevitable. No Algonquian community had yet been willing to challenge Puritan dominance, nor did they know how the Puritans would respond if they did. The test was not long in coming.

4

War with the Pequots

1636 to 1637

NATIVE COMMUNITIES ON both sides of Long Island Sound chafed at their domination by the Pequots. When English colonists moved into the Connecticut Valley, some tribal leaders saw an opportunity to weaken their Pequot overlords. Among them was an upstart sachem named Uncas, son-in-law of the recently murdered Pequot sachem Tatobem and brother-in-law of Tatobem's successor, Sassacus. Uncas's Mohegan people lived around the headwaters of the Pequot (modern-day Thames) River. Although the Mohegans and Pequots were closely related, Uncas repeatedly rebelled against Sassacus. But he had only about fifty warriors and was easily defeated.[1]

Seeking allies, Uncas sought to ingratiate himself to the English. In June 1636 he informed Plymouth's Connecticut Valley agent, Jonathan Brewster, that the Pequots were planning to raid English settlements. They were also, he claimed, lying about the men who had killed the trader John Stone. Five, including Sassacus, were still alive. There was every reason to doubt Uncas's credibility, given his ulterior motives, but several colonists had recently been killed on Long Island, and colonists suspected the Pequots of that too. Brewster relayed Uncas's warnings to Winthrop Jr., governor at Fort Saybrook, imploring that all boats coming upriver be armed and alert.[2]

Processing such intelligence in Boston was an inexperienced new governor named Henry Vane. Just twenty-three and fresh from England, Vane owed his election to the prominence of his father, comptroller of the king's house.[3] He and John Winthrop, now Massachusetts's deputy governor, decided to confront the Pequots. They sent Winthrop Jr. to charge the Pequots with a host of infractions: breaking the previous year's treaty by refusing to surrender Stone's killers and failing to send all the wampum their ambassadors had promised (never mind that their sachems had not consented to it), killing three colonists on Long Island, and conspiring against the English. Winthrop Jr. should explain, they said, that the English did not "take revenge" for injuries "until the parties that are guilty have been called to answer fairly for themselves." If the Pequots could "clear themselves," Massachusetts would renegotiate the treaty. But if they were found guilty and refused to deliver the murderers, Winthrop Jr. was to return the original payment of wampum, declare the treaty void, and announce that Massachusetts would "revenge the blood of our countrymen."[4]

Vane and Winthrop probably had Boston minister John Cotton's encouragement. Back in 1630, Cotton had preached that if Natives wronged colonists and refused to offer recompense, the English had the right to conquer them. But what Vane and Winthrop were proposing was an ultimatum rather than a serious effort at diplomacy, and it betrayed their attitude of moral superiority. If the sachems accepted their terms, they would essentially be surrendering their sovereignty over their own people. That was exactly what the Puritan magistrates believed Natives should do, if they knew what was best for themselves.

Lieutenant Gardener, the commander at Fort Saybrook, was horrified. He considered the ultimatum a virtual declaration of war. Neither Saybrook nor the Connecticut Valley settlements were remotely prepared for a conflict. If Massachusetts risked their destruction for the sake of a despicable Virginian like Stone, he protested, they must "love the Virginians better than us."[5]

If Winthrop Jr. ever met with Pequot leaders, the meeting was swiftly overtaken by events. On July 20 a Connecticut trader named John Gallop was navigating his twenty-ton bark toward Long Island when a sudden shift of wind forced him off course. As he neared Manisses, which Europeans called Block Island, he spotted a small vessel, called a pinnace, owned by trader John Oldham. He signaled his approach.

When he drew near, he saw that the deck of the pinnace was full of Indians: fourteen by Gallop's count, armed with guns, swords, and pikes. Other Indians were paddling a canoe laden with goods toward shore. Startled at Gallop's appearance, the Indians attempted to sail the pinnace toward the Narragansett mainland. Gallop and his crew of three opened fire, sending Indians scurrying under the hatches. Catching a good wind, Gallop then rammed the pinnace, nearly capsizing it. Six Indians panicked and leaped off. Gallop pulled back, fitted his anchor to his ship's bow, and rammed the pinnace again, punching a hole through its bow.

At this point four or five more Natives jumped overboard, so Gallop boarded the pinnace. Two Indians surrendered, while two others held out below deck. Deciding it was too dangerous to keep two prisoners, he bound and tossed one into the sea, drowning him. He found Oldham's body under an old fishing net, "stark naked, his head cleft to the brains, and his hand and legs cut as if they had been cutting them off, and yet warm." Gallop then cut the pinnace loose and sailed away.[6]

Oldham had been sailing with two Narragansetts and two English boys. About a week later, the two Narragansetts arrived in Boston with a letter from the exiled Roger Williams. The Narragansetts were "grievously" afflicted by Oldham's murder, Williams explained on behalf of their sachem, Canonicus.

They blamed the Manisses, fellow members of the Narragansett confederation. Canonicus had already dispatched his nephew Miantonomo with two hundred warriors to take revenge.

Governor Vane and the magistrates were skeptical. When they interrogated Gallop's remaining prisoner, he claimed that all the Narragansett sachems except Canonicus and Miantonomo had conspired in Oldham's murder, resenting him for trading with the Pequots, their traditional enemies. The two Narragansetts were also involved. Vane then wrote to Williams demanding the return of the captive boys. Although Massachusetts would not detain the two Narragansetts since they had come as diplomats, he instructed Canonicus to be ready to hand them over to English justice. He knew the sachems would regard this as a violation of their sovereignty, and he cautioned Williams that war might be imminent.

Canonicus and Miantonomo proved cooperative. They admitted that many Narragansett sachems had been involved in the attack and ordered the sachem Ninigret, Canonicus's nephew and Miantonomo's cousin, to recover the boys and send them to the English. They also secured some of Oldham's property, including nearly one hundred fathoms of wampum. Massachusetts then demanded that the perpetrators be surrendered to the colony, including six "under-sachems." The colony wanted justice by English standards, not Algonquian.[7]

This was the same domineering line Massachusetts was taking toward the Pequots, and it threatened to put the colony at war with New England's two most powerful Agonquian peoples. To avoid this, and if possible to recruit the Narragansetts against the Pequots, Massachusetts sent a delegation to Canonicus. The delegation included the Massachusett sachem Cutshamekin, a tributary of the Narragansetts. The delegates were "entertained royally," feasting on sweet boiled chestnuts and boiled pudding made with corn and blackberries. Then they were led into a fifty-foot wigwam for an audience with Canonicus and Miantonomo. The elderly Canonicus "lay along upon the ground on a mat, and his nobility sat on the ground, with their legs doubled up, their knees touching their chin."

The sachems listened gravely to the interpreter's words. Canonicus exhibited "marvelous wisdom in his answers . . . clearing himself and his neighbors of the murder and offering assistance for revenge of it, yet upon very safe and wary conditions." Delegates were surprised at "how solidly and wisely these savage people did consider of the weighty undertaking of a war, especially old Canonicus."

Miantonomo pointed out that his warriors outnumbered the English by a wide margin and controlled the woods and swamps, giving them a decided advantage. But he respected English weaponry, "especially their guns, which were of great terror to his people," and knew there were many more people where they came from. As for the cruel Pequots, with their "aptness to make war," Miantonomo feared the peaceable Narragansetts would suffer grievously from their "sudden incursions." It was safest for his people to remain neutral. Canonicus warned Pequot ambassadors not to alienate the English, "laying before them the sad effects of war." Surely it was wise to surrender men who had shed English blood, if that was necessary to appease them.[8]

That was what the English wanted to hear.

MASSACHUSETTS WAS ALREADY concluding that the time for negotiation was over. On August 25, 1636, the magistrates asked the ministers for advice "about doing justice upon the Indians for the death of Mr. Oldham." The Puritan elite deliberated. The proper authority, all agreed, was scripture. Most relevant were the laws God gave Israel through Moses. But which laws applied to the case at hand? For example, God's command to the Israelites to conquer Canaan by slaughtering men, women, and children did not authorize the Puritans to do the same in America. Israel's mission was unique and never to be repeated.

Other laws, however, such as those found in Deuteronomy 20, reflected binding Christian principles. If one party harmed another, for example, it should pay restitution and the offender be "severely punished." But if the Indians denied the English this right, as John Cotton would write, "and it will not stand with the honor of God and safety of our nation that the wrong be passed over, then war is to be denounced and undertaken." They were authorized to "smite every male thereof with the edge of the sword," but they were to temper violence with justice, compassion, and respect for creation. Thus fruit trees and crops were to be preserved, and "women (especially such as have not lain by man), little children, and cattle are to be spared and reserved for spoil." Furthermore, Christians should not form alliances with pagans, for their armies were the armies of God.[9]

Cotton's views were typical among seventeenth-century Europeans. Killing civilians was common in war, especially if they were considered traitors, criminals, or simply non-Christians. And while slavery had largely been abolished in England, it remained lawful in certain circumstances. The great jurist Sir Edward Coke, Roger Williams's mentor, affirmed that a person "taken in battle should remain bound to his taker forever, and he to do with him [and] all that should come of him [according to] his will and pleasure, as with his beast or any other cattle, to give, or to sell, or to kill."

Massachusetts believed the Natives needed a lesson in justice. It ordered former governor John Endecott to lead ninety soldiers and two Indian guides, including the Massachusett sachem Cutshamekin, "to put to death the men of Block Island but to spare the women and children, and to bring them away and to take possession of the island." The message would be loud and clear: Indians who refused justice for murdered colonists would be killed, their families enslaved, and their land occupied. Next Endecott was to "go to the Pequots to demand the murderers of Captain Stone and other English and one thousand fathom of wampum for damages . . . and some of their children as hostages." If they refused these exorbitant demands, he was authorized to use force, warning that the longer they resisted, the more severe English terms would become.[10]

Massachusetts ensured that its orders would be carried out aggressively, for Endecott was known for his religious zeal, and his soldiers would be volunteers whose only pay came from plunder. Captain John Underhill, his second-in-command, was equally zealous. Just shy of forty, he had grown up in the Netherlands and served in the Prince of Orange's guard before emigrating to New England and becoming a militia officer. He believed God had "stirred up the heart" of the magistrates to order this expedition. John Oldham was a martyr whose blood "called for vengeance."[11]

⁂

NINE MILES FROM the mainland, Block Island encompassed just under ten square miles "full of small hills" and "overgrown with brush-wood of oak." The Manisses inhabited several villages totaling about sixty wigwams and were beginning to harvest their corn when, in late August, they spotted Endecott's three approaching pinnaces.

Underhill and a dozen men boarded a small vessel, called a shallop, to head for shore. He wore a helmet in deference to his wife, though he would have preferred to forgo its weight and heat. While struggling to navigate the heavy surf, the men anxiously scanned the bank for signs of the enemy. Suddenly fifty or sixty "men straight as arrows, very tall, and of active bodies," emerged from the woods and launched a hail of arrows at the shallop. One penetrated a soldier's neck "as if it had been an oaken board." Another struck a soldier's leg. An arrow tore through Underhill's sleeve and a second slammed into his helmet, confirming his wife's good sense. But while arrows were "flying thick," they failed to penetrate the armor the soldiers wore over their chests and upper legs.

The turbulence of the surf prevented the English from firing their muskets, but finally they were able to jump out of the shallop into waist-deep water. There they could dodge incoming arrows and return fire. The Manisses soon realized they were outmatched and withdrew into the woods. Once on shore, Underhill's men united with Endecott's, who had landed further downshore. They posted guards, and that night the anxious soldiers tried to sleep, "expecting hourly they would fall upon us."

They moved inland in the morning, scanning the woods for signs of the enemy. Eventually a detachment penetrated a swamp where the Manisses had hidden their women and children. (Algonquians believed Manitou, the

force that permeates the world, and associated spiritual guardians were especially powerful in swamps.) The warriors were dismayed to see a Massachusett
among the soldiers, carrying a gun and wearing English clothes. "What are you,
an Indian or an Englishman?" they cried. "Come hither and I will tell you," he
retorted, before killing an Indian with a musket shot.

Endecott feared losing his men in such terrain, so he turned them against the
islanders' villages and crops, a tactic the English had often used against the Irish
(but that Cotton had condemned). All day, soldiers "burned and spoiled both
houses and corn in great abundance." They even killed the Manisses' dogs. After
taking some "well-wrought mats" and "several delightful baskets," they destroyed
everything else, including seven canoes.

But Endecott failed in his primary mission: killing the Manisses warriors
and capturing their families. Although Underhill claimed they killed fourteen
Indians, the Narragansetts later reported only one islander killed. Still, Endecott
doomed them to a winter of famine and hardship while avoiding significant
casualties. Deciding his work was done, he set sail for Fort Saybrook.[12]

WHEN HE FIRST heard of the orders given to Endecott, Saybrook's Lieutenant
Gardener was aghast. He had no doubt the Pequots "plotted our destruction,"
but a raid on Pequot country would provoke devastating counterattacks in
the Connecticut Valley. "You come hither to raise these wasps about my ears,"
he scolded, "and then you will take wing and flee away." Knowing his protests
were futile, he urged Endecott to seize enough Pequot corn to feed his garrison
through the war, offering men, boats, and bags for the task.[13]

Roger Williams claimed the Pequots knew the expedition was coming but
believed "a witch amongst them will sink the pinnaces by diving under water and
making holes," something he probably heard from the Narragansetts. "I hope
their dreams, through the mercy of the Lord, shall vanish," he wrote, "and the
Devil and his lying sorcerers shall be confounded."[14]

In fact, as Endecott sailed east toward the Pequot River, the Pequots' Western
Niantic tributaries ran along the shore shouting greetings. "What cheer
Englishmen, what cheer, what do you come for?" Clearly they had no idea that
the English "intended war." According to Underhill, the officers decided not to
answer so that "we might drive them in security, to the end we might have the
more advantage of them." But this made them suspicious. "What Englishman,
what cheer, what cheer, are you hoggery, will you cram us?" they asked. The
English knew what they meant: "Are you angry? Will you kill us, and do you
come to fight?"

Endecott entered the Pequot River late that day. As darkness fell, Pequots lit
signal fires along the banks, and all that night soldiers heard the "most doleful
and woeful cries . . . so that we could scarce rest." Underhill believed the Pequots

were "giving the word from place to place, to gather their forces together, fearing the English were come to war against them."

The next morning, a canoe approached carrying a Pequot ambassador, "a grave senior, a man of good understanding, portly, carriage grave, and majestic in his expressions." When he asked why they had come, they explained that Massachusetts demanded the heads of Captain Stone's killers, since "it was not the custom of the English to suffer murderers to live." If the sachems "desired their own peace and welfare," they should readily comply.

The emissary replied that his sachems saw things differently. True, Pequots had killed Captain Stone and his crew, but on legitimate grounds. Dutch traders had treacherously murdered their sachem Tatobem, and "suddenly after came these captains with a vessel into the river and pretended to trade with us as the former did," he explained. Assuming Stone was Dutch and that his intentions were equally nefarious, Tatobem's son entered Stone's cabin, found him passed out drunk, and "knocked him in the head" with a hatchet. Stone's crew then blew themselves up when they accidentally set fire to their gunpowder. "Could you blame us for revenging so cruel a murder?" the ambassador asked. "For we distinguish not between the Dutch and the English, but took them to be one nation, and therefore we do not conceive that we wronged you, for they slew our king, and thinking these captains to be of the same nation and people as those that slew him made us set upon this course of revenge."[15]

Such words might have given Endecott pause. Algonquian justice was not English justice, but that hardly justified war. He could have taken the ambassador's explanation to Boston and let the magistrates pursue further diplomacy. But that was not the sort of man Massachusetts had chosen to lead this expedition. The officers retorted that the Pequots "were able to distinguish between Dutch and English, having had sufficient experience of both nations." Stone and his crew were the king's subjects, and Massachusetts was "liable to account for them." It was a simple matter of justice.

The ambassador insisted they had not grasped Stone's identity. "We crave pardon. We have not willfully wronged the English," he pleaded.

But Endecott would not yield. Give us the heads of the men who killed Stone and his crew, he replied, "or else we will fight with you."

The ambassador finally requested permission to relay this message to his sachems. "If you will stay aboard," he promised, "I will bring you a sudden answer." This was wise advice, for disembarking on Pequot land drastically increased the likelihood of violence. Nevertheless, when the ambassador went ashore, Endecott quickly followed with his soldiers, determined to be in position to strike before the Pequots organized their forces.

The portly Pequot rushed back and begged them "to come no nearer" but remain by the bank. But Endecott suspected a trap, for the ground rose from the river to "high, rugged rocks," leaving his soldiers extremely vulnerable. He organized a line of battle and "marched up to the ascent." There he held his position while the ambassador departed. When he returned, he claimed the sachems had gone to Long Island and were expected within a few hours. This the officers refused to believe. If the sachem Sassacus did not show up soon, they threatened, "we will beat up the drum and march through the country and spoil your corn."

The ambassador promised to try again, so Endecott waited another hour before word arrived that a lesser sachem had been located. Another hour passed before a messenger explained that he was gathering a council to determine who had slain Stone and his crew. Endecott's anxiety grew. His armored soldiers stood in the blazing summer heat while hundreds of unarmed Pequots gathered nearby, some talking with Gardener's men, whom they knew. Endecott became convinced they were simply stalling while they whisked their vulnerable population to safety, hid their valued possessions, and gathered their forces.

Thus, when a messenger finally indicated that the Pequots were ready to talk, requesting that both sides lay down their weapons, Endecott refused. He told the Pequots to "be gone and shift for themselves, for they had dared the English to come fight with them, and now they were come for that purpose." He allowed them to withdraw, as he thought honor demanded. Then, with drums beating and flags waving, his soldiers advanced. The Pequots kept their distance, though Underhill claimed they "laugh[ed] at us for our patience." Exasperated, Endecott unleashed his men, who began shooting at any Pequots they saw. A few Pequots fired arrows from behind thickets and rocks, but they did little damage. The soldiers devastated a Pequot town, "firing their wigwams, spoiling their corn," and digging up valuables.

By afternoon, Endecott was anxious to get back to his pinnaces. Somehow, his men embarked without notifying Gardener's men, who were busy gathering corn and suddenly came under attack from furious Pequots. Fortunately for them, they "could easily see and avoid" the Pequots' arrows, and only two were wounded as they executed a fighting retreat to their boats. Endecott's soldiers raided Western Niantic territory the next day before returning to Boston.[16]

John Winthrop considered it "a marvelous providence of God" that not a single soldier was killed. Narragansetts reported that thirteen Pequots had been killed and forty wounded. Cutshamekin, the Massachusett sachem, sent a Pequot scalp as tribute to the Narragansett sachem Canonicus. Pleased at the defeat of his rivals, Canonicus passed the scalp among his sachems, summoning them to war. He "returned many thanks to the English and sent four fathoms of wampum to Cutshamekin."[17]

◈

MASSACHUSETTS ASSERTED THE right to subjugate Indians who refused to submit to English justice and assumed Endecott's raid would be sufficient to intimidate them. But the Pequots had their own principles of justice and honor, which required them to avenge their people. Gardener understood this and diligently prepared to defend Fort Saybrook. He took men to harvest the fort's corn, located two miles away on Long Island Sound, posting five men in a small blockhouse nearby. Three guards foolishly went bird hunting and were ambushed. One, with an arrow through his leg, fought his way back to the blockhouse. The others were wounded, captured, and tortured. As the survivors sailed for the fort, they saw the blockhouse go up in flames.

Not long after, men from Wethersfield went to harvest hay on Six Mile Island, upriver from Saybrook. Warriors "rose out of the long grass and killed three," captured a fourth, "and roasted him alive." A corpse washed up near the fort, "an arrow shot into his eye through his head."[18] What was supposed to be a righteous display of Christian justice was devolving into New England's greatest nightmare: full-scale Indian war.

When a report reached Boston that the Pequots were negotiating with the Narragansetts, Governor Vane urged Roger Williams to use his "utmost and speediest endeavors to break and hinder the league." Believing Jesus called him to be a peacemaker even though Massachusetts had exiled him, Williams embarked in his canoe despite "a stormy wind" and paddled thirty miles through "great seas," every minute in "hazard of life," until he reached Canonicus and Miantonomo, the Narragansett sachems. Much to his dismay, there he found "bloody Pequot ambassadors, whose hands and arms (me thought) reeked with the blood of my countrymen murdered and massacred by them on Connecticut River." That night he lay in terror, fearing he might find a knife at his throat.

The Pequot ambassadors labored to convince the Narragansetts that the Pequot cause was their own. The English were not like them, they warned. They had begun "to overspread their country" and would eventually take their land "if they were suffered to grow and increase." "And if the Narragansetts did assist the English to subdue them, they did but make way for their own overthrow, for if they [the Pequots] were rooted out, the English would soon take occasion to subjugate them [the Narragansetts]." Together, however, they might defeat the English. True, the English had vastly superior weaponry, but this would only benefit them in open battle, which the Pequots had no intention of waging. Instead, they would "fire their house[s], kill their cattle, and lie in ambush for them ... without any or little danger to themselves." The English would "either be starved with hunger or be forced to forsake the country."

It was a prescient argument, but Williams reminded the sachems that while the English had never attacked them, the Pequots had done them "much wrong."[19] And after Endecott's successful raid, the Narragansetts were less afraid of the Pequots. Spurning Pequot entreaties, Miantonomo traveled to Boston with twenty-five men, arriving on October 21, 1636. Vane invited Miantonomo and his counselors to dine with him while the others ate at the inn. After dinner, Miantonomo addressed the magistrates and ministers. The Narragansetts had always "loved the English" and wanted peace, he declared. Thus, Winthrop summarized, "they would continue in war with the Pequots and their confederates till they were subdued, and desired we should do so [also]." Miantonomo worried about heavy-handed English justice, however. English cattle damaged Narragansett crops, and Narragansetts sometimes retaliated by killing the animals. He requested that the English "not kill" the Narragansetts in return, "but cause them to make satisfaction."

The English raised their own concerns, including the tendency of servants to run away to Narragansett country. Then they drew up a treaty. Winthrop admitted they lacked an adequate interpreter and "could not well make them understand the articles perfectly," but Massachusetts promised to send a copy to Williams, "who could best interpret" the treaty to the Narragansetts. As usual, the sachems had to sign trusting that what was written matched what was spoken. The treaty itself has been lost. As recorded by Winthrop, the parties promised not "to make peace with the Pequots without the other's consent." The Narragansetts agreed not to harbor Pequots and promised to kill or deliver "murderers" to the English, provide guides for colonial troops, return "fugitive servants," and allow free trade.[20] But Williams highlighted a stipulation favorable to the Narragansetts that Winthrop failed to record: Pequots could "not be sheltered nor disposed of without mutual consent of the English and the two Narragansett sachems."[21] It would prove to be an important discrepancy.

The treaty was a watershed in Puritan-Algonquian relations. Massachusetts had not only thwarted the Pequots' efforts to forge a pan-Algonquian alliance; it had recruited the mighty Narragansetts to defeat them. The Narragansetts clearly valued peace with Massachusetts and a chance to defeat the hated Pequots more than they feared English domination. Like the Wampanoags, they were betting their future on English friendship.

Ironically, while the Narragansetts supported the war, Plymouth would not. Plymouth governor Edward Winslow considered Massachusetts the aggressor for "provoking the Pequots," which meant the war was unjust, and Plymouth resented Massachusetts's aggression in the Connecticut Valley, among other grievances. Winthrop countered that Massachusetts had not sent Endecott to wage war "but to do justice." That the Pequots refused to submit showed that God had "deprived them of common reason."[22]

THE PEQUOTS HAD FORT Saybrook under siege by November. Warriors raided its food supply, killing two oxen, a ram, and twenty-two pigs and destroying abandoned warehouses. Gardener secured sheep and cattle but was running out of hay and fodder and did not know how long he could hold out. "The Indians are many hundreds off both sides of the river and shoot at our pinnaces as they go up and down," he reported. They occasionally fired muskets at the fort. Gardener had predicted the unfolding disaster, he angrily reminded Winthrop Jr., yet Massachusetts was not doing anything about it.[23]

As winter set in, the Pequots focused on hunting and fishing, relieving pressure on the fort. On February 22, 1637, Gardener took ten men to secure timber and burn weeds and reeds from the neck of land connecting Saybrook with the mainland. Much to their surprise, four Indians dashed out of the burning reeds into the far woods. Sentries warned that others were emerging from the far side of a marsh. Gardener tried to organize his men, but two terrified soldiers threw down their guns and ran toward the fort. Indians began firing and moving to cut them off. Gardener formed his men in the shape of a "half-moon" and commenced a fighting retreat. Thomas Hurlbut was shot "almost through the thigh," and John Spencer took an arrow "in the back into his kidneys." Then Gardener was hit in the thigh. Two soldiers were killed, but the rest fought on until they reached the fort. A furious Gardener wanted to hang one of the shirkers as an object lesson, but the fort's young chaplain, John Higginson, persuaded him to show mercy.

A few days later, they retrieved the body of a soldier with an "arrow going in at the right side, the head sticking fast half through a rib at the left side." Bitter at Massachusetts's confident assurances that arrows were harmless, Gardener sent the arrow-embedded rib to Boston.[24]

One day, Indians hiding behind a small rise near the fort signaled a desire to talk. Gardener armed himself with a sword, pistol, and carbine, ordered his men to cover him, and passed through the gate, accompanied by a trader and interpreter named Thomas Stanton. Neither party dared approach too close. The Indians were incredulous that Gardener was alive. Had he not been shot with many arrows? Yes, Gardener admitted, but his buff coat protected him.

The Indians may have hoped to negotiate peace. As they saw it, blood had been shed on both sides, satisfying the demands of honor and justice. They asked if the English would fight against Western Niantics, "for they were our friends and came to trade." But Gardener was in a foul mood and sarcastically retorted that the English did not know one Indian group from another and would not trade with any of them.

"Have you fought enough?" the Indians asked.

Gardener said he did not know.

This could only mean the war would continue, so they posed another question: Did the English kill women and children?

It was a critical moment. Algonquian warriors often spared women and children, capturing them in hopes of incorporating them into their communities. But would the English do the same? Had Gardener attempted to set their minds at ease, things might have turned out differently. But he was not interested in calming Native fears. He simply replied that "they should see that hereafter."

The implied threat left the Indians "silent a small space." When they responded, it was with anger: "We are Pequots and have killed Englishmen and can kill them as mosquitoes, and we will go to Connecticut and kill men, women, and children, and we will take away the horses, cows, and hogs." One Native, wearing an English coat, boasted that he had killed three colonists and was wearing their clothes. Outraged, Stanton urged Gardener to "shoot that rogue." But Gardener attempted damage control. If they ravaged Connecticut for women and plunder, he argued, "it would do them no good, but hurt, for English women are lazy and cannot do their work. Horses and cows will spoil your cornfields, and the hogs their clam banks, and so undo them." He taunted them to try to take the fort, which was full of trade goods, instead. This made them "mad as dogs," ending the conversation. After both parties had withdrawn, Gardener opened fire with his artillery. He sent warning to the towns upriver to take precautions.[25]

The disastrous meeting signaled a more terrible phase of the war. The Pequots were determined to send a message that would force the English to treat them honorably.

WHILE THE PEQUOT War consumed Gardener's attention, Massachusetts was distracted by a religious controversy most Puritans considered much more serious. Military conflict threatened their bodies, but spiritual warfare threatened their very souls. Known to historians as the Antinomian Controversy, the crisis stemmed from the teaching of a Boston woman named Anne Hutchinson, who was hosting large gatherings in her home. At the heart of the Puritan faith was the conviction that salvation is a gift of God. No human being deserves it or can earn it by good deeds. But most pastors preached that by acts of love and righteousness true Christians exhibited evidence of their salvation, and Hutchinson challenged this as a form of legalism contrary to the gospel. She taught that assurance of salvation came directly from the Holy Spirit. Many found her persuasive. One colonist described her as a woman who "would show me a way, if I could attain it, even revelations, full of such ravishing joy that I should never have cause to be sorry for sin, so long as I live."[26]

The controversy exploded when the Boston church voted to call Hutchinson's brother-in-law, Thomas Wheelwright, as a minister. Winthrop blocked the proposal, which required unanimity. Then, while Boston pastor John Wilson was leading a worship service, Hutchinson's followers "contemptuously" turned their backs and marched out of the meeting house. In December 1636, Governor

Vane, who supported Hutchinson, attempted to resign because he feared "God's judgments" on Massachusetts, though he was dissuaded. Then, in a fast-day sermon in Boston on January 19, Wheelwright called the faithful to "prepare for a spiritual combat." As for their opponents, "we must kill them with the word of the Lord," for they were "the greatest enemies to the state that can be." The General Court convicted Wheelwright for "contempt and sedition," but Vane protested and the Boston church appealed. The controversy threatened to dominate the annual May elections.[27]

By contrast, the occasional killing of a soldier or farmer in the Connecticut Valley seemed a distant nuisance. All Massachusetts did in response was dispatch Captain Underhill to Fort Saybrook with twenty men, and even this was largely because it feared an attack by the Dutch. Meanwhile, Pequots taunted the garrison that the Christian god was a mere fly: "Come and fetch your Englishmen's clothes again! Come out and fight if you dare! You dare not fight. You are all one like women. We have one amongst us that if he could kill but one of you more, he would be equal with God, and as the Englishman's God is, so would he be." Such "blasphemous speech troubled the hearts of the soldiers," Underhill admitted. Many concluded that God was preparing the Pequots for destruction.[28]

Finally, on April 18, 1637, the Massachusetts court went into special session to deal with the Pequot crisis. Resolving that it had "just ground" for war, it called the towns to enlist or impress 160 soldiers that it might be "seriously prosecuted." This time they would be paid.[29] According to colonist Edward Johnson, colonists felt "full assured that the Lord would deliver them [the Pequots] into their hands, to execute his righteous judgments upon these blasphemous murderers."[30] They never doubted this was what God wanted them to do.

Five days later, in the Connecticut Valley, everything changed. For the first time, Pequots attacked an English settlement: Wethersfield.

5

Massacre at Mystic

April 1637 to October 1637

WETHERSFIELD WAS NESTLED on the west bank of the Connecticut River, about five miles south of Hartford. Until now its people had lived peacefully alongside the local Wangunks, from whom they had purchased the land in 1634. The sachem Sequin had agreed to the sale because it specified that his people could continue living there, and he hoped the English would protect them from the Pequots. But in the spring of 1637, Wethersfield had a change of heart and drove the Wangunks off their land. Sequin entreated the Pequots for aid, and the Pequots were all too willing to oblige. Embarking in "a great many canoes," they ascended the river, approaching the town on the night of April 22.[1]

Around dawn, Wethersfield's unsuspecting inhabitants roused themselves and headed out to their fields to work. Suddenly, two hundred warriors were upon them, killing people and animals. By the time the bloodletting was over, six men and three women lay dead. Two girls, the older of whom was about sixteen, were taken captive. The victorious war party descended the river until they were spotted by sentinels at Fort Saybrook. Dismayed to see the Indians using the white shirts of colonists as sails, the fort's commander, Lieutenant Gardener, ordered his artillery to fire "two round shot." One crashed through the nose of a canoe. The warriors paddled to shore, "drew their canoes over a narrow beach with all speed, and got away." Only after firing did the officers realize the Wethersfield girls were in the canoes. It was a "special providence of God" the shot did not hit them, marveled Captain Underhill.[2]

The raid shattered the complacency of the valley settlements. Guards were posted day and night. Men carried muskets at all times. It was reported that warriors massacred sixty people at William Pynchon's nascent trade settlement upriver at Springfield. Although the report proved false, the terror was real.[3]

Representatives from Hartford, Windsor, and Wethersfield convened the Connecticut General Court on May 1. Later, colonial authorities would rule that Sequin's attack on Wethersfield was justified because his people had been wrongfully evicted, but at this moment there was no such judicious reflection.[4] The court declared "an offensive war against the Pequots." Although Connecticut's three towns had scarcely 250 people, it called them to muster ninety soldiers, to be commanded by Captain John Mason. In his late thirties, Mason was a veteran of the war in the Netherlands and would prove an aggressive and ruth-less commander.[5]

Rage against the Pequots rose to unprecedented heights. Puritans believed all enemies of the gospel—Catholic, Protestant, or pagan—were under Satan's con-trol, and many thought the Devil had raised up the Pequots to destroy Christ's kingdom in New England. The "old Serpent, according to his first malice, stirred them up against the Church of Christ," Captain Underhill vented. The "wicked imps" had grown so insolent "that like the Devil their commander, they run up and down as roaring lions, compassing all corners of the country for a prey, seeking whom they might devour." Colonists "[hardly dared] rest in their beds."[6]

Lieutenant Gardener had ordered Saybrook's inhabitants not to go ashore, but a trader named Joseph Tilley ignored him, casting anchor three miles up-river to hunt fowl. Indians killed his partner and captured Tilley.[7] They "tied him to a stake, flayed his skin off, put hot embers between the flesh and the skin, cut off his fingers and toes, and made hatbands of them."[8] He survived three days, earning their respect because he never cried out.[9]

FOR THE CONNECTICUT VALLEY clergy, the Wethersfield raid was a turning point. Killing traders on distant waters was one thing. Attacking God's people in their towns was another. It was time for the faithful to act, and it was ministers' responsibility to rouse them. They preached sermons and wrote letters, stirring magistrates and soldiers to action. They called for the aggressive prosecution of what they considered a religious war in defense of Christ's kingdom.

John Higginson, Saybrook's chaplain, wrote that his garrison was scared, discouraged, and felt abandoned. He too was "afraid to die." Mindful that Massachusetts was distracted by controversy, he penned a long letter to Deputy Governor Winthrop, arguing that God had sent "the Indians upon his servants to make them cleave more close together and prize each other." Colonists had boasted that ten Englishmen could whip a hundred Pequots. God was showing how foolish such self-confidence was. Pequot attacks were "heavenly warnings" to prosecute the war "more seriously."

Higginson apprised Winthrop that the crisis was far worse than he thought. Wounded men were crying out in agony. Others were "gasping and dying and breathing out their last." How could Massachusetts be so apathetic? Its people should be opening their purses and extending their hands to defend not only their "lives and liberties" but "the glorious gospel of Jesus Christ." They should not delude themselves that the war would not reach the bay, he warned, "for this seems to be a universal deluge creeping and encroaching on all the English in the land." The Pequots were experienced fighters with significant advantages in agility and arms. They would marshal their resources, "providing retreats at Long Island, fortifying upon the mainland, gathering new supplies of forces, confederating with former enemies, [and] giving large rewards to those amongst them who are most skillful to destroy."

The next stage of the war was critical, for "the eyes of all the Indians in the country are upon the English, to see what they will do." Unless they humbled the "insulting Pequots" speedily, they were "like to have all the Indians in the country about our ears." It was time for God's servants to turn from theological disputes and economic endeavors. It was time for ministers "to press upon the conscience, charge as a duty, [and] command in the name of the Lord from heaven . . . the serious and speedy prosecution of this war."[10]

Connecticut's leading clergyman, Thomas Hooker, reported that Indians who hated the Pequots were pressing for action. If the English delayed, they would attribute it to "base fear and cowardice" and "turn enemies against us." God called the English to strike now, he admonished Winthrop. "I hope you see a necessity to hasten execution and not . . . do this work of the Lord's revenge slackly."[11]

It was probably Hooker who preached to Mason and his ninety soldiers at Hartford. They had not been summoned rashly, nor were they called to acts of "rape, theft, and murder," he declared. They had been "picked out by the godly grave fathers of this government" to "execute those whom God, the righteous judge of all the world, hath condemned for blaspheming his sacred majesty and murdering his servants." The war was a judicial exercise. "Every common soldier among you is now installed a magistrate." The Pequots have "large conceptions against you and all the people of Christ in this wilderness," he continued, but they were cowards who relied on "nimbleness of foot and the inaccessible swamps and nut-tree woods" to protect themselves. Through hard work and clever tactics, the English would defeat them.

Many soldiers fought for plunder and gold, but this army had a nobler purpose: "to maintain [that] which is far more precious: the lives, liberties, and new purchased freedoms, privileges, and immunities of the endeared servants of our Lord Christ Jesus." They were fighting for their loving wives and "harmless prattling and smiling babes." Even more important, they were fighting for "the enjoyment of Christ in his ordinances." They should have no doubts. They were called to "execute vengeance upon the heathen."

Some would die. But "let every faithful soldier of Christ Jesus know that the cause why some of his endeared servants are taken away by death in a just war, as this assuredly is . . . is not because they should fall short of the honors accompanying such noble designs, but rather because earth's honors are too scant for them, and therefore the everlasting crown must be set upon their heads forthwith." They could march firm in the confidence that God went with them. He would crush their enemies, and "your feet shall soon be set on their proud necks."[12]

INSPIRED BY THE righteousness of their crusade, the troops boarded a flotilla of three boats. Uncas, the Mohegan sachem whose reports helped alienate the English from the Pequots, offered to accompany them with at least sixty warriors. Mason accepted his offer, despite misgivings about his trustworthiness.[13]

It was just fifty miles to Saybrook, but crosswinds and shallow water slowed progress to a crawl. Impatient, the Mohegans secured permission to continue on foot. As hours dragged into days, officers worried that this was a mistake. Was Saybrook in danger? Their chaplain, Samuel Stone, prayed that God would provide a sign of the Mohegans' fidelity. No sooner had he finished than Captain Underhill, having traveled upriver from Saybrook, stepped aboard and announced that God already had.

Uncas had reached Saybrook on Sunday. Gardener, knowing the Mohegans "had but that year come from the Pequots," challenged Uncas to prove his loyalty. The next morning, the Mohegans returned with five Pequot heads (or scalps) and two prisoners. Thrilled, Gardener rewarded them with fifteen yards of trading cloth. The Mohegans then took a prisoner, named Kiswas, "tied one of his legs to a post, and twenty men, with a rope tied to the other [leg], pulled him in pieces." Appalled, Underhill put Kiswas out of his misery with a pistol shot.[14]

Mason's flotilla arrived on Wednesday. As usual, Gardener objected to Mason's orders. Mason's force was not remotely large enough to invade the Pequot homeland, he protested. A raid would not be enough; they had to destroy the Pequots. He urged Mason not to attack "unless we that were bred soldiers from our youth could see some likelihood to do better" than Captain Endecott's Massachusetts forces had the year before.[15]

Meanwhile, Dutch traders, having conferred with Gardener, sailed up the Pequot River in hopes of negotiating the release of the Wethersfield girls. The girls had suffered a harrowing few weeks, being taken from one village to another, but the kind wife of the sachem Mononotto protected them. Pequots invited the girls to join their celebrations, but the terrified girls refused. Men solicited the older girl for sex, and she bravely spurned their advances. Much to her surprise, they respected her wishes. The girls felt certain that God was punishing them but remained confident of his love. As the older girl put it, "He hath said he will never leave me, nor forsake me. Therefore I will not fear what man can do to unto me, knowing God to be above man, and man can do nothing without God's permission."

When the Dutch asked the Pequot sachem Sassacus if he would sell the girls, he refused. They were more valuable as captives than anything the Dutch could offer in exchange. So the Dutch resorted to trickery. They invited seven Indians onto their bark, seized them, and threatened to drown them unless Sassacus released the girls. To prove their resolve, they sailed for the mouth of the river. Sassacus finally backed down. Pequots brought the girls, "almost naked," and the Dutch released the Pequots. Providing the girls "their own linen jackets," the traders brought them to Saybrook. Mason, Gardener, and Underhill interviewed them. Had they been mistreated? Were they raped? The girls assured them that the Pequots had not been abusive. Underhill considered them heroes of faith whose rescue testified to God's loving care for his people.[16]

The commanders still had to figure out the best way of getting at the Pequots. Mason's orders required him to attack straight up the Pequot River, as Endecott had done, but Pequot scouts watched the river day and night, and their warriors would bitterly contest a landing. Marching overland from Saybrook was out of the question, for they would inevitably march into an ambush. Eventually someone proposed a third possibility: Why not bypass Pequot country, sail into Narragansett Bay, and surprise the Pequots from the east?

Some questioned whether Mason had the authority to ignore his orders, so Mason asked Chaplain Stone to "commend our condition to the LORD that night, to direct how [and] in what manner we should demean ourselves." The next morning, Stone told Mason that he had prayed and was "fully satisfied to sail for Narragansett." Underhill offered his twenty Massachusetts soldiers for the campaign. Mason gladly accepted, for it enabled him to send back twenty Connecticut men to protect the towns upriver.[17]

Those towns were paralyzed by anxiety. There were not enough men for a decent watch, let alone to plant crops. "My spirit is ready many times even to sink within me . . . upon alarms, which are daily," Windsor colonist Roger Ludlow confided to William Pynchon of Springfield. "I must confess both you and ourselves do stand merely by the power of our God."[18]

MASSACHUSETTS, MEANWHILE, ACTED so lethargically that the Narragansetts questioned whether they could trust its promises. Their sachem Canonicus had become "very sour" toward the English, Roger Williams reported. Canonicus had never been enthusiastic about the war, and now he accused the English of "sending the plague amongst them and threatening to kill him." Williams told him God controlled the plague and inflicted it on the English when they sinned too. It was not the English Canonicus should fear, but God.

Miantonomo, the younger Narragansett sachem, was steadier. His warriors constantly skirmished with Pequots, and he had devised a plan for their defeat. The problem was that any time the English approached the Pequot River, the Pequots would withdraw to Ohomowauke Swamp, three or four miles inland, as they had done when Endecott invaded. Miantonomo suggested the English use Narragansett country as a base from which to launch a surprise attack. He knew two renegade Pequots who could guide them, and they could strike at night, when the Pequots felt secure. One force could launch a direct attack, while another cut off the Pequots' retreat.

He had two requests, however. First, he wanted Massachusetts to support a Narragansett attack against some of the Nipmucs who were subject to Pequot control. The Nipmucs inhabited a scattering of communities in the rolling hills of New England's highlands, and the Narragansetts and Pequots had long competed for domination over them. Second, Miantonomo said, "it would be pleasing to all Natives that women and children be spared." He hoped to incorporate them into his community.

Two weeks later, he was still urging a strike. Pequots had moved to the coast to fish and plant, their usual spring pattern, and were vulnerable. But Massachusetts remained distracted by the controversy over Anne Hutchinson's teaching.[19] The colony's only significant effort was an attempt to persuade Plymouth to join the war, lest "all the Indians in the country" rise up "to root out all the English." Plymouth did not buy it.[20]

Not until May 17, 1637, could Massachusetts act with any sort of unity. That day, in a tumultuous election, the colony chose Winthrop as governor in place of Vane (who soon returned to England). Not one of Hutchinson's supporters was elected as a magistrate. The new General Court acted decisively. It called a synod to address the Hutchinson controversy, dispatched forty soldiers under Captain Daniel Patrick to help Miantonomo raid the Pequot coast, and called for an additional 160 soldiers. Much to the chagrin of the Boston-Hutchinson faction, it honored the unpopular Boston pastor John Wilson as chaplain of the new force. Boston displayed its bitterness by refusing to commission any prominent men, selecting a few "whom they cared not to be rid of" and "of the most refuse sort." Wilson's congregation would not even bid him farewell.[21]

ON FRIDAY MORNING, MAY 19, Captain Mason and his army sailed from Fort Saybrook, launching the campaign that would decide the outcome of the Pequot War. They arrived at Narragansett Bay in time to observe the Puritan Sabbath, but poor weather kept them from disembarking until sunset on Tuesday, May 23. Most soldiers were seeing Narragansett country's miles of cleared, fertile flatland for the first time. It would one day be the most hotly contested acreage in New England.

Miantonomo was surprised to see them but eagerly shared his plan to defeat the Pequots. Mason readily adopted it, though he would never acknowledge his debt. Miantonomo's only concern was that Mason's army was too small, for the Pequots had "very great captains and men skillful in war." He recommended his kinsman sachem Ninigret's fort at Niantic, near the Pequot frontier, as a launching point. The next morning, Mason marched almost twenty miles to Niantic. But Ninigret refused to allow him inside, perhaps fearing that Mason meant to punish him for trader John Oldham's murder. Such temerity insulted the proud Mason. Convinced of the "falsehood of Indians" and fretting that they would betray his presence to the Pequots, with whom they had kinship ties, he surrounded the fort and forbade anyone from leaving "upon peril of their lives."

Tension eased in the morning after several hundred of Miantonomo's Narragansett warriors arrived, accompanied by the Pequot Wequash, whom Miantonomo had recruited as a guide. Seeing that Miantonomo supported Mason, Ninigret's men, known as Eastern Niantics, gathered in a circle where, "one by one," they made "solemn protestation how gallantly they would demean themselves, and how many men they would kill." Thanks to Miantonomo and Ninigret, Mason now had nearly six hundred men: sixty from Connecticut, twenty from Massachusetts, about sixty Mohegans, two hundred Eastern Niantics, and more than two hundred Narragansetts. They informed him that the Pequots had two "almost impregnable" forts a few miles apart, Weinshauks and Mystic. Mason decided to march all day to be in position to attack Mystic at dawn on May 26. Afterward they would march to Pequot Harbor, where he had ordered his flotilla to meet them.[22]

They began marching at 8:00 a.m., and it quickly became evident that they lacked sufficient food or water for such a grueling march. As mile followed mile and the late May sun rose overhead, men passed out from heat or exhaustion. Some Narragansetts and Eastern Niantics deserted. About a dozen miles in, at the Pawcatuck River, Mason permitted a rest. Narragansetts fretted that it was a Pequot fishing site. Pequots were no doubt tracking them and might be massing for an attack. But Uncas, the Mohegan sachem, disparaged Narragansett concerns, vowing that he and his men would prove more steadfast.

Resuming the march, after about three miles they came to a recently planted cornfield. Mason gave orders for strict silence. Darkness fell, providing merciful relief from the heat. An hour later, they reached a swampy lowland between two hills. They stopped, "much wearied," Mason recalled, "supposing we were very near the fort, as our Indians informed us." Scouts could hear Pequots singing in Mystic. The sky was clear and the moon bright. Mason posted guards and ordered the men to rest.

Against all odds, the Pequots failed to detect their presence. A few days earlier they had watched Mason's flotilla sail eastward. Convinced that the English had abandoned their campaign, they had been celebrating their victory late into the night.[23] Mason could scarcely have dreamed of a better opportunity to unleash God's vengeance. His soldiers and their Algonquian allies waited, knowing the Pequots had no idea what was coming. Dawn was a few hours away.

MASON MUST HAVE been exhausted because, by his own account, he slept in. When he woke up, he was mortified to discover that it was "very light" and "we might have lost our opportunity." (Underhill claimed that his Massachusetts troops were up around 1:00 a.m.) Mason roused his troops, who gathered for a brief prayer, commending their operation to God. Then, following their Native guides, they rushed down the path toward the fort.

It was further away than expected, and Mason's anxiety grew with each step. Suddenly they emerged from the trees into a cornfield at the foot of a hill. Open ground lay all around. Mason summoned Uncas and Wequash, the Pequot guide. Where was the fort, he demanded? At the top of the hill, they replied. Where were his Algonquian warriors? To the rear, "exceedingly afraid," they admitted. Nearly half had deserted. Only about three hundred remained. Mason instructed them to form a perimeter around the fort to prevent any Pequots from escaping. His English soldiers would make the attack.[24]

The fort covered more than two acres of ground. Logs "as thick as a man's thigh or the calf of his legs" had been pounded three feet into the ground to form a palisade ten to twelve feet high. Between the logs were loopholes for shooting arrows. There were two entrances, both barricaded with branches and bushes, making them so narrow that a man had to turn sideways to pass through. Inside, Mystic was crowded with wigwams containing at least four hundred men, women, and children.[25]

The colonists decided to strike from two directions. Underhill would pass around to the south gate, while Mason attacked from the northeast. Although Miantonomo had requested that women and children be spared, the officers agreed to "destroy them by the sword and save the plunder." After more prayer, they moved into position. Mason crept within twenty feet of the fort when a dog started barking. A Pequot cried, "Owanux! Owanux!" (Englishmen!), and Mason ordered a charge. Soldiers rushed forward, shooting through holes in the palisade. Screams and cries pierced the air, jarring the inexperienced soldiers, most of whom were farmers, tradesmen, or servants. "If God had not fitted the hearts of men for the service, it would have bred in them a commiseration towards [the Pequots]," Underhill believed. But they merely had to recall "the blood they had shed of our native countrymen, and how barbarously they had dealt with them."

Mason reached an opening and clambered over a chest-high obstruction of branches, hollering for his men to follow. A lieutenant struggled to obey before deciding on a better approach. Stepping back, he pulled the branches out of the way and slipped through. Sixteen men followed, one by one.

Had the Pequots been prepared, Mason would have been killed the moment he stepped inside the fort. As it was, he did not see a single Indian. He ducked into a wigwam and was "beset with many Indians waiting all opportunities to lay hands on him." Another soldier followed, tripping over a dead Pequot. Some Pequots fled the wigwam. Others cowered in fear. Mason stepped outside and chased some down a lane before several of his soldiers intercepted and killed them. He walked back up the lane, "very much out of breath." Approaching the gate, he saw two soldiers, their swords lowered as if they had no idea what to do.[26] The fort was so crowded they had no "foot-room to grapple with their adversaries."[27]

On the south side, Underhill's men had more trouble. When Underhill tried to dismantle the branches blocking the entrance, he found them locked in place. A detachment led by a man named Hedge finally cleared a way through, but the delay had given the Pequots precious time. A "sturdy Indian" defended the opening, firing an arrow into Hedge's arm. Hedge killed him, only to be confronted by another, whom Hedge ran through with his sword. As soldiers poured into the fort, Pequot warriors shot several at point-blank range, and Hedge took an arrow in the other arm. Underhill recalled entering the fort soon after, "our swords in our right hand and our carbines or muskets in our left hand."

As soldiers barged into wigwams and fought off warriors, casualties mounted. Soon nearly twenty soldiers, a quarter of Mason's English force, had been wounded, "some through the shoulders, some in the face, some in the head, some in the legs." Multiple arrows hit Mason's helmet. Underhill took one in his left hip, though his buff coat prevented serious injury, and another was lodged in the linen of his helmet between his neck and shoulders. Two soldiers were dead.

The commanders held a brief conference. They had not expected the Pequots to fight so well. "We should never kill them after that manner," Mason declared. "We must burn them." He dashed into a wigwam, fought off several Pequots, and grabbed a firebrand. The walls were covered with mats made from "rushes and hempen threads" that lit easily. Underhill used gunpowder to start a fire on the south side. Wind swept the flames through the fort, engulfing the dry, tightly packed houses. The palisade became an inferno, Mason recalled, "to the extreme amazement of the enemy and great rejoicing of ourselves." Women and children screamed, yet some were so terrified of the soldiers that they ran "into the very flames."

The colonial soldiers withdrew from the palisade, taking their wounded. Mason ordered them to prevent any Pequots from escaping. Warriors fought desperately. "Some of them climbing to the top of the palisade, others of them running into the very flames, many of them gathering windward, lay pelting at us with their arrows," Mason remembered. They fired through the palisade even as "they were scorched and burnt with the very flame." Soon their bows became ineffective because "fire burnt their very bowstrings." Their lungs choked and skin burned, bands of "twenty and thirty," including women and children, poured through the gates. Soldiers cut them down with swords.

The Mohegans, Narragansetts, and Eastern Niantics "left the whole execution to the English" and spared a few fortunate Pequots who broke through the English cordon. "Down fell men, women, and children," Underhill recalled. "Not above five of them escaped out of our hands." Soldiers would never forget the horror, according to William Bradford's account, "to see them thus frying in the fire and the streams of blood quenching the same, and horrible was the stink and scent." Men who had never experienced battle were shocked "to see so many souls lie gasping on the ground, so thick in some places that you could hardly pass along."[28]

Mason relished the massacre as an act of divine judgment. "God was above them, who laughed his enemies and the enemies of his people to scorn, making them as a fiery oven," he crowed. "Thus did the LORD judge among the heathen, filling the place with dead bodies!" Underhill estimated that four hundred Pequots were killed in little over an hour, but Mason claimed Pequots later informed him six or seven hundred died. He thought scarcely seven had escaped. Seven more were taken prisoner, and these owed their lives to the Algonquians. As for the English, Mason reported two killed and twenty wounded.[29]

MASON HAD WON a stunning victory, but his situation remained critical. They were at least six miles from Pequot Harbor, where they were supposed to meet their flotilla that afternoon, and many of the wounded could not move without help. (Shockingly, the army's surgeon had remained at Narragansett Bay.) "Most were thirsty but [we] could find no water," Mason added. "The provision we had for food was very little." Ammunition ran low. Meanwhile, the Pequot sachem Sassacus had hundreds of warriors at Weinshauks who might counterattack any moment.

Sure enough, three hundred warriors were discovered approaching the battlefield. Mason dispatched a detachment to hold them off, but he knew they would succeed for only so long. He asked the Algonquians to cover their withdrawal and help carry wounded. Observing as the warriors moved against the Pequots, Underhill was not impressed. The two sides shot arrows from such a distance and "after such a manner, as I dare boldly affirm, they might fight seven years and not kill seven men," he marveled. European warfare was far more effective. Nevertheless, they gave Mason the cover he needed to extricate his men.

As Pequots occupied the battlefield, they discovered what the English had done. Hundreds of corpses littered two acres of smoldering ruins. Men and women, young and old, children, infants, mothers, warriors: the stench of burning flesh was nauseating. These were their people, their kin. Mason watched as warriors, "coming up to the place where the fort was and beholding what was done, stamped and tore the hair from their heads." Eventually they turned toward the departing English. Throwing caution to the wind, they charged down the hill.

The rearguard turned and fired a volley, cutting warriors down. That stunned the enraged Pequots. They continued running "to and fro, and shooting their arrows at random," but English muskets kept them at a distance. Slowly, the English made their way toward the river, burning wigwams along the way. Pequots harassed them, lying in "ambush behind rocks and trees," but their arrows were ineffective. Occasionally they blocked the English path through a swamp or thicket, but musket fire dispersed them. Each time, Mason's Algonquian allies gave "a great shout," rushed forward, and scalped the dead and wounded.[30]

But the soldiers were exhausted and discouraged, and their Narragansett and Eastern Niantic allies kept slipping away. When fifty such Narragansetts were attacked, they begged Mason and Underhill for assistance. "How dare you crave aid of us," the officers retorted, "when you are leaving . . . us in this distressed condition, not knowing which way to march out of the country?" Nevertheless, Underhill led thirty soldiers to their relief, driving the Pequots back. Finally, about two miles from the river the Pequots abandoned their pursuit. Ascending a hill, the soldiers saw their vessels in the harbor, which produced "great rejoicing." With a new burst of energy, they finally reached the river. Relieved, famished, and utterly exhausted, Mason recalled, "we sat down in quiet." Underhill eventually sailed to Fort Saybrook with the wounded. Mason returned overland, destroying wigwams and fields on the way.[31]

The exiled Roger Williams waited anxiously for news, the Narragansett sachems nearby. The first Narragansetts who returned claimed Mason had been defeated. Then Williams heard that a great victory had been won. But this was followed by news that Mason's army had been cut off. In Boston, Winthrop received the dismal report that "all the English and two hundred of the Indians were cut off in their retreat for want of powder and victuals." At last Williams learned the truth. "I have received tidings (Blessed forever be the Lord of Hosts!)," he wrote Winthrop, "that the Narragansetts . . . all came safe home" and "the English were all safe." The victory had come the day after Massachusetts had observed a colony-wide fast, so Winthrop considered it a direct answer to prayer.[32]

ALGONQUIANS HAD NEVER experienced anything like it. Their bows and arrows were no match for English muskets and armor, and the English were willing and able to annihilate their opposition, much as armies had done in Europe for decades. Although the Narragansetts and Eastern Niantics "much rejoiced" at the defeat of their traditional foes, they considered English tactics far too brutal. "*Mach it, mach it* [it is evil]" they cried, "because it is too furious and slays too many men."

The day after, the Pequot sachems held a council. Furious at the Mohegan sachem Uncas's betrayal, they killed some of their Mohegan neighbors. They now realized that Canonicus was right: they could not stand up to English power. They faced the loss of everything they held dear, and many blamed Sassacus, their leading sachem. Most agreed that it was time to flee.[33] Sassacus and eighty men headed for the Mohawks. A hundred people made for Long Island. About seventy took their chances with the Narragansetts, to Sassacus's disgust.[34]

Connecticut responded swiftly to the news that Pequot power was broken, claiming the Pequots' land and on June 2 dispatching thirty soldiers to "maintain our right that God by conquest hath given to us."[35] Three days later, Plymouth entered the war, with its governor Winslow urging "such revenge" on the Pequots as might discourage, for all time, any "barbarians to rise against us."[36]

Not all colonists supported such ruthlessness. John Humfrey advised Winthrop to make peace while English casualties remained low. "Our nation, the gospel, [and] the blood of those murdered persons of ours seems to triumph in the present success," he opined. "The honor and terror of our people to all the Natives is abundantly vindicated and made good." Why not make peace while they had the upper hand, lest a short war devolve into a "perpetual" one?[37]

He need not have worried. Pequot allies and tributaries were so desperate for peace that they were betraying erstwhile allies. The Montauk sachem Wyandanch, from Long Island, delivered five Pequot heads to Saybrook, promising to "give you tribute as we did the Pequots."[38]

The Narragansetts reiterated their request that Pequot captives "be not enslaved like those which are taken in war, but . . . be used kindly, [and] have houses and goods and fields given them." They expected a say in the matter, as stipulated by the treaty their sachem Miantonomo had signed in Boston. But English officers did not treat them as equals. In late June, Narragansett and Massachusett forces captured a hundred Pequots and delivered them to Israel Stoughton, Massachusetts colony's commander in the field. Stoughton executed twenty-two Pequot men, sparing two sachems because they promised to help find Sassacus. He gave thirty women and children to the Narragansetts and three to the Massachusetts.[39] But he sent forty-eight to Boston as slaves, he and his officers claiming several for themselves. One "is the fairest and largest that I saw amongst them, to whom I have given a coat to clothe her," he wrote the governor. "It is my desire to have her for a servant, if it may stand with your good liking."[40]

When Miantonomo showed up, Stoughton's soldiers refused to let him see the captured sachems. "I was thrust at with a pike many times," the sachem complained, "that I durst not come near the door." To make matters worse,

Stoughton appropriated a canoe his officers had promised to Miantonomo's brother, and his soldiers talked openly about attacking the Narragansetts. Disgusted, Miantonomo and Cutshamekin, the Massachusett sachem, returned home with their men. "Did ever friends deal so with friends?" Miantonomo asked Roger Williams. Williams took such tensions seriously. "Little sparks prove great fires," he warned John Winthrop.[41]

Stoughton admitted that the Narragansett alliance was strained but declared churlishly that the colonists did not need Narragansett help. "The heathen shall not say our dependence is on them," he avowed. "So we look up to God."[42] In fact, the Narragansetts were doing more for the English than he knew. That summer, Miantonomo's warriors and their Nipmuc tributaries defeated a force of Pequots and Nipmucs, sending them fleeing across the Connecticut River.[43]

AS PEQUOTS FLED IN every direction, colonists worried the war might spread. Sassacus and his warriors had moved west, killing three colonists on the Connecticut River, and Roger Williams feared they might secure an alliance with the Mohawks, dreaded for their savagery and cannibalism. Stoughton set out in pursuit in July, sailing west along the north shore of Long Island Sound with 160 Massachusetts soldiers and 40 Connecticut troops. Uncas's Mohegans kept pace on land, seizing Pequots who fell behind "by reason of their children and want of provisions."[44] They took women and children alive, but soldiers executed at least seven men, including two sachems.

On July 13, they discovered a body of Pequot warriors at a Sasqua village bordering the Munnacommock Swamp (present-day Fairfield). More than one hundred soldiers moved to surround the swamp. "I judged best, while the terror was upon them, to fall in upon them," wrote the impetuous Salem officer Lieutenant Richard Davenport. That was a mistake, for the ground was "so thick with shrub wood and so boggy" that soldiers' feet "stuck fast" in muck. Davenport discovered "a man and a sachem's child and thrust him through" twice with his pike. Only then did he realize that only three soldiers had followed him. Within moments, all were wounded by arrows. Struck near his left armpit and on the right side of his chest, Davenport thought it might be the end. "Now all had left me," he later wrote, "but God stood to me." Reinforcements arrived, forced the Pequots back, and carried out the wounded.

Soldiers formed a thin perimeter around the swamp, about a mile in circumference, occasionally firing their muskets while dodging arrows. Officers agonized over what to do next. It was about 3:00 p.m., and they were sure the Pequots would try to break out come nightfall. Gaps between soldiers were so large that such an attempt would probably succeed. Captain Daniel Patrick advocated cutting down the swamp, but this was rejected. Others proposed building a barrier around it. This was deemed impractical. Captain Mason's soldiers did manage to cut their way through a narrow part of the swamp, reducing the length of the perimeter.

Mason claimed that because the English were "loath to destroy women and children," they decided to negotiate. Thomas Stanton, who had interpreted during the previous year's meeting at Saybrook, offered to make contact. It was not long before he returned with the village sachem and a trickle of women, children, and old men at his heels. More came throughout the evening. By dark the number of refugees totaled almost two hundred. "It was lamentable to see into what condition they have brought themselves," the wounded Davenport observed, "everyone crying out." Had the English agreed to spare the lives of warriors, further bloodshed might have been avoided, but they would not. The warriors alerted Stanton that "they would sell their lives there" and commenced shooting.

The violence resumed, unseen arrows slicing through the darkness amid the flash of musket fire. Soldiers hacked their way through underbrush, confining the Pequots "into so narrow a compass as they could easier kill them through the thickets." Gaps between soldiers were reduced to about twelve feet. But all night Pequot warriors launched counterattacks, "coming up behind the bushes very near" the soldiers. Arrows "pierced their hat brims and their sleeves and stockings and other parts of their clothes," but the soldiers wore armor, and none were fatally wounded.

About an hour before dawn, it "grew very dark." The Pequots attempted to break through Captain Patrick's sector, but the Massachusetts troops beat them back. The warriors attacked again, making a "great noise," but were driven back a second time. Their war cries unnerved the officers on other parts of the line, and with "the tumult growing to a very great height," Mason pulled his Connecticut troops out of their place on the perimeter and marched to Patrick's relief. As they rounded a curve in the swamp, Mason's men were attacked. They sent the Natives reeling into the underbrush with a volley of small shot, then braced for a second attack. But the Pequots, taking advantage of their interior lines, slipped back toward Patrick's exhausted soldiers. Some officers later claimed they sneaked past the soldiers, but according to Mason, the Pequots "pressed violently upon Captain Patrick, breaking through his quarters." Others no doubt slipped through the part of the line abandoned by Mason.

The officers put the best spin on it, claiming that fewer than twenty warriors escaped, but the reality was that when they combed the swamp, they found only nine Indian bodies. Almost the entire Pequot force had gotten away.[45]

Even so, it was a victory, and soldiers relished its spoils, gathering "kettles, trays, [and] wampum." The village sachem and his people were freed, but captured Pequots were parceled out to Connecticut and Massachusetts as slaves. Among them was the sachem Mononotto's wife, "of a very modest countenance and behavior," who requested that they "not abuse her body and that her children might not be taken from her." Because she had protected the Wethersfield girls during their captivity, she and her children were entrusted to Governor Winthrop. They would be freed within two years.[46]

Wounded soldiers were brought to the pinnaces. Davenport suffered "great pain," as an arrowhead lodged deep in his arm was removed, but he was grateful to be alive. "My humble request to you is that you remember my case and soul to the Lord," he implored his pastor, "that he that teacheth his people to profit will teach me how to use this special deliverance." He asked him to "cheer up the spirit of my poor wife, who I fear will apprehend worse than the thing is."[47]

Stoughton gave up pursuing Sassacus. Instead, he sailed to Block Island, killed a couple of Natives, and burned wigwams before the local Manisses sued for peace. Their sachems agreed to pay one hundred fathoms of wampum, surrender John Oldham's killers, and become tributaries of Massachusetts. "Indians in all quarters [are] so terrified," Winthrop wrote, that they refused to protect Pequot refugees. They pledged friendship or submission to Massachusetts by sending Pequot heads and hands and wampum in exchange for protection.[48]

On August 5, colonists from Connecticut arrived in Boston with the most valuable trophies of all: "part of the skin and lock of hair of Sassacus" and the scalps of six other Pequot leaders. All were gifts from the Mohawks, who had decided that friendship with the English and Narragansetts was more valuable than with the defeated Pequots.[49] Over the coming weeks Indians delivered Pequots "almost daily to Windsor or Hartford." Mason exulted, "The Pequots now became a prey to all Indians. Happy were they that could bring in their heads to the English!"[50]

In Massachusetts, the end of the war coincided with the conclusion of the synod called to resolve the colony's theological dispute. On October 12, 1637, the churches observed a day of thanksgiving "for our victories against the Pequots and for the success of the assembly." (Embittered members of Anne Hutchinson's faction boycotted the festivities.) After a sermon, the magistrates and ministers paraded with veterans before all joined in a feast.[51]

THERE IS NO record of Puritan hand-wringing over the massacre at Mystic. Boston minister John Cotton's prewar writings forbade killing women and children in war, but he wrote nothing about what happened there. There was ample precedent for such brutality in recent European wars, especially against enemies considered notorious, such as rebels, heretics, and pagans, or towns that refused to surrender. The Pequots fell into both categories.[52]

Captain Underhill faced accusations of brutality head-on. "It may be demanded, 'Why should you be so furious?' as some have said. 'Should not Christians have more mercy and compassion?' But I would refer you to

David's war," he explained, invoking the Old Testament Israelite king. "When a people is grown to such a height of blood and sin against God and man, and all confederates in the action, there he hath no respect to persons, but harrows them, and saws them, and puts them to the sword and the most terrible death that may be. Sometimes the scripture declareth women and children must perish with their parents. Sometimes the case alters, but we will not dispute it now. We had sufficient light from the word of God for our proceedings."[53]

Mason defended the massacre as an act of God. "Thus was God seen in the mount, crushing his proud enemies and the enemies of his people," he boasted. The Pequots had been "a terror to all that were round about them," having "resolved to destroy all the English and to root their very name out of this country." The fact that destruction fell "upon their own heads in a moment," and by "such weak means, even seventy-seven [soldiers]," proved that God was at work, "burning them up in the fire of his wrath and dunging the ground with their flesh," Mason insisted. "It was the Lord's doings, and it is marvelous in our eyes!"[54]

Governor William Bradford of Plymouth echoed this rhetoric, though none of his colony's troops were at Mystic. "The victory seemed a sweet sacrifice," he wrote, and the soldiers "gave the praise thereof to God, who had wrought so wonderfully for them, thus to enclose their enemies in their hands and give them so speedy a victory over so proud and insulting an enemy."[55]

Not a single minister went on record criticizing what had happened. One, Philip Vincent, celebrated it. He acknowledged that Indians were fundamentally equal to Englishmen, though uncivilized. But he insisted that as long as the English maintained peace with them, the Pequots posed a threat. Now, however, "having once terrified them by severe execution of just revenge," the English "shall never hear of more harm from them" but "have those brutes [as] their servants, their slaves."[56]

Only Roger Williams questioned the killing and enslavement of women and children, in large part because he rejected the Puritan belief that the Old Testament offered a model for Christian states. In a private letter to Winthrop, he respectfully stated his "fear that some innocent blood cries at Connecticut." True, God once commanded Israel to kill Amalekite women and children (a precedent Protestants often applied to Roman Catholics), but this command was "extraordinary and mystical." In the second book of Kings, by contrast, mercy was shown to children of "treacherous servants that slew their lord and king." Should not similar mercy be granted to the children of Pequots, whose crime was not nearly so great?

"I observe our countrymen have almost quite forgotten our great pretenses to king and state and all the world concerning their souls," Williams lamented, reminding Winthrop of New England's stated purpose. Pious talk of evangelizing the Natives had given way to plotting their destruction. Hope of welcoming them into Christ's kingdom had succumbed to an intense desire to purge them from the region. "The general speech is, all must be rooted out." What Puritans imagined as an enterprise of peace and liberation had devolved into a bloody struggle for power and land.[57]

6

Miantonomo

1637 to 1644

MASSACHUSETTS AND CONNECTICUT claimed the spoils of victory. A just war, they believed, brought rights of conquest and enslavement. The Narragansetts, Eastern Niantics, and Mohegans also sought to secure captives and control over former Pequot tributaries. These maneuvers provoked tensions that left the region constantly on the brink of war.

The colonies enslaved at least 260 Pequots. Leading Puritans like Salem minister Hugh Peter and former governor John Endecott requested boys or girls as slaves. Roger Williams claimed a boy whose mother and siblings had been taken to Boston. Massachusetts shipped seventeen boys to the Caribbean in exchange for Africans. Many colonists thought servitude would benefit Pequot captives by exposing them to Christianity, but John Mason, who had led the attack on Fort Mystic, admitted that women enslaved in Connecticut "could not endure that yoke, few of them continuing any considerable time with their masters." Some who escaped Massachusetts were restored to the English by allied Indians and "branded on the shoulder." A few were delivered to Williams "almost starved," one having been raped and "beaten with firesticks." Williams returned them to Massachusetts, pleading for better treatment.[1]

Williams protested that permanent enslavement violated the Christian principle of mercy. The Pequots were, after all, "our brethren by nature." While Puritans justified the practice by drawing on Old Testament law, Williams insisted that Jesus's life and death made God's commands to Israel regarding the treatment of enemies obsolete. "Since the Most High delights in mercy, and great revenge hath already [been] taken," why not allow the Pequots to settle as English subjects?[2] Williams's protests were ignored. In 1641, Massachusetts confirmed that it was legal to enslave "captives taken in just wars," "strangers as willingly sell themselves or are sold to us," and persons convicted of crimes, as long as they received "all the liberties and Christian usages" prescribed by Old Testament law.[3]

The Narragansetts believed their 1636 treaty with Massachusetts entitled them to a fair share of captives, as well as hunting rights east of the Pequot River and control of former Pequot tributaries. But their relationship with Massachusetts was rapidly breaking down. The English accused them of abandoning colonial forces in the field and illegally harboring Pequot captives. Williams defended them, writing Massachusetts governor Winthrop that although they were barbarians, "if I mistake not, I observe in Miantonomo some sparks of true friendship." If Massachusetts assured the sachem that it would not "despoil him of the country," he might even become a powerful ally.[4]

Yet Winthrop played hardball, insisting that Williams present the Narragansett sachems with Massachusetts's "grievances and threatenings." Williams reluctantly did so, using a symbolic Algonquian gesture: he broke "a straw in two or three places" to represent the Narragansetts' purported treaty violations. The elderly Canonicus was unimpressed. "I have never suffered any wrong to be offered to the English since they landed, nor never will," he retorted. If the alliance failed, it would be because the English proved false. But as long as the English were faithful, "then shall I go to my grave in peace and hope that the English and my posterity shall live in love and peace together." Williams countered that Canonicus had "long experience of their friendliness and trustiness." But Canonicus picked up a stick, broke it into ten pieces, and "related ten instances" of English perfidy, "laying down a stick to every instance."[5]

Canonicus and Miantonomo watched with dismay as rivals snatched up Pequot captives. Their kinsman Ninigret welcomed dozens to Niantic and protected about 120 on Pequot land along the Pawcatuck River. Even worse, it was said that Uncas, the Mohegan sachem, had three hundred new men, mostly Pequots and their tributaries. It was not just a matter of numbers. Pequots were wampum producers whose labor enhanced the economic power of their adoptive communities.

The Narragansetts proposed to seize the Pawcatuck Pequots, but Massachusetts forbade it. Miantonomo retorted that the 1636 treaty hardly required them to tolerate "so many of their enemies" living "so near them." Tensions rose when Mohegan warriors seized some Narragansetts.[6] At last Miantonomo traveled to Boston, where he negotiated an agreement. He acknowledged that Pequot country belonged to Massachusetts by right of conquest, while Massachusetts authorized him to apprehend the Ninigret's Pequots.[7]

Miantonomo seemed satisfied. But Connecticut, now an independent colony, denied that it was bound by Massachusetts's treaties and threatened war unless Miantonomo came to Hartford to negotiate a treaty with Connecticut. Meanwhile, believing Uncas's support would strengthen its own claims over Pequot land, Connecticut allowed Uncas to accumulate captives and marry the Pequot sachem Sassacus's widow and sister, an obvious attempt to position Uncas as Sassacus's successor.

The frustrated Narragansetts demanded that the Pequots be removed from rival sachems' control. Williams warned that Connecticut was "marvelously deluded" by Uncas.[8] He urged Massachusetts to honor its 1636 treaty, observing that whenever Narragansetts suspected him of breaking his word, they would object, "Do you know God, and will you lie?'"[9]

But Uncas played Governor Winthrop skillfully. In June 1638, he traveled to Boston, gave Winthrop twenty fathoms of wampum, and promised to submit to Massachusetts's adjudication. "This heart," he told Winthrop, his hand on his chest, "is not mine but yours. I have no men; they are yours. Command me any difficult thing; I will do it. I will not believe any Indians' words against the English. If any man shall kill an Englishman, I will put him to death, were he never so dear to me." Deeply moved, Winthrop gave him a "fair, red coat" and defrayed his expenses. After Uncas departed, Winthrop cast further accusations at Miantonomo, the Narragansett sachem.[10]

Disgusted at Winthrop's gullibility, Williams protested that one of Uncas's men was a Pequot who had murdered and tortured colonists. Soon after, Williams reported that two of Winthrop's female slaves, who had gone missing, had joined Uncas's collection of wives; Uncas had allegedly arranged the escape. Williams tried to make Winthrop understand how foolish it was to insult Miantonomo. The Narragansett sachem had invested considerable prestige in his relationship with Massachusetts, yet now it was "all dashed in a moment." Lesser sachems, less friendly to the colony, were eager to undermine him. Williams admitted that Miantonomo was "proud and angry and covetous and filthy, hating and hateful." But, he reminded Winthrop, apart from God's grace, so were the English.[11]

Ninigret, the Eastern Niantic sachem who was suddenly defying Narragansett authority, also acted aggressively. Determined to bring the Pequots' former Long Island tributaries under his control, he went "up and down the island robbing and pillaging." In response to Montauk protests that they were English tributaries, Ninigret replied, "Englishmen are liars. They do it but only to get your wampum." Connecticut held the Narragansetts responsible for Ninigret's behavior and dispatched Captain Mason with eight men to demand satisfaction.[12]

In late July, the situation reached a breaking point. Arthur Peach, an English veteran of the Pequot War, and three companions were fleeing Plymouth, where they faced charges of fornication. On the way, they encountered a Nipmuc trader carrying beaver pelts and wampum for the Narragansetts. After inviting him to smoke tobacco by their fire, Peach boasted to his friends that he had killed many Indians during the war and would kill this one too. Then he ran his rapier through the man's leg and belly.

Indians found the Nipmuc in agony and bleeding profusely. When Roger Williams set out to treat him, he encountered Indians fleeing on the road, convinced that the English planned a "general slaughter of the Natives." Williams tried to assuage their fears, promising that justice would be done. But when the

Nipmuc died, many Narragansetts were "ready to rise in arms." The Pequots had been right about the English, some said. It was time to retaliate.

Peach and his comrades were captured, and although Governor Winthrop suggested they be turned over to the Narragansetts, Plymouth claimed jurisdiction. Miantonomo ordered his people to desist from violence, insisting that Plymouth would "see justice done," and he warned the English to "be careful on the highways." But his Pokanoket rival, the sachem Ousamequin, declared that the Nipmuc was "not worthy another man should die for him," and some colonists protested "that any English should be put to death for the Indians."

As the region teetered on the brink of war, Mason arrived from Connecticut to confront Ninigret over his raids on Long Island. Desperate to "save blood, whether the Natives' or my countrymen's," Williams persuaded Ninigret to pay satisfaction. Plymouth, meanwhile, was determined to prove that Indians could receive justice from an English jury. It tried Peach and two accomplices (one had escaped) for murder, convicted them, and executed them.[13] That calmed matters somewhat.

But Connecticut was not finished with its power play and demanded that Miantonomo come to Hartford. Miantonomo set out overland with more than 150 men as well as his wife and children. He took Roger Williams with him, since he did not trust Connecticut's Thomas Stanton as an interpreter. Along the way, he was informed that Mohegans and Pequots were attacking Narragansetts and their Nipmuc tributaries and planning to ambush his entourage. Williams urged him to turn back, but Miantonomo refused. Posting warriors in the woods on each side of the trail, he pressed on, even stopping for a day so Williams could observe the Sabbath. They reached Hartford on September 20, 1638.

The summit was tense, with Narragansetts and Mohegans lobbing accusations at each other. Williams thought it served "to give vent and breathing" to both sides. Eventually Miantonomo and Uncas were induced to shake hands, but Uncas refused Miantonomo's invitation to eat with him and had to be coerced into revealing how many Pequots he was harboring.[14]

On September 21, Connecticut persuaded the two sachems to sign what became known as the Treaty of Hartford. In it, they pledged "all former injuries and wrongs offered to each other remitted and buried and never to be renewed anymore." They promised not to fight over future grievances but submit them to Connecticut's adjudication. The treaty divided up the Pequots and their families: eighty to the Narragansetts, eighty to the Mohegans, and twenty to Ninigret, each of whom were required to pay annual tribute for them. They would "no more be called Pequots, but Narragansetts and Mohegans," and were forbidden to live in Pequot country.[15]

For Miantonomo, it was a stunning surrender. Massachusetts had treated him as an equal, at least formally, but Connecticut claimed the right to dictate his foreign relations and impose tribute on him. Miantonomo obviously valued an equitable division of the Pequots and may have reasoned that Massachusetts would protect him. But the ultimate effect of the treaty was to confirm the up-start Uncas, just two years removed from being a Pequot subject, as the region's rising Algonquian power and Miantonomo's equal, and to ratify Connecticut's conquest of Pequot country. Its message was as clear as it was alien to tradi-tional Christian rules of just war. Any Algonquians who waged war against the English would suffer cultural genocide, their identity erased and their land occupied.[16]

THE NARRAGANSETT SACHEMS continued lobbying Massachusetts to honor the 1636 treaty by allowing them to hunt in Pequot country and take the Pawcatuck Pequots as captives. In May 1639, they sent Winthrop thirty fathoms of wampum and a basket for his wife, Margaret, from Miantonomo's wife, expressing their "sincere affection" and desire for "the continuance of your an-cient and constant friendship." But Winthrop suspected them of harboring a large number of Pequots and insulted them by accepting the gift while ignoring their pleas.[17]

By contrast, Connecticut worked closely with Uncas, the Mohegan sachem. On August 26, it dispatched Captain Mason and Uncas with forty English soldiers and one hundred Indians to destroy the Pequot community Ninigret was protecting at Pawcatuck. The force sailed into Pawcatuck Bay, entered a "small river," and fell upon the village, plundering wigwams and stockpiles of freshly harvested corn. When sixty angry warriors confronted them, Mason outflanked and dispersed them, capturing seven. These were Ninigret's men, and Mason prepared to cut off their heads, only for the Narragansett Miantonomo's brother to arrive and announce that they belonged to Miantonomo. The Narragansett offered to purchase them with the heads of seven Pequots who had killed colonists. Mason agreed and handed them to Uncas pending the transfer.

The next morning, more than three hundred warriors, probably Eastern Niantics and Narragansetts, appeared across a creek, demanding an explana-tion for Mason's depredations. Mason explained that the Pequot settlement was illegal under the Treaty of Hartford. The Indians replied that the Pequots were "good men, their friends," and that "they would fight for them and protect them." Mason called their bluff, daring them to do so. But having seen what Mason did at Mystic, they told him "they would not fight with Englishmen, for they were Spirits, but would fight with Uncas." Mason retorted that they could do what they pleased, but he would be "burning wigwams and carrying corn aboard all that day." The Indians bitterly jeered at the pillaging soldiers until Thomas Stanton, Mason's interpreter, silenced them by shooting one in the thigh.

After loading their vessels with corn, kettles, mats, and other plunder, Mason and Uncas departed the ruined town. Mason viewed the raid as the final campaign of the Pequot War. God had destroyed the wicked and would "cut the remembrance of them from the earth," he reflected. "Thus the Lord was pleased to smite our enemies in the hinder parts and to give us their land for an inheritance," just as he had done for Israel.[18]

The raid merely intensified the crisis. Ninigret refused to surrender seven Pequots, having promised to protect them, but vowed that if Uncas harmed his seven Eastern Niantic hostages, Ninigret would retaliate against English settlers. The Narragansett sachems Canonicus and Miantonomo had been estranged from Ninigret, but in the face of Mohegan aggression, they closed ranks. They assured Roger Williams they were trying to reason with Ninigret, but English favoritism toward Uncas was "so great and the consequences so grievous" that it was like shooting arrows at a stone wall. When Williams urged them "to desert the [Eastern] Niantics," they reminded him that they were "their brethren" who had "never hurt the English but joined with them against the Pequots."[19]

Connecticut considered going to war against the Narragansetts, with tentative support from Plymouth. On June 29, 1640, Governor William Bradford of Plymouth informed Winthrop of "good intelligence" that the Mohawks had promised to support the Narragansetts against the English, though Bradford would not reveal his source, "lest it should be suspected."[20] Similar reports came from Connecticut, and colonists complained that the Narragansetts' Massachusett tributaries were acting suspiciously.[21] Uncas warned Miantonomo that if he approached the Mohegan fort at Shantok, Connecticut troops would "fall upon him."[22] Bradford was not sure what to think about Connecticut going to war. "I wish they may go upon good grounds, lest they bring evil upon themselves and their neighbors," he wrote, but "if justice or necessity compel them," they should strike quickly, before the Narragansetts harvested their corn.[23]

Williams continued to intercede. Christians were not modern-day Israelites called to wage war against the heathen, he chided Winthrop. They were called to seek the kingdom proclaimed by the prophets, in which nations "beat their swords into plowshares and their spears into pruning hooks. Nation will not take up sword against nation, nor will they train for war anymore." War was sometimes justified to secure "justice upon malefactors" or defend one's people, as in the Pequot War, but this was no such case.[24]

Thankfully, the colony of Massachusetts discredited reports of a Narragansett attack, aware that the Narragansetts had plenty of enemies inclined to stir up false rumors about them. But to be safe, it ordered the Massachusett sachem Cutshamekin to surrender his people's ammunition and summoned Miantonomo to Boston. Miantonomo agreed to come if Williams could serve as his interpreter. Winthrop had suggested that Williams's exile from Massachusetts be revoked as a reward for his diplomatic service, but Boston minister John Cotton objected, and the council refused Miantonomo's request.[25]

Miantonomo swallowed the insult and traveled to Boston. As he did so, a wave of racist hostility swept through the colonial population. Colonists said Indians belonged to the "cursed race of Ham" and should be "rooted out" of the land. (In the Bible, Ham was one of Noah's three sons. Noah cursed Ham's son Canaan, and some Christians believed the curse extended to Ham's descendants.) Such talk alarmed officials, who maintained that Indians had to be won over "by justice and kindness."[26]

The Boston summit was an opportunity to prove they could do so, but the colony botched it. Winthrop had been replaced as governor by Thomas Dudley, a strict Puritan, who not only insisted on using an interpreter Miantonomo mistrusted but imperiously informed the General Court that while traveling to Boston Miantonomo had been rude, disrespectful, and ungrateful. Dudley would not allow any discussion or let Miantonomo eat with him until he apologized. Miantonomo reminded him that when colonists "came to him, they were permitted to use their own fashions." Why did not they extend such hospitality to him? Nevertheless, he humbled himself and "acknowledged his failing." The two parties then reaffirmed the 1636 treaty, but Winthrop feared the sachem would "carry [Dudley's insult] home in his breast."[27]

The Mohegan Uncas, in contrast, further ingratiated himself with Connecticut, taking a female sachem as at least his seventh wife and selling some of her land. Then he entrusted all the land he claimed to Connecticut (including much that had belonged to the Pequots), reserving for his Mohegans "that ground which at present is planted and in that kind improved by us." It was a calculated move. At the cost of submission, he secured Connecticut's support for his lofty ambitions. Connecticut, in turn, strengthened its claims to Pequot country.[28]

⟨ ❧ ⟩

IN LATE AUGUST 1642, a sachem nervously approached colonist Roger Ludlow while he was harvesting hay near New Haven, a new colony on the northern shore of Long Island Sound. Requesting anonymity for fear of his life, the sachem warned that Miantonomo, the Narragansett sachem, was recruiting the Long Island sachems for a war against the English. The conspiracy included "all the sachems upon the mainland, from the Dutch to the [Massachusetts] bay, and all the Indian sachems from the eastward." According to the informant, when sachems protested that the English were too strong, Miantonomo argued that they only defeated the Pequots because they had Algonquian support, much to his regret. The English "did get possession of all the best place in the country and did drive the Indians away and were likely to take away the country from them," Miantonomo warned. All Indians, including Uncas, needed to unite as "one man" before it was too late. The plan was to approach English towns after harvest under pretense of trade, only to kill the colonists.

Ludlow took the alarming report to New Haven, where he discovered that a Long Island Indian "had declared the same to them verbatim." He traveled to Connecticut, where he learned that a third "Indian of note" had reported the conspiracy, apparently after suffering an injury that convinced him the "Englishman's God was angry with him." It was as if God had confirmed the evidence "with a threefold testimony."[29]

Lieutenant Lion Gardener, having left Fort Saybrook to settle on a small island off Long Island, was informed by the Montauk sachem Wyandanch that Miantonomo was recruiting Montauks behind his back. "You know our fathers had plenty of deer and skins, our plains were full of deer, as also our woods, and of turkeys, and our coves full of fish and fowl," Miantonomo allegedly told them. "But these English having gotten our land, they with scythes cut down the grass, and with axes fell the trees. Their cows and horses eat the grass, and their hogs spoil our clam banks, and we shall all be starved." The English were strong because they were unified, he continued, "so must we be one as they are, otherwise we shall be all gone shortly." All the sachems "from east to west," including the Mohawks, must "fall upon them all, at one appointed day." In forty days they would light three signal fires, Miantonomo supposedly said. "The next day, fall on and kill men, women, and children."[30] The Dutch likewise reported that Miantonomo was "passing through all the Indian villages, soliciting them to a general war against both the English and the Dutch."[31]

Connecticut relayed the intelligence to Massachusetts and called for a preemptive strike. Winthrop, reelected governor of Massachusetts, called the General Court for an emergency session in early September. Meanwhile, he ordered that the Massachusetts and Pennacooks, Narragansett tributaries, be disarmed "to strike some terror into the Indians." Cutshamekin, the Massachusett sachem, "came willingly" and was quickly released after interrogation revealed "no ground of suspicion." The attempt to disarm the Pennacooks was a fiasco, however. Unable to locate their sachem Passaconaway, forty soldiers arrested his son and his son's wife and child. When the son "slipped his line" and dashed for freedom, a soldier shot at him. It was more than three weeks before Passaconnaway received satisfaction and surrendered his people's weapons. Such heavy-handed tactics threatened to provoke the very hostility they were supposed to prevent.[32]

The General Court, assembling on September 8, was more careful. Its members agreed that although the evidence presented by Connecticut rendered a conspiracy "very probable," it was hardly "sufficient ground for us to begin a war, for it was possible it might be otherwise." They had learned not to believe every tale of an Indian conspiracy. "We considered also of the like reports which had formerly been raised almost every year since we came," Winthrop wrote, "and how they proved to be but reports raised up by the opposite factions among the Indians." Indeed, the testimony of the various informants was so similar that the court suspected "all this might come out of the enmity which had been between Miantonomo and Uncas, who continually sought to discredit each other with the English." Even if Miantonomo *was* building an alliance, its purpose might simply be defensive, and its target might be Uncas.

For Puritans who wanted their society to reflect Christ's kingdom, the moral and spiritual costs of an unjust war were too high. If they went to war on "a false report," they worried, "we might provoke God's displeasure and blemish our wisdom and integrity before the heathen." War might prove costly and catastrophic, and while soldiers "well assured of the justice of the cause" would endure its perils, this cause was doubtful at best. The court decided to pursue diplomacy. It sent envoys to summon Miantonomo to Boston, threatening that "if he refused to come," it "would give us occasion to right ourselves."[33]

But while Massachusetts investigated (the Narragansetts were, after all, their allies), Connecticut "resolved to make war" and pressured Massachusetts "to delay no longer." Even Plymouth ordered preparations for a "defensive and offensive war." With time running out, Winthrop assembled available magistrates, deputies, and clergy. All day the Puritan elite sifted through reports, but they found the evidence lacking. If the colonies went to war over every alleged conspiracy, they argued, "we should never be free from war." Winthrop duly wrote Connecticut "to dissuade them from going forth," warning that to attack in the midst of negotiations was base treachery.

Massachusetts's diplomacy was rewarded when Miantonomo agreed to come to Boston. The magistrates prepared carefully, anxious to avoid a repeat of the toxic meeting of 1640. Since Winthrop was moderate and tactful, they decided he alone would speak to the sachem. The suspense was palpable as Miantonomo appeared before the court. Everything was arranged to make him as comfortable as possible. He was assigned a seat across the table from Winthrop, and the meeting did not begin until all his counselors were present. Then Winthrop began to question him.

"In all his answers he was very deliberate and showed good understanding in the principles of justice and equity and ingenuity," Winthrop recorded. Charges that had seemed terrifying now appeared flimsy and disingenuous. Disgusted that his accusers were anonymous, Miantonomo charged Uncas with defamation and demanded an investigation. If his accusers could not prove their charges, they should suffer the very punishment they sought against him: death. When

Winthrop assured him that the court did not believe the reports, he replied, "If you did not give credit to it, why then did you disarm the Indians?"

The two-day summit was not without insult. When colonists prepared a separate table for the Narragansetts, Miantonomo refused to eat until Winthrop invited him to his own table. Nevertheless, the sachem departed in excellent spirits. Bidding farewell, "he returned and gave his hand to the governor again, saying, 'that was for the rest of the magistrates who were absent.'" Colonists returned the Massachusetts' and Pennacooks' guns, which they needed for hunting, deciding it was "better to trust God with our safety than to save ourselves by unrighteousness."[34]

Historians debate whether Miantonomo was actually organizing a conspiracy. The evidence is inconclusive, but Massachusetts's skepticism gives ample reason for pause. Fort Saybrook's former commander Lion Gardener, however, was convinced that Miantonomo would have struck if Wyandanch and Uncas had not revealed his plans—and that one day he would try again. The Pequot War "was but a comedy in comparison of the tragedies which . . . may yet come," Gardener predicted, "if God do not open the eyes, ears, and hearts of some that I think are willfully deaf and blind." One day Indians "would easily destroy us, man and mother's son," and God would judge the colonies for their "extreme pride and base security, which cannot but stink before the Lord."

Over the years, Gardener grew more fearful. One morning, he imagined, as colonists stirred from their beds, offered morning prayers, and headed to their fields, Indians would be upon them. He dreaded the moment when he might "have a sharp stake set in the ground and thrust into my fundament [buttocks], and to have my skin flayed off by piecemeal and cut in pieces and bits, and my flesh roasted and thrust down my throat, as these people have done, and I know will be done to the chief [people] in the country by hundreds, if God should deliver us into their hands, as justly he may for our sins."[35]

The crisis united the Puritan colonies. Enduring fear of a conspiracy and alarm at their failure to coordinate their response invigorated calls for a confederation to handle future crises. In May 1643, Massachusetts, Connecticut, Plymouth, and New Haven established the United Colonies of New England. "Whereas we all came into these parts of America with one and the same end and aim, namely, to advance the kingdom of our Lord Jesus Christ and to enjoy the liberties of the gospel in purity with peace," they declared, now they were joining together so that "as in nation and religion, so in other respects, we be and continue one." The confederation would be responsible "for offence and defense, mutual advice and succor upon all just occasions, both for preserving and propagating the truth and liberties of the gospel, and for their own mutual safety and welfare."

It was a distinctly Puritan union, so Providence, Roger Williams's colony, was excluded. The agreement required the colonies to defend one another against

attack, sharing the economic and military burden of "all just wars" in proportion to their populations. No colony could launch an offensive war without
permission from the confederation. The governing body would consist of two
commissioners from each colony, each a faithful church member. Binding
decisions required the agreement of six. They were to ensure that Indians were
treated justly and received "due satisfaction" when injured. The colonies also
pledged to return fugitive servants to their masters.[36] From now on, they hoped,
hostile Indians would face a Puritan confederation that acted as one.

EVEN AS REPORTS circulated of Miantonomo's purported conspiracy,
Massachusetts recklessly antagonized him by expanding its jurisdiction into
Narragansett country. Puritans had watched with alarm as Roger Williams
provided refuge in Providence to exiles from Massachusetts, including Anne
Hutchinson and William Coddington, on whose behalf he negotiated the acqui-
sition of Aquidneck Island from Miantonomo. Williams himself rejected infant
baptism and no longer believed a true church existed. He even refused to pray
with anyone other than his wife. By annexing the region, Puritans reasoned, they
could suppress such radicalism, promote Massachusetts's prosperity and defense, and evangelize the Natives.

Their opportunity emerged from the actions of a contentious religious leader
named Samuel Gorton. Gorton rejected Puritan views of church and state and
challenged every authority he encountered. He had already been driven from
Plymouth and Newport (on Aquidneck Island) and was now, complained
Williams, "bewitching and bemadding poor Providence." Two ambitious
landholders, William Arnold and William Harris, had recently settled four miles
south of Providence at Pawtuxet and wanted to break free of Providence's control. Using Gorton's presence as a pretext, in September 1642 they petitioned to
join Massachusetts.[37]

Massachusetts leaped at the opportunity and proceeded to annex Pawtuxet.
Not only could it "rescue these men from unjust violence," Winthrop explained,
but it wanted to "draw in the rest in those parts, either under ourselves or
Plymouth." The "place was likely to be of use to us, especially if we should have occasion of sending out [military expeditions] against any Indians of Narragansett,
and likewise for an outlet into the Narragansett Bay."[38] Providence and Newport
were so alarmed that, in 1643, they sent Williams to England to procure a charter
confirming title to their lands.[39]

Further opportunity for expansion came when Algonquian communities
solicited Massachusetts's help in escaping Narragansett dominion. When
Miantonomo forced a lesser sachem named Pomham to sell Gorton sixty thousand acres at Shawomet, south of Pawtuxet, William Arnold persuaded Pomham
and the Pawtuxet sachem Sacononoco to appeal to Massachusetts, offering
their people as subjects in exchange for protection. They arrived in Boston

with his son Benedict Arnold (great-grandfather of the famous traitor) in May. Massachusetts summoned Miantonomo.[40]

Massachusetts quickly demonstrated how little it valued the Narragansett alliance. It ordered Miantonomo to surrender a Pequot convicted of attempting to assassinate Uncas, the Mohegan sachem. It received testimony from Cutshamekin, the Massachusett sachem, whose allegiance to the Narragansetts was weakening, denying that Pomham and Sacononoco were Narragansett subjects, even though they regularly gave them gifts. And it nullified the sale. Furious, Miantonomo declared he "would come no more to Boston."[41]

"The General Court considered how offensive it would be to the Narragansetts" to annex the wampum-producing regions of Shawomet and Pawtuxet, Winthrop conceded, "and so likely to engage us in a war with them," but decided it was worth the risk. "The thing being lawful and expedient for us and giving hope of opening a door to the conversion of some of them, they would not let slip the opportunity of such advantages for the fear of doubtful dangers."[42]

Massachusetts informed Pomham and Sacononoco that their people had to submit to the Ten Commandments and Christian teaching. "We desire to speak reverently of Englishman's God," the sachems agreed, "because we see the Englishman's God doth better for them than other gods do for others." Massachusetts's commissioners explained that they could no longer swear falsely or do unnecessary work on the Sabbath within English town limits. The sachems replied that this would be no trouble. Would they allow their children to be taught "knowledge of the true God and to worship him in his own way?" the commissioners asked. "As opportunity serveth by the English coming amongst us, we desire to learn their manners," they replied.

Puritan leaders were thrilled. "We looked at it as a fruit of our prayers and the first fruit of our hopes," Winthrop wrote, "that the example would bring in others, and that the Lord was by this means making a way to bring them to civility, and so to conversion to the knowledge and embracing of the gospel, in his due time." The sachems ratified the treaty on June 22 in the presence of magistrates and ministers. "[We], of our own free motion, put ourselves, our subjects, lands and estates under the government and jurisdiction of . . . Massachusetts," they declared. Afterward they dined with the governor, sitting "at a table by themselves." They departed with gifts, and Winthrop thought them "joyful and well-satisfied."[43]

Events would prove them to be less interested in Christianity than Winthrop hoped, but Massachusetts had sent Miantonomo a clear message: English power and English Christianity would march hand in hand at the expense of Narragansett dominion.

IN THE LONG RUN, Narragansett efforts to maintain their powerful position were doomed by colonial support for Uncas and the Mohegans, whose numbers had probably increased to more than twenty-five hundred. Claiming that his enemies were trying to kill him, Uncas obtained permission from Connecticut to attack a Connecticut Valley sachem named Sequassen, a Narragansett ally. When Miantonomo protested, Connecticut washed its hands of the affair. So Miantonomo asked Massachusetts governor Winthrop for permission to intervene, as required by treaty. Winthrop assured him that "if Uncas had done him or his friends wrong and would not give satisfaction, we should leave him to take his course."

Miantonomo gathered a thousand warriors and set out for Mohegan country wearing chain mail he had received from one of the disputatious Samuel Gorton's followers. Although Uncas had fewer than half as many warriors, the battle was catastrophic for Miantonomo. Thirty Narragansetts were killed, including Miantonomo's brother and two of the sachem Canonicus's sons, and many more were wounded. Worst of all, Miantonomo was betrayed by two of his own men, captured, and brought before Uncas. He refused to beg for mercy, but Uncas did not kill him. Surprised, Miantonomo entreated Uncas to turn him over to Connecticut. The Narragansetts tried to ransom him, sending Uncas a large quantity of wampum. Gorton threatened in Winthrop's name that if Uncas refused to release Miantonomo he would find himself at war with Massachusetts. The bluff apparently worked, for Uncas brought Miantonomo to Hartford. Connecticut referred the case to the United Colonies, whose commissioners met in Boston in September 1643.[44]

If the commissioners had any doubt about what was at stake, all they had to do was look at New Netherland, where Dutch governor William Kieft's misguided policies had triggered escalating ethnic violence not long after Miantonomo passed through. The brutality of Kieft's War surpassed even the Pequot War. In February 1643, Dutch soldiers massacred 120 men, women, and children in a Native village. "Infants were torn from their mother's breasts," according to one account, "and hacked to pieces in the presence of their parents."[45] Algonquians "set upon the Dutch with an implacable fury and killed all they could come by, and burnt their houses and killed their cattle without any resistance," Winthrop recorded. Among the victims were Anne Hutchinson and her family, who had migrated there in 1642. The Dutch governor and "such as escaped" were practically besieged at Manhattan. Defeated colonists returned to the Netherlands in droves. Roger Williams witnessed the crisis firsthand on his way to England.

The commissioners feared Kieft's War would spill into New England. Rumor had it that the Mohawks were but a day away, waiting for Miantonomo's release before they attacked. "It was now clearly discovered to us," Winthrop claimed, "that there was a general conspiracy among the Indians to cut off all the English, and that Miantonomo was the head and contriver of it." Puritan leaders accused the sachem of treachery, cruelty, and malice, claiming his "turbulent and proud spirit" "would never be at rest." But Winthrop admitted there was no proof. It seemed unsafe to free Miantonomo, but neither was there "sufficient ground for us to put him to death." Perplexed, the commissioners asked "five of the most judicious" ministers for advice: "all agreed that he ought to be put to death." If for no other reason, "Uncas cannot be safe while Miantonomo lives."

The problem was, killing New England's greatest sachem might provoke the very uprising they feared, much as Massachusetts's earlier crusade for justice provoked the Pequot War. So the commissioners decided on a solution that would deflect blame from themselves. They authorized Uncas to kill Miantonomo.[46]

They sent the elderly Canonicus an explanation, charging the Narragansetts with repeated treaty violations in the face of English "love and integrity." They accused Miantonomo of attacking Uncas without Connecticut's consent (despite permission from Winthrop), a violation of the Treaty of Hartford. "However his death may be grievous at present," they patronized, "yet the peaceable fruits of it will yield not only matter of safety to the Indians, but profit to all that inhabit this continent." As if that were not infuriating enough, they declared their intent to restore to Ousamequin's Pokanokets land the Narragansetts had taken years before and authorized Massachusetts colony to seize Samuel Gorton's community from the land Miantonomo had sold them at Shawomet.[47]

Somewhere between Hartford and Windsor, outside Connecticut's jurisdiction but with colonial representatives standing by, Uncas's brother stepped behind Miantonomo and "clave his head with a hatchet."[48] For the Narragansetts, it was cold-blooded murder, and all the more treacherous since Uncas had accepted wampum for Miantonomo's redemption. Narragansetts blackened their faces and "mourned continually." Morning and evening, their "mourning women" were "upon their knees with lamentations and many tears."

Gorton saw Miantonomo's wife "praying, sighing and lamenting with abundance of tears" at her wigwam. Her son Canonchet was probably too young to grasp what was happening, but perhaps he watched as an esteemed Narragansett reminded distraught warriors of their obligation to avenge his father's "blood, else would it so lie upon their own heads as to bring more miseries and evils upon them."[49] Soon after, Massachusetts troops marched to Shawomet and captured Gorton and his associates. The court in Boston condemned them to slave labor.[50]

Miantonomo's twenty-year-old brother, Pessicus, took his place as sachem. Having no desire to alienate Massachusetts, Pessicus sent Governor Winthrop wampum and an otter coat, professed "peace and friendship," and requested permission to attack Uncas "in revenge of his brother's death." Winthrop replied that the English wanted friendship with all Indians and would not accept the gift unless Pessicus kept the peace.[51] Winthrop also refused to get involved in Kieft's War, "doubting of the justice of the cause." But soldiers under Captain John Underhill, the Pequot War commander who had been recruited by the Dutch

after departing Massachusetts under a cloud of heresy, adultery, and insubordination, used tactics reminiscent of the Mystic massacre to kill more than a thousand Indians.

The Narragansetts refused to abandon their campaign for justice. Reports
had them sending the Mohawks massive quantities of wampum, and rumor
had the Mohawks promising a thousand warriors in return. Benedict Arnold
of Pawtuxet reported such rumors, but neither he nor Massachusetts believed
them. He knew the aging Canonicus did not want war, and other sachems'
alliance-building efforts proved futile. The Narragansetts lobbied so hard for
permission to fight Uncas that Arnold accused them of bribery.[52] Pessicus did
send Winthrop wampum, as was expected in Algonquian diplomacy, but he also
argued that the Narragansett cause was just. Winthrop self-righteously replied
that even if Pessicus sent a thousand fathoms of wampum and a thousand pelts,
"yet we would not do that which we judged to be unjust." If the Narragansetts
attacked Uncas, "the English would all fall upon them."[53]

THE PURITAN COLONIES' EGREGIOUS treatment of the Narragansetts was
rationalized by notions of justice but driven by fear, opportunism, and a desire for domination. Concerns about justice led Massachusetts to prevent
Connecticut from launching a war against the Narragansetts, but eventually it
bowed to arguments that Miantonomo threatened colonial security and had to
be executed. In doing so, it needlessly antagonized a valuable ally and set the
stage for decades of tension and conflict.

PART II
MISSION

7

The Conquests and Triumphs of Christ

1640 to 1648

THE INDIAN ON the Massachusetts colony seal begged the English to "come over and help us," but more than a decade after its founding, few Indians had converted to Christianity and New England lacked a single missionary. Military conquest far outpaced spiritual conquest. "The Indians are wholly subjected," reported Pastor Edmund Brown of Sudbury in 1639. "Both wolves and Indians are afraid of us (the Lord be praised)."[1] Yet colonial domination cleared the way for evangelization, and the minister John Eliot, whose missionary work would earn him the moniker "Apostle to the Indians," was waiting in the wings.

John Cotton offered a theological explanation for the lack of evangelization. He argued that according to biblical prophecy, the widespread conversion of pagan Gentiles would not take place until the Antichrist was defeated and the Jews converted. Until then, conversion numbers would remain at a trickle.[2] Another reason was the Puritan belief that civilization must precede evangelization, and civilization required Indians to submit to Massachusetts.

In truth, most colonists were focused on establishing homes, farms, towns, and churches. By 1640 Massachusetts had more than twenty towns and twelve thousand inhabitants. Plymouth established towns along the coast and inland, including Taunton, at Cohannet, and Rehoboth, near Sowams. Connecticut expanded along the Connecticut Valley, annexing Saybrook to the south. Although Connecticut did not make church membership a condition for voting, its culture remained decidedly Puritan.

Colonists were also distracted by dramatic events in England. War with Scotland finally forced King Charles, desperate for revenue, to summon Parliament in 1640. Parliament pushed reform, Charles stubbornly resisted, and by 1642 England had spiraled into a civil war between parliamentarians and royalists. Puritans supported the parliamentary cause, hoping they were witnessing "the day of Antichrist's great overthrow at Armageddon." A Massachusetts minister told his congregants that although they could not fight, "churches of praying believers are terrible as so many armies with banners." Parliamentary leaders urged Cotton and other ministers to return to England to help reform the church. Cotton did not, but many prominent colonists did go back, including a majority of Harvard's graduates over the next decade. Immigration to New England slowed to a trickle, straining its economy.[3]

Massachusetts dispatched two ministers, Hugh Peter and Thomas Weld, to represent its interests and raise support in London. (The governor's son John Winthrop Jr. accompanied them.) Mindful of criticism that so few Indians had become Christians, Peter and Weld wrote a tract titled *New England's First Fruits* to show that God was nevertheless at work among the Indians. They called for "mercy upon those miserable souls, the very ruins of mankind," claiming that they were pained "to see them go down to hell by swarms." They identified various obstacles to success. The Indians "have ever sat in hellish darkness, adoring the Devil himself for their God," the ministers explained. They stood at an "infinite distance from Christianity, having never been prepared thereunto by any civility at all," and their language was extremely difficult to understand.

Nevertheless, there had been progress. Boys and girls, including Pequot captives, who were being raised in English households were "long since civilized," could speak and read English, "and begin to understand in their measure, the grounds of Christian religion." Some of these children lamented their sinfulness, attended worship, and were "much in love with us, and cannot endure to return anymore to the Indians."[4]

The most prominent convert was Wequash, the Pequot leader at Pawcatuck. It was he who had guided Captain Mason's army to Fort Mystic during the Pequot War, and the ensuing massacre left him terrified by "the mighty power of God in our English forces." He had viewed the English God as "but a mosquito God, or a God like unto a fly." Now he considered him "a most dreadful God, and that one Englishman by the help of his God was able to slay and put to flight a hundred Indians." Mason's 1639 raid against Pawcatuck must have intensified Wequash's fear. "He went up and down bemoaning his condition and filling every place where he came with sighs and groans." He took every opportunity to inquire about Christianity. Sometimes colonists spent "more than half the night in conversing with him." It was said he would "smite his hand on his breast," declaring it "much machete [very evil]." He said, "Wequash, no God. Wequash, no know Christ." He began attending church, grew less violent and provocative, and paid restitution to people he had wronged. When abused, Peter and Weld claimed, he lay at his abusers' feet. When struck, he turned the other cheek. To honor Christian teachings against polygamy, he divorced all his wives but the first. He even evangelized fellow Indians, warning them "to flee from the wrath to come."

Then he fell deathly ill. Ministers claimed that his evangelistic efforts so disturbed the Devil that "Indians, whose hearts Satan had filled," had poisoned him. Indians urged him to send for a powwow, but he refused. "If Jesus Christ say that Wequash shall live, then Wequash must live. If Jesus Christ say that Wequash shall die, then Wequash is willing to die and will not lengthen out his life by any such means." He left his child to the care of colonists, to learn "more of Christ then its poor father ever did." After he died, minister Thomas Shepard wrote that Wequash was "certainly in heaven," for "he knew Christ, he loved Christ, he preached Christ up and down, and then suffered martyrdom for Christ."[5]

Peter and Weld claimed Indians like Wequash were open to Christianity because they had experienced English kindness and justice. Colonists did not come into the land "with violence and intrusion, but free and fair, with their consent and allowance," they argued. The leading sachems declared them "much welcome," and colonists did not take a single acre without the Natives' consent. They treated Indians "fairly and courteously, with loving terms, good looks, and kind salutes," and procedures were in place to resolve disputes.

It was a highly idealized picture. A few years earlier, according to John Winthrop, Indian servants had reported that the spirit Hobbomock warned them "to forsake the English and not to come at the assemblies nor to learn to read." Indians who visited English homes were so turned off by Christianity, according to a minister, "that if any began to speak of God and heaven and hell and religion unto them, they would presently be gone." Indeed, "it was a received and known thing" that if you wanted to get rid of an Indian, you simply had to talk about religion. Peter and Weld admitted that colonists were wary: "We are wont to keep them at such a distance, knowing they serve the Devil and are led by him, as not to embolden them too much or trust them too far." Thankfully, "God hath so kept them (excepting that act of the Pequots . . .) that we never found any hurt from them, nor could ever prove any real intentions of evil against us."

Still, they warned that if colonists failed to evangelize them, "these poor Indians will certainly rise up against us and with great boldness condemn us" on the day of God's judgment. God had not brought "so many thousands of his people into the wilderness" for no purpose. He wanted them to "pity those poor heathen that are bleeding to death, to eternal death, and to reach forth a hand of soul mercy, to save some of them from the fire of hell." This required prayer and material support. New England's ministers had their hands full serving their congregations, but with proper funding, men could be recruited for missionary work.[6]

The truth, as Peter and Weld presented it, was that death and conquest had paved the way for evangelism. The ministers praised God for "sweeping away great multitudes of the Natives by the small pox . . . that he might make room for us," and for extending his hand so "that the name of the Pequots (as of Amalek) is blotted out from under heaven, there being not one that is, or (at least) dare call himself a Pequot." As the English grew in power, they believed, Christ's kingdom was advancing. The result was that more Natives would be saved.[7]

THE EXILED ROGER WILLIAMS, who was in England to contest Massachusetts's claims to Narragansett Bay, challenged Peter and Weld's rosy picture. He had once held "great hopes . . . of many a poor Indian soul inquiring after God."

Narragansetts told him they believed in at least thirty-eight gods, naming "all they could remember," but he claimed to have persuaded hundreds that they lacked the truth. "I hope the time is not long that some shall truly bless the God of heaven that ever they saw the face of Englishmen," he wrote in 1638.[8]

Now he had become more skeptical, toward both Massachusetts's intentions and Puritan Christianity, and he cast serious doubts on their claims of Indian conversions. In 1643, Williams published *A Key into the Language of America*, a treasure trove of observations about Algonquians' language, religion, politics, and culture informed by his innumerable hours among them. He described it as a resource for people who wanted to civilize and evangelize Indians, and it quickly emerged as a rival interpretation to *New England's First Fruits*. He contended that Indians were more civilized and better prepared for Christianity than most English assumed, possessing a "savor of civility and courtesy" many colonists lacked. They were so hospitable that "if any come to them upon any occasion they request them to come in." He was sure God would eventually convert them in fulfillment of biblical prophecy regarding the Gentiles. But he questioned whether converts like Wequash truly understood God's grace. Williams had spent long hours talking with Wequash about sin, judgment, repentance, and salvation. On his deathbed, Wequash told Williams, "Your words were never out of my heart." But when Wequash said he prayed regularly, Williams warned that many unsaved English also prayed. This discouraged Wequash, who admitted his heart was evil and hard.[9]

Williams claimed he could easily persuade Indians to practice formal Christianity, which he considered worthless. "I know it to have been easy for myself, long ere this, to have brought many thousands of these Natives, yea the whole country, to a far greater antichristian conversion than ever was heard of in America," he boasted. Their awe of English clothing, books, and letters left them "easily persuaded that the God that made Englishmen is a greater God, because he hath so richly endowed the English above themselves." They hoped he might do the same for them. But given language and culture barriers, it was unrealistic to expect many true conversions anytime soon. Colonists knew enough Algonquian to communicate about trade or law, but explaining complicated spiritual truths required a nuanced understanding of Native culture.

To be sure, Williams doubted most English were true Christians. In his pamphlet *Christenings Make Not Christians*, published in 1645, he argued that despite their sense of superiority over heathen Indians, most professed Christians had "no more of Christ than the name." From God's perspective, Indians were no worse and perhaps better. "There is no respect of persons with him, for we are all the work of his hands," Williams wrote. "If we respect their sins, they are far short of European sinners. They neither abuse . . . corporal mercies, for they have them not, nor sin they against the gospel light, which shines not amongst them."

They were "intelligent, many very ingenuous, plain-hearted, inquisitive," and held "many convictions." As he put it in the *Key*, drawing on Acts 17, "Boast not, proud English, of thy birth and blood. Thy brother Indian is by birth as good. Of one blood God made him, and thee, and all."

Williams also shared the minister John Cotton's belief that the heathen would not embrace Christianity until Christ defeated Antichrist and the Jews returned to Palestine. "The prophets are deep concerning this," he admitted. Yet while Cotton believed the church could still evangelize Indians, Williams thought no true church would exist until God sent apostles to establish one. As for the Indians, Williams would wait until God revealed his hand.[10]

THE ONLY PLACE WHERE missionary efforts had commenced was Martha's Vineyard, where about three thousand Wampanoags lived off Plymouth's southern coast. Colonist Thomas Mayhew had procured a patent to the island and nearby Nantucket in 1641, purchasing land from the sachem Tawanquatuck. There his twenty-two-year-old son, Thomas Mayhew Jr., pastored about a hundred colonists. The younger Mayhew befriended a Wampanoag outcast named Hiacoomes, who had "a sad and a sober spirit" and believed the English held superior means of "attaining the blessings of health and life." Mayhew taught him to read, while Hiacoomes taught Mayhew Algonquian.

It came at a cost for Hiacoomes. "Here comes the Englishman," Wampanoags would say, to peals of laughter. When a sagamore named Pakeponesso railed at him for submitting to the English, Hiacoomes replied that he was "gladly obedient to the English, neither was it for the Indians' hurt he did so." Furious, Pakeponesso struck him in the face, and colonists had to protect Hiacoomes from further violence. Hiacoomes predicted that God would judge the sagamore. Soon after, Pakeponesso was seriously injured by lightning.

In 1643 and 1645 epidemics killed as many as half the island's Wampanoags. Many blamed the illness on their departure from traditional ways, but others pointed out that the disease did not afflict the English. A sachem named Myoxeo invited Hiacoomes to speak, so Hiacoomes explained everything he knew about the Christian God. When Myoxeo protested that it made little sense to throw away "thirty-seven gods for one," Hiacoomes replied, "I have thrown away all these, and a great many more some years ago, yet am preserved as you see this day." Upon reflection, Myoxeo declared that he would also serve the one God.[11]

Mayhew gained credibility by treating sick Indians the powwows were unable to help. Powwows gave up a sixty-year-old named Ieogiscat for dead, but when Mayhew prayed for him, he recovered. In contrast, a man named Saul, who ignored Mayhew's warnings not to rely on powwows, died. Tawanquatuck's son recovered after Mayhew bled him and prayed for him, leading the grateful sachem to ask why Mayhew waited so long to share his knowledge of God. Mayhew began teaching his people every other week.[12]

⊙⋙⊙

WHAT FINALLY TRIGGERED missionary work in Massachusetts was the weakening of Narragansett dominion after the sachem Miantonomo's death. Following the example of Pomham and Sacononoco, the Shawomet and Pawtuxet sachems, in 1644 six sachems pledged allegiance to the colony of Massachusetts in exchange for protection. Several, perhaps all, had been Narragansett tributaries, including the Massachusett Cutshamekin, Passaconnaway of the Pennacooks, and Wassamequin and Showanon of the Quaboag and Nashaway Nipmucs. Showanon, eager to make Nashaway a hub in the burgeoning fur trade, sold colonists eighty square miles in the fertile Nashua Valley, where they established a trading post and the town of Lancaster.[13]

"We now began to conceive hope that the Lord's time was at hand for opening a door of light and grace to those Indians," Governor Winthrop wrote.[14] On June 10, the government ordered each town to select men "whose hearts God shall stir up" to teach local Indians how to submit to "the scepter of the Lord Jesus."[15] The towns proved slow to act, so on November 13 Massachusetts ordered county courts to civilize local Indians and "have them instructed in the knowledge and worship of God." A year later, it was still urging ministers to submit a plan to evangelize and civilize Indians "as speedily as may be."[16]

It was John Eliot, Roxbury's forty-two year-old minister, who finally took action. A Cambridge graduate, Eliot had arrived in Massachusetts in 1631, married soon after, and was raising four sons to be ministers. He later recalled that God filled him with compassion for Indians and a desire to teach them "to know Christ and to bring them into his kingdom." He met an "ingenious" Pequot War captive named Cockenoe who spoke and read English, and Cockenoe began tutoring him in Algonquian.[17]

In September 1646, Eliot preached to Cutshamekin's Massachusett people at Neponset, near Dorchester. He emphasized God's law, for Puritans believed a person had to experience intense guilt for sin before they could appreciate the gospel. It did not go well. As Eliot put it, "They gave no heed unto it, but were weary and rather despised what I said." When he asked if they had any questions, their response discouraged him: "What was the cause of thunder?" one asked. What caused "the ebbing and flowing of the sea?" What of the wind?

Soon after, he learned that the Massachusetts at Nonantum, near Watertown, wanted to adopt "English fashions and live after their manner." Their leader, Waban, had sent his son to Dedham to receive schooling and be taught Christianity. They thought it inevitable that "Indians would be all one English" someday but "despaired that ever it should come to pass in their days." Eliot told them the English and Indians "were already all one." The only differences were that the English "know, serve, and pray unto God" and "labor and work in building, planting, clothing ourselves," and so forth, and the Indians "do not." Yet this could be remedied. If Indians were civilized and became Christians, they "would be all one with Englishmen."[18]

Eliot and other ministers visited Nonantum on October 28, 1646. Men, women, and children gathered in Waban's large wigwam. Waban's son, wearing English clothes, stood by his father. Eliot prayed in English, hoping to convey that prayer was "serious and sacred" and wanting to be free with his words. Then he preached in Algonquian, with Cockenoe's help, for seventy-five minutes. He could "but stammer out some pieces" of scripture, relying on "many circumlocutions and variations of speech," but he made himself understood. The minister Thomas Shepard thought "it was a glorious, affecting spectacle to see a company of perishing, forlorn outcasts, diligently attending to the blessed word of salvation." Eliot explained the Ten Commandments, conveying the "dreadful wrath of God" against those who disobeyed even "the least" of them. Algonquians believed that after death the souls of decent people rested in the house of the god Kiehtan, while those of murderers, thieves, and liars would "wander restless abroad," but what Eliot described was judgment on a whole new level, and actions he described as sins were common among Indians. Having terrified his audience, he spoke winsomely about Jesus, calling him "the only means of recovery from sin and wrath and eternal death." He portrayed "the blessed estate" of all who "believe in Christ, and know him feelingly," contrasting the "joys of heaven and the terrors and horrors of wicked men in hell."

This sermon went much better than the one at Neponset. Afterward, he asked his audience if they understood him.

Numerous voices called out that they did. "How may we come to know Jesus Christ?" one wondered.

Eliot pointed to the Bible. They could not read it, but he could teach them what it said. They could also pray that God would reveal himself to them. Even "if they did but sigh and groan," asking God to help them know Jesus "again and again with their hearts," God would answer them, for he heard "the prayers of all men, both Indians as well as English." They simply had to confess their sins, recognizing that God did not owe them salvation.

A Massachusett said that an Indian told him his prayers were useless because Jesus could not understand their language.

Eliot replied that God "knew all that was within man and came from man, all his desires and all his thoughts."

Others wondered whether the English had ever been ignorant of God.

Eliot affirmed that they had, but came to know God "by reading his book and hearing his word and praying to him." Even now, however, there were "two sorts of Englishmen." Some were wicked and no better off than Indians. Others had repented and turned to Christ, much as Indians could do.

He used analogies to help them understand the Christian concept of God. If they saw a great wigwam, "would they think that raccoons or foxes built it?" Or "would they think that it made itself?" In the same way, someone must have created the world. And just as the sun's light shone in many places at once, so God was present everywhere.

He took questions for over an hour and a half. Although they wanted to hear more, he was exhausted and wanted to "leave them with an appetite." He closed with prayer and dispensed gifts—apples for the children and tobacco for the men. Some expressed a desire for regular instruction, so the ministers promised to propose this to the Massachusetts General Court.[19]

Within a month, the General Court declared that since many Indians had "become subjects to the English and have engaged themselves to be willing and ready to understand the law of God," land should be set aside where they could "live in an orderly way amongst us" under "rules for their improvement." New laws would punish idolatry, powwowing, and pagan worship, subject to a fine of twenty shillings. Anyone, "whether Christian or pagan," who "wittingly and willingly" blasphemed God's name would be subject to death as stipulated by the Law of Moses (though this was never enforced). At the same time, the court affirmed the principle, recognized by Boston minister John Cotton in a debate with Roger Williams, that no Indian could be compelled "to the Christian faith ... either by force of arms or by penal laws." Laws could instill Christian morality, but only the gospel could change hearts.[20]

That was Eliot's task. That month, he and Shepard returned to Nonantum and addressed a much larger crowd than before. Eliot used a simple catechism to teach younger children.

"Who made you and all the world?"

Answer: "God."

"Who do you look should save you and redeem you from sin and hell?"

Answer: "Jesus Christ."[21]

Next, Eliot preached for an hour. God was terribly angry with sin, he explained, and would inflict "dreadful torment and punishment" on those who broke his "holy commandments." Nevertheless, God "sent Jesus Christ to die for their sins" and would "love the poor miserable Indians if now they sought God and believed in Jesus Christ."

During the question-and-answer session an elderly man asked if it was too late for someone as old as he to be saved.

Eliot assured him that no matter how long he had lived in sin, God would forgive him.

Why did the English know so much more about God than Indians? one asked.

"Englishmen seek God, dwell in his house, hear his word, pray to God, instruct their children out of God's book," Eliot answered. "But Indians' forefathers were a stubborn and rebellious children and would not hear the word, did not care to pray nor to teach their children, and hence Indians that now are, do not know God at all." Not all Englishmen knew God, he reminded them. Many were as wicked as "Cutshamekin's drunken Indians."[22]

He held their attention all afternoon and beyond. When he closed with fifteen minutes of prayer, many looked upward, lifting their hands. A man broke down, Shepard reported, and his tears "forced us also to such bowels of compassion that we could not forebear weeping over him also." Indians said they could not sleep that night, as their minds were racing about what they had heard, though others resented what the ministers were doing.

The ministers committed themselves to the long haul. By giving gifts and forcing baptisms they could have converted thousands, Shepard argued, but genuine conversions would take years of diligent labor. First, Indians had to be civilized, for they were "the dregs of mankind and the saddest spectacles of misery." In time, Lord willing, a few would be converted. They, in turn, would be trained and sent to teach their people. "God is wont ordinarily to convert nations and peoples by some of their own countrymen," Shepard explained, for they could "best speak and most of all pity their brethren."[23]

Eliot made two other visits to Nonantum that year, and several Indians professed sorrow at their sin and a desire to know Christ. A powwow declared that he and his wife were resolved "to hear the word and seek the devil no more." Men offered themselves for service in English households, and parents presented their children to be raised by English families or attend English schools. On November 26, Nonantum's leader Waban proposed a set of laws, drafted with English help. Some enforced scriptural teachings, while others reflected English cultural conventions. One law prohibited sex outside of marriage. Another punished husbands for beating their wives. Women were required to keep their hair tied up and cover their breasts. Men had to keep their hair short and work their fields. Indians were forbidden to crush lice between their teeth.[24]

A Pennacook sachem named Attawans expressed a desire to "become more like . . . the English" and establish a town with similar laws near Concord. Attawans had probably been exposed to Christianity by the ambitious trader Simon Willard. Born in 1605, Willard had immigrated to Massachusetts in 1634, helped found Concord, and became the dominant fur trader in the Merrimack Valley.[25] On Attawans's behalf, he drew up an ambitious code prohibiting drunkenness, powwowing, lying, fighting, polygamy, fornication, wife-beating, and Sabbath-breaking. Bestiality, adultery, and murder carried a death sentence, while theft required fourfold restitution. The code prohibited Algonquian customs such as greasing skin, isolating women during menstruation, and various games. Indians could no longer wear masks or "keep up a great noise by howling" when mourning a death. They were required to pray before and after meals and knock before entering English homes.

But Attawans's efforts provoked stiff opposition from his leading men as well as from Concord colonists who objected to Indians living nearby. To his men, Attawans argued that while higher sachems (presumably the Pennacook Passaconnaway) exploited them for pelts, kettles, and wampum, "you may evidently see that the English mind no such things, care for none of your goods, but only seek your good and welfare, and instead of taking away, are ready to give to you." To colonists, he replied that Indians who remained distant "would not so much care to pray, nor would they be so ready to hear the word of God, but they would be all one Indians still." His arguments proved unpersuasive, and the code was not implemented. Shepard attributed the opposition to "a special finger of Satan."[26]

Governor Winthrop and other officials visited Nonantum and were deeply impressed by the "appearances of a great change." Natives observed the Sabbath and adopted "civil fashions." Young men worked hard fencing their land. Women took up spinning. "They begin to grow industrious, and find something to sell at market all the year long," Eliot reported. In winter they sold brooms, staves, pots, baskets, and turkeys; in spring they brought cranberries, fish, and strawberries; by summer it was hurtleberies, grapes, and fish; and in autumn, venison. During hay season and harvest they labored for colonists for wages. Shepard was amazed "to see so many Indian men, women, and children in English apparel," such that "you would scarce know them from English people." More important, they prayed "constantly in their families, morning and evening." Shepard wished "many English who profess themselves Christians" showed equal piety, musing that they would do well to "become Indians, excepting that name."

Natives may have especially appreciated prayer because it enabled each man, woman, and child to have regular, direct access to God, in sharp contrast to Algonquian religion, in which visions and rituals were primarily the prerogative of powwows. They called themselves "praying Indians" and called Nonantum a "praying town."

They asked difficult questions. Ministers did not allow women to speak publicly, but one posed her question through a spokesman. Her husband was often angry and abusive, she said; was it right for him to pray with her? Since God was all-powerful, others asked, why did he not give people good hearts so they stopped sinning? Why did he not destroy the devil? An old powwow could not understand why it took the English twenty-seven years to teach them about God. "Had you done it sooner," he said, "we might have known much of God by this time, and much sin might have been prevented." The embarrassed ministers replied that the Indians "were never willing to hear till now."[27]

THE PRAYING TOWNS REQUESTED permission to establish their own courts, so in May 1647 Massachusetts authorized sachems to hold monthly court sessions to adjudicate minor civil and criminal matters and appoint officers to serve warrants and enforce rulings. Massachusetts claimed jurisdiction over major cases, stipulating that each quarter a magistrate would serve as a circuit judge. Meanwhile, ministers would teach "the principles of reason, justice and equity" that informed the laws.[28]

By late summer, even the reluctant Massachusett sachem Cutshamekin had accepted a legal code at Neponset. Eliot took up the practice of censuring misconduct during his regular meetings. Once, an Indian named Wampooas was brought forward for beating his wife. As he confessed his sin, he "turned his face to the wall and wept, though with modest endeavor to hide it." Colonists were "much affected" to observe such repentance "in a barbarian," according to Shepard, "and all did forgive him," though he still had to pay a fine.

Cutshamekin's son, about fifteen, was admonished for getting drunk and dishonoring his parents. He protested that his father did all sorts of things the ministers considered sinful. Why should he be any different? The ministers urged Cutshamekin to "remove that stumbling block out of his son's way by confessing his own sins." When Cutshamekin expressed openness, Eliot pressed him: "Are you now sorry for your drunkenness, filthiness, false dealing, lying, [and other sins]?" Cutshamekin, in front of his people, declared that he was and "condemned himself." The ministers then turned to his son. After much laboring by Boston minister John Wilson, the boy yielded, "entreated his father to forgive him, and took him by the hand." Cutshamekin "burst forth into great weeping." Then the boy turned to his mother, who was also reduced to tears. Even the English "fell a weeping, so that the house was filled with weeping on every side."[29]

Emotional as such moments were, many Algonquians reviled their kin for accepting Christianity, cutting their hair, and adopting English ways. Powwows, who found themselves denounced as "great witches" who worshiped "the old serpent," departed Nonantum and Neponset and warned their people against Christianity. When Eliot learned how many opposed the mission, even "threatening death to some if they heard any more [teaching]," he told the Nonantum Indians it was the Devil's doing but that they need not fear "the reproaches of wicked Indians, nor their witchcraft and powwows and poisonings," for God would protect them.[30]

Opponents argued that Christianity did not benefit them. "You go naked still, and you are as poor as we," they told praying Indians, yet "we take more pleasure than you." Eliot could not deny their poverty. They lacked "so much as meat, drink, or lodging" to offer visiting ministers. It struck him that while Jesus appeared to first-century Gentiles as "a poor underling, and his servants poor," to Indians he was "rich, potent, above them in learning, riches, and power." As a result, they came seeking not only spiritual blessings but material gifts. Ministers affirmed that it was better to be poor with Christ than rich without him, but they also highlighted Christianity's material benefits, exhorting that if praying Indians worked hard like the English, they would receive greater rewards.[31]

One day, Eliot prayed with a woman who lay dying from a difficult childbirth. She told him that although God afflicted her, she loved him and believed he would forgive her sins because of Jesus's death. Calling two grown daughters to her side, she warned that their grandparents and uncles would pressure them to leave the praying town. "I charge you, never hearken unto them nor live amongst them," she exhorted, "for they pray not to God, keep not the Sabbath, commit all manner of sins, and are not punished for it. But I charge you, live here, for here they pray unto God, the word of God is taught, sins are suppressed and punished by laws." Eliot shared her concern. If Indians were to be evangelized, they had to live in praying towns. They could not be trusted to form congregations while living "so unfixed, confused, and ungoverned a life, uncivilized and unsubdued to labor and order."[32]

Hoping to expand his work, in the spring of 1647 Eliot visited Pawtucket Falls, "a great fishing place" on the Merrimack River, where Pennacooks gathered every spring to catch "salmon, shads, lamprey eels, sturgeon, bass," and other fish and to play games, dance, and observe various rituals, many of which Puritans condemned. Passaconnaway, their sachem, was renowned for his powwowing. Indians claimed he could "make the water burn, the rocks move, the trees dance, metamorphise himself into a flaming man," and bring dead plants and animals to life. But he had not forgotten how Massachusetts colony soldiers had seized his son, daughter-in-law, and grandchild five years before, so he and his sons left before Eliot arrived, leading minister Thomas Shepard to mock that he fled a man who "came only with a book in his hand," proving "that Satan is but a coward." Other Pennacooks listened carefully to Eliot's preaching, however. Eliot decided to return the following year.[33]

Later that year, Eliot, Shepard, and Wilson preached to Nausets on Cape Cod. A sachem sent most of his men fishing to prevent them from hearing the sermon, though he himself attended with "a dogged look and a discontented countenance." Other Nausets responded in surprising ways. An old man claimed "they had heard some old men who were now dead to say the same things." Others said "their forefathers did know God, but that after this, they fell into a great sleep, and when they did awaken they quite forgot him." One claimed that during the dark days of the plague, before the Pilgrims arrived, he had a dream. In it, "he saw a great many men come to those parts in clothes just as the English now are appareled." Among them was "a man all in black, with a thing in his hand," which he now realized was the Bible. The man preached that "God was *moosquantum*, or angry with them, and that he would kill them for their sins." When the Nauset asked what God would do to him and his family, the man in black smiled and promised that they would be safe.[34] The ministers struggled to make sense of such stories. Had God revealed himself to Indians before the English arrived?

Eliot believed that if he could convert Ousamequin, many Wampanoags would follow, but the great Pokanoket sachem steadfastly opposed Christianity. Eliot had better success elsewhere. He traveled to Nashaway four times in 1648, reporting that its sachem Showanon "doth embrace the gospel and pray unto God." He also returned to Pawtucket Falls. This time Passaconnaway stayed to hear him preach on Malachi 1:11, which prophesied that God's name would be great among the Gentiles. Eliot translated "Gentiles" as "Indians," telling Passaconnaway that the prophecy foretold their conversion. But a Pennacook was disturbed to hear that people who did not believe the gospel were punished forever in hell. "If it be thus as you teach," he reflected, "then all the world of Indians are gone to hell to be tormented forever, until now, [when] a few may go to heaven and be saved. Is it so?" Eliot confirmed that it was. At last, Passaconnaway spoke. He had never heard of God, he admitted, but he believed Eliot preached truth, so from now on he would pray to God. His sons said the same. He asked Eliot to settle nearby so he could teach them regularly. Simon Willard, who had introduced Eliot to Passaconnaway, could establish a trading post.[35]

"Sundry in the country in diverse places would gladly be taught the knowledge of God and Jesus Christ and would pray unto God if I could go unto them and teach them where they dwell," Eliot lamented. "But to come to live here among or near to the English, they are not willing." One reason, the recent convert Wampooas complained, was that while their kin despised them for accepting Christianity, the English "suspect us and fear us to be still such as do not pray at all." Eliot knew he was right, though he replied that "others of us, who know you and speak with you, we do not so think of you." Another reason was that Indians who lived near English towns lost control of their land. Cattle invaded their hunting grounds and devoured their cornfields, yet colonists insisted Indians were responsible for fencing their own fields. Indians countered that they had "neither tools, nor skill, nor heart to fence their grounds." Eliot admitted, "It's a very great discouragement to them and me."

The solution, he thought, was to establish a new praying town, "somewhat remote from the English, where they must have the word constantly taught and government constantly exercised, means of good subsistence provided, encouragements for the industrious, means of instructing them in letters, trades, and labors [such] as building, fishing, flax and hemp dressing, planting orchards." Unfortunately, he lacked resources for such a scheme.[36]

Despite such difficulties, Puritan missionary work had taken giant strides and was poised to make more, largely because, as Narragansett power declined, former Narragansett tributaries were submitting to Massachusetts. "Surely there is some conquering power of Christ Jesus stirring among them," Shepard wrote in a tract to England. True, after the initial high, many converts lost their early zeal. Plenty attended services and went through the motions to curry ministers' favor, just as many colonists did. But others were different. "I think it might make many Christians ashamed, who may easily see how far they are exceeded by these naked men in so short a time," Shepard reflected. He argued that unlike the Spanish Empire, responsible for the deaths of millions of "poor innocent Natives," Christ's kingdom was advancing in New England not by force of arms but by Christ's word and Spirit. "Christ can and will conquer by weak and despicable means, though the conquest perhaps may be somewhat long," he wrote. They simply needed to be patient.[37]

8

Reparations

1644 to 1650

PURITAN LEADERS BELIEVED that expanding their dominion throughout New England was in not only their interests, but the Indians' as well. Ideally this would be a peaceful conquest: sachems would voluntarily surrender their sovereignty to embrace "civilization" and Christianity. They expected the Narragansetts to toe the line, and when the Narragansetts sought justice for the killing of their leader, Miantonomo, the colonies denied them in the name of their own vision of justice. The key question was whether Puritan views of justice would prevent war or provoke it.

The Narragansetts were surprised when, half a year after colonial troops seized Samuel Gorton from the land controversially sold to him by Miantonomo, Gorton returned to Narragansett country. How, they asked, had he escaped harsher punishment? Gorton explained that it was because he was a subject of England, where he intended to travel to appeal his case. The sachems wondered whether they might pursue a similar strategy. At Gorton's urging, they held a great council and with "unanimous consent" agreed to become subjects of England.[1]

Gorton drafted a letter, dated April 10, 1644, in which they formally submitted their people and land to King Charles and the "laws and customs" of England. Their only condition was that the king extend his "royal protection, and righting us of what wrong is, or may be done unto us" by "His Majesty's pretended subjects." The sachems attached their signatures: a downward facing bow and arrow for Pessicus, an upside-down T for Canonicus, and a tomahawk for Canonicus's son Mixanno. Gorton agreed to represent them in London.[2]

Oblivious to these developments, that spring Massachusetts summoned the sachems to Boston. Much to the colonists' surprise, Canonicus and Pessicus politely declined. Justice demanded they avenge Miantonomo's death, otherwise "we should fear his blood would lie upon ourselves," they explained. The colonies could try to persuade them that war was a bad idea, but they were no longer bound by such judgments, for they were now subjects of the crown. With newfound confidence that must have infuriated the Puritan magistrates, the sachems assured them that "the former love that hath been betwixt you and us" would surely increase now that they were subjects "unto the same king and state."[3]

The General Court dispatched envoys demanding to know whether the sachems really "did own that letter." How could they follow the counsel of "such evil men [Gorton], and such as we had banished from us?" Canonicus left the envoys waiting in the rain for two hours before welcoming them into his wigwam. Then he "lay upon his couch" and ignored them, aside from a few adversarial comments, until Pessicus arrived, four hours later. During a conference that lasted all night, the Narragansetts declared their intent to go to war against Uncas and the Mohegans to avenge Miantonomo's death—with or without Massachusetts's permission.[4]

War parties began raiding Mohegan territory, and the sachems summoned their tributaries to war by sending them Mohegan body parts. They sent Pomham, the Shawomet sachem who had pledged his loyalty to Massachusetts, two hands and a foot, but he boldly rejected their overture and invoked the colony's protection. Massachusetts dispatched fourteen soldiers to construct a fort at Shawomet, recognizing that "if we fail them, we break our covenant with them, whereby the name of God will suffer, and religion will be evil spoken of, and the whole nation will be odious in their sight."[5]

The commissioners of the United Colonies summoned both Uncas and the Narragansett sachems to Hartford in September. The Narragansetts sent a lesser sachem. Uncas admitted that he had discussed releasing Miantonomo and had accepted wampum from the Narragansetts but denied making any ransom agreement. Predictably, the commissioners took him at his word, dismissed contrary testimony, and vowed to defend Uncas. The Narragansett sachem refused to accept the ruling. All he would promise was peace "until after the next planting of corn" and that the Narragansetts would provide thirty days' notice of an attack. They did not want to alienate the colonies, but neither would they give up their quest for justice.[6]

THE PURITAN COLONIES SUFFERED another blow that month when the banished Roger Williams arrived in Boston from London carrying a patent dated March 14, 1644, establishing the colony of Providence Plantations in the Narragansett Bay (eventually known as Rhode Island). Approved by the Committee on Foreign Plantations headed by the Earl of Warwick, its territory included Aquidneck Island and Providence and was said to be bordered on the west by Narragansett country, "the whole tract extending about twenty-five English miles unto the Pequot River and country." This made no sense, because the Pequot River was on the far side of Narragansett country, some forty miles from Narragansett Bay.

Massachusetts's agent, Thomas Weld, had contested the patent, securing signatures from several committee members for a conflicting patent that gave Narragansett country to Massachusetts. Its booming population needed more land, they argued, and "the gospel may be speedier conveyed and preached to the Natives that now sit there in darkness." But Weld's efforts fell short, for several committee members, including former Massachusetts governor Henry Vane, sympathized with Williams's cause.

The committee also found Williams's vision for English–Indian relations more compelling than Weld's. One of the reasons they gave Williams the charter, they informed Massachusetts, was because of "his great industry and travels in his printed Indian labors in your parts (the like whereof we have not seen extant from any part of America)." Yet Williams's patent said nothing about evangelizing Indians. It simply acknowledged that colonists had settled alongside the Narragansetts, "which may in time by the blessing of God upon their endeavors lay a surer foundation of happiness to all America." To those who wondered how Williams justified procuring a charter after having condemned Massachusetts for doing the same, Williams would have replied that the Narragansetts had granted this land by deeds of friendship.[7]

Massachusetts continued to contest the patent. Not only did the colony claim Shawomet and Pawtuxet and covet Narragansett country; it also cast its eyes toward the Pequot River, thanks to the initiative of John Winthrop Jr. In recent years, Winthrop Jr. had pursued one manufacturing venture after another. He tried to develop means of extracting salt from sea water. He established an ironworks. When he discovered black lead ore at Tantiusque, in Nipmuc country, he decided to establish two plantations, one near the prospective mine and another at the mouth of the Pequot River, which offered a deep-water harbor. His objectives were not merely entrepreneurial; he envisioned the settlement as a destination for alchemical scholars and a post for evangelizing Indians.

Both Massachusetts and Connecticut claimed Pequot country, but Massachusetts granted Winthrop, Jr. the land. His agents purchased the mine and surrounding area from Nipmuc sachems. He already owned Fisher's Island, near the river mouth, where he kept hogs and goats and planned to plant English grasses, rye, winter wheat, indigo, and fruit trees.[8] To procure land on the mainland, he sought out Robin Cassacinamon, leader of a group of Pequots assigned to the Mohegan sachem Uncas, who had established a town there called Nameag. Cassacinamon, who had formerly served Winthrop Jr.'s father in Boston—he was suspected of having helped Winthrop's female Pequot servants escape— had reason to welcome English settlement and the protection it might bring: he wanted independence from Uncas.[9]

Winthrop Jr. was in the area with Thomas Peter when the Narragansett-Mohegan war resumed. In February 1645, the Narragansetts notified Boston that unless Uncas paid them 160 fathoms of wampum as recompense for their sachem Miantonomo's death, or agreed to a new hearing, they would attack him. Canonicus preferred a less militant posture but conceded that "the young sachems, being but boys, will need war." Narragansetts sieged Uncas's fort at

Shantok. Connecticut and New Haven rushed troops to Uncas's defense, while Massachusetts demanded the Narragansetts cease their attacks, "promising their grievances should be fully and justly heard."[10]

As soon as colonial troops returned home, a thousand Narragansetts again invaded Mohegan territory. The Mohegans drove them back but suffered at least forty casualties. Winthrop Jr. and Peter rushed to Shantok, where Peter tended the wounded. "The Lord pardon our neglect of Uncas and charge not the blood on our faces," Peter lectured Winthrop Jr.'s father a few days later. He thought it long overdue for the English to act with the spirit of the Israelites who conquered Canaan, for "I fear we shall be in flames, ere we are aware."[11]

Roger Williams implored the senior Winthrop to show restraint. He had tried to convince the Narragansetts to stop fighting, but "there is a spirit of desperation fallen upon them," Williams explained. "[They are] resolved to revenge the death of their prince and recover their ransom for his life . . . or to perish with him." Williams appealed to "the common bonds of humanity" shared by English and Indians alike. "My humble requests are to the God of Peace that no English blood be further spilt in America." The colonies should pursue "loving mediation or prudent neutrality."[12]

The United Colonies commissioners met in Boston in July, with Governor Winthrop serving as president. They called the sachems to send delegates, promising to judge their case "without any partial respect to either party," seeking "peace between them for their mutual safety and advantage." They warned the Narragansetts that if they failed to appear, the colonies would go to war on Uncas's behalf.[13]

Pessicus, the Narragansett sachem, received the envoys graciously, agreeing to send representatives, but then Ninigret showed up. Although he was formally the Eastern Niantic sachem, Ninigret was growing influential among younger Narragansetts, who were tired of bowing to English demands. Stiffened by Ninigret, Pessicus declared that they "were resolved to have no peace without Uncas's head." The meeting quickly soured. Ninigret rejected the Puritan claim that whoever initiated the war was necessarily in the wrong, insisting that the English had violated the Treaty of Hartford by supporting Uncas without cause. If they continued to do so, he threatened, the Narragansetts would call on the distant Mohawks, who "would lay the English cattle on heaps as high as their houses." A colonist would not be able to "step out of doors to piss, but he should be killed."[14]

The commissioners were faced with a monumental decision: Did the Narragansett-Mohegan war justify an invasion of Narragansett country? Emmanuel Downing, Governor Winthrop's brother-in-law, advocated war on two grounds. First, he feared it was sinful "to suffer them to maintain the worship of the devil, which their powwows often do." Second, "If upon a just war the Lord should deliver them into our hands, we might easily have men, women, and children enough to exchange for Moors [Africans]." The colony desperately needed slaves, he argued, for English servants "desire freedom to plant for themselves, and [will] not stay but for very great wages." Twenty African slaves were cheaper to maintain than one English servant.[15]

The Puritan elite agreed that they were obligated to intervene. On August 11, the commissioners issued a declaration defending their decision. They had pursued peace and arbitration, they contended, but the Narragansetts had rejected their overtures. Failure to defend Uncas as required by treaty would "dishonor and provoke God" and expose them to "contempt and danger from the barbarians." Indeed, "no Indians will trust the English . . . either in the present or succeeding generations." Instead, Indians would return their allegiance to the Narragansetts, forging an overwhelming coalition against the English. Much as the Devil once raised the Amalekites and Philistines against Israel, they claimed, so now Satan was stirring up the Narragansetts as "his instruments against the churches of Christ." The conclusion appeared inescapable: "God calls the colonies to a war."[16]

They called for three hundred soldiers and proclaimed a day of prayer and humiliation. Soldiers from New Haven and Connecticut under Captain John Mason, of Mystic fame, joined Mohegan forces at Shantok to strike from the west. Plymouth and allied Wampanoag forces mustered under Miles Standish, hero of Wessagusset, to invade from the east. Massachusetts forces, alongside their Shawomet and probably Massachusett allies, would descend from the north. "We see ourselves called to a war in the full compass and extent," the commissioners explained to Mason. He must seize every opportunity "to weaken the Narragansetts and their confederates in their number of men, their corn, canoes, wigwams, wampum, and goods," taking as many captives as possible for enslavement, "men, women, or children."[17]

Some Puritans may have questioned the justice of the march to war, for a few days later, when appointing Edward Gibbons of Massachusetts commander-in-chief of colonial forces, the commissioners expressed their "earnest desires . . . if it may be attained with justice, honor and safety, to procure peace rather than to prosecute war." But they proposed steep terms. The Narragansetts would have to pay substantial reparations, promise not to attack Uncas or other English allies, and provide sachems' sons as hostages or cede "some considerable part of the country." If war proved necessary, Gibbons was to make sure the army observed rigorous discipline and conducted faithful worship, for otherwise God would not bless them. "You are to make fair wars without exercising cruelty," they ordered, "and not to put to death such as you shall take captive." While cooperating with Indian allies, he should preserve appropriate distance "betwixt Christians and barbarians."[18]

The envoys presenting these terms tried to recruit Benedict Arnold of Rhode Island as an interpreter, but he was no friend to the Narragansetts and refused to go without an escort of one hundred soldiers. Roger Williams went in his place. Desperate for peace, Williams shrewdly used his power as interpreter to manipulate the two sides to the bargaining table. He did not inform Pessicus and Ninigret, the Narragansett leaders, about the colonies' draconian terms, knowing it would make them more likely to resist. Heeding Williams's advice and hoping to avoid war, Pessicus, Canonicus's son Mixanno, and a representative of Ninigret set out for Boston to negotiate. The envoys reported this to Mason, who postponed his invasion.

When they learned what had happened, the frustrated commissioners accused the envoys of exceeding their orders by recruiting Williams. According to the exiled Samuel Gorton, Boston minister John Cotton preached that relying on Williams was akin to seeking advice from a witch. For their part, the sachems were dismayed to discover that the United Colonies were demanding the exorbitant sum of two thousand fathoms of wampum within two years, which would require some fifteen thousand to twenty thousand individual working days to produce. (To put this in perspective, Winthrop and Williams had purchased Prudence Island for only twenty fathoms.) They also balked at the commissioners' insistence that they acknowledge their guilt in provoking the crisis. Nevertheless, with colonial armies poised, they had little choice. After "long debate and some private conference," they signed a treaty on August 27. Among other stipulations, they agreed to send four sons to Boston as hostages until the wampum was paid and to accept a binding judgment on their dispute with Uncas. Although they avoided ceding any land, they also pledged not to alienate their land to anyone else without the United Colonies' consent.[19]

"The Lord framed the hearts of the Indians to submit," Springfield trader William Pynchon exalted to the senior Winthrop. "Surely this was the Lord's doing, and it ought to be marvelous in our eyes and to be acknowledged with all thankfulness." In fact, the treaty made mockery of Narragansett sovereignty, hamstrung their economy, and embittered their people for a generation to come. Many bristled that so much had been surrendered without a fight. They had not been defeated, and they knew it. Mohegans warned that while Pessicus would honor the treaty, Ninigret, who had not signed it, would not.[20]

Williams lamented English bellicosity: "How oft have I heard both the English and Dutch (not only the civil, but the most debauched and profane) say, 'These heathen dogs, better kill a thousand of them than that we Christians should be endangered or troubled with them. They have spilt our Christian blood, the best way [is] to make riddance of them, cut them all off, and so to make way for Christians.'" Williams considered such religious rhetoric pure hypocrisy. Colonists assumed they were Christians and that Natives were irreparably heathen. They distorted Christianity by conflating it with nationality in order to justify oppression and violence. The problem, he believed, was that the English viewed themselves as a new Israel, God's chosen people. God had commanded the Israelites to destroy and enslave heathen nations, so the English thought they could do the same.

Like most Christian theologians, Williams viewed Israel as a type or symbol of Christ and his kingdom. Once Christ came, Israel no longer held special status, for Jesus's disciples, the church, were the new Israel. But that was where his agreement ended. Nearly all Protestants believed a nation could be Christian, and if so, it was in covenant with God, much like Old Testament Israel. Also like Israel, from time to time it would have to fight God's enemies. Williams, by contrast, believed only faithful followers of Jesus were God's "holy nation." England, Massachusetts, and Rhode Island were as much "the heathen" as the Narragansetts or Mohegans.[21]

Williams's intervention prevented war but did not change prevailing colonial attitudes. It was a fragile peace.

THE NARRAGANSETT-MOHEGAN CONFLICT PERSISTED, in part because no matter what the Mohegan sachem Uncas did, the United Colonies treated him gently. Uncas had watched with alarm as some five hundred Pequots eager to escape his control settled under the Pequot sachem Robin Cassacinamon at Nameag. Even worse, Winthrop Jr. brought colonists to the area. They settled in wigwams and tents alongside their Pequot hosts and began constructing permanent homes. In 1646, when Pequots hunted on land Uncas claimed, he and three hundred warriors attacked them and pursued them into Nameag, "tearing up their wigwams, cutting and slashing and beating." They stole wampum, pelts, and whatever else they wanted, tearing the Pequots' "breaches [and] their hose from their legs [and] their shoes from their feet." They drove some into the river and opened fire on them. Some of Uncas's fighters invaded English dwellings, seizing terrified Pequots and "frightening the women and children." They drove off English cattle, stole English corn, and one threatened to shoot a colonist in the back. Winthrop Jr. was in Boston, and much of his wampum was stolen.[22]

Governor Winthrop was outraged. "You know what the English have done for your safety against the Narragansetts," he berated Uncas. "If you go on to take this course, we shall leave you and your brother to shift for yourselves, and then we know the Narragansetts will be well pleased and do what we will require of them."[23] The Nameag settlers petitioned the commissioners, meeting in New Haven, for redress. Winthrop Jr. sent Thomas Peter to represent him. He urged Peter to make the case that if the Pequots were freed from Mohegan control and made subject to the English, they would help defend English settlements. If they were left under Uncas, on the other hand, "there will be no living for the English."[24]

Uncas's appearance in New Haven triggered a bevy of charges and countercharges. Called to account for his raid, he insisted he was "vindicating his own right." Amazingly, the commissioners merely lectured him not to launch raids without their permission, especially against a town with English inhabitants, and ordered him to apologize. Then they ruled that Nameag was part of Connecticut, whose land extended to the Pequot River by "patent, purchase, and conquest." A delighted Uncas boasted on his way home, "Did [I] not tell you I would do well enough there? I am the victor!"[25] Meanwhile, 130 warriors led by his brother Nowequa raided the Nipmucs near Winthrop Jr.'s mine at Tantiusque, seeking to enforce their allegiance to Uncas. They stole "thirty-five fathoms of wampum, ten copper kettles, ten great hempen baskets, many bear skins, deer skins, and other things to a great value."[26]

While letting Uncas off gently, the commissioners maintained heavy pressure on the Narragansetts, who had managed to pay only 170 fathoms of wampum. Though it is possible the Narragansetts were stringing the colonies along, since they considered the 1645 treaty invalid, it is also likely that, given the intensive labor required, they were unable to produce the quantity demanded. When the Narragansetts declined to appear in New Haven, the commissioners declared them "perfidious and treacherous" and asserted "a clear way open to right themselves according to justice by war." Nevertheless, to "show how highly they prize peace" and "their forbearance and longsuffering to these barbarians," they gave the Narragansetts more time.[27]

At the same meeting, the commissioners called for a stricter policy toward those Indian communities that protected Indians from English justice. They encouraged magistrates to punish such communities by seizing male hostages. If the Indians remained recalcitrant, the hostages could be enslaved or "sent out and exchanged for Negroes." The commissioners realized this might incite retaliation but insisted it was the best way to keep the peace. The Devil ruled most of America, but New England was "Emmanuel's land," where Christian justice must prevail.[28]

FOR A BRIEF MOMENT in early 1647, the Pequot leader Cassacinamon reached an agreement with Uncas. Governor Winthrop and Roger Williams encouraged Winthrop Jr. to do the same.[29] But then Uncas's brother raided Winthrop Jr.'s farm on Fisher's Island, and Mohegans lurked suspiciously around Nameag, terrifying the inhabitants. In July the Pequots petitioned to be released from Uncas's authority. They acknowledged that their nation had "done very ill against the English" during the war, "for which they have justly suffered and been rightfully conquered," but insisted they themselves "had no consent nor hand in shedding . . . English blood." They had taken refuge with Uncas, yet he oppressed them, demanding excessive wampum, forcing them to fight his wars, and even taking their women.

The commissioners knew many of these complaints were true, including the "lustful adulterous carriage of Uncas," but they doubted there were "any such innocent Pequots." After hearing Uncas's perspective, they rebuked his "tyrannical," "outrageous" behavior, ordered him to pay Nameag one hundred fathoms of wampum, and ordered his brother to pay restitution to the Nipmucs. But they denied the Pequots' petition for independence.[30]

Meanwhile, an unexpected event hampered further talks with the Narragansetts. Canonicus, always the voice of moderation and restraint, had died. For Williams, it marked the end of an era. As long as Canonicus lived, the Narragansetts considered Williams "their right hand, their candle and lantern, the quencher of their fires." Now that changed.[31] Pessicus, now the leading Narragansett sachem, was obligated to mourn Canonicus's death for many days and claimed he was too sick to meet with the commissioners. He sent Ninigret, the influential Eastern Niantic sachem, in his place. "It is true . . . I have broken my covenant these two years," Pessicus conceded, "and it is and hath been the constant grief of my spirit." At the same time, he protested that the treaty had been forced on him.[32]

Ninigret seemed entirely unpredictable. Five months earlier, he had told Winthrop Jr. that he was coming to realize "the English do justly and never begin [war] with any till they are provoked." He wanted to know how he could "enjoy" their "love" and had urged Pessicus to pay the wampum he owed.[33] But after Ninigret arrived in Boston, on August 3, he "pretended ignorance, as if he had not known what covenant had been made." The meeting devolved into haggling over how much wampum had been paid before it was discovered that Cutshamekin, the Christian Massachusett sachem, had not relayed everything the Narragansetts sent him. After this, Ninigret said he felt betrayed by Pessicus and was "resolved to give the colonies due satisfaction in all things." He even promised to remain in Boston to prove his good faith while his men procured the remaining wampum.[34]

By August 16 they had delivered only another two hundred fathoms, so Ninigret took personal responsibility for completing payments by spring. If he failed, he promised, the English could "take his head and seize his country." Fed up, the commissioners threatened that if he did not submit one thousand fathoms within twenty days, they would "take course to right themselves." He "cheerfully accepted" these terms, according to the commissioners, so they released the children they had been holding hostage.[35] Within four days, Ninigret was requesting another month. Roger Williams discerned "nothing but reality and reason in his request," but the commissioners suspected base treachery.[36]

AMID RISING TENSIONS, calls for Massachusetts to assert jurisdiction over Indians in the upper Connecticut Valley threatened to provoke a full-blown crisis. In 1648, the Quaboag Nipmucs who had submitted to Massachusetts four years earlier called on the colony for help. Several of them had been murdered by Norwottucks from the Connecticut Valley, they claimed. Governor Winthrop sent men to investigate and arrest suspects. They were unsuccessful, but he hoped the Quaboags "saw our care of them and readiness to protect them and revenge their wrongs."[37]

But Quacunquasit, the Quaboag sachem, was not satisfied. He sent Cutshamekin, the Christian Massachusett sachem, to persuade John Eliot, the missionary, to mediate. Eliot informed the magistrates that both the victims and their killers were Massachusetts subjects. By bringing them to justice, Massachusetts could solidify its authority among the Quaboags, making them more likely to accept Christianity. Winthrop instructed William Pynchon, western Massachusetts's sole magistrate, to arrest the suspects. Eliot urged Pynchon to pursue justice as "with a command of God." He need not worry about resistance, for the Norwottucks feared English power.[38]

Pynchon was aghast. He had worked hard to establish friendly relations with the local Agawams and Norwottucks, his trading partners, and carrying out Winthrop's instructions would surely alienate them. Nor could it come at a worse time, for the two Connecticut Valley peoples were allied with the Narragansetts and on the verge of war with Uncas and the Mohegans. In 1646 the United Colonies had authorized Uncas to seize the valley sachem Sequassen for allegedly attempting to assassinate Connecticut's governor. Uncas seized Sequassen in a raid against the Pocumtucks, Norwottuck allies further up the valley, only for Connecticut to release him for lack of evidence.[39] The enraged Pocumtucks began building a large fort and gathering warriors, including Mohawks. Reports suggested that after harvest, their Narragansett allies would initiate war against Uncas.

Pynchon implored Winthrop to consider the consequences. The Norwottucks, Pocumtucks, and Mohawks sought "the utter ruin of the Mohegans," he warned, "and the English will, I fear, be embroiled in the war." Massachusetts needed to avoid antagonizing them. He also pointed out that, contrary to Eliot, the Norwottucks were not Massachusetts subjects. True, they fell within its patent, but "you cannot say that therefore they are your subjects, nor yet within your jurisdiction, until they have fully subjected themselves to your government (which I know they have not), and until you have bought their land. Until this be done, they must be esteemed as an independent, free people." Here Pynchon agreed with Roger Williams. A royal charter alone could not give the English jurisdiction over Native peoples and land. "These Indians of Quaboag have dealt subtly in getting Cutshamekin to get Mr. Eliot to be their mediator," he chided, for it was not even clear that the victims were Massachusetts subjects.[40]

Pynchon's desire for peace with still-sovereign Natives proved more compelling than Eliot's appeal. Massachusetts deputy governor Thomas Dudley produced a significant memorandum confirming Pynchon's view that Massachusetts lacked "ground and warrant" to intervene because, its charter notwithstanding, neither the victims nor the Norwottucks were Massachusetts subjects. If Massachusetts provoked a war, "we shall incur blame at home and with our confederate English," Dudley warned, and forfeit "help from heaven." Once again, concern for justice held Puritan Massachusetts back. Winthrop withdrew Pynchon's instructions.[41]

By September as many as a thousand warriors had amassed at Pocumtuck, in the upper Connecticut Valley, including four hundred Mohawks with guns. Winthrop Jr. reported that the Narragansetts were moving women, children, and the elderly into swamps, hiding corn, and preparing for battle. Their emerging leader, Ninigret, warned him that if the English defended Uncas, Mohawks would attack settlements in the lower Connecticut Valley.[42] As usual, Roger Williams's interpretation of Narragansett activity was more nuanced. He reported that the sachems were divided over whether to attack Uncas. One Narragansett was doing everything he could to foment an offensive alliance with the Mohawks, but the sachems had not committed themselves. Uncas was as belligerent as anyone, daring the Mohawks to attack and threatening "to set his ground with gobbets of their flesh."[43]

Even John Mason, Connecticut's aggressive military commander, thought English fears were overblown, believing the Mohawks would not dare attack the English, while the Pocumtucks would not act without the Mohawks. Nevertheless, Connecticut sent interpreter Thomas Stanton to meet with the Pocumtucks and confirm the colony's commitment to Uncas. The Pocumtucks admitted having received wampum from the Narragansetts "to invade Uncas." However, they had called off the attack, and the Mohawks had returned home to deal with an unrelated crisis. This was a relief, but it left the United Colonies commissioners angry that the Narragansetts were using wampum to recruit allies while failing to pay their reparations. Connecticut sent envoys to the Narragansetts bearing these latest charges.[44]

Their sachems, Pessicus, Ninigret, and Mixanno, swore in the name of the English God "they gave not a penny to hire the Mohawks against the Mohegans." All they did was send gifts, an essential practice in Native relationships. They also had to use wampum to purchase corn because of severe food shortages, in part because they lacked access to sufficient hunting grounds. The sachems also protested that the English shielded Uncas from justice. In the previous three years, they charged, he had gotten away with thirteen murders. The envoys explained that they supported Uncas because he was always cooperative.[45]

Controversy over hunting rights added another layer to the conflict. Ever since the war, Ninigret maintained, Massachusetts had promised the Narragansetts they could hunt on Pequot land "till the English came to make use of the country." The Mohegans also had such rights, but Ninigret thought the Mystic River, midway between the Pequot River and Narragansett country, formed a logical boundary between the two groups. Massachusetts had left the matter up to Winthrop Jr., who offered no objections. But this infuriated Connecticut, whose governor John Haynes expressed "vehement suspicion" that Ninigret was colluding with the Mohawks to attack Uncas. Commissioner Edward Hopkins denied that Ninigret ever received permission to hunt in Pequot country, but even if he had, "his non-performance of covenants and treacherous designs" disqualified him from "favors or encouragements from any who love the peace of the colonies." Mason angrily told Winthrop Jr. to give Ninigret fair warning: "For I am almost resolved, God assisting, if they go on, to give them a visit which I suppose will not be very pleasing to them."

Winthrop Jr. could not understand why Mason was so upset about "so trivial a matter [as] who should range over a vast country without inhabitants." They could not stop Ninigret from hunting east of the Mystic River, and it was "better for him to have it by a supposed allowance." All that mattered was for "the English to maintain their right" and Ninigret to acknowledge that right. In this way, he argued, "we may obtain peace."[46] Roger Williams was even more sympathetic. "These sachems, I believe, desire cordially to hold friendship with both the English and the Mohawks," he wrote. "I am confident . . . they never intended hurt against the English."[47]

Meanwhile, the commissioners gave Uncas free rein. When Uncas complained that the Nameag Pequots were not submitting to him, they authorized him to assert control by "violence," instructing Connecticut to ensure he was not "opposed by any English, nor the Pequots," and that he did not harm any colonists.[48] So it was that in the dead of winter Uncas and his warriors arrived at Nameag, accompanied by Captain Mason and bearing a commission from the United Colonies to subdue the Pequots by force. Mason had already warned Winthrop Jr. not to in "any way hinder Uncas in the prosecution of this service."[49]

Mohegans plundered the Pequots' wigwams, stealing "coats, shoes, stockings, corn, beans, [and] hatchets." They burned kettles and shattered pots. They stole or wrecked "trays, dishes, mats, bags, sacks, baskets . . . and all their wampum." They even stripped Pequots of their clothes. Several Pequots were wounded.

Outraged at "so inhumane an action," colonists feared the Mohegans might turn on them. A constable's attempt to intervene proved futile.

Winthrop Jr. and his fellow colonists drew up a formal grievance. "We are most barbarously, injuriously, and unchristianly dealt withal to have such a people, whose tents are yet amongst us, to be unnecessarily provoked and forced upon a condition of absolute despair," they wrote. The Pequots had been utterly deprived of "their necessaries for their very life in this very depth of winter."[50] Roger Williams could not comprehend "how it stands with religion and reason that such a monstrous . . . affrightment should be offered to an English town, either by Indians or English, unpunished." Governor Winthrop denounced Uncas's "outrage" and expressed hope that the commissioners would "take some stricter course with him."[51]

The dire situation weighed heavily on the elder Winthrop even as he fell dangerously ill early in 1649. On March 14, Adam Winthrop informed Winthrop Jr. that their father had hardly left his bed during the past month and was "weaker than ever I knew him." But the old man had a final wish: "He would request you, as if it were his last request, that you would strive no more about the Pequot Indians, but leave them to the commissioners' order."[52] Twelve days later, the great John Winthrop died.[53]

THE MOHEGAN-NARRAGANSETT CONFLICT CONTINUED to simmer, exacerbated by rival claims to the Pequots and their hunting grounds. The Pequots who had settled at Pawcatuck strengthened ties with Uncas and Connecticut's John Mason in hopes of breaking free from Ninigret and the Narragansetts, while the Nameag Pequots sought help from Ninigret and Winthrop Jr. (hereafter simply Winthrop) to break free from Uncas and the Mohegans. Each cast bitter accusations and recriminations at the other.[54] Uncas accused a Narragansett trader named Cuttaquin of stabbing him in the chest with a sword. After Mohegans tortured him, Cuttaquin told Mason the Narragansetts had promised him one thousand fathoms of wampum if he killed Uncas. The Narragansetts dismissed the charge as "childish." They were on the verge of paying off their reparations, after which the English had promised they could bring charges against Uncas, securing "English justice, in a legal way." Why would they jeopardize this? Obviously, Uncas was trying to make them "odious to the English and prevent his trial."

Roger Williams was tired of it. "I believe nothing of any of the barbarians on either side," he admitted. Then he learned that Uncas had been accused of stabbing himself, which suggested the Narragansetts might be telling the truth. "Many circumstances look earnestly toward a plot of Uncas," he told Winthrop. He knew Cuttaquin and doubted he was capable of murder. And who would assault a sachem "at noonday in the midst of his own [men]?"[55]

Mason, on the other hand, decided it was time for the Narragansetts to face English wrath. "If nothing but blood will satisfy them, I doubt not but they may have their fill," he told Williams. "I perceive such an obstinate willfulness, joined with desperate malicious practices, that I think and believe they are sealed to destruction." Such words were "terrible to all these Natives," Williams admitted. Everyone knew about Mason's brutality at Mystic.[56]

Mason submitted a letter to the commissioners, gathering in Boston in July, declaring that although he hoped for "peace with righteousness," it was time to consider military action. When Ninigret arrived, the commissioners rehearsed accusations that had piled up against him over the years: protection of runaway Indian servants, unpaid tribute for Pequot captives, unpaid reparations, conspiracies, assassination attempts, and trespassing on hunting grounds. They accused him of conspiring to marry his daughter to a brother of the late "malignant furious Pequot" Sassacus in an attempt to "reunite the scattered conquered Pequots" under his control. (Uncas wanted the Pequot to marry *his* daughter, but the Pequot declined "because of her sore eyes.") Ninigret defended himself, but the commissioners no longer believed a word he said. They even retracted their promise of a fair hearing of Narragansett complaints against Uncas, which Ninigret could only have viewed as base treachery. They vowed to secure "the peace of the country and preservation of Uncas according to their covenants" and advised the colonies to prepare for war.[57]

To prevent Ninigret from winning the allegiance of the Nameag Pequots, they reconsidered Winthrop's request that the Pequots be received to "live under . . . English justice." Winthrop argued that the Pequots could work as hired laborers and would serve as a defensive bulwark for the English. They would also be more likely to receive "the glorious gospel."[58] Concluding that it was better to have the Pequots as allies than as enemies, the commissioners ordered that land be granted them "to settle and plant," though they formally remained subject to Uncas.[59]

Soon after, under cover of night, Mohegans attacked a community of Pequots living under Narragansett protection. One person was killed on each side. Winthrop blamed the commissioners for empowering Uncas, "setting up new monarchs of the treacherous heathen, and such as have been already by the mighty hand of the Lord subdued to the English." The Narragansetts itched to retaliate, arguing they could hardly keep the peace, let alone focus on producing wampum, if Uncas attacked them. Roger Williams advised them to force their tributaries to provide wampum, but the sachems countered that they lacked power to do so. To Williams, it showed how weak they had become and how little the colonies had to fear from them. He hoped their weakness would force them to draw "nearer to civility."[60]

THE COMMISSIONERS IGNORED Uncas's latest depredation, but the Narragansetts, who still owed 308 fathoms of wampum, were a different matter. The commissioners ordered Captain Humphrey Atherton to take twenty men and force them to pay, even at the risk of war. If they refused, he was to seize property of equal value, plus additional reparations to pay for his expedition. If they resisted, he was authorized to seize Ninigret, "Pessicus or his children," or other leading persons.[61]

The Narragansetts would come to rue the name Humphrey Atherton. On the last day of September, the captain arrived at Roger Williams's trading post at Cocumscussoc and asked him to arrange a meeting with Pessicus. After Williams brought him to the sachems, Atherton demanded the 308 fathoms of wampum, plus 200 for his expenses, or two sachems as hostages. The Narragansetts requested time; two days later, negotiations remained at an impasse.[62] Winthrop dashed off a letter to Atherton, urging him "to accept any reasonable terms" rather than "begin a war of such doubtful hazard." That morning, he explained, a prominent Narragansett known to be faithful to the English had reported that they "did really intend to pay the peage [wampum] as fast as they could gather it." But they would "rather hazard all, wives and children and lives and all that they had," than surrender their sachems.[63]

Winthrop's letter came too late. Tired of negotiating, Atherton summoned his twenty soldiers and brazenly surrounded the sachems' wigwam. Two hundred warriors, "ready with guns and bows," rushed to the sachems' defense, surrounding Atherton's men. The captain refused to stand down, telling Williams to inform them he intended to take Ninigret and Pessicus by force. Williams refused, lambasting Atherton for betraying his trust. "I would not have hazarded life or blood for a little money," he scolded. "I would not be desperate with so few men to assault kings in the midst of such guards about us, and I had not so much as a knife or stick about me." English soldiers and Narragansett warriors stared each other down "upon the ticklish point of a great slaughter." Williams tried to forestall a bloodbath, offering ten fathoms of his own wampum to help the Narragansetts. Finally, after "long agitations," Atherton offered them four more days.

The soldiers returned to Cocumscussoc, occupying Williams's trading post. Williams fled to a wigwam, pulled out pen and paper, and vented his frustrations to Winthrop. "I told the captain he had desperately betrayed me and himself," he scrawled. "I hope the Lord will show him and show the country what dangerous counsels the commissioners produce."

A few days later, the Narragansetts paid the full debt, finally bringing the five-year crisis to an end. Williams was relieved but ruminated over the commissioners' reckless policy. Uncas could steal "many horses" and get away with it, he groused to Winthrop, but if Ninigret did so much as "look over the hedge" they were ready with punishment. Uncas got away with repeated raids on Nameag, yet the commissioners threatened war against the Narragansetts over three hundred fathoms of wampum. How could they be so shortsighted? War was a fearful judgment that would "dispossess many a planter" and "hazard much blood and slaughter and ruin to both English and Indian."[64]

Few knew how close to war the Puritan determination to punish and control the Narragansetts had pushed them. Even fewer appreciated Williams's role in preventing it. During sixteen years of exile from Massachusetts, Williams wrote, "scarce a week hath passed but some way or other I have been used as instrumental to the peace and spreading of the English plantings in this country."[65] "The whole country are much obliged to you," Winthrop agreed, "which they cannot be so sensible of, who do not fully understand the nature and manner of the Indians."[66]

Puritan concerns for justice had occasionally restrained the colonies from waging the sort of war of conquest some ambitious colonists hoped for, but the harshness of the justice they imposed, combined with their favoritism toward the Mohegans, nearly triggered war anyway. The fact that war did not break out owed much to Narragansett forbearance, fueled by the dark memory of the Pequot War. It also owed something to the Puritan desire to impose colonial dominion by peaceful means whenever possible. Most Puritan leaders did not want war, as much as their policies threatened to provoke it. They wanted Indians to submit voluntarily to their authority so they might be civilized and evangelized. They never doubted that this would be for the Indians' own benefit.

9

Natick

1649 to 1662

Although the colonists and major Algonquian tribes were often on the brink of war, missionary work progressed among Native communities that accepted Massachusetts's dominion. The volume of invitations that the missionary John Eliot received indicated that many Natives were attracted to Christianity, for one reason or another. Praying Indians had to overcome significant obstacles, including formidable opposition from their kin, sachems, and powwows, but with Eliot's guidance they began to forge a vibrant, self-sustaining Christian Algonquian community.

An elderly Quaboag sachem, appreciating Eliot's earlier mediation on Quaboag's behalf, invited Eliot to teach and even live among the Nipmucs at Quaboag. Fear of war prevented this for a time, but Eliot was able to visit Quaboag when Showanon, Nashaway's sachem, provided a twenty-warrior escort. Incessant rain made the journey exhausting. "We were extreme wet, insomuch that I was not dry night nor day from the third day of the week unto the sixth," Eliot recalled. Stream crossings left him even more soaked. Each night, "pull off my boots, wring my stockings, and on with them again." His horse broke down. But he endured it as a "good soldier of Christ" and found Quaboag "hungry after instruction." Soon after, a Nipmuc sachem "submitted himself to pray unto the Lord" and urged Eliot to send a permanent teacher.[1]

Eliot made annual visits to the Pennacook town of Pawtucket and was encouraged by the result. Where formerly he witnessed gaming, immorality, and "open profaneness," now he saw "praying to God and good conference, and observation of the Sabbath by such as are well minded." But the Pennacook sachem Passaconnaway complained that annual visits were insufficient, because people quickly forgot what Eliot taught, and many "would not believe him that praying to God was so good." "We like it well at the first sight," Passaconnaway explained, but "we know not what it is within. It may be excellent or it may be nothing. We cannot tell, but if you would come unto us and open it unto us, and show us what it is within, then we should believe that it is so excellent as you say." Indians from north of the Merrimack River occasionally heard Eliot preach and wanted him to visit their communities, but he was reluctant to travel so far into the wilderness. "Truly my heart much yearneth towards them," he confessed.[2]

A growing number of praying Indians requested baptism, the Lord's Supper, and other elements of church life, but Eliot did not think they were ready. "I declared unto them how necessary it was that they should first be civilized by being brought from their scattered and wild course of life unto cohabitation and government before they could, according to the will of God revealed in the scriptures, be fit to be trusted with the sacred ordinances of Jesus Christ, in church communion."[3] Otherwise any Indian who sinned "could easily run away, as some have done, and would be tempted to do so, unless he were fixed in a habitation and had some means of livelihood to lose and leave behind him."[4] The solution was to establish another praying town, he thought. But this required tools and supplies. "Want of money is the only thing in view that doth retard a more full prosecution of this work," he informed supporters.[5]

Eliot hoped for funding from England. The Civil War had taken a radical turn in 1648 when parliamentary forces captured King Charles, and the brilliant Puritan general Oliver Cromwell purged Parliament of its more conservative members. The remaining "Rump Parliament" put the king on trial, and he was beheaded for treason on January 30, 1649. Soon after, Parliament abolished the monarchy. Eliot, who like some other Puritans believed Charles had fought for the "Antichristian principle for man to be above God," interpreted these developments as a sign of Christ's imminent victory over Antichrist. Eliot even hoped Parliament could inaugurate the millennial kingdom many believed would precede Christ's second coming, when Jews, followed by many Gentiles, would convert to Christianity.[6]

Edward Winslow, the prominent Plymouth colonist whom Massachusetts had sent to London to defend its claim to the Shawomet region, published missionary reports and lobbied Parliament for financial support. He urged Parliament to consider "how these poor creatures cry out for help, 'Oh come unto us, teach us the knowledge of God . . . come and dwell amongst us.'" Tapping into growing millennial fervor, he speculated that Indians might be the lost tribes of Israel, which meant their conversion could be imminent. (Eliot also entertained this view.) The time was ripe, Winslow claimed, because Indians were attracted to Christianity by "the justice, prudence, valor, temperance, and righteousness of the English," both in peace and "in such wars they had unavoidably drawn upon themselves."[7]

Massachusetts tried to persuade the Committee on Foreign Plantations, led by the Earl of Warwick, that nascent missionary work at Shawomet would "be dashed" if the contentious Samuel Gorton won his appeal regarding the sale of Shawomet land and the committee allowed him to return there. The committee did not agree. The Gortonists were permitted to return to Shawomet, where they gratefully named their settlement Warwick. Winslow's efforts to procure funding were more successful. On July 27, 1649, Parliament established the Society for Propagation of the Gospel in New England, eventually known as the New England Company, to raise funds for missionary work. The United Colonies commissioners would oversee spending, even though their primary mission was defending the colonies against Indian threats. Puritans considered the two missions complementary.[8]

Eliot was filled with excitement, convinced he was about to see the fulfillment of biblical prophecy that "all kingdoms and nations shall become the kingdoms of Christ." Surely his work would help inaugurate the millennium among Christian Indians, who had the opportunity to "set up the kingdom of Jesus Christ so fully, so that Christ shall reign both in church and commonwealth, both in civil and spiritual matters." Other nations, like England, had "been adulterated with their Antichristian or human wisdom" and were reluctant to give up their traditions. By contrast, he imagined, the Indians "have no principles of their own, nor yet wisdom of their own (I mean as other nations have) . . . and therefore they do most readily yield to any direction from the Lord, so that there will be no such opposition." With government in the hands of godly Indians, they would be "wholly governed by the scriptures in all things." "They shall have no other lawgiver. The Lord shall be their lawgiver. The Lord shall be their judge. The Lord shall be their king, and he will save them."[9]

It would take time before funding reached New England, but Eliot wanted to bring praying Indians together as quickly as possible, for they faced considerable pressure to abandon Christianity. Nashaway, which initially embraced his teaching, had already taken up powwowing again. And when a group of non-Christian Indians lingered near Neponset, Eliot feared Satan was using them "to seduce" younger praying Indians. He credited divine intervention when the lingerers fell ill with smallpox. Bringing praying Indians together would help them forge new loyalties, he realized. "What is the reason that when a strange Indian comes among us, whom we never saw before, yet if he pray unto God, we do exceedingly love him?" one asked. "But if my own brother, dwelling a great way off, come unto us, he not praying to God, though we love him, yet [it is] nothing . . . [like the way] we love that other stranger who doth pray unto God?"[10]

Yet another motivation to get praying Indians settled was to protect them from the negative influence of non-Puritan colonists. Rhode Islanders told praying Indians that heaven and hell were not real places, that they did not need ministers, and that English magistrates had no right to punish them. Roger Williams told them they did not need to observe the Sabbath. Other colonists acted so deplorably that it threw Christianity into disrepute.[11]

Ministers urged Eliot to create a settlement for praying Indians despite his lack of funding. "Go on, and look to the Lord only for help," encouraged Boston minister John Cotton. So Eliot submitted a proposal to his congregation, which devoted a day to prayer and fasting. That night he received what seemed a clear reply: letters from England promising support.

The first task was to select a site. Neither of the existing praying towns Nonantum nor Neponset would do, for the Massachusett sachem Cutshamekin had sold nearly all their land, and many Indians refused to live so near the English. Eventually they identified land along the Charles River about eighteen miles from Boston, owned in part by another Massachusett sachem, Josias Wampatuck (Cutshamekin's nephew). Indians had lived there "longer than the oldest man alive can remember," but Massachusetts had granted the land to the colonists of Dedham, about seven miles away, so Eliot reached out to Dedham's pastor, John Allen. They visited the site, and although some Dedham inhabitants objected, Allen assured Eliot that a majority was inclined to support his plan. As Eliot later recalled, then Wampatuck "did solemnly in God's presence, give up his right in these lands unto God, to make a town, gather a church, and live in civil order in this place." They called it Natick.

Eliot paid Indians to mow grass, make hay, and cut timber. In autumn, they broke up ground for planting and, through "hard and tedious labor in the water," constructed a footbridge eighty feet long and "nine-foot high in the midst," over the Charles River. This time, Eliot claimed, he offered to pay them, adding that "if they should do all this labor in love, I should take it well," and they cheerfully declined pay.[12]

Sachems watched with dismay. Uncas, the Mohegan sachem, traveled to Hartford to ask the commissioners not to force his people to accept Christian teaching. "The sachems of the country are generally set against us and counterwork the Lord by keeping . . . their men from praying to God," Eliot admitted. "They plainly see that religion will make a great change among them and cut them off from their former tyranny." As he saw it, the sachems held "their people in an absolute servitude" much as King Charles had in England. They demanded tribute and threatened violence until they received it. When a subject defied them, they hired an assassin to kill him. People did not work hard to accumulate property, knowing their sachems could easily take it.

This was hardly a fair assessment, but praying Indians did prove more likely to defy their sachems. "If a man be wise, and his sachem weak, must he yet obey him?" one asked. "We are commanded to honor the sachem, but is the sachem commanded to love us?" Christian Indians paid far less tribute than before, Eliot realized, and "instead of seeking his favor with gifts, as formerly, they will admonish him of his sin," telling him "that is not the right way to get money, but he must labor."[13] Since Eliot believed monarchy was anti-Christian, he applauded this development.

Cutshamekin resolved to challenge Eliot. In front of his people, he declared that he and "all the sachems in the country" opposed Natick's establishment. It had the desired effect. "Indians were filled with fear, their countenances grew pale, and most of them slunk away," Eliot recalled. Knowing he had to respond, he told Cutshamekin "it was God's work I was about, and he was with me, and I feared not him nor all the sachems in the country; and I was resolved to go on, do what they can, and [neither] they nor he should hinder that which I had begun." On hearing this, he claimed, Cutshamekin's "spirit shrunk and fell before me." Praying Indians regarded the confrontation as a decisive test of will. Eliot insisted he did not intend to humiliate the sachem, "but the Lord carried me beyond my thoughts and wont."

But Cutshamekin was not finished. He complained that praying Indians no longer paid tribute. Eliot replied that he taught them to pay tribute to those in authority as commanded in scripture. Upon investigation, he concluded that Cutshamekin received substantial payments and was simply bitter that he could no longer collect tribute without his subjects' consent. Eliot also argued that Indians were justified in withholding tribute when sachems did not "govern well by justice and as the word of God taught." He preached a sermon on Matthew 4 in Cutshamekin's presence, describing how the Devil tempted Jesus by offering him all the kingdoms of the world if Jesus would worship him. "I did apply it wholly to his case, showing him the Devil was now tempting him as he tempted Christ," Eliot reported. Satan's lie was that Cutshamekin would lose everything if he served Christ when, in fact, the opposite was true.

Cutshamekin received the sermon surprisingly well, but other formerly sympathetic sachems distanced themselves. Eliot was not surprised, for he believed the Devil would do everything he could to prevent "these poor creatures" from seeking God. Fearing Satan would instigate an attack against Natick, he proposed that it be fortified and asked his supporters for guns, ammunition, and swords.[14]

EPIDEMICS REMAINED THE gravest threat the Indians faced. Smallpox swept through Nonantum during the winter of 1650–1651. Among those stricken was Wampooas, who had repented for beating his wife and now expressed hope that his sons would be trained to "teach their countrymen." To his family and friends, he declared, "I now shall die, but Jesus Christ calleth you that live to go to Natick, that there the Lord might rule over you, that you might make a church and have the ordinances of God among you, believe in his word, and do as he commanded you." Eliot thought Wampooas "did more good by his death than he could have done by his life."

Many Nonantum Indians relocated to Natick that spring. Many Neponset Indians did not, hoping they would receive their own town at Punkapoag. Those at Natick laid out streets, measured and divided lots, planted orchards, and constructed a palisade. Work on a meeting house was delayed because their carpenter died from smallpox and they lacked tools.[15] At last, the first New England Company shipment arrived, containing nails, hatchets, axes, hoes, spades, saws, augers, chisels, knives, hammers, adzes, and gimlets. Indians got to work chopping down trees and squaring and sawing timber into boards. They constructed the meeting house with two floors, a large room for meetings downstairs and a large chamber with a smaller room enclosed upstairs. The small room had a bed where Eliot could sleep when visiting. There was also a wardrobe for hanging skins, pelts, and other merchandise. They built a chimney, making "groundsells and wall-plates, and mortising and letting in the studs into them artificially."[16]

The Indians continued living in wigwams, which were easy to build, warmer than English houses (due to their centralized fireplaces), and portable. It was one of many ways they maintained Algonquian customs. While many attended Eliot's teaching sessions, their reasons varied. Some feared that if they did not become praying Indians they would lose their land. Others came for social reasons or to preserve ties with kin. Most felt conflicted, afraid of what it would cost them and aware that many Indians strongly opposed it. But enough were enthusiastic to make it work. Disease and colonization had devastated their communities, and Christianity offered a fresh foundation on which to rebuild, with material English support.[17]

Eliot's next goal was to establish a government in which "the Lord above shall reign over them and govern them in all things by the word of his mouth." He followed the great reformer John Calvin in arguing that God's preferred form of government was found in Exodus 18, where Moses chose godly men to serve as rulers of one hundred, of fifty, and of ten men, to govern in accord with God's commands. Exodus did not say it, but Eliot thought these leaders should be elected. Like England, Natick would give up monarchy (rule by sachems) for republican government by the godly, according to scripture. But it was telling that Natick elected the Massachusett sachem Cutshamekin, whom Eliot considered "constant in his profession, though doubtful in respect of the thoroughness of his heart," as its chief ruler. Here too, traditional Algonquian norms endured.

The plan was for Natick to enter a covenant like the ones that governed English Puritan towns, but before that could happen, a series of disasters convinced Eliot that God was calling Natick to repent. First, a vessel bringing supplies shipwrecked, its cargo "much spoiled." Then Cutshamekin traveled to Warwick, where he purchased alcohol and some of his men got drunk. The sachem was required to repent publicly, demonstrating that even sachems were accountable. He confessed that Satan had tempted him, begged forgiveness, and prayed that God's Spirit might transform him.

Natick enacted its covenant on September 24, 1651. "We and our forefathers have a long time been lost in our sins, but now the mercy of the Lord beginneth to find us out again. Therefore, the grace of Christ helping us, we do give ourselves and our children to be his people." They vowed to submit to Christ, "not only in our religion and affairs of the church . . . but also in all our works and affairs in this world. . . . Oh Jehovah, teach us wisdom to find out thy wisdom in thy scriptures. Let the grace of Christ help us, because Christ is the wisdom of God. Send thy Spirit into our hearts, and let it teach us. Lord, take us to be thy people, and let us take thee to be our God."[18]

Eliot was so confident about Natick's government that he wrote a manuscript titled *The Christian Commonwealth: or, The Civil Policy of the Rising Kingdom of Jesus Christ*, addressing it to Christ's servants "who manage the wars of the Lord against Antichrist in Great Britain." Having defeated Antichrist, he argued, they needed to establish "the peaceable kingdom of Christ," in which Jesus was "the only right heir of the crown of England." Their task was to discern from scripture the "form of government by which Christ meaneth to rule all the nations on earth." This, he believed, was the system established at Natick. It simply needed to be expanded for a larger population.[19]

Many colonists questioned whether the praying Indians' faith was genuine. The United Colonies commissioners lectured Eliot not to be too generous with gifts, lest Indians "only follow Christ for loaves and outward advantage, remaining enemies to the yoke and government." They complained that praying Indians consorted with pagan Indians and violated the Sabbath.[20] John Endecott, who as Massachusetts's first governor had been instructed to make Indian conversion a primary goal and was now governor again, decided to investigate for himself. He arrived in October with twenty men, including Boston minister John Wilson. He marveled at the footbridge and meeting house but was even more inspired by the service he witnessed. A hundred Natives, most wearing English clothing, gathered inside the palisade. Men and women sat separately, some under shelters. Eliot and some Indians were under a "large canopy of mats upon poles."

A middle-aged Indian led in prayer. Then he sat on a stool and taught in Algonquian for about forty-five minutes, impressing the visitors with his "great devotion, gravity, decency, readiness, and affection." His text was Jesus's parable in which a man sold his possessions to purchase a field containing buried treasure. The treasure represented God's kingdom, he explained. Jesus was calling them "to part with all their sins, and to part with all their old customs, and to part with their friends and lands, or anything which hindereth them from coming to that place where they may gather a church and enjoy all these pearls." Eliot then preached in Algonquian for an hour. After time for questions, they concluded by singing Algonquian psalms set to English tunes.

"Every one of us [was] much refreshed in our spirits in what we saw," Wilson reported. Endecott was thrilled. "I could hardly refrain tears for very joy to see their diligent attention to the word first taught by one of the Indians," he wrote. They put many English Christians to shame. "Truly I account it one of the best journeys I made these many years."[21]

A few days later, the General Court granted Natick two thousand acres within Dedham's bounds, on the condition that its people "lay down all claims in that town elsewhere and set no traps in unenclosed land."[22] "It is no small humbling to me that the Lord hath made my poor labors to find such acceptance in the hearts of states," Eliot gratefully wrote Massachusetts's London agent, Edward Winslow.[23]

⟨⟡⟩

ELSEWHERE, TOO, MISSIONARY work progressed. Thomas Mayhew Jr. continued to win converts among the Wampanoags of Martha's Vineyard by discrediting powwows. When a powwow threatened to kill every Indian who attended Christian meetings, the Wampanoag teacher Hiacoomes called his bluff. He dared the powwows to "do their utmost they could against him, and when they did their worst by their witchcrafts to kill him, he would without fear set himself against them." Their failure made him living proof that God protected Christian Indians. Two powwows accepted Christianity, confessing "they had served the devil, the enemy both of God and man." A third converted after admitting that his attempts to heal the sick were not working.

One night, an Indian shot a "broad-headed arrow" at the Christian sachem Towanquatick from six paces away, piercing his eyebrow and cutting his nose from top to bottom. The sachem survived, "praising God for his great deliverance," and Indians took note. Mayhew considered him an exemplary witness, who "bears in his brow the marks of the Lord Jesus." Towanquatick's conversion pitted him against the high Wampanoag sachem Ousamequin. When Ousamequin asked what gifts the English had given to attract them to Christianity, praying Indians replied, "We serve not God for clothing, nor for any outward thing." The truth was, they felt relatively little pressure from colonists, for few were on the island, and unlike Eliot, Mayhew made little effort to alter their way of life, though he required them to observe some basic Christian moral imperatives. Christianity's apparent power had persuaded them of its truth. Soon some two hundred were meeting, in two groups, twice every Sunday.[24]

Across the sound, the minister William Leverich was winning converts at the base of Cape Cod. Wampanoags built a wigwam outside Sandwich where they could stay when they came for services, even though their kin threatened to expel them their community. Another minister was preparing to work with the Quinnipiacs north of Long Island Sound, and John Winthrop Jr. sought one to evangelize the Pequots. A sachem invited colonists to settle in the Quinebaug Valley and teach his people. Natick had received such requests from several Nipmuc towns and began sending Indian teachers "to teach them to pray unto God."[25]

During the spring of 1652, dysentery swept through Natick. Monequassun, its schoolteacher, fell ill, and his wife and child died. A man named Nishohkou watched as his young child cried in extreme pain, "God and Jesus Christ, God and Jesus Christ, help me!" The child died, as did Nishohkou's wife. When Nishohkou asked why God punished him so, Eliot suggested it was because he "refused to do God's work" as an elected ruler. Robin Speen lost three children and reeled from the blows. "I fear God is still angry because great are my sins, and I fear lest my children be not gone to heaven," he later confessed.

Once the disease passed, more Indians arrived, including some Nipmucs. Eliot paid them to work, though he had trouble keeping them occupied. They built more than a thousand rods of fencing and were continually mowing, making hay, and building barns for cows and goats. "We have sundry buildings in hand," Eliot wrote, "but want of skill and experience maketh them slower in dispatch then the English be." While they learned skills necessary to adapt to the colonial world, Eliot pursued his own purpose: "to civilize the wild people, thereby to prepare them for religion." He requested "strong linen cloth, canvas, and other good hempen cloth, and lockrams," noting that on hot days Indians preferred to work, "if in any garment, only a linen garment, if they can get it." They had tremendous "ingenuity and ingeniosity," he wrote later, "only it is drowned in their wild and rude manner of living."

During a trip to the Pennacook town of Pawtucket, whose sachem Passaconnaway again requested a regular teacher, Eliot was dismayed to see that English traders were selling "strong liquors in such plenty as to cause drunkenness," which he considered Satan's dealing. "I greatly wish that such as travel and set up houses of trading among them might be such as had an heart also to teach them," he lamented. "When God's time is come," he hoped, "he will bow men's minds, who may do it."

He visited the Quinebaug Valley with Governor Endecott's son and intended to go farther, but heavy rains made the rivers impassable. Even so, he reported, in fifty miles of riding "all the Indians we met with and came among had some savor of the gospel and had at sometimes come and heard the word, and our coming unto them was very gladly accepted." Satan discouraged many from settling at Natick, he believed, but this merely left potential converts scattered among more communities. Thus "by that means which Satan hoped to have broken our work, the same is a means to multiply it."

But it was telling that the region's most powerful sachems resisted Christianity. At John Winthrop Jr.'s suggestion, Eliot sent praying Indians with a coat as a gift to Ninigret, the Narragansett leader. Narragansetts told them they were willing to pray but doubted their sachems would do so "because they were so proud."

True enough, Eliot reported, Ninigret "did little less than despise the offer, though he took the present."[26] "There be two great sachems in the country that are open and professed enemies against praying to God," he wrote later: the tyrannical Uncas and the raging Ninigret. He hoped for their downfall, for "whenever the Lord removeth them, there will be a door open for the preaching of the gospel in those parts."[27] Praying Indians allegedly threatened Ninigret that if the Narragansetts "would not pray, they should be destroyed by war." Alarmed, Ninigret recruited Roger Williams to petition the English government "that they might not be forced from their religion, and for not changing their religion, be invaded by war."[28]

THE NEXT STEP AT Natick was establishing a church. It was no easy task, for Puritans believed church members must be able to articulate Christian teaching and narrate God's work in their lives. This bar proved too high for many colonists, let alone Indians, who had to overcome considerable linguistic and cultural barriers. In 1652, Eliot had some Indians profess their faith and provided a summary to his fellow clergy. They were sufficiently impressed that they gathered in person to hear the Indians on October 13. Eliot and his interpreter translated the Indians' words as faithfully as they could, but it was a painstaking process, and he admitted that the translations were imperfect.

The first speaker, Wampooas's brother Totherswamp, admitted that when the English first told him about God, he was not interested. Later, however, some of his family members were dying, so he decided to pray. He became convinced he was a sinner who deserved hell. "I cannot deliver myself, but I give my soul and my flesh to Christ, and I trust my soul with him, for he is my redeemer, and I desire to call upon him while I live," he said. Pastor Allen of Dedham asked if he had repented in his heart. "I am ashamed of all my sins," Totherswamp replied. "My heart is broken for them and melteth in me. I am angry with myself for my sins, and I pray to Christ to take away my sins, and I desire that they may be pardoned."

The next candidate was Waban, former sachem of Nonantum and now a ruler of fifty. He too confessed to being angry when he first heard Christian teaching. Then came the devastating epidemic, to which colonists seemed impervious. "I thought I shall quickly die, and I feared lest I should die before I prayed to God." But praying was difficult. "I do not know how to confess, and little do I know of Christ. I fear I shall not believe a great while, and very slowly. I do not know what grace is in my heart. There is but little good in me. But this I know, that Christ hath kept all God's commandments for us, and that Christ doth know all our hearts, and now I desire to repent of all my sins." By the end, he was in tears: "This day I do not so much desire good words, as thoroughly to open my heart. I confess I can do nothing, but deserve damnation. Only Christ can help me and do [it] for me. I have nothing to say for myself that is good. I judge that I am a sinner, and cannot repent, but Christ hath deserved pardon for us."

The ministers found Waban's testimony insufficient, so Eliot explained that Waban was not gifted "in expressing himself this way" but was "patient, constant, and prudent" and had drawn many Indians to the faith. Pastor Wilson thought the Indians were nervous, having never spoken before "so great and grave an assembly." It did not help that Eliot repeatedly interrupted them for clarification as he translated.[29]

Netus, a Nipmuc the English knew as William of Sudbury, had been outraged when colonists told him he served the Devil. But gradually he accepted their judgment, especially when he learned that the sachems Waban and Cutshamekin had become praying Indians. When he told Sudbury pastor Edmund Brown that he would pray as long as he lived, Brown challenged him to prove it by cutting his hair. Netus did so and stuck with it: "I cannot get pardon of my sins, for my sins are great in thought, word, and deed, and no man can cast off his own sins, but that is the work of Christ only to work it in us," he said. "A man cannot make a right prayer but when Christ assisteth him. Then we shall do all things well. I believe that Christ is God and the Son of God, because when he died he rose again, and he died for our sins. And I believe he is in heaven and ever prayeth for us and sendeth his gospel unto us." This was promising, but suddenly Netus undermined his own testimony. "I am angry with myself," he said, "because I do not believe the word of God and gospel of Jesus Christ."[30]

Next came Monequassun, the schoolteacher. He had thought about running away when Christianity came to Cohannet, he acknowledged, but he loved his home, so he pretended. He went to Natick, even though "my heart disliked that place," only for his wife and child to die of "the bloody flux," filling him with anger. Anger turned to fear, and fear provoked openness to Christianity. Although he resisted teachings that were contrary to Algonquian culture, such as the Apostle Paul's statement "it is a shame for a man to wear long hair," after much agonizing, he cut it off. Like many Puritans, he struggled through cycles of faith, unbelief, sin, and repentance. "Satan hath power in me," he confessed, "but I cry to God, 'Oh! Give me faith and pardon my sin, because Christ alone can deliver me from hell.'" He understood the basics of Puritan covenant theology. "The first covenant is broke by sin, and we deserve hell," he explained, "but Christ keepeth for us the new covenant, and therefore I betrust my soul with Christ." But he too seemed uncertain, constantly repeating, "I desire to believe in Christ."

As his testimony dragged on, colonists awaiting Eliot's translation grew restless. Some walked out, "others whispered, and a great confusion was in the house." Finally, Eliot cut Monequassun off. One more Indian spoke before the ministers ended the session. They were unwilling to spend the night in wigwams and wanted to get going. Establishing a church would have to wait.[31] Dorchester minister Richard Mather defended this decision, arguing it would take time to build "a church out of such rubbish as amongst Indians," especially since they lacked anyone capable of serving as pastor or elder. They could join English congregations, but it was another thing entirely to organize an Indian church "invested with all church power."[32]

Eliot was disappointed but persuaded himself that the delay was for the best. Truth be told, he felt relieved, given the heady responsibility of entrusting a church to Indians. "I cannot express what a load it took off my heart," he later confessed. He published fifteen testimonies in the tract *Tears of Repentance*, adding written testimonies from Robin Speen and Nishohkou. Taken together, the testimonies show that many praying Indians had sincerely internalized Puritan ideas about sin and guilt. They interpreted the epidemics as judgment for their sins (including Algonquian cultural practices), and their confessions of hypocrisy, doubt, lust, and lack of love reflected genuine fear of a God who would judge their most inward thoughts (an idea foreign to Algonquian religion). But they were deeply conflicted. More even than most Puritans, they questioned whether their faith was genuine and whether God would forgive them. As Nishohkou put it, "I know I deserve to go to hell because [of] all these sins I have committed. . . . If I truly believe, then he will pardon. But true faith I cannot work. Oh Jesus Christ, help me and give it [to] me!"[33]

For all their ambivalence, Eliot considered their testimonies an important sign of Christ's advancing kingdom. A year earlier, Oliver Cromwell, now England's Lord Protector, had asked Boston minister John Cotton, "What is the Lord a doing? What prophesies are now fulfilling?" Eliot consulted regularly with Cotton before Cotton died in 1652, and in *Tears of Repentance* he offered his own answer to Cromwell's question. Christ had empowered Cromwell "to overthrow Antichrist by the wars of the lamb" and establish his kingdom in England, and Indian testimonies revealed "the kingdom of Christ rising up in these western parts of the world." Clearly the time was coming when God's kingdom would "fill all the earth."[34]

PURITAN LEADERS VIEWED Natick as a blueprint for incorporating praying Indians into an English Christian commonwealth. In October 1652, therefore, Massachusetts issued instructions clarifying the status of Indian land. Citing scripture (Genesis 1:28 and 9:1, Psalm 115:16), the General Court affirmed that as people made in God's image, Indians had as much right to the earth as Englishmen. Any lands they held "by possession or improvement," including fishing places, were theirs by "just right," from which they could not be dispossessed without their consent. Indians driven from such lands should receive "relief in any of the courts of justice among the English, as the English have."

But to encourage them to be civilized and accept Christianity, the court declared that Indians who desired to settle "civilly and orderly" in English towns would "have allotment amongst the English." And it offered any "competent number of the Indians brought on to civility" who desired it, such as those at Natick, a land grant "for a plantation, as the English have." The court also confirmed English rights to unused land granted by the court or settled by "invitation of the Indians."[35]

The policy envisioned the settlement and integration of Indians under English law, with the same rights as Englishmen, freeing unoccupied land for colonial settlement. But it defined ownership, improvement, and civility in English terms and subjected disputes to English courts. In practice, colonists were required to purchase even unused land from Indians who claimed it, and courts consistently upheld "native right" when it was overtly violated. But pressure on Indians to sell was often substantial. The opportunity to protect land with a legal title via a land grant was a powerful incentive to form praying towns.

It was not long before several communities did so. In May 1653, Massachusetts authorized a Pennacook praying town at Wamesit, where the Concord River entered the Merrimack. Eventually, it would receive twenty-five hundred acres bordering the new English town of Chelmsford.[36] By October, following the United Colonies' offer of tools for Indians who formed praying towns, the Cohannet and Neponset Indians had established a praying town south of Dorchester at Punkapoag, the traditional seat of the Massachusett "sachems of the blood." Josias Wampatuck, who became the leading Massachusett sachem when Cutshamekin died, vowed before the magistrates that he would pray to God "all the days of his life." Eventually, Punkapoag was granted up to six thousand acres. While not particularly fertile, this included a stretch of the Neponset River, excellent fishing ponds, and a cedar swamp rich in timber.[37]

The following May, Massachusetts authorized three more praying towns. Hassanamesit, a Nipmuc town on the Blackstone River, would receive eight thousand acres. It lay midway on the Connecticut Path, an Indian trail connecting the Connecticut River with Massachusetts Bay.[38] Okommakamesit was a Nipmuc town eight miles west of Sudbury. It received six thousand acres, including some of the region's "best" farmland and "most considerable meadow," "well wooded and watered." Sudbury, which had been eyeing the land for itself, would contest Okommakamesit's grant in court. Nashobah, between Okommakamesit and Wamesit, was led by Attawans, the Pennacook sachem who had wanted to form a praying town in 1647. It was granted eight thousand acres "well stored with meadows and woods" and "good ponds for fish."[39]

The United Colonies commissioners feared Eliot was being *too* aggressive in recruiting praying Indians, alienating their sachems. "We desire you would be slow in withdrawing Indian professors from paying accustomed tribute and performing other lawful services to their sagamores till you have seriously considered and advised with the magistrates and elders of . . . Massachusetts, lest the passage and spreading of the gospel be hindered," they warned.[40]

Massachusetts did not hesitate to get involved. When the praying Nashaway sachem Showanon died in 1654, it worried about who might replace him. Like many Algonquian communities, the Nashaways were divided over their response to colonization, some supporting a leader named Shoshanim, whom the General Court viewed as a debauched, "drunken fellow, and no friend to the English," others supporting a Christian Nashaway named Matthew, who was "very hopeful to learn the things of Christ." The court dispatched Eliot to influence the decision by "persuasion or counsel, not by compulsion," and Matthew was chosen. But Massachusetts had not heard the last of Shoshanim.[41]

❦

JOHN ELIOT LAUNCHED his second attempt to establish a church at Natick when he asked the clergy to gather on June 13, 1654, to interview Indian converts. They would meet in Roxbury, making it easy for ministers to attend, and Eliot invited many interpreters. Churches prayed for the event during fast-day services, but before it took place, Natick suffered another scandal. Totherswamp, a Natick ruler who had testified to the ministers two years earlier, had sent his eleven-year-old son to purchase corn and fish at Watertown. On the way, the boy encountered three inebriated Natick men, including Eliot's interpreter. They persuaded the boy to try some alcohol and got him drunk. "Now we will see whether your father will punish us for drunkenness," they laughed, "seeing you are drunk with us!"

Eliot thought about canceling the interviews, just ten days away. "The tidings sunk my spirit extremely," he confessed. "I did judge it to be the greatest frown of God that ever I met withal in the work." At Natick, he met the distraught Totherswamp. Puritan discipline was harsh by Algonquian standards, and the tearful father felt forced to choose between obeying Christ by punishing the boy and loving his son by showing mercy. Moved to tears himself, Eliot said the boy's sin was not as severe as those who had gotten him drunk, but Totherswamp replied that he should not have ignored his father's counsel and fallen into bad company. Natick's court sentenced the men to twenty lashes and time in the stocks. The boy spent a short time in the stocks, and Totherswamp whipped him in front of his classmates. Eliot decided the ordeal was beneficial, for it demonstrated how serious Natick was about discipline.

On examination day, Eliot opened the floor to anyone who wanted to ask the Indians a question.[42] What good things do you see in the English? a colonist asked.

"I see true love that our great sachems have not, and that maketh me think that God is the true God," an Indian replied.

Why do you believe the Bible is the word of God?

"I believe it to be the word of God, because when we learn it, it teacheth our hearts to be wise and humble."

Another asked about humanity's fall: "When Adam sinned, what befell him?"

"He lost the image of God."

"What is the image of God, which he lost?"

"Wisdom, holiness, and righteousness."

"To whom is man now like?"

"He is like unto Satan."

Another asked what Christ had done for human beings.

"He hath died for us," an Indian replied.

What did he earn for us by this death?

"Pardon of all our sins because he paid a ransom, the favor of God, and eternal life."

The exam lasted much of the day, and this time the ministers encouraged Eliot to go ahead and establish a church. Praying Indians had wanted this for years, yet suddenly Eliot hesitated. He worried that they had not given "sufficient proof and experience of their steadfastness." What if they abused their authority and defiled Christ's name "among their barbarous friends and countrymen"? He decided to wait and focus on training ministers and elders.[43]

The Natick Indians had done everything the Puritans asked of them, abandoning their homes, submitting to Massachusetts, and transforming their way of life, but it was not enough. Eliot believed Christ had liberated them from Satan and brought them into his kingdom, but he did not trust them enough to release them from English control.

THE PACE OF MISSIONARY work accelerated as the New England Company established an annual budget of £600 for missionary work. The process was not always smooth. Donors expressed concerns about how their money was being spent. Colonists cast aspersions on missionary work by their "malicious, profane, careless and envious tongues and pens." Massachusetts agent Hugh Peter told his successor Edward Winslow "he heard the work was but a plain cheat and that there was no such thing as gospel conversion amongst the Indians." There were constant disputes between Eliot, the commissioners, and the company. Eliot regularly complained to supporters in England about insufficient funds and fretted that the commissioners failed to support him. The company suspected the commissioners of misappropriating supplies, including guns and ammunition that were supposed to be auctioned for funds but were instead divided among the colonies.[44]

Company funds paid the salaries of Eliot, Thomas Mayhew Jr., and other missionaries. The commissioners spent £200 educating Connecticut interpreter Thomas Stanton's son for missionary work, though it proved a complete waste. They paid the salaries of Indian teachers and magistrates and procured tools, clothing, and other supplies for praying towns. They supported a school for boys and girls at Natick and grammar schools at Cambridge and Roxbury where about twenty Indians, including a woman, studied. They even built an Indian College (or dormitory) at Harvard, where a few Indians had already studied in pursuit of its stated mission to educate "English and Indian youth." But only a few Indians would occupy it, and it was also used to house Cambridge's printing press.

While many of those efforts proved disappointing, the commissioners accomplished more by funding Eliot's pioneering efforts to translate the Bible and other literature into Wôpanâak, or Massachusett, which had no written form. A skilled Indian team assisted him, including longtime assistant Job Nesutan, John Sassamon, a "man of eminent parts and wit" who briefly studied at Harvard, and James Printer, who may have studied at Harvard and later worked for the Cambridge press. The press published Eliot's Massachusett catechism and a primer in 1654. The next year it released translations of Genesis and Matthew. The psalms followed in 1658 and another catechism in 1659. In 1660 the press began printing fifteen hundred New Testaments, and at Governor Endecott's urging, it followed with the Old Testament. Popular Puritan books came later, including Richard Baxter's *Call to the Unconverted* and Lewis Bayly's *Practice of Piety*.[45] By 1660, about a hundred praying Indians in Massachusetts could read these works. Surviving copies contain their handwritten notes and marginal comments. The effort was highly significant, not only for the long-term survival of the Massachusett language but because it enabled the maturation of an indigenous Algonquian Christianity, which no longer depended on an English Bible or English teachers.[46]

The missionary movement repeatedly endured setbacks. Plymouth missionary William Leverich abandoned the Nausets to work on Long Island, although his work was eventually taken up by others. Eliot suffered from sciatica in 1656–1657, leaving him bedridden and unable to travel for months. "I do bless the Lord, he hath in some measure recovered me and enabled me to attend my work," he finally wrote in late 1657, "though not without pain. . . . I can pretty well endure my travel, but if I travel either in wet or cold it doth shake me much and is ready to lay me quite up again." Later that year, Thomas Mayhew Jr., New England's most successful missionary, was killed in a shipwreck. "The Lord hath given us the amazing blow, to take away my brother Mayhew," Eliot lamented.

The elder Mayhew would take up the work on Martha's Vineyard, but he was not a minister and could hardly fill his son's shoes.[47]

Around the same time, Massachusett sachem Josias Wampatuck apostatized from the faith. Wampatuck "had considerable knowledge in the Christian religion" and had donated the land at Natick, but now he abandoned the praying town of Punkapoag and settled with Massachusett Indians who rejected Christianity.[48] The Connecticut Podunks also proved wary of Christianity when Eliot preached to them in 1657, complaining "that the English had got away their lands and were now seeking to make servants of them." As it turned out, they had heard that Sudbury colonists were building a settlement on land granted to the praying town Okommakamesit. "These actings of the English do make the profane Indians laugh at the praying Indians and at praying to God," Eliot warned.[49]

Eliot wanted Massachusetts to take a more active role in praying towns, so in 1656 he petitioned the colony to appoint agents to help establish governments and procure teachers. Surprisingly, he recommended Humphrey Atherton, who had nearly provoked war with the Narragansetts in 1650. Atherton had since become a magistrate, and Eliot was grateful to him and other Dorchester inhabitants for providing land for Punkapoag at a time when "our poor Indians are much molested in most places." Massachusetts appointed Atherton as Indian superintendent in 1658, instructing him to "take care that all . . . Indians live according to our laws as far as they are capable." He was to appoint Indian commissioners to adjudicate civil and criminal cases and officers to enforce their decisions. The Indians would remain largely autonomous, but Atherton would join them as a "county court" for major cases.[50]

THESE WERE DISCOURAGING times for Natick. "We are called to fasting this day," the Massachusett John Speen announced during a service on November 15, 1658, "because of the great rain and great floods and unseasonable weather, whereby the Lord spoileth our labors. Our corn is much spoiled with the wet, so that the Lord doth threaten us with want of food. Also our hay is much spoiled, so that God threateneth to starve and kill our cattle. Also, we have great sickness among us, so that many are dead. The burying place of this town hath many graves, and so it is in all our towns among the Praying Indians. . . . And what maketh him angry? We may be sure it is our sins, for we are great sinners."

Waban, Natick's leader, declared that spiritual diseases, such as laziness, Sabbath-breaking, and "passion," were more serious than physical illnesses. He urged them to seek Christ, the "physician of souls." Piumbubbon invoked hope from Jesus's beatitude "Blessed are the poor in spirit, for theirs is the kingdom of heaven." It was good news for Indians, Piumbubbon declared, for "we are the most poor, feeble, despicable people in the world."[51]

The clergy decided that until Natick had its own church, its inhabitants could join Eliot's congregation in Roxbury. Eight professed their faith there on April 15, 1659. Roxbury took the unprecedented step of inviting representatives of ten churches to attend a final examination on July 5.[52] On both occasions, Natick's Indians described their struggles to accept and understand a faith delivered by people who dominated them in so many ways. They made the faith their own, invoking poignant scripture passages to make sense of their experiences. They emphasized their need for the Lord's Supper and baptism to strengthen their faith.

One, Anthony, had run away when he heard his brothers Wampooas and Totherswamp had become praying Indians, but he eventually converted be- cause he could not bear to alienate them. He apprenticed himself to a Roxbury smith, yet his master refused to teach him certain skills, "lest Indians learn to make locks and guns," and he angrily resolved to "cast off praying." Again, his family persuaded him to stay. When family members fell sick, he prayed that God would heal them, only to see them die. "Then my heart said, 'sure it's a vain thing to pray to God, for I prayed, yet my friends die,'" he admitted. He remained in Natick, but only to earn money by helping build the meeting house. One day he was in a sawpit directing the placement of a freshly sawn plank when it slipped, slamming into his head and fracturing his skull. He was taken up "half dead," but Eliot found a surgeon to attend to him at New England Company expense. That proved a turning point. Anthony recalled, "That winter God broke my head. I knew but little. I was almost dead. Then my heart said, 'Now I know God is angry with me for my sins, and hath therefore smote me. Then I prayed hard, when I was almost dead. I remembered my sins much, and considered them much." Now he wholeheartedly embraced faith in Christ.[53]

A teacher named Ponampam described the pivotal role epidemics had played in his conversion. When he was eight, he recalled, his father rebuked him for playing, warning that "we shall all die shortly." Ponampam thought he got this idea from hearing John Wilson preach that in Noah's day "God drowned all the world for the sins of the people." He tried to forget about it, but that winter, smallpox killed "almost all our kindred," including his father. His mother took him to Cohannet, where he grew up, married two wives, and had children. He considered fleeing when the missionaries arrived, but Eliot's sermon on Malachi 1:11, which prophesied that the Gentiles would worship God, convinced him that Christianity would follow him wherever he went. So he took up the life of a praying Indian, only to face a new crisis when asked to become a teacher. "I feared, and durst not for fear of the sachems, yet they urged me, and I did," he recalled. Satan tempted him to flee to where there was "land enough, and riches [in] abundance," much as the Devil tempted Christ in Matthew 4. But after his mother and two children died, he fully committed to Christianity.[54]

Many Indians testified to Waban's influence in their conversion stories, but Waban admitted that he had initially scorned the new religion. He recalled being furious when colonists told him he loved the Devil. "You know the devil. I do not know the devil," he retorted. Later, however, he attended the ministers' teaching because they gave him good food, and he began wondering whether they were telling the truth. "Sometimes I thought if we did not pray, the English might kill us." Other times he concluded, "The English love us, and therefore it is like[ly] that is true which they say of God, and I desire to live forever where they do." Though he struggled daily with "contrary and misbelieving thoughts," he emerged as a stalwart of the praying community. John Speen, whose family had owned some of the land that became Natick, expressed similar motivations: "I saw the English took much ground, and I thought if I prayed, the English would not take away my ground." Whatever their initial motivations, both men now embraced Christianity out of conviction.

Another who spoke was the Nipmuc sachem Wuttasacomponom, later known as Captain Tom, whose leadership would prove critical in future years. When Pastor Brown of Sudbury first urged him to become a Christian, he recalled, "I did not like it, nor to hear of praying to God." Eventually, however, under Waban's influence, he came to Nonantum to hear Eliot. Eliot's warning that God would judge those who failed to repent and believe in Christ terrified him, especially when his wife and children died, followed by a second wife. "Then my heart said, surely God is angry with me, who doth thus afflict me." Fear finally drove him to faith: "I now confess my sins before God, and I beg mercy from God in Jesus Christ."

When the last Indian had spoken, the ministers interviewed them about "grace, ordinances, sacraments, baptism and the Lord's Supper, about repentance and faith, all which they readily answered." The ministers then approved them for membership.[55] A year later, in 1660, an Algonquian church was finally established at Natick.[56]

NATICK'S ORDEAL WAS hardly over. A short time after the General Court issued Natick's land grant, the people of Dedham challenged its use of land south of the Charles River, claiming that in oral agreements it had specifically excluded that land from the grant. Eliot countered that the south bank was included in the agreements and always belonged to Natick's people. Dedham hoped to settle out of court, but Eliot and Natick considered it a question of justice and refused.[57] As Eliot explained, Massachusetts's "general practice hath been to purchase of the Natives what we enjoy, and not only so, but it is frequent also with them to invite the English unto fit places for towns because of the benefit they receive by our neighborhood." It was only under these terms that colonists had any right to Native land.[58]

Thus Massachusetts always acknowledged that "where the Indians have a right, we do religiously take care that it be lawfully alienated," but this had not happened at Natick. Dedham claimed it had received the land from Chickataubut, a Massachusett sachem, but Natick countered that it belonged to another Massachusett sachem, Josias Wampatuck, who with his people had, "in a solemn fast, given up their right in these lands unto God, here to begin a town and gather a church." If Dedham prevailed, Eliot warned, Indians would abandon Natick. "Now if Natick also be overthrown, let wise men look upon the consequences in respect of God and man," he warned. Indians everywhere were watching.[59]

English mediators urged the parties to compromise, "forbearing and forgiving one another," as commanded in Colossians 3:12–13. They criticized Eliot for encouraging Indians to settle south of the river without clear legal title and for supporting their rejection of Dedham's "reasonable motions." On the other hand, they conceded "how grievous it will be to those poor Natives to be put from the lands which they have so long possessed." They therefore urged Dedham, "for Christ's sake, lovingly to grant unto the Indians the lands now possessed by them" in exchange for a compensatory grant elsewhere, not because of the "right of any Indian title" but for the "gracious gospel principles of self-denial, love, peace, and desire to further Christ's work among the Indians."[60]

Dedham refused. Soon they were determined to reclaim Natick's land on both sides of the river. In 1661 they sued Natick's leaders, including Waban and John Speen. The Suffolk County Court issued three rulings in Dedham's favor. But, much to Dedham's dismay, the Court of Assistants overturned the rulings.[61] In May 1662 the General Court issued a final ruling. It acknowledged that Dedham's "legal right . . . cannot in justice be denied" but asserted that the Indians had a more basic "native right" to the land on which they lived, strengthened by the fact that they had developed it, which "cannot, in strict justice, be utterly extinct." Thus, in accord with Massachusetts law, they could "not [be] dispossessed of such lands as they are at present possessed." Dedham would receive compensatory land elsewhere.[62]

It was a significant vindication for Natick and praying Indians everywhere. Over the previous twelve years, as Christianity spread to more Algonquian communities, Natick had come to embody the Puritans' grandest hopes for America's first people. While it maintained many aspects of Native culture, it also embraced elements of English civilization and law. It had an independent congregation of faithful, increasingly educated Indians committed to an Algonquian form of Puritan Christianity. But the journey had been fraught with frustration, misunderstanding, and conflict. Natick would strive to preserve its Algonquian community within the colonial system, but non-praying Indians were alarmed, Dedham was resentful, and many colonists doubted praying Indians' sincerity and coveted their land. Such tensions boded ill for the future.

10

The Pocumtuck War

1652 to 1661

NEW ENGLAND IN 1652 was a place of relative optimism. The Narragansetts and Mohegans were at peace, and missionary efforts heralded a future in which English and Algonquians might live side by side as Christians. Over the next decade, however, competition over trade, tributaries, and land pushed Algonquians into a series of destructive wars. At first, Puritan concerns about justice prevented the United Colonies from intervening, but as the violence escalated, they decided to impose their will. It became all too easy to confuse the cause of justice and peace with the colonial desire for power, dominion, and land.

The first hint of trouble emerged when England prohibited Dutch merchant ships from entering English ports. A naval war soon broke out between the two colonial powers. The United Colonies were already engaged in territorial disputes with New Netherland and resented Dutch traders for selling guns and ammunition to Indians. Tensions increased when the English intercepted a letter from the Dutch West India Company to New Netherland's governor Peter Stuyvesant. While it ordered him to keep the peace, the letter counseled him to "make use of the Indians" if New England attacked New Netherland.[1]

English suspicion centered on Ninigret. That winter, the Narragansett leader fell ill and sought help from John Winthrop Jr., whose services as a healer were known throughout New England.[2] Winthrop directed him to a French doctor in New Netherland, so Ninigret traveled there bearing wampum for the doctor and Governor Stuyvesant. "I stood a great part of a winter day knocking at the governor's door," Ninigret later claimed, but "he would neither open it nor suffer others to open it to let me in." Ninigret visited the doctor and various sachems across the Hudson River before returning home. When he sent men back with wampum and gifts, Mohegans captured them. Uncas, the Mohegan sachem, claimed that two of them "freely confessed" that Ninigret and other sachems were conspiring with the Dutch. Outraged, Ninigret asked Winthrop to intervene on his behalf. He had proven his goodwill by paying the tribute the colonies demanded. Why would he suddenly turn treacherous?[3]

By then the region was erupting with alarms of a conspiracy. A Native woman warned the colonists of Wethersfield, Connecticut, that the Dutch and Indians were conspiring "to cut them off," observing that they had foolishly ignored her similar warning during the Pequot War. One report had Stuyvesant selling guns and ammunition to Uncas. Another had the Showamet sachem Pomham conspiring with Ninigret, despite Pomham's estrangement from the Narragansetts. It was said that Ninigret was procuring guns, ammunition, and "wildfire from the Dutch, which, being shot with their arrows, will kindle and burn anything." Indians warned that warriors would strike on land while a Dutch fleet attacked from the sea. Sachems from Long Island and Manhattan claimed the Dutch offered them guns and ammunition and encouraged them to attack English settlements.

Such stories were hardly new. Many colonists were quick to believe the worst about Indians, and there was no shortage of Indians who delighted in scaring colonists or using false information to discredit their Native rivals. Moreover, linguistic differences easily bred confusion and exaggeration. But this time, the war between the English and the Dutch made the stories seem credible.[4]

Worried colonists lashed out at praying Indians, though missionary John Eliot found their fears "utterly groundless." The government was skeptical but yielded to the pressure and dispatched soldiers to disarm Natick. The soldiers interrupted a Sunday church service and demanded the Indians' guns. Natick leaders Cutshamekin and Nishohkou were outraged. Had God not said, "Keep the Sabbath day holy?" Shocked at English hypocrisy, Nishohkou concluded, "God is not, the Sabbath is not, it is not the Lord's Day, for were it so, the soldiers would not have . . . come." In despair, he turned to drink and landed in court for drunkenness.[5]

Massachusetts governor John Endecott called an emergency session of the United Colonies in April 1653. Meanwhile, he dispatched envoys to the Narragansetts. "We have never injured any of you, but have been ready at all times to do you justice according to our best understanding," the emissaries claimed. "We have been and are very slow to give credit to what we hear or to engage in a war against you, till evident grounds appear." Still, they had to make sure, so they asked the sachems to send representatives to Boston. Even if the Narragansetts had conspired with the Dutch, they promised, it was not too late to back out.[6]

The sachems defended themselves. "Do you think that we are mad and that we have forgot our writing that we had in the bay, which doth bind us to the English, our friends?" Pessicus asked. "Shall we throw away that writing, and ourselves too?" Why would they support the Dutch, who were far away, against the English, who were nearby? "Have we not reason in us?" They would keep their covenant "firmly to our dying day," he pledged. "And when we are dying and going out of the world, we will leave it in special charge to ours to carry it well to the English and their children." Ninigret denied hearing any talk of a conspiracy in New Netherland, nor did he "know any wrong the English hath done him" to justify one. "What do the English think, that I think they be asleep and suffer me to do them wrong? . . . Do they think we are mad, to sell our lives and the lives of our wives and children and all our kindred, and to have our country destroyed for a few guns, powder, shot and swords? What will they do us good when we are dead?"[7]

Narragansett representatives traveled to Boston, where the commissioners, including Endecott and Plymouth's William Bradford, convened on April 19. The Narragansetts accused Uncas of spreading malicious reports and demanded that he be punished for abusing Ninigret's men. The commissioners promised to investigate the matter but complained that Ninigret had not been paying tribute for his Pequot captives. It did not help when a Narragansett man boasted to colonists that the Dutch had informed him they planned to "cut off the English on Long Island."[8]

The commissioners drafted a long statement of grievances that they planned to send to New Netherland. That the Indians should be hostile ("who know not God, but worship and walk after the prince of the power of the air, serving their lusts, hateful and hating one another") was not surprising, they wrote, but they expected better from a Protestant colony. New England sought what was best for the Indians, but the Dutch poisoned Indians against them. Evidence for a conspiracy was overwhelming, including "many concurrent strong and pressing testimonies," which they proceeded to summarize. They warned that they would do whatever was necessary to defend the honor and safety of the United Colonies.[9]

The statement was so belligerent that Massachusetts's commissioners balked. Did the evidence warrant such a response, and did it befit a Christian people? They sent the document to the clergy for advice. The ministers found the evidence of a conspiracy to be "very strong, and such as we cannot deny," but while some thought it "sufficient proof" to justify war, others were skeptical. They urged the magistrates to consider whether "a people professing to walk in the spirit of the gospel of peace" owed the Dutch governor an opportunity to defend himself.[10] Seventeen years earlier, Governor Endecott had led the opening strike of the Pequot War, and perhaps that experience sobered him. "I greatly doubt a clear ground for a war, because it's not certain there hath been such engaging of the Indians [in a conspiracy]," he declared, "and [I] fear the testimonies of the Indians may be defective for want of due interpreters. I therefore cannot advise to a war."[11]

Acceding to Massachusetts's desires, in May the commissioners dispatched three agents and interpreter Thomas Stanton to meet the Dutch governor and investigate the reports. Two weeks later, they called the United Colonies to raise five hundred soldiers. But the investigation proved a farce. The agents failed to meet with Governor Stuyvesant and rejected his demand that they cooperate with Dutch officials and follow Dutch principles of law. Instead, they accumulated sworn testimony from Indians, Dutch, and English alleging that Stuyvesant and Ninigret were conspiring against New England. Many accusations came from English colonists eager to end Dutch rule over western Long Island. The restless Indian-fighter John Underhill was a ringleader, enthusiastically urging the commissioners to "vindicate the common cause of England against the Dutch," for "the cause is God's and ours."[12]

The agents returned to Boston on May 21 and delivered their report. But Massachusetts remained skeptical. When a joint committee of magistrates and commissioners worked through the evidence, it produced conflicting reports, one for war and another against. Again, the colony turned to its ministers. On May 27, after earnest prayer and extensive debate, the clergy delivered their assessment of "what the Lord calleth [us] to do." There was not "sufficient clear ground of war at present," they argued. Evidence for a plot was substantial, and they were inclined to believe it, but "upon serious and conscientious examination," it was not "fully conclusive." "Therefore we humbly conceive it to be most agreeable to the gospel of peace which we profess, and safest for these colonies, to forbear the use of the sword till the Lord by his providence and by the wisdom of his servants set over us, shall further clear up his mind." God would not forsake them because "tenderness of conscience" made them "slow to shed blood."[13]

Unfortunately for Massachusetts, its commissioners were outvoted 6–2. New Haven, Connecticut, and Plymouth advocated war. But Massachusetts refused to submit, protesting that it was a "scandal in religion that a general court of Christians should be obliged to act and engage upon the faith of six delegates, against their conscience," a "bondage hardly to be borne by the most subjective people."[14] Given that Massachusetts was by far the largest colony, the commissioners were unwilling to act without it and postponed the matter to their September meeting.

Not all ministers were pleased. Edward Norris of Salem worried that inaction would make the "Indians and infidels . . . intolerable insolent," leading them to "blaspheme and despise both our God and ourselves." Then God's judgment would fall upon the country, and innocent people would die.[15] "They have concluded, no war," complained Hartford minister Samuel Stone, a former Pequot War chaplain. "I wish we may not love our skins too well but be ready to adventure in time of need."[16]

ALL THAT SUMMER, NARRAGANSETTS heard rumors that the English were recruiting the Mohegans and Long Island's Montauks and Shinnecocks to invade

Narragansett country. Amid widespread fear and mistrust, a man who claimed to be acting on orders from the Narragansett leader Ninigret attempted to assassinate a Shinnecock sachem. With Connecticut's permission, the Montauks and Shinnecocks executed him and burned his body. Roger Williams later claimed that Massachusetts governor John Endecott gave Ninigret "implicit consent to right himself." In a retaliatory raid, Ninigret killed some Indians and captured at least fourteen women, including the daughter of Wyandanch, the Montauk sachem.

Wyandanch had paid the colonies tribute since the Pequot War and confirmed a treaty of friendship in 1644, although the colonies had not promised him protection. So when the Montauks appealed for help, the commissioners dispatched envoys summoning Ninigret to Boston. John Winthrop Jr. warned Ninigret that Wyandanch was his friend, so if Ninigret was Winthrop's friend, he would release Wyandanch's people.[17]

The interpreter Thomas Stanton, who had recently established a trading post at Pawcatuck, set out for Ninigret's fort. He was quickly accosted by warriors shouting that "they cared not for the English, nor did they fear them." Never one to tolerate such behavior from Indians, Stanton struck a warrior in the head with his rapier, dared them to retaliate, and insisted on proceeding. The irritated men brought him to Ninigret, but they "expressed themselves very tumultuously, and would hardly suffer any speech" between them.

Stanton joined the commissioners' envoys in another attempt to reach Ninigret on September 16, 1653. This time as many as fifty warriors confronted them, and more kept arriving as they rode, running along the path and jeering at them. When they found Ninigret, he was holding a pistol, accompanied by more armed men. They sat on the ground, and Stanton relayed the commissioners' message over the warriors' shouts and interruptions. Ninigret denied the commissioners' right to challenge his actions. Why did they always slight his authority? Indians respected him, yet the English did not. Did they not know the Montauks had murdered his man? Did he not have the right to protect his people? He refused to go to Boston. "If the English say that we have broken covenant," he charged, "they lie."

The commissioners bristled upon hearing of Ninigret's "proud, peremptory and offensive answers" and his warriors' "rude and hostile affronts," which they interpreted as part of a legacy of Narragansett treachery going back to Miantonomo. Most argued that they had to hold Ninigret accountable for murdering the "innocent" Montauks, for if they failed to defend their allies, no Indians would trust their promises, and Ninigret would be emboldened. Declaring themselves "called by God" to make war, they ordered the mobilization of 250 soldiers.

But Massachusetts demurred yet again. Commissioner Simon Bradstreet denied that the colonies were "obligated to protect the Long Island Indians." This was simply another Indian quarrel, "the grounds whereof they cannot well understand," he argued, and justice required English neutrality. Massachusetts's executive council declared that it did "not see sufficient grounds [for war], either from any obligation of the English towards the Long Islanders, or from the usage the messengers received from the Indians."

The other commissioners believed that Massachusetts simply wanted to avoid the cost of war and accused it of having "broken their covenant," effectively wrecking the confederation. But Bradstreet denied that Massachusetts was obligated "to act in any offensive war according to the determination of the commissioners further than the same is just and according to God," and he urged them to respect their Christian "judgments and consciences." When they faced God's judgment, he added, no one would regret that "we have neither shed blood causelessly, nor drawn others to do it upon grounds not clear to them." The other commissioners retorted that God would judge them for failing to vindicate "the blood of innocents—who depend on us for safety and probably suffer for their faithfulness to the English." Plymouth later accused Massachusetts of allowing their enemies "to reproach the name of God and his ways."[18]

But Massachusetts would not be moved. For the second time in a year, Puritans invoked Christian principles of justice to prevent the colonies from going to war.

BY 1654 THE NARRAGANSETT-MONTAUK war was escalating into a regional conflict. Uncas reportedly offered the Montauks Mohegan support in exchange for seven hundred fathoms of wampum.[19] Ninigret, the Narragansett leader, released his Montauk captives in an attempt at peace, according to Roger Williams, but the Montauks treacherously killed thirty of Ninigret's men, including his nephew.[20] So Ninigret resumed his raids against Long Island, now with support from the Connecticut Valley Pocumtucks and other upland Indians. When the Quinebaug Nipmucs plundered one of Uncas's towns, the furious Mohegan threatened retaliation unless Massachusetts rendered satisfaction. His Connecticut patron John Mason charged that if the colonies refused to restrain Ninigret and his allies, "I shall then fear that we have not [only] lost the hearts of men, but almost of Christians."[21]

The commissioners summoned the belligerents to Hartford in September. The Pocumtucks sued for peace, claiming they had not realized the war was "offensive to the English." But Ninigret denied the commissioners' right to interfere. "If your governors' son were slain, and several other men, would you ask counsel of another nation how and when to right yourselves?" he demanded. "I do but right my own quarrel which the Long Islanders began with me." Of course, the colonies did not believe he had the authority to right his own quarrel, for various treaties prohibited him from waging war without their consent. By refusing to honor such treaties, he had proved himself a treacherous rebel. Even Massachusetts commissioner Simon Bradstreet now believed colonial "forbearance and lenity" had increased Ninigret's "insolency and our danger."

They decided to send Major Simon Willard, now a Massachusetts magistrate, with sixty soldiers to force Ninigret to not only cease his attacks but surrender his Pequots, for whom he had not been paying tribute, and pay the tribute he owed. Captain Mason would gather another 310 soldiers at Pawcatuck, and in the event that Ninigret refused, Willard was "to make fair war without exercising cruelty and not to put to death any you have taken captives."[22]

Even Massachusetts supported the decision, no doubt in part because England and the Netherlands had agreed to peace that spring, but also because escalating conflict was devastating the trade in wampum and furs. The Massachusetts government made the moral case for war in a declaration to be read in the colony's churches. It acknowledged the Montauks as allies who were deserving of English protection and accused Ninigret of unprovoked aggression and of having rejected a peaceful resolution. It called churches to observe October 12 as a "day of solemn humiliation," asking the Lord to "to go out with our forces, preserve peace in our borders, and give good success to our endeavors."[23]

Roger Williams, whose Rhode Island was excluded from the United Colonies, remained unconvinced. "I have been more or less interested and used in all the great transactions of war or peace between the English and the Natives," he declared in a lengthy protest letter, "and have not spared purse, nor pains, nor hazards (very many times), that the whole land, English and Natives, might sleep in peace securely." How was Massachusetts honoring Christ's command to seek peace with all people? They claimed that Ninigret was the aggressor, but all warring nations "labor to maintain their wars to be defensive." He urged them to consider "whether it be not only possible, but very easy for the English to live and die in peace with all the Natives of this country."

In sharp contrast to the Pequots, Mohegans, and Montauks, he observed, the Narragansetts had never "stain[ed] their hands with any English blood." Their worst offenses were mere "matters of money" or "petty revengings" against Indian rivals. Hundreds of Rhode Islanders experienced their tendency "to peace and love with the English nation," safely trading and enjoying hospitality in their towns. How was it faithful to Jesus's teachings "to take hold of some seeming occasions [as a pretext] for their destruction?"

War threatened everything colonists held dear, Williams warned. All it would take was one English defeat, and Indians across New England might rise up against them. "England and other nations ring with the glorious conversion of the Indians of New England," but that would change quickly if they learned of "unnecessary wars and cruel destructions of the Indians." Had colonists forgotten the founding generation's evangelistic vision? "How much more noble were it, and glorious to the name of God and your own," if they brought the Narragansetts "from barbarism to civility," and then to Christianity? It was hardly worth hazarding this for the Montauks, "a few inconsiderable pagans and beasts wallowing in idleness, stealing, lying, whoring, treachery, witchcrafts, blasphemies, and idolatries," Williams argued.[24]

Williams's letter did not reach Boston in time, though he shared it with Major Willard.[25] As Willard advanced into Narragansett country, Ninigret withdrew his people into a swamp and demanded to know what crime he had committed "that they came so against him round about." Willard sent allied Pequots to solicit their kin to abandon Ninigret, and although some responded belligerently, 109 surrendered over the following days. With Mason's army menacing from Pawcatuck, Ninigret finally agreed to negotiate. Protesting bitterly that he had every right to fight for his people, he signed a document promising to surrender his Pequots, but he refused to pay tribute for them, let alone additional reparations. When Willard's men threatened to mount Ninigret's head on a spike if he launched further attacks, Ninigret remained silent. Willard was mindful of his instructions to avoid war if possible. He decided he had accomplished enough and returned to Boston.[26]

The following year, to prevent Ninigret from reasserting control over the Pequots, the United Colonies issued a stunning reversal of long-standing policy. They recognized the Pequots as a distinct people subject to English rule and free from Narragansett or Mohegan control. The Pequot sachems would serve as governors subject to colonial oversight, enforcing Christian laws against blasphemy, Sabbath-breaking, witchcraft, adultery, and drunkenness. The 1638 Treaty of Hartford had banned the Pequot name; now the Pequots were protected English subjects. To soften the blow against Uncas, the commissioners stipulated that the Mohegans and Pequots were "to assist and defend each other in all just cases." But there was no softening the blow against Ninigret.[27]

MAJOR WILLARD'S EXPEDITION failed to stop the drift toward a regional Algonquian war. A chorus of voices protested Ninigret's "murderous attacks" on Long Island, and the Montauks warned that they might have to "yield up themselves and their country to the Narragansetts." The commissioners blamed Willard for failing to impose their full demands. "Ninigret, through the fear that then possessed him," would surely have yielded. They sent the Montauks powder and shot and dispatched an armed vessel to prevent Narragansetts from crossing Long Island Sound.[28] By 1656 Uncas's Mohegans were fighting the Connecticut Valley Podunks, who had ties with the Narragansetts. Connecticut's exasperated governor John Webster begged them to make peace but made it clear that Connecticut would not intervene as long as they steered clear of English property.[29] Uncas began baiting the Narragansett sachem Mixanno by "jeering his dead ancestors."

The frustrated Narragansetts protested to the United Colonies. Ninigret submitted a long list of grievances, but his primary complaint was that the Montauks treacherously attacked his men after negotiating peace. The commissioners were hardly inclined to believe him, especially since the Montauks denied agreeing to peace. They were more sympathetic to Mixanno's complaint. "We know that Uncas, out of his pride and folly, is apt to speak that many times which he ought not," they admitted. "We shall let him know . . . that we will not in any measure countenance any such carriage and behavior in him towards you or any other of our friends." But despite their patronizing description of the Narragansetts as "long friends to us," they refused to allow retaliation.[30]

When Mohegans drove the Podunks from their villages, the Podunks appealed to the Narragansetts and Pocumtucks for aid.[31] Several Narragansett and Pocumtuck sachems requested permission from Massachusetts to attack Uncas in May 1657, but Massachusetts toed the commissioners' line. The colony acknowledged their "friendship" and praised them for asking. It denied having done them "any wrong or injury" and promised everlasting love and friendship. But it rejected the petition. While "Uncas may be in fault," the magistrates conceded, they did "not fully understand the ground" of the conflict, "not having heard both parties together." The dispute had to be adjudicated by the United Colonies.[32]

The Pocumtucks and Narragansetts invaded Mohegan country anyway. "We are at this time in a disturbed way in respect of the Indian wars managed round about, nay, at our very doors," Captain Mason anxiously wrote Winthrop from Connecticut. Indians "continually lie skulking near our towns." They even killed a pregnant Native woman near an English house. "I look at it as a matter unreasonable, as also very unsafe, to suffer Indians to manage and maintain a seat of war at and in our very bowels," he continued. "In my apprehension, we act like men either asleep or afraid. Certainly there is a very great . . . confusion among us, and if the Lord help not, we may soon feel the smart of it." Narragansetts threatened Uncas's home at Shantok, across the river from a trading post recently opened by Jonathan Brewster, and soon ran into colonial interference. Colonists alerted the Mohegans every time enemy warriors approached. Connecticut even authorized Brewster to garrison Shantok with twenty men. This forced the frustrated Narragansetts, unwilling to fight colonists, to withdraw.[33]

Connecticut's intervention angered the commissioners. Many considered Uncas the aggressor, and they had just promised the Narragansetts they would "protect no man in his proud and sinful miscarriages." Furthermore, the presence of English soldiers at Shantok risked dragging the colonies into the war. They ordered the colony to remove Brewster's men, but they could not agree on how to restrain the warring parties. When Uncas failed to appear in Boston as summoned, Connecticut's commissioners defended his absence. All they would do was order him to allow the Podunks back to their villages. When the commissioners voted to send Ninigret a threatening rebuke, on the other hand, Massachusetts commissioners Bradstreet and Daniel Denison protested that such blatant favoritism was "unreasonable," made the colonies "contemptible" to the Narragansetts, and risked "a dangerous and unnecessary war upon Indian quarrels, the grounds whereof we can hardly ever satisfactorily understand." But the majority insisted that "God and the peace of the country called them" to hold Ninigret accountable. If it were not for Massachusetts's waffling, they added, Ninigret would have submitted long ago.[34]

With Connecticut favoring Uncas and Massachusetts sympathizing with the Narragansetts, the commissioners were unable to orchestrate a coherent policy, let alone bring the sachems to the negotiating table. Their struggle was complicated by significant leadership transitions as the founding generation of colonists passed from the scene. William Bradford, who had long dominated Plymouth politics, died in 1657. Rising in prominence was John Winthrop Jr., whose services were solicited by Providence, Hartford, New Haven, and even New Amsterdam. Winthrop had relocated to New Haven, but on May 21, 1657, Connecticut elected him governor. He hesitated, and for six months Connecticut was reduced to begging him to take up the office while war raged all around. Not until December did he arrive in Hartford.[35]

Another emerging figure was John Pynchon, who inherited his father's Springfield-based fur-trading enterprise in 1652 and emerged as the dominant trader, lender, entrepreneur, landowner, militia officer, and magistrate in the upper Connecticut Valley. Trading tools, clothing, food, and wampum with valley Indians in exchange for furs, he exported nine thousand beaver pelts for a profit of nearly £7,000 between 1652 and 1658 and shipped more than a thousand bushels of wheat to Boston annually. In 1653 he purchased land from the Norwottucks and financed the new town of Northampton. Over time he employed more than half the English population in the valley and rented land, housing, or livestock to more than a third. He owned Springfield's store and mill and an enormous amount of land.[36]

His enterprise required good relations with the valley Indians, but war was crushing profits. At one point, the Mohegans and Pocumtucks appeared to make peace, but Uncas failed to deliver promised wampum, and Pynchon vented to Winthrop that Uncas and his patron John Mason had antagonized the Pocumtucks with inflammatory rhetoric.[37] When the Pocumtucks and Narragansetts resumed their siege of Shantok in 1658, Uncas sent men bearing wampum to Pocumtuck, accompanied by Connecticut representatives. But the enraged Pocumtuck sachem, Onopequin, threw "an axe, horn, and the wampum" at a Connecticut representative, swung a gun at another, and told his warriors "to kill their horses."[38]

Meanwhile, Mohegans launched retaliatory raids against the Quinebaug Nipmucs and other Narragansett allies. The missionary John Eliot claimed they killed eight "unarmed poor people" and seized twenty-four women and children, including praying Indians, and "did not only abuse the women by filthiness, but . . . sold away (as I hear) some or all of those captives." "The poor bereaved Indians wait to see what you please to do," he implored Massachusetts.[39] Uncas, however, complained that the commissioners were abandoning him "for the crow and wolves to feed upon" and insisted that the people Eliot claimed were so innocent had attacked his people. It was said the commissioners were like gods, he declared. If so, they should "show themselves so that the sky may be cleared" and Indians might "conclude that they are so indeed."[40]

The violence drew ever closer to colonists. Pocumtucks allegedly stole corn from a Wethersfield farm and seized an Indian man and two children who had lived alongside colonists for decades. During a skirmish, stray bullets whistled through Farmington, west of Hartford. Connecticut retaliated by expelling local Indians from their land.[41] In March 1659 Jonathan Brewster's wife was working in a field with three Indian servants when a dozen Narragansetts emerged from the bushes. A terrified Mohegan servant "ran to Mrs. Brewster and held fast about her," but the Narragansetts "violently took him from her and shot him by her side, to her great affrightment." Pocumtucks killed a trusted Mohegan servant at another farm.[42]

That summer Pocumtucks sieging Shantok were informed that twenty Mohegans were at Brewster's trading post. When shots were fired from that side of the river, they crossed, entered Brewster's house, and plundered trade goods and corn, though they did not find any Mohegans. Captain Mason vented that colonial passivity had emboldened the Pocumtucks beyond belief. The commissioners again summoned the warring sachems, but Uncas ignored the appeal, and the Pocumtucks replied that no treaty obligated them to obey. They insisted they had "charged their men to do no wrong to any English or their cattle" and offered satisfaction for abuses. The commissioners in turn escalated their accusations and threatened war. They were harshest toward the Narragansetts, ordering them to pay ninety-five fathoms of wampum for killing Brewster's Mohegan servant.

The Pocumtucks protested the colonists' double standard. Indians often suffered abuses from colonists, they pointed out, but they did not blame all the English because they knew such behavior was "not countenanced by the governors." Similarly, the actions of "young and foolish" Pocumtucks "should not break the league betwixt us and the English, seeing we do not countenance our men for so doing." They had returned Brewster's goods and rebuked their men, having no desire to fight the English, but neither would they make peace with Uncas, "for though he promiseth much, yet he will perform nothing. We have experience of his falseness."[43]

The final straw came in early 1660, when Narragansetts committed an act that would have grave consequences for their people. In the middle of the night, warriors opened fire on a house near Shantok where John Mason lay sleeping, riddling it with bullets. Colonists claimed to hear them boast of having killed the Connecticut magistrate, though he survived unscathed.

"All candidness and clemency toward these beastly minded and mannered creatures seems rather to embolden them," Connecticut's outraged government charged. If the commissioners did not take control, Connecticut would do "what God requires" toward the "uncircumcised heathen" on its own. As Connecticut saw it, years of appeasement had softened colonists and emboldened Indians, many of whom were too young to remember the massacre at Mystic. "We entreat you to consider how incongruous and cross it would have been twenty years ago to an English spirit, to bear such things as now we are forced to bear," thundered the magistrates. "It is high time to renew upon the memory of these pagans the obliterate memorials of the English."[44]

Plymouth commissioner Josiah Winslow, son of the late Edward Winslow, agreed. Then in his early thirties, Winslow was one of the first colonial leaders to have been born in America. "We deeply resent the insolencies and affronts done to any of yours (as if to ourselves)," he told Connecticut governor John Winthrop Jr. "I perceive that such is the lowness and baseness of their spirits, that our clemency and gentleness is but abused and contemned by them, and doubtless it will be very dishonorable to the English to let such miscarriages pass without full satisfaction, such as may make them fearful to offend for the future." While the colonies should not be "prodigal of blood and expense in an unnecessary war," he admitted, neither should they be "timorously sparing when God or our own honor and safety calls for it."[45]

The Narragansett sachems blamed the attack on renegade warriors, explaining "they did neither consent to nor allow of such practices." They offered to meet with the commissioners, but the commissioners refused, claiming they had "plentiful experience" of the sachems' "frequent breach of promise and neglect of the commissioners' orders, and especially of the insolency of Ninigret." Even Massachusetts's commissioners abandoned their support for neutrality.

The commissioners sent the sachems an ultimatum: surrender those responsible for the attack or pay five hundred fathoms of wampum in restitution. No
foot-dragging would be tolerated. If they failed to pay within four months,
Connecticut was authorized to invade Narragansett country and "seize their
persons, goods, and lands, and force them to make full satisfaction."[46]

If there was one thing colonists had learned, it was that sachems were never
willing to compromise their sovereignty by surrendering their men to colonial
justice. Nor could they collect so much wampum in so little time. But that was
the point. The Narragansett sachems were forced to draw upon the resource the
commissioners really wanted: land. On September 29, threatened with invasion,
the sachems signed a political mortgage promising to grant "our whole country"
to the United Colonies should they fail to pay the 595 fathoms they owed within
four months.[47]

⁕

PRESSURE ON INDIANS to sell their land had risen dramatically during the
1650s. The English population was booming, thanks to a high birth rate and
low mortality, increasing the demand for acreage. At the same time, Native
populations, drastically reduced by disease, needed less farmland than before. Many were eager for English tools, clothing, and other trade goods and
lacked other resources to sell. They were losing access to furs (due to war and
overhunting of desired animals), and the inflation of wampum was ruining its
value as currency. They could purchase goods on credit, but land was typically
required as collateral, and inability to pay debts led to further sales.

The Narragansetts faced additional pressure because the fields west of
Narragansett Bay were among the most fertile in the region. They were ideal
for cattle grazing, and cattle had become one of New England's most lucrative
exports. Thousands of animals were shipped to the West Indies every year, especially from Rhode Island. Corporations formed by wealthy entrepreneurs
mobilized to procure these lands for settlement.[48]

Like other Algonquians, the Narragansetts did not interpret land sales as un-
conditional property transfers. As they saw it, they offered colonists the right
to settle and farm while reserving rights to hunt, fish, and receive tribute. That
colonists were typically slow to settle encouraged this belief. When they sold
most of their best land over a period of four years, therefore, the Narragansetts
did not believe they were giving up their land forever. In 1657 the sachem
Pessicus's brother Cojonoquant sold land around Pettaquamscut to Rhode
Island speculators. The following year, Pessicus and other sachems sold twelve
miles square to what became the Pettaquamscut Company, founded by several
Rhode Islanders and a Boston merchant. The influential Ninigret consented to

these transactions. In 1660 Rhode Islanders purchased land running from the Pawcatuck River to within several miles of Ninigret's home town of Niantic, eventually founding the town of Westerly.[49]

The United Colonies, which denied Rhode Island's jurisdiction over Narragansett country, coveted the same land. Massachusetts colonists had been settling along the Pawcatuck River, and Massachusetts recognized the community on the west bank as Southertown in 1658.[50] But the most aggressive acquisitions came from the Atherton Company. Led by Humphrey Atherton, Massachusetts's praying town superintendent, who had led several diplomatic and military expeditions to Narragansett country, the company's shareholders included a who's who of colonial leadership, including commissioners Winthrop, Winslow, Bradstreet, and Denison. Atherton tried to recruit Roger Williams, but Williams objected that Atherton's enterprise was illegal because it lacked Rhode Island's authorization.

Taking a page out of Williams's book, Atherton tried to earn the Narragansetts' trust by advocating on their behalf to the United Colonies. Meanwhile, he acquired two tracts totaling six thousand acres from Cojonoquant, who deeded them as a gift conveying his "great love and affection" for Englishmen. One of the tracts was north of Williams's old trading post, Cocumscussoc, now owned by Atherton Company partner Richard Smith. The other overlapped the Pettaquamscut Purchase further south. Critics accused Atherton of making Cojonoquant drunk to get him to sign the deal. But the Narragansett sachems Pessicus and Scuttup (son of Mixanno, who had died) confirmed the purchase in a procedure witnessed by John Eliot's praying Indian assistant, John Sassamon. Atherton set about dividing the land, nearly seven hundred acres per shareholder. Rhode Island denounced the enterprise as illegal, but the commissioners, who were Atherton's partners, ignored these protests.[51]

It was in this context that the commissioners imposed their massive fine on the Narragansetts. Atherton immediately perceived an opportunity to gain the region for his shareholders. He claimed he found the sachems "in a very sad condition, not knowing how to discharge their engagement to the commissioners," and that they entreated him for help. So he offered to pay their debt (now 735 fathoms due to various expenses) if they mortgaged Narragansett country to him. If they failed to pay him back within six months, their land would default to the Atherton Company. He promised to protect them from invasion and possibly from Rhode Island, several of whose land purchases they contested. They probably believed he would protect their land, much as Connecticut's John Mason did for Uncas and the Mohegans.

Desperate, the sachems Ninigret, Pessicus, and Scuttup signed Atherton's mortgage on October 13, 1660. The company acknowledged that the Narragansetts "put a great deal of trust" in Atherton "and expect kindness from him," and its shareholders promised not to "take the land from them for five or six years," to allow them "privileges of royalties," and to provide "planting ground for them and their successors forever."[52]

How exactly events unfolded remains obscure, but the result was decisive. The Narragansetts later claimed they "sent to know where they would have the money paid, before the time in the mortgage was expired," but were told the company "could not receive it now, because Mr. Winthrop was in England." But Winthrop did not leave for England until July, and payment was due in April. By August the company was claiming possession of Narragansett country and urging Connecticut to establish jurisdiction over it. Atherton did not live to see this. He fell off his horse on Boston Common, suffered severe head trauma, and died on September 16.[53]

Some historians have characterized the Atherton mortgage as a blatant case of fraud, but this was not how Puritans like Winthrop, Bradstreet, Winslow, and Denison viewed it. They believed they were imposing justice by fining the Narragansetts, that they were promoting the Natives' ultimate welfare by acquiring dominion over them (in however manipulative a manner), and that there was nothing wrong with turning a profit in the meantime. It was not by abandoning their principles of justice that they exploited the Narragansetts. It was by applying them.

MOHEGANS AND WAMPANOAGS also faced growing pressure to alienate their land and submit to English dominion. Between 1658 and 1661 Uncas sold several Mohegan tracts between Nameag (now renamed New London) and Shantok. John Mason and other Connecticut settlers founded Norwich just north of Shantok. Uncas's relations with New London were testy, but his alliance with Mason meant he had it better than most. He deeded all his land to Mason in 1659, and Mason deferred authority over sales back to Uncas, recognizing Uncas's "native right" to the land. Connecticut acknowledged the arrangement, and Mason benefited, for Uncas later granted him half the proceeds from sales.[54]

Ousamequin's Wampanoags lacked such a patron, and multiple colonies competed over their land. During the 1650s, a Rhode Islander purchased land on Pocasset Neck from the Pocassets' female sachem Weetamoo. When Plymouth protested, Ousamequin replied that Weetamoo was free to do as she wished with her own land. Frustrated, Plymouth purchased the neck from a lesser sachem with no authority to sell it. A few years later, when Weetamoo married Ousamequin's son Wamsutta, Plymouth colonist Josiah Winslow and some partners persuaded Wamsutta to mortgage some of Weetamoo's land to pay a debt. As the years passed, Wampanoag sachems sold more and more land. A new settlement emerged at Dartmouth in 1652, Bridgewater was recognized as a township in 1656, and settlers purchased land at Nemasket in 1661–1662, eventually founding Middleborough.[55]

As Plymouth's English population grew, colonists and Wampanoags increasingly lived side by side. Tensions rose over contested boundaries, English cattle trampling Native crops, various crimes, and Puritan missionary work. The town of Rehoboth built a five-mile fence across the base of Mount Hope peninsula, where the Pokanokets lived, but it proved ineffective in stopping cattle. Whatever the dispute, Plymouth insisted that its courts do the adjudicating. Ousamequin tried to leverage land sales to his benefit, allegedly asking Plymouth "never to attempt to draw any of his people . . . to the Christian religion" as a condition for a deal, but without success. He died in 1660, leaving his son Wamsutta as the Pokanoket sachem and the leading Wampanoag sachem. Wamsutta decided to change his name in accord with Algonquian custom and asked Plymouth to give him an English name. They offered the name Alexander. They also renamed his brother, Metacom, who would now go by Philip.[56]

Alexander was in Plymouth when the commissioners asked him to testify regarding one of the final clashes of the Mohegan-Pocumtuck war. On March 12, 1661, Uncas's son led a Mohegan raid against the Nipmucs at Quaboag, killing three people and capturing six. The Nipmuc sachem Wassamequin, who had submitted to Massachusetts in 1644, and the Quaboag sachem Quacunquasit appealed to the missionary John Eliot for help, complaining that the Mohegans acted with impunity because Uncas's patron John Mason protected them. Massachusetts had every reason to be concerned, for twenty English families had recently established a new settlement, financed by the Springfield-based trader John Pynchon, near Quaboag. But when Massachusetts governor John Endecott sent messengers to confront Uncas, he "insolently laughed them to scorn."[57] Massachusetts dispatched Major Willard with several soldiers to Quaboag in June. (Hoping to evangelize the Quaboags, Willard asked them to send some children to be educated by colonists.)[58] Finally, Massachusetts deferred the matter to the United Colonies, and Mason apparently persuaded Uncas to cooperate. Uncas insisted that the people his men killed were Pocumtucks but released the captives, and Alexander testified that the Quaboags were allied with the Pocumtucks against Uncas. The commissioners let Uncas off lightly.[59]

As sachem, Alexander sold Wampanoag land at breakneck pace, alarming his own people. A group of Martha's Vineyard Wampanoags even reversed their opposition to Christianity, hoping conversion would help them protect their land. When Alexander sold Pocasset and Sakonnet land to a Rhode Islander in 1662, the female Pocasset and Sakonnet sachems, Weetamoo and Awashonks, protested that he had no authority to do so. Fearing Rhode Island's encroachment, Plymouth confronted Alexander about "estranging land and not selling it to our colony" and made sure the sachems were not removed from it.[60]

Exactly what happened next is murky. According to accounts written a decade and a half later, Plymouth learned that Alexander "was plotting or privy to plots against the English" and ordered Josiah Winslow to bring him to Plymouth. It was Josiah's father, Edward, who, nearly thirty years earlier, had won the dying Ousamequin's everlasting friendship by nursing him to health. Now Josiah—accompanied by William Bradford Jr., son of Plymouth's other founding father, and ten soldiers—set out to apprehend Ousamequin's son. According to one account, Winslow surprised the Wampanoags, seized their guns, and warned Alexander that "if he stirred or refused to go, he was a dead man." According to another, perhaps more reliable account, they found Alexander eating breakfast, and he "freely and readily, without the least hesitancy, consented to go." Once in Plymouth, Alexander assuaged the court's concerns. Afterward he went to Winslow's house, only to fall seriously ill. But Winslow proved unable to do for Alexander what his father had done for Ousamequin. Wampanoags brought Alexander home, and within days he was dead. Pokanokets suspected foul play.

When Philip succeeded his brother as Pokanoket sachem and the leading Wampanoag sachem, Indians "from all parts" came to congratulate him, leading to "great feasting and rejoicing at Mount Hope," his home. Once again, Plymouth suspected a plot.[61] Philip was summoned to Plymouth, where he expressed his earnest desire to maintain the friendship Plymouth had long enjoyed with his father and brother. He promised to "remain subject to the king of England" and not to wage war or "dispose of any lands" without Plymouth's permission.[62]

Philip's submissive posture was typical of the dynamic emerging throughout New England following the Mohegan-Pocumtuck war. The United Colonies were asserting dominion over Indians like never before, convinced that justice and peace demanded they rule the barbarians with a heavy hand. Even great sachems like Ninigret and Uncas were becoming dependent. As they sold more and more land and their people lived ever closer to the English, the potential for conflict increased. And the Puritans, mindful of their growing strength and confident about the blessings they were offering, were less and less likely to back down.

11

God, King, and Land

1660 to 1666

THE PURITAN CAUSE suffered a devastating blow on May 25, 1660, when Charles Stuart returned to England to reclaim the throne as Charles II. England's Puritan regime had been in a state of crisis since the death of Lord Protector Oliver Cromwell in 1658, and Parliament finally invited Charles to reestablish the monarchy. Bishops returned to the Church of England. The Act of Oblivion and Indemnity nullified all laws enacted by the Puritan Commonwealth. Puritan leaders were removed from power, and those involved in Charles I's execution were hunted as traitors. Some fled to New England. Others, including former Salem minister Hugh Peter and former Massachusetts governor Henry Vane, were executed.

The king's Council for Foreign Plantations placed New England under heavy scrutiny. Charters, treaties, and legal judgments were invalidated, including the act incorporating the New England Company, which had raised nearly £16,000 for missionary work. Meanwhile, a plethora of conflicting petitions, appeals, and complaints flowed from New England to London. Colonies sought charters to confirm their contested claims. Critics lobbied the crown to curb Massachusetts's autonomy or revoke its charter. Everything seemed up for grabs, leaving the future of the Puritan colonial enterprise in doubt.[1]

Massachusetts reminded Charles that his father had issued its charter in hopes of saving Indian souls. Its sixty-year-old governor, John Endecott, informed Parliament that Massachusetts was converting more Indians than any other English colony. To appease the king, the General Court banned the missionary John Eliot's recently published antimonarchical tract, *The Christian Commonwealth*. Eliot, yielding, conceded that monarchy was defensible from scripture.[2]

Charles confirmed the Massachusetts charter in 1662 but ordered the colony to expand access to church membership and allow all upstanding "freeholders of competent estates" to vote and hold office. These demands arrived as New England's churches were already vigorously debating whether to relax baptism requirements. Many younger colonists were not becoming full church members because membership requirements were so demanding, meaning their children were not getting baptized. Fearing that a generation would grow up outside the church, the clergy proposed that baptized parents who affirmed the church's teaching, accepted its covenant, and submitted to its government could have their children baptized. The proposal provoked a maelstrom of controversy, yet the king's demands were much more radical. The colonial government was determined to resist them.[3]

The king also addressed Massachusetts's policy toward Quakers, adherents of a radical sect that had recently emerged in England. Quakers believed that God revealed himself directly to men and women. They also rejected social hierarchy and the established church and were notorious for their abrasive public demonstrations, which landed many in jail. As dozens of proselytizing Quakers arrived in New England during the 1650s, most settling in Rhode Island or on Plymouth's frontier, the United Colonies expelled them, whipping and mutilating repeat offenders (despite reservations from men like John Winthrop Jr.). Massachusetts went farthest, executing four who defied sentences of banishment. The king had no problem with imprisoning Quakers, but he ordered executions and mutilations to stop. Massachusetts complied.[4]

CONNECTICUT PERCEIVED ROYAL rule as an opportunity. The colony's claims had always been dubious because they rested on its purchase of the 1632 Warwick Patent, of which no one had a copy. Governor Winthrop agreed to travel to London to seek a charter confirming Connecticut's boldest ambitions: jurisdiction over New Haven, Narragansett country, and part of New Netherland.[5] He drafted a glowing address to the king, emphasizing that Connecticut was founded for "very pious and public ends: the propagation of the blessed gospel of the Lord Jesus amongst the heathen," and for "the honor and further extent of the British monarchy." He argued that its land had been purchased fairly from sachems with their people's consent or occupied by right of conquest in the justly fought Pequot War.[6]

Winthrop's Atherton Company associates urged him to make sure Narragansett country was assigned to Connecticut. The validity of their holdings depended on it, but they also claimed pious motives. Rhode Island had no established church, its government was chaotic, and, they argued, the "vileness of opinions and corruptness of manners" it tolerated were "a dishonor to the English" and "a scandal to poor heathen Natives, whose civilizing is so acceptable, whose Christianizing will be so glorious to our renowned sovereign." Under Connecticut, by contrast, Narragansett country could be settled by "a sober and considerable people, knit together in the beautiful order of a well-managed government." Nor, they insisted, did Rhode Islanders have valid title to the land. They had "by fraud, pretending a deed, and by force, seized on possessions to which they had no right, though the Indians constantly refused to sell the land unto them." Indeed, the Atherton associates claimed, "Had not we restrained [them], the incensed heathen had ruined their houses and burnt their hay as a sharp correction to their violent intrusion."[7]

Winthrop strengthened Connecticut's case by proposing a plan to civilize and evangelize the Narragansetts and Pequots. These Indians were "more civil and active and industrious" than others, he argued. Many "wholly adhere" to the English "and are apt to fall into English employment." He suggested that a reauthorized New England Company pay them to produce "hemp, flax . . . pitch, tar, wheat, prairie grass," and other commodities. Their wages would enable them to purchase "necessaries as may make their lives more comfortable, establishing a market for English goods. For example, thousands "would willingly wear English apparel if they knew how to purchase it." They would also be more likely to "hearken to the gospel." After an initial five-year loan of £5,000, the enterprise would be self-sustaining and even help fund the company.[8]

But would Charles reauthorize an organization founded by Puritans? The United Colonies petitioned him to do so, dedicating John Eliot's Massachusett New Testament to him. (Company president Robert Boyle presented it to the king in his bedchamber.) They had come to America to spread the gospel "to the poor barbarous heathen," they wrote, and Charles's father declared this "his principal aim" in Massachusetts's patent. Thanks to the company's work, many "wild Indians" were embracing Christianity, some could read and write, and a few were attending Harvard. Surely the king should act for the sake of "the poor Indians, who only receive the benefit."[9]

Winthrop arrived in London with ample money and an influential network of contacts. On February 7, 1662, Parliament incorporated the Company for Propagation of the Gospel (or New England Company) to finance "educating, clothing, and civilizing the poor Natives." Soon after, the Council for Plantations granted Winthrop a charter recognizing Connecticut's territory as extending west from the "Narragansett River, commonly called Narragansett Bay," and including New Haven.[10]

Upon learning of these developments, the commissioners praised the king heartily. Thanks to his compassion, Indians made in God's image, "among whom Satan hath had his throne," could "now become the Lord's." Connecticut's charter, furthermore, would prevent Rhode Island from "corrupting . . . the heathen" and hindering the gospel, "to the great dishonor of God and reproach of the English nation."[11]

NARRAGANSETT COUNTRY HAD become a vortex of intercolonial conflict. Colonists from Massachusetts and Connecticut urged the United Colonies to stop Rhode Islanders from occupying land purchased by the Pettaquamscut Company along the Pawcatuck River. The Narragansett sachems Ninigret, Pessicus, and Scuttup protested Rhode Islanders' "forcibly" taking their land "by building and bringing cattle" and even shooting at them and requested a "fair trial" before the commissioners "or some other indifferent judges." If the Rhode Islanders refused such arbitration, the sachems wanted permission "to drive their cattle away or take any course whereby we [might] dispossess them."

The commissioners were hardly "indifferent." On their behalf, Plymouth governor Thomas Prence notified Rhode Island that former Pequot lands along the Pawcatuck River were "the undoubted right of those English colonies that conquered that bloody nation." If Rhode Island did not "keep your people from injuring the heathen or others," he threatened, it "may draw upon yourselves and us uncomfortable consequences."[12]

Hostilities intensified in 1662. Rhode Island ordered colonists to surrender their land east of the Pawcatuck. The commissioners rejected their authority to do so. The Atherton Company, now led by Edward Hutchinson, an extensive landholder and son of the once-exiled Anne Hutchinson, moved to strengthen its claims. Hutchinson and some partners met Ninigret and Scuttup at Pettaquamscut where, in the presence of two hundred to three hundred Indians, Scuttup transferred ownership of the area by symbolically offering them "turf and twig." They sent documentation to the king, complaining that "turbulent spirited fanatics" from Rhode Island had disturbed lawful settlers "by cutting down their houses in the night." They enclosed a copy of the sachems' protest against Rhode Island.[13]

Hutchinson warned Governor Winthrop that the Narragansetts might be playing both sides. Rumor had it that they had sent agents to the king "to complain against the English, and in special against ourselves, for taking away their lands." Perhaps they intended to submit to the king's protection, as in 1644. He did not believe it, but it was best to be prepared.[14]

In fact, the rumor was true. Neither would Rhode Island be bullied out of Narragansett country. Connecticut received a rude awakening when Rhode Island representative John Clarke persuaded the crown to reconsider Connecticut's charter since it "injuriously swallowed up half our colony." Hutchinson urged Winthrop to defend Connecticut's claims tooth and nail, but Winthrop was loath to ruin relationships with Rhode Islanders like Roger Williams. "They are friends that I always did and do respect and love, and [I] had not the least intent of wronging them," he told Hutchinson.[15] Arbitrators helped him and Clarke reach a compromise on April 7, 1663. In favor of Rhode Island, they agreed that the Pawcatuck River would be its western boundary. (They called it the Narragansett River to satisfy Connecticut's charter.) In favor of Connecticut, they agreed that settlers on Atherton land around Richard Smith's trading post at Cocumscussoc could "choose to which of these colonies they will belong."[16]

Winthrop sailed for home, having been away for two years. The Atherton proprietors met at Cocumscussoc on July 3, Winthrop's sons Fitz-John and

Wait among them, and voted unanimously to join Connecticut. Connecticut quickly recognized the settlement, named Wickford after Mrs. Winthrop's birthplace.[17]

Back in England, however, the crown betrayed its confusion in a series of contradictory rulings. An Atherton Company agent persuaded it to declare that the company's "laudable endeavors" to establish a colony on justly acquired land were being "unjustly molested" by Rhode Island and call the United Colonies to protect its right and title.[18] A few weeks later, the crown granted Rhode Island a charter that nullified the Winthrop-Clarke agreement, received the Narragansetts under the king's protection, and placed Narragansett country in Rhode Island. It also gave Rhode Island jurisdiction over Wampanoag land claimed by Plymouth three miles northeast and east of Narragansett Bay. Even more infuriating to Puritan sensibilities, it declared that Rhode Island was settled with "religious intentions," including evangelizing "poor ignorant Indian Natives," and that it procured its land "by purchase and consent of the said Natives, to their full content." It also forbade the United Colonies "to invade or molest" the Narragansetts, "they having subjected themselves unto us, and being by us taken into our special protection."[19]

While London promulgated conflicting decisions, the colonies attempted to impose their will on each other. Connecticut asserted jurisdiction over New Haven, Long Island, and Southertown. New Haven had little choice but to accept annexation, which was completed in 1665. Massachusetts eventually ceded Southertown, renamed Stonington in 1666.[20]

Rhode Island attempted to enforce its jurisdiction east of the Pawcatuck, where settlers tried to drive off competitors by harassment, vandalism, and the occasional kidnapping. It arrested several Atherton men at Wickford. Roger Williams knew such contention over land made mockery of Christianity in the eyes of the Narragansetts and wrote Winthrop in hopes of finding a way forward. Long gone was the "model of love" Winthrop's father had practiced, he lamented. "I fear that . . . God-Land will be (as now it is) as great a god with us English as God-Gold was with the Spaniards." Winthrop proposed negotiations, but diplomacy proved futile as long as Connecticut refused to recognize Rhode Island's jurisdiction over Narragansett country.[21]

THE ENDLESS CONTENTION PERSUADED the king that he needed representatives on the ground in New England. He dispatched four commissioners—Colonel Richard Nicolls, Sir Robert Carr, Colonel George Cartwright, and Samuel Maverick—with "full power and authority" to investigate colonial affairs and adjudicate "all complaints and appeals." The choice of Maverick, a Massachusetts expatriate, bitter critic of New England Puritanism, and advocate of direct royal rule, did not bode well for Massachusetts. The king informed Massachusetts of his intent to investigate the Narragansetts' complaint about "breach of faith and acts of violence and injustice." He lectured that such injustice brought Christianity "into prejudice and reproach with the Gentiles and inhabitants of those countries who know not God, the reduction of whom, to the true knowledge and fear of God, is the most worthy and glorious end of all those plantations."

The king had decided to occupy New Netherland, so the royal commissioners arrived with some five hundred soldiers in four frigates. Governor Winthrop helped persuade his friend Governor Stuyvesant to accept the generous terms offered by the crown, and New Netherland surrendered on August 29. Reconstituted as a proprietary colony and renamed New York, its borders were extended to include Long Island (a check to Connecticut's ambitions), Nantucket, Martha's Vineyard, and part of Maine. Colonel Nicolls remained in New Amsterdam as governor, while the other royal commissioners proceeded to Plymouth, then Rhode Island. Winthrop braved snow, ice, and cold to meet them at Pettaquamscut on March 16.[22]

Edward Hutchinson, the Atherton Company's executive, presented a deposition supporting his claim that the Atherton Company was the Narragansetts' protector. It was signed by the Narragansett sachem Scuttup and his sister, their counselors, and the Christian Indian John Sassamon. "I, Scuttup, together with the rest of the Narragansett sachems, sold and made over all our lands in the Narragansett, Niantic, and Cowesett countries unto Major General Atherton and his friends," it declared. Scuttup affirmed that the company "have been always friends to me" and asked that "they will continue to be friends to my sister after me, and to all the Indians under me." The signatories then declared, "We all do so well approve of the government and manners of the English in the United Colonies that we voluntarily and of our own accord do desire to be governed by the English laws and governors, and desire to be no longer under the Indian government."[23]

It sounded impressive, but Scuttup was a junior sachem who had no right to speak for Ninigret or Pessicus. These senior sachems presented a copy of the Narragansetts' 1644 submission to Charles I, reaffirming their submission "to the king's protection." The royal commissioners needed little convincing. They declared Narragansett country "the King's Province" and authorized Rhode Island to govern it on his behalf. They gave the sachems two "scarlet, silver-laced coats," a sword, and a belt as gifts from the king. The sachems gave "two caps of peag [wampum] and two clubs inlaid with peag" for the king and "a feather mantle and a porcupine bag" for the queen. They promised two wolf skins annually as symbolic tribute.

The sachems then offered a "long petition" summarizing their mistreatment by the United Colonies.[24] They complained about Atherton's purchases from Cojonoquant, asserting that Cojonoquant was "simple" and lacked authority to make such transactions. Furthermore, "he was seduced, being made drunk and kept so for some days, and carried to Boston, where this sale was made, about 6,000 acres of the best in that province, for about £25 (300 fathoms of wampum)." Winthrop professed surprise at this, protesting that Atherton had used his name "without his consent and without his knowledge."

The sachems also complained about the mortgage. "The Indians never knew what selling of land or mortgaging meant till the English taught them," the royal commissioners concluded. "Yet it was proved before the commission that the Indians sent to know where they would have the money paid before the time in the mortgage was expired, and answer was returned, they could not receive it now, because Mr. Winthrop was in England, yet after that [the company] seized upon the country as forfeited."[25]

The royal commissioners voided the Atherton transactions on March 20. They instructed the Narragansetts to repay 1,035 fathoms of wampum they had received from the company and ordered colonists to remove themselves from the disputed lands by September.[26] They extended the order to settlers east of the Pawcatuck River, observing that while the United Colonies claimed that land by right of conquest, "the Narragansett had conquered it first" and "sold it to the Rhode Islanders."

The royal commissioners also tackled the long-standing dispute between Pomham's Shawomets and the town of Warwick, founded by Samuel Gorton and his followers. Pomham still refused to give up Warwick Neck, maintaining that the Narragansett sachem Miantonomo had possessed no authority to sell Shawomet land in 1643. Roger Williams insisted that Miantonomo had the right and that the "wild" Shawomets could be removed from the neck "with little more trouble and damage than the wild beasts of the wilderness." Shawomet "is a very den of wickedness, where they not only practice the horrid barbarisms of all kind of whoredoms, idolatries, and conjurations," he claimed, "but living without all exercise of actual authority and getting store of liquors," it attracted "the wildest and most licentious Natives and practices of the whole country." He claimed the conflict cost Warwick £60 to £100 annually and blamed Massachusetts, which the Shawomets invoked as their patron.

A Massachusetts magistrate, by contrast, described the Shawomets as an "active, laborious and ingenious people" who performed excellent labor for colonists. (Warwick, additionally, was notorious for its illegal liquor trade.)[27] But the royal commissioners were biased against Puritan Massachusetts and ordered Pomham to leave Warwick Neck in exchange for a mere £20 worth of wampum, even though wampum was rapidly losing value and had been demonetized as legal currency.[28]

Massachusetts, fearful that the king would curtail its autonomy, treaded carefully. Shortly before he died on March 15, Governor Endecott protested that the king had given his commissioners arbitrary and unrestrained power and implored him to preserve Massachusetts's liberty of self-government, lest the "good work of converting the Natives [be] obstructed" and the colony "ruined." At the same time, Massachusetts repealed its law limiting voting rights to church members.[29] But the royal commissioners' ruling on Narragansett country provoked an immediate appeal. Pawcatuck landowners argued that they occupied their land by "consent of the Indians" who lived there and had spent years improving it, "not doubting the justness of the title, being both conquered and long possessed." Forwarding their appeal, Massachusetts denounced their expulsion as a violation of the basic rights of Englishmen going back to the Magna Carta. It rehashed old arguments about the justice of the Pequot War and insisted that, for the sake of security, Pequot country had to be settled by colonists. By nullifying the United Colonies' authority, it added, the royal commissioners were undermining an institution that had maintained peace for nearly two decades. Already "savage Natives" were growing insolent as fear of Massachusetts "turned into contempt." With the Narragansetts freed from the United Colonies' bridle, "what else could be expected but trouble from them?"[30]

Much to the settlers' relief, chief royal commissioner Nicolls agreed that the time frame for removal was "too short." He permitted them to remain pending an appeal to the king, and while he left Narragansett country subject to Rhode Island, his stay fed hope that this too might be reversed. As it turned out, the king was distracted, and the royal commissioners' decisions proved unenforceable. The Atherton and Pawcatuck settlers retained their land. Narragansetts retaliated by burning hay, killing horses, and driving off Atherton settlers. They accosted travelers, "throwing many stones at them" and "beating their horses . . . with clubs and staves." Massachusetts berated the Narragansett sachems Ninigret and Pessicus for behavior "not only contrary to humanity, but to the covenants made with us."[31]

Nor would Pomham give up Warwick Neck, even when royal commissioner Carr offered double the original payment. Carr tried to bypass Pomham by dealing with his son, but when a constable attempted to evict the Shawomets, forty warriors prevented him. Pomham appealed to John Eliot, who was always willing to mediate for potential converts. "It is his Majesty's pleasure to command us to deal well with the poor Indians," Eliot lectured Carr. "Pomham and his people have suffered much hard and ill dealings by some English, and there hath been both force and fraud used towards them to drive them or deceive them out of their lands." Carr dismissed Eliot's intervention as yet another example of Puritan insubordination.[32]

Sixty-two-year-old Roger Williams, whose hair had recently whitened, learned that Pomham was recruiting "great numbers" of Indians to defend his land. Williams offered to mediate. Since Pomham was "the ancient possessor" of Warwick Neck, Williams now questioned "whether it be just to dispossess him (not only without consent, which fear may extort, but without some satisfying consideration)." If there was violence, he feared, Ninigret and Pessicus might intervene, triggering a regional war. "Barbarians are barbarians," he warned Carr. "They are a melancholy people and judge themselves . . . oppressed and wronged. You may knock out their brains and yet not make them peaceably to surrender. . . . Yet with patience and gentle means [they] will rise, and draw, and do good service."[33]

Williams proved unable to negotiate a solution. One day Pomham's bitterness would drive him into just the sort of anti-English alliance Williams dreaded.

AS THE DUST SETTLED from the royal commissioners' visit, Puritan leaders chafed at the Narragansetts' newfound autonomy and sought opportunities to reassert control. During the winter of 1668–1669, Connecticut was alarmed to learn that longtime foes Ninigret and Uncas, sachems of the Narragansetts and Mohegans, respectively, along with many other Algonquians, were attending a dance hosted by Pequot leader Robin Cassacinamon at Noank, where the Pequots had received a five-hundred-acre reservation. The hot-headed Thomas Stanton, the Pequots' supervisory agent, found it terribly unnerving considering Ninigret and Uncas "durst not look each upon [the] other this twenty years but at the muzzle of a gun or at the pile of an arrow."[34] Deciding that nothing good could come of it, he brazenly marched soldiers into Noank and demanded Cassacinamon hand over Ninigret, blustering that he would not leave without him even if he had to "die in that place."

Narragansett warriors rallied to their sachem's defense, and Cassacinamon knew he had to act fast. "I then saw Ninigret's men, almost one hundred of them, have clubs in their hands, and the Englishmen laid their hands upon their swords ready to draw," he later reported. Should there be violence, Ninigret's men "might have fried Englishmen's houses and . . . a great deal of hurt might have come of it." Cassacinamon cried out, demanding of Stanton what would satisfy him.

A "great deal of wampum," Stanton replied.

Wampum "was like the grass," Cassacinamon admonished. "When it was gone, it would come again, but if men be once killed, they will live no more." He offered £20 worth at the Indian exchange rate. Thankfully, Stanton accepted, and the crisis was averted, though Stanton eventually insisted on £40 worth. "I hope you will consider my great love I have to the English and to the saving of men's lives," a relieved Cassacinamon informed Connecticut.[35]

But it was not over. The following spring, Long Island colonists reported that Montauks were warning about "an extensive Indian conspiracy for the destruction of the English." Supposedly the Montauks were part of it, having sent Ninigret two hundred to three hundred fathoms of wampum. The Pequots were too. They expected guns and ammunition from Rhode Island, and even the French had offered to "help them to destroy the English, and then they should have their land again" and all would be as "in former times before the English came." Indians were moving "incredible sums" of wampum, warned Connecticut's John Mason. They were probably only waiting for Mohawk support, and while the Mohawks remained friendly, Mason urged the colonies "to kill such birds in the egg."[36]

Reports emerged of militant rhetoric from Pequots who had been driven from their land at Caussatuck, near the Pawcatuck River, by Stanton and other Connecticut settlers. A woman claimed the Indians were conspiring "to kill all the English" as soon as "green Indian corn was ripe enough to make their bread." A man boasted that "if there was a war, the Indians would run down out of the woods and would first knock them of the head with their tomahawks . . . because they hated them for living on Causattuck land." It was probably just talk, but what if it was not? "The truth is, they are very high of late and slight all authority of the English," Stanton claimed. Ninigret's messengers were running "to and fro with great speed," inviting all manner of Indians to "the greatest dance . . . that ever was," and many were promising warriors and wampum. "That is their last shift," he predicted. "If they do anything it will be within these few days, and if God prevent them not, our town is like to undergo the first of their cruelties."[37]

Mason had often warned of such dangers, but this time he was sure the threat was real. "If I am not stark blind in Indian matters," he postulated, "it's not far from as great a hazard as ever New England yet saw." It was imperative that Ninigret be "seized and examined" and the Narragansetts and Pequots "compelled to surrender their arms." He even ordered the Mohegans to surrender some muskets. Connecticut ordered Captain Wait Winthrop, the governor's twenty-seven-year-old son, "to summon Ninigret before them for examination." But Rhode Islanders intercepted Winthrop at the Pawcatuck River on July 19, declaring that Rhode Island "protested against any such illegal or unlawful proceedings."

Ninigret would "answer before the government under whom his majesty have put him," Rhode Island.[38]

Having been alerted of a potential Indian conspiracy by a skeptical New York governor Francis Lovelace, Rhode Island issued a warrant for Ninigret's arrest. But it treated him gently, lodging him in Newport at colony expense. Appearing before the council on July 28, Ninigret expressed amazement at their credulity. Four years earlier, the king had acknowledged the Narragansetts as loyal subjects. The royal commissioners' exhortation to "be faithful to all his majesty's subjects" was "rooted in his heart," Ninigret declared, and he intended to honor it as long as he lived. A French alliance was manifestly ridiculous, and "he had quarrels" with the Mohawks. Colonists should not believe the rumors, for they came from a disgruntled Montauk, who was upset that his people had resumed paying Ninigret tribute.

To each of the magistrates' questions, Ninigret offered a plausible response. Wampanoags had come to Niantic "to bark cedar trees and to make bark houses, which his men had not good skill in," he explained. Another came to teach a dance. He did not understand how this could be "taken for a plot." When asked why he was holding such a "great dance," he replied, "It is known to you it is no unusual thing for us so to do, but that it is often used from the time after the weeding of our corn till such time as we do eat of it." It was "a kind of invocation" that "they might have a plentiful harvest."[39]

The council dismissed Ninigret and reported his "fair and reasonable answers" to New York and Connecticut. Four Montauks corroborated Ninigret's testimony. Governor Lovelace congratulated Rhode Island for the "care you have shown in settling the minds of some over-credulous persons amongst us." Fearmongering simply animated "the heathens who, taking courage from our fear, might be apt to break forth into extravagances not to be redressed without a war and all the miseries attending it."[40]

Rhode Island had protected Ninigret from another disastrous confrontation with the United Colonies, but it did not protect the Narragansetts from the Atherton Company. In 1668, after the sachem Scuttup died, his mother Quaiapin, her counselor Potuck, and the sachem Cojonoquant's son Quinnapin confirmed the company's title to land around Pettaquamscut. Four years later, in an obvious attempt to secure the company's allegiance and preempt Connecticut's claim to the region, Rhode Island declared the Atherton transactions valid, as if they had never violated Rhode Island law or been overturned by the royal commissioners. It did so, the government explained, to protect the Atherton settlers from "barbarous Indians so ready to war."[41]

Royal intervention alarmed Puritans, but it proved fleeting, and colonial expansion proceeded apace. New England now had some eighty towns with a population rapidly surpassing fifty thousand, dwarfing the Algonquian total of about fifteen thousand. With the local fur trade collapsing and the English trading directly with the Mohawks through New York, many Algonquians found it necessary to work for colonists for wages, even as their sachems sold more and more land. Some decided the best hope of prosperity came from submitting to the English and accepting Christianity. Others bitterly resented English domination and the destruction of their way of life.[42]

12

Praying Towns

1665 to 1675

ON A SEPTEMBER afternoon in 1665, residents of Cambridge, Massachusetts, were stunned to see five Mohawks arrive at the home of the Taylor family. Each had "a firelock gun, a pistol, an helved hatchet, a long knife hanging about their necks," and a "pack, or knapsack, well furnished with powder and bullets." They did not resist arrest and were brought before the General Court in Boston a couple of days later.[1]

Their presence was terrifying, especially for local Indians. For several years, the Mohawks had been fighting a coalition of Algonquians on New England's northern frontier. They had driven the upper Connecticut Valley Sokokis from their fort at Squakeag, and when a Mohawk sachem and his entourage were treacherously murdered at Pocumtuck, they destroyed that town too, killing Uncas's rival sachem Onopequin.[2] Mohawks also attacked the Pennacooks of the Merrimack Valley, and it was during one such raid that five warriors ventured as far as Cambridge.

They had no desire "to do the least wrong to the English," the Mohawks informed the court, "but to avenge themselves of the Indians, their enemies." The magistrates retorted that they were "more like wolves than men, to travel and wander so far from home, merely to kill and destroy men, women, and children," and it was "base and ignoble" to "do this in a secret, skulking manner, lying in ambushment, thickets, and swamps." "Men of courage, valor, and nobleness of spirit . . . would fight with their enemies openly and in a plain field."

Local Indians poured into Boston, urging the court to kill the Mohawks. "These Mohawks are unto us as wolves are to your sheep," they explained. "They secretly seize upon us and our children, wherever they meet us, and destroy us." The magistrates discussed how to handle the situation "as became wise and Christian men." They were anxious to avoid war with the Mohawks, but they were also obligated to protect their Indian subjects. Three considerations informed their decision. First, it was neither honorable "nor suitable to the Christian profession to begin a war with a people that had not killed or slain any Englishmen." Second, it was immoral to join an Indian conflict, "the cause whereof we knew not, or which party were the aggressors." Third, to execute men who had surrendered and "not done us any wrong" would be a "great injustice."

They sent the Mohawks home with coats and a letter asking their sachem not to attack Indians under Massachusetts's protection or within forty miles of an English town.[3] A few days later, the United Colonies appropriated £5 worth of "powder and shot" for the praying Indians.[4] Massachusetts authorized more a year later.[5]

Spearheading Massachusetts's involvement was the devout Captain Daniel Gookin, a magistrate since 1652 and superintendent of the praying towns since 1661. Born in 1612, Gookin had lived in Virginia and Maryland before his Puritan beliefs led him to Massachusetts. He owned extensive lands in all three colonies. He briefly returned to England during the 1650s, where Cromwell tasked him with recruiting colonists for Jamaica, but the restoration of the monarchy drove him back to Massachusetts. He was close with the missionary John Eliot and passionate about missionary work.[6]

Arming Indians was controversial, but Gookin and his fellow magistrates were committed to protecting Christian Indians. Eager to benefit from such protection, more Algonquian communities began accepting Christianity, while a troop of Indian teachers trained by Eliot prepared to instruct them. The result was a rapid increase in the number of praying towns.

MOHAWK WAR PARTIES terrorized Pennacooks and Nipmucs. They ambushed Indians traveling along forest paths. They shot men fishing or collecting eel pots in the Merrimack. Praying Indians like those of Nashobah abandoned their cornfields and wigwams for the safety of a fort recently built at the Pennacook praying town of Wamesit, where they labored in the employ of local colonists for wages. Captain Gookin sent soldiers to garrison Wamesit. But he forbade Wannalancet, the Pennacook sachem at Pawtucket Falls, from sheltering his people at Wamesit unless they became praying Indians. So Wannalancet built his own fort. Gookin considered Wannalancet "loving and friendly" and suspected that he rejected Christianity due to pressure from his family and leading men. Colonists had jailed his brother for two years for debt, and Wannalancet had to sell a valued tract of land to secure his release. His bitterness must have been substantial.[7]

In 1669 members of the Abenaki tribe from Maine began recruiting Pennacook and Massachusett men to invade Mohawk country. Gookin and John Eliot dissuaded most praying Indians from participating, but Wamesit's sachem, Numphow, whose brother had been killed by Mohawks, decided to go. So did the apostate Massachusett sachem Josias Wampatuck, who had given up Christianity out of concern that his subjects would forsake him. As many as seven hundred warriors marched two hundred miles to Caughnawaga, where they attacked a Mohawk fort on August 18, only to be repulsed. They sieged it "some days" before illness and lack of food and ammunition forced them to return home. Twenty or thirty miles down the trail, Mohawks ambushed them, killing Wampatuck and "fifty of their chief men." The survivors returned "with lamentation and mourning," only to discover that Wamesit "was for the most part scattered, and their corn spoiled."

Eliot and Gookin interpreted the catastrophe as God's judgment on the Pawtucket Pennacooks for rejecting Christianity. They considered it a boon for the faith. "Indians take notice of [it]," Eliot told Robert Boyle of the New England Company. Algonquians grew ever more dependent on English protection. The following year, Mohawks attacked some Wamesits north of the Merrimack, killing some and scalping a teenage girl, fracturing her skull. An English woman from Woburn extracted skull fragments and nursed her back to health. The Pawtuckets finally yielded to the pressure and became praying Indians. Wannalancet, their sachem, did not become a Christian but agreed to observe the Sabbath and attend teaching, so Eliot sent him an Indian teacher named Peter Jethro.[8]

Mohawks were not the only ones driving Indians into Massachusetts's arms. In August 1667, at least 125 Narragansett warriors raided Quantisset, a Nipmuc town of a hundred inhabitants. They did not kill anyone, but they tore mats from wigwams and plundered guns, powder and shot, swine, wampum, deer skins, coats, kettles, food, and other items worth about £130. They had been sent by Ninigret's sister, the female Narragansett sachem Quaiapin, who was determined to demonstrate her power over her erstwhile tributaries following the deaths of her husband Mixanno and son Scuttup. When the Quantissets appealed to Eliot for help, he told them God was punishing them "for standing off so long from praying to God." So they offered to become praying Indians and submit to Massachusetts in exchange for protection, and Eliot urged the government to intervene on their behalf.[9]

Massachusetts summoned the parties to appear in court in October, reminding Quaiapin that the 1645 treaty prohibited her from waging war without their consent. Quaiapin affirmed the treaty but insisted she had not violated it; the raid, she believed, was well within her rights as sachem. The Quantissets had been her family's subjects "time out of mind" and had robbed her men, insulted her late son, and refused to pay tribute, she argued. Still, she sent deputies who professed "great love and respects to the Massachusetts government and a readiness to be directed by them in all these matters." But the Quantissets denied being her subjects. True, they had often given the Narragansetts gifts, but "in a way of love and as a present unto them, and not by way of right or due." So the court ordered Quaiapin to restore what her men had stolen and find trustworthy witnesses to prove that the Quantissets were her tributaries.[10]

She turned to Roger Williams, who submitted a letter attesting "abundant and daily proof" that Quantisset was "unquestionably subject to the Narragansett sachems." It was "as plain and clear as that the inhabitants of Ipswich or Newbery . . . are subject to the government of . . . Massachusetts." Massachusetts was right to discourage the Narragansetts from oppressing tributaries, he conceded, but it had to recognize their God-given authority over the Quantissets, having no right to change Indian "laws and customs."[11]

The parties were instructed to appear again on May 8, but due to "misreports carried to them," the Narragansetts did not make it. Many Nipmucs did, and not just from Quantisset. Tom Wuttasacomponom, the "grave and pious" sachem who had professed his Christian faith in 1659, was there, as was Job Kattenanit, brother of Eliot's assistant. So were eight sachems representing the towns of Quantisset, Manchage, Chabanakongkomun, Hassanamesit, Magunkog, and Wabquisset, a Mohegan tributary. These Nipmuc sachems formally submitted to Massachusetts on May 9. "[We are] convinced of our great sins and how good it is to turn unto the Lord and be his servants by praying and calling upon his name," they declared. "We do solemnly, before God and this court, give up ourselves so to God." They had learned from experience "how good it is to live under laws and good government, and . . . how much we need the protection of the English."

Narragansetts arrived four days later with "something in way of proof" that the Nipmucs, especially Quantisset, were their subjects, but by then the Nipmucs had departed. According to court records, the Narragansetts generously conceded that "if the Nipmucs were real in their profession to serve God and to live under the government of the English, they were willing it should be so." The court then announced a trial period for the Nipmucs to prove the sincerity of their submission. It assured the Narragansetts that it considered them "friends," promising to treat them with "righteousness and equity."[12]

Considering that the royal commissioners had ruled the Narragansetts free from the United Colonies, this was an aggressive move by Massachusetts. It set the stage for the rapid expansion of the Puritan mission. But to sachems like Quaiapin and the Mohegan sachem Uncas, who were losing tributaries, it was further evidence that they needed to resist Christianity.

JOHN ELIOT AND the praying Indians of Natick were well prepared to take advantage of the Nipmucs' submission. Every two weeks during summer Eliot taught logic, theology, and rhetoric at Natick. Indians practiced their preaching under his tutelage, and he was satisfied that many could "speak methodically and profitably unto any plain text of scripture." Thus while many Indians who studied at Harvard or the grammar schools dropped out or died of various causes— Daniel Gookin considered them casualties in "the wars of the Lord against sin and Satan"—Eliot had trained a generation of teachers. Now Natick sent them "to sundry parts of the country, to call in their countrymen to pray unto God."

While some colonists doubted the Natives' capabilities or sincerity, Eliot believed they made the best missionaries. The work was difficult, paid poorly, and received little encouragement; few colonists were willing to endure it. Gookin added that missionaries had to be "very much mortified, self-denying, and of a public spirit, seeking greatly God's glory, and these are rare qualities in young men." More important, Indians appreciated the nuances of Algonquian language and culture. Many of their people were deeply suspicious of Christianity (and the colonial domination it fostered), so if the gospel had any hope of success, it had to be delivered by their own people.[13]

To help train missionaries, Eliot published his *Indian Dialogues* in 1671. The book presented a series of "partly historical" conversations in which Indians presented objections against Christianity, and Indian missionaries responded to them. Some were based on real conversations; others were fictional. In one dialogue, an Indian asked his Christian relatives if the English invented Christianity to terrify the Indians "that they might wipe us off our lands." A Christian Indian replied that God gave human beings the Bible before the English knew God. Indians should "be thankful to the English" and "thank God for them," he added. "For they had a good country of their own, but . . . they heard of us, and of our country, and of our nakedness, ignorance of God, and wild condition. God put it into their hearts to desire to come hither and teach us the good knowledge of God." He added, "We gave them leave freely to live among us." "They have purchased of us a great part of those lands which they possess. They love us, they do us right, and no wrong willingly. If any do us wrong, it is without the consent of their rulers, and upon our complaints our wrongs are righted." True, the English were great sinners, so God sometimes punished them. But the Indians should imitate their faith, not their sin.[14]

In Eliot's book, Indians protested that those who became Christians alienated family and friends and had to give up cherished customs, including "pleasures and sports and delights and joys in this world." The Christian assured them that the gospel was worth it. "But if you so love your old company, as that you choose rather to feed on trash and venture to perish among them, then perish you shall, and thank yourself for your foolish choice." A powwow retorted that they had their own gods. But the Christian replied that they worshiped the devil, for which they deserved to be "damned in hell and to be tormented among the devils forever." Faith in Jesus could save them from this terrible fate. Jesus had pacified God's wrath and reconciled God toward humans by dying on the cross. Now, by his Spirit, he had begun "to conquer the world" by leading people to faith. "Christ Jesus taketh possession of the heathen and utmost ends of the earth," Natick's leader Waban said, "and this is one description of our country."[15]

Whether or not many praying Indians actually spoke this way, it reflected how Eliot wanted them to think about colonization.

᝔ᨏ᝕

AS MASSACHUSETTS'S SUPERINTENDENT OF praying Indians, Daniel Gookin was responsible for organizing praying towns among the Nipmucs who had recently submitted to the colony. A "pious magistracy and Christian government is a great help and means for promoting, cherishing, encouraging, and propagating the Christian religion among any people," he explained, especially "rude, uncultivated, and barbarous Indians." John Eliot had abandoned his strict views of biblical government, and Gookin was flexible about the process. In each town, Indians elected their own rulers, ideally wise and godly men. Gookin's task as chief magistrate was to confirm their selections and supervise their work. He made sure they prevented powwowing and punished drunkenness. He promoted "morality, civility, industry, and diligence," believing "idleness and improvidence are the Indians' great sin, and . . . a kind of second nature to them." He trusted that "by good example and wholesome laws, gradually applied with God's blessing," such flaws would be rooted out. He made sure they observed the Sabbath, attended worship, and supported teachers and rulers by paying a tithe. And he would help them establish schools for their children.[16]

It was equally important to protect their land from acquisitive colonists. Massachusetts did this by issuing land grants, as stipulated by the 1652 law. Gookin knew that some critics, especially in England, considered this improper since "it was all their native country and propriety before the English came into America." He summarized Massachusetts's position in a tract he wrote around 1674. Indians had a *native* "title" to their lands according to Genesis 1:28 and 9:1 and Psalm 115:16, he argued. Thus colonists could not dispossess them of "lands they have subdued, or from their fishing places." All land Indians plausibly claimed had to be purchased, subject to the government's approval. But *civil* jurisdiction was a different matter. The king claimed New England by right of discovery, and the region's sachems had "long since" submitted to Massachusetts. Thus Massachusetts legally possessed "most of the land within this jurisdiction, either by purchase or donation from the Indian sachems." Indians who wanted civil title to their land required a grant.

This policy helped Indians preserve their land, Gookin argued. After all, many sachems, "being poor, as well as improvident, are very prone to sell their land to the English and thereby leave themselves destitute." This problem was only intensifying, for the English were "a growing and potent people," and grants were essential to "prevent differences and contention among the English and Indians in future times about the propriety of land." The policy also had moral value, Gookin claimed. Abandoning their traditional way of life with its seasonal migrations, Christian Indians would settle in towns, "without which neither religion or civility can well prosper." By planting crops, raising cattle, and producing trade goods, they would learn to live as civilized Christians.[17]

Indians who rejected Christianity saw it differently. Why should the strength of their land rights depend on whether or not they became praying Indians? And what did it suggest about the future of those who did not? Debates within Algonquian communities must have been long and bitter. While some believed Christianity would secure their future, others viewed it as a scheme to rob them of their land. For them, the expansion of the praying town system was deeply disconcerting.[18]

Quantisset was recognized as a praying town in 1669. There must have been resistance, since Eliot admitted that Indian teachers "received too much discouragement" there. Nevertheless "the seed is alive," he wrote. "There doth only want strength to bring [it] forth."[19] Another praying town was founded at recently established Magunkog, a "place of great trees" about twenty-four miles southwest of Boston. It was granted three thousand acres encompassing a large, fertile hill.[20]

In 1671 an Indian church was established at Hassanamesit, which joined Natick as a base for missionary work. Eliot's biggest problem was lack of funds to pay Native teachers and officials. There were many things he wanted to do, he complained to the New England Company, "but I cannot come at them for want of means." He needed reimbursement of his considerable debts, and "if it should be refused, then my hands are tied. I can do little." Nevertheless, he continued, "I am resolved through the grace of Christ, I will never give over the work so long as I have legs to go. . . . If no man help me, yet mine eyes are to the Lord, who hath said he will never leave me nor forsake me."[21]

The following year, about forty-five Nipmucs from Chabanakongkomun, twenty miles northeast of Quantisset, formed a praying town. Chabanakongkomun lay north of "a very great pond, about five or six miles long," and was "well-accommodated with upland and meadows." Hassanamesit sent Joseph Petavit, "a sober, pious, and ingenious person" who could speak and read English, to serve as its teacher. Thanks to him, Gookin thought, its people were "better instructed in the worship of God than any of the new praying towns." The following year, Gookin appointed Black James of Chabanakongkomun, whom he considered "diligent and courageous, faithful and zealous to suppress sin," as constable of the new towns.

Pakachoog became Massachusetts's tenth praying town, located on "a fertile hill" south of the new road from Boston to Connecticut.[22] Gookin was especially interested in it because in 1665 he and several entrepreneurs purchased thirty-two hundred acres southeast of Quinsigamond Lake from its sachem, Sagamore John, where they were attempting to establish an English town.[23]

CONNECTICUT LAGGED FAR behind Massachusetts in missionary work. The United Colonies paid ministers to evangelize the Pequots, but they accomplished little.[24] However, Norwich's pastor James Fitch achieved a breakthrough that John Eliot thought he would never see, persuading Uncas to let him teach the Mohegans. The key was Uncas's patron John Mason.[25] Fitch had been Mason's pastor at Saybrook before following him to Norwich in 1659. He married Mason's daughter, and his son and daughter from a previous marriage married two of Mason's other children.[26]

Connecticut supported Fitch's efforts, promising to "encourage" Mohegans who faithfully attended his teaching, while displaying "an unpleasant countenance" toward those who "interrupt or hinder" it.[27] This was not mere rhetoric, for the Mohegans depended on Connecticut to preserve their land. Even now, Connecticut governor John Winthrop Jr. was arguing that when Mason was entrusted with Uncas's land, it was in his capacity as Connecticut's agent, meaning it belonged to Connecticut. Uncas faced growing pressure for land from towns like New London.[28]

By September 1671 Fitch was teaching at his house every two weeks, and Uncas and his son Owaneco had promised to attend. "Uncas's coming in is a great matter," Eliot informed the United Colonies commissioners. "I desire the work may be countenanced and supported."[29] Then, in January, Mason died suddenly, leaving a gaping hole in Connecticut–Mohegan relations.[30] Fitch assumed Mason's role as mediator, but Fitch and Uncas never trusted each other, and his work suffered.[31] Nevertheless in 1673 Uncas signed a remarkable agreement, promising to "attend upon" Fitch "at all such seasons as he shall appoint for preaching to and praying with the Indians," and to command his people to attend "in a constant way and solemn manner." He vowed not to "affright or discourage" them from this "good work . . . upon penalty of suffering the most grievous punishment that can be inflicted upon me." Time would tell whether or not he was sincere.[32]

THE MOHAWK WAR PETERED out during the early 1670s, but it left the Pennacooks devastated. Their population was perhaps 1,250, half of what it had been a generation earlier. This did not stop praying town superintendent Daniel Gookin from criticizing the praying town of Wamesit's lack of spiritual progress. He praised its sachem Numphow and Numphow's son Samuel, a teacher who could read and write fluently in English and Algonquian. But Gookin complained that every spring at fishing time Wamesit was inundated with "vicious and wicked men and women, which Satan makes use of to obstruct the prosperity of religion." He was equally frustrated at Wamesit's failure to channel its resources into meaningful prosperity. "These Indians, if they were diligent and industrious . . . might get much by their fish, especially fresh salmon, which are of esteem and good price at Boston," he claimed. But "their idleness and improvidence" prevented it.

Gookin was at the Pennacook town of Pawtucket in 1674 when John Eliot challenged Wannalancet, its sachem, to stop wavering and accept Christianity. After "some deliberation and serious pause," he recalled, Wannalancet "stood up and made a speech to this effect: 'Sirs, you have been pleased for four years past, in your abundant love, to apply yourselves particularly unto me and my people, to exhort, press, and persuade us to pray to God. I am very thankful to you for your pains. . . . I have all my days used to pass in an old canoe . . . and now you exhort me to change and leave my old canoe and embark in a new canoe, to which I have hitherto been unwilling. But now I yield up myself to your advice and enter into a new canoe, and do engage to pray to God hereafter."

A colonist replied that "while he went in his old canoe he passed in a quiet stream, but the end thereof was death and destruction to soul and body." Now, although "perhaps he would meet with storms and trials," he should "persevere, for the end of his voyage would be everlasting rest." Later they heard that Wannalancet prayed regularly with his family, lived soberly, and traveled two miles each Sunday to attend services at Wamesit. It came at a cost, for several of his people rejected his leadership.[33]

Weshakim, a Nashaway town, was moving in the opposite direction. Although Massachusetts had ordered Major Simon Willard to arm the Nashaways, the war had so ravaged Weshakim that a population of about three hundred in the 1640s had been reduced to scarcely fifteen families. As the fur trade declined, many found themselves indebted to regional traders like Willard, who sought payment in land, while the nearby English town of Lancaster flourished and expanded at the Nashaways' expense. Local traders sold them alcohol illegally, with dire consequences. A Nashaway told Gookin some were "desirously willing . . . to pray to God," but others were "very wicked and much addicted to drunkenness, and thereby many disorders were committed." Their Christian sachem, Matthew, had been succeeded by the bitter Shoshanim, whose leadership Eliot had openly opposed.

Gookin blithely informed Shoshanim of his mission to govern Weshakim, promoting "religion and civility." He sent him the praying Indian Peter Jethro, promising that if the Nashaways obeyed Jethro's teaching, observed the Sabbath, and abstained from "drunkenness, whoredom, powwowing, and all other evils," they would find "temporal and eternal happiness." But Shoshanim wanted nothing of it, and when Gookin tried to appoint a constable at Weshakim, his candidate admitted that it was futile without support from other Nashaways.[34]

Gookin and Eliot recognized four new Nipmuc praying towns in 1674, raising the number in Massachusetts to fourteen. Gookin appointed Tom

Wuttasacomponom, who had orchestrated the Nipmucs' 1668 submission, as ruler of the new towns. They called him Captain Tom because he led a well-known Indian militia unit. Gookin, Eliot, and several Indian teachers set out on a tour to organize the new towns in September. The first was Manchage, about ten miles southwest of Hassanamesit. Most of its sixty inhabitants were absent, but Eliot left them a teacher. From there they traveled to Chabanakongkomun. After Eliot preached, they prayed, sang psalms, and discussed civil and religious polity well into the night. Next they traveled seven miles west to Maanexit, a town of one hundred people near the Quinebaug River, where Eliot assigned another teacher. They bypassed Quantisset, crossed the river, and pressed another six miles to Wabquisset, a Mohegan tributary.[35]

With 150 people, Wabquisset was the largest of the new towns, and its rich soil produced "not less than forty bushels [of corn] upon an acre." The sachem was not home, but his wife generously welcomed them into her wigwam, which, at sixty-by-twenty feet, doubled as a meeting house. Sampson Petavit, Wabquisset's Nipmuc teacher, had an interesting story. He had been "dissolute" and "lived very uncomfortably with his wife" in recent years, but Gookin punished him, and now he was, "through grace, changed and become sober and pious," and they lived "very well together." Gookin found him "very thankful to me for the discipline."

As Eliot and Petavit led the people in prayer, psalm singing, and preaching, one Indian sat sullenly. Afterward he informed them that the Mohegan sachem Uncas was "not well pleased that the English should pass over Mohegan River to call his Indians to pray to God." He "challenged [Massachusetts's] right to and dominion over this people of Wabquisset." Eliot offered his usual misleading reply that it was "his work to call upon all men everywhere as he had opportunity, especially the Indians, to repent and embrace the gospel, but he did not meddle with civil right or jurisdiction." Gookin told the Mohegan agent to inform Uncas that Wabquisset was under Massachusetts's jurisdiction. Nevertheless, they had no intention of robbing "the Indian sachems of their just and ancient right over the Indians in respect of paying tribute or any other dues." Massachusetts's purpose "was to bring them to the good knowledge of God in Christ Jesus and to suppress among them those sins of drunkenness, idolatry, powwowing or witchcraft, whoredom, murder, and like sins." This would hardly satisfy Uncas, but Gookin held court anyway.

From Wabquisset they continued to Pakachoog, where Sagamore John "kindly entertained" them. Ephraim Curtis had established a trading post nearby at Quinsigamond, where several families were building houses, and Gookin had agreed to pay Sagamore John and other sachems £12, "two coats and four yards of trading cloth valued at twenty-six shillings" for an additional eight-mile-square tract. After Eliot preached and Pakachoog's teacher James Speen led in singing a psalm, Gookin and Captain Tom held court, recognizing the town's leaders as "clothed with the authority of the English government." They chose a "grave and sober" man named Matoonas as constable. In 1671 the colony had executed Matoonas's son for murder; his head still hung "upon a pole" in Boston. Matoonas admitted he had wanted revenge, his heart "so big hot within him," but now he was "resolved to abide a faithful friend to the English." Time would show he had not forgotten his grievance, nor were Sagamore John's people entirely happy about Gookin's land deal.[36]

The traveling party did not reach Waeuntug, where Eliot's former assistant James Printer was pastor, near the recently established English town of Mendon. Nor did they visit Quaboag. The General Court had authorized a four-thousand-acre grant for Quaboag in 1664, and Gookin believed it was "coming on to receive the gospel," but it had not become a praying town. Events would reveal that its opposition to Christianity was growing.[37]

In one respect, Gookin and Eliot's tour was detrimental. Alarmed by their actions at Wabquisset, Uncas discouraged Mohegans from attending Norwich minister James Fitch's teaching sessions. "These Indians do suffer much" from "reproaches, revilings, and threatenings," Fitch lamented about the thirty or so who persisted. He secured more than three hundred acres for a praying town, promising it would be theirs "so long as they go on in the ways of God." At that point Uncas became interested in his teaching again, but Fitch was under no illusions about his motives.[38]

THE OLDER PRAYING TOWNS struggled to practice Christianity while maintaining something of their traditional way of life. The town of Punkapoag found a measure of prosperity raising cattle and hogs, fishing, and producing goods for sale in Boston and other markets. Its people earned "many a pound" cutting trees in a large cedar swamp and manufacturing shingles and clapboards. Nashobah was resettled by about fifty people after the war. They planted corn and apple trees, fished, hunted, and labored in nearby towns, but Gookin lamented the problem of drunkenness. "I have often seriously considered what course to take to restrain this beastly sin," he admitted, "but hitherto cannot reach it." Even if he could stop English traders from illegally selling alcohol, Indians produced their own from apples, grain, or barley. Nothing could "conquer this exorbitance but the sovereign grace of God in Christ," he concluded. Hassanamesit, on the other hand, was thriving. It had "rich land and plenty of meadow, being well tempered and watered," producing "plenty of corn, grain, and fruit" from "several good orchards." Raising cattle and hogs, its inhabitants did "better than any other Indians," though "very far short of the English, both in diligence and providence." It had a meeting house and several other English-style structures, though its twelve families lived in wigwams. John Eliot's former assistant James Printer's brothers, Annaweekin and Joseph Tuckawillipin, served as ruler and teacher, and their father, Naoas, was a deacon.

Natick remained the model. Every Sunday morning and evening the beating of a drum summoned inhabitants to the meeting house. A teacher opened with prayer, followed by scripture and the singing of a psalm. Then the minister catechized the congregation, prayed, and preached. After further prayer and another psalm, the people were blessed and dismissed. "They demean themselves visibly with reverence, attention, modesty, and solemnity, the men-kind sitting by themselves and the women-kind by themselves, according to their age, quality, and degree," Gookin wrote.[39] Despite substantial cultural differences, the churches of Natick and Hassanamesit functioned much like English Puritan churches. When it came to discipline, Eliot claimed, they were "so severe" that he had to "bridle them to moderation and forbearance."[40]

Massachusetts's fourteen praying towns had a total population of eleven hundred, by Gookin's count, and were growing rapidly. True, most praying Indians were not baptized and had not become church members. Most "are catechized, do attend public worship, read the scriptures, pray in their family morning and evening," Gookin wrote, but have "not yet come so far as to be able or willing to profess their faith in Christ and yield obedience and subjection unto him in his church." Many English Puritans put off church membership for similar reasons. Yet, Gookin claimed, all of them, young and old alike, could "readily answer any question of the catechism, which, I believe, is more than can be said of many thousands of English people."[41]

Eliot tried to be positive about relations between Natives and colonists. Indians "have a deep sense of their own darkness and ignorance and a reverent esteem of the light and goodness of the English," he claimed, "and ordinarily in their prayers, they thank God for them and pray for them as the instrument of God for their good." When Indians and English celebrated the Lord's Supper together as brothers and sisters in Christ, it represented the community of which Eliot dreamed. Christian Indians frequented English homes, and dozens were educated in English schools. One even purchased a home in Boston.

But Eliot lamented that even pious colonists often viewed Indians as "the worst of men." (Harvard president Charles Chauncy, who supported Eliot's work, requested a special allowance for teachers of Indian students by explaining that they "have to deal with such nasty savages" who require "greater care and diligent inspection.") Eliot had to persuade some ministers that since God received Indians into his church, they were obligated to do the same, and it was telling that his funding came almost exclusively from England. Another problem was the English obsession with land. Puritan ministers recognized the problem, but they viewed the primary sin as materialism or worldliness rather than injustice toward Indians. For Indians, Eliot confessed, "the business about land giveth them no small matter of stumbling."[42]

There were many other problems. For example, Massachusetts offered praying Indians the same legal rights as colonists, but juries and judges did not always treat them equally in practice. While they usually suffered the same punishments for the same crimes, prejudice left them vulnerable to discrimination and less likely to receive mercy, and they often lacked the resources to file appeals or pay fines.[43]

Despite such challenges, Gookin was optimistic that New England's first people were on the verge of embracing Christianity wholesale and thought hard about how to integrate them into English society. The best approach, he thought, was to teach Indian children "to speak, read, and write the English tongue." History demonstrated that "changing . . . the language of a barbarous people into the speech of a more civil and potent nation that have conquered them" gradually transformed them "unto the civility and religion of the prevailing nation." Once Algonquians spoke and read English, they would essentially become English.

One way to accomplish this was to place Indian children with English families. Boys could learn a trade and girls could learn "good housewifery," while being educated at their masters' expense. Colonists might support such a program because New England was desperate for labor. The harder part was persuading Indian parents to part with their children. A second approach was to establish free, integrated schools in which English and Indian children could study side by side. Indian children would learn the "arts and sciences," form friendships with English youth, and be evangelized. The funds could be raised in England, supplemented by minimal contributions from colonists and Indians. Gookin and Eliot reported that "most of the known and pious Indians earnestly desired it" and drafted a proposal for the United Colonies and New England Company.

Gookin envisioned the praying town of Okommakamesit as an ideal location because it bordered the English town of Marlborough. In between were 150 acres that could support a school, schoolmaster's house, and farm whose proceeds could pay the schoolmaster's salary.[44] But Gookin's judgment was naïve, for relations between the two towns were as troubled as those between Dedham and Natick. In 1656 Massachusetts had granted Marlborough's founders land belonging to Okommakamesit. Eliot appealed, and two years later the General Court ruled in Okommakamesit's favor. The ruling left the towns practically on top of each other and Marlborough embittered at losing prime land. While Okommakamesit grew "plenty of corn" and "several good orchards," it languished under the shadow of the larger English town with its many livestock. Marlborough resented Okommakamesit's presence, and there was no chance that it would accept an integrated school.[45]

Undaunted, Gookin urged readers of his 1674 tract to embrace the glorious opportunity and sober responsibility of building God's kingdom among the Indians. They could see in the "poor forlorn" Indians, "as in a mirror or looking glass, the woeful, miserable and deplorable estate that sin hath reduced mankind unto," he wrote, for aside from their rational souls, they were "not many degrees above beasts." Yet the English were no better by nature. The only difference was that by God's grace they were "born and bred among civilized and Christian nations." Was God not exhibiting the same grace to many Indians? Had he not brought the English to America for this very purpose? God was fulfilling his promise in Psalm 2 to give Christ "the heathen for his inheritance and the uttermost parts of the earth for his possession," and it was past time to get serious about evangelizing Indians. This involved acting righteously to prevent any stumbling block from hindering "Indians in their travel towards the heavenly Canaan." They had to lure the Indians to salvation by love and justice.[46]

For all its hubris about English cultural superiority, Gookin's proposal was the most specific and hopeful plan for English-Indian integration yet produced by a New England Puritan. But it came too late. Although many Algonquians had accepted Christianity, there were already many stumbling blocks in the way of their seeking a heavenly Canaan. Within a year, Gookin's hope of an integrated society would be shattered amid the fulcrum of war. Many colonists would abandon all thought of a heavenly Canaan that included Indians, instead envisioning an earthly Canaan whose first people needed to be destroyed.

DESPITE MISSIONARY PROGRESS, by the late 1660s many ministers were convinced that the colonies were straying from their covenant with God and losing their way. The evidence of God's displeasure seemed manifold. Severe droughts were followed by destructive floods. Caterpillars and mildew devastated wheat crops. Fire and smallpox claimed property and lives. Conflict consumed communities, and prominent churches suffered schism, including the first churches of Boston and Hartford. In 1664 a comet blazed across the sky, and three years later a "zodiacal" light appeared, shaped like a spear and pointed at New England.[47] It troubled many that the esteemed ministers of the founding generation were dying. "Is not the Lord packing up the chief goods he hath and removing them away?" asked Northampton pastor Eleazer Mather. "When God dismisseth his righteous ones, it is a sign that he himself will be gone ere long."[48]

Ministers concluded that God had a "controversy" with New England. They used special occasions such as elections or fast days to warn that God was disciplining his people and that if they did not repent, discipline would lead to judgment. Such sermons became known as "jeremiads" because, like the ancient prophet Jeremiah, they warned of God's looming judgment.[49] They were sure God had a covenant with New England, similar though not identical to his ancient covenant with Israel. "The Lord hath said of New England, surely they are my people," William Stoughton preached. God "singled out New England . . . above any nation or people in the world." True, "God had his creatures in this wilderness before we came, and his rational creatures too, a multitude of them, but as to sons and children that are covenant born unto God, are not we the first such a relation?"[50]

To be God's first people meant being held to a higher standard. If they obeyed God, he would bless them, but if they disobeyed, he would punish them. "God hath given New England many days of prosperity," warned Simon Willard's son Samuel, "but meanwhile sin hath been growing upon us." As God's watchmen, ministers had to warn the people, identify their sins, and call them to repentance.[51]

Unfortunately, ministers did not always agree about what those sins were. Many ministers lamented congregations' failure to bring young adults into church membership. "You may fear that your children one day will curse you and wish that they had been the children of Indians," warned Eleazar Mather.[52] They fretted that the founding generation's passion for God's kingdom had given way to obsession with land and economic prosperity, resulting in pride, conflict, and exploitation. They complained about lack of financial support and challenges to their authority and about the increasing toleration of Baptists and other dissidents, which produced such "diversity of opinions" that people "know not what to believe." Towns petitioned for a formal investigation of "the causes of God's displeasure against the land," triggering intense debate among the colony's leaders. They did not say much about evangelizing America's first people, let alone injustice toward Indians. Samuel Danforth, Eliot's colleague in Roxbury, did not even mention missionary work when discussing New England's purpose.[53]

Urian Oakes preached one of New England's most memorable jeremiads in 1673. Like Israel, he declared, God had granted colonists a Canaan that once belonged to the heathen. Was it not his "almighty arm that vanquished the Pequots and put the dread and terror of you into the hearts of the Natives?" New England had become "a little model of the kingdom of Christ," "a city upon an hill," and by God's blessing the New England Way would "spread over the face of the earth." But this made their sin all the more grievous. "We are making God our enemy," Oakes warned. "Our defense and glory is departing from us. That strong hedge of protecting providence that hath been about us is breaking down."[54]

A year later, thirty-five-year-old Increase Mather, who would become Massachusetts's most influential minister, delivered an even more notable sermon. A son of Richard Mather, Increase had experienced an intense religious conversion at Harvard before heading to England for higher studies. He returned to Massachusetts, married the famous John Cotton's daughter, and became pastor of Boston's North Church.[55]

Convinced that cataclysm was just around the corner, Mather assumed the role of a prophet. He selected Ezekiel 7:7 as his text: "The time is come, the day of trouble is near." God's ministers had been warning of imminent judgment, he argued, and "if the Lord's watchmen do with one voice cry, 'The day of trouble is near' . . . it is so indeed." "War is determined in heaven against us," he warned. "Your enemies will come and make a general slaughter among you." Even now God was "numbering many of the rising generation for the sword, as if the Lord should say, 'I will bring a sword to avenge the quarrel of a neglected covenant.'"

"This is Immanuel's land," he reminded them. "Christ by a wonderful providence hath dispossessed Satan, who reigned securely in these ends of the earth for ages." God "caused, as it were, New Jerusalem to come down from heaven. He dwells in this place." He would not abandon them, and if they repented, "it is possible that this cloud may blow over." Then, even if "all the nations of the earth should be gathered together against [us], they shall be broken in pieces." But they needed to pray like never before. "Why then, up and be doing," Mather exhorted. "If thou has but one tear in thy eyes, if thou hast but one prayer in thy heart, spend it now."[56]

His troubling prophecy was more accurate than he knew. War was coming to New England.

13

The Wampanoags

1665 to 1675

As COLONISTS ACQUIRED more and more land and settled ever closer to Native communities, and as growing numbers of Indians accepted Christianity, tensions escalated. Nowhere was this truer than in Plymouth colony. Plymouth had long maintained a stable relationship with the Wampanoags, but during the 1660s it began to deteriorate. Christianity lured Wampanoag communities away from control of the Pokanoket sachem Philip, son of the great Ousamequin, while Plymouth aggressively asserted its power, triggering a series of crises that pushed the region to the brink of war.

English entrepreneurs who bought up vast tracts of land were among the sources of tension. While fourteen land transfers had been recorded during the 1650s, there were sixty-one during the 1660s. Even Philip sold prime land north of his home at Mount Hope, sometimes over the protests of Indians who lived there yet received no compensation. While Philip and other sachems sold land voluntarily and usually knew what they were doing, they did so under enormous economic, political, and demographic pressure and often regretted the results.

Most sales presupposed that Wampanoags could continue hunting, fishing, and living on purchased land, but growing English populations increasingly crowded them out. This was especially true north of Mount Hope. Cattle devoured or trampled Native crops, dug up storage pits and clam beds, and ate the plants, nuts, and berries that sustained wild game. Each year more Wampanoag complaints poured into colonial courts. The courts ordered colonists to honor shared-use agreements, help Indians build fences, or pay compensation for damages, but enforcement fell short. When Indians retaliated against cattle, colonists responded harshly. When Wampanoags raised cattle, colonists fearing competition enacted laws discouraging it.[1]

A growing number of Indians worked for English employers. The more that colonists and Indians came into contact, the more occasions there were for conflict, and the more frequently colonial courts asserted jurisdiction over Wampanoags. Courts tried to adjudicate fairly, but the power imbalance and cultural misunderstanding made abuses inevitable. Punishment often took the form of fines that Indians could pay only by entering servitude. In areas like Taunton and Middleborough, colonists lost patience with shared-use agreements and pressured Wampanoags to move or sell their rights, leading to further legal battles. It did not bother them that the Wampanoag way of life was being destroyed, because they did not consider it worth preserving. As they saw it, sensible Indians would become Christians, settle in praying towns, and adapt to English society.[2]

On Martha's Vineyard, Nantucket, and Cape Cod, where Wampanoags vastly outnumbered colonists and suffered less from colonization, many did become Christians. They had long resisted Ousamequin's dominion and willingly shifted their loyalty to the English. Sometimes they turned to Christian missionaries to protect their land from sachems overly eager to sell it. The wealthy lay missionary Richard Bourne, who acquired substantial tracts of land, petitioned the General Court to establish a praying town at Mashpee in 1665. The court consented on condition that Mashpee continue paying homage to "any superior sachem."[3]

Bourne, the missionaries John Eliot and Thomas Mayhew, Plymouth governor Thomas Prence, and other ministers and magistrates met the Mashpee Indians the following summer. A minister preached before they interviewed converts and received their testimonies. "I saw myself as all Indians lost, but I continued to hear and read the word, looking to Jesus Christ for mercy," a man declared in "broken English." Another confessed, "First I heard Mr. Eliot preach, but I liked not to hear him. My heart said, I like it not, therefore I went away to strange places." Later, however, he was impressed by the "many wise actions and works" of praying Indians. He occasionally attended services, and after three of his children died, he recalled, "At last I said to my wife, I will harken no more to what men say, dissuading me from prayer, but I will hear what God saith." After hearing such testimonies, the ministers agreed that Mashpee was ready for a church and called Bourne as its pastor.[4]

A similar process unfolded on Martha's Vineyard, where the energetic John Cotton Jr. began a tumultuous, short-lived partnership with Mayhew. Despite his famous father, Cotton's ministerial career had a rocky start when he was excommunicated for "lascivious unclean practices" with several women and for lying to cover it up. He repented, was restored, and became a missionary.[5] Wampanoags, who preferred his teaching to Mayhew's, took the opportunity to ask him "whether it be a righteous thing for Mr. M[ayhew] to buy away so much of the Indians' lands." They complained that Mayhew required them to submit to their current sachems rather than giving them Christian rulers. But they also knew Mayhew helped them protect their community. He negotiated with a sachem to set aside land for a praying town in 1669, and he gave freer rein to Wampanoag customs than Eliot did.[6]

The Pokanoket sachem Philip's influence among Wampanoags diminished as Christianity advanced, but it remained strong among western Wampanoags, especially the Nemaskets of the Titicut Valley and the Sakonnets and Pocassets along the Sakonnet River. Eliot hoped they too would accept the gospel. His son began visiting the Pokanokets at Mount Hope, and in the winter of 1663–1664, Philip asked Eliot "for books to learn to read, in order to praying unto God." Eliot sent books and gifts, as well as the teacher John Sassamon. Sassamon would prove a fateful choice. A Massachusett born around 1620, he had helped build Natick and became one of its first schoolteachers. He went on to study at Harvard with prominent young colonists like Increase Mather and later helped Eliot translate the Bible. He had worked on several major land deals as an interpreter, including the controversial Atherton mortgage and several of Philip's sales. He also served Plymouth, surveying land alongside entrepreneur Josiah Winslow. If Philip ever turned against Plymouth, Sassamon would surely be caught in the middle.[7]

THE FIRST CRISIS UNFOLDED in 1667. Anxiety was high because England was at war with the Netherlands and France, and English authorities feared that their rivals might provoke an Indian uprising. When a Rehoboth colonist warned of suspicious activity at Mount Hope, Philip's seat of power, the colonies took immediate precautions. Rhode Island imposed a curfew on Indians, disarmed those on Aquidneck Island, and summoned the Narragansett sachems.[8] Plymouth dispatched Josiah Winslow to investigate. A Pokanoket told Winslow that Philip was discussing joining the war to recover his lands and enrich his people with English goods. He provided names and details, but Philip "stiffly denied" them and accused his rival Ninigret, the Narragansett sachem, of hiring the Pokanoket to turn Plymouth against Philip. To prove his loyalty, Philip agreed to surrender his people's weapons and come to Plymouth.

Appearing before the court on June 4, he professed "love and faithfulness" and presented two letters as evidence of Ninigret's treachery. The first, from a Narragansett sachem, claimed that Ninigret had hired the Pokanoket "to break that long continued love and amity" between Plymouth and Philip. The second, from Roger Williams, described the Pokanoket as "a very vile fellow." Unfortunately, the Narragansett sachem "utterly disclaimed that he had [said] or could say any such thing concerning Ninigret." Still, Philip insisted that the Pokanoket's accusations were absurd. Philip's people owed their freedom from Narragansett domination to Plymouth's friendship, he pointed out, so to jettison it would be "little less than a death to him, gladding his enemies." Why would he "desert his long experienced friends" for the French or Dutch? Plymouth concluded that while Philip had probably been running his mouth, a conspiracy was unlikely.

Plymouth might have taken pause from the alleged cause of Philip's hostility: his frustration at losing so much land. Instead, the court tightened the economic pressure by fining Philip £40 to defray the costs of Winslow's expedition.[9] Meanwhile, Philip's Pokanokets found themselves even more hemmed in when

Baptists seeking freedom from Rehoboth established the town of Swansea at the mouth of Mount Hope peninsula.[10]

The crisis did not slow Christianity's spread. In 1670, Eliot helped establish Plymouth's first Wampanoag church at Mashpee and another on Martha's Vineyard. Two more were in the works there and another on Nantucket.[11] John Cotton Jr., now pastor of Plymouth's English church, began preaching in Algonquian at Manomet, seven miles south of Plymouth, and claimed thirty converts within a year. "In one meeting after another, they have encouraged my heart to be constant in the work with them," he wrote. "I do find that every sermon leaves them with desires of another." Cape Cod Wampanoags also attended teaching sessions, often by Wampanoag teachers.[12]

Eliot remained so hopeful about Philip's conversion that he wrote about the possibility in his *Indian Dialogues*. Though *Indian Dialogues* was partly fictional, it was also "partly historical" and probably reflects the type of conversations Christian Indians had with Philip in their attempts to win him to Christianity. The two missionaries featured in *Indian Dialogues*, Anthony from Natick and William Ahawton from Punkapoag, almost certainly visited Mount Hope. Ahawton was a "studious and industrious" young man who "prayeth and preacheth well," according to Eliot, but his visit to Mount Hope would have been painful. A few years earlier, he had become suspicious that his wife, Sarah, was having an affair with an Indian named Joseph. Though she denied it, he beat her several times, and his fears became reality when, at the suggestion of her parents from the praying town of Wamesit, she and Joseph took refuge at Mount Hope. Haunted by her conscience, she eventually returned, accepted punishment, and reconciled with Ahawton, but he may have encountered her former lover at Mount Hope.[13]

In *Indian Dialogues*, Anthony and Ahawton tell Philip that many Wampanoags want to pray to God and urge him to do what is best for them. "It will be a joy to all the English magistrates and ministers and churches and good people of the land to hear that Philip and all his people are turned to God and become praying Indians," they say.

"God hath afflicted and chastised me," Philip replies, "and my heart doth begin to break. And I have some serious thoughts of accepting the offer and turning to God to become a praying Indian, I myself and all my people." Still, he has "great objections." Most important, "you praying Indians do reject your sachems and refuse to pay them tribute." Wampanoag Christians always rejected Philip's authority.

Ahawton counters that Christianity requires submission to authority. For example, praying Indians honored, obeyed, and paid tribute to the Massachusett sachem Cutshamekin as long as he lived. They even obeyed his apostate successor, Josias Wampatuck.[14]

In reality, of course, Cutshamekin complained that praying Indians did *not* obey him as before. Anthony admits as much by telling Philip that praying Indians would "not easily be abused." So Philip approaches the question from the other side. If he becomes a Christian, he worries, his people will forsake him. "I shall be empty and weak."

Becoming a Christian requires "much self-denial and faith," Anthony admits, but he urges Philip, "Try the Lord. It may be he will make all your men to stick the closer to you." Surely Philip would only lose "the worser sort." Josias Wampatuck rejected Christianity, only for his heathen warriors to abandon him to the Mohawks, "which his praying subjects would not have done."

Ahawton adds that while Cutshamekin and Wampatuck embittered their people by selling so much land, "Mr. Eliot procured [land] for us after we prayed to God." Similarly, Christianity would restore to Philip much that he had lost. It would restore the friendship of praying Wampanoags from the islands, Mashpee, and Cape Cod and "a more intimate love of the Governor and magistrates and good people of Plymouth, who were ever good friends to your father." The United Colonies and the king would embrace him as a brother. "And what are a few of your subjects that hate praying to God in comparison of all these?"

Philip then complains that "all are brought to an equality" in churches. "The vote of the lowest of the people hath as much weight as the vote of the sachem."

"We must all be ruled by the word of God, both sachems and people," Anthony replies. "And here is a great point of self-denial in sachems and chief men, to be equal to his brethren in the things that appertain to Christ, who is no respecter of persons." But Anthony hastens to assure Philip that such spiritual equality does not affect civil order. Indeed, "it obligeth all godly hearts the more to honor him in his civil order."

Philip objects that he will still have to submit to the church's discipline. "I know not how I shall like that."

Church discipline is medicine for the soul, Anthony counters. It is a gift, not a burden.[15]

Eventually, despite his people's reluctance to abandon their ancestral faith, Philip comes around. "I desire wholly to give myself to the knowledge of and obedience to the word of God," he declares.

"You shall see better days than ever you have yet seen," a delighted Anthony predicts. He promises that Natick will send a teacher.[16]

It is impossible to know how much of these conversations was fiction. They certainly include the types of objections Philip would have raised to Christianity, but did he find Anthony's and Ahawton's answers persuasive? Was he really so close to accepting Christianity? The test was not long in coming.

THE SECOND CRISIS CAME in 1671. Hugh Cole and two other colonists were heading to Mount Hope in February to summon some Pokanokets to court when they encountered twenty or thirty Indians, some armed with clubs. The Indians told Cole they had no intention of going to Plymouth. When he arrived at Mount Hope, Cole was shocked by what he found. "I saw the most part of the Indians that I knew," he reported, "generally employed in making of bows and arrows and half pikes, and fixing up of guns." Then more Indians arrived, "better armed than I usually have seen them." A few days later, the Pokanoket sachem Philip was reported to be marching from Mount Hope with sixty men.[17]

By late March it was said that "multitudes" of warriors were gathering, "instigated by the devil and evil-minded English and French." Josiah Winslow reported intelligence of a plot to kidnap him and Governor Prence for ransom, though it had been called off at the last hour. Philip and a female sachem were said to have sent the Narragansetts wampum, and settlers were fleeing Narragansett country, claiming the Narragansetts were engaged in "warlike preparation" and threatening "to kill the men first and then flay the women alive." One Narragansett demanded of colonists "why they came from their own country" and threatened to "slay them as they do cattle" if they did not leave. Rhode Island went on full alert. Plymouth magistrate Thomas Hinckley urged Prence to consider preemptive military action.[18]

John Eliot and Massachusetts praying town superintendent Daniel Gookin implored restraint. Eliot informed the governor of Massachusetts, "with some confidence," that Philip and his men were "in a way to receive the gospel." Gookin exhorted colonists not to wage war over "horses and hogs, as matters too low to shed blood." Governor Prence agreed with Gookin that "Christian prudence" required negotiation, but Philip refused to come to Plymouth, and Hinckley warned Prence against traveling "into the country of so treacherous a people that surely have not the fear of God" and might "take the opportunity to quench the light of our Israel." Hinckley proposed a more heavy-handed tactic: announce that all Wampanoags who refused to disarm in submission to Plymouth would be considered enemies. This would isolate Philip's militant supporters from Wampanoags loyal to the colony.[19]

Prence decided to risk meeting Philip at Taunton. He did so on April 12, accompanied by representatives from Massachusetts and probably a substantial military escort. Somehow he persuaded Philip to sign a document with shocking implications. In it, Philip confessed that he and his predecessors, Alexander and Ousamequin, had subjected themselves not only to the king (as the records show) but to Plymouth. He admitted having "violated and broken this my covenant with my friends by taking up arms with evil intent against them, and that groundlessly." Agreeing to his people's temporary disarmament, he then reaffirmed the "covenant with my ancient friends and my father's friends." In a passage Puritan leaders would never forget, he declared, "This [treaty] may testify to the world against me, if ever I shall again fail in my faithfulness towards them."[20]

By signing the document, Philip appeared to forfeit his moral authority and sovereignty, but he had done so under duress. Historians debate whether he was actually preparing for war, as he confessed. If so, why come to Taunton, where he was so vulnerable? Was he hoping to buy time? It is impossible to know.

Governor Prence praised God for defeating "Satan's design" and leading "the barbarous Indians to peace," but his optimism proved short-lived. Philip surrendered only about sixteen muskets and claimed that Wampanoags who refused to surrender theirs were not his subjects. Plymouth duly adopted the hardline tactics proposed by magistrate Hinckley, demanding that all Wampanoags surrender their guns and sign treaties of subjection.[21]

As expected, the ultimatum widened the breach between eastern Wampanoags, who largely accepted Christianity, and western Wampanoags loyal to Philip. On June 7 several Cape Cod sachems signed a treaty pledging loyalty to Plymouth "to the shedding of our blood or the loss of our lives." Kinship need not determine their allegiance, they declared, for scripture taught in Acts 17:26 that "the English and we, the poor Indians, are of one blood." "We do confess we poor Indians in our lives were as captives under Satan and our sachems," they continued, but they had learned from "the word of God that it is better to trust in the great God and his strength." The gospel had led them to peace in fulfillment of Isaiah 11:6: "We were like unto wolves and lions [seeking] to destroy one another. But we hope and believe in God. Therefore we desire to enter into covenant with the English."[22]

Eliot could hardly believe it. There were "greater motions about the Indians than ever were since I began to teach them," he informed the English minister Richard Baxter. "I never found such violent opposition by Satan; and yet the Lord doth outwork him in all, and the kingdom of Christ doth spread and rise the more by his so violent opposition."[23] But while he encouraged Governor Prence to pursue Wampanoags who refused to disarm "with speed and vigor," he urged him to "immediately" return the weapons of those who cooperated, beginning with Philip. This would communicate that the English were not afraid of them—and Eliot reminded Prence that colonists had far more to fear from their own sin than from Philip—and "open an effectual door to their entertainment of the gospel."[24]

More eastern Wampanoags submitted in July, including the praying Indians of Mashpee and Manomet. "We poor Indians were a people delighting in war," they confessed. But they had learned "the benefit of peace by your favorable protection towards us for these many years past." Some, "having received the faith of the gospel of Christ," had been "taught to seek for peace and cast off our lion-like spirits," as prophesied by Isaiah. They were no longer "strangers and foreigners" to the English, but in accord with Ephesians 2:9, "we hope to be of the household of God." They too promised their lives in loyalty. In return, they requested protection from enemies who sought their "destruction, not for any hurt that we have done unto them, neither for . . . lands or what we possess besides, but only for that we are seeking after the knowledge of the true God and his ways."[25] The Wampanoags of Martha's Vineyard, now subject to New York, pledged allegiance in August. The island's proprietor and lay missionary Thomas Mayhew took the opportunity to establish a formal Christian government among them.[26]

But non-Christian western Wampanoags held out, including those Sakonnets led by the female sachem Awashonks. Plymouth increased the pressure on July 8, ordering Josiah Winslow to lead one hundred English troops and forty Wampanoags to "reduce them to reason." It called on the churches to observe "a solemn day of humiliation" to seek God's favor for the expedition. Winslow had plenty of motivation, for he and other entrepreneurs coveted Awashonks's land. But Awashonks came to Plymouth and submitted on July 24, blaming her brother, sons, and other insubordinate men for the delay. The court made her pay, drawing up a treaty in which Awashonks agreed to "the disposal of her lands to the authority of this government," allegedly so that Plymouth would bolster her authority over her men. It also imposed a £50 fine, no doubt hoping she would have to sell land to pay it.[27]

As disgruntled warriors gathered at Mount Hope, Plymouth prepared to march against Philip. But it was reluctant to fight without support from other colonies. The United Colonies had ceased functioning because of constitutional conflict, so Plymouth sent letters to Massachusetts and Rhode Island soliciting advice and support. "We have extended great patience and tenderness towards [the Wampanoags]," Governor Prence claimed, "being unwilling either to shed their blood or to embroil the country, might it be avoided without dishonor to God and our nation, and hazard to our people." But Philip was uncooperative, refused to come to Plymouth, and was extremely "insolent and provoking in his speeches and carriages." Having sent the letters, Plymouth held its soldiers in readiness "until we shall see the mind of God further."[28]

Waban and other Natick praying Indians were alarmed to learn that Plymouth was impressing soldiers for war, "for what cause we know not." An unjust war, they knew, would be devastating for the cause of Christ among their nonbelieving kin. "Though they yet pray not to God," Natick declared, "yet we hope they will, and we do mourn and pray for them and desire greatly that they may not be destroyed, especially because we have not heard that they have done anything worthy of death." Observing that peacemaking was the "glory of Christ's kingdom," the Natick church deputized Anthony and William Ahawton (the Indians featured in Eliot's *Indian Dialogues*) to join John Sassamon in mediating the quarrel.

Eliot wrote their commission on Natick's behalf. He instructed them to exhort Philip to obey two key texts. In the first, Deuteronomy 20:10–11, God commanded the Israelites to offer their enemies peace before going to war. In the second, 1 Corinthians 6:1–6, the Apostle Paul instructed Christians to seek arbitration amid conflict. The mediators were to urge Philip to refer his quarrel with Plymouth to arbitration by Massachusetts. If Philip agreed, they were to inform Governor Prence that the Natick church had commissioned them as mediators and implore Plymouth "for God's sake, who is the God of peace, and for Christ's sake, who is the king of peace and our great peacemaker in heaven, that they would accept this offer and submission unto peace."[29]

Some days later, colonists James Brown and Harvey Walker brought a letter to Mount Hope offering Philip one more chance to come to Plymouth. They recruited Roger Williams to assist them, but an illness delayed him. They arrived as a dance was ending, and Philip was drunk and in no disposition to receive them. Offended by Brown's words and refusal to remove his hat (upholding a Quaker principle), Philip struck it from his head. Insult triggered insult. Thankfully, the following day Williams arrived and Philip was sober, enabling Brown and Walker to present their letter. But when he heard the summons to Plymouth, Philip explained that John Eliot had invited him to appeal to Massachusetts, and he intended to do so.[30]

A few days later, Philip and a large entourage traveled to Boston by way of Punkapoag. Philip wore a coat and buckskin "thick" with beautifully designed wampum and a broad wampum belt. He informed the court that the Pokanokets had not broken the Taunton treaty and were not Plymouth's subjects. The old treaties affirmed friendship, not subordination. He must have been gratified when Massachusetts wrote Plymouth questioning its handling of the crisis. "We do not understand how far he hath subjected himself to you," Massachusetts chided, "but the treatment you have given him and proceedings toward him do not render him such a subject as that, if there be not present answering to a summons, there should presently be a proceeding to hostilities." Nor did the Articles of Confederation obligate Massachusetts to support Plymouth in an unjust war. Plymouth should be careful, for "the sword once drawn and dipped in blood may make him as independent upon you as you are upon him."

Plymouth must have been frustrated, but it agreed to a meeting of colonial representatives, including Connecticut governor John Winthrop Jr., with Philip.[31] Perhaps Philip was hopeful as he traveled to the September 24 meeting, but his hopes were cruelly dashed. Plymouth convinced Massachusetts that Philip

had acted "insolently and proudly" at every turn, and the Massachusetts delegation concluded that Philip's testimony was full of "lies and false stories." They
agreed that either Philip had to sign a treaty of submission, or there would be
war. Betrayed and outnumbered, Philip had little choice but to sign the humiliating document on September 29. "We, Philip, my council, and my subjects, do
acknowledge ourselves subjects to his majesty the king of England, etc., and the
government of New Plymouth, and to their laws." He promised not to sell land
or wage war without Plymouth's permission, to submit all Pokanoket-English
disputes to its adjudication, and to pay an annual tribute of five wolf heads.
Plymouth also imposed a burdensome fine of £100.[32]

At face value, the treaty indicated that the proud Pokanokets, on whom
Plymouth once depended for survival, had been reduced to servility. But Philip
would never view it as legitimate. Nor would he forget how the mediation of
Natick, Eliot, and Massachusetts led to his betrayal. He would never let himself
be this vulnerable again. Eliot's dream that praying Indians might advance the
cause of Christianity by reconciling Plymouth and the Pokanokets had suffered
a devastating blow.[33] As for Governor Prence, he warned those who continued
to resist Plymouth's dominion, "Do they think themselves so great as to disre-
gard and affront his majesty's interest and authority here, and the amity of the
English? ... [I] wish they would yet show themselves wiser, before it be too late."[34]

THE 1671 CRISIS SHOULD have persuaded Plymouth's magistrates and
entrepreneurs to give the Wampanoags space. It did not. Instead, they increased
the pressure, using every possible strategy to manipulate sachems into legally
alienating their land. The sachems had new reasons to sell. They needed the
proceeds to pay their fines. They needed funds to purchase guns and ammunition and build alliances in preparation for the next confrontation. They sold
land to Rhode Islanders, perhaps hoping to avoid Plymouth's domination, but
Plymouth voided such sales.

Much of the remaining Wampanoag land was sold between 1670 and 1675.
Philip sold large tracts north and east of Mount Hope peninsula, isolating the
Pokanokets and threatening their fishing rights. His brother-in-law Tuspaquin,
known as the "Black Sachem," sold land around Nemasket to Middleborough.
Josiah Winslow was as aggressive as any colonist, suing Tuspaquin's son for
failing to pay for a horse and forcing him to sell land worth much more to cover
it. After Winslow became Plymouth's governor in 1673, Plymouth authorized the
mortgage of land for payment of debts, making such manipulation easier.[35]

Plymouth pursued a strategy of divide and conquer to obtain coveted
Sakonnet land. It had promised to uphold the Sakonnet sachem Awashonks's authority over her insubordinate sons, but it reneged when it became evident that
her son Mammanuah, who had heard Plymouth minister John Cotton Jr. teach

and expressed his desire to be a praying Indian in 1673, was more pliable. A faction of Sakonnets declared Mammanuah their "chief sachem," and soon he and Awashonks had sold competing deeds to overlapping land. Furious, Awashonks seized Mammanuah and demanded that he renounce his authority to make the sale. Instead, he appealed to Plymouth, and the court declared him Sakonnet country's "chief proprietor." Soon settlers were establishing farms on Sakonnet land and planning a town. Mammanuah even sold Awashonks's homeland south of Sakonnet Point.[36]

Settlers also moved onto Pocasset Neck on the basis of deeds and surveys that the Pocasset sachem Weetamoo rejected. With "great fear of oppression," she appealed to Rhode Island's Quaker deputy governor John Easton. "I take myself as much engaged that they should not be wronged as if they were my countrymen and I of their nation," Easton told Governor Winslow. "It appeareth to me [they] desire only of you what is their reasonable due." Declaring that Weetamoo's claims were supported by many witnesses, he urged Winslow to grant the Pocassets their "right according to English law," lest they be provoked to "do wrong."[37]

Plymouth insisted that every square foot was acquired legally. When it judged that Indians had been cheated, especially by Rhode Islanders, it voided the transactions. But while the deeds were technically legal, the circumstances were often manipulative and exploitative. Under enormous economic, political, and legal pressure, sachems signed documents forfeiting their homelands and stirring their impoverished people's resentment. Colonists had little trouble with this, believing that the sooner Wampanoags settled in praying towns, the better.

More Wampanoags than any other Indians were accepting Christianity. By one estimate, as many as thirty-four hundred had become praying Indians, nearly half from the mainland. So many could read and write in Algonquian that Cotton professed a "very great" need for Indian primers and Bibles. There were four Wampanoag churches and ten praying towns (one of each on the mainland), nearly all led by Wampanoag pastors.

Christianity made inroads among western Wampanoags too. Mammanuah was the first Sakonnet sachem to confess his faith and took every opportunity to listen to Christian teaching. Many, including Philip and other Pokanokets, heard Cotton preach in Plymouth on court days. "Some of his chief men, I hear, stand well inclined to hear the gospel," Daniel Gookin wrote of Philip, "and himself is a person of good understanding and knowledge in the best things. I have heard him speak very good words, arguing that his conscience is convicted, but yet, though his will is bowed to embrace Jesus Christ, his sensual and carnal lusts are strong bands to hold him fast under Satan's dominions."[38]

Cotton occasionally preached to Tuspaquin's people at Nemasket, and Natick sent John Sassamon, Tuspaquin's son-in-law, to serve there as a teacher.

As Philip's former teacher, interpreter, and nephew by marriage, Sassamon might also continue to influence Philip. Colonists from nearby Taunton were impressed with Sassamon. Massachusetts minister William Hubbard claimed he was "better gifted" and conformed "more to the English manners than any other Indian."[39] But all was not as it seemed. Relations between Sassamon and Philip had soured beginning in 1671, when Sassamon enraged Philip by telling Plymouth that Narragansetts were at Mount Hope. Later Philip complained that when Sassamon drafted a legal document for him, he wrote it such that "a great part" of Philip's land became his.[40]

❧

THE THIRD CRISIS BEGAN in 1675. One day in January, Sassamon arrived in Plymouth with a disturbing report: Philip, the Pokanoket sachem, was "endeavoring to engage all the sachems round about in a war" against Plymouth.[41] Governor Winslow did not believe it, for as Increase Mather put it, it came from an Indian, "and one can hardly believe them when they speak truth."[42] But Sassamon was clearly worried, fretting that if Philip knew he had revealed the plot, he would kill him. By February, Sassamon was missing. An Indian search party grew suspicious when it spotted a gun, hat, and two dead ducks lying on the ice of Assawompsett Pond. They found Sassamon's body under the ice.[43]

According to an autopsy ordered by Winslow, Sassamon's head was "extremely swollen" and "his neck was broken by twisting of his head round." The search party reported that no water came from his lungs when they pulled the body from the pond, so it was concluded that he must have been dead before he entered the water. Suspicion grew when the body started "bleeding afresh" after a Nemasket Wampanoag named Tobias, one of Philip's counselors, came near. Although there was a natural explanation, Europeans had long regarded this as a supernatural sign of guilt.[44] But Wampanoags pointed out that it was not the Indian way to murder a man and cover it up.[45]

Philip took no chances. Before the court could summon him, he traveled to Plymouth and denied any responsibility for Sassamon's death. The suspicious magistrates told him they would continue their investigation, and he left on friendly terms.[46] As gossip proliferated, Punkapoag minister William Ahawton reported that a praying Indian named Patuckson had witnessed the murder. Called before the court, Patuckson claimed he was "standing unseen upon a hill" when he saw Tobias and two other Wampanoags murder Sassamon. They had bribed him to keep quiet with a coat, and he had initially done so out of fear.[47]

Plymouth regularly tried Wampanoags for murdering colonists, but it had never tried Wampanoags for murdering Indians on Wampanoag land, leaving such cases to sachems. In this case, the relevant sachem was the Nemasket Tuspaquin, who had close ties to both Tobias and Sassamon. But Sassamon was a Christian who had faithfully served colonial interests, and Plymouth now regarded all Wampanoags as subjects. So, in an unprecedented decision, the court asserted jurisdiction, scheduling a trial for June. Murder suspects were not permitted bail under English law, but the court made an opportunistic exception, allowing Tuspaquin, his son, and Tobias to "bind over all their lands to the value of £100 unto the court."[48] (Tuspaquin may have hoped to influence the court's handling of the case, because a few days before the trial he sold Assawompsett Neck and adjacent land. If so, he would be sorely disappointed.)[49]

Three months offered ample time for fearmongering. Puritans speculated that Sassamon was murdered for his missionary work. "No doubt but one reason why the Indians murdered John Sassamon was out of hatred against him for his religion," Boston minister Increase Mather later wrote. "[He] was wont to curb those Indians that knew not God on the account of their debaucheries."[50] Gookin later called Sassamon "the first Christian martyr of the Indians, for tis evident he suffered death upon the account of his Christian profession and fidelity to the English." In April and again in May, Waban, leader of the praying town of Natick, warned that colonists and Christian Indians were in danger. Four years earlier Natick had played the role of peacemaker, but now it predicted Philip would strike as soon as "the woods were grown thick with green trees."[51]

Philip worried that if Tobias was found guilty, Plymouth would come after him next. He gathered warriors at Mount Hope and marched them toward the colonial town of Swansea at the northern end of the neck as a display of strength. When settlers asked why, the Wampanoags said "they were only on their own defense, for they understood that the English intended to cut them off." Confident that Philip's mobilization was purely defensive, Governor Winslow resolved not to provoke him. Hopefully once Philip "saw the court broken up and he not sent for, the cloud might blow over."[52]

Since it was unprecedented to try Wampanoags for killing another Indian, Plymouth selected six "of the most indifferent, grave, and sage Indians" from praying communities to serve as advisory jurors. The court charged that Tobias, his son Wampapaquan, and Mattashunnamo "did with joint consent . . . of malice forethought, and by force and arms, murder John Sassamon, another Indian, by laying violent hands on him and striking him, or twisting his neck, until he was dead."[53]

The three Wampanoags denied the charges. Tobias charged his accuser Patuckson with fabricating his story to avoid paying a gambling debt and to make the English "think him a better Christian."[54] It was one man's word against three, and Plymouth law, following the Old Testament, required at least two witnesses, "or that which is equivalent thereunto."[55] Nevertheless, the jury delivered a unanimous verdict. "We of the jury, one and all, both English and

Indians, do jointly and with one consent agree upon a verdict, that Tobias and his son Wampapaquan, and Mattashunnamo . . . are guilty of the blood of John Sassamon." It sentenced them to die by hanging on June 8.

John Cotton Jr. preached to Indians in Plymouth on the day of execution. A crowd watched as Tobias and Mattashunnamo were executed, but when it was Wampapaquan's turn, the noose snapped. With sudden hope, Wampapaquan revised his story and blamed his dead partners for killing Sassamon while he stood by. Plymouth granted him a reprieve, but not for long. A month later he was shot to death.[56]

Governor Winslow believed a crisis had been averted, for Philip would hardly go to war for the sake of three Wampanoags.[57] "Praised be God the storm is over," wrote Roger Williams.[58] But it was not over. Philip, furious at the violation of Wampanoag sovereignty, regarded the trial as a sham. That praying Wampanoags played such a major role made it that much worse. A rumor reached Mount Hope that the convicted men had accused Philip of ordering them to kill Sassamon. Many Wampanoags concluded that Plymouth coerced their confessions as a pretext to kill Philip and seize his land.[59]

THREE DAYS AFTER the hanging, colonist John Brown of Swansea alerted Governor Winslow that sixty warriors were occupying the way to Mount Hope. "One reason, say they, is because they hear you intend to send for Philip." Many Pokanokets had sent their wives to Narragansett country, and young Narragansetts, Shawomets, Cowesetts, Pocassets, and Nemaskets were flocking to Philip. A Wampanoag told his English employer he was leaving, for "he was sent for to fight with the English within two days." Indians were said to be patrolling the road to Taunton, and they alarmed Swansea by shooting guns at night and constantly beating drums. "The truth is," Brown concluded, "they are in a posture of war."[60]

Winslow trod carefully, warning Philip's sister-in-law Weetamoo, the Pocasset sachem, that Philip was causing trouble "upon no provocation . . . in the least from us, but mostly from his own base groundless fear." His attempts to recruit Pocassets were based on "notorious falsehoods, as if we were secretly designing mischief to him and you." If she remained faithful and provided intelligence of Philip's plans, Plymouth would overlook the actions of her insubordinate "young men" and protect her. When Philip's "pride and treachery have wrought his own ruin," she would be rewarded.[61]

The council also wrote to Philip, urging him "to dismiss his strange Indians and command his own men to fall quietly to their business, that our people might also be quiet," for they "intended him no wrong, nor hurt."[62] Not trusting Plymouth's messenger, Philip enlisted Samuel Gorton Jr. to draft his reply. He admitted that his people had "great fears and jealousies" toward Plymouth.

Accepting Winslow's assurance that those concerns were groundless, he asked Winslow not to disarm or punish the Pokanokets for taking precautions. He wanted peace, but given the "harsh threats" he had received, it was not safe for him to go to Plymouth.[63] The humiliation of 1671 loomed large.

The Sakonnet sachem Awashonks initiated her own diplomacy by reaching out to a rising entrepreneur in his mid-thirties named Benjamin Church. Church's version of events, written four decades later by his son based on Church's notes, should be received cautiously, but as he told it, he had built a house and barn in Sakonnet country and was "disposing of his affairs" when two Sakonnets invited him to meet Awashonks at a dance. He arrived to find hundreds of Indians and Awashonks leading the ritual "in a foaming sweat." She sat down, summoned her counselors, and informed Church that Philip, fearing an English attack, had sent six men "to draw her into a confederacy." The purpose of the dance was to discern what to do.

Church assured her that Philip's fears were false. Would Church "have brought up his goods to settle" in Sakonnet if war was imminent? Awashonks summoned Philip's men, "their faces painted and their hair trimmed up in comb-fashion, with their powder-horns and shotbags at their backs." She told Church, he claimed, that Philip threatened to target English property in Sakonnet country to provoke the English into attacking the Sakonnets. Church urged her to kill Philip's men then and there, for they were "bloody wretches and thirsted after the blood of their English neighbors who had never injured them but had always abounded in their kindness to them." He warned her not to join a "rebellion which would certainly prove fatal to her."

She asked him to intercede with Governor Winslow, and he agreed. He traveled to Pocasset, where he met the Pocasset sachem Weetamoo and her husband Peter Nunnuit, just returned from Mount Hope. Nunnuit believed war was imminent, according to Church, for Philip was convinced that Plymouth intended to arrest him and was gathering "young men from all parts of the country." Many yearned for war and had wanted to kill Winslow's messenger, but Philip forbade it. Instead, he promised that on Sunday, when colonists were in church, they could "rifle their houses" and kill cattle. Weetamoo lamented that many Pocassets were at Mount Hope against her wishes. She "much feared there would be a war." Church urged her to submit to Plymouth.

Church left for Plymouth and met Winslow the next morning. Contrary to his assurances, Plymouth had formed a war council and was mobilizing for action.[64]

REALIZING HOW DIRE the situation had become, Rhode Island's deputy governor John Easton invited Philip to a conference. He and two other magistrates met Philip's entourage on June 17. "We sat very friendly together," Easton recalled. They told the Pokanoket sachem their goal was to ensure he did "not receive or do wrong."

The Pokanokets replied that "they had done no wrong." Rather, "the English wronged them."

"The English said the Indians wronged them, and the Indians said the English wronged them," the Rhode Islanders replied, "but our desire was the quarrel might rightly be decided in the best way, and not as dogs decided their quarrel."

War was the worst way to resolve the crisis, the Pokanokets agreed, but they would never get justice from Plymouth.

The Rhode Islanders proposed arbitration.

The Pokanokets retorted that they knew from experience how that would play out. Four years earlier the praying Indians of Natick had persuaded Philip to seek arbitration from Massachusetts, but "all English agreed against them, and so by arbitration they had had much wrong. Many miles square of land" had since been "taken from them." The English would force them to surrender their weapons and impose a massive fine. The Pokanokets would lose "all their livelihood" and may "as good be killed."

The Rhode Islanders suggested a different approach. Why not select a team of arbitrators, including the governor of New York and a prominent sachem chosen by the Indians?

This intrigued the Pokanokets. They then explained why they were frustrated with Plymouth's handling of John Sassamon's death. They were willing to accept colonial jurisdiction in English townships, but this was an exclusively Indian affair that should have been left to the sachems. They also complained that when Indians were "called or forced to be Christian Indians" they stopped submitting to their sachems and became "in everything more mischievous, only dissemblers."[65]

But Philip's grievances went far beyond that. When the English first arrived in 1620 they were "as a little child," he explained, while his father Ousamequin was a "great man." Yet Ousamequin prevented "Indians from wronging the English and gave them corn and showed them how to plant." He gave them plenty of land. But they had not responded in kind. The more powerful they became, the more they exploited Wampanoags. They even poisoned Philip's brother Alexander. Indians never received justice in court, for if twenty Indians "testified that an Englishman had done them wrong, it was as nothing," but "if but one of their worst Indians testified against any Indian . . . when it pleased the English, it was sufficient." Tobias, Mattashunnamo, and Wampapaquan, Sassamon's supposed killers, had been executed on the testimony of a single witness.

Plymouth used every available trick to defraud Wampanoags of their land, Philip continued. Colonists produced documents asserting the sale of larger tracts than Indians had agreed to verbally. They pressured sachems to sell the land on which their people depended for sustenance. Sometimes "the English made them drunk and then cheated them." When sachems refused to sell, they purchased the land from others who had no right to sell it. Wampanoags "had no hopes left to keep any land," and the land they still had was overrun by cattle. Then there was the problem of alcohol. Colonists sold Indians liquor, only to hold sachems responsible when drunk Indians committed crimes.

Philip said he would think about their arbitration proposal. The Rhode Islanders warned that war would be disastrous, for the colonies would unite against him and were too strong for him. If the English were so strong, Philip bitterly replied, "the English should do to them as they did when they were too strong for the English."

Easton departed hopeful, only to receive a letter from Governor Winslow indicating that Plymouth planned to force Philip's submission.[66] Further diplomacy might have paid off, but Plymouth considered Philip's militancy a dire threat and was determined to teach him a lesson. Philip expected this all along, but this time he would not submit. In the words of one witness, "If he must die," he was resolved to "die on his own land."[67]

The tinderbox was Swansea, a cluster of three scattered settlements with thirty English families. Several lived near the Baptist meeting house of pastor John Miles on the Palmer River toward Rehoboth. Others lived six miles southeast at Mattapoisett. The third group lived closest to Mount Hope, just east of the Kickemuit River.[68]

On June 18, Rehoboth settlers were traveling toward Mount Hope to retrieve some horses at Philip's request when Wampanoag warriors "presented their guns at them" and forced them back. The next day, Indians looted the home of Job Winslow, the governor's cousin. On Sunday, June 20, warriors marched toward Swansea with drums beating as if they intended an assault. A few demanded that a colonist sharpen a hatchet for them. He declined, observing that it was the Sabbath, but they retorted that "they knew not who his God was" and would sharpen it whether he liked it or not. They stole food, set two houses on fire, and briefly seized a colonist, lecturing that "he should not work on his God's day, and that he should tell no lies."

Terrified colonists abandoned their homes for stronger buildings known as garrison houses and appealed for help. The next morning, Governor Winslow ordered 70 men from Taunton and Bridgewater to Swansea's relief, followed by 150 the next day. He dashed off a letter to Massachusetts governor John Leverett. Plymouth had not wronged the Pokanokets, he insisted; their own pride was to blame. He asked Leverett to prevent the Narragansetts and Nipmucs from aiding Philip, which he believed they intended to do. But he was confident he would not need Massachusetts's help. "If we can have fair play with our own," he wrote, "we hope with the help of God we shall give a good account of it in a few days."[69]

Figure 1 Edward Winslow (1595–1655) won Ousamequin's enduring friendship by nursing him to health from a serious illness. He later served as Plymouth's governor. As Massachusetts's agent to England, he advocated on behalf of missionary work to the Indians.

Source: Portrait painted in 1651 in London, artist unknown. Image from Mayflower 400 UK, mayflower400uk.org. Public domain.

Figure 2 John Endecott (1600–1664) was Massachusetts's first governor and later commanded colonial forces in the aggressive opening campaign of the Pequot War. He later served again as governor and promoted the early missionary work of John Eliot.

Source: Portrait painted by Francis D'Avignon (1813–1871) in 1843. National Portrait Gallery, Smithsonian Institution. Public domain.

Figure 3 John Winthrop (1588–1649) led the great migration to Massachusetts and became the colony's most influential governor. He was convinced that God called the Puritans to settle in America and bring the gifts of Christianity and civilization to the Natives.

Source: Portrait by unknown artist, thought to be a follower of Anthony van Dyck. Image from Wikimedia Commons. Public domain.

Figure 4 The Massachusetts Bay Seal (1629) featured a friendly Indian imploring the English, "Come over and help us." It spoke to the early Puritans' conviction that evangelizing Native Americans was a primary purpose of colonization.

Source: Image from Wikimedia Commons. Public domain.

Figure 5 John Winthrop Jr. (1606–1676) was an energetic entrepreneur who served as governor of Saybrook colony and later Connecticut. He pursued close economic and political ties with Indians and advocated diplomacy with the Narragansetts during King Philip's War (Massachusetts Historical Society).

Source: Portrait painted by an unidentified artist of the school of Sir Peter Lely or William Dobson, 1634–1635. Collection of the Massachusetts Historical Society. Reproduced with permission.

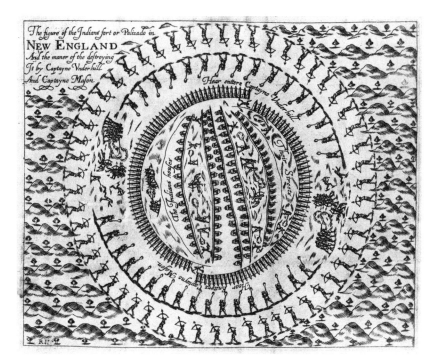

Figure 6 This engraving of the 1637 Mystic massacre was published in John Underhill's *Newes from America* (London, 1638). Notice that as fighting rages inside the palisade, concentric circles of English troops and allied Narragansetts, Niantics, and Pequots surround it.

Source: Image from Wikimedia Commons. Public domain.

Figure 7 This model of Algonquian wigwams inside a palisade, constructed by the Mashantucket Pequot Museum & Research Center, offers a realistic portrayal of a fortified Algonquian village such as the Pequot village of Mystic, destroyed by colonial forces in 1637.

Source: Mashantucket Pequot Museum. Reproduced with permission.

Figure 8 John Eliot (1604–1690) became known as the Apostle to the Indians for his missionary work. He proved a consistent advocate for the rights of Christian Indians and petitioned against selling Algonquian captives into the slave trade during King Philip's War.

Source: Artist unknown. Image from Meisterdrucke, at meisterdrucke.com. Public domain.

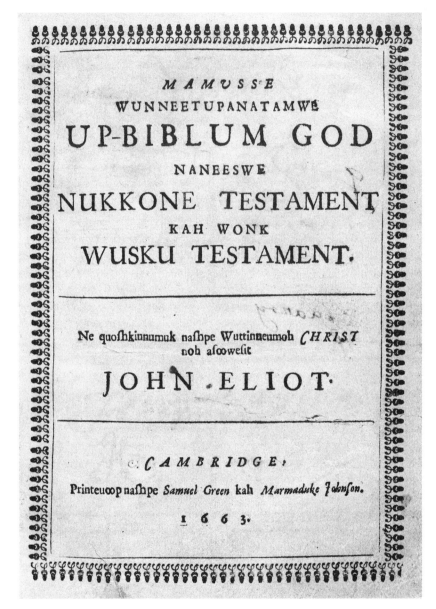

MAMVSSE
WUNNEETUPANATAMWÉ
UP-BIBLUM GOD
NANEESWE
NUKKONE TESTAMENT,
KAH WONK
WUSKU TESTAMENT.

Ne quoſhkinnumuk naſhpe Wuttinneumoh *CHRIST*
noh aſooweſit

JOHN . ELIOT.

CAMBRIDGE:
Printeuꝏp naſhpe *Samuel Green* kah *Marmaduke Johnſon.*
1 6 6 3.

Figure 9 John Eliot's Massachusett Bible, published in Cambridge in 1663, was the most significant of Eliot's many religious publications in the Wôpanâak Algonquian dialect which enabled Indians to make the Christian faith their own. The Algonquian language had existed only in oral form until then.

Source: Image from Wikimedia Commons. Public domain.

Figure 10 Josiah Winslow (1629–1680) was the governor of Plymouth during King Philip's War and commanded colonial forces in the invasion of Narragansett country. He steadfastly defended the justice of Plymouth's actions toward Philip and his Wampanoags, both before and during the war.

Source: Portrait painted in 1651 in London, artist unknown. Pilgrim Hall Museum. Public domain.

INCREASE MATHER. D.D.   1639-1723.

Figure 11 Increase Mather (1639–1723) was a leading pastor in Boston at the time of King Philip's War. Warning even before the war that Massachusetts faced God's judgment for its sins, he led the wartime movement for repentance and reform as a means of restoring God's favor. His postwar histories interpreted the conflict in distinctly religious terms.

Source: Portrait painted by Gustavus Ellinthorpe Sintzenich (1821–1892). Mansfield College, University of Oxford. Public domain.

Figure 12 This medal (front and back) was awarded by Massachusetts to an Indian company in 1676 for its faithful service in King Philip's War. Notice the similarities to the Massachusetts Bay seal, as well as the inscription praising the Indian soldiers for their service against "the Heathen Natives of this Land, they giving us peace and mercy at there hands."

Source: Image from Smithsonian National Museum of the American Indian. Public domain.

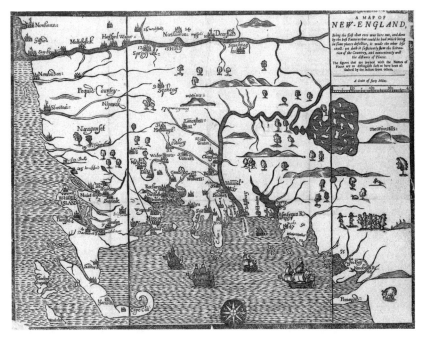

Figure 13 This map of New England, attributed to John Foster, was originally published in William Hubbard's *The Present State of New England* (London, 1677). It is the first map known to have been published in the English North American colonies. Notice the colonizing perspective: the western edge is at the top, and the northern edge is at the right.

Source: Image from Wikimedia Commons. Public domain.

Figure 14 This Algonquian sachem has traditionally been identified as the Eastern Niantic and Narragansett sachem Ninigret, but some scholars argue that it is actually one of Ninigret's descendants, or even the Pequot sachem Robin Cassacinamon. Notice the wampum headdress and jewelry (c. 1700).

Source: Artist unknown. Image from *World History Encyclopedia*, original from Rhode Island School of Design Museum. Public domain.

Figure 15 Wampum, such as these beautiful buttons, beads, and tubes photographed by the Mashantucket Pequot Museum & Research Center, was produced by Algonquians from the shells of whelks and clams. Highly valued, it was used for diplomatic, judicial, and social rituals. It became the leading currency of trade between Europeans and Indians during the mid-1600s.

Source: Mashantucket Pequot Museum. Reproduced with permission.

PART III
WAR

14

Who Are Friends and Who Are Foes?

June 1675 to August 1675

PLYMOUTH AND THE Wampanoags were on the brink of war. As long as the fighting remained confined to Mount Hope, colonists could feel relatively secure. But a regional war would be disastrous. So the colonies worked to keep Philip's potential allies, the Narragansetts and Nipmucs, from entering the conflict. But heavy-handed colonial policies threatened to provoke the very hostility they sought to prevent.

Rumors of a Narragansett–Wampanoag alliance had circulated for years, but the notion was unlikely on its face. The two peoples had been rivals for at least half a century, and in recent years Philip had repeatedly opposed Narragansett interests.[1] A Nipmuc–Wampanoag alliance was even less likely, since despite ties between Philip's Pokanokets and the Quaboag Nipmucs, many Nipmucs were praying Indians. Nevertheless Massachusetts would take no chances. It sent the Atherton Company's Edward Hutchinson to secure Narragansett neutrality and thirty-three-year-old Ephraim Curtis, whose trading post was near the praying town of Pakachoog, to deal with the Nipmucs. It also dispatched Captain Thomas Savage to meet with Philip in hope of avoiding conflict altogether.

Hutchinson's delegation reached Providence on June 22, 1675, where he recruited seventy-two-year-old Roger Williams as an interpreter and advisor. Continuing that night, they met Canonchet, youngest son of the great Narragansett sachem Miantonomo, who had been executed by Uncas so many years before. They presented Canonchet with a letter from Governor Leverett, and Canonchet "readily and gladly assented to all the governor's desires." Canonchet called the other major Narragansett sachems—Ninigret, Pessicus, Quaiapin, and the late Cojonoquant's son Quinnapin—to meet the envoys at Wickford, where Richard Smith Jr. ran his late father's trading post. But the sachems were wary and asked to meet "near the great pond" ten miles from Wickford instead.

There, having heard Leverett's letter, the sachems said they held "no agreement with Philip in this his rising against the English." They had forbidden warriors to travel to Mount Hope and encouraged Narragansetts married to Wampanoags to return to Narragansett country. If any of Philip's warriors came to them, they promised to "deliver them to the English." They also warned that Uncas, the

Mohegan sachem, had sent twenty warriors to help Philip. Nevertheless, they wondered why Plymouth was being so aggressive.

Massachusetts's envoys replied that Philip "broke all laws and was in arms of rebellion against that colony, his ancient friends and protectors."

But why were Massachusetts and Rhode Island supporting Plymouth rather than letting them fight it out on their own? the Narragansetts wondered.

The envoys replied that the colonies "were subject to one King Charles" and were obligated "to stand to the death by each other, in all parts of the world." They warned the sachems how disastrous an alliance with Philip would be. He could not win; the colonies would go after him with "thousands of horse and foot."

The Narragansetts raised their own "vehement" frustration. Uncas's son Owaneco had killed a Narragansett sachem, but Connecticut had released Owaneco with a mild rebuke on a plea of self-defense. "I am my father Miantonomo's son, as Owaneco is to Uncas," Canonchet had earlier reminded Roger Williams. "If there should partiality be showed to him ... then all we young sachems shall have a temptation laid before us to kill and murder in the hope of the like impunity." The envoys sensed an opportunity. If the Narragansetts were "permitted to right themselves" against the Mohegans, neither group would be able to aid Philip. Williams sent the suggestion to Connecticut governor John Winthrop Jr.[2]

Meanwhile, Massachusetts agent Ephraim Curtis and two Christian Indians reached the praying town of Hassanamesit on June 24, where they met Captain Tom Wuttasacomponom, the praying Indian ruler. Captain Tom assured Curtis that Hassanamesit would not support Philip. Nor did he believe any of his men would go to Mount Hope, for as Christians, they "accounted themselves as the English, and they would not fight against themselves." Curtis also visited the praying towns of Manchage, Chabanakongkomun, Quantisset, Wabquisset, Maanexit, and Pakachoog. Each assured him they remained loyal to Massachusetts. On June 25 Curtis reached Quaboag, a former Pokanoket tributary. Its sachem Konkewasco promised to "continue our subjection unto the English of the Massachusetts colony, neither will I suffer any of my men to go" help Philip. Curtis returned home with signed pledges from no fewer than thirteen Nipmuc leaders.[3]

PLYMOUTH CALLED ON its churches to observe June 24 as a fast day. John Cotton Jr. wrote the proclamation, observing "the awful hand of God upon us in permitting the heathen to carry it with great insolency and rage against us, appearing in their great hostile preparations and also some outrageous carriages." The English needed to humble themselves for their sins, entreating God "to go forth with our forces and bless, succeed, and prosper them, delivering them from the hands of his and our enemies, subduing the heathen before them, and returning them all in safety to their families and relations." None doubted that Plymouth's enemies were God's enemies.[4]

While Philip's men looted abandoned houses and killed cattle around Swansea, English soldiers fortified garrison houses. Seventeen from Bridgewater marched to Mattapoisett, ignoring pleas from fleeing colonists to turn back.[5] But despite claims of an Indian uprising, Philip's men had not harmed a single colonist. While many historians echo colonial claims that Philip had been planning an uprising for years, the evidence is circumstantial. He was certainly trying to forge an Algonquian alliance, as had Miantonomo and Ninigret before him, but its purpose may have been defensive. He was resigned to war with Plymouth, but that does not mean he wanted it. He even advised local colonists to flee their isolated homes since "they were in danger to be killed." Many young Wampanoags wanted war, yet they held their fire. Rhode Island deputy governor John Easton later suggested their powwows warned that if they started the war "they should be beaten, and otherwise not." Perhaps Philip hoped that if Plymouth was the aggressor, its allies would withhold support, while Indians would rally to the Pokanoket cause.

Whatever the case, it was a colonist who fired the first shot. On June 23 two colonists, "an old man and a lad," approached a house that Indians were plundering. When three Indians dashed out, the older colonist told the younger to shoot. He pulled the trigger and an Indian fell, mortally wounded. Angry warriors approached a garrison house and demanded an explanation. A young colonist retorted that the man's death "was no matter." Wiser colonists interjected that "it was but an idle lad's words," but the damage was done.[6]

On Thursday, June 24, Plymouth's fast day, Rehoboth's pastor Noah Newman preached on Psalm 46:10, "Be still and know that I am God: I will be exalted among the heathen." But the day would be calamitous for the English. Bridgewater troops marching to Mattapoisett encountered thirty Indians shouting and firing guns into the air. They warned colonists in a nearby garrison house, but the colonists foolishly took carts to retrieve corn from a barn a quarter-mile away. Soon the soldiers heard gunfire. They galloped toward the barn and chased away the attackers, but six colonists lay dead or dying.[7]

Six miles northwest, Baptist minister John Miles led an afternoon prayer service. As worshipers returned to his garrison house, Indians opened fire, killing one man and wounding three others, including Miles's African slave, who later died. When two men went to find a surgeon, they were ambushed. Thomas Savage's delegation, en route from Boston to meet with Philip, discovered their bodies on the road. "The men were stripped of their upper garments, one having his head cut off and carried away, the other his head flayed, the skin and hair off from his skull and both their right hands cut off and gone," an officer reported. At least ten colonists were killed or mortally wounded that day, including the young man who fired the opening shot. More than a dozen buildings were burned. With their men pinned down in garrison houses, officers called for reinforcements. Rumor had it that Uncas, the Mohegan sachem, had promised that if Philip sent him six English scalps, "all the Indians in the country" would rally to him.[8]

News of the attack shocked Massachusetts. Tales of atrocities staggered belief. One writer told of a man who went with his wife and son to recover possessions from their home. The Indians shot and killed the man, raped his wife, and killed and scalped her and her son. The story was almost certainly false, but it was widely believed because it fit colonial stereotypes about heathen barbarians.[9] Boston minister Increase Mather, who had predicted God's judgment a year earlier, found it significant that the attack occurred on a fast day, "the Lord thereby declaring from heaven that he expects something else from his people besides fasting and prayer."[10]

Massachusetts debated whether to send troops. The justice of Plymouth's war was "much questioned" by some, council secretary Edward Rawson admitted. They debated whether Plymouth had jurisdiction over Mount Hope. When warriors captured some Massachusetts colonists, Philip released them, and it was tempting for Massachusetts to avoid "the trouble, charge, and loss" war would entail. Nevertheless, Governor Leverett had promised troops to Plymouth's Governor Winslow, and the magistrates decided that since Plymouth had been attacked, its prior conduct was irrelevant. The United Colonies' "solemn league and covenant" required mutual aid in defensive wars, and failure to send it would be a serious sin against God.[11] The General Court ordered the impressment of one hundred infantry and fifty cavalry, to be led by Captains Daniel Henchman and Thomas Prentice. Both were reliable supporters of John Eliot's missionary work.[12]

Former commissioner and Atherton Company member Major General Daniel Denison was placed in command of Massachusetts forces. His orders were "to kill, burn, and destroy the enemy, unless they shall yield themselves your prisoners." His objective was "taking or destroying the head of them, Philip and his chief counsellors," responsible for the "treacherous and barbarous in-surrection." At stake was nothing less than "the honor of God, the good of his people, and . . . the interest of our Lord Jesus Christ in his churches." To secure God's blessing, Denison was to ensure that his troops worshiped daily, attended preaching when possible, and conducted themselves as Christians.[13] Observing a colony-wide fast, Mather prayed that God would "subdue the heathen, blessing [the] present expedition for that end."[14]

But the court was not scrupulous in selecting soldiers. Four months earlier, a former privateer in his mid-thirties named Samuel Mosely had captured some Dutch privateers and brought them to Boston. Several were sentenced to death, but now they were offered freedom in exchange for service in a company of horsemen led by Mosely. Mosely filled out the rest of the unit, 110 men, by enlisting his old "Jamaica privateers" and an assortment of indentured servants and underage youths. As an incentive, Massachusetts offered them the right to enslave any Indians they captured.[15]

RHODE ISLANDERS WERE terrified that the conflict would spread beyond Mount Hope. Canoes were reportedly passing between Mount Hope and Narragansett country, and when a hundred Narragansetts approached Warwick, Roger Williams feared their sachems' assurances of neutrality were "falsehood and treachery." Colonists in Narragansett country, seeking safety, ferried their families to Aquidneck Island amid pouring rain. Narragansetts plundered their abandoned houses. Rhode Island governor William Coddington asked the Narragansett sachem Pessicus to come to Newport, but Pessicus declined, explaining that his son was sick. He said he "sorrowed for the English" and admitted his people were divided. He and his nephew Canonchet wanted peace but "could not rule the youth and common people." Philip had sent messengers bearing three scalps in a bid for Narragansett support, but while the female sachem Quaiapin welcomed the messengers, Pessicus persuaded his people to reject the scalps. He warned the English to be vigilant: abandon isolated homes, fortify garrison houses, and avoid the roads.

"Many wish that Plymouth had left the Indians alone, at least not to put to death the three Indians upon one Indian's testimony," Williams complained on June 27.[16] The next day, unidentified warriors raided Williams's hometown of Providence, burning eighteen outlying buildings and wounding three colonists, and losing five or six of their own men.[17] Panic spread to Connecticut's eastern frontier, with rumors of Wampanoags near the Pawcatuck River. Colonists traveled to Shantok to interview Uncas, sachem of the Mohegans. He assured them he had no communication with Philip, but they suspected "most of his men are gone that way." Connecticut dispatched troops and called its General Court into emergency session.[18]

Plymouth's forces around Swansea were scattered among six different posts, making joint operations impossible. Their commander, Captain James Cudworth, proposed abandoning all but two positions so he could adopt a more aggressive strategy. He would dispatch squads of twelve or fifteen men, each squad within supporting distance of two or three others, to ambush Wampanoags in the woods. Whatever happened, they had to prevent Philip from escaping the peninsula. Governor Coddington promised that Rhode Island would patrol the peninsula's western coast, but Cudworth worried that the female Pocasset sachem Weetamoo, who had nearly twenty canoes, one of which could carry forty men, might ferry the Wampanoags across the Sakonnet River to Pocasset. "Sir, if they may take their flight towards Pocasset, it may be the demise of our plantations," Cudworth warned Plymouth's governor Josiah Winslow. He suggested that forces at Taunton seize the canoes.[19]

It was good advice, but Winslow objected that it was "dishonorable giving ground to the enemy" and would result in further property damage. He also feared "that base skulking way of engaging them may be our disadvantage." Instead, he urged Cudworth to wait for reinforcements from Massachusetts and make "a more honorable and resolute charge on the enemy's quarters." He did order Taunton forces to disarm the Pocassets and seize their canoes.[20]

The Massachusetts forces, accompanied by five Christian Indian volunteers, arrived at the Miles garrison house on June 28. Many were rattled, having witnessed a lunar eclipse that they considered a divine portent. Some claimed "in the center of the moon they discerned an unusual black spot, not a little resembling the scalp of an Indian." Others saw "the form of an Indian bow." Did it signify victory or defeat?

Indians hidden in the foliage across the river harassed the garrison, mocking soldiers and shooting two sentinels. A dozen troopers boldly crossed the bridge to disperse them, only to suffer a deadly volley from the camouflaged warriors. The scout William Hammond went down, and Quartermaster Joseph Belcher was shot in the knee. The troopers returned fire, then beat a hasty retreat. Benjamin Church of Plymouth, who always portrayed himself as the hero, claimed that he and two others rode to rescue Hammond, only to discover that he was dead. They recovered his body and withdrew under fire that wounded yet another soldier. "The Lord have mercy on us if such a handful of Indians shall thus dare such an army!" Church vented.[21]

Captain Cudworth ordered an advance on June 29. He divided his army into three parts in hopes of sweeping the peninsula and forcing a battle. Jittery soldiers feared the presence of Indians behind every bush and tree. A mile be-yond the bridge, some thought they saw Indians to their right and opened fire, only to wound twenty-year-old Perez Savage, son of Major Thomas Savage of Massachusetts, in the thigh. With rain falling and recriminations likely flying, the army withdrew to the garrison house. Embarrassment must have been high when the sixty-seven-year-old Major Savage arrived from Boston to take com-mand. A member of the first generation of immigrants, Savage had married Anne Hutchinson's daughter and was exiled from Massachusetts before repenting and returning. He must have been distressed about more than just his son's wounding. The colonial army, four hundred strong, was floundering and mo-rale was plummeting. One soldier, shocked at the profanity of Samuel Mosely's privateers, broke under the strain and declared that God was against the English. His officers sent him home.

Major Savage led the army across the river late the next morning, after the rain had dissipated. Cavalry moved ahead of each wing. A mile and a half out, they passed burned-out houses. A Bible lay on the ground, its pages torn and scattered. A few miles further, they encountered a grisly sight: poles along the road adorned with the bloody scalps and severed hands and heads of eight Englishmen. Savage ordered the remains taken down and buried before the outraged soldiers continued their march. They eventually discovered three hundred acres of "stately corn" and a hundred wigwams, but not a Pokanoket to be found. Items scattered along the ground suggested the Pokanokets had departed in haste. Soldiers continued to the coast, but the reality was all too obvious: Philip had escaped, probably across the Sakonnet River to Pocasset country. Some officers expressed delight at the easy conquest (one man estimated the peninsula's value at £10,000), but Savage knew better. Philip's warriors were now at large, free to strike anywhere from Providence to Dartmouth. Savage's men spent a miserable night under heavy rainfall before returning to Swansea. A small garrison was left to build a fort at Mount Hope.[22]

Colonists had imagined they would "easily . . . chastise the insolent doings and murderous practices of the heathen," Daniel Gookin later wrote, but the Wampanoags easily eluded them. While English soldiers were loud and clumsy, Indians were "subtle and wily," keeping "deep silence in their marches and motions." While English formations sought open fields where they could fire European-style volleys, Indians hid in the foliage and relied on marksmanship honed by years of hunting. Unfamiliar with the woods and swamps, the colonial officers had no idea how to respond to the Wampanoags' "skulking way of war."

Some officers urged the conscription of praying Indians, who understood Indian tactics. Massachusetts quickly ordered Gookin to recruit a company. Fifty-two praying Indians were equipped at New England Company expense and dispatched to Swansea on July 6, having been promised a coat for each Indian head they delivered and two per captive. It was controversial, for as Gookin noted, many colonists were "filled with animosity against all Indians without exception." Seasonal Wampanoag laborers had already been forced to leave the colony. As a precaution, the Indian soldiers' families were held hostage in Boston.[23]

Meanwhile, Wampanoags began raiding English towns while colonial forces struggled to respond. "We are a distressed people," a lieutenant scribbled from Taunton, a town of about ninety-six families. "We hear nothing since from the army. We find the enemy is dispersed through the wilderness. They are, as we judge, round about us. This morning, three of our men are slain, close by one of our courts of guard, houses burnt in our sight, our men being so picked off out of every bush. . . . We see their design is not to face the army but to keep a flying army about the woods, to fall on us and our army as they have advantage." He urged that allied Indians be recruited to "hunt them out for us, or else our English will be disheartened to travel about in the woods, and get nothing but a clap with a bullet out of every bush. The Lord humble us for our sins, which are the procuring causes of God's judgments, and remember mercy and bestow it on us."[24]

Indians burned several buildings around Rehoboth. Prentice's Massachusetts cavalry pursued them, killing four Indians, but a soldier named John Druce died from a wound to his bowels. A praying Nashaway, Thomas Quanapohit, killed one of Philip's leading men.[25]

Plymouth's Captain Cudworth marched toward Dartmouth and ordered Captain Matthew Fuller to lead thirty-six men into Pocasset country in an attempt to seize hostages and thereby force Weetamoo and her Pocassets to join forces with the English. Crossing the Sakonnet River on the night of July 7, Fuller divided his forces. One group, led by Benjamin Church, marched to Pocasset Neck, where they were ambushed, pinned down on the beach, and had to be rescued by a passing sloop. Fuller's group was also attacked, and two men were wounded before they too were rescued. In addition, five Rhode Islanders were wounded while attempting to rescue cattle from Pocasset Neck. Weetamoo had clearly chosen sides.[26]

Church claimed he had hoped to meet the Sakonnet sachem Awashonks but was unable to do so. She requested refuge from Rhode Island, but although Deputy Governor John Easton offered to shelter her at his expense, his colleagues, "in fury against all Indians, would not consent." Narragansett sachems told Rhode Island they doubted that Awashonks supported Philip, so Rhode Island encouraged the Narragansetts "to get her and as many [of her people] as they could from Philip."[27]

COLONIAL AUTHORITIES WORKED vigorously to win Algonquian support. "It is absolutely necessary to engage some Indians with us, whereby we may understand the motions of Philip and the Narragansetts," Springfield magistrate John Pynchon warned Governor Winthrop.[28] They would use carrots and sticks: taking hostages to guarantee loyalty and rewarding warriors for military service. Massachusetts urged that all Indians "speedily be put to the test of their fidelity, that so we may forthwith know who are our friends and who are our foes."

Uncas approached Norwich's minister James Fitch and pledged two hundred Mohegan warriors, while predictably accusing the Narragansetts of sheltering Philip's women and children. Fitch replied that time would tell "who are friends and who are foes." But he wrote a letter on Uncas's behalf and sent it to Boston with six Mohegan envoys. Pequot sachem Robin Cassacinamon, John Winthrop Jr.'s old friend, offered similar assurances. Like the Mohegans, the Pequots had come to depend on Connecticut, which had granted them two thousand acres at Mashantucket. In response to Cassacinamon's petition, Connecticut had just issued a body of laws subjecting the Pequots to typical Christian regulations and requiring them to attend Christian teaching. Fitch believed they were sincere in their loyalty to the colonists but cautioned that "if they doubted of the victory, they would be in hazard of joining with the strongest."[29]

Massachusetts remained worried about the Narragansetts. Doubting the pledges of their sachems, it ordered its agent Edward Hutchinson to coerce them into signing a formal treaty. Hutchinson would be aided by Captain Samuel Mosely's soldiers, with Major Savage ready to supply more troops if necessary. Hutchinson arrived at Wickford on July 7, where a deeply apprehensive Roger Williams joined him. Williams understood the depth of Narragansett grievances. "What God can that be," they said, "that is followed by such extortioners, cheaters, and liars as his servants and worshipers?" Williams feared the Narragansetts' intentions and realized that the colonists' heavy-handed tactics made war even more likely. It would take a miracle to keep the peace.[30]

Ninigret, the Eastern Niantic and Narragansett sachem, assured Connecticut colonists he had nothing to do with Philip's war and that King Charles had won his heart when the royal commissioners ruled in his favor in 1665, but he refused requests to surrender his people's guns, which would leave them defenseless against the Mohegans. He claimed Uncas had accepted wampum and coats from Philip's messengers, while he himself "received nothing from Philip" and refused communication with him.[31] He did concede that six of his men had joined Philip. Wait Winthrop, commanding colonial forces on Connecticut's eastern frontier, warned his father that "thirty or forty of Philip's men" had sought refuge with a Narragansett sachem who in turn asked Ninigret whether to "deliver them to the English or let them go." Meanwhile, renegade Narragansetts were pillaging abandoned houses. Wait called for reinforcements, arguing that a "considerable force" would keep the Narragansetts in line.[32]

Approaching his seventieth birthday and afflicted by "troubles and pains," Governor Winthrop had no desire for war. His wife had died two years earlier, and he wanted to return to England to restore his health and manage his affairs. He had tried to resign repeatedly since the 1660s, most recently just two weeks prior.[33] He advised Wait to be gentle with Ninigret. "I think it would not be good to have them sent back to Philip," he suggested of Philip's men, "but to have them in hopes of good quarter if delivered to us." If they were treated kindly, perhaps others would surrender.[34] On the other hand, he fretted about his son marching into Narragansett country and cautioned him to be careful, meeting the sachems on "open ground to prevent that treachery and surprise which they use in dark and mountainous places." Wait should use Mohegans and Pequots as scouts to avoid ambushes, but it was also wise "to suspect them a little, although no good reasons appear for it."[35]

Ninigret agreed to meet at a "great pond" near Thomas Stanton's farm on July 8, but he feared enemy raids and warned Wait not to bring any Mohegans. Wait did recruit some of Cassacinamon's Pequots. In an ironic reversal of Mason's march thirty-eight years earlier, 120 Connecticut soldiers and 60 Pequots marched as allies past the site of the Mystic massacre and into Narragansett country. There they found Ninigret wearing the coat he had received from King Charles. Friendship with the king was all he wanted to talk about, insisting he "had engaged his heart to the English." He promised to deliver Philip's men if they came to him, but he rejected Wait's request for a hostage and protested the presence of Pequot warriors on his land.[36]

Hutchinson met the other Narragansett sachems at Wickford that same day. They responded to his show of force by bringing "all the force they were able," which the English hypocritically interpreted as a "great deal of insolency." Hutchinson presented Massachusetts's ultimatum: the Narragansetts had to provide hostages, or the colony would view them as "enemies and abettors with Philip." The sachems refused, insisting they were not subject to Massachusetts but to the king. Tempers rising, they broke off negotiations. Warriors shot several of trader Richard Smith Jr.'s hogs with arrows on their way out. Outraged, Hutchinson and Mosely prepared to attack the next morning.

Wait Winthrop arrived just in time to dissuade them: Why not seek instructions from Boston and give the sachems time to consider the consequences of their decision? He warned his father that Massachusetts and Plymouth were pursuing a reckless policy. The Narragansetts had seven hundred warriors, he estimated. "I fear [it] will be found more difficult than is imagined to hunt such wolves, unless God help by some eminent providence."[37]

Rhode Island protested the invasion of Narragansett country, suspecting that Massachusetts and Connecticut intended to claim the region by right of conquest. Hutchinson was, after all, the Atherton Company's executive and denied Rhode Island's jurisdiction there. A Rhode Island official confronted Hutchinson, declaring that the army had no right to be there because the Narragansetts "had given no cause of war" and that its presence would do "more hurt than good." Hutchinson arrested him for "mutinous" conduct and sent him to Connecticut.[38]

Governor Winthrop was alarmed for different reasons. The Narragansetts had always been friendly to the English, he reminded Major Savage, and were "very helpful" in the Pequot War. To demand hostages of a neutral nation was unprecedented, and the sachems probably could not persuade their people to yield them even if they wanted to. Nor should Massachusetts be "too strict in inquiry about persons fled to them from Philip, whether old men or soldiers, much less women and children," for it was unrealistic to expect them to deny protection to refugees, especially their own kin. Was it not wiser to seek "such engagements of amity as can be attained freely and willingly, than that the most potent of all our neighboring heathen should be made open, professed enemies because we may have suspicion of them? . . . I believe there is difficulty enough with that one enemy [Philip]," he added. Why "stir up another before an issue with the first?" "To have an open breach with Narragansett may be of worse consequence than they are aware," he told Wait. Better to keep the peace, even if it required "bearing some of their ill manners and conniving at some irregularities."[39]

When Savage led the rest of Massachusetts's army to Wickford, however, the sachems capitulated. Four Narragansetts arrived, claiming to represent the Narragansett sachems Pessicus, Ninigret, Quaiapin, Canonchet, and even the Shawomet sachem Pomham, and on July 15 they signed another humiliating treaty. It required the sachems to surrender any Wampanoags who fell into their hands, including women and children, exercise their "utmost ability" to "kill and destroy" the enemy, render satisfaction for property damages, and provide four prominent persons as hostages. It reaffirmed all previous treaties and transactions, including, presumably, the Atherton deals voided by the royal commissioners a decade earlier. The Narragansetts were made to vow in the name of the Christian God that they would "remain true friends to the English government." In exchange, the colonies promised them two coats for every live Wampanoag they delivered and one for every head.[40]

What should have given colonial authorities pause was that no sachem personally signed the treaty. Pessicus and Ninigret had already shown that they considered coerced treaties nonbinding. But the sachems had fair warning that the English would not tolerate neutrality. The colonies would hold this treaty over their heads as a sacred covenant. Any violation would be considered base treachery and evidence that they were in league with Philip.

WHILE MASSACHUSETTS'S ARMY was in Narragansett country, Wampanoag warriors unleashed terror on Plymouth's exposed towns. They burned dozens of homes, slaughtered hundreds of cattle, tore down fences, and ruined corn and hay. On July 9 warriors assaulted Middleborough, which had recently acquired so much of the sachem Tuspaquin's Nemasket land. Residents watched helplessly from a fort as most of the town was torched. "Towards night," an officer wrote, warriors "returned to the top of Tuspaquin's hill with great triumph and rejoicing."[41] Other Indians destroyed nearly all of Dartmouth, killing at least six people.[42]

The English raged at Wampanoag atrocities, real or imagined. A colonist falsely charged that the Indians raped every woman they found and tortured people by "skinning them all over alive . . . cutting off their hands and feet."[43] Boston minister Increase Mather later wrote that they scalped the dead, leaving bodies "in the open field as naked as in the day wherein they were born."[44] Few noted displays of Wampanoag compassion, as when warriors nursed and released a wounded Dartmouth woman because she had once cared for an Indian child. It was easier to ignore Wampanoag humanity.[45]

The colonial response remained futile. Plymouth struggled to send supplies for fear Wampanoags would intercept them, forcing Captain Cudworth's Plymouth troops to march back to Plymouth to procure them. When an allied Pocasset revealed the location of the Pocasset sachem Weetamoo's camp, handpicked volunteers crossed the Sakonnet River to attack it, only for Wampanoag scouts to sound the alarm, enabling the Pocassets to flee into a cedar swamp. The soldiers followed the cries of women and children until their officer lost his nerve and called a retreat. Warriors harassed them back to their sloop, wounding three or four men, though the soldiers claimed to have killed between fifteen and twenty Indians.[46]

The crisis spread to the interior, where alarmed Nipmucs abandoned several praying towns and sought refuge at the praying town of Okommakamesit. There they built a fort, from which forty praying Indians ranged as scouts, protecting towns further east.[47] Massachusetts learned that Philip had sent two English scalps to the Nipmuc towns of Quaboag and Wabquisset. The Nipmucs had rejected them, but the colony remained concerned, especially after Nipmucs led by Matoonas, the Christian constable of Pakachoog, robbed Ephraim Curtis's trading post at Quinsigamond. Massachusetts dispatched Curtis to reconfirm the Nipmucs' allegiance.[48]

When Curtis reached Okommakamesit, Indian scouts advised him against continuing, for Nipmucs of doubtful loyalty were gathering and might shoot him on sight. He decided to press on anyway, reinforced by two additional horsemen and an Okommakamesit Indian just returned from the interior. They passed through the praying towns of Hassanamesit, Manchage, Chabanakongkomun, Maanexit—all abandoned—and Wabquisset. Turning north, they traveled several miles further but found no Indians. Eventually they took a prisoner who told them where the Nipmucs were gathering. Curtis sent his Okommakamesit guide ahead to announce that "the messenger of the Massachusetts governor was a coming with peaceable words." As they rode toward the camp, he observed that the Nipmucs occupied a four-acre island, "being compassed round with a broad miry swamp on the one side and a muddy river, with meadow on both sides of it, on the other side." There was "only one place that a horse could possibly pass," and that only "with a great deal of difficulty by reason of the mire and dirt."[49]

They were intercepted by "at least forty Indians" posing menacingly, "some with their guns upon their shoulders, others with their guns in their hands, ready, cocked, and primed." Curtis tried small talk with those he recognized, but they did not respond. When he declared himself a representative of "the great sachem of the Massachusetts English," they began shouting and arguing. His Algonquian guides wanted to turn back, but Curtis refused. Only later did they tell him that the Nipmucs had been debating whether to kill him.

After they crossed the river and a boggy meadow beyond, more warriors surrounded them, pointing guns and shouting "with such noise that the air rang." His guides tried "to still the tumult," but only after "much threatening and persuasion" did the uproar subside. They took Curtis to a council of sachems, including Muttaump and Konkewasco of Quaboag, Keehood of Wabquisset, and Shoshanim of Nashaway. Keehood was a praying Indian, and most of the sachems had recently reaffirmed their allegiance to the English. Curtis asked why their men acted so rudely. They explained that they had been warned the English intended "to destroy them all." He assured them this was not true; Massachusetts simply wanted to confirm their loyalty. This appeared to satisfy them, but Curtis departed without any formal agreement. In his disconcerting report to Boston, he estimated that he had seen two hundred warriors at the Nipmuc camp.[50]

Suddenly, on July 14, Indians attacked Mendon, Massachusetts, killing three men, a woman, and two children. The news set Boston astir, for the colony had never been the target of a raid before, and Mendon was as close to Boston as to Mount Hope. Increase Mather heard about it while preaching a midweek sermon on Isaiah 42:4: "Who gave Jacob to the spoil, and Israel to the robbers? Did not the Lord, he against whom we have sinned?" Mather had warned of God's judgment, but the colony had not listened. "Had we amended our ways," he lamented, "this misery might have been prevented." He would have been even more alarmed had he known that it was a praying Nipmuc, Matoonas, who had led the attack.[51]

PLYMOUTH TROOPS PROBED Pocasset country, but finding Philip proved an impossible task, as he and his forces had taken refuge in a swamp seven miles long and knew every foot of it. Wampanoag scouts could hear the soldiers coming, observe them from the foliage, and move their people to safety. Soldiers discovered a village on July 14, Major William Bradford reported to his pastor John Cotton Jr., but most of the Indians had fled. Frustrated, the colonists burned it and killed two old men.[52]

Two days later, Captain Cudworth led 120 men into the swamp. A captive pointed them toward Weetamoo's camp, but as the soldiers approached, Indians opened fire from seemingly every direction. Soldiers panicked, confused each other for the enemy, and killed one of their own men. The Pocassets escaped, and all the soldiers could do was plunder and burn the empty town. They had killed seven Indians, but two soldiers were killed and four wounded.[53]

As the expense of operations increased beyond expectation, Plymouth's vexed governor Josiah Winslow cast about for a cost-saving strategy that would allow most soldiers to return home. Surely one hundred soldiers from each colony and allied Indians would be sufficient to harass and contain Philip in the swamp, "from whence he cannot easily make his escape." Lord willing, he told Massachussets governor John Leverett, God would "get himself a glorious name by the overthrow of his blasphemous enemies and the establishment of his poor people." Leverett, a former cavalry officer under Cromwell, agreed to the plan.[54]

Major Savage's Massachusetts army, having returned from Narragansett country, joined Plymouth forces for a final foray into the Pocasset swamp on July 19. Wampanoags fired at them, then withdrew. Colonial soldiers pursued, only to fall into a trap. Indians "betook themselves [to] trees and thickets [and] fired thick upon us," Major Bradford recalled. "Suddenly the hand of God seemed to be against us." Five men were killed and six wounded before the Wampanoags were driven off. Among the dead was John Eliot's Indian assistant Job Nesutan, who had helped translate the Bible into Massachusett. Savage pressed on until they found a village of a hundred wigwams. The only person there, an old man, claimed Weetamoo had been there that day and that Philip was half a mile away. Savage duly ordered his men to search the area, but the men were exhausted and night was coming fast. With soldiers "ready to fire upon every bush they see move," the danger of friendly fire, to say nothing of an ambush, was high. So Savage ordered a retreat. Men grumbled that half an hour more would have "utterly subdued Philip."

The officers struggled to discern "what the Lord calls us further to do," Bradford admitted. "We are waiting upon him, desiring to lay ourselves low before him who will exalt us in his due time." He thought that God was punishing them for their self-confidence. An exasperated Captain Cudworth lamented, "We shall never be able to obtain our end in this way, for they fly before us from one swamp to another." The men were ill equipped and worn out. They dreaded the swamps where, Ipswich minister William Hubbard later explained, "their eyes were muffled with the leaves, and their arms pinioned with the thick boughs of the trees, as their feet were continually shackled with the roots spreading every way in those boggy woods."[55]

As most soldiers returned home, Captain Daniel Henchman and 125 Massachusetts troops began building a fort southwest of the swamp, while one hundred Plymouth troops scattered among several outposts to respond to Wampanoag raids.[56] By all indications, the Wampanoags were "reduced to great straits," for on July 26 about a hundred men, women, and children turned themselves in at Dartmouth. "God ... help us to distinguish aright between the innocent and the guilty if they are distinguishable," Plymouth's governor Winslow wrote.

Nevertheless, Winslow acceded to Massachusetts's advice that he call an emergency meeting of the United Colonies. The war was lasting "longer than we sometimes hoped," he admitted, because the Indians fought in a "skulking, unmanly way," hiding in "the most hideous swamps they can find, wherein we cannot engage them but at extreme disadvantage." A friend informed him that many Bostonians considered Plymouth's war unjust. But while Winslow conceded that God was using the Indians to punish his people, and that Plymouth's punishment was "less, far less, than our iniquities have deserved," he insisted the war itself was just. Plymouth could "appeal to God" and prove to critics "that we stand as innocent as it is possible for any person or people to be towards their neighbor." He even claimed that the Wampanoags executed for murdering John Sassamon had thanked Plymouth for a fair trial. Philip's attacks, he believed, were treacherous and unprovoked.[57]

While nearly everyone agreed the war was God's judgment, ministers struggled to discern the cause. Barnstable pastor Thomas Walley wondered, echoing the prophet Jeremiah, "Who is the wise man, that may understand this? And who is he to whom the mouth of the LORD hath spoken, that he may declare it, for what the land perisheth and is burned up like a wilderness, that none passeth through?" There were many opinions about it. "A Quaker told me it was for my saying in my sermon they were blasphemers and idolaters, and for the persecution they have had from us," Walley told Cotton, "but I judge we may as well fear it is our suffering in the public exercise of their false worship." Had God not punished Israel for tolerating idolatry? Another cause was covetousness and "love of the world," which ministers failed to rebuke for fear of offending those who provided their livelihood. "We . . . have not been so faithful to God and them as we ought to have been," he admitted. Unfortunately, Plymouth's churches were too independent for concerted action. If the war "should continue till we could agree in our humiliations and for a reformation," he worried, "I fear it would last long and cost dear." He expected Plymouth's magistrates to guide them, but the pious founding generation had died off. Would their sons measure up to the task?[58]

Few ministers questioned the justice of the war, but John Eliot did. Aware of Connecticut governor John Winthrop Jr.'s careful diplomacy toward the Narragansetts, Eliot praised him for displaying "the very spirit of a Christian governor, striving for peace, making war the last and unavoidable remedy." Eliot awaited Plymouth's explanation of "the causes of the war." "I know them not, but betwixt God and us, I think that our sins have ripened us for so severe a scourge as the war hath, and is likely to prove. We were too ready to think that we could easily suppress that flea [Philip], but now we find that all the craft is in catching of them, and that in the meanwhile, they give us many a sore nip."

Eliot was one of the only ministers who sympathized with Indian grievances over land. Perhaps "one effect of this trouble may be to humble the English to do the Indians justice and no wrong about their lands," he hoped. "Our doing them justice about their lands may, by the blessing of God, open their hearts to the word of God, to bring them to religion, which I do earnestly desire may be another effect of this great motion." Until then, English hypocrisy made it all too easy for Indians to reject Christianity. "The Indians have very sinfully refused praying to God, but they do too much justify themselves by the example of the English. For when I have exhorted them to keep the Sabbath and pray unto God, they have answered me, 'Why do you speak so to us, why do you not speak to your own countrymen? We do but as they do.'" Colonists needed to wake up. "We had need be serious in this matter, lest God chastise us seven times more by his next visitation."[59]

⁂

WITHIN DAYS OF Massachusetts agent Ephraim Curtis's return from Nipmuc country, the colony sent him on a third visit. This time he found the Nipmuc sachems much friendlier. Muttaump of Quaboag was away, but Curtis met Keehood of Wabquisset and Shoshanim and Monoco of Nashaway. "We had pretty good quarter with them," he informed Governor Leverett. "There was no abuse offered to us. I read your honor's letter deliberately to them. They seemed to accept of it very well." They revealed that it had been Black James, constable of the new praying towns, who told them "the English would kill them all without any exception because they were not praying Indians." Clearly the zealous constable had overstepped his bounds. Curtis encouraged them to send sachems to Boston where Leverett would treat "them kindly, and well fill their bellies, and answer all their questions." They apparently agreed to do so. A dozen miles down the road, however, an Indian guide told Curtis that a man in the Nipmuc camp "had been with Philip." Was it possible the Nipmucs were playing Massachusetts? Or were they divided, some advocating peace and others war?[60]

By July 27 no sachem had arrived in Boston, and Massachusetts had learned that the Nipmuc praying Indian Matoonas had led the raid against Mendon. There was also a rumor that one hundred Narragansett warriors were with the Nipmucs. The colony decided it was time for a display of strength. Atherton executive Edward Hutchinson had imposed the treaty on the Narragansetts, so Massachusetts told him to take twenty horsemen led by Captain Thomas Wheeler and do the same with the Nipmucs. Curtis and three praying Nipmucs would go as interpreters, including the brothers Sampson and Joseph Petavit, pastors of Wabquisset and Chabanakongkomun. If the sachems refused a treaty, Hutchinson was to inform them that Massachusetts considered them "aiders and abettors" of Philip. "If you should meet with any Indians that stand in op-position to you or declare themselves to be your enemies," the colony instructed

Hutchinson, "then you are ordered to engage with them if you see reason for it and endeavor to reduce them by force of arms."[61] The Nipmucs would have to choose sides.

Hutchinson arrived at the isolated English town of Brookfield, near Quaboag, on August 1. He sent Curtis to inform the Nipmucs, gathered about ten miles northwest at a swampy area called Menameset, that he had come to negotiate a treaty. Curtis found many warriors "stout in their speeches and surly in their carriages," but three sachems agreed to meet Hutchinson on a plain three miles from Brookfield. Hutchinson's team traveled to the designated place on August 2, accompanied by three Brookfield men. No Nipmucs showed up. The Petavit brothers, who had kin at Menameset, warned that the Nipmucs could not be trusted and implored Hutchinson not to continue toward the swamp. But the Brookfield colonists assured him they had good relations with the Quaboag Nipmucs and were confident of their fidelity. Fatefully, Hutchinson decided to proceed.[62]

BACK AT POCASSET, Captain Daniel Henchman of Massachusetts had nearly finished constructing a fort of forty-nine hundred square feet with two long houses, a magazine, a smith's forge, and large flankers. By July 30 they were just finishing the southeast flanker.[63] That evening, just after 9:00, Lieutenant Norman Thomas arrived from Rehoboth with shocking news: Philip and his Wampanoags had escaped the Pocasset swamp.[64] Colonists from Taunton reported that "a considerable party of Indians, great and small," had ferried themselves across the Taunton River on rafts and were moving north. "It is not unlikely that they have conveyed away their women and children," wrote Rehoboth's pastor Noah Newman, so the men "may be at more liberty to play their parts." Lieutenant Peter Hunt urged Henchman, "Come with your soldiers to our town [Rehoboth] with all speed." Perhaps they might catch the slow-moving Wampanoags the next day.[65]

At 11:00 p.m. another letter reported that the Wampanoags were fording the Pawtucket River, the last significant barrier before Nipmuc country. Philip and Weetamoo, the Pocasset sachem, were part of the group. Their men were "much disheartened," had little ammunition, and were burdened with women and children. Newman urged "that no time be lost, if possible, to apprehend them before they swamp themselves, and while their weariness is upon them."[66] Here was the moment the English had been waiting for, as if "ordered by the divine hand." Narragansetts and Mohegans, having provided hostages to ensure their loyalty, were at hand to help. Ninigret, the Narragansett sachem, had 120 warriors in action, having already delivered a Wampanoag head to Connecticut. Uncas's son Owaneco was in Rehoboth with fifty Mohegans. Troops from Mount Hope,

Swansea, Taunton, and Rehoboth, accompanied by Mohegans and praying Indians, set out in pursuit of Philip.[67]

The next evening around sunset, scouts discovered a Wampanoag camp in rolling terrain a dozen miles north of Providence. Marching through the night, officers positioned their men in an Indian field known as Nipsachuck, about 550 yards from the camp. They had around 130 men. They faced perhaps 500 Wampanoags, but most were women and children. Just before dawn, as officers spoke in hushed tones, they were startled to see five Indians approaching from the Wampanoag camp. Soldiers fired, killing two. Then they charged.

Startled awake by gunfire, Wampanoags took their children in their arms and fled. Pursuing soldiers killed several until they found their way blocked by Philip's warriors, who had taken position on hilly ground surrounded by wet swampland. For several hours colonial forces battled to flush them out. Mohegans and praying Indians probably played the decisive role, and toward midmorning the Wampanoags withdrew. They left behind fourteen dead, whom the Mohegans stripped and scalped. Not a single English soldier was killed, and only three were wounded.

Allied Indians collected spoils: "kettles, coats, meat dressed and undressed, some ammunition as lead and slugs, and other goods" abandoned by the Wampanoags. Little did the officers know that most of the terrified Wampanoags were hiding in a swamp less than a mile away. A captive revealed that they had struck Weetamoo's camp. Philip and the Nemasket sachem, Tuspaquin, had been in another camp, as had the brother of the Sakonnet sachem Awashonks, though Awashonks herself had gone to Narragansett country. He also shared the disturbing news that Nipmuc sachems had invited Philip to take refuge near Quaboag. That was Philip's destination.

Captain Henchman arrived an hour later with seventy reinforcements, becoming the ranking officer on the field. The day was hot, the men were exhausted and low on provisions, and Lieutenant Thomas was taking the wounded to Providence, so Henchman decided to let the men rest. Not until the next day, August 2, did he pick up the Wampanoag trail. Disgusted Rehoboth soldiers complained that he had given the Wampanoags a day's head start. Even worse, on August 3 Henchman gave up the pursuit and turned west toward Wabquisset to obtain supplies from Norwich. Catching up with him that evening, Thomas marveled at the "great quantities of special good corn and beans and stately wigwams as I never saw the like," but "not one Indian to be seen." Scouts reported that the Wampanoag tracks diverged. One set led south toward Narragansett country. The other continued north toward Quaboag.[68]

MASSACHUSETTS AGENT EDWARD Hutchinson knew none of this as he and his twenty-seven men rode toward the Nipmuc camp at Menameset on August 2. If he had, he might have heeded the warnings of his Christian Nipmuc scouts. About ten miles from Brookfield, the path narrowed. Horses had to pass "in a single file, there being a very rocky hill on the right hand, and a thick swamp on the left." Dense underbrush obscured the hillside. Suddenly the quiet was shattered by a hail of bullets. Men reeled in their saddles as Indians dashed across the path behind. A colonial soldier shot an Indian, but moments later bullets slammed into his shoulder and tore off part of his thumb. The only option was to "fly for the safety of our lives," Captain Thomas Wheeler decided. They drove their horses up the "steep and rocky hill."

Wheeler realized that some men had been left behind. "I wheeled about upon the Indians," he recalled. But a bullet tore into him. Another brought down his horse, "faltering and falling." His son Thomas, though wounded in his midsection, rode over to help. A bullet ripped into his arm, but he managed to get his father on his own horse and send it galloping. He himself dashed through the smoke and underbrush, mounted a riderless horse, and rode into the woods. Eight colonists had been killed, including all three Brookfield men. Five were wounded, including Hutchinson, and a praying Indian was captured. But there was no time to tend wounds. Someone spotted Nipmucs moving through the woods, so they wheeled in the other direction. The Petavit brothers, both Nipmuc pastors, faithfully guided the survivors ten anxious and painful miles back to Brookfield. The colonists would never have made it without them.[69]

The survivors rode exhausted and bleeding into the hilltop settlement, alerting its twenty families that the Nipmucs might attack at any moment. Securing whatever supplies they could, the stunned colonists headed for the tavern house, one of Brookfield's "largest and strongest" buildings. About twenty-six able-bodied men and fifty women and children crammed inside.[70]

The nearest English town was thirty miles away. Ephraim Curtis and Henry Young attempted to ride for help, but when they saw Nipmucs looting abandoned houses, they fired two shots and beat a hasty retreat. The Nipmucs launched an immediate assault. The "barbarous heathen pressed upon us in the house with great violence, sending in their shot among us like hail through the walls and shouting as if they would have swallowed us up alive," recalled Captain Wheeler. The English returned fire through windows and doors. Henry Young was seriously wounded. A young man named Prichard, whose father had died in the ambush, foolishly attempted to retrieve items from his father's home and was captured. Nipmucs cut off his head and kicked it around in full view of the tavern. Then they mounted it on a pole at his father's door, a grisly warning to the beleaguered colonists.

The colonists were alone. No one knew of their plight. Wheeler admitted that "all hope that we should be saved was in the eye of reason taken away, and we were in continual expectation of death."

That night the Nipmucs attacked again, roaring "like so many wild bulls" and riddling the house with shot. Around 3:00 a.m., with the moon high in the night sky, warriors piled hay, wood, and flammable materials by a corner of the tavern. To the horror of the English, they lit the pile on fire before withdrawing. A soldier named Simon Davis called for cover while he and some men ventured outside to extinguish it. "God is with us and fights for us," he exhorted, "and will deliver us out of the hands of these heathen." Nipmucs heard him. "Now see how your God delivers you!" they shouted. They opened fire, wounding two of Davis's men, but the colonists succeeded in dousing the flames. With ammunition running low, Captain Wheeler asked Ephraim Curtis to make another attempt for help. Curtis slipped outside, only to find "so many Indians everywhere thereabouts that he could not pass without apparent hazard of life." Toward morning he made a third attempt. Crawling on his hands and knees, he eluded Nipmuc sentries, and by morning he was gone. But even if he made it, would help come in time?

Nipmucs "continued shooting and shouting" all the next day. Although some were praying Indians, they mocked the colonists' faith, "blaspheming the name of the Lord and reproaching us, his afflicted servants, scoffing at our prayers as they were sending in their shot," Wheeler recalled. Some gathered in the meeting house, about a hundred yards from the tavern. "Come and pray and sing psalms," they taunted. Then colonists heard what Wheeler called a "hideous noise somewhat resembling singing." They retaliated by firing a volley at the meeting house.

More Indians arrived that night until colonists imagined there were as many as five hundred. Suddenly the tavern was pelted with flaming arrows. Nipmucs had fastened brimstone wrapped in rags to their arrows, lit them on fire, and were shooting them onto the roof. Colonists cut holes to clear away the burning projectiles. Next, Nipmucs carried flax and hay to the walls of the tavern and set it on fire. To prevent soldiers from extinguishing it, warriors hid outside the door. With growing desperation, colonists broke down an outer wall to smother the flames. Nipmucs fired a "ball of wild fire" into the attic, igniting a heap of flax. A soldier doused the flames. But the colonists were running out of water, either to drink or to put out fires. Thomas Wilson, from Brookfield, volunteered to fetch more, but as he stepped outside, bullets slammed into his upper jaw and neck. He cried out, and the Nipmucs "rejoiced and triumphed."[71]

Thirty miles away, in Springfield, local Indians informed magistrate John Pynchon that Nipmucs had attacked Brookfield. A colonist rode through the night to confirm and observed several burned-out buildings before returning.

"How soon their Indians may be upon this town," Pynchon worried, "we know not." Connecticut dispatched forty soldiers, but it would be noon on August 6 before they reached Springfield, let alone Brookfield. "The Lord grant they may be able to hold out till our soldiers come to their relief," Pynchon prayed.[72]

Wednesday, August 4, was the third day of the siege. The Nipmucs prepared their next attack, filling a cart with "flax, hay and candlewood and other combustible material." They spliced poles together and attached wheels, forming movable tracks seventy-five yards long. Using this ingenious device, they could roll barrels of kindling right up to the tavern. That evening, they moved their equipment toward the tavern and commenced setting fires. What happened next would always be remembered by Puritans as divine intervention. It began to rain. Rain quenched the flames and drenched the tavern. It soaked the hay, flax, and kindling. It provided precious drinking water. It bought precious time.

About an hour after sunset, dark forms approached. Men prepared to fire, only to hear English voices. Captain Wheeler ordered a trumpet call to prevent friendly fire, and Massachusetts soldiers dashed toward the tavern. The surprised Nipmucs "spared not their shot, but poured it out on them," wounding two, but all made it inside. For the exhausted men, women, and children who had endured more than forty-eight harrowing hours, it was a sight they would never forget. The esteemed Major Simon Willard had come to their relief with forty-six English soldiers and five praying Indians. Willard explained that colonists traveling the bay path to Connecticut had seen Indians killing cattle and burning houses on the Brookfield hill. They had hastened back to Marlborough, which in turn alerted Willard, whose Massachusetts company was in the area.

The Nipmucs burned the meeting house, but as night wore on it became eerily quiet. When the sun rose, colonists cautiously ventured outside. They found their homes in ashes, property destroyed, and cattle gone, but the Nipmucs had departed, and they had survived. Not all would recover; Edward Hutchinson died of his wounds on August 19. But it could have been much worse. "Had not the Lord been on our side when these cruel heathens rose up against us," Wheeler marveled, "they had then swallowed us up quick."[73]

Philip's haggard Wampanoag band, reduced to fewer than fifty warriors (plus women and children), arrived at nearby Quaboag that day. The following day he reached the main Nipmuc camp, where he gave Muttaump, Monoco, and another sachem "about a peck of unstrung wampum." He confessed that had the English pressed their offensive in Pocasset country "one or two days more," or had they "pursued him closely" as he moved northward, "he must needs have been taken."[74]

A campaign Plymouth's governor Winslow believed would be quick, punitive, and decisive had escalated into the sort of regional war colonists had dreaded for decades. While Massachusetts's heavy-handed efforts to prevent the war from spreading had succeeded with the Narragansetts, such tactics backfired disastrously with the Nipmucs. Still, Puritan leaders never wavered in believing that their policies were justified. The Indians were treacherous and malicious, and their rebellion had to be crushed.

15

God Does Not Go Forth
with Our Armies

August 1675 to September 1675

COLONISTS LAMENTED THE incompetence that had enabled Philip and his Wampanoags to escape their clutches and join forces with the Nipmucs. Now "the war is likely to continue with the Nipmuc and Narragansett as [well as] the rest who are fled to them," Lieutenant Norman Thomas lamented. "But what shall I say? However was the neglect of man, the Lord is to be looked at in the matter."[1] Some took solace from Brookfield's deliverance, which suggested that God remained compassionate toward his people. Leading a service of humiliation in Boston on August 12, Increase Mather observed that no established church had yet been destroyed. He prayed that God would preserve Boston and the troops, "causing his enemies to fall before him," and that God would use "these awful dispensations of his holy providences" to sanctify his people.[2] But as disaster piled on disaster, Puritans worried that God had abandoned them and was unleashing the Indians against them. They believed that without God on their side, they could not win.

Many severely denounced the Nipmucs' treachery. "The Lord avenge the blood that hath been shed by these heathen who hate us without a cause," cursed Captain Thomas Wheeler, whose unit had been ambushed north of Brookfield. Although he and his men had been saved by Nipmuc pastors, the Petavit brothers, he coldly ignored them in his account.[3] The minister William Hubbard later condemned the "horrible perfidiousness and treacherous dealing of these Nipmuc Indians, who of all others had the least reason as to any pretense of injury, yet did most deceitfully and barbarously join with Philip and his Indians, after they had been several times sent unto by the governor and . . . faithfully promised not to meddle in the quarrel."[4]

Few had any sympathy for Philip. "The English took not a foot of land from the Indians, but bought all, and although they bought for an inconsiderable value, yet they did buy it," reasoned merchant Nathaniel Saltonstall. Philip simply resented that by hard work and God's blessing they had made the wilderness so fruitful.[5] The English "by their great industry have of a howling wilderness improved those lands into cornfields, orchards, enclosed pastures, and towns inhabited, which hath considerably advanced the value," a colonist agreed, and Philip regretted losing them.[6]

For Philip, successful flight and Nipmuc intervention offered a new lease on life. The region north of Quaboag contained virtually endless tracks of forest crisscrossed by streams and rivers, hills and mountains. Here, hidden from colonial forces, he could build up his strength, expand his alliance, and extend the war indefinitely. According to one report, he cut his famous wampum coat in pieces and distributed it among the sachems "to the eastward and southward, and all round about."[7]

Some of the Nipmuc sachems who welcomed him were praying Indians who had pledged their loyalty to Massachusetts a few weeks earlier. Why had they suddenly shifted course? One reason was that the colonies' aggressive military expeditions lent credibility to the praying Indian Black James's threats and Philip's purported claim "that the English had a design to cut off all the Indians round about them, and that if they did not join together, they should lose their lives and lands." Edward Hutchinson's expedition had forced them to choose sides, and they had chosen Philip.[8]

But many young Nipmucs were itching for war even before Hutchinson's expedition. Like Philip, their grievances ran deep. Some resented the establishment of praying towns, which divided their people, appropriated their land exclusively for praying Indians, and subjected their sachems to colonial jurisdiction. It is telling that Muttaump, whose Quaboag people never accepted praying-town status, became the militants' leading sachem. Some—such as the praying Indian Matoonas, whose son had been executed for murder—were embittered by punishments handed down by colonial courts. Others, like the Nashaways, were devastated by the decline of the fur trade and owed huge sums to English traders. Their sachem, Shoshanim, had long opposed the English. And while the Nipmucs felt far less pressure to sell land than did the Wampanoags, recent sales suggested such pressure was coming.[9]

Colonists wondered whether any Indians could be trusted. What town would be next to suffer Brookfield's fate? As the dominant trader and landowner in the upper Connecticut Valley, Massachusetts magistrate John Pynchon was the primary broker with the valley Indians, including the Agawams near Springfield and the Norwottucks, Pocumtucks, and Sokokis upriver, each a community of several hundred people. From them he had purchased most of the land that became Northampton, Hadley, and Hatfield, near Norwottuck; Deerfield, at abandoned Pocumtuck; and a new settlement at recently abandoned Squakeag. He believed they could be trusted, and as Massachusetts's regional commander, he recruited them for military service.

This alarmed many colonists. When Massachusetts agent Ephraim Curtis accused a Norwottuck of having fought with the Nipmucs, Pynchon provoked fury by releasing the suspect because Indians Pynchon trusted vouched for him. "I wonder at such a spirit in people," Pynchon marveled. On the other hand, Pynchon deferred to local Indians who accused an Algonquian of fighting for Philip because he was wearing an English coat, linsey-woolsey stockings, tightly woven breeches, and hogskin moccasins with hog hair still on them, which they claimed he plundered from the colonial town of Swansea. "It being a most clear and evident case," Pynchon reported, "all the Indians also desiring he might be killed, I bid two of our men take him out and shoot him."[10]

Connecticut agreed that their security depended on their Indian allies and ordered that those serving be "well provided for, and that they receive no affront from any English." It sent Uncas's son Joshua with thirty Mohegans to join colonial forces at Brookfield.[11] Connecticut's deputy governor William Leete advocated a decisive blow to persuade neutral Indians to cast their lot with the English, but this was easier said than done.[12] When colonial forces ventured north from Brookfield, they accomplished little more than burning dozens of empty wigwams and killing a few Indians. Their failures triggered further suspicion of allied Indians. Connecticut's Captain Thomas Watts charged that Indians accompanying his troops were "fearful or false or both." The Mohegans, who had fought the valley Indians during the Pocumtuck War, claimed they never captured anyone because the valley Indians "would always give some shout when they came near the enemy." "The English were blind if they could not see that our Indians made fools of them," declared Joshua.[13]

Northampton's thirty-one-year-old pastor, Solomon Stoddard—who would be the grandfather of Jonathan Edwards, America's greatest colonial theologian—was convinced that the Norwottucks could not be trusted. Many had gone to Quaboag that summer, he warned, deserting their corn, packing up their wigwams, and removing property they stored in English towns. An Indian woman reported "with great earnestness" that two of Philip's men were at Norwottuck, and a Frenchman passing through claimed they were soliciting the Norwottucks to fight. Then, when word of Hutchinson's ambush reached the Norwottuck fort, colonists heard them erupt with eleven joyful shouts, one for each slain colonist. After that, Stoddard claimed, Norwottucks talked about killing colonists, taking their homes, and making them servants, while objecting to fighting their Nipmuc "mothers and brothers and cousins." They predicted that in battle allied Indians would stab the English in the back. Some were accused of shooting at colonists.

Captain Thomas Lathrop of Massachusetts proposed disarming the Norwottucks, since he was authorized "to disarm all the Indians that were not manifest friends to the English." Other officers and local leaders—including Stoddard, but not Pynchon—agreed. While he shared their concerns, Pynchon feared an attempt to disarm the Norwottucks would drive them into the arms of the enemy. Connecticut also warned that forced disarmament might back-fire. But Lathrop was already acting. On August 24, 1675, he met a Norwottuck sachem and demanded that his people surrender their weapons. The sachem agreed to try to persuade them. When colonists followed up that day, how-ever, the Norwottucks said they would answer in the morning. When a colonist inquired that evening, they told him to "kiss."[14]

Lathrop decided to march against the Norwottuck fort. When scouts approached it that night, however, they found it abandoned, save for the dead body of the Norwottucks' elderly chief sachem Sopus, who had advocated submission to the English. Lathrop and one hundred men followed Norwottuck tracks north toward Pocumtuck, catching up ten miles north of Hatfield, near Sugarloaf Mountain. (The Indians called it the Great Beaver because, according to myth, it was the remains of a giant beaver killed by the spirit Hobbomock for greedily consuming the people's resources.) The des-perate Norwottucks dropped their belongings and opened fire, taking cover in a nearby swamp. Lathrop counterattacked, but his tactics proved futile. According to Stoddard, "After a while our men, after the Indian manner, got behind trees and watched their opportunities to make shots at them." After a three-hour fight, the Indians slipped away. Lathrop suffered nearly thirty casualties, nine of whom were dead or dying. A captive later claimed that twenty-six Indians were killed.[15]

With the Norwottucks and apparently Pocumtucks now hostile, Stoddard begged Connecticut governor John Winthrop Jr. for help: "We send in all haste to you. If you can forthwith send us some supplies of men it may save the lives of many."[16] He defended their decision to disarm the Norwottucks, declaring a need for "utmost caution in our dealing with such persons in whom is no faith."[17] But Connecticut blamed Captain Lathrop for provoking the Norwottucks. It urged Springfield not to make the same mistake with the Agawams. (Instead, it persuaded the Agawams to provide hostages.)[18] Pynchon was equally frustrated but came to believe Lathrop was right. "The truth is, when I recollect things, I can't but conclude that this was a contrived business of the Indians. For how suddenly they all removed and secured their women is beyond imagination, had it not been before afoot."[19]

The reality was that the Norwottucks and Pocumtucks were traditional Nipmuc allies and Mohegan foes and shared many Wampanoag grievances. Many had accumulated substantial debts to Pynchon since the collapse of the fur trade and had sold nearly all their best farmland. The Pocumtucks were es-pecially distressed, for after the Mohawks destroyed their town, Massachusetts awarded it to Dedham as compensation for the land Dedham had lost to Natick. Pynchon then purchased it from Indians whose authority to sell was doubtful, enabling the establishment of Deerfield in 1670.[20]

Even so, the Norwottucks had been divided, and it was Captain Lathrop's bull-headed attempt to disarm them that united them against the English. Algonquians were learning that they either had to submit or fight.

SOME INDIANS TRIED to avoid the conflict by giving themselves up. About 120 Nipmucs surrendered to Uncas in August. Soon after, Wabquissets brought in 111 Wampanoags, whom Connecticut ordered sent to Boston.[21] Two Christian Indians petitioned Massachusetts on behalf of the Wabquissets, who were praying Indians, claiming they had been at Quaboag only because hostile Nipmucs "threatened to kill them" if they submitted to the English. The wife of the Wabquisset sachem Keehood was a "wise and godly woman," they claimed, and Keehood's sons were promising young men, one of whom read the Bible ably. The petitioners urged Massachusetts to receive the Wabquissets in a "Christian manner" and spare their cornfields, for why "famish those that are your friends and submit themselves to you and to the Lord?" They also petitioned that three Wampanoag women not be exported as slaves, because "they desire to pray to God."[22]

Plymouth's war council met on August 4 to decide the fate of 112 Wampanoags taken at Dartmouth, most of them women and children. Plymouth officer Benjamin Church later claimed that most had surrendered after they were promised good terms thanks to the efforts of a friendly Indian, but Plymouth governor Josiah Winslow was informed they came in "without any assurance or invitation from us." After questioning them, the council concluded that several had participated in raids and that the rest had either supported them or violated their covenant by failing to report Philip's conspiracy. After "serious and deliberate consideration," it sentenced most to be sold abroad. A dozen or so were "otherwise disposed of" on "special consideration." A few weeks later, fifty-seven more Wampanoags who had surrendered were condemned to slavery by Plymouth.[23] Another eighty brought in by Captain Samuel Mosely were sold in Boston.[24]

John Eliot, the missionary, was horrified. He could hardly imagine a policy more likely to encourage Native hostility than the "terror of selling away such Indians unto the [Caribbean] islands for perpetual slaves," he wrote in a petition to the Massachusetts government. It was certain to prolong the war, leading to unimaginable "evil consequences." Even worse, it contradicted the gospel. "Christ hath said, blessed are the merciful, for they shall obtain mercy," he reminded them, yet this fate was "worse than death," since those sold would never hear the gospel. Christ's goal was to evangelize the heathen, not destroy them, turning "the kingdoms of this world" into "the kingdoms of the Lord and of his Christ."

"When we came [to America]," he continued, "we declared to the world . . . that the endeavor of the Indians' conversion, not their extirpation, was one great end of our enterprise." God had blessed this mission richly. True, many Indians rejected the gospel and were now at war. Psalm 2 prophesied that the nations would thus rage and plot against the Lord. But Psalm 2 also promised them the opportunity to flee to Christ for refuge. "My humble request is that you would follow Christ's design in this matter, to promote the free passage of religion among them and not to destroy them," Eliot implored. To sell them abroad was to condemn them to "perpetual darkness, to the eternal ruin of their souls." How could Christians cast away "souls for whom Christ hath . . . provided an offer of the gospel? To sell souls for money seemeth to me a dangerous merchandize." Even Old Testament law prohibited sending a slave back to a heathen master. The English condemned the Spanish for "destroying men and depopulating the land," yet they were in danger of doing the same thing, and Eliot believed he knew why: they desired the Indians' land. "The country is large enough," he pleaded. "Here is land enough for them and us too."[25]

But his petition made little difference. Although some captives were sold locally, in September the *Sampson* set sail from Boston with 178 captives destined for sale in Spain. They would not be the last.[26]

CONNECTICUT, LIKE PLYMOUTH and Massachusetts, viewed the war as a religious struggle against the heathen, while at the same time acknowledging that God was using the heathen to judge his people for their sins. It called on counties to take turns observing weekly fast days, praying that God would reveal the sin "that troubles Israel and effectually purge it out, that he might yet go forth with our armies and his own right hand may make peace in the land, guiding, blessing, and saving his poor people." It ordered its military commander, fifty-one-year-old magistrate Major Robert Treat, to ensure that his soldiers conducted themselves "before the heathen" in accord with the gospel so that God's name would not be "dishonored by ourselves while we are endeavoring to vindicate the same against the heathen's wickedness and blasphemies."

When Indians shot at a colonist near Hartford, Connecticut authorized colonists to apprehend armed Indians traveling without an escort, shooting them if they failed to show themselves friendly. But it forbade towns to disarm or provoke local Indians. Instead, they should protect them.[27]

Upriver, all was chaos. On September 1 Algonquians descended on Deerfield, where Pocumtuck used to be, a dozen miles upriver from Hatfield. While its 125 inhabitants huddled in garrison houses, Indian warriors killed a soldier and burned most of the houses, barns, corn, and hay. The following day, Algonquians attacked the nascent English settlement at Squakeag, killing at least eight colonists. Captain Richard Beers of Massachusetts, a Pequot War veteran, set out with thirty-six men bearing supplies for Squakeag's relief. But on September 4 hundreds of warriors ambushed Beers's force about three miles from Squakeag. Nearly twenty English soldiers were killed, including Beers. One, who was captured, watched Algonquian warriors get drunk that evening while they mourned the loss of a leader (among twenty-five Indians allegedly killed). A praying Indian later helped the soldier escape.[28] "It's sad news," wrote lay missionary Thomas Mayhew of Beers's death. "He was one I loved much. He is with God, who I hope will arise in the behalf of those that call upon him for aid, to confound their enemies."[29]

Major Treat, fresh from Connecticut, marched for Squakeag with one hundred men the following morning. Soldiers grew solemn as they passed the scene of Beers's ambush. A soldier's body was hanging from a tree by a chain hooked through his lower jaw. Poles mounted with dismembered heads lined the road. Treat ordered them to press on. They drove a band of Indians away from Squakeag and were relieved to find the remaining settlers alive. They left the dead unburied, abandoned cattle and property, and led them south, ever fearful of ambush.[30]

The string of disasters left Puritans in shock. "You cannot be enough sensible how these Indians here do rage," wrote a despairing John Pynchon, now a major in command of Massachusetts forces in the upper Connecticut Valley, to Massachusetts governor John Leverett. "Is the Lord about to ruin us and leave us to be destroyed?" Men discussed evacuating more towns. "The little success of our forces speaks [to the fact that] we are not yet truly humbled," Pynchon concluded. Overwhelmed by responsibility, he begged to be relieved of command.[31] "If the Lord give not some sudden check to these Indians," pastor Solomon Stoddard fretted, "it is to be feared that most of the Indians in the country will rise [against us]."[32]

THE NIPMUC ATTACKS ON Brookfield and Mendon provoked an equally heavy-handed reaction toward Indians—including praying Indians—in eastern Massachusetts. Many colonists doubted that the praying Indians were real Christians anyway. In mid-August, Massachusetts's Major General Daniel Denison ordered Major Richard Waldron and Captain Mosely to march to Pawtucket, "supposed to be the great rendezvous of the enemy," and demand that the Pennacooks surrender their guns or provide hostages to ensure their loyalty. If they refused, the troops were to "pursue, kill, and destroy them."[33]

The Pennacook sachem Wannalancet was a praying Indian. His late father, Passaconaway, had warned him to "never engage with any other Indians in a war against [the English]," for "though you may do them much mischief, yet assuredly you will all be destroyed." Wannalancet had no desire to fight the English, but neither did he trust them, so as Mosely's company approached, he prudently withdrew his people into a swamp. Mosely commenced burning wigwams and destroying stores of dried fish. Outraged warriors implored Wannalancet for permission to resist, but he refused to be provoked.[34]

Many Christian Indians were eager to prove their loyalty. Scouts from the praying town of Okommakamesit invited Massachusetts troops to join them patrolling the woods, providing what Gookin called "a living wall to guard the English frontiers."[35] But when Sudbury colonists threatened some Natick scouts, the scouts began to worry that colonists would hold them responsible for enemy raids. "We humbly request that if such a thing should be done by them, that you would not suffer a jealousy to rise in your hearts against us," they implored Massachusetts's council.[36]

John Eliot's former assistant James Printer and other praying Indians captured a local Indian named Andrew, as well as Andrew's son-in-law. They accused them of participating in Hutchinson's ambush and turned them over to Mosely, who separated them for questioning. Andrew, tied to a tree, insisted he was a praying Indian who had simply been out hunting but asserted that his son-in-law had fought in the ambush. Unsatisfied, Mosely played a trick. A soldier fired a gun, and Andrew was led away. Then they brought his son-in-law to the tree. They had shot Andrew, they lied, and he would share the same fate if he did not confess everything he knew. Terrified, he blamed Andrew for everything, only to learn that Andrew was still alive. Eventually both confessed to fighting Hutchinson, even claiming that the son-in-law actually shot him. Mosely had them executed.[37]

Praying Indians' fears became reality when Algonquian warriors attacked Lancaster on August 22, killing seven colonists, including a four-year-old girl, an infant, and their parents. Sure enough, colonists blamed praying Indians. "The animosity and rage of the common people increased" to the point that "the very name of a praying Indian was spoken against," Gookin recalled. Many pressured the government to round them up. The town of Marlborough had long resented Okommakamesit for occupying land it coveted, and its militia marched to the Indians' fort and demanded their guns and ammunition. The Indians hastily complied, but those recruited by Massachusetts secretly withheld their guns.

On August 30 Massachusetts ordered that since the heathen waged war "by stealth and skulking in small parties," contrary to the "practice of civil nations," Indians could no longer travel without an English escort. Furthermore, for the "security of the English and Indians in amity with us," praying Indians would be resettled in five praying towns under colonial supervisors: Natick, Punkapoag, Nashobah, Wamesit, and Hassanamesit. Colonists who encountered them more than a mile from these towns were authorized to kill them unless they surrendered on demand. They would hardly be able to travel for trade or work, let alone hunt or fish. Gookin claimed many magistrates felt pressured to enact this policy "against their own reason and inclination," if only for praying Indians' safety. But some shared the prevailing paranoia. The Okommakamesits would be moved to Hassanamesit, gratifying Marlborough. Envoys would seek to persuade Wannalancet to settle his Pennacooks at Wamesit.[38]

That same day, Mosely apprehended an Okommakamesit named David, the recently executed Andrew's brother, who was accused of shooting at a colonist. Mosely tied David to a tree and threatened to shoot him unless he revealed what he knew. Terrified, David accused eleven Okommakamesits, including the scouts who had captured his brother, of attacking Lancaster. "I did not see it done, neither was I there, but I heard some of them speak so," he said. That was enough for Mosely. He and his men ransacked Okommakamesit, discovering more guns and ammunition. Then he marched the eleven men David had accused, plus two from Natick, "pinioned and fastened with lines from neck to neck," to Boston. Among them were James Printer and Old Jethro, the teacher Peter Jethro's father.[39]

Their arrival stirred Boston into an uproar. Colonists expected them to be executed or sold into slavery and were agitated when the council ordered a trial. Daniel Gookin and John Eliot rose to the Indians' defense. Although people could accept this from Eliot, a missionary, it was another matter for Gookin, a vocal magistrate. During one meeting, a colonist declared Gookin insolent and complained that the council let him talk so much. Gookin's fellow magistrate, the merchant James Oliver, declared that Gookin "ought rather to be confined among his Indians than to sit on the bench. His taking the Indians' part so much hath made him a byword among both men and boys."[40]

"I have been lately abroad in the country's service and have ventured my life for them and escaped very narrowly," a veteran of Beers's ambush vented, "but if they clear those Indians they shall hang me up by the neck before I ever serve them again."[41] Captain Mosely publicly called for the Indians to be hanged (eliciting a friendly rebuke from Governor Leverett).[42] When Captain Daniel Henchman was assigned command of a company, the men refused to serve under him because he was friendly to praying Indians. They requested Oliver instead.

Passions were further inflamed when the two Natick prisoners were quietly released. Around 9:00 p.m., thirty or forty men, including prominent citizens, marched to Oliver's house and summoned him to lead them to the jail to lynch the other Indians before they too were released. Oliver shared their concerns, but he was not in favor of mob rule. He "took his cane and cudgeled them stoutly" before alerting the justice of the peace. For all their prejudices, Puritan leaders were committed to law and order and determined that Indians should receive a fair trial.[43]

"The clamors and animosity among the common people increased daily, not only against these Indians, but against all such English as were judged to be charitable to them," Gookin recalled. People called him and Eliot traitors, as if they supported the enemy. Men known for their piety denounced anyone who described any Indians as genuine Christians. Gookin informed the council that he "was afraid to go along the streets."

"You may thank yourself," a magistrate retorted. But Gookin refused to be intimidated. "I cannot join with the multitude that would cast them all into the same lump with the profane and brutish heathen, who are as great enemies to our Christian Indians as they are to the English," he later declared. Some colonists supported him. They prayed fervently that the judges and jurors would pursue justice and avoid "bringing innocent blood upon the land."[44]

Some recognized that praying Indians were crucial to their security. The English town of Mendon, which had been attacked in July, petitioned that the Indians relocated to Hassanamesit be permitted to settle and build a fort at Mendon, "both for the security of the English and Indians." On September 17 the council authorized the Indians to do so after they harvested their corn, and to continue ranging the woods for the enemy, accompanied by English soldiers. It also ordered Marlborough to return the arms and ammunition seized from Okommakamesit.[45]

A week later, Plymouth's Captain John Gorham and Massachusetts's Lieutenant Phineas Upham were dispatched to Nipmuc country with eighty-eight soldiers to destroy enemy cornfields and prevent the enemy from gathering food for the winter. They were ordered to spare the praying towns of Hassanamesit, Chabanakongkomun, and Manchage. They marched to Hassanamesit to find a guide, but "the Indians were all gone." The next day they reached Pakachoog, a praying town whose leaders, Sagamore John and Matoonas, had joined the enemy. It too was abandoned, but they found "a field of good corn, and well fenced." They left it intact, hoping local colonists might harvest it. From there they moved to Manchage and Chabanakongkomun, also unoccupied. Violating their orders, they torched corn, wigwams, and whatever else they found.

In his report, Lieutenant Upham suggested that the people of Hassanamesit had joined the enemy. But they had done no such thing, nor had they abandoned their town. Gookin later complained that the soldiers destroyed loyal praying towns while sparing hostile ones like Quaboag. The enemy would have plenty of corn that winter, while loyal Indians were doomed to famine.[46]

The trial of James Printer and his fellow praying Indians taken from Okommakamesit commenced on September 21. But the case against them suffered a severe blow when David, the key witness, admitted that he had falsely accused them to save his life. (They *were* the men who captured his brother.) Colonists produced evidence superficially linking the accused with the attack on Lancaster, but in each case the defense offered plausible explanations. Moreover, many witnesses testified that on the Sunday of the attack, the accused were attending worship services in Okommakamesit. The charges collapsed when two Indians testified that Monoco of Nashaway led the attack on Lancaster. While some Nashaways were Christians, their sachem Shoshanim opposed Christianity.[47]

The court acquitted all but three Indians, though it sentenced Old Jethro to thirty lashes for "abusive speeches." Two, including David, were condemned to be sold abroad. The third was convicted of murder.[48] According to the merchant Nathaniel Saltonstall, he was "led by a rope about his neck to the gallows. When he came there, the executioners . . . flung one end over the post, and so hoisted him up like a dog, three or four times, he being yet half alive and half dead," until a sympathetic Indian stabbed him in the heart. "Thus with the dog-like death . . . of one poor heathen was the peoples' rage laid in some measure," Saltonstall wrote, ignoring the fact that the executed man was a Christian.[49]

The acquittals demonstrated the Puritan magistrates' commitment to justice for Indians but left many colonists outraged. One declared, "All the Indians . . . pretend favor to the English. However, we trust them not, as knowing they wait a fit occasion against us." It was blatant racism, but Gookin believed the ultimate cause was "the malice of Satan against Christ's work among those Indians." The devil was using the war to poison colonists' minds so they would treat Indians with contempt and alienate them from Christianity. Hostile Indians shrewdly spread misinformation portraying praying Indians as treacherous in hopes that the English would retaliate.[50]

THE UNITED COLONIES COMMISSIONERS, including Governors Winslow and Winthrop, assembled in Boston in September. Plymouth submitted a lengthy justification for going to war against Philip, and on September 9 the commissioners voted unanimously that the war was "defensive" and therefore "just and necessary." They called the colonies to provide troops proportional to their population: Massachusetts 527, Connecticut 315, and Plymouth 158.[51]

Then they turned their attention to a growing object of English fears: the powerful Narragansetts, longtime allies of the Norwottucks and Pocumtucks and enemies of Uncas and his Mohegans. The Narragansett sachem Pessicus's warriors had delivered seven Wampanoag heads to trader Richard Smith Jr. at Wickford in August, but they were also sheltering many Wampanoag refugees in violation of the July treaty, including Awashonks and her Sakonnets (at Rhode Island's encouragement) and Weetamoo with some hundred Pocassets.

Weetamoo was "kind" to Pessicus, so he asked Connecticut to show her favor, hoping the colonies would relax the stipulations of the treaty.[52] Connecticut replied graciously, praising the Narragansetts' "good endeavors and actions against the enemy" and indicating that Pessicus's service, friendship, and concern for his Wampanoag kin would receive the highest consideration.[53] But then, in a night raid against the Wabquissets, Narragansetts seized the Wampanoag captives Connecticut had ordered sent to Boston. They killed the men, delivering seven additional heads to Smith, but kept the women and children to spare them from slavery.[54]

Narragansett representatives arrived to confer with the commissioners, but so did Uncas's son Owaneco, who protested the Narragansett raid on Wabquisset. It did not help when one of the Narragansett representatives was arrested on his way home for having killed a colonist while fighting with Philip. He was tried and executed in violation of his diplomatic immunity.[55]

Samuel Gorton of Warwick, Rhode Island, who had long cooperated with the Narragansetts, warned Connecticut's governor Winthrop that colonists near Narragansett country were succumbing to panic. "Many people in these parts are like souls distracted, running hither and thither for shelter." Families were packing up their livelihood and abandoning their homes. "People ... give credit to every flying and false report, and not only so, but they will report it again." Many claimed that all Indians were conspiring to wipe out the English, "as though God brought his people hither to destroy them by delivering them into the hands of such barbarians, a people of the curse." Gorton thought the English had been naïve, even arrogant, to assume that they could make the Narragansetts into Christians. He did not consider most colonists true Christians. But that did not mean the Narragansetts were hostile. After all, they had willingly submitted to the crown. Gorton cautioned that if the colonies treated them belligerently, however, the Narragansetts would have no choice but to take up arms in self-defense.

The real cause of the crisis, Gorton argued, was colonial desire for Narragansett land, "a great and universal grudge among the Indians." They knew the king had forbidden colonists to seize land without the sachems' consent, but colonists did so anyway, perhaps paying a trivial sum to "some base inferior fellow." This "makes the sachems afraid, lest by this means in short time they shall be spewed out of the country for want of land to reside upon," Gorton wrote.[56]

Richard Smith Jr., writing from Wickford, in Narragansett country, urged caution for different reasons. He had his doubts about the Narragansetts, but he recognized that, like all Algonquian groups, they were divided. Their leading sachems Pessicus and Ninigret were inclined to peace, while lesser men recklessly advocated war and killed English cattle. A "great body" of Narragansetts was gathering, and it was essential not to provoke them. Nor did he think they would give up the "many inland Indians" who had taken refuge with them, especially the Wampanoags. Nevertheless, Pessicus had delivered fourteen scalps and Ninigret two. They believed they had proven their fidelity and requested the return of their hostages and permission to keep their refugees.[57]

Connecticut's deputy governor William Leete urged the colonies to cultivate the Narragansetts as allies by persuading them that it was in their best interests for the English to win the war. Pressuring them to surrender refugees would do precisely the opposite. The sachems had explained their policy toward captives in a way that made sense, Leete argued. They distinguished warriors captured in war from those who surrendered in hope of mercy. Many of the latter were their kin, and to yield these to the English "for slaughter or foreign captivity doth run hard against the grain of nature." If the sachems turned over enemy warriors, surely the colonies could permit them to redeem the others. Why alienate the Narragansetts and expand the war when the English could not defeat the enemies they already had? English soldiers could not match the enemy's tactics, but Narragansetts could, and Leete proposed offering them an incentive: for every one of Philip's "Philistines" they took, award them captives and plunder, "life for life." English soldiers could assume a secondary role, saving much "blood and treasure."[58]

But before Leete's advice reached them, the commissioners asked Smith to persuade the sachems to surrender their captives. Smith met Pessicus, Ninigret, Quaiapin, Canonchet, and Quinnapin at Wickford around September 22. "We found a great strangeness in the spirits of the sachems here," a colonist reported, "as I never observed... before." Only Ninigret proved fully cooperative, offering to surrender his Wampanoags and to encourage his fellow sachems to do the same, if the English promised to treat them fairly and return them in the future. It helped that he trusted Governor Winthrop as "a man of peace and wisdom" and despised Philip. He refused to risk his people's well-being "for a company of bloody persons that have not only killed the English, but killed his people likewise."[59]

The young sachem Canonchet and Corman, Ninigret's counselor, traveled to Boston to confirm the July treaty. Soldiers led by Captain James Oliver escorted them into the city, but they encountered bitter hostility on Boston's streets. A colonist in his thirties walked up to the elderly Corman, slammed him with his elbow and threw him violently to the ground "so his back and head came first to the ground, his heels flying up." The court fined the assailant fifty shillings, ten of which went to Corman. There is no record of what Canonchet and Corman agreed to, and events would reveal that the diplomatic standoff was not over, but on September 30 Connecticut released the hostages it had received from Ninigret.[60]

WHILE MASSACHUSETTS STRUGGLED to preserve justice and the rule of law, Boston pastor Increase Mather vented at the magistrates for holding court while his church was observing a service of humiliation on September 1, 1675, "when the Lord did so visibly call them and all the country to fasting and mourning." "I was troubled at this and expected to hear more sad news," he wrote in his diary. Sure enough, word arrived that on September 1 Indians had attacked Deerfield, where Mather's nephew was pastor. "This day Amalek prevailed over Israel!" he lamented, invoking a well-known Old Testament story. "For Moses' hands were not held up [in prayer], as should have been!"[61]

Indians attacked Deerfield again on September 12. They captured a soldier, burned houses, "killed many horses, [and] carried away horse loads of beef and pork." Fearing further destruction, Major Pynchon, commander of Massachusetts forces in the Connecticut Valley, ordered Captain Lathrop to secure three thousand bushels of corn and other goods from Deerfield. Meanwhile, Captain Mosely, whose company had arrived from the east, would march up the west side of the river, while Major Treat led one hundred Connecticut soldiers and sixty Mohegans and Pequots up the east side.

Lathrop was a Pequot War veteran who believed the English had to fight like Indians to defeat them. But on the morning of September 18, as he and between fifty and eighty men escorted half a dozen carts loaded with corn, wheat, and other goods from Deerfield to Hadley, Lathrop let his guard down. Soldiers left their guns in wagons and casually stopped to pick grapes. They had just crossed Muddy Brook, about five miles south of Deerfield, when the Algonquians fell on them. They killed Lathrop and massacred his men. They plundered carts, cut open mattresses and bags of grain, and stripped the dead.

Survivors reported the disaster to Captain Mosely, who marched to the site at once. Arriving around 11:00 a.m., he formed his seventy men in ranks and ordered them forward. They "desperately charged through the enemy" and drove them into a swamp, recovering some of Lathrop's wounded soldiers. But the Algonquians recovered the initiative. "Come Mosely, come," they taunted, "you seek Indians, you want Indians, here's Indians enough for you!" Warriors began encircling the English soldiers, pressing "upon them with great numbers, so to knock them down with their hatchets." For five exhausting hours the soldiers held them off, despite rising casualties. Weary to the point of collapse, Mosely turned command over to some lieutenants. His company would not last much longer.

It was Major Treat, with the Mohegans and Pequots, who saved them. Confronted by Treat's force, the Algonquians withdrew northward. "Our Indians fired upon them, made many shots at them, and called them to stay, but they went away over Pocumtuck River," a colonist reported. Treat did not pursue because rain had made the river difficult to cross.

It was "the saddest [day] that ever befell New England," the minister William Hubbard observed. At least seventy men were dead, and probably twenty wounded. Lathrop's company, "the very flower" of Essex County, was wiped out almost to a man. In one town alone, the battle produced eight widows and twenty-six orphans. Eighteen Deerfield men were killed, including a father and three sons. Soldiers claimed they killed ninety-six Indians, but such estimates were unreliable. The English returned early the next morning to bury the dead in a mass grave. They found a soldier named Robert Dutch, shot in the head, scalped, and stripped, but somehow still alive. One day, Hubbard wrote, the valiant men who died for God and country at Bloody Brook would rise up to receive a martyr's crown.

But religious comfort could not save Deerfield, where Algonquians taunted the remaining garrison by hanging the tattered garments of dead soldiers in plain view across the river. A few days later, Deerfield was abandoned and reoccupied by the Pocumtucks.[62]

COLONIAL FORCES SEEMED powerless to contain the enemy, and misguided attempts to intimidate Indians into remaining neutral were actually causing the war to spread. Fighting even spread to Maine, where Wabanakis devastated English settlements.[63] Spurred by Increase Mather and other ministers, on September 17 the Massachusetts council issued a proclamation acknowledging that God was punishing the people for ingratitude, worldliness, "ill entertainment of the ministry," apostasy from truth to heresy, and many other "scandalous sins." He was "not going forth with our armies as in former times" and even seemed "angry with the prayers of his people." It called for churches to observe October 7 as a "day of public humiliation," to seek God's face and discern what needed to be done for a "thorough reformation."[64]

Not everyone agreed. One morning, on market day, Bostonians discovered a newly erected pillar at the grave of the four Quakers executed in 1659–1661, near the highway into town. It bore following inscription:

Though here our innocent bodies in silent earth do lie,
Yet are our righteous souls at rest, our blood for vengeance cry.

The authorities ordered it demolished, but people shared written copies. The message was clear: the war was God's judgment on Massachusetts for killing Quakers.

While some Quakers supported the war and others refused military service on the principle that all war was unchristian, nearly all Quakers sharply criticized the Puritan perspective on it. "The Indians, I hear, insult very much and tell the English warriors that God is against them and for the Indians," wrote Edward Wharton, who had constructed the pillar. "Our rulers, officers, and counsellors are like as men in a maze, not knowing what to do." The clergy "spur them on, telling them the Indians are ordained for destruction, bidding them to go forth to war, and [saying] they will fast and pray at home in the meantime, yet their general, with some other officers, complain and say with tears, they see not God go along with them." Indians boasted of driving the English to Boston and other coastal towns where they would starve to death. Unless God showed mercy, Wharton concluded, the Indians "would destroy and roll up the rest of our nation as a burdensome and menstruous cloth, and cast it out of their land."[65]

On one point, Puritans and Quakers agreed: God was not showing New England much mercy.

16

No Indians Can Be Trusted

September 1675 to December 1675

THE MORE FREQUENTLY colonists suffered from Algonquian raids, especially by formerly neutral Indians, the more they suspected *all* Indians of treachery. That suspicion extended even to those who supported the colonial cause. The distinction that once mattered most, between Christian and heathen, was eclipsed by a racial distinction between English and Indian.

Events in the Connecticut Valley spurred these trends. No one was more concerned about the valley's security than John Pynchon, whose prosperity depended on it. As a military commander, however, Major Pynchon was in over his head. He knew this better than anyone, which is why he repeatedly asked to be relieved of command. Governor Leverett of Massachusetts exhorted him to take inspiration from biblical figures like Moses, David, and Isaiah, who also felt unworthy of God's calling, and look to "the Lord Jesus, the captain of the Lord's hosts, to be your mighty counsellor." He advised Pynchon to be careful of ambushes and order his men to study "the enemy's method, which though it may seem a rout [compared] to ours, is the best way of fighting the enemy in this bushy wilderness."[1]

The Massachusetts government had its own problems, not least of which was impressing unwilling men into military service. "The slaughter in your parts has much damped many spirits for the war," Secretary Edward Rawson admitted to Pynchon. "Some men escape away from the press, and others hide away after they are impressed."[2] The United Colonies commissioners ordered five hundred soldiers to the valley, instructing Pynchon not to leave them in garrison but to pursue the enemy "vigorously."[3] The problem was that Pynchon had no idea where the enemy was. The Mohegans and Pequots had returned home, unwilling to fight "upland Indians" without good cause, and English scouts were decidedly inferior. Officers constantly feared being attacked. On September 28, 1675, two men were found dead and scalped near Northampton, "two bullets apiece shot into each of their breasts." Indians raided Pynchon's Springfield farm, burning barns, killing cattle, and destroying corn. His wife, Margaret, "almost overwhelmed with grief and trouble," urged him to come home. He again begged to be relieved of command so "the interest of God and his people may be better managed and defended" by "some more able and fit person."[4]

In early October, scouts finally located a significant number of enemy Indians, so on October 4 Pynchon called all available troops to concentrate near Hadley. Leaving towns undefended bothered him, but he interpreted the commissioners' instructions as a "strict order" to "leave no soldiers in garrison, but call out all." At the same time, Connecticut relayed intelligence to Springfield that the local Agawams had welcomed Philip, the Pokanoket sachem, and five hundred enemy warriors into their fort. Springfield's leaders were skeptical, observing that the Agawams had given "the firmest assurances and pledges of their faithfulness and friendship that could be imagined or desired." They did not know that the Agawam hostages, held to secure their loyalty to the English, had escaped. When Pynchon received the intelligence in Hadley, he took it more seriously. With five hundred inhabitants, Springfield was second only to Hartford in importance among valley towns. He called off his offensive and started south with two hundred men.

The next morning, Springfield's Lieutenant Thomas Cooper and several colonists rode toward Agawam. Indians ambushed them a quarter mile from town, shooting Cooper off his horse and killing a companion. The lieutenant remounted, galloped back, and sounded the alarm, only to be shot again—this time fatally. While colonists scurried to their garrison houses, as many as a hundred warriors descended on the town, shooting and burning. One boasted that he had helped burn Brookfield and would do the same to Springfield.

Around midday, Major Robert Treat arrived on the other side of the river with troops from Connecticut. But when he attempted to cross by boat, Indians fired from the riverbank, shooting a soldier through the neck. Treat's soldiers beat a hasty retreat. Not until mid-afternoon did Pynchon's exhausted men approach, leading the Indians to withdraw.

"We came to a lamentable and woeful sight," Pynchon wrote. "The town in flames, not a house nor barn standing, except old Goodman Branch's, until we came to my house." A few houses near the meeting house survived, but "then from Goodman Mirick's downward, all burnt, to two garrison houses at the lower end of the town." Inhabitants emerged from the garrison houses, "full of fear and staggering in their thoughts." More than thirty houses and roughly twenty-five barns had been destroyed. In the town proper, only about thirteen houses were unburned. The town's pastor, Pelatiah Glover, lost his large library. Three people were dead, including a woman, and four were wounded, two of whom would eventually succumb to their wounds.[5] "The Lord hath spared my dwelling house, but my barns and outhousing [are] all burnt down, and all my corn and hay consumed, and not anything have I left of food either for man or beast," Pynchon informed his son. "All my mills, both corn mills and sawmills, burnt down."

Soldiers tried to salvage the remaining corn. They grumbled about lack of bread and "comfortable lodging," having to share the remaining houses with forty destitute families, but Pynchon was loath to abandon the town that represented his and his father's life's work, arguing that to do so was "to quit the cause of God and the interest of his people." Colonists blamed him for the disaster, but he blamed the commissioners for ordering him to put Springfield's garrison in the field. "To speak my thoughts," he informed Governor Leverett, "all these towns ought to be garrisoned, as I have formerly hinted, and had I been left to myself, I should, I think, have done that which possibly might have prevented this damage."

He was a beaten man. He argued that an offensive would require no fewer than one thousand soldiers and should be delayed until winter. To "go out after the Indians in the swamps and thickets is to hazard all our men," he explained. When the leaves fell and the swamps froze, the Indians would lose their advantages. Even then, he wanted no part of it. "I am not capable of holding my command," he admitted, "being more and more unfit and almost confounded in my understanding." The council had better remove him quickly, unless "you intend to let all fail, as of necessity it must, by my management."

His losses were staggering. It was not just his personal property that was lost—he was Springfield's leading financier and employer. "Naked came I [into the world] and naked shall I return, and blessed be the name of the Lord," he mourned, quoting the famously miserable Job. Why did God disappoint "all our hopeful designs"? Why was he "answering all our prayers by terrible things"? How long would he be angry? "Surely he will [take] revenge [on the Indians] for their falsehood in his time and send defense to his people, when it may make most for his glory and their good." Pynchon concluded that God had commissioned the "heathens" to "destroy his people" until they fully repented. Like so many Puritans whose lives were unraveling, he took refuge in his faith. "Oh dear son," he wrote Joseph Pynchon, "how sweet is an interest in Christ Jesus in these distracting times. They are trying times, and it is good knowing [he] in whom we have believed and treasured in heaven is abiding."[6]

NEWS OF THE disaster reached Boston on Massachusetts's fast day, October 7. It was the first time that a town with an established church had been attacked, reminding Boston minister Increase Mather of God's warning in Leviticus that if Israel did not repent after he took its children and cattle, he would destroy its sanctuaries. "New England is in the most lamentable state that ever was," Mather wrote in his diary. "The Indians risen almost round the country. God doth not go forth with our armies. Many cut off by the enemy." The meaning seemed clear: "Praying without reforming will not do."[7]

Mather's fellow minister, William Hubbard, whose daughter was married to Major Pynchon's son, was outraged. Springfield never should have trusted "those perfidious, cruel, and hellish monsters," he later vented. The Agawams' treachery proved that Indians were "children of the devil, full of all subtlety and malice."

They had received nothing but friendship from Springfield for forty years, but like the wicked in Psalm 55, "though their words were smoother than oil, yet they were drawn swords."[8]

To hear the news "with a still spirit is very difficult," Governor Leverett admitted, and trusting God was "[more] easily spoken than practiced." The disaster was all the more troubling given the "prayers and . . . solemn humiliation of churches and people," for it suggested God was even "angry with our prayers."[9] Ironically, Massachusetts had relieved Pynchon of command on October 4, before the attack, though the news had not reached him at the time.[10] Now Leverett chided Pynchon for trusting the Agawams: "I doubt not but you see how [foolish] confidences are in such, who cannot be truer than [the devil] whom they serve." Nevertheless, "the will of the Lord is done," and "[I will not] add affliction by blaming you or any for what was not done."[11]

The attack triggered another wave of hostility against praying Indians, for it was said that forty of the Agawam assailants had been praying Indians often seen in Springfield. Many agreed with a Boston bookseller who punned that praying Indians deserved their name because they "made prey of much English blood."[12] Determined not to make the same mistake, Massachusetts forbade Indians to enter Boston unless they had express government permission, were escorted by soldiers at all times, and were either out of town or in jail by nightfall.[13] The House of Deputies, responding to popular demands, passed a bill for "removing the praying Indians from their plantations." The Court of Assistants objected that it failed to specify a destination for those removed, so a joint committee was appointed to study the issue.

Daniel Gookin, who served as both a magistrate and the superintendent of the praying towns, produced a paper arguing that removing Christian Indians was a terrible idea that reflected poorly on "the piety and prudence of the government." Evangelizing Indians was one of Massachusetts's primary purposes and praying Indians were its legacy. Furthermore, Massachusetts had signed treaties promising to protect them. Even if Indians were analogous to the Canaanites Israel was ordered to destroy, as some colonists claimed, the biblical story of the Gibeonites proved that a covenant with Canaanites was "a very binding thing, and the breach of it sorely punished by the Lord." Massachusetts law promised Christian Indians the same basic rights as Englishmen. And while many colonists denied that praying Indians were real Christians, Massachusetts had informed the king that "not a few" were members of Christ's kingdom. Removal was unjust even on secular grounds, for Indians had a "natural right" to their land and "legal title" from the General Court. It would be one thing if they had been disloyal, but most had displayed "constant faithfulness." Their men served as trusted soldiers, some even sacrificing their lives for the colony. Removing them in a fit of prejudice and paranoia would destroy Christ's work and raise disturbing questions about the sincerity of the colony's Christianity.

The committee admitted that Gookin's paper offered solid arguments and assured him that it would follow its principles. Nevertheless, to appease the people's demands, it recommended that the government relocate praying Indians to various towns around Boston. This solution was unsatisfactory to many members of the General Court, and the towns affected flat-out refused to have Indians settled nearby. Some protested that Gookin cared more about Indians than about them.

Alarmed, the praying Indians of Natick sent their supervisor John Watson to implore the government not to be suspicious or harsh toward them or credit misinformation about them. They begged the court, in Gookin's words, "not to fetch them off from their dwellings, which would expose them, especially the aged and weak, to very much sorrow and misery, both for want of food and apparel, especially considering that the winter was approaching." They offered hostages. Gookin heard Watson say he used to feel "much animosity, prejudice, and displeasure" toward praying Indians, but having lived at Natick, he now felt "ashamed of himself for his harsh apprehensions of them only upon common fame." They had demonstrated nothing but fidelity toward God and the English.

But many found Watson's testimony offensive, and Natick's petition was not favorably received.[14]

WHILE BOSTON DEBATED the fate of praying Indians, Increase Mather was carefully crafting a sermon for the General Court. He felt enormous pressure, for he intended to call for a reform program to turn aside God's wrath, and he expected opposition.[15] "I prayed with tears in my study . . . that the Lord would be with me, and own and bless my labors for glory to his name," he reported in his diary. Then he made his way to the meeting house, where "God . . . gave me acceptance beyond expectation."[16]

The court appointed him to a committee to address "those evils which have provoked the Lord to bring the sword upon us, and to withdraw from our armies from time to time." The committee was unified and efficient, submitting its report on October 19, just five days later. The court then appointed another committee to draft corresponding legislation. The cause of the war was not injustice against Indians, ministers and magistrates agreed. It was their sin against God. None doubted that when God was satisfied with their repentance, he would grant them victory.[17]

The same day that Mather's committee submitted its report, word arrived that Lieutenant James Richardson's haystack at Chelmsford had been burned. Chelmsford blamed the praying Indians at nearby Wamesit, but Richardson was skeptical. He was Wamesit's supervisor and told Gookin that the Wamesits loved him as their friend. Gookin also knew the Wamesits had been helping

Massachusetts pursue reconciliation with the Pennacook sachem Wannalancet. Wamesit's teacher, Samuel Numphow, had traveled north with a guarantee of safe conduct from Massachusetts to persuade Wannalancet to meet with Gookin and the missionary John Eliot. Unfortunately, he did not find Wannalancet, and some Pennacooks told him they were afraid to come to Wamesit because of the English.

Despite Numphow's service, the magistrates succumbed to what Gookin called "a hurry of temptation" and dispatched forty troopers to Wamesit. The troopers rounded up 145 people and marched them, poorly clothed and with little food, toward Boston on October 20. Learning of these conditions, the magistrates exercised "more deliberate consideration" and ordered that all but thirty-three who were men of military age be returned home. Troops also arrested the praying Indians of Punkapoag, but Punkapoag's Indian pastor, William Ahawton, obtained the release of all but three or four.[18]

Six days later, the council learned that an old barn was burned near Dedham. It was not worth ten shillings, according to Gookin, but that did not stop Dedham from blaming the praying town of Natick, which it still resented for having won the land dispute between the two towns. Gookin suspected that colonists had deliberately set the fire to provoke Natick's removal. "God, who knows all, will I hope one day awaken and convince the consciences of those persons," he wrote. Yielding to popular pressure, on October 30 the General Court ordered that Natick's people be interned on Deer Island in Boston harbor, in part for their own safety. Troopers led by Captain Thomas Prentice arrived with carts and informed residents to be ready to leave in about an hour. A dozen fled, but most of the two hundred residents "quietly and readily submitted." Those too old or sick to travel were permitted to remain, as were a few scouts. The rest packed what they could, "some few" taking their Bibles, and followed the soldiers into the night, terrified that they would "never return more to their habitations, but be transported out of the country."

They left behind the meeting house where they had worshiped for more than a decade. How many testimonies of God's grace had emerged from this place? How many young men had been educated here before setting off to teach other Indians? How loyally had they served the English in crisis after crisis? None of it mattered to colonists who wanted them gone. Prentice led them to an embarkation point on the Charles River, where they were met by seventy-one-year-old John Eliot. He prayed with them and exhorted them to continue in faith, recalling Jesus's teaching that "through many tribulations we must enter into the kingdom of heaven." Observers were struck by "how submissively, innocently, and Christianly and affectionately these poor souls carried it, taking encouragement and encouraging and exhorting one another with prayers and tears." Around midnight, three boats carried them to Deer Island.

The desolate island offered no shelter and little food, and its owner, merchant Samuel Shrimpton, would not let them cut down trees or butcher his sheep.[19] The court instructed the treasurer to ship them provisions and investigate conditions "from time to time." But the Indians were prohibited from leaving "upon pain of death." Those who escaped could be shot on sight, and anyone who transported them would be charged with "man stealing," a crime subject to death.[20]

THE COURT HELD THE thirty-three praying Indians taken from Wamesit for ten days before questioning them. Colonists' hostility toward them was palpable, for a Wamesit had been spotted among warriors attacking an English settlement in Maine, and as Massachusetts's General Denison observed, "It is hardly imaginable the panic fear that is upon our upland plantations and scattered places." But despite their accusers' "bitter words," the Wamesits adamantly denied burning the haystack. Evidence was lacking, but the House of Deputies voted them guilty anyway. The Court of Assistants rejected the verdict. In effect, the people's representatives channeled popular racial prejudices, while the magistrates countered with calls for justice and the rule of law.

Eventually they agreed to release twenty men known to be from Wamesit while condemning three, who seemed unable to explain their presence there, to foreign slavery. The rest remained in custody. Lieutenant Richardson, who was Wamesit's supervisor, and a group of soldiers escorted those released back to Wamesit. About halfway they approached Woburn, where colonial militia were engaged in drills. Fearing a confrontation, Richardson raised a flag of truce. The militia commander ordered his men to let the Indians pass, but as they did so, a young militiaman named Knight fired his gun, killing a "stout young" Wamesit. Five years earlier, a Woburn woman had saved a Wamesit girl whose skull was fractured by Mohawks. Now a Woburn man murdered a Wamesit in cold blood.

In his trial, Knight claimed the shooting was accidental, and witnesses were afraid to speak about what they had seen. So the jury ruled there was insufficient evidence to convict Knight. Dissatisfied, the magistrates demanded a retrial. "The jury was sent out again and again by the judges," magistrate Daniel Gookin lamented, but they kept returning the same verdict. Knight was cleared of all charges. A month later, the General Court discovered how careless its own judgments had been: two of the men it sentenced to be sold abroad were envoys from the Pennacook sachem Wannalancet and carried a letter of safe conduct from the council. They were released, but any hope of a treaty with the Pennacooks was dashed. It was later confirmed that Richardson's haystack had been burned by hostile Indians in a deliberate attempt to antagonize the English against Wamesit.[21]

NO ONE KNEW WHERE Indians would strike next or what company of soldiers might be massacred. Philip's strategy was to lure colonists into places "full of long grass, flags, [and] sedge," an Indian declared, to greet them with "fire, smoke, and bullets." While giving the young Narragansett sachem Canonchet a lift in his canoe one day, Roger Williams lambasted Philip's warriors as "so cowardly that they have not taken one poor fort from us in all the country, nor won, no, scarce fought, one battle since the beginning."

Many colonists, including Providence militia commander Arthur Fenner, predicted that the Narragansetts would emerge as the greatest threat yet. "I am between fear and hope," Williams admitted to Governor Leverett of Massachusetts, but God wanted his people to pursue peace, not "cut off the barbarians or subdue" them without just cause. Even so, Williams warned Canonchet that if the Narragansetts violated their treaties "we would pursue them with a winter war, when they should not, as mosquitoes and rattlesnakes in warm weather, bite us."[22]

But the English continued to antagonize the Narragansetts. One night, colonists kidnapped several Narragansetts on Prudence Island, including a man named Jack and his wife, confining them on a ship belonging to Plymouth captains Matthew Fuller and John Gorham. A local merchant protested that he had known Jack to be loyal for many years and had promised to protect him. He called for a careful investigation, observing that colonists often confused Indians, "as it is hard to distinguish of them," and warned that God would avenge the innocent. Pessicus, the Narragansett sachem, also appealed on their behalf. Richard Smith Jr., whose trading post was in Narragansett country, was under no illusions about the sympathies of many Narragansetts, having witnessed their delight at English defeats, but he knew Pessicus opposed war and so relayed his appeal. Nevertheless, the captives were carried to the Azores and sold.[23]

Many frontier settlers clamored for a preemptive strike against the Narragansetts. A woman named Mary Pray, from Providence, Rhode Island, complained to Massachusetts magistrate James Oliver that the Narragansetts, "false treacherous imps," boasted openly about English disasters, stole swine from nearby farms, and taunted colonists about slaughtering their cattle and plundering their crops. "We every day expect to be assaulted by them and look for nothing but treachery from them." They were fighting in the Connecticut Valley, she believed. Some had returned home wounded after the August Battle of Nipsachuck, and it was only a matter of time before they openly joined Philip's coalition. One informant said they planned to attack during winter, "when you English think you are at quiet." Another claimed they would strike in the spring.

Mary Pray could not understand why the colonies did nothing about it. "This false peace hath undone this country," she protested. Everyone in Providence agreed that "now is the time to try what the Lord God of power and mercy will do for us against them." There would be a narrow window of opportunity in late fall when the Indians were robbed of their cover yet the weather remained good for campaigning. Come spring, the enemy would be brimming with confidence, their numbers swelling with new allies. "Sir, can you think we can subsist another summer?" she asked. "No, we cannot, if these [Narragansetts] live. We are forced now [to have] ten men to go about two men's work. We have lost our crop, many of us our hay time. We are forced to destroy all or most of our cattle and hogs because we have not corn and hay for to keep them alive." Eventually, colonists would starve.

Pray lamented the endless diplomacy while so many lives were being lost. "Oh what cause hath Captain Hutchinson's family and hundreds more to rue the treatings with the Indians!" she exclaimed; better to have attacked the Indians all at once. She claimed that wealthy traders like Smith pursued peace out of greed. Smith was expecting one hundred barrels of pork from the Indians, and "some here conclude he staved off war with them for his pork's sake." Equally at fault were colonists beguiled by praying Indians, who, she claimed, repeating common accusations, acted treacherously in battle. "We have experience of them that they are as bad as any other [Indians], and it is reported by the Indians themselves that Captain Gookin helps them to powder, and they sell it to those that are employed by Philip." They even urged the Narragansetts to attack the English, saying "they are sure that if they do not, the English will fall upon them suddenly." Pray hoped that God "doth purpose utterly to destroy these wretches."[24]

But the United Colonies continued negotiating, demanding that the Narragansetts turn over all refugees. Under enormous pressure, the sachem Canonchet and the counselor Corman, representing Ninigret, signed a new treaty on October 18, 1675, promising to surrender all refugees within ten days. The commissioners made no promises about the refugees' welfare, only that they would be "disposed . . . for the best security and peace of the United Colonies." Nor did they make exceptions for those, like Awashonks, the Sakonnet sachem, who never supported Philip.[25]

On October 27, however, Richard Smith Jr. reported that only Ninigret would meet the deadline. The sachems said they were "willing," but it was "not feasible . . . at present," for many men refused to surrender their kin, and any attempt to seize them by force would fail. Also, many Wampanoags were out hunting. The sachems pleaded for time, "very fearful at the news" of an English invasion. Praying Indians from Massachusetts had informed Pessicus that "all the praying Indians" had been seized and "killed by Boston men. Only they escaped." The English "intended a war with the Narragansetts suddenly," they warned. Given what Massachusetts *was* doing with praying Indians, Pessicus had every reason to believe them.[26]

SIMILAR RUMORS OF colonial atrocities must have reached the two hundred or so praying Indians at Hassanamesit, many of whom had been resettled from the praying towns of Magunkog, Chabanakongkomun, Okammakamesit, and Pakachoog. The Petavit brothers, who had helped save the survivors of Hutchinson's ambush, were there, as was Captain Tom Wuttasacomponom, ruler of the new praying towns. So were John Eliot's former missionary assistant James Printer and his brothers: Joseph Tuckawillipin, Annaweekin, and Job Kattenanit. Anxiety must have been high as men and women threshed recently harvested corn and buried it in storage pits.

Suddenly, some three hundred warriors arrived, many of whom were their Nipmuc kin, and offered to take them north to the Nipmuc refuge at Menameset. It was only a matter of time before the English carried them off to Deer Island, they warned, where they would probably die or be sold abroad. Tuckawillipin, Hassanamesit's pastor, protested, but many conceded that the warriors were right. James Printer and others had already been jailed once and nearly lynched. Many had been forced from their homes, their corn and wigwams destroyed by soldiers. All were prohibited from leaving Hassanamesit to hunt or trade, and Natick's people had already been taken away. At least the Nipmucs would protect and feed them. Captain Tom should have been leading Indians in the field alongside colonial forces, but Massachusetts had dismissed all but a few Indians from service. He decided his people's safety required going with the Nipmucs. Tuckawillipin wept, eliciting mockery from the warriors.

Two praying Indians—Magunkog pastor Job Kattenanit, a widower, and Pakachoog pastor James Speen—escaped detection and fled to Mendon, leaving Kattenanit's three children behind. When they reported what had happened, the Massachusetts council did not know what to make of it. Had the praying Indians been captured, or had they treacherously joined the enemy? Daniel Gookin later wrote that Captain Tom "should rather have suffered death than have gone among the wicked enemies of the people of God."[27] The council ordered Captains Daniel Henchman and Joseph Sill to rescue the captives and execute God's "just judgment" on his "bloodthirsty and cruel" enemies. Their mission became all the more urgent when Nipmucs raided Marlborough, scalping one boy and capturing another.

Captain Henchman passed through Mendon, whose demoralized inhabitants were anxious to evacuate. He urged them to obey the court's orders not to do so, for "breaking up a town" and "rending a church" would encourage the enemy. He reached Hassanamesit a few days later. There he found signs of chaos: "apples, corn, nuts and other things lying up and down," sixty bushels of corn in storage pits, and some partially constructed wigwams. He pressed on to Pakachoog, where he found a large quantity of corn and evidence of recent Indian presence. After departing, he realized he was missing his letter-case and sent the Nashaway praying Indian Thomas Quanapohit and two soldiers to retrieve it. They stumbled upon six Nipmucs and were lucky to escape with their lives, only to discover that it was for nothing. Henchman, after "searching diligently, had found his letter-case."[28]

A few days later, Henchman learned that forty Nipmucs had returned to Hassanamesit. He decided to surprise them. Taking twenty-two men on horseback, he had them dismount before approaching an occupied wigwam. But as they crept through a thicket, a dog started barking. Henchman ordered covering fire, dashed forward, and called his men to surround the wigwam, only to realize that just five were with him. When he ordered them into line, they panicked. "I cried of them for the Lord's sake to stay," he reported, "for in retreating as we did, I gave up myself and them with me for lost." Instead they fled, and with warriors pouring out of the wigwam, Henchman had no choice but to follow. Reaching his horse, he "threatened to run them through" if they did not stop and fight, but they were more terrified by the Nipmuc war cries piercing the night than of their angry captain. They rode hard for Mendon, leaving two wounded men behind. When they returned the next day, in front of the wigwam they found a "crotched pole" bearing the heads of the two soldiers "faced against each other."[29]

Job Kattenanit, the Indian pastor who had escaped Hassanamesit, remained distraught about his children and asked Gookin for a pass to travel into Nipmuc country to find them. "God sparing my life," he promised, "I may bring you some intelligence of the residence and state of the enemy." Gookin wrote an order declaring that Kattenanit was trustworthy and that soldiers who encountered him should "not misuse him, but secure him and convey him to the governor or myself."

Unfortunately, Henchman's soldiers captured Kattenanit before he reached his family. One wanted to kill him, but others insisted on bringing him to Henchman, who sent him to Boston. There he was confined to a jail overcrowded with Indians. Colonists argued that since he was found without an English escort, he should be executed. Some accused Gookin of using him to send intelligence to the enemy. After three weeks, the magistrates sent Kattenanit to Deer Island.[30]

CAPTAIN SAMUEL APPLETON, a deputy from Ipswich, was John Pynchon's replacement as commander of Massachusetts forces in the Connecticut Valley. Though reluctant to accept command, he was confident in the cause. "We shall not, cannot fail," he wrote, for God's people were "lifting up their hands and hearts" in prayer. Just as God enabled Israel to destroy the cursed Canaanites, "so our Israel may in his time prevail against this cursed Amalek, against whom I believe the Lord will have war forever until he have destroyed them."[31]

He set about planning an offensive but ran into the same problems as Pynchon: his scouts could not locate the enemy, and he lacked sufficient troops. To make matters worse, the attack on Springfield frightened Connecticut into recalling its forces from the upper valley. Connecticut warned that its Indian allies were wavering in the face of colonial defeats. It would take a miracle to save the upriver towns, Connecticut added, unless Massachusetts sent five hundred fresh troops.[32]

Fear gripped the towns amid a barrage of reported Indian sightings. The infamous Captain Samuel Mosely captured an old woman who claimed that Indians were building a fort fifty miles north of Hadley. He rewarded her by ordering her "torn in pieces by dogs, and she was so dealt with." A few days later, scouts reported that Indians were constructing a fort at Pocumtuck, near the ruins of abandoned Deerfield. Captain Appleton wanted to strike, but Connecticut protested that the enemy was threatening Norwich, the Narragansetts were preparing to join the war, and the Mohegans and Pequots needed to defend their homes. Exasperated, Appleton explained that the enemy was threatening Hadley, then launched a futile expedition on his own. "We have wearied ourselves with a tedious night and morning's march," he reported on October 17, "without making any discovery of the enemy."[33]

Connecticut finally sent Major Treat's forces back upriver, just in time. On October 19 scouts spotted bonfires north of Hatfield, a town of about three hundred inhabitants. Captain Mosely sent nine horsemen to investigate, but Indians ambushed them, killing five and capturing three. One, an Indian, escaped to report the disaster, enabling Mosely to summon reinforcements, so colonial forces were ready when hundreds of warriors converged on Hatfield at around 4:00 p.m. The attackers set fires at three locations before heavy casualties forced them to withdraw. Colonial troops pursued them to a creek where desperate warriors abandoned guns and ammunition, but not the bodies of their slain, to swim to safety. Several drowned.

The battle of Hatfield was a desperately needed boost for English morale. Ten men were wounded in addition to those lost in the ambush, but officers claimed to have killed over a hundred enemy warriors. William Hubbard, the Ipswich minister, later described it as "the first check to the rage of the heathen." Increase Mather considered it a "signal victory" from God, since it happened the same day that Massachusetts voted to draft the reform legislation he was calling for.

Later, frustrated Indians executed a prisoner, "cutting a hole below his breast, out of which they pulled his guts and then cut off his head," to the horror of fellow captive Thomas Warner, who survived to tell of it. Two days later they tortured Warner. They "burned his nails and put his feet to scald them against the fire."

Then they "drove a stake" the size of his finger "through one of his feet to pin him to the ground."[34]

The boost to colonial morale proved short-lived, as officers bickered over authority and strategy. Connecticut officers complained that Captain Appleton was heavy-handed, failed to consult them, and refused to take the offensive. Appleton deemed Connecticut's officers insubordinate. On October 25 an Indian war party burned houses and barns around Northampton. The following day, Indians killed three men and burned several houses at Westfield. They hit Northampton again on October 29, killing two men and a boy working in a field.

Soldiers exhausted themselves in futile marches and countermarches. Awakened during the night of October 30, Appleton was informed that Indians were attacking Hatfield. But when he arrived, he found no Indians. The following night, Major Treat responded to a similar alarm at Northampton. On November 1 Appleton's troops marched more than ten miles through the woods, and the following night he and Treat marched all the way to Pocumtuck and ranged the area the day after, but they failed to discover the enemy. On November 5, Indians showed up at Northampton again, only to disappear into thin air.

Fed up, Treat requested permission to return to Connecticut. Appleton refused. But with winter approaching, the situation grew desperate. So much hay had been lost that people could not feed their cattle, let alone the army's horses. Settlers began abandoning the towns, leading Appleton, who needed every man, to forbid anyone to leave without permission. But by then, most believed the Indians had withdrawn northward for the winter. The colonies were shifting their focus to the Narragansetts, and Appleton knew his army would be summoned to fight them. He authorized Treat's departure on November 19, organized his garrisons, and ordered the construction of palisades. Then he headed east.[35]

INCREASE MATHER INTERPRETED every defeat as a "sore rebuke" to the General Court for taking so long to pass reform legislation. Finally, on November 9, the Court of Assistants passed a bill. The next day, wrote a vindicated Mather, "as I was sitting alone in my study, I was suddenly moved by the spirit of God and wonderfully melted into tears, with a firm persuasion that God would make me his mouth and own the words I should speak in his name." The reform bill became law on November 15, and its preamble endorsed Mather's interpretation of events. For several years, it declared, God had used his ministers and various judgments to warn the people to repent, but they had refused. Therefore, he gave "commission to the barbarous heathen to rise up against us … burning and depopulating several hopeful plantations, murdering many of our people." The Indians were God's instrument of judgment, yet it was he who had abandoned his people, "seeming as it were to cast us off, and putting us to shame, and not going forth with our armies."

The law did everything Mather's committee recommended. It called on churches to train and discipline young people to bring them into church membership. It targeted casual oaths, drunkenness, partying, idleness, immodest hairstyles and clothing, and disrespect for authority. It cracked down on "shopkeepers and merchants who set excessive prices" and "mechanics and day-laborers" who failed to fulfill their responsibilities. It ordered the abolition of trading houses that sold alcohol to Indians. It decreed stiff penalties against Quaker meetings.[36] Mather was more hopeful than he had been in months. If Massachusetts enforced the laws, he believed, victory over the Indians would surely follow.

Meanwhile, Massachusetts continued sending praying Indians, including those of Punkapoag, to Deer Island. Their confinement was "reasonable" and "much to a general satisfaction," argued merchant Nathaniel Saltonstall, for it distinguished "our friends the Christian Indians and our enemies the heathens" by securing the former from violence.[37] "Most of our mischiefs have flowed from pretended friends who have demeaned themselves exceedingly fairly with us till they have had the opportunity secretly and suddenly to endamage us, and then they fly to our avowed adversaries," another colonist explained. "Many of our commonalty would have all Indians . . . declared enemies, but our soberest sort justly fear to condemn the innocent with the guilty . . . nor would they draw on themselves the guilt of blotting out the interest of the gospel among the Indians." Thus the Christian Indians were "placed and provided for on certain islands, where they are out of harm's way."[38] Daniel Gookin, Christian Indians' leading advocate, agreed that the praying Indians were being held for "their and our security, but not with any purpose of doing them wrong."[39]

The praying Indians of Wamesit and Nashobah, who remained on the mainland, faced more danger from colonial vigilantes than from hostile Indians. When a barn full of hay and corn went up in flames near Chelmsford, fourteen Chelmsford men marched to Wamesit and summoned the people from their wigwams. Two colonists then opened fire with pistols. They wounded five women and children, including a woman named Sarah, whose father, grandfather, and successive husbands were Christian sachems. They killed her twelve-year-old son, whose grandfather Attawans had been one of the first sachems to embrace John Eliot's mission. "Lord, thou seest that we have neither done or said anything against the English," Sarah cried, raising her hands, "yet they thus deal with us." The surviving Wamesits fled into the wilderness, taking "little or nothing with them." There, Indian teacher Symon Betokom preached from texts like Psalm 35. "Cruel witnesses did rise up," the psalm declared, "they asked of me things that I knew not. They rewarded me evil for good."

Puritan leaders denounced the violence. "I much lament that rash cruelty of our English toward innocent Indians," wrote Barnstable pastor Thomas Walley. But while the murderers were put on trial, the other Chelmsford men refused to testify against them, and the jury released them for "want of clear evidence." When the council tried to persuade the Wamesits to return, their leaders sent a letter declaring that they would seek refuge with Wannalancet, the Pennacook sachem. The government's promise of protection was worthless, they insisted. Nor were they willing to go to Deer Island, "because many English be not good, and maybe they come to us and kill us." "We are sorry the English have driven us from our praying to God and from our teacher," they added. "We did begin to understand a little of praying to God."[40]

They must have failed to reach Wannalancet, for in December many "half-starved" Wamesits returned. The council ordered Major Simon Willard, Gookin, and Eliot to determine whether they should be removed to Deer Island or left at Wamesit. Either way, they were to be disarmed and "kept to labor." The three men visited Wamesit on December 13. Chelmsford colonists implored them to consider the threat the Wamesits posed to their "lives and estates." But instead of authorizing removal, they exhorted Chelmsford to "be more friendly" and assigned guardians to protect Wamesit "night and day." Eventually about a hundred Indians returned, including Sarah.[41]

The council also ordered Willard, Gookin, and Eliot to inspect the Nashobah praying Indians, who had been resettled near Concord. "There was no man in Concord [who] appeared willing to take care of and secure those Indians but Mr. John Hoar," Gookin admitted. A lawyer from a prominent family—his brother was president of Harvard—Hoar constantly argued with his fellow citizens and was rebuked for profanity and failure to attend worship. Nevertheless, the council authorized him to house and employ the Nashobahs on his property. Colonists threatened to shoot them and harassed Hoar, and he expressed concern to the General Court, but despite what had happened at Wamesit, the court took no action.[42]

The council did take steps to improve conditions on Deer Island. It commissioned colonists to make sure no one attacked the Indians, "nor that they suffer want of necessaries." It ordered that they be provided tools so they could labor for provisions and ease the colony's financial burden. And it forbade colonists from stealing property left at the praying towns.[43]

But conditions were dire when Gookin and Eliot visited in late December. "The island was bleak and cold, their wigwams poor and mean, their clothes few and thin," Gookin observed. Corn shipments were woefully inadequate, reducing them to surviving on clams and shellfish. They "suffer hunger and cold," Eliot reported. "There is neither food nor competent fuel to be had, and they are bare in clothing." Still, Eliot thought they were safer on Deer Island than on the mainland. "I praise God that they be put out of the way of greater perils, dangers, and temptations." What impressed Gookin was their loyalty. "I observed in all my visits to them that they carried themselves patiently, humbly, and piously, without murmuring or complaining against the English for their sufferings, which were not few," he later recalled. "I may say in the words of truth . . . there appeared among them much practical Christianity in this time of their trials." He would not say the same for many colonists.

Eliot returned home discouraged. "The profane Indians prove a sharp rod to the English," he admitted, "[but] the English prove a very sharp rod to the praying Indians." "I have much to write of lamentation over the work of Christ among our praying Indians," he informed the New England Company's Robert Boyle. It "is under great sufferings," indeed, "greater than I can, or in modesty or meekness is fit for me to express." He had no idea what became of the praying Indians taken from Hassanamesit and feared the worst. But he had not given up hope. The mission to evangelize the Indians is "dead, but not buried," he wrote. "It is killed in words, wishes, and expression, but not in deeds." Like Jesus, it would rise again. "My care and labor is to exhort them to humiliation and re-pentance, to be patient and meek in the sight of both God and man." God was using the English and their unjust wrath to discipline his Indian people, but they remained precious to him, and eventually he would reward them.[44]

17

The Narragansetts

November 1675 to February 1676

DESPITE THE DISASTERS unfolding from Plymouth to the Connecticut Valley, many colonial leaders remained convinced that their greatest threat came from the neutral Narragansetts. True, the Narragansett sachems Ninigret and Pessicus expressed "much joy" when confirming the October 1675 treaty, but except for Ninigret, no other sachems surrendered their Wampanoags by the October 28 deadline as agreed.[1] Equally concerning, the young sachem Quinnapin had strengthened Narragansett–Wampanoag ties by marrying Philip's sister-in-law, the Pocasset sachem Weetamoo, whose former husband remained loyal to the English. Colonial leaders believed that Narragansetts were fighting alongside Philip and his upland allies. They suspected Philip was in Narragansett country and that Narragansetts helped capture the praying Indians at Hassanamesit. They pushed for a preemptive strike against the Narragansetts, which risked expanding the war dangerously.

"The Narragansetts still make pleas and excuses for their not performance of their covenant to deliver up our enemies," Massachusetts magistrate Daniel Gookin told Wickford trader Richard Smith Jr., who had contact with the Narragansetts. If they did not surrender the Wampanoags "very speedily," he threatened, "they must expect to hear from us [in] another manner besides words." The colonies would no longer "suffer themselves to be baffled and abused by those Narragansetts." By "God's assistance," they would "reduce them to reason."[2]

On November 2 five United Colonies commissioners met in Boston (one of Connecticut's failed to arrive) and prepared an ultimatum: unless the Narragansetts surrendered their captives immediately, they would be "prosecuted as the abettors and friends of our enemies." An ailing Governor John Winthrop Jr., Connecticut's commissioner, drafted a statement asking the colonies for one thousand fresh troops.[3] But Winthrop hesitated. Like his deputy governor, William Leete, he advocated a gentle approach to the Narragansetts and refused to approve the ultimatum without Connecticut's second commissioner. It was an ironic reversal of past crises, when Connecticut advocated invading Narragansett country while Massachusetts vetoed it. Plymouth governor Josiah Winslow and the other commissioners remonstrated that delay was hazardous.[4]

On November 5 they denounced Winthrop's obstruction as an "absolute violation of the main ends of the Articles of Confederation," one with potentially disastrous consequences. Winthrop held firm.

After his son Wait, Connecticut's second commissioner, arrived, however, he reluctantly fell into line. On November 12 the commissioners voted unanimously to send an expedition to force the Narragansetts to deliver "those of our enemies that are in their custody," demand reparations, and secure hostages. If, as expected, the Narragansetts refused, the army would commence "subduing and destroying" them (with the exception of Ninigret's Eastern Niantic faction, if Ninigret cooperated). To those who considered this unprovoked aggression, they declared that it was essential to winning "the present defensive war," since the Narragansetts were the "secret and constant abettors and principal succor of all our more open enemies, notwithstanding their reiterated covenants to the contrary."[5]

They selected Winslow to lead the expedition, scheduled for December 10. His commission warned him not to trust the Narragansetts, "nor take their words or subscription to any engagement without further assurance of arms, good hostages, etc." He was to "vanquish and subdue the cruel, barbarous and treacherous enemy" by endeavoring "silently and suddenly to surprise" them. Nothing less than "the honor of God, the good of his people, and the security of the interest of Christ in his churches" was at stake, so Winslow was to ensure that the army conducted itself according to Christian principles.[6]

The king had forbidden the colonies to invade Narragansett country, placing it under Rhode Island's jurisdiction, so the commissioners notified Rhode Island of their intent. They were not asking permission. Under "pretense of friendship," they claimed, the "false and perfidious" Narragansetts were supporting the king's enemies to the point that Narragansett country had become "the very rendezvous and seat of the war." Since "God calls all the colonies to use their utmost endeavors to defend his majesty's interest," they expected Rhode Island to provide troops and boats as necessary.[7]

Rhode Island's political situation was fractious, with towns on the mainland occasionally defying the colony's authority and power lurching back and forth between rival factions. Quakers had substantial influence (despite Roger Williams's bitter opposition), and the colony exempted men from military service for reasons of conscience.[8] Most Rhode Islanders believed the Narragansetts were treacherous, but they were also suspicious of the United Colonies' intentions. Deputy Governor John Easton, a Quaker, conceded that the Narragansetts were sheltering hostile warriors and that "some of their men did assist Philip," which the sachems were powerless to prevent. Still, he thought both sides exaggerated the danger. "The English were jealous that there was a general plot of all Indians against English, and the Indians were in like manner jealous of the English." On each side, certain men clamored for war while wiser men tried to prevent it. But he believed the real reason for the looming invasion was that the Puritan colonies coveted Narragansett land.[9]

Roger Williams supported the invasion. While he usually labored strenuously for peace and interceded on behalf of the Narragansetts, he was not close to the current sachems and believed they posed a genuine threat. He later told a doubting Winthrop that while he appreciated how hard Winthrop worked for peace, "it is not possible at present to keep peace with these barbarous men of blood, who are as justly to be repelled and subdued as wolves that assault the sheep." He even used religious rhetoric he usually deplored, claiming God was hardening the Narragansetts for destruction like the Old Testament Canaanites. But he urged colonial authorities to distinguish defiant warriors from those who surrendered, to "spare the conquered, though we strike down the proud."[10]

The response of Rhode Island's governor William Coddington reflected the colony's ambivalence. He promised boats and other assistance but no troops, and he urged the colonial commanders to sort the innocent from the guilty and grant generous terms to all who cooperated.[11]

Over the following weeks, Massachusetts, Plymouth, and Connecticut prepared the largest military operation in New England history. Hundreds of soldiers were impressed into service. Gunpowder, ammunition, food, and supplies for a winter campaign were stockpiled and prepared for transport. December 2 was proclaimed a fast day, that God might grant the soldiers success in "repelling the rage of the enemy."[12] Most ministers endorsed the invasion. Increase Mather later described it as "the vengeance of the Lord upon the perfidious and bloody heathen."[13] Thomas Walley, a Plymouth minister, praised the choice of Winslow as commander, though he worried about Winslow's health. "I know no man fitter for this great service," he wrote. "Who knows but God will make him a savior to this poor distressed land, set[ting] aside his weakness?"[14]

Some raised questions. John Bishop, a pastor in Stamford, Connecticut, later admitted that many doubted "whether our English were wholly innocent" toward Philip and the Wampanoags. There were "uncomfortable and dishonorable reports" about Plymouth's handing of the initial crisis, and it was "very difficult, dissatisfying, and uncomfortable" for "conscientious" people to send their loved ones to fight and die in a war whose justice they questioned. They knew "dishonor would redound to the name of God if New England should go to war for a bad cause."[15]

To answer such doubts, on December 7 Massachusetts issued a declaration defending its conduct since the beginning of the war. It emphasized "how studious this government hath been to preserve peace." Time and again it had pursued diplomacy, only for Indians to respond treacherously. Now, it claimed without solid evidence, Philip had gone to the Narragansetts, "who, we do conclude, have favored, abetted, and assisted him." The invasion was therefore essential to "the just defense of the glory of God . . . king, country, and ourselves." As the colony's governor John Leverett explained in a letter to the king, the enemy had slain three hundred colonists, destroyed numerous towns, and laid waste to the northern frontier. It was time to defend the colonies "against the barbarous rage and inhumanity of the pagans."[16]

BY DECEMBER 10 TWO companies of Plymouth troops under Major William Bradford and six companies of Massachusetts troops, 690 men in all, had concentrated at Rehoboth. Massachusetts's commanders included Appleton and Mosely, fresh from the Connecticut Valley, and Captain James Oliver, the Massachusetts magistrate. Also present was Joseph Dudley, representing the Massachusetts government, and Plymouth veteran Benjamin Church, now a captain serving as an aide to the overall colonial commander, General Winslow.

They knew they were fighting not only for their people and for justice but for land. Many colonial leaders had a stake in Narragansett, Pocasset, or Sakonnet land, and Plymouth pledged "that the lands and other profits of the war" seized "by the blessing of God" would be set aside for soldiers. A proclamation was read to Massachusetts troops promising that if they conquered Narragansett country they would be rewarded with land in addition to wages. The merchant Nathaniel Saltonstall thought that Weetamoo's Pocasset lands alone would "more than pay all the charge we have been at in this unhappy war."

Most of Winslow's army was ferried to Providence on December 11. Mosely's company disembarked at Wickford.[17] The following day, scouts reported that Pomham's Shawomets, whose long-standing conflict with Warwick, Rhode Island, had pushed them into an alliance with the Narragansetts, were on the Pawtuxet River, perhaps a dozen miles away. Winslow marched through the "bitter cold night" to capture them, but despite clear skies and a bright moon, his guides got lost. He finally led his exhausted soldiers to Wickford. Near dawn, Mosely's forces surprised about thirty-five Indians. As a rule, they killed men while capturing women and children to sell as slaves. One old man was so decrepit that his son had to carry him. Soldiers wanted him "devoured by dogs," but others urged compassion, so they cut off his head instead. Captain Church claimed that he presented eighteen captives to Winslow, including two boys. Smiling, Winslow said he had no doubt Church "would supply them with Indian boys enough before the war was ended."[18]

A Narragansett named Peter preserved his life by serving as an informant. He claimed that the Narragansetts had three thousand warriors, though many were poorly armed. They were gathering at Pessicus's fort in the great Narragansett swamp. He revealed the location of two Narragansett towns, including the female sachem Quaiapin's. Making no attempt at negotiation, Winslow unleashed his troops against the towns on December 14. They killed seven Indians and captured nine, burning 150 wigwams in Quaiapin's town alone. Only one colonial soldier was wounded. That same day, scouts killed two men and a woman and captured three others. Perhaps a fifth of all captives were Wampanoags. Success left soldiers "very cheerful," despite the cold. "Thus far our God hath been pleased to appear for us," pastor Noah Newman wrote from Rehoboth. "We are eagerly waiting to hear what God hath further to do."

The following day, a Narragansett named Stonewall John showed up at Wickford and informed the colonists that the sachems had sent him to negotiate. He warned that the colonies would regret provoking a war. Rather than pursue an agreement, however, the annoyed officers sent him away and told him to return with the sachems. Less than fifteen minutes later, Narragansett warriors ambushed Massachusetts troops within a mile of Winslow's headquarters. Others attacked soldiers occupying a house three miles away. Warriors even fired at three companies marching out of Wickford. Five colonial soldiers were killed, convincing the furious officers that Stonewall John's visit was simply a ruse.

General Winslow wanted to strike Pessicus's fort, but Major Robert Treat's Connecticut forces had not arrived yet, so he lacked the manpower. Winslow sent Captain Thomas Prentice's Massachusetts cavalry to meet them at Jireh Bull's garrison house at Pettaquamscut, nine miles south, on December 16. Narragansetts got there first. When Prentice arrived, he found Bull's house burned to the ground and at least seventeen colonists dead, including five women and children, no doubt in retaliation for Winslow's unprovoked attack. Major Treat, with five Connecticut companies totaling three hundred soldiers, plus 150 Mohegans and Pequots, approached Pettaquamscut the following night, taking a dozen Narragansetts on the way. Winslow arrived late the next afternoon and called a council of war.

The colonial army numbered about 1,140 men. The temperature was plummeting, it was snowing, and there was no available shelter. With provisions dwindling, the officers agreed that they had no choice but to attack Pessicus's fort or abandon the campaign. They ordered the men to prepare to march at dawn and arranged for the shipment of forty-seven captives by Captain Nathaniel Davenport. "That night was very stormy," Oliver recalled. "We lay, one thousand [men], in the open field that long night." They huddled around fires to keep warm as snow piled around them. The next day would be the Puritan Sabbath. Many believed it would bring the greatest battle of the war.[19]

THEY MUSTERED BEFORE dawn and commenced their march at around 5:00 a.m. Massachusetts forces led the way, guided by Peter, the Narragansett informant. Plymouth followed, and Connecticut took up the rear. The storm had taken its toll. Men with severe frostbite of the hands or feet had to be left behind.

The blizzard had left two or three feet of snow, one of the heaviest snowfalls in years, but although the march was exhausting, General Winslow did not permit them to stop and cook food. They marched seven or eight hours through a forest of "mighty oaks, maples, and ashes," covering as many as fifteen miles.

Peter guided them to the edge of a thick cedar swamp, where Mosely's troops exchanged fire with Indian scouts. They pursued the scouts, rushing over frozen wetlands that were ordinarily impassable, until they came upon a massive palisade: five or six acres of slightly elevated ground, strengthened with flankers and numerous blockhouses. In front were downed trees and brush, forming an obstruction five yards deep. There was only one gate, and approaching it required traversing a single narrow log. It was the most formidable Algonquian fortification they had ever seen.

However, officers discovered that near one corner, next to a blockhouse, the palisade was incomplete. All that obstructed the gap was a fallen tree resting four feet above the ground. That would be their point of attack.

Captains Isaac Johnson and Nathaniel Davenport led their Massachusetts companies forward, but the Narragansetts were ready and greeted them with a withering fire. Men attempting to climb over the fallen tree were cut down, including Johnson, who was killed. Davenport led a few men into the fort before he was riddled with bullets. With his last breaths, he called a lieutenant to take command. Lieutenant Phineas Upham, who had plundered the praying towns during an earlier expedition, was mortally wounded. Survivors scrambled for cover. Captains Mosely and Joseph Gardiner brought up their companies, but they too failed to break through. For about an hour, four Massachusetts companies lay pinned down by "many thousand shot."[20]

Finally, the last Massachusetts companies, commanded by Appleton and Oliver, were committed. "They run! They run!" an officer cried, and several hundred soldiers surged forward. This time they broke through, only to suffer heavy fire from the blockhouse to the right and a flanker on the left. They drove the warriors out of the flanker and exchanged fire with Indians further down the palisade. Winslow sent in Treat's three hundred Connecticut troops, but no one warned them that the Narragansetts still held the blockhouse. They paid dearly, with many gunned down as they entered the fort. A soldier named Samuel Hall was shot twice in each thigh. Captain John Mason Jr., whose father had led the attack on Mystic thirty-eight years before, fell next to him. Hall grasped Mason's hand, but the wounded captain gathered his strength and continued forward.

While officers fell with galling frequency, the soldiers slugged it out, gradually driving the enemy from one position after another, "first into the middle, and then into the upper end of the fort."[21] Accounts are confusing, but at some point, according to Joseph Dudley, Massachusetts's representative, the Narragansetts reorganized and "fell on [us] again, recarried and beat us out of the fort." Many soldiers remained inside, however, so Winslow committed his reserve, the Plymouth troops. Dead and wounded piled up as fighting raged both inside and outside the palisade. Major Bradford was shot "in the back, a little under one shoulder."[22]

Captain Church secured permission to join the fight. Leading thirty men inside the palisade, he was dismayed to see "many men and several valiant captains lie slain." He spotted Captain Gardiner among the wigwams and walked toward him. Suddenly the captain dropped, blood streaming down his cheek from a bullet wound to the head. Church cried his name, but all he received was a silent stare. Believing the bullet had come from outside the fort, he sent a courier to alert General Winslow that soldiers were suffering from friendly fire. Narragansetts were also fighting outside the palisade, so Church led his men back toward the swamp. When an Indian tried to surrender, one of Church's men shot him.

Suddenly they heard "a great shout" behind them. Indians were running through the trees to fire on soldiers in the fort. The soldiers prepared to return fire, only for a sergeant to yell "for God's sake not to fire," for the Indians were allies. Church hesitated but decided the sergeant was mistaken. His men fired a volley, scattering the surprised warriors. They pursued some into the fort, but suddenly Church went down, a bullet piercing his leg and another glancing off the joint of his hip-bone. A soldier who tried to move him took an arrow in the shoulder.[23]

Winslow grew concerned. Night was approaching, casualties were mounting, and the enemy kept coming. He decided to adopt the tactic John Mason had used at Fort Mystic during the Pequot War: burn the wigwams, even though women, children, and elderly remained inside. The wounded Samuel Hall recalled the moment: "I lay bleeding there in the snow, and hearing the word commanded to set fire on the wigwams, I considered I should be burned if I did not crawl away." Despite excruciating pain, "it pleased God to give me strength to get up and get out, with my cutlass in my hand."[24]

Captain Church later claimed he objected to Winslow's order because the wigwams were full of provisions and could offer shelter during the long cold night. He believed the enemy was nearly defeated, so burning the fort was unnecessary. A doctor countered that if they did not return the eighteen miles to Wickford that night, many wounded would die.[25] Whether or not Church actually protested, Winslow gave the order. His men burned an estimated five hundred wigwams, despite "many living and dead persons in them, great piles of meat, and heaps of corn." They also destroyed a blacksmith's forge. The Narragansetts, out of ammunition, were unable to stop them.

The consensus among officers was that they had killed "at least two hundred men," not including hundreds who perished in the wigwams. But the English also suffered grievously: 218 soldiers were casualties—about 20 percent of the army. At least twenty of them were dead. Seven company commanders were dead or mortally wounded. Nearly half the casualties were from Connecticut.

Fearing a counterattack, General Winslow gave his men little time to rest or treat the wounded. The exhausted, hungry, and shivering troops were on their way before dark, flames raging behind. Many wounded had to walk, as there were not enough horses to carry them. If the Narragansetts had attacked, Dudley believed, the English would have been gobbled up like "a morsel." "One signal mercy that night, not to be forgotten," Captain Oliver admitted, was "that when we drew off with so many dead and wounded, they did not pursue us." Even so, many did not survive that "long, snowy, cold night." Winslow and forty men went missing. The rest trudged on, soldiers dying every hour. The wounded Samuel Hall had lost his coat and knapsack, but he was better off than many. By the time they reached Wickford, ten hours later, thirty-four more soldiers had died. At least twenty-eight would succumb over the following weeks, raising the confirmed colonial death toll to eighty-two.

Winslow showed up around 7:00 a.m. The army was "much disabled," Dudley reported. In addition to the wounded, about two hundred were laid low from exhaustion, sickness, or frostbite. Suffering men filled Richard Smith Jr.'s house, but most had "no lodgings." A soldier named John Bull recalled being "laid in a cold chamber [with] a wooden pillow. My covering was the snow the wind drove on me." Hall lay on straw for days, with nothing but icy water to drink. Eventually he was transported to Rhode Island, first by cart, then by boat, as were the rest of the wounded.[26]

Their ordeal was all the worse because there were not enough surgeons. One, Simon Cooper, extracted fragments from Captain Mason's shattered skull. He treated a Connecticut soldier "shot through the mouth, and his upper jaw broke, which the [other] surgeons would not dress because they said he was a dead man." He helped one whose shoulder blade was "shot to pieces," and another, "his jaw broke and many pieces taken out."[27]

Pastor Newman visited the wounded, including his friend William Bradford. Bradford would recover, though the projectile that struck him remained in his body for the rest of his life. Mason lingered for months but eventually died. John Bull returned home to Hingham, where for two years he was unable to work. After that he could labor "with much pain," but thirty years later he still suffered "upon every little cold or change of weather."[28]

Many Narragansetts wanted to attack the retreating English, but their sachems refused because they lacked ammunition. The following day, Ninigret's men, who had stood by while the English battled their kin, began burying charred and mangled corpses. A person who had been with the sachems claimed they counted ninety-seven killed and forty-eight wounded, not including those burned in the wigwams. Narragansetts informed the Nipmucs that forty warriors, one sachem, and "about 300 old men, women, and children" were killed. Captives later estimated the number at 300 warriors plus 350 women and children. Later claims were inflated to more than a thousand deaths. Among the wounded was the young sachem Quinnapin, shot through the thigh.

Their homes were destroyed, their food stores devastated. Many would suffer severely that winter. Nevertheless, Narragansett power had not been broken. They still had at least seven hundred warriors, some said thousands. Thanks to the colonies' invasion, Philip's coalition was stronger than ever before.[29]

NEWS OF THE bloodbath and Winslow's dismal retreat shocked colonists. Had the Narragansetts "pursued our soldiers . . . when upon their retreat, they might easily have cut off the whole army," Increase Mather realized. Had God punished the army for fighting on the Sabbath?[30] "It appears [that] though the enemy have received considerable damage," Rehoboth colonist George Shove wrote John Cotton Jr., "his power is not yet broken. The Lord's hand is yet against us. We are not prepared for mercy. Pray, pray, pray."[31] "I wish I could hear you prophesy good to this land," a distraught Cotton wrote Mather. "I should then believe these wars may have an end. . . . If we lose Captain Bradford, we lose a great part of our glory, and I, most of my comfort as to man. I beseech you, pray earnestly for his life, if it be not too late."[32] "Philip still lives!" another colonist mourned, and "by his subtlety proves a more forcible and perilous enemy to us than ever we could have imagined."[33]

Rhode Island deputy governor John Easton was mortified when he learned that Winslow had attacked without offering fair terms, for he had "often informed the Indians that Englishmen would not begin a war," since "it was brutish so to do." He had also promised many Narragansetts that if they minded their own business, the English would leave them alone. "I am sorry the Indians have cause to think me deceitful," he mourned. He was baffled by the decision to attack a neutral people more powerful than any the English had yet fought, provoking their inevitable vengeance. How many innocent people would suffer for it? As a Quaker, he blamed the Puritan clergy. "They have been the cause that the law of nations and the law of arms have been violated in this war," he charged. The magistrates were merely their "pack horses."[34]

Others focused on what had been accomplished. Leaders in Connecticut were saddened by "the loss and suffering of so many worthy and deserving men" but "thankful for the success and victory of our armies over our blasphemous and bloody heathen adversaries."[35] Wait Winthrop wrote a thirty-two-stanza poem eulogizing New England's slain. Like his father, the governor, he recognized that

Algonquians were fighting for freedom, but he had no doubt New England's cause was God's.

> It grieves my heart, and makes it smart
>> I cannot choose but weep
> To think on those, who on the snows
>> are forced to take their sleep.

God was using the Indians to discipline his people, Wait believed, but once his wrath was appeased, they would be eradicated like a plague of rats,

> Lest they do boast of their great host,
>> and praise their god the Devil,
> From whom indeed, this doth proceed
>> the author of all evil.

Until then, New Englanders had to arm themselves with ammunition and prayer, confident that God rewarded soldiers who died in Christ's service:

> Though here they die immediately,
>> yet they shall go to rest,
> And at that day the Lord will say,
>> happy art thou, and blessed.[36]

It was, after all, a war for Christ's kingdom, which in the long run, they could not lose. On that, Puritans were agreed.

THE COMMISSIONERS REACTED TO Winslow's campaign by announcing that God was calling them "aloud" to defeat the Narragansetts before spring and requesting an additional one thousand soldiers.[37] But Winslow's army struggled to even feed itself. Soldiers consumed Richard Smith Jr.'s cattle, goats, and hogs and dismantled his fences and buildings for fuel. They raided Indian stores and burned sixty wigwams at Shawomet. Connecticut soldiers began to desert, so Major Treat led his contingent back to New London. Reinforcements arrived from Massachusetts, but many suffered frostbite or were "sick and disheartened," and eleven died.[38]

Colonists tried to encourage the troops. One wrote an eloquent letter invoking the New Testament's exhortations to "put on the whole armor of God" and not "do the work of the Lord negligently," for "He shall tread down your enemies and make you more than conquerors through Jesus Christ our Lord." Those exhortations were metaphorical and had nothing to do with military conflict, but that was ignored. Most Puritans had no doubt their soldiers were Christian heroes executing God's justice in service of Christ.[39] The reality was more troubling. Connecticut's Deputy Governor Leete complained that Massachusetts soldiers provoked God's wrath by "uncivil, if not inhumane deportment towards the living and dead," and he feared that if such behavior continued, God would no longer "go forth with the armies of Israel."[40] On one occasion, soldiers tortured an Indian by wrapping a cord around his head, inserting a thin device, and gradually twisting the cord to inflict excruciating pain.[41]

On December 23, Narragansett representatives arrived at Wickford to discuss peace terms. General Winslow acquiesced, hoping for time to rebuild his army, but with the English demanding the surrender of all refugees, discussions went nowhere. A Narragansett pointed out that the English were the aggressors, having invaded Narragansett country without even a declaration of war. But Winslow refused to debate questions of justice. How did the sachems like losing so many men? he taunted. If they were real men, they should come speak to him in person. They could bring an escort and would be permitted to leave in peace.

Pessicus, the senior Narragansett sachem, still wanted peace, but younger sachems refused to sign another humiliating treaty. Canonchet suggested agreeing to a meeting to buy time. Pessicus declined, saying he was old and "would not lie to the English." "If you will fight, fight, for tis a folly for me to fight any longer." Canonchet replied that even if he went to Wickford, no one else would support him. A commander added that "he would not yield to the English so long as an Indian would stand with him." He had fought "English and French and Dutch and Mohawks and feared none of them," and he knew if "they yielded to the English, they should be dead men or slaves."

Nevertheless, on January 5, 1676, the sachems graciously sent Winslow a three- or four-year-old English child Pomham's Shawomets had taken from Warwick. But when they claimed they had misunderstood the treaty Canonchet signed in October, the officers decided they were merely stalling. This impression was confirmed a week later when Pessicus requested a month's delay before confirming a treaty. Winslow finally broke off negotiations, although the commissioners encouraged him to persevere.[42] As Rhode Island's Deputy Governor Easton wryly observed, "the English dare not trust the Indians' promises, neither the Indians to the English's promises, and each have great case."[43]

Winslow felt ready to resume the offensive, but Connecticut's forces protested having to return to Wickford, and some still urged Winslow to seek "an honorable peace."[44] The opportunity for a decisive victory was rapidly slipping away. On January 14 Rhode Island forces were pursuing a Narragansett war party near Providence when they wounded and captured a colonist named Joshua Tift. Captives claimed Tift had lived with the Narragansetts and fought along-side them in Pessicus's fort, killing several soldiers, but Tift insisted Canonchet had captured him at Pettaquamscut. He claimed the Mohegans and Pequots betrayed the English during the battle and that forty of Ninigret's men fought with the Narragansetts. He also revealed that the main body of Narragansetts was heading for Quaboag, in Nipmuc country. "A sad wretch, he never heard a sermon but once, these fourteen years," Captain Oliver concluded after Tift was turned over to Winslow. The minister William Hubbard claimed Tift had "turned Indian, married one of the Indian squaws, [and] renounced his religion, nation and natural parents." When asked about Christianity, "he was found as ignorant as a heathen." The officers condemned him as a traitor, and he was exe-cuted on January 18.[45]

NOT LONG AFTER THE swamp battle, Massachusetts ordered Daniel Gookin to recruit two praying Indians as spies. Gookin selected Job Kattenanit, whose children the Nipmucs held captive, and James Quanapohit, a Nashaway scout.[46]

They started out on December 30, carrying hatchets and "a little parched meal," with the aim of discerning enemy intentions. Encountering Nipmucs near Maanexit, they were brought to the Nipmuc refuge at Menameset on January 4. Wigwams housing about nine hundred people were scattered over an area about "three miles compass." Kattenanit was greatly relieved to find his children among the 120 praying Indians taken from Hassanamesit. They had been well-treated. The praying Indian ruler Captain Tom Wuttasacomponom and his son Nehemiah said they had refused attempts to recruit them to fight, leading Nipmucs to scoff that they "cried when they were carried away, more like squaws than men." Lame from injury and having lost a son to illness, Captain Tom declared that he yearned to escape if the English would accept him. Kattenanit's father, Naoas, and brother, Tuckawillipin, said reading the Bible daily was their "greatest comfort."[47]

Many Nipmucs, especially the praying Indian Matoonas, suspected that Kattenanit and Quanapohit were spies, and Tuckawillipin warned Quanapohit that Philip had ordered him killed. So Quanapohit was relieved when he encountered his friend Monoco, a Nashaway with whom he had served in the Mohawk War. Monoco was glad to see him. "I know thou art a valiant man," he said, "and therefore none shall wrong thee nor kill thee here, but they shall first kill me. Therefore abide at my wigwam, and I will protect thee." When men threatened Quanapohit, Monoco fired his gun and threatened to kill anyone who touched him.

To earn the enemy's trust, Quanapohit and Kattenanit painted their faces and participated in a multi-night dance. They went on hunting expeditions. They gleaned valuable intelligence. Monoco revealed that Philip was near Albany seeking ammunition and allies. The valley Indians were in Sokoki country, and a valley sachem had attempted to assassinate Philip for starting a war that "brought great trouble upon them." The Nipmucs also remained divided. The "chief men and old men" wanted peace, but the young men were not interested. "We are all or most of us alive yet, and the English have killed very few of us last summer," some said. "Why shall we have peace [only] to be made slaves and either be killed or sent away to sea to Barbados? Let us live as long as we can and die like men and not live to be enslaved."

Contrary to English suspicions, the Narragansetts had not been the Nipmucs' allies. In fact, the Nipmucs had regarded the Narragansetts as English allies until the English invaded Narragansett country. Since then, the Narragansetts had sent them a dozen English scalps, which Quanapohit saw hanging on trees. The Nipmucs had large quantities of corn, beef, pork, and venison, but they had not anticipated needing to feed hundreds of Narragansetts. They intended to raid English towns, beginning with Lancaster, for corn and livestock.[48]

In mid-January, Quanapohit discovered that the Quaboag sachem Muttaump wanted to bring him to Philip to discuss "the breach between the English and Narragansetts." Fearing Philip would kill him, Quanapohit convinced Muttaump to let him first "kill some Englishmen" to earn Philip's trust. Meanwhile, he and Kattenanit plotted their escape. Their opportunity came during a hunting trip. They had shot four deer and spent the evening of January 19 dressing and eating venison. Around 3:00 a.m., Quanapohit suggested they slip away. But Kattenanit hesitated, loath to abandon his children. He asked Quanapohit to meet him at Natick in three weeks, when he hoped he could take them with him. Quanapohit protested, but Kattenanit was resolved. "If God please, he can preserve my life. If not, I am willing to die." They prayed before Quanapohit departed. Walking on snowshoes nearly eighty miles "through the woods, night and day," he arrived in Natick on January 23, "very weary, faint, and spent."

His report to the council, two days later in Boston, confirmed what they had already learned from New York governor Edmund Andros. If Philip had been near Narragansett country that winter, it was not for long, for he and several hundred warriors were near Albany seeking Mohawk support. When Thomas Danforth asked "whether the Narragansetts had aided and assisted Philip," Quanapohit told him they had not. The Nipmucs had always viewed them "as friends to the English" and as "their enemies."

The truth was painfully obvious. Although many Narragansetts had wanted to fight the English, and some were doing so, their sachems had done everything they could to remain neutral while protecting Wampanoag refugees from captivity. Attacking them had not disrupted a Narragansett-Wampanoag-Nipmuc alliance; it had created it. The enemy expected "to carry all before them," Quanapohit warned. They would hit Lancaster within three weeks.[49]

ON JANUARY 21 A warm front brought what Increase Mather described as "strange warm weather, like April," rapidly melting the heavy snow.[50] The main body of Narragansetts was about ten miles northwest of Providence. Prentice's Massachusetts cavalry took eleven Indians that day. Six days later, Narragansetts led by the recently wounded Quinnapin raided William Carpenter's farm near Warwick. They burned corn, hay, and farm buildings and seized two hundred sheep, fifty cattle, and fifteen horses.[51] They also raided William Harris's farm. An ambitious landholder who had helped found Providence, eventually becoming a magistrate, Harris was a bitter rival to Roger Williams, who accused him of defrauding the Narragansetts of a substantial tract of land. Now Indians who accused him of "Commootin [theft]" burned his house, barns, and "above fifty load of hay." They also drove off fifty cattle and eighty horses and killed his thirty-year-old son and an enslaved African. Already willing to shift his loyalty to Connecticut to defend his interests, Harris became all the more bitter at Rhode Island for failing to protect him.[52]

Rage over Indian depredations was rising in Connecticut too. Two half-starved Pequots allied with the Narragansetts had been jailed at New London. When word arrived that two colonists were killed and a teenage boy missing at Norwich, two Connecticut soldiers went to the jail and shot the Pequots to death. Guards refused to reveal the culprits, and New London would not punish them.

Finally, on January 28, forty days after the swamp battle, General Winslow launched his pursuit of the Narragansetts. He had as many as fourteen hundred troops, including Major Treat's Connecticut forces.[53] Mohegan and Pequot scouts flushed war parties from the woods and swamps to prevent ambushes, enabling the army to kill some seventy Indians, including women and children. On February 1 they reached the camp where the Narragansetts had spent the better part of a month. "There were many wigwams in sight, but an icy swamp lying between them and the wigwams prevented their running at once upon it," recalled Captain Church, whose wounds left him unable to mount a horse without help. But the Narragansetts got away. Soldiers burned nearly five hundred wigwams and discovered the remains of sixty horses the Indians had eaten.

Winslow continued almost as far as Quaboag, but morale plummeted with every mile. Soldiers would remember it as "the hungry march." Rations ran so low that they too were reduced to eating horses. Many, including Winslow, suffered from dysentery. Some Plymouth soldiers deserted. At a council of war on February 3, most officers advised retreat. Winslow allowed Connecticut's troops to return south and marched the rest of the army eastward.[54]

His critics were many. "Mutineers and renegades filled the spirits of people with base prejudice against the general," John Cotton Jr. complained. "God's anger burns against this poor land. What will become of us?"[55] Equally frustrated, pastor Thomas Walley defended Winslow. "We know no man in the place he hath sustained that could have preserved his honor in the service of this country better than he hath done."[56]

Increase Mather believed God was judging Massachusetts for failing to enforce its reform legislation. "We have often carried it before the Lord as if we would reform our ways," he wrote, "and yet when it hath come to, we have done nothing."[57] Famine seemed imminent, and smallpox was reported in Plymouth and Boston. A Quaker nailed a note to Mather's meeting house declaring that its ruin was at hand. Mather considered the Quakers "false prophets" but feared this prophecy might come true.

During a lecture in Boston on January 27, he mentioned that visitors reported seeing "more drunkenness in New England in half a year than in England in all their lives." Afterward, over dinner, Governor Leverett, who had spent time in England, told Mather this was ludicrous and that drunkenness was actually less common than in years past. Magistrate William Stoughton amiably declared that Mather would have to "preach a recantation sermon." "No," Mather retorted, "but if men would not accept my labors, God will." The next day, frustration turned to despair. "Sad thoughts in my heart with respect to the state of this poor country, fearing yet greater judgment and ill success as to armies," he wrote in his diary. The magistrates had "no heart to do what they might in order to reformation," he added, "especially the governor. Nor will they call upon the churches to renew their covenant with God." A week later, when he read the reform legislation from his pulpit, two church members accused him of abusing his authority.

Mather also feared another cause of God's wrath: colonists were consumed with "unreasonable rage against the enemy," and "there is guilt upon the land in respect of the Indians, yea guilt of blood in respect of the Indian so treacherously murdered at Chelmsford."[58]

WITH WINSLOW'S RETREAT, the colonies had abandoned a vast corridor of New England, from Narragansett country north through Nipmuc territory to the upper Connecticut Valley. Algonquians, their numbers bolstered by the Narragansetts, could roam undetected through this wilderness, suddenly assaulting Massachusetts towns to the east and west, or turning south toward Connecticut, Rhode Island, or Plymouth. If pursued, they could easily withdraw northward, where the English would never find them.

Thomas Eames and his wife, Mary, had settled near the praying town of Magunkog in 1669. There Eames built a two-story house where they lived with a dozen children. On February 1, while Eames was in Boston, eleven mostly praying Indians came to retrieve corn from Magunkog. One was Netus, who had confessed his faith before the Puritan clergy in 1652. Another was Job Kattenanit's brother Annaweekin, whom John Eliot described as a godly and penitent Christian. When they discovered their corn missing, Netus and Annaweekin suspected Eames. According to the praying Indian William Wannukhow, they "earnestly moved to go to Goodman Eames's farm for to get corn." Wannukhow and his sons objected, "but they by their persuasion and threatening carried us with them." They killed Mary Eames and several children and torched the farm. While some plundered corn and provisions, according to Wannukhow, "one of us carried one boy upon our backs rather than let them be killed." They took the surviving children to Menameset.[59]

Fearing retaliation, the praying Indians at Wamesit petitioned Massachusetts to move them to a safer location. But most fled north, unwilling to wait, leaving six or seven elderly people behind. Soon after, colonial vigilantes furtively approached their wigwam, set it on fire, and burned them to death. The suspects were never brought to trial.[60]

New England was spinning out of control, and everything the United Colonies did seemed to make it worse. The invasion of Narragansett country had been an unmitigated disaster. With the Narragansetts now on Philip's side, the worst was yet to come.

18

New England in Flames

February 1676 to March 1676

THE ALGONQUIAN ONSLAUGHT began in February, 1676. It unfolded just as the Christian Nashaway James Quanapohit had warned it would, though Massachusetts foolishly ignored his warning. Within weeks, it brought New England to its knees.

Quanapohit's fellow spy, Job Kattenanit, had remained with the Nipmucs so he could escape with his children, but upon learning that four hundred warriors were marching for Lancaster, he knew he could not wait any longer. Leaving his children behind, he reached Major Daniel Gookin's Cambridge home at around 10:00 p.m. on Wednesday, February 9. Gookin was in bed, but Kattenanit was ushered into his bedroom. Within moments Gookin was up and conferring with his neighbor, fellow magistrate Thomas Danforth. They dispatched couriers to warn Lancaster and ordered 120 soldiers to march there from Marlborough and Concord. Captain Samuel Wadsworth set out from Marlborough with forty men shortly after dawn. Lancaster, with its 350 inhabitants, was ten miles away.[1]

Mary Rowlandson, the thirty-nine-year-old wife of Lancaster's pastor, heard the first shots around sunrise. Rushing to the window, she saw houses burning. Colonists scrambled for cover while warriors cut them down with hatchets or bullets, some shooting from the roof of a barn. A wounded colonist offered money if they spared his life. They "knocked him in the head and stripped him naked and split open his bowels." Warriors entered a house and bashed in the heads of a man, his wife, and their nursing infant.

Mary's husband, Joseph, had gone to Boston seeking reinforcements, but clearly he was too late. Warriors shot at the Rowlandson home, an unfinished garrison house, from every direction, "so that the bullets seemed to fly like hail." Three men inside were wounded, but they held the Indians at bay for about two hours, until the warriors used flax and hemp to ignite the house. "Some in our house were fighting for their lives," Mary Rowlandson recalled, "others wallowing in their blood, the house on fire over our heads, and the bloody heathen ready to knock us on the head if we stirred out." Mothers and children cried, "Lord, what shall we do?"

To remain in the blazing inferno was certain death, so Rowlandson called her children, picked up her six-year-old daughter, Sarah, and opened the door. Bullets rattled against the wall "as if one had taken a handful of stones and threw them," so she retreated, but not for long. "Out we must go, the fire increasing and coming along behind us, roaring, and the Indians gaping before us with their guns, spears and hatchets to devour us." A bullet tore through her side and, to her horror, "through the bowels and hand of my dear child in my arms." Another killed her brother-in-law, and a third shattered her nephew William's leg. Warriors finished William off with a blow to the head and began stripping the dead. "Lord, let me die with them," her sister muttered, and was immediately killed. "Thus were we butchered by those merciless heathen," Rowlandson remembered, "with the blood running down to our heels." One person had been "chopped into the head" and stripped naked but was still "crawling up and down." It was "a solemn sight to see so many Christians lying in their blood," "stripped naked by a company of hell-hounds, roaring, singing, ranting and insulting, as if they would have torn our very hearts out."

Warriors led some captive children away, though Sarah was left with Rowlandson. Rowlandson had always said she "would choose rather to be killed by them than be taken alive," but now she changed her mind. "Their glittering weapons so daunted my spirit that I chose rather to go along with those, as I may say, ravenous beasts, than that moment to end my days." She and twenty-three other colonists, including her three children, were marched into captivity.[2]

Meanwhile, Captain Wadsworth's company from Marlborough approached the burning town undetected. The bridge over the Nashua River was burning but passable, so they moved into town.[3] At least fifty of Lancaster's people were dead, wounded, or missing. At least five of those killed were under eleven years old. Joseph Rowlandson arrived to discover that almost his entire extended family was gone.[4]

Mary Rowlandson's captors included Wampanoags, Narragansetts, and local Nashaways led by Shoshanim and Monoco, who knew that as a pastor's wife and the daughter of a prominent landowner, she would prove a valuable bargaining chip.[5] They walked a mile before stopping on a high hill overlooking the town. When she requested permission to sleep in an abandoned house, they mocked her, "Will you love English men still?" They feasted on plundered "horses, cattle, sheep, swine, calves, lambs, roasting pigs, and fowl," but she received nothing. "Oh the roaring and singing and dancing and yelling of those black creatures in the night, which made the place a lively resemblance of hell!" she later wrote. It was "the dolefullest night that ever my eyes saw."

They resumed their march in the morning. "One of the Indians carried my poor wounded babe upon a horse," and she "went moaning all along, 'I shall die, I shall die.'" Rowlandson carried her for a while, but she too was wounded and eventually collapsed in exhaustion. The Indians then allowed her to ride bare-back with Sarah in her lap. Once, as the horse descended a steep hill, she lost her grip and both "fell over the horse's head" to the ground. Indians burst into laughter. It snowed, and that night she struggled to warm herself by a small fire. Sarah had a "violent fever" and called repeatedly for water, but Rowlandson was so stiff she could hardly "sit down or rise up."

The next day, an Indian allowed her to sit behind him on his horse with Sarah in her lap, which provided welcome relief. But now she and Sarah suffered the agony of hunger, having had nothing since the night before the raid "except only a little cold water." Indians offered food, but not the sort she was willing to eat. They reached Menameset, the Nipmuc refuge, early that afternoon. There were praying Indians there, but she considered them all heathen. "Oh the number of pagans, now merciless enemies, that there came about me," she thought. She was sold to the Narragansett sachem Quinnapin, who by marriage to Weetamoo was Philip's brother-in-law. He was a primary English target, for he had once been jailed in Newport, had escaped, and had since emerged as a leading Narragansett commander.

The next day was the Puritan Sabbath, and Rowlandson despaired that God was punishing her for wasting Sabbaths past. Much to her surprise, an English soldier approached: Robert Pepper, who had been captured by Shoshanim at Beers's ambush in September. He told her that Indians used oak leaves to treat his wounded leg and suggested she try it. Much to her surprise, the remedy worked, and her wound began to heal. But Sarah did not. "I sat much alone with a poor wounded child in my lap," she later recalled, while Sarah "moaned night and day." Exasperated Indians threatened that Quinnapin would "knock your child in the head" and told her to take the moaning girl somewhere else. With a "very heavy heart," she fled their presence and sat on the ground, her daughter "the picture of death in my lap." Two hours into the night on February 18, Sarah's suffering ended: "My sweet babe like a lamb departed this life."

Rowlandson considered taking her own life as she clung to Sarah's body that horrible night. But again she chose life over death. In the morning, Indians told her to return to Quinnapin's wigwam. "I went to take up my dead child in my arms to carry it with me, but they bid me let it alone. There was no resisting, but go I must and leave it." Later they showed her where they buried Sarah's body. "There I left that child in the wilderness and must commit it, and myself also in this wilderness condition, to him who is above all."[6]

She had two other children in captivity, however, and she managed to find ten-year-old Mary. Upon seeing her mother, the traumatized girl burst into tears. Her constant weeping annoyed Indians, and again they forced Rowlandson to leave, eventually forbidding her from visiting Mary at all. "I had one child dead, another in the wilderness I knew not where, [and] the third they would not let me come near to." She prayed that God might give her "some sign and hope of some relief." Soon after, her son Joseph found her. He inquired tearfully about Sarah, and Rowlandson gave him the awful news.[7]

"THIS NEWS FROM Lancaster is exceeding sad and should greatly humble us," pastor Thomas Walley mourned. That a pastor's family had been targeted was especially disconcerting. Increase Mather concluded that God was threatening to withdraw his gospel. Others took it as evidence of Indians' "damnable antipathy . . . to religion."[8] Colonists accused Quanapohit and Kattenanit of treachery, even though they had warned of the attack. One colonist claimed Indians were saying that in the spring warriors would rescue praying Indians from Deer Island, when "they will make Boston, especially the magistrates, pay dear for sundry hours they have been kept there." Colonial vigilantes discussed going to Deer Island to "kill all the praying Indians," and it was more than idle chatter. A man testified under oath that he had been solicited to join a night raid against the island. The council summoned the ringleaders and warned them to desist.[9]

Terror consumed the frontier. Medfield's pastor John Wilson Jr. begged for reinforcements "by the soonest, by the soonest that possibly can be, lest Medfield be turned into ashes." The town of about eighty homes had one hundred militiamen commanded by Lieutenant Henry Adams, known for his hostility to Christian Indians, and the governor sent one hundred reinforcements under Captain John Jacob. Guards were posted, but Medfield had cleared too much land, and its fields were overgrown, enabling some three hundred enemy warriors to approach undetected during the predawn hours of February 21. When unsuspecting colonists stepped outside that morning, Indians gunned them down. A man named Dwight looked to see what the noise was and was shot in the shoulder. Joshua Fisher was hit after leaving his grandmother's home, the bullet "passing through some flesh about his collar bone" and grazing his throat. Lieutenant Adams, stepping over his threshold, "was shot through the windpipe and fell down dead."

Indians torched buildings and shot colonists who fled the flames. A husband and wife took off in different directions, each carrying a child. One was killed, the other survived. A hundred-year-old man burned to death in his home. It was like the terrible Day of the Lord, Rehoboth's pastor Noah Newman later reflected, "fires being kindled round about them, the enemy numerous and shouting so as the earth seemed to tremble, and the cry of the terrified persons very dreadful." Sergeant Thomas Thurston's wife was holding the hands of two children when all three were struck down. Warriors stripped her and left her for dead. Later she came to, found a blanket, and ran to Pastor Wilson's house. Although they did not recognize her, "her hair hanging down and her face covered with blood," the occupants pulled her to safety. Samuel Smith's wife, "big with child and another child in her arms," was killed fleeing to a garrison house.

Struggling to organize his scattered men, Captain Jacob accidentally discharged his gun, sending a bullet through the ceiling and mortally wounding Lieutenant Adams's wife upstairs. Only after soldiers fired a cannon several times did the Algonquians withdraw across the Charles River, laden with plunder. Surviving inhabitants were stunned by the death and destruction. Samuel Smith's child was found standing by the body of his slain wife. Two Thurston children were recovered, one wounded in the head and a daughter shot through both thighs. A third was missing. At least seventeen colonists were dead or dying, and many others were wounded. About fifty buildings were burned, including twenty-nine homes. A trooper found a chilling note posted on the Charles River bridge, probably written by a praying Indian: "Know by this paper that the Indians that thou hast provoked to wrath and anger will war this twenty one years if you will. There are many Indians yet. We come three hundred at this time. You must consider the Indians lost nothing but their life. You must lose your fair houses and cattle."[10]

Mary Rowlandson could hear the triumphant warriors returning to Menameset. "Oh! The outrageous roaring and whooping that there was," she marveled. "By their noise and whooping they signified how many they had destroyed, which was at that time twenty-three." At each cry, Indians shouted so loud "the very earth rung." The warriors paraded to a sachem's wigwam, proudly displaying scalps. Much to Rowlandson's surprise and delight, one gave her a plundered Bible. She turned to Deuteronomy 28, which listed the curses Israel would suffer for disobeying God, including starvation, disease, violence, conquest, captivity, and death. Such curses had become the story of her life. But she took comfort from Deuteronomy 30, in which God promised that "if we would return to him by repentance . . . the Lord would gather us together and turn all those curses upon our enemies."[11]

FEAR AND RACIAL hostility intensified with every attack. On February 22, nearly a hundred Boston colonists petitioned the General Court for drastic security measures, including "the removal of those Indians that dwell in and amongst our plantations."[12] The next day, amid rumors that hostile Indians were just ten miles from Boston, colonists proposed that the court have the praying Indians killed or sold abroad. Daniel Gookin fought back, providing example after example of their fidelity and arguing that the 1644 treaty obligated Massachusetts to protect them. Others disagreed, forcing someone to retrieve a copy of the treaty. The court rejected the extreme proposals, but what would happen if the government lost control?[13]

Fifty-eight praying Indians on John Hoar's property at Concord faced daily harassment, especially after two colonists were killed nearby. Since the government refused to remove them, colonists asked the Indian-hating Captain Mosely to do it. He arrived during a Sunday church service, addressing the congregation after it was over. He had heard some "heathen" were troubling Concord, he declared, and he was willing to take them to Boston. Most congregants sat silently, but a few told him to go ahead, so he marched his company to Hoar's home with more than a hundred congregants in tow. Hoar objected that Massachusetts had left the Indians under his care. Mosely posted his soldiers anyway, and they taunted the Indians that night. The next morning, when Hoar demanded that Mosely produce a warrant, Mosely said he had been commissioned to destroy the enemy. Hoar countered that the Nashobahs were not the enemy, but Mosely ordered his men to break down the door. They seized the Indians, stole their clothes, shoes, and dishes, and marched them to Charlestown.

Mosely's actions were lawless, but the populace supported him, and the magistrates knew it. The General Court declined to censure him and sent the Nashobahs to Deer Island.[14] The last of Massachusetts's praying communities was now removed from the mainland. The General Court offered £3 for every Indian killed or captured moving forward.[15]

Resentment festered toward magistrates who defended Indians. A note was passed around Boston, purportedly written by a secret society, "ABCD," which vowed death to Gookin and Thomas Danforth, "those traitors to their king and country": "As Christians we warn them to prepare for death, for though they will deservedly die, yet we wish the health of their souls."[16] A drunk veteran, Richard Scott, ranted that Gookin was an "Irish dog that was never faithful to his country, the son of a whore, a bitch, a rogue, God confound him, and God rot his soul.... If I could meet him alone I would pistol him. I wish my knife ... were in his heart." He and others planned to kill the Indians on the island, he continued, but "some English dog discovered it, the devil will plague him." Determined to maintain order, the court fined Scott a staggering £150.[17]

The council tried to tamp down anxiety while keeping the approximately four hundred praying Indians on Deer Island fed and safe from vigilantes, who occasionally shot at them. On February 29 it ordered Captain Henchman to post six or eight soldiers to prevent Indians from leaving the island "so the people in those parts that are fearful of them may be quieted." At the same time, admitting that Deer Island lacked soil suitable for growing corn, it ordered him to redistribute the Indians over several islands, contracting with their English owners to provide sufficient land for planting. He was to ensure the Indians lived "soberly and religiously" and were employed in spinning, fishing, or other labor to pay for their confinement.[18]

Samuel Shrimpton, who owned Deer Island, allowed a hundred Indians to "abide and plant" free of charge, but Henry Mayes, who owned land on Boston harbor's Long Island, protested that his aged mother and wife lived in "exceeding fear and dread of the Indians," having "lost their all by the barbarism of the heathen." The council instructed Henchman to seize Mayes's house, and Mayes quickly relented.[19] But Henchman realized much more needed to be done, for the Indians were "in great distress for want of food." They had only one fishing boat, so the council ordered him to impress another, making sure a colonist always escorted Indians using it and that its oars were secured at night.[20]

All the while, colonists clamored for the removal of the few Indians remaining on the mainland, including some living in Dorchester. Such persons might assist the enemy, they claimed, "being their own nation, to the great detriment if not utter ruin of our plantation." The council agreed to remove them.[21]

THE COLONIES WERE IN dire straits. Unless things changed quickly, a merchant reported to England, "the colonies will soon be ruined" and forced to submit "upon any terms to any that will protect them." Massachusetts's treasury was exhausted. Food was so scarce that "without foreign supplies many must starve."[22] The minister Thomas Cobbet later claimed that around this time Algonquian leaders held a council at Mount Wachusett, the two-thousand-foot summit overlooking the hills of northern Massachusetts. Canonchet, the young Narragansett sachem, recommended that they avoid fighting large bodies of colonial troops and instead dispatch war parties to burn towns and devastate food supplies, forcing Massachusetts to seek peace. But the confident sachems resolved to battle English forces wherever they found them.[23]

Philip himself remained near the Hoosick River, north of Albany, seeking guns and ammunition from Dutch or French traders via Indian middlemen. Indians claimed he gave the Mohawks three hundred fathoms of wampum to enlist their support. The captive Thomas Warner witnessed a gathering of what he estimated were twenty-one hundred Indian warriors, including five hundred "French" Indians "with straws in their noses" who appeared to be planning an offensive down the Connecticut Valley. If so, their plans were disrupted. Urged by the United Colonies, New York governor Edmund Andros persuaded the Mohawks to attack Philip. Some three hundred Mohawks assaulted Philip at Hoosick in early March, driving him away from his crucial ammunition supplies.[24]

Connecticut, like New York, was eager to cooperate with Indian allies. Governor Winthrop encouraged Thomas Stanton to reward allied sachems, as another magistrate put it, for their "service to Christ and his gospel in this war." Uncas, the Mohegan sachem, and Ninigret, whose Eastern Niantics formed the core of a Narragansett faction that supported the English, should be encouraged to accept refugees, for "many of the common people may have been unwillingly involved" in the war and would surrender if promised good treatment. Connecticut sought to treat local Indians gently, "wisely and warily, that God may be with us." When Connecticut forces seized plunder from Ninigret, the council ordered it restored. Such efforts helped keep the colony's Indians loyal.[25]

Plymouth took a more heavy-handed approach. The island Wampanoags had pledged allegiance to the king, and those on Cape Cod and around Mashpee and Manomet promised loyalty to Plymouth, but colonists still feared them. In December, Plymouth confined them to the Cape, prohibiting them from coming any nearer than Sandwich "on pain of death or imprisonment."[26] After Indians raided Weymouth in February, 1676, the colony ordered the Nemasket Wampanoags, including some praying Indians, to be interned on Clark's Island "upon pain of death." It did recruit twenty Cape Wampanoags to serve in a company under Captain Michael Pierce.[27]

Too late, Massachusetts recognized that its harsh policy regarding refugees had made the enemy "desperate" and helped escalate the war. In a remarkable about-face, it agreed that Indians who surrendered to Ninigret and Uncas would not "be sold for slaves or . . . lose their lives." But it still refused to recruit many praying Indians, except six scouts requested by Major Thomas Savage for an offensive against Menameset.[28]

One of those scouts, Job Kattenanit, petitioned Massachusetts to let him travel to Hassanamesit to meet some praying Indians who had agreed to escape the Nipmucs with his children.[29] Permission was granted, but when General Denison and Major Savage authorized him to proceed from the army's base at Marlborough, an irate Captain Mosely objected that Kattenanit would alert the Nipmucs of the army's approach. His protests so inflamed the troops that the officers sent horsemen to bring Kattenanit back.

As it turned out, Kattenanit had reached Hassanamesit too late, and his family was not there. Disappointed, he returned to the army, which had marched west from Marlborough. Soon after, soldiers discovered eleven fugitives in the woods: Kattenanit's children, a widow taking care of them and her grown daughter, Kattenanit's eighty-year-old father Naoas and brother Joseph Tuckawillipin, and Tuckawillipin's wife and three children (including a three-month-old).[30] Soldiers stole their blankets, kettles, dishes, and a pewter communion cup John Eliot had given Tuckawillipin, a pastor. One, Jonathan Fairbanks, claimed Tuckawillipin's preteen daughter as a servant, pending a petition to the General Court.

They brought the prisoners to Major Savage, who realized who they were and relayed them to Marlborough. English women gathered outside their quarters, taunting and threatening them. Terrified, Tuckawillipin's wife, twelve-year-old son, and the widow and her daughter fled into the woods. A captain admitted being ashamed of what the English women did, saying if he was "an Indian and so abused," he would have run away too. The remaining captives were brought to Boston and lodged in the home of Captain Nicholas Page, who provided milk for Tuckawillipin's starving infant. Eliot and Daniel Gookin visited them.

"I am greatly distressed this day on every side," Tuckawillipin confessed. "The English have taken away some of my estate, my corn, cattle, my plough, cart chains, and other goods. The enemy's Indians have also taken a part of what I had, and the wicked Indians mock and scoff at me, saying, 'Now what is become of your praying to God?' The English also censure me and say I am a hypocrite." "Now my dear wife and eldest son are, through the English threatenings, run away, and I fear will perish in the woods for want of food. Also, my aged mother is lost." He still had faith in God, he said, but not in the English.

Page questioned him. Had he "assisted the enemy"? The Nipmucs "often solicited me," Tuckawillipin replied, "but I utterly denied and refused it. I thought within myself, 'it is better to die than to fight against the churches of Christ.'" He refused to demonize the Nipmucs, however, explaining that most simply wanted peace and would soon "be in great straits for food."

The authorities sent the group to Deer Island. The four who had escaped tried to survive in the wilderness, but Tuckawillipin's son died. It was two months before the others were rescued by a Christian Indian named Tom Nepanet. (Kattenanit eventually married the widow who had cared for his children in captivity.)[31]

SAVAGE'S MASSACHUSETTS ARMY rendezvoused with Major Robert Treat's Connecticut forces at abandoned Brookfield before turning north toward Menameset. But the Algonquians were already preparing their getaway. Rowlandson found her fellow captive, Goodwife Joslin, who was nine months pregnant and caring for a two-year-old, contemplating escape. Rowlandson protested that she would never survive the wilderness and exhorted her from Psalm 27: "Wait on the Lord. Be of good courage, and he shall strengthen thine heart." Indians later described what happened next. Joslin tried the patience of her captors by constantly begging to go home. Eventually they stripped her and formed a circle around her, her toddler in her arms. While she prayed, and captive children watched, they sang and danced. Then they attacked her and the toddler with hatchets. They threw the bodies onto a bonfire, threatening the children that if they tried to escape, they would suffer the same fate.

Some praying Indians apparently escaped Menameset, including Captain Tom Wuttasacomponom, the former ruler of the Nipmuc praying towns, and his son Nehemiah. Afraid that soldiers would consider them hostile, they traveled toward Natick and Magunkog in hopes of meeting someone they knew. Rowlandson was led north into a seemingly endless wilderness. They "marched on furiously with their old and with their young," she recalled. "Some carried their old decrepit mothers. Some carried one, and some another. Four of them carried a great Indian upon a bier, but going through a thick wood with him, they were hindered and could make no haste." So they took turns carrying him on their backs. Hungry, wet, and cold, Rowlandson felt dizzy, her knees weakening. She forced herself to eat but found it "very hard to get down their filthy trash." Lowering herself to the cold ground, she opened her Bible to Jeremiah 31:16, where God told Israel not to weep, for they would return from captivity. She "wept sweetly over this scripture," pouring out her heart to God.

They reached the Paquaug River (present-day Millers River) on Friday afternoon. Indians cut down trees, constructed rafts, and began ferrying people across that night. On the far side, Rowlandson ate a broth boiled with an "old horse's leg." She even enjoyed it. The crossing continued Saturday and Sunday. There were "many hundreds, old and young, some sick and some lame. Many had papooses [young children] at their backs," and women were laden with baggage. It was a snail's pace, but Indians teased her about the slower pursuit of the English army. "It may be they will come in May," they joked. When her mistress Weetamoo, the Pocasset sachem, ordered Mary to knit a pair of cotton stockings, Mary asked permission to rest, since it was Sunday, and do twice the work on Monday. Weetamoo replied that if she did not work, they would "break" her face.[32]

Meanwhile, ignoring the advice of their Indian scouts, Major Savage and his officers frittered away their time on a series of false trails, skirmishes, and ambushes. Not until Monday, when the Algonquians had finished crossing, did they approach the river. Nor did they attempt to pursue, to Rowlandson's disgust. "God did not give them courage or activity to go over after us," she lamented, exhibiting "strange providence . . . in preserving the heathen." The Algonquians continued west on the Mohawk Trail, Rowlandson's heart sinking with every step, until they made camp at a "great swamp." "Indians were as thick as the trees," she observed from a hill. "It seemed as if there had been a thousand hatchets going at once. If one looked before one, there was nothing but Indians, and behind one, nothing but Indians, and so on either hand, I myself in the midst, and no Christian soul near me." The next day, they continued into the foothills until they reached Squakeag. The sight of English fields and roads encouraged her, but not for long. "A solemn sight me thought it was to see fields of wheat and Indian corn forsaken and spoiled, and the remainders of them to be food for our merciless enemies."

Two days later they crossed the Connecticut River and joined Philip's people, who had been driven from New York. "When I was in the canoe," she recalled, "I could not but be amazed at the numerous crew of pagans that were on the bank on the other side. When I came ashore they gathered all about me, I sitting alone in the midst." They laughed and talked excitedly while she wept. When a warrior asked why, she expressed fear that they would kill her. "None will hurt you," he promised. They gave her peas and meal and brought her to Philip. "He bade me come in and sit down and asked me whether I would smoke," she remembered, "but this no way suited me." He asked her to make a shirt and hat for his son and afterward invited her to dinner. He gave her a pancake "made of parched wheat, beaten and fried in bear's grease." It tasted better than anything she had ever eaten.[33]

Savage's army arrived at Hadley around March 12. Soldiers accused his Indian scouts of alerting the enemy to their approach, but chaplain Samuel Nowell countered that if officers had listened to the scouts, they might have overtaken the enemy. Much to Nowell's disgust, Hadley colonists forced the scouts to pay for their own food, unlike English soldiers.

Two days later enemy warriors assaulted nearby Northampton, penetrating its palisade at three points. They burned buildings and seized horses and sheep before colonial forces drove them off. Five colonists were killed and six wounded. Perhaps a dozen Indians were killed. Major Savage now found himself in the same unenviable position as the upper Connecticut Valley commanders Pynchon and Appleton before him. Colonists lived "in very great fear" amid constant Indian sightings, but whenever soldiers went after them, the Algonquians slipped away. He believed the enemy was desperate for food and would attempt to destroy the valley towns so they could safely plant and fish upriver.

Hadley's pastor, John Russell, prepared his people for the onslaught. Colonists across New England were "crying for their lives and all that is dear to them," he admitted. But they could entrust themselves to God, "always pleading his covenant grace and mercy in taking us to be his people . . . to keep and comfort us when he leads us into the darkest valley of the shadow of [death] . . . to heal our backslidings and love us freely." This hope "is all we have to live on in this evil day," Russell acknowledged. "My desire is we may be willing to do or suffer, live or die, remain in or be driven out from our habitations, as the Lord our God would have us."[34]

ATTACKS ACCELERATED AS hungry Algonquians sought corn and cattle. During the night of March 2, Indians rummaged in abandoned houses and stole cattle at Groton, many of whose sixty families had fled. A few days later, Indians returned for corn, swine, and poultry, leaving a dead colonist "stripped naked, his body mangled and dragged into the highway and laid on his back in a most shameful manner."[35] On March 13 two Indians were spotted on a nearby hill. Soldiers pursued and walked into an ambush that left one dead and three wounded. Warriors then counterattacked, seizing corn, cattle, and provisions and setting fire to the meeting house and other buildings.

That night, as Algonquians celebrated within earshot of Groton's garrison, Monoco, the leading Nashaway warrior, called out to Groton's Captain James Parker, his former neighbor, suggesting they negotiate a peace treaty. Rumor had it that Monoco had forced Mary Rowlandson to marry him, and colonists despised him. The two men debated who was to blame for the war until a frustrated Monoco began mocking Christianity. "What will you do for a house to pray in now we have burnt your meeting house?" He had burned Lancaster and Medfield, he boasted, and if they rejected peace, he would do the same to Chelmsford, Concord, Watertown, Cambridge, Charlestown, Roxbury, and even Boston. "What me will, me do," he vowed.

Only after the Algonquians withdrew did Major Simon Willard, the regional commander, arrive with reinforcements. His home was among forty that were burned, and only the four garrison houses remained. The head of a colonist was mounted on a pole facing his land, his naked body nearby. Indians had dug up another man buried several days before and mounted his head and a leg on poles, and they had cut up a dead infant and fed it to pigs. Increase Mather brooded that another church had been destroyed by those who boasted of their opposition to God. "They have cast fire into the sanctuary," he later quoted from Psalm 74. "O God, how long shall the adversary reproach? Shall the enemy blaspheme thy name forever?"[36]

Disasters came in rapid succession, "fresh messengers (like Job's servants) hourly arriving to bring the doleful tidings of new massacres, slaughters, and devastations committed by the brutish heathens," reported merchant Nathaniel Saltonstall.[37] Andover, Chelmsford, and Concord were hit in the east; Westfield in the west. Ipswich minister William Hubbard blamed the Wamesits for killing two men at Chelmsford, claiming that Chelmsford's hostility had alienated them.[38] Troops intended for the Connecticut Valley were rerouted to protect the eastern towns, but General Denison complained that Major Willard did little to "prosecute the enemy." Men who were desperately needed for spring planting were consumed with garrison duty, transporting supplies, and improving fortifications. Massachusetts even explored the feasibility of building a twelve-mile stockade between the Concord and Charles rivers.[39]

Warriors returned to Narragansett country, burning most of Warwick on March 17 (which Pomham's Shawomets, who had long resisted Warwick's efforts to seize their land, surely viewed as justice). A few days later, they destroyed what was left of Wickford, the site of Richard Smith's trading post. The claims of the Atherton Company and Rhode Island meant little now.[40] Rhode Island advised

Providence's inhabitants to take refuge on Aquidneck Island and ordered that Indians be escorted by day and "locked up" at night.[41] Connecticut ordered fresh troops to prevent Narragansetts from reoccupying Narragansett country, promising recruits whatever persons or property they seized as plunder.[42] Plymouth dispatched Captain Pierce's company to protect Rehoboth.

Indians raided within three miles of Plymouth town. A month earlier, William Clark had openly wished that all Indians might be hanged. When Increase Mather replied that "their innocent blood would cry out," Clark invoked the words the Jews used when crucifying Christ: "Their blood be upon me and my children." On March 12 Wampanoags led by the local sachem Tatoson, who had "received many kindnesses" from the Clarks, attacked Clark's house while he was in Plymouth, killing eleven people, including his wife and children. Mather remembered Clark's words.[43]

Sunday, March 26, 1676, marked the New Year in the colonists' Julian calendar and typically heralded spring, but this year it brought death and destruction. In Connecticut, warriors burned much of Simsbury.[44] Further north, in Massachusetts, eight Indians targeted several English families and eighteen soldiers escorting them to a church service in Springfield. Ambushing the tail of the column, they killed a man and a young woman, wounded two others, and captured two mothers, each with a small child. Soldiers tracked the warriors to the edge of a swamp the next day. The warriors tried to hack their captives to death with hatchets before fleeing, but one woman survived. She told her rescuers that according to the warriors, three thousand Indians, including the praying Indian ruler Captain Tom, were at Pocumtuck, well supplied and reconciled with the Mohawks.[45]

Other Indians descended on Marlborough, Massachusetts's eastern supply base. A colonist suffering a painful toothache stepped outside the meeting house during the afternoon service when he saw them coming and sounded the alarm. The garrison commander, Captain Samuel Brocklebank, focused on protecting the army's supplies, enabling Indians to burn about thirty buildings and kill or wound three colonists. That night, after reinforcements arrived, Lieutenant Richard Jacob and forty men attacked the Algonquian camp, killing or wounding about thirty Indians. Among the dead was Netus, one of Eliot's first converts, who had led the February attack on the Eames farm.[46]

The greatest disaster that day occurred along the banks of the Blackstone River, north of Providence. Captain Michael Pierce's Plymouth company had damaged an enemy force near the Pawtuxet River the previous day, and he set out with eighty men, including twenty allied Wampanoags, to finish the job. He sent a message to Providence requesting reinforcements, but it was not delivered, and he had no idea he faced more than a thousand warriors. As his men marched through the woods, they spotted wounded Indians and took off in pursuit.

Within minutes, hundreds of Algonquians were upon them, triggering some of the bloodiest fighting of the war. For a while Pierce held his own, but he was gradually forced to withdraw toward the river to avoid being surrounded. Warriors had crossed to the far side, however, so he organized his men in a circle facing outward. One by one they were cut down. Pierce was shot in the leg. A praying Indian named Amos stood by him until the situation was hopeless, then slipped away. Pierce died with about sixty of his men, including eleven Wampanoags. According to informants, who claimed that 140 Indians were killed, warriors tied two captives to trees and "Indian women whipped them almost to death." Then they "cut off some of their flesh and put therein hot embers." It took Pastor Newman and Rehoboth colonists three days to bury the dead, filling Rehoboth "with an awful expectation of what further evils" were in store.[47]

Plymouth called for three hundred fresh troops and one hundred Wampanoags, and Governor Winslow implored Massachusetts for aid, fearing "our people will be cut in pieces." But Massachusetts was also under attack and had no troops to spare.[48] On March 28 hundreds of shouting warriors swept into Rehoboth, burning houses, barns, and mills and taunting residents. They seized corn and fowl and drove off cattle, swine, sheep, and horses. What they could not take, they destroyed. Colonists discovered cattle with their hindquarters cut off. About sixty-six buildings, including forty homes, were burned, and one colonist was killed. The elderly John Kingsley lost his home and all his animals except one pig. "Had not our God restrained them, they were enough to have swallowed us all up," he wrote a Connecticut pastor. "I am not able to bear the sad stories of our woeful days, when the Lord made our wolfish heathen to be our lords."[49]

The following morning, the Algonquians moved on to Providence, though few of its five hundred residents remained. As warriors pillaged and burned, an Indian called for colonist Valentine Whitman to speak with them. Old Roger Williams hastened after Whitman. "The town cried out to us not to venture," Williams recalled. "My sons came crying after me." Whitman turned back, but, "my heart to God and the country forced me to go." Williams spoke with three Indians, including Potuck, counselor to the Narragansett sachem Quaiapin, for an hour. "This [is] my ground which you have got from me," an Indian declared. They mocked that Englishmen fought like women and that "the great God" opposed them. They had fifteen hundred Narragansetts, Nipmucs, Wampanoags, and valley Indians, and they intended to burn "all the towns about Plymouth."

Williams asked why they assaulted colonists who had always been kind "neighbors to them." He looked back. "This house of mine now burning before mine eyes hath lodged kindly some thousands of you these ten years." They replied that Providence had proven itself their enemy by "entertaining, assisting, [and] guiding" colonial forces. Williams retorted that Providence had "entertained all Indians, being a thoroughfare town, but neither we nor this colony had acted [in] hostility against them." They "forgot they were mankind and ran about the country like wolves tearing and devouring the innocent and peaceable." They had no regard for their families, who would suffer the consequences, "nor to God."

Potuck and his companions confessed they were "in a strange way" but insisted the English had "forced them to it." Furthermore, they were sure "God was [with] them and had forsaken us," Williams recalled, "for they had so prospered in killing and burning us far beyond what we did against them." Williams retorted that the English "had driven the Wampanoags and Philip out of his country and the Narragansetts out of their country and had destroyed multitudes of them," and "God would help us to consume them." But Williams urged them to negotiate. "I told them they knew many times I had quenched fires between the Bay and them, and Plymouth and Connecticut and them. And now I did not doubt, God assisting me, to quench this and help to restore quietness to the land again."

They proposed that he cross the river to talk further, agreeing to a ceasefire and exchange of hostages. But back at the garrison house, Williams's neighbors tried to dissuade him. "Some came running and affirmed that J. Lapham's house," on the way to the rendezvous, "was full of Indians." When more homes went up in flames, Williams ventured out and accused the Indians of breaking their word. They replied that their warriors ignored their orders to desist. Eventually several came over, including the Narragansett Stonewall John, a Nipmuc sachem, and a stout Connecticut Valley sachem named Kutqen.

Williams said the Narragansetts were responsible for the war because they broke the treaty requiring them to surrender their Wampanoag captives. Stonewall John replied that they "heartily endeavored" to surrender the captives, but the people "were divided and could not effect it." That hardly justified a colonial invasion. "You have driven us out of our own country and then pursued us to our great misery and your own," John continued. Threatened with starvation, they had no choice but to raid English towns for food.

Williams tried a different approach. "I told them if their sachems would propound something and cause a cessation, I would presently write . . . to Boston." They could plant corn and feed their people. But Kutqen retorted that "they cared not for planting these ten years" and would "live upon" the English. God was with them, and they had killed hundreds of colonists while losing few of their own people. Just look at Pierce's soldiers lying dead along the Blackstone River. Williams replied that it was no surprise that so many warriors could overcome "half a hundred" soldiers, but "they were a cowardly people" who dare not approach English strongholds and achieved success only by cheating and stealth. Given a fair chance, one hundred Providence men could whip them that night. Kutqen accepted the challenge. "We will meet you a hundred to a hundred tomorrow on the plain." Williams then boasted that Massachusetts could raise ten thousand soldiers, and if the Indians killed them, the king would send thousands more.

The conversation was going nowhere. The Indians said they would talk again in a month. Meanwhile, they would move on to Plymouth. Williams lashed out that "God would stop them or plague them hereafter except they repented of these their robberies and murders." But they remained courteous as he walked away, warning him to "not go near the burned houses," where Indians might harm him, "but go by the waterside."

So Providence burned. A pacifist named Wright, known for "great knowledge in the scriptures" but "of no particular professed sect," refused to shelter in a garrison house, believing that as long as he held his Bible, he was safe. Warriors "ripped him open and put his Bible in his belly." A woman named Elizabeth Sucklin was "killed and laid in a barbarous manner not fit to be told." Having burned about thirty houses, the Indians left for Pawtuxet. "We see smoke rise from Pawtuxet and from my daughter Mercy's house in the woods," reported Williams.[50] (Soon after, out of sympathy, Massachusetts offered Williams refuge as long as he kept his controversial beliefs to himself.)[51]

With the towns around Narragansett Bay in ruins, Plymouth anticipated the imminent destruction of Taunton and Bridgewater. Frustrated that Massachusetts would not send aid, Plymouth magistrate Thomas Hinckley warned Massachusetts governor John Leverett that the Indians might deliberately be spreading misinformation about a concentration at Pocumtuck, while "breaking in like a flood now upon us." If so, the flood would "reach very quickly to your frontiers next [to] us." Plymouth was doing its best to raise troops, but its towns remained virtually defenseless. "If God should please to put it into your hearts to join with us with some of your forces, it may do well," he pleaded. "However, if we be left to be a prey in their hand, God is righteous. Yet we desire to trust in his name when all other help fails."

There was little Massachusetts could do, for its own towns were nearly as vulnerable as Plymouth's. Times had never been darker for New England's Puritans, and there was no end in sight.[52]

19

Negotiations

March 1676 to May 1676

THE INVASION OF Narragansett country had backfired spectacularly. Hundreds of colonists were dead, dozens were in captivity, and towns across New England were now smoldering ruins. War parties roamed freely, killing soldiers and seizing cattle and corn while colonists cowered in garrison houses. Reports came like Job's messengers, wrote William Harris of Rhode Island, telling of Indians "burning houses, taking cattle, killing men and women and children, and carrying others captive, and the enemy triumphing and boasting that God was departed from the English and was with them." They said that "because we so sinned against God, God would and did deliver us into their hands." For the English, thoughts of conquest gave way to a desperate struggle for survival. They even opened negotiations with the sachems.

Their Indian allies complained that the English were cautious and inept. Harris was inclined to agree. "All the houses in the Narragansett country burnt, all at Warwick, all at Pawtuxet, and almost all burnt at Providence," he lamented. They had lost at "least a thousand horses," "two thousand cattle and many sheep." Yet Rhode Island did nothing to defend its territory. The "wisest men" were "at their wits end, to think what might become of themselves and families and the whole country."[1]

Connecticut, which coveted Narragansett country, was doing something about it. It was also the only colony enjoying success. Beginning in March 1676, it regularly sent companies of English and Indian troops to hunt Narragansetts, offering plunder as a reward. They were usually led by Captain George Denison, a veteran cavalryman who had served under Oliver Cromwell in England. On March 30 Denison set out with seventy-nine English and one hundred Indians, including Pequots under Robin Cassacinamon, Mohegans under Uncas's son Owaneco, and twenty of Ninigret's men led by the warrior Catapazet. They captured two elderly women who revealed that the Narragansett sachem Canonchet, son of the great Miantonomo, was nearby. Scouts confirmed he was at the Blackstone River, supposedly "diverting himself with the recital of Captain Pierce's slaughter." Denison ordered a strike.

Detecting Denison's approach at the last moment, Canonchet cast aside his blanket, a belt of wampum, and the "red coat laid with silver lace" that the English had given him in October. Then he fled. Catapazet recognized him and urged his men forward. Canonchet dashed into the river, but his foot slipped on a stone and he tumbled into the water. He recovered, waded to the far bank, and ran. He made it another 150 yards before a Pequot overtook him. Exhausted, Canonchet did not resist.[2] Breathless soldiers and warriors caught up. Few would forget the moment.

Thomas Stanton's twenty-two-year-old son Robert asked Canonchet a question. "You much child, no understand matters of war," Canonchet replied, mindful of his honor. "Let your brother or your chief come. Him I will answer." Finally Denison and other officers arrived. They offered Canonchet his life if he submitted, but he insisted his people would not surrender and he would rather die than face captivity. He simply asked to be killed by Owaneco, his equal. Having taken at least forty-five Narragansetts (he killed "the stoutest men"), Denison brought Canonchet to Stonington. He should have sent him to Hartford, but officers and sachems protested that Connecticut might use him as a bargaining chip, and if it released him, he would wreak vengeance. So Denison turned him over to the Mohegans and Pequots for execution, knowing it would cement their loyalty and shatter any possibility of their reconciliation with the Narragansetts. Canonchet expressed gladness that he would die "before his heart was soft or had spoken anything unworthy of himself." He refused to take any blame for the war and predicted that it would continue long after his death.

Thirty-three years earlier, Uncas had executed Miantonomo at the behest of the English. Now Uncas's son Owaneco stood to kill Miantonomo's son at the behest of the English. He denounced Canonchet as a "rogue . . . whereupon Canonchet at once flung open his garment and stretched out his arms" before the Mohegan shot him. The Pequots quartered him, cut off his head, and sent it to Hartford. Ninigret's men buried the body.

William Harris considered it fitting that God had "given the father into the hands of Uncas and the son into the hands of Uncas's son," for both were "monstrous proud" and always treacherous. "So O Lord let all such thine enemies be defeated," he wrote. Ipswich minister William Hubbard later described Canonchet as a "damned wretch" who "often opened his mouth to blaspheme the name of the living God," "the ringleader of almost all this mischief, and [a] great incendiary between the Narragansetts and us." Increase Mather thought it "humbling" that Canonchet was captured and killed by Indians but rejoiced that "it is now their interest to be faithful to the English, since their own countrymen will never forgive them."[3]

Canonchet's killing offered colonists their first glimmer of hope in months, but it came amid further blows. On April 6 an epidemic claimed the life of

Connecticut governor John Winthrop Jr. Acclaimed for his "wisdom, real moderation and charity," he was buried in Boston alongside his father with, in merchant Nathaniel Saltonstall's words, "universal lamentation and all the honors that our distresses and distractions would allow."[4] Benjamin Thompson spoke in tribute, praising Winthrop as a governor, scientist, and human being. To describe his virtue, humility, and justice was to write God's moral law, Thompson eulogized, for "all the law . . . had its impression in his spotless heart."[5] The epidemic also killed the esteemed Major Simon Willard. Willard had been an advocate for praying Indians, and John Eliot lamented that his death left a serious void in Massachusetts's leadership.

Eliot and magistrates Daniel Gookin, Thomas Danforth, and William Stoughton were heading to the islands to visit praying Indians on April 7 when a fourteen-ton shallop "turned head" and crashed into their smaller boat. "I so sunk that I drank in salt water twice and could not help it," Eliot recalled. All were rescued, but some colonists suspected the crash was intentional, an attempt to assassinate the praying Indians' leading advocates. The shallop's captain received a hefty fine for negligence.[6]

Meanwhile, Massachusetts's armies flailed about trying to find the enemy. "We cannot meet with any body of them, their manner being to remove from place to place almost every day," its council reported to London, "leaving their women and children in hideous swamps and obscure unaccessable places . . . and the men sometimes dispersing themselves in small parties all over the country. . . . And then again on a sudden multitudes of them gathering together falls upon our out towns."[7] On April 1 Massachusetts ordered Major Thomas Savage to march his army from the Connecticut Valley back to the east, attacking the Algonquian stronghold at Mount Wachusett on the way.[8] But when his Indian scouts reported that the enemy camp was "very difficult to have access to by reason of thick woods and rocks and other fastnesses," the officers decided not to attack, pleading exhaustion and lack of supplies. When they reached Marlborough, colonists were so abusive toward Savage's Indian scouts that the scouts refused to lodge indoors.[9]

Attacks continued almost daily. At Hadley, Indians killed three men and captured a fourth. Near Andover, they killed a colonist and captured his brother. They shot at colonists at Billerica, burned two houses near Braintree and razed fifteen at Chelmsford. Warriors raided Bridgewater in Plymouth colony, torching a house, barn, and lumber, pillaging homes, and seizing horses and pigs. Sometimes they displayed their antipathy toward English cattle. Once, according to Increase Mather, "They took a cow, knocked off one of her horns, [and] cut out her tongue." Another time they put a horse, ox, and other animals "into a hovel and then set it on fire."

Massachusetts had prohibited colonists from abandoning towns without permission, but now it urged the evacuation of frontier settlements. Groton,

Lancaster, Mendon, and Marlborough were abandoned (a garrison remained at Marlborough), but not without incident. On April 16 warriors ambushed a two-mile column of sixty wagons carrying provisions from Groton, mortally wounding two soldiers. A few days later, warriors killed two colonists at Weymouth and Hingham, killed a colonist and burned ten houses at Scituate, and killed or wounded four colonists south of Medfield. Fields lay unplanted, and colonists dreaded the specter of famine.[10]

Officers had been urging Massachusetts to recruit more praying Indians, but the council had refused, mindful of the public mood. But it could not fail to notice that the only colonial forces enjoying success were Connecticut's combined Indian-English forces. On April 14 the council finally reversed its self-defeating policy. It ordered Captain Samuel Hunting to recruit a company of praying Indians and deploy them to the Merrimack Valley.[11]

PLYMOUTH HAD CALLED up three hundred English troops and one hundred Wampanoags for an expedition to relieve Rehoboth, but too few showed up, forcing the council to call it off.[12] "I am exceedingly afflicted to think that we should so reel and stagger in our counsels as drunken men, and that so precious a people as Rehoboth should be so forsaken by us, for our own selfish interests," John Cotton Jr. wrote his fellow minister Thomas Walley.[13] Walley shared Cotton's despondency but pointed out that Wampanoags who "might have proved faithful and been a help to us" had been "much grieved" and alienated when Plymouth sold Wampanoag women into slavery. "They see we cannot so easily raise arms as send away poor squaws. The country about us is troubled and grieved at this action, accounting it very unreasonable. . . . Some fear we have paid dear for former acts of severity, and how dear we may yet pay, God knows."[14]

Unable to defend Rehoboth, Taunton, and Bridgewater, Plymouth reversed long-standing policy and encouraged residents to evacuate the towns. Surprisingly, they refused. Rehoboth declared that evacuation would jeopardize the "interest of Christ amongst us." God had called them to this land, and abandoning it would expose his name and people to reproach from "the blasphemous heathen, who will much embolden themselves hereby to get more ground of us." They were also loath to lose a "considerable quantity of English grain" and feared being ambushed on the road. In any case, the ultimate cause of their suffering was their sin, and they could hardly leave that behind. "What will you do with our sins?" they wrote. "Should we bring them with us? Will not both yourselves and us be endangered thereby?"[15]

Taunton echoed these arguments, declaring that abandoning their land would "give the adversary occasion to triumph over us, to the reproach of that great and fearful name of our God." And would not his wrathful hand "follow us and find us out withersoever we flee?" They had no choice but to trust God.

"Here we have sinned, and here we submit ourselves to suffer."[16] Bridgewater's pastor James Keith implored Plymouth magistrate Thomas Hinckley to "pray hard for us," for "prayer must be our battle-axe," and "we are in expectation every day of an assault."[17]

Privately, Rehoboth pastor Noah Newman admitted that his town was not as unified as their letter implied. "Sundry amongst us upon the desolation by fire began to conclude there was no subsisting [here]," he admitted. Yet "a removal will involve us in such new cares and hurries that we shall forget the Lord's controversy with us." Although their homes lay "in ashes," he thought they should have been more concerned about repenting for the "sins, which occasioned" such judgment. He boldly requested prayer "that God would not cease afflicting us" until they were transformed according to his will.[18]

Plymouth's efforts to raise troops were so futile that when Massachusetts suggested a joint deployment of praying Indians along their common frontier, as proposed by the Punkapoag Indian pastor William Ahawton, it had to decline. Not only did it fear its Wampanoags would "be corrupted by the enemy," but it was unable to provide enough English soldiers to accompany them. "We must at present do no more but scout about our towns with what diligence we can," it conceded. "We are in a very sore condition, and the spirits of our people begin to run low."[19]

IN CAPTIVITY, MARY ROWLANDSON saw firsthand how enemy Algonquians experienced the war. Often their kindness surprised her. When it rained, they allowed her to sleep in a wigwam even as many Indians had to remain outside. Once, she got lost traveling to visit her son, Joseph, but "though I was gone from home and met with all sorts of Indians, and those I had no knowledge of, and there being no Christian soul near me, yet not one of them offered the least imaginable miscarriage to me." Quinnapin, her Narragansett master, eventually brought her to Joseph. Another time, a woman generously gave her bear meat and allowed her to cook it in her kettle. Others gave her part of an unborn fawn, "so young and tender that one might eat the bones as well as the flesh."[20]

Sometimes Indians refused to give her food or allow her inside their wigwams. One evening she was excluded from a fire circle, and when she protested, a man threatened to run her through with his sword. She was turned away from wigwam after wigwam until an elderly couple welcomed her to their fire and fed her. Another time, when she moved some burning wood, an angry woman flung a "handful of ashes" in her eyes. The pain was intense and she briefly feared she might never see again. Sometimes Indians made up terrifying stories, saying they had eaten her son or killed her husband, or that he had remarried. "There is not one of them that makes the least conscience of speaking of truth," she later vented.

She was encouraged when Quinnapin confided that he planned to sell her to her husband. The realization that they were heading south "much cheered my spirit," she recalled, "and made my burden seem light and almost nothing at all." But her hopes were dashed when Weetamoo, her Pocasset mistress, turned back (possibly because Weetamoo's son was sick), taking Rowlandson with her. Rowlandson felt she would have rather died, for Quinnapin "seemed to me the best friend that I had of an Indian." "I began to think that all my hopes of restoration would come to nothing."

She despised Weetamoo, describing her as "a severe and proud dame" who spent "every day in dressing herself neat as much time as any of the gentry of the land, powdering her hair and painting her face, going with necklaces, with jewels in her ears and bracelets upon her hands." Weetamoo was a prominent sachem, but Rowlandson never acknowledged this, perhaps because Weetamoo was female. One Sunday morning, Weetamoo discovered Rowlandson reading her Bible instead of helping with preparations for the day's journey. Furious, she threw the book outside the wigwam. When Rowlandson complained that her load was too heavy, Weetamoo slapped her face. Another time, when Rowlandson disobeyed, Weetamoo swung a large stick at her head. Rowlandson felt no sympathy when Weetamoo's son died. Longing for family, friends, and home, she was callous toward Indian suffering.[21]

Suffer they did, especially from hunger. They ate "nuts and acorns, artichokes, lily roots, ground beans, and several other weeds and roots," and things "a hog or a dog would hardly touch," she recalled. "They would pick up old bones and cut them to pieces at the joints, and if they were full of worms and maggots, they would scald them over the fire to make the vermin come out, and then boil them and drink up the liquor, and then beat the great ends of them in a mortar, and so eat them. They would heat horse's guts and ears and all sorts of wild birds which they could catch; also bear, venison, beaver, tortoise, frogs, squirrels, dogs, skunks, rattlesnakes, yea, the very bark of trees." Yet she was impressed at their ability to survive, for she never saw an Indian die of starvation. It discouraged her that "instead of turning his hand against them, the Lord feeds and nourishes them up to be a scourge to the whole land."[22]

The Indians would not last long this way. Ordinarily, during spring they migrated to fishing places; they would catch and store enough fish to feed them until they could harvest their corn, beans, and squash. But what if the English prevented them from fishing or planting crops? No matter how many towns they destroyed or soldiers they killed, if they could not eat, they would lose. This convinced some sachems that it was time to use Rowlandson and other captives as bargaining chips to negotiate peace. Philip had nothing to gain from this, but other sachems blamed him for the war and decided to act without him. They would bargain from a position of strength. As it happened, Joseph Rowlandson had been trying to recover his wife, but no praying Indians were willing to risk their lives carrying a message. Finally, in late March, John Hoar, the Concord colonist who had tried to protect the Nashobah praying Indians from being moved to Deer Island, recruited Tom Nepanet and Peter Tatiquinea of Nashobah to deliver a letter from Massachusetts governor John Leverett to the sachems.

Three sachems, including Shoshanim of Nashaway and Kutquen from the Connecticut Valley, dictated a response to the praying Indian teacher Peter Jethro. They were willing to negotiate, they explained, because they knew the English were on their "backside." "Because you know and we know your heart [is] great sorrowful with crying for your lost: many hundred men and all your house and all your land and woman, child and cattle."[23]

Meanwhile, Weetamoo finally headed east toward Mount Wachusett, where Quinnapin was. Hunger had severely weakened Rowlandson, now an experienced beggar. Sometimes "I got enough and did eat till I could eat no more, yet I was as unsatisfied as I was when I began," she later wrote. Recrossing the Paquaug River almost proved too much. "The water was up to the knees, and the stream very swift and so cold that I thought it would have cut me in sunder. . . . I was so weak and feeble that I reeled as I went along and thought there I must end my days at last." Afterward, when she was informed of the governor's letter, she could scarcely believe it. "My strength seemed to come again and recruit my feeble knees and aching heart." When she saw men with "hats, white neckcloths, and sashes about their waists, and ribbons upon their shoulders," she momentarily hoped they were colonists come to redeem her. But "there was a vast difference between the lovely faces of Christians and the foul looks of these heathens," she later wrote.

After three days and "many weary steps," she saw Mount Wachusett. But as they traversed a swamp, "up to the knees in mud and water," she feared she might sink and never rise again, only for Philip himself to take her hand. "Two weeks more and you shall be mistress again," he promised.

Was it really true, she asked?

"Yes, and quickly you shall come to your master again."

She would never forget his compassion.

After they arrived at Wachusett, Quinnapin brought her water to wash and then a mirror to see how she looked. One of his older wives gave her "a mess of beans and meat and a little ground nut cake," leaving her "wonderfully revived." Weetamoo even gave her a sleeping mat and a "good rug" for a blanket, which Rowlandson claimed was "the first time I had any such kindness" from her. She figured that Weetamoo was hoping for a reward when her captive was redeemed.

When Nepanet and Tatiquinea arrived with another letter from the governor, Rowlandson nearly forgot herself. "Though they were Indians, I got them by the hand and burst out into tears. My heart was so full that I could not speak to them. But recovering myself, I asked them how my husband did, and all my friends and acquaintances." The sachems called her into their council and asked what they should request for her ransom. Shoshanim instructed a praying Indian, probably John Eliot's former assistant James Printer, what to write. "I am sorrow that I have done much wrong to you," he declared, taking a less strident tone than before, "yet I say the fault is lay upon you, for when we began quarrel at first with Plymouth men, I did not think that you should have so much trouble as now is." They offered to release Rowlandson for £20. Massachusetts's council received this letter on April 27 and quickly dispatched John Hoar with £20 and other goods.[24]

Rowlandson despised praying Indians like Peter Jethro and James Printer for helping the enemy. She was even more vitriolic toward praying Indians who fought the English. One, she recalled, wore a necklace "strung with Christians' fingers." But she did not regard such people as Christians. When one confided that eating horsemeat had violated his brother's conscience, she scoffed that his conscience was "as large as hell," for he killed "poor Christians."

While awaiting Massachusetts's response, the Algonquians held a powwow. Rowlandson watched as a man kneeled on a deerskin while others kneeled around him. "At the end of every sentence in his speaking they all assented, humming or muttering with their mouths and striking upon the ground with their hands" and sticks. Next to him stood an Indian with a gun. "Then they bade him with the gun go out of the ring, which he did, but when he was out, they called him in again. But he seemed to make a stand. Then they called the more earnestly, till he returned again. Then they all sang." They gave him a second gun and repeated the ritual. This time when they called, "he stood reeling and wavering as if he knew not whither he should stand or fall, or which way to go." "Then they called him with exceeding great vehemency, all of them, one and another. After a little while he turned in, staggering as he went, with his arms stretched out, in either hand a gun." All "sang and rejoiced exceedingly," assenting to his words.[25]

Rowlandson did not know it, but they had decided to attack Sudbury.

TWENTY MILES FROM Boston, Sudbury lay on the road to Marlborough and the Connecticut Valley. Most of the town lay east of the Sudbury River, but a few garrison houses and a mill were to the west. It had about eighty soldiers. Captain Samuel Wadsworth and fifty soldiers passed through on their way to Marlborough on April 20. Had he known that hundreds of Algonquians were approaching, he might have stayed.

The following morning, around first light, Indian warriors set fire to buildings on both sides of the river and attacked Deacon Haynes's two-story brick garrison house on the west bank. They charged "with great force and fury," killing two soldiers, but suffered "considerable slaughter" before falling back.[26] When news of the attack reached Concord, twelve men set out to investigate. Spotting Indians in a meadow near the Haynes house, they brazenly attacked. Indians killed or captured them all. Three miles west of town, eighteen cavalrymen under Captain Edward Cowell were marching from Marlborough to Boston when "hundreds of Indians" ambushed them, killing four soldiers and wounding another.[27]

It was reported that fifteen hundred warriors were involved in the attack, and nearby towns scrambled to send reinforcements. A few dozen marched from Watertown, while Major Daniel Gookin dispatched Captain Hunting's praying Indians and troopers led by Corporal Solomon Phipps. Captain Wadsworth, who had relieved Lancaster in February, had his exhausted soldiers retrace their steps from Marlborough, accompanied by troops under Captain Samuel Brocklebank. A mile from town, they spotted a hundred Indians moving through the trees and pursued them toward some wooded hills. Suddenly as many as five hundred Indians rose around them, yelling and shooting. The soldiers struggled to the top of Green Hill where, surrounded, they held out desperately.[28]

Their approach may have helped Sudbury, because around 1:00 p.m. warriors pulled back from the Haynes house and began withdrawing from the east side of the river. The Watertown soldiers arrived, joined some Sudbury men, and drove two hundred Indians over the river in a "running flight," recapturing most of their plunder and seizing the bridge near the Haynes house. Smoke and gunfire around Green Hill, half a mile distant, indicated that Wadsworth's men were fighting for their lives. Hoping to rescue them, officers launched an attack across the river. They encountered tenacious resistance. When they attempted to fight through, warriors moved around their flanks, threatening to cut them off from the river. "We stayed so long that we were almost encompassed," soldiers Daniel Warren and Joseph Pierce recalled. The English finally withdrew to the Goodenow garrison house, a quarter mile southeast of Green Hill.[29]

By then it was nearly dark. Wadsworth's men had been fighting for almost four hours. Five were dead, though the Indians also suffered heavy casualties. Now the Algonquians changed tactics, lighting fires in the dry underbrush. As flames licked their way up the hill, the heat and smoke became too much to bear. Soldiers broke in disorder, fleeing southwest toward Noyes' Mill, half a mile away. Warriors cut down soldier after soldier, including Wadsworth and Brocklebank. A soldier hiding in the underbrush saw a comrade captured. A warrior mocked him: "Come Lord Jesus, save this poor Englishman, if thou canst, whom I am now about to kill." He then proceeded to "knock him down and leave him dead." Fewer than fifteen Englishmen made it to the mill. Corporal Phipps impetuously rode to their relief with six troopers, but the enemy blocked his path. Further slaughter seemed imminent until Captain Cowell arrived with reinforcements. The Indians withdrew, enabling the soldiers to rescue Wadsworth's wounded and weary survivors.[30]

Hunting's praying Indians, including the former pastor and spy Job Kattenanit, arrived that evening. They were ordered to scout the west side of the river the next day. In preparation, they removed their English clothing and painted themselves. But when they crossed in the morning, the enemy was gone. According to Gookin, some "wept when they saw so many English lie dead," some of whom they knew personally. Soldiers arrived to bury the bodies, including those of Wadsworth and Brocklebank. Warren and Peirce searched for the Concord men. "We went in the cold water up to the knees, where we found five [bodies], and we brought them in canoes to the bridge foot and buried them there."[31]

The Algonquians passed by Marlborough on their way back to Mount Wachusett. Lieutenant Richard Jacob heard gunfire, then watched as "they gave a shout and came in sight upon the Indian hill, [in] great numbers." They signaled how many men they had killed, one calling and others whooping seventy-four times in response. All that day they plundered, seized cattle, and burned buildings, while Jacob's forty-six soldiers watched helplessly. "The town is wholly consumed, excepting four garrisons," he reported. Soon Marlborough too would be abandoned.[32]

The battle of Sudbury was one of the largest of the war, with two hundred colonial soldiers fighting more than a thousand Algonquians. At least fifty-five soldiers were dead or missing, and more were wounded. They claimed to have killed more than a hundred Indians, but the Algonquians denied that there were more than a handful of casualties.[33] They sent a scornful message, warning colonists that "they intended to dine with us upon the election day." That was May 3.[34]

Mary Rowlandson was present when Quinnapin and his warriors returned, boasting of their exploits. An English prisoner admitted they "made sad work at Sudbury." But Rowlandson thought the warriors seemed subdued. "They came home without that rejoicing and triumphing over their victory which they were wont to show at other times," "but rather like dogs . . . which have lost their ears. . . . When they went, they acted as if the devil had told them that they should gain the victory, and now they acted as if the devil had told them they should have a fall." A warrior gave her pork and ground nuts. While she was eating, an Indian warned, "He seems to be your good friend, but he killed two Englishmen at Sudbury, and there lie their clothes behind you." She turned and saw "bloody clothes, with bullet holes." But the warrior and his wife were kind to her. "If I went to their wigwam at any time, they would always give me something, and yet they were strangers that I never saw before."

She feared that the battle would jeopardize her ransom. On the last day of April, however, Indians suddenly ordered her inside a wigwam, and warriors rushed off with guns. A colonist rode up. "They shot over his horse, and under and before his horse, and they pushed him this way and that way at their pleasure, showing what they could do." It was John Hoar, and he had come with Tom Nepanet to ransom her. She feared for his life, but the Indians did not harm him, which she credited to God's "power over the heathen." He brought gifts from Joseph, including a pound of tobacco.[35]

The following evening, the Indians held a dance in a large wigwam. Quinnapin "was dressed in his Holland shirt, with great laces sewed at the tail of it; he had his silver buttons, his white stockings, his garters were hung round with shillings, and he had girdles of wampum upon his head and shoulders." Weetamoo "had a kersey coat, and [was] covered with girdles of wampum from the loins upward. Her arms from her elbows to her hands were covered with bracelets. There were handfuls of necklaces about her neck, and several sorts of jewels in her ears. She had fine red stockings and white shoes, her hair powdered and face painted red." Two people were "singing and knocking on a kettle," and others "kept hopping up and down, one after another," tossing wampum to bystanders in a display of generosity.

After several hours, Rowlandson lay down in Quinnapin's wigwam. James Printer brought word that Quinnapin would release her if Hoar added a pint of liquor to her redemption price. Hoar consented, knowing the sachems still had to approve her ransom. Philip promised to put in a good word for her if she secured him "two coats and twenty shillings in money, and half a bushel of seed corn and some tobacco." "I thanked him for his love," she later recalled. Late that night, Quinnapin "came ranting into the wigwam." He toasted Hoar as a "good man," only to exclaim soon after that he was a rogue who should be hanged. Rowlandson had not seen an Indian drunk before and trembled when he bid her approach, but he merely offered her a toast. Then he chased his younger wife around the wigwam, "money jingling at his knees." Eventually he contented himself with an older wife, so Rowlandson and Hoar were "no more troubled." But anxiety kept her awake. What would the sachems decide? What would become of her children?[36]

The sachems held a council the next day. Rowlandson claimed that Philip refused to attend, but if so, he eventually came around. Philip, Shoshanim, the female Narragansett sachem Quaiapin, the Shawomet sachem Pomham, and others wrote a letter offering to suspend their attacks if Massachusetts promised to let them plant at Quaboag, Mendon, Groton, and other abandoned towns. They would "fight no more but in their own defense," as Hoar later put it, and would free Rowlandson as a gesture of good faith. She was surprised that "they seemed much to rejoice" in her release, no doubt confident their peace offer would be accepted. They shook her hand, requested bread or tobacco, and gave her "a hood and scarf" for her journey.[37]

After eighty-two days in captivity, she could hardly believe she was going home. Tears flowed freely. But she grew solemn when her party reached burned-out Lancaster. "There had I lived many comfortable years amongst my relations and neighbors, and now not one Christian to be seen, nor one house left standing." Arriving in Concord the next morning, she was filled with "joy to see such a lovely sight, so many Christians together." But "I was not without sorrow, to think how many were looking and longing, and my own children amongst the rest, to enjoy that deliverance that I had now received, and I did not know whether ever I should see them again." There were many anxious inquiries about loved ones. She had to inform a brother-in-law that his wife was dead, her body consumed by the flames that had devoured the Rowlandson house.

She was reunited with her husband in Boston, grateful to be among "tender-hearted and compassionate Christians." But she admitted that the Indians had treated her far better than expected. "I have been in the midst of those roaring lions and savage bears that feared neither God nor man nor the Devil, by night and day, alone and in company, sleeping all sorts together," she would write, "yet not one of them ever offered me the least abuse of unchastity to me, in word or action."

Her return was celebrated as an answer to prayer and the "smile of providence," an impression strengthened when Thomas Eames's son also escaped captivity. That very day, however, Indians killed Thomas Kembal and another man near the Merrimack River and captured Kembal's wife and five children. Rowlandson knew that Indian morale remained high. "They would boast much of their victories, saying that in two hours' time they had destroyed such a captain and his company at such a place, and such a captain and his company in such a place, and such a captain and his company in such a place, and boast how many towns they had destroyed, and then scoff and say they had done them a good turn, to send them to heaven so soon." They intended to kill all the English, "drive them into the sea, or make them fly the country."[38]

CONNECTICUT ALSO INITIATED negotiations in late March 1676, though it insisted to the sachems that it had not "wronged the Indians nor injured them in the least so as to cause them to take arms against us." Requesting an exchange of captives, Connecticut promised that if any Indians "desire any treaty with us and can make appear that they have been wronged by any of the English, we shall endeavor to have that wrong rectified and hear any propositions." It guaranteed their safe conduct, for "we are men of peace and willing to farther peace with all our neighbors."[39]

Connecticut negotiated from a stronger position than did Massachusetts. Captain George Denison's English-Indian force killed or captured seventy-six Indians in Narragansett country in late April without losing a single soldier. When Connecticut learned that Massachusetts wanted to abandon Westfield, Hatfield, and Northampton to focus on defending Springfield and Hadley, it protested that the Indians "have a great ambition to possess those parts" and would quickly commence planting. "We would be loath to see that day and to lose such good neighbors, Christian, for heathen."[40]

The Connecticut Valley now had an unlikely commander. Captain William Turner was a tailor who had immigrated to Massachusetts in 1643. His role establishing a Baptist church in Boston got him imprisoned for thirty weeks in 1668 before a public outcry led to his release, and he was briefly imprisoned again in 1670. When war broke out, Turner, now in his fifties, organized a company of volunteers, but the colony denied him a commission. Finally, the government decided it needed all the help it could get, and Turner found himself a captain.[41]

Like his predecessor, John Pynchon, Captain Turner wanted to be relieved of command. His 150 men were "in great distress" for want of "shirts, stockings, shoes, and drawers." His health was poor, and his wife, Mary, was impoverished at home. "I should be glad if there might be some fitter person found for this employment, for I much doubt my weakness of body and my often infirmities will hardly suffer me to do my duty," he wrote his government.[42] It did not help that three thousand Indians were reported at Pocumtuck, who though "bare of provisions and clothing," were well "furnished with ammunition from the Dutch." On the other hand, an Indian captive claimed most wanted peace. Some were even willing to "bring in Philip's head" to end the war.[43]

On April 29 an envoy reached Connecticut from the senior Narragansett sachem Pessicus at Squakeag, saying Pessicus "was thankful" that the English desired peace and wanted to hear what they had to say. He had long been "a friend to the English" and still did not understand why they attacked his people. He believed many Indians would surrender in exchange for freedom.[44]

Upriver, Captain Turner, pastor John Russell, and Hadley's leaders were eager to attack. "It is strange to see how much spirit . . . appears in our men to be out against the enemy," they reported. "They are daily moving for it and would fain have liberty to be going forth this night. The enemy is now come so near us that we count we might go forth in the evening and come upon them in the darkness of the same night. . . . It is the general voice of the people here that now is the time to distress the enemy, and that could we drive them from their fishing and keep out though but lesser parties against them, famine would subdue them."[45]

Nevertheless, Connecticut wanted to attempt peace. It wrote Pessicus on May 1, promising that if the sachems brought their captives to Hadley within eight days, colonial representatives would negotiate with them. Connecticut had good relations with its Indians, it pointed out: "They know we never use to break our promises to Indians." It warned colonial leaders at Hadley not to attack "whilst the treaty with them is in hand," lest it endanger the lives of captives.[46]

The previous few months had been devastating, but negotiations offered a glimmer of hope. With both colonists and Indians desiring peace, perhaps New England's agony would finally come to an end.

20

New England's Reckoning

May 1676

THERE WAS ONLY one way to interpret the cataclysm destroying New England, as far as colonists were concerned: it was God's judgment. "Various are men's thoughts why God hath suffered it," one later wrote. "All acknowledge it was for sin."[1] But what sins? There was no shortage of opinions, yet all could agree that the Indians were God's enemies and would ultimately be defeated.

Edward Perry, a Quaker, brooded on the "horrible cruelty, bloodshed and torment" inflicted by Indians as he warmed himself by his hearth one morning in March 1676. It reminded him of how the colonies once whipped, mutilated, and executed Quakers. "Come New England," he declared in a tract written in God's voice, "thou that accountest thyself to be my people . . . hast thou lived according as thou hast professed?" Had not the clergy "turned thee from my power into the power of Satan, the grand original of all cruelty?" The war was New England's punishment, "and my hand will I not withdraw until I have avenged the blood of my servants."[2]

Few Puritans took such rhetoric seriously, for they believed persecuting the Quakers was God's will. But neither did everyone agree with the young Boston minister Increase Mather's calls for strictly enforced moral reforms, including laws prohibiting Quaker meetings, and for churches to formally renew their covenants. The fifty-five-year-old William Hubbard, Ipswich's minister, doubted that anyone could discern precisely why God was angry. And it was Hubbard, not Mather, whom the General Court invited to preach its annual election sermon on May 3, 1676.

Much of Hubbard's sermon summarized the Puritan view of society: governments should protect true religion; disparities of wealth, education, and vocation were essential to order and prosperity; liberty to elect their rulers was "one of the highest civil privileges a people can enjoy," and they should elect wise men who feared God, loved justice, and rejected extremism. He rebuked those who were contentious about religious matters. "For all necessary and fundamental truths, we cannot be too resolved in contention," he admitted, but "wise and good men" needed freedom to disagree about "opinions of less certainty and moment." For example, Baptists were "orderly and peaceable" and deserved lenience.[3]

The most important matter facing voters was management of the war. "There is nothing more easy than to begin a war," he observed, but "nothing more diffi-cult than to manage it aright or bring it to a good issue." He delicately questioned whether the colonists had provoked God's wrath by seeking war too eagerly, but he did not press the issue. "I judge charitably of the present auditors and dare not censure others." But he returned to the subject later. Governments should take "great care" to avoid "unnecessary war," for "war is on one side an heinous evil or murder, [and] on both it is a judgment," he declared. Perhaps "imprudences, indiscretion, and want of faith in God's promises, not asking counsel at God's or-acle" had caused the war. "We must do no wrong to the innocent, be they Indians or English."

He urged colonial leaders not to seek a spiritual explanation for every defeat (as Mather was wont to do). "Upon serious thoughts, the sad losses and slaughter that have befallen this poor country in the present war can be imputed to nothing more than to the contempt of our enemies, or overweening thoughts of our own skill and courage." Soldiers were ambushed because they lacked the skill of their opponents, who shrewdly used the woods to their advantage.[4]

He also warned them not to jump to false conclusions, making "God speak that by his providence which never entered into his heart." No one should con-fuse God's truth with "the private apprehensions of ourselves or our own party." Some men claimed New England was too tolerant, others claimed the con-trary, and Hubbard urged humility. Practicing charity was unlikely to provoke God's wrath. There were many commonplace sins, but state and church already combatted these "by executing wholesome laws and church censures." And while younger colonists were often criticized for their spiritual failures, they had gen-erously given themselves "to the work and service of their generation."

He pointed out that God's people sometimes suffered for reasons other than sin. For example, the early church had been faithful amid horrible persecution, and such faithfulness persuaded many of the truth of the gospel. God might have a similar purpose in mind for "his servants in the first planting of the gospel in the West." Perhaps he was using hardship to train them in virtue or military skill. There were other possible causes. "There hath been some things objected against the proceedings with the Indians," he admitted, "relating both to the present war and former peace." But he shrank from assertions that might antago-nize the magistrates. "I intend not to meddle with things out of my line or above my sphere."[5]

What, then, should they do? Obviously "God hath a controversy with New England," but how could they repent if they did not know the cause of his wrath? Hubbard suggested they repent of what all agreed was sinful: spiritual pride and worldliness, which "neither civil nor ecclesiastical censures can reach." Pride provoked conflict, turning magistrates and people against each other. Left unchecked, it would "make them turn Indians." Worldliness spurred obsession with land and wealth: "They that first came over hither for the gospel could not well tell what to do with more land than a small number of acres, yet now men more easily swallow down so many hundreds and are not satisfied." Hunger for land led them into the wilderness where there were no churches. Like the biblical Lot, who chose to live among the Canaanites, they were "too ready to exchange the kingdom of heaven for earthly possessions." No wonder God was using "a foolish nation" they "despised" to cut them off "from the world and from new plantations." They spoke "contemptibly of the Indians, as if one of us could drive hundreds of them," and perhaps they once could, "when God put the dread of us upon them." No more. "These things may seem harsh, yet when the Lord is crying aloud in his providence . . . who can but prophesy?" he asked, quoting the biblical prophet Amos.[6]

It all came down to lack of love. Echoing John Winthrop's forgotten discourse on charity, Hubbard called on colonists to "put off this private selfish worldly spirit and put on humility and charity and manifest a public spirit." Love "would heal all our divisions, reform all our vices, root out all our disorders, make up all our breaches." He finally reached his climax: "I tell you, if we could set up such a bank of Christian charity in New England, it would prove a richer storehouse than all the Spanish mines or banks of Venice or Amsterdam. . . . It would make our forces, however weak in themselves, become a host like the host of God— though not in numbers, yet in virtue and power—against which our enemies should not be able to stand up. Were our Jerusalem thus compacted together, the gates of hell with all their instruments would never be able to undermine it or prevail against it."[7]

The sermon was well received. The court approved it for publication. Many appreciated its message that they simply had to stay the course, trusting that God would crush his enemies under their feet.[8] Voters reelected most magistrates and deputies, with one prominent exception. For the first time in twenty-four years, Daniel Gookin, widely resented for his advocacy for praying Indians, was turned out of office.[9]

HUBBARD'S UNWILLINGNESS TO advocate legislative reform and covenant re-newal frustrated Mather. "New England is in sad estate," Mather wrote in his diary on May 9, 1676, "the war with the Indians still having little success" and the people demonstrated no "fitness for deliverance."[10] The latest calamity was the "epidemical diseases, which sin hath brought upon us," he later wrote. "I cannot hear of one family in New England that hath wholly escaped the distemper." "We in Boston have seen a sad and solemn spectacle, coffins meeting one another, and three or four put into their graves in one day. In the month of May, about fifty persons are deceased in this town."[11] Stamford, Connecticut, buried six people in one week and had "about a hundred sick at once," according to John Bishop. "The sword bereaved abroad. At home here was death."[12]

Mather was writing a book in which he intended to show that the war was God's judgment on New England for breaking its covenant. But Hubbard's sermon so roiled him that he set it aside to write a tract, "An Earnest Exhortation to the Inhabitants of New England, to Hearken to the Voice of God in His Late and Present Dispensations." He worked on it almost every day, finishing on May 16.

The situation was far graver than people realized, he argued. God was warning New England to repent, or he would forsake them and leave the land "desolate without an English inhabitant." Had God's judgment been in vain? "Is it nothing that widows and fatherless have been multiplied among us? That in a small plantation we have heard of eight widows, and six and twenty fatherless children in one day? . . . How can we speak of such things without bleeding lamentations!" It was utterly humiliating "that New England should be brought so low in so short a time . . . by such vile enemies, by the heathen, yea *the worst of the heathen*." And "when there are so many evils visible and manifest, it is the subtlety of Satan to persuade men that this judgment cometh for some one secret sin," he argued, in a thinly veiled critique of Hubbard. "Do not say that the ministers of God cannot tell you why this judgment is come. How then could they give you faithful warning thereof long enough before it came?" God had "confirmed the word of his servants" so people would know they spoke for him.[13]

Mather suggested that since God was using the heathen to punish them, their sin was probably heathenism. How many people claimed to be Christians but were "no better than heathens in heart and in conversation? How many families that live like profane Indians without any family prayer?" How many settlements lacked churches? He enumerated their manifold sins, including conflict, perjury, Sabbath-breaking, economic exploitation, failure to support their ministers, religious formalism, sensuality, drunkenness, pride, immodesty, and ostentatious clothing. The prophet Isaiah warned that God would strip the daughters of Israel because of their pride. "Hath not the Lord fulfilled this threatening when the Indians have taken so many and stripped them naked as in the day that they were born?" Isaiah said God would make them stink. "Is not this verified when poor creatures are carried away captive into the Indians' filthy and stinking wigwams," where they were "exposed to the burning heat of the sun, and burnt and tanned thereby till they become of an hue like unto these Indians"?

On one point he agreed with Hubbard: "Land! Land! hath been the idol of many in New England. Whereas the first planters . . . were satisfied with one acre for each person, as his propriety, and after that with twenty acres for a family, now have men since coveted after the earth, that many hundreds, nay thousands, of acres have been engrossed by one man." Men built settlements without churches, leaving their children unchurched. "Let there then be no more plantations erected in New England where people professing Christianity shall live like Indians . . . without instituted worship." Here too the punishment fit the crime: "Do men prefer their farms and merchandize above the gospel? Here is the reason why armies are sent forth against us and our cities are burnt up." Was it not greed that built the "unhappy Indian trading houses, whereby the heathen have been so woefully scandalized" with alcohol, "and was it not from the same root of all evil that the Indians have been furnished with arms and ammunition?" As for the sins of English youth, Mather thought it significant that "old Indians were very unwilling to engage in a war with the English, but the young men would do it whether their fathers would or no."[14]

While Hubbard only hinted at it, Mather explicitly charged colonists with "the guilt of Indian blood" for their treatment of praying Indians, alienating them "against the English interest, yea against the interest of Christ in this land." "What madness and rage hath there been against all Indians whatsoever? Yea, what willingness to destroy those that . . . are proselytized to the faith and have put themselves under the protection of the English Israel in this land, though they never did us hurt?" He quoted an accusing letter from a Christian Indian: "When any hurt is done, you say that we have done it, though we never did wrong to Englishmen and hope we never shall. You have driven us from our houses and lands, but that which most of all troubles us is that whereas we began to know Jesus Christ, you have driven us away from serving God." Terrible as it was, Mather admitted, the charge was true. "Truly when I think of what things have happened at Chelmsford my heart doth ache and bleed within me."

Forgetting that God desired the heathen's conversion, colonists "slighted, scorned, [and] vilified" the mission that was once "one of the glories of New England." Christian Indians were God's chosen people, "yet how many with us have condemned all praying Indians?" True, some were hypocrites, but "are not some praying English as perfidious, as hypocritical, in heart as profane as some praying Indians? Shall we therefore condemn all?"

Mather had put his finger on the problem: Puritans professed to value faith above ethnicity, but ethnicity had come to trump faith. He warned that many colonists might be disappointed on the Day of Judgment: "I do believe that many Englishmen that look with a disdainful eye upon these poor praying Indians shall see a number of them sitting down with Abraham, Isaac and Jacob in the kingdom of God when, I pray God, they may not see themselves shut out." He implored, "Confess your sin before him, pray that it may not be imputed to you or to your families, or to the land for your sakes." Their ancestors had come to "set up the kingdom of the Lord Jesus among the heathen," yet not nearly enough had been accomplished. How would they view "the present generation, who will neither believe that there is any good work begun amongst the Indians, nor yet desire and pray that it might be so?" Was it any wonder God used Indians to afflict them?[15]

Mather did not doubt the justice of the war, for they were defending Christ's kingdom. "Jesus Christ hath by a wonderful hand of providence dispossessed Satan who reigned in these dark corners of the earth in ages that are past, and hath taken possession of this land for himself. Now shall we think that Christ will suffer the devil to drive him out of his possession?" It might be gradual, as with the Canaanites, but surely God would ultimately destroy Indians who rejected Christianity. "I do believe that if the Lord had not had a righteous design utterly to destroy those of the heathen nations who have refused and horribly contemned the gospel, they had not been permitted to do what they have done, that so they might bring swift destruction upon themselves," he concluded.

He suggested that New Englanders pray the words of Psalm 79: "'Pour out thy wrath upon the heathen that have not known thee . . . for they have devoured Jacob and laid waste his dwelling place.'" "Certainly those prayers and tears will come pouring down at last in streams of blood and fire and vengeance upon the heathen," he declared. God used disease to kill Indians in their fathers' day, and he would kill them again. Only for Indians who embraced the gospel would it be different. One day, Mather believed, for Christian Indians and English alike, peace and prosperity would fill the earth like a mighty river.[16]

MANDATED BY THEIR government to investigate the causes of God's wrath, Connecticut's ministers followed their Massachusetts counterparts by calling for repentance and reformation. They confessed that God had rejected their prayers, covering them with "shame in the sight of the heathen" and "slaying many of the chosen young men of our Israel." They discussed the many sins of which the people were guilty, singling out young people for failing to become church members and churches for not disciplining wayward members. James Fitch led his church through the sort of covenant renewal ceremony Mather advocated, and Connecticut passed reform legislation in May 1676.[17]

As young men fought and died, as town after town was torched, some questioned Plymouth's role in starting the war. Mather was sufficiently alarmed to write Governor Josiah Winslow about it. Winslow insisted that Plymouth always acted "justly and faithfully" toward the Wampanoags, "and friendly beyond their deserts. I think I can clearly say that before these present troubles broke out, the English did not possess one foot of land in this colony but what was fairly obtained by honest purchase of the Indian proprietors." True, many colonists *wanted* to cheat Indians, but Plymouth did not allow it: "Because some of our people are of a covetous disposition, and the Indians are in their straits easily prevailed with to part with their lands, we first made a law that none should purchase or receive of gift any land of the Indians without the knowledge and allowance of our court." Plymouth even prohibited the sale of "Mount Hope, Pocasset," and other valuable tracts, otherwise sachems would have "sold them long since." Whenever Wampanoags brought complaints, they "had justice impartial and speedily, so that our own people have frequently complained that we erred on the other hand in showing them overmuch favor." Winslow did acknowledge some guilt on Plymouth's part. They had failed to seek the Wampanoags' "enlightening and conversion" and "taught them new sins that they knew not." For these failures, God was just to punish them. But as Winslow knew, these were not the failures that drove Indians to arms.[18]

FRONTIER SETTLERS STRUGGLED to make sense of all the destruction, disease, and death. "I can say truly that since our war's begun my flesh is so gone with fear, care, and grief, and now this sickness, my skin is ready to cleave to my bones," wrote elderly John Kinglsey from Rehoboth. "To tell you what we have [suffered], and how we are like to suffer, my heart will not hold to write, and sheets would [not] contain." They had planted crops, but it was too little: "famine stares us in the face." When they sought food from Rhode Island, they were charged exorbitant prices. "It is better to die by sword than famine," he wrote friends in Connecticut. "I beg in my Lord's name, to send us some meal."

"Ah, the burden that I bear night and day, to see the blessed and loving God thus angry, and we have not a prophet to tell how long, and to say this or these are New England's sin," Kingsley lamented. He tried to exhibit the spirit of Job, who responded to cataclysmic tragedies by declaring, "The Lord gave and the Lord has taken away; blessed be the name of the Lord" (Job 1:20), but it was harder than expected. "I prayed seven years to be fitted to suffer common calamity, so the thing I feared is come on me, but alas, I am ready to faint in the day of adversity."[19]

Rehoboth deacon Philip Walker expressed his bitterness through poetry. In a poem dedicated to Captain Pierce's Plymouth troops, whom he considered martyrs, he described Indians as "savage, sneaking, brutish" hunters, "heathen Canaanite[s]" from the devil's "hellish nest," whom colonists should send to hell. He supported recruiting friendly Indians, for it made sense to "employ a wily rogue to catch a thief," but thought their families should be held hostage.[20] In another piece, he portrayed the enemy as following Satan's orders from that "dark place where all the rabblement of devils" assembled. "Him they only adore and serve, and he by their powwows, as Baal priests, proscribes them to his law."[21]

In yet another poem, Walker rehearsed how God brought his people to America not for pleasure or ease, but freedom "to practice what God did reveal by grace and Spirit from holy writ." God was now using the Indians to discipline his people for forgetting that mission.

> We came to wild America,
>> whose native brood to devils pray.
> A savage race, for blood that thirst,
>> of all the nations, most accursed.

Some hoped Indians could be civilized, but Walker compared this to putting a jewel in a pig's snout. Philip's warriors were "incarnate devils sent from the infernal lake" and "hellish monsters," and allied Indians were no better than "rogues and serpents in our breast" who threatened the ruin of "all the rest." Walker relished the thought of the Narragansett sachem Canonchet burning in hell, where he "must yell and cry and lie . . . gnash, gnaw, and fry eternally."[22]

Like many Puritans, Walker spoke a religious language, but his bitterness deformed it into racist vitriol.

BENJAMIN THOMPSON'S *New England's Crisis* was better known. Thompson, who had given the eulogy at John Winthrop Jr.'s funeral, waxed nostalgic about New England's founding, when men and women were more devoted to piety and virtue than material prosperity and defeated their enemies with prayer.[23] Now "New England's hour of passion" was at hand. Thompson questioned why Philip and his "pagan slaves" rebelled:

> Whether our infant thrivings did invite,
> Or whether to our lands pretended right,
> Is hard to say; but Indian spirits need
> No grounds but lust to make a Christian bleed.

Thompson vividly imagined the horrors of an Indian raid:

> Here might be seen the infant from the breast
> Snatched by a pagan hand to lasting rest:
> The mother, Rachel-like, shrieks out "My child!"
> She wrings her hands and raves as she were wild.
> The brutish wolves suppress her anxious moan
> By cruelties more deadly of their own.
> Will she or nill, the chastest turtle must
> Taste of the pangs of their unbridled lust.
> From farms to farms, from towns to towns they post,
> They strip, they bind, they ravish, flay, and roast.

It was pure fabrication; there were no credible reports of Indians raping women. Yet Thompson went even further, describing supposed atrocities toward pregnant women:

> ... mothers' bodies ripped for lack of aid.
> The secret cabinets which nature meant
> To hide her masterpiece is open rent.
> The half-formed infant there receives a death
> Before it sees the light or draws its breath.[24]

Thompson described warriors "besmeared with Christian blood" who bashed out "New England's brains." The "midnight shrieks and soul-amazing moans" of colonists blended in cacophony with the shooting and shouting of warriors as "towns and churches" were reduced to ashes. He concluded by expressing confidence that God would judge the Indians and raise up New England like a Phoenix, more glorious than before.[25]

In a subsequent edition, he added a few lines about the praying Indians:

> These are confined under Christian wings,
> And hopes we have never to feel their stings.
> A natural prison walled with sea and isles,
> From our metropolis not many miles,
> Contains their swarms.[26]

Puritans might not agree on the precise cause of God's anger, but they agreed that they were still God's people and that their enemies were his enemies. More suffering was to come, they knew, much of it deserved, but in the long run, God would destroy the Indians just as he would destroy all the devil's servants. Christ's kingdom would triumph, and America's first people would be conquered.

21

Turning Point

May 1676 to July 1676

As THE WAR entered its eleventh month—with no end in sight—Puritans' distress approached new heights, driving them to desperation. Unable to defeat Algonquian warriors on the battlefield, they entered into negotiations with their sachems. The problem was that the colonies negotiated from a position of weakness.

In these dire straits, colonists began to believe that praying Indians might be the key to winning the war. It was no coincidence that the colony that had fared best militarily—Connecticut—was the one that had cooperated most extensively with Indians. The other colonies began to see the wisdom in that policy, not only because they were desperate but because of the distinguished service that praying Indians provided the army. On May 5, 1676, praying Indians encountered a large body of Indians northwest of Mendon. They reported it to Captain Thomas Brattle, who launched an immediate assault. Most of the Indians escaped, but his troopers killed twenty, including four women.[1] Increase Mather noted that "many who had hard thoughts of them begin to blame themselves and to have a good opinion of the praying Indians, who have been so generally and so sinfully decried."[2]

Such exploits made the plight of their family members on the islands all the more egregious. Despite Massachusetts's orders, the interned Indians had not received adequate fishing boats. Many suffered from dysentery and other illnesses, including Waban, Natick's elderly leader, who was laid "extreme low." To make matters worse, although they cleared and broke up ground, colonists prevented them from planting. The New England Company provided aid, but not enough. They were "ready to perish for want of bread and incapacitated to make provision for the future," the General Court admitted. If something was not done soon, many would die.[3]

On May 10 a proposal was introduced to return the Indians to the mainland so they could plant crops and provide security and support for "both English and Indians against the common enemy." Able-bodied men would be recruited for military service, while others would work their fields, returning to assigned locations at night. Perhaps it was to sway hesitating deputies that the final version of the measure forbade Indians from leaving their assigned garrisons "on pain of death" and provided that any Indian "impeached by name by any English" had to remain on the islands until the council decided his fate. The Indians would be transported "at their own charge," which meant the New England Company's missionary funds would be used to pay for it. Most deputies still opposed the proposal, but enough joined the magistrates in support that it passed.

Transportation commenced on May 12, overseen by Daniel Gookin with help from John Eliot. Some were settled on land provided by Cambridge's Thomas Oliver, who had "a very loving, compassionate spirit" toward them. The site was spacious, "convenient for fishing," and offered plenty of wood for fuel. "This deliverance from the island was a jubilee to those poor creatures," Gookin wrote. Those who were strong enough began planting crops. About forty were assigned to a company under Captain Daniel Henchman. Even the Indian-hating Captain Samuel Mosely realized their value, securing permission to recruit sixty Indians for his independent company.[4]

A TURNING POINT IN the negotiations came a week later. When the sachems proposed a truce in early May, the General Court consulted the clergy for advice. The ministers supported peace talks but suggested that "war be vigorously prosecuted" in the meantime. They seemed more concerned with urging churches to renew their covenants and the government to enforce its laws.[5]

The sachems had intended Mary Rowlandson's release as a gesture of good faith, but Massachusetts was hardly satisfied. They insisted that the sachems immediately release all their captives. "Our mind is not to make bargain with you for one and one, but for all together," the court wrote on May 5. "Unto this, which was our chief business, you send us no answer, which we do not take kindly." As for a truce, "this is a great matter and therefore cannot be ended by letters without speaking to one another. . . . If you will send us home all the English prisoners, it will be a great testimony of a true heart in you to peace, which you say you are willing to have, and then, if any of your sachems and counsellors will come to us at Boston or else to Concord or Sudbury to meet with such chief men as we shall send, we will speak with you about your desires and with true heart deal with you." To its envoy, Seth Perry, the court explained that if the sachems "demur at the delivery of our captives before the treaty, yet you shall somewhat insist thereon as a real testimony of their true meaning," but it should not be a deal-breaker.[6]

Indians released a few captives over the following days, including the mother and five children they had captured the previous week. Colonists were encouraged by a report that Mohawks were assailing Philip's forces and Indians were suffering from "fluxes and fevers."[7] But no response came from the sachems.

So Massachusetts sent another letter, promising, "We [are of] very true heart, and you tell your people so." It instructed its envoys that if the sachems had "any reasonable offers" to help end the war, "you shall let them know we will hear and consider what they have to say." But the sachems should know "the English are resolved to make war their work until they enjoy a firm peace."[8]

The sachems finally agreed, and a meeting was held around May 11 at a place between Concord and Groton. The sachems brought a man and two women and explained that more would be released when Shoshanim, the Nashaway sachem, retrieved them from the Connecticut Valley.[9] It was a substantial step toward peace.

Unfortunately, the sachems' promises were overtaken by catastrophic events in the Connecticut Valley. Despite Connecticut's offer to negotiate with Pessicus, the Narragansetts' senior sachem, no Indian envoys had arrived at Hadley. Connecticut had declared that Indians who surrendered within thirty-six days would receive their lives and freedom and be settled on land where, like the Pequots, they could live as Connecticut's subjects.[10]

During the night of May 13, however, Indian warriors seized at least eighty horses and cattle from Hatfield. Two days later, soldier Thomas Reed returned from captivity reporting that many Indians and captives were at Peskeompscut Falls, a fishing place five miles north of Pocumtuck where the river narrowed, rushing among rocks and small islands before plunging over a forty- or fifty-foot waterfall. He did not think more than seventy were warriors. "We think the Lord calls us to make some trial what may be done against them suddenly, without further delay," Hadley minister John Russell goaded Connecticut. "I verily fear God will charge it upon us for sloth and neglect of following his guiding providence when he hath been leading [us] to advantageous ways of coming upon them, such as we cannot expect at another time. They sit by us secure, without watch, busy at their harvest work, storing themselves with food for a year to fight against us, and we let them alone to take the full advantage that the season would afford them, [as] if there were no enemy." "We need guidance and help from heaven. We humbly beg your prayers, advice, and help."[11]

Captain William Turner and other officers decided they could not wait. Turner rode north with 150 men on the evening of May 18. They must have been anxious as they traversed battlefields where previous expeditions had ended in disaster. But they made the twenty miles to Peskeompscut without mishap. A captive later claimed that the Indians had celebrated a rare meal of roast beef and fresh milk that evening. They slept unconcerned as Turner deployed his men.

When the soldiers opened fire, the camp exploded in chaos. Hundreds of men, women, and children poured out of wigwams screaming "Mohawks! Mohawks!" and rushed toward the river, even as bullets brought many down. Those few intrepid warriors who resisted were overpowered. Indians crammed into birch canoes, only for the overcrowded boats to capsize amid the rushing current. Others attempted to swim. Some were shot, and the current swept dozens more over the falls to the treacherous rocks below. Still others clung to the riverbank, hiding among rocks and bushes until soldiers slew them with swords. Lieutenant Samuel Holyoke killed five, "young and old, with his own hands." Soldiers destroyed food, ammunition, wigwams, and a forge critical for repairing guns. They cast two large pigs of lead into the river. A sergeant who scoured the area counted more than 100 dead Indians. Others reported seeing 120 get swept over the falls, though Indians claimed many of these survived. Still others estimated more than 200 bodies, "some in the river and some cast ashore." Turner's forces suffered only three casualties.[12]

Captain Turner knew they had to get away quickly, since Indians were swarming the riverbanks. A liberated English captive claimed that Philip was nearby with a thousand warriors. So Turner ordered his men to retrieve their horses and ride for Hadley. About twenty men, including sixteen-year-old Jonathan Wells, found that the soldiers who were guarding their animals were already under attack. They drove off the assailants, mounted, and spurred their horses. A bullet slammed into Wells's horse. Another shattered Wells's thigh, but he clung to the horse's mane and kept riding. Turner and the main body of soldiers rode toward the Green River, harassed the whole way. As word circulated that Philip was upon them, the ailing captain lost control. Wells caught up and warned that the rearguard was in danger of being cut off, but Turner refused to delay. "Better save some, than lose all," he declared. A scout cried, "If you love your lives, follow me!" Another urged the men in a different direction.

Indians caught Wells's party in a swampy area, inflicting heavy casualties. About ten soldiers got away, but Wells and a wounded man named John Jones could not keep up. Wells concluded that Jones's wound was mortal and abandoned him. Wells would spend several harrowing days in the wilderness before he found his way to Hatfield. Captain Turner was fording the Green River when bullets tore into his thigh and back. Enemy warriors stripped him and left him dying on the bank. Lieutenant Holyoke assumed command, exhorting the men to keep close and stay calm. "God hath wrought hitherto for us wonderfully," he cried. "Let us trust in him still!" Then he went down, his horse shot beneath him. Warriors charged, but he cut them down with pistol shots until a soldier rescued him.[13]

The enemy abandoned the chase after about five miles. By the time the soldiers straggled into Hadley, forty-five were missing, most presumed dead. Many more were wounded. Indians claimed no more than 60 warriors were killed, though others put the number at 170. Over the next few days, six missing soldiers returned, including Hope Atherton, Hatfield's pastor.[14] He claimed he had repeatedly tried to surrender, but Indians refused to take him, which was so bizarre he wondered if he had imagined it. As he explained to his congregation, he decided "it tends to the glory of God in no small measure if it were so as I believe it was: that I was encompassed with cruel and unmerciful enemies, and they were restrained by the hand of God from doing the least injury to me." He struggled to understand why God spared him, when so many others died.[15]

Turner had dealt the enemy a crushing blow at what became known as Turner's Falls, but the cost was staggering. The most devastating consequence was that it shattered hope of a peace treaty. That very day, Shoshanim had been on his way to Peskeompscut to retrieve captives as promised by the sachems. "I went to Connecticut about the captives that I might bring them into your hands," he later wrote, "and when we were almost there, the English had destroyed those Indians. When I heard it, I returned back again."[16] His heart must have sunk with every step.

LOCAL LEADERS WERE eager to strike again, so Connecticut abandoned diplomacy, suggesting that it and Massachusetts launch a major offensive against Pocumtuck and Peskeompscut. Some sachems were inclined to peace, the colony conceded, but "surely those Indians up the river . . . most encourage the war." Major Robert Treat had been elected Connecticut's deputy governor, so Connecticut ordered Major John Talcott, a forty-five-year-old magistrate, to organize a new force, reminding him that it was "God whose battles you are to fight."[17] Massachusetts agreed to the plan, having decided that the Indians were not serious about peace and that it was imperative to prevent them from stockpiling food. It ordered Captain Henchman to lead five hundred soldiers to attack Mount Wachusett and Quaboag en route to joining Talcott in Hadley.[18]

The Algonquians struck first, seizing cattle and killing nine horses at Hadley on May 25.[19] Four days later, hundreds of warriors descended on Hatfield, torching a dozen buildings outside the palisade and rounding up sheep, cattle, and horses. Twenty-five men from Hadley boldly crossed the river to relieve Hatfield, only to come under fire as they disembarked. Five were killed and three wounded as they fought their way to the palisade. Other reinforcements proved reluctant to follow, and when the Indians withdrew, it was of their own accord. Colonists claimed to have killed twenty-five.[20]

Meanwhile, Major Talcott found it difficult to persuade the Mohegans and Pequots, who were not happy with the rewards they had received for earlier expeditions, to march with his Connecticut forces. Ninigret's Narragansett warriors, who had assisted Connecticut up to this point, refused to serve at all. Tensions between them and the Mohegans had been rising, each accusing the other of various crimes. During an expedition in Narragansett country, one of Ninigret's people was killed, and Mohegans stole two hundred fathoms of wampum from Ninigret's family. "Uncas's pride and arrogance and covetousness" were beyond belief, Thomas Stanton protested regarding the Mohegan sachem. "It will be well if he prove not as bad as Philip to the English, and that it be not proved against him that he had a great hand with Philip." Connecticut merely urged the Algonquians to "lay aside all controversies for the present" and focus on the war. Alienated from all sides, Ninigret's embittered warriors withdrew from the war.[21]

Many Indians clung to hopes of peace. Even before Talcott left Norwich, eighty-eight Wabquissets, some of whom were praying Indians, turned themselves in.[22] The Narragansett sachems Quinnapin and Quaiapin, at Mount Wachusett, attempted to jump-start negotiations with Massachusetts. Escorted to colonial authorities by the praying Indian Peter Ephraim on June 1, their representative asked if they might return to Narragansett country in peace. The council replied that as treaty-breakers they could not be trusted. But the Narragansett emissary insisted that "they never intended to kill English." He blamed the slain Canonchet for breaking the treaty and waging war, maintaining that neither they nor their senior sachem Pessicus supported it.

Massachusetts hardly believed such claims, but it commissioned Ephraim to meet the sachems and receive their proposals. The timing could not have been worse. Unaware that Major Talcott was marching north with 240 Connecticut soldiers and 200 Mohegans and Pequots (accompanied by an ailing James Fitch, serving as chaplain), the sachems arranged to meet Ephraim near Chabanakongkomun. On June 5, just before they arrived, Talcott's forces captured Ephraim and fifty-one other Indians. Only Ephraim's pass from Massachusetts spared him the fate of twenty men who were shot. Two days later, Talcott's troops surprised a band of Indians near Quaboag. They killed twelve men, though only two, laden with "as much fish as they could carry," were enemy warriors. Colonial aggression had again thwarted Algonquian efforts toward peace.[23]

Captain Henchman's Massachusetts forces, now including a company of praying Indians, found the enemy in disarray and desperate for peace. The praying Indian Tom Nepanet led them to some Nashaways fishing near Weshakim Pond on June 7. According to one account, a praying Indian offered to let the Nashaways live if they surrendered, but they replied with a volley. Colonial forces killed seven men and captured twenty-nine mostly women and children, including the sachem Shoshanim's wife.[24] Four days later, praying Indians found the praying Indian ruler Captain Tom Wuttasacomponom, his daughter, and two grandchildren. Captain Tom explained that after escaping the Nipmucs they had avoided English soldiers for fear they would be killed. They had gone to Captain Thomas Prentice's farm, but Prentice was not there. They also revealed that many Indians knew Shoshanim was negotiating a treaty and intended to take refuge with him, which another Indian source confirmed.[25]

By then Talcott's army had reached Hadley, where Indians remained combative. On June 12 warriors fatally wounded three colonists outside Hadley's palisade. Colonial forces counterattacked but encountered hundreds of warriors emerging from the foliage. Soldiers fired a cannon at a house that warriors had occupied and sent them fleeing. They pursued for about two miles, reportedly killing thirty Indians.[26]

After Captain Henchman's Massachusetts force joined Talcott a few days later, the two armies marched north with more than a thousand men, Henchman east of the river, and Talcott west. Though drenched by a massive thunderstorm, they reached Pocumtuck, only to find that the Algonquians had left. Peskeompscut was also abandoned, though there were large quantities of fish and other food. The next day, another storm brought cold wind and more rain. Shivering, exhausted soldiers stumbled upon one discouraging sight after another. Near the Green River they found Captain Turner's naked body. Occasionally they discovered charred remains between stakes, where, they conjectured, Indians had roasted captives to death. Scouts ranged as far as Squakeag but could not find the enemy. They returned downriver on June 18, demoralized that the "Lord .. . seemed to fight against them by the storm." Talcott departed for Connecticut. Ten days later, soldiers returned upriver, destroyed wigwams and a fort and seized or ruined fish, canoes, and other property.[27]

Had they known the reason for the Algonquian retreat, the colonists would have been encouraged. Mohawks had attacked from the west, killing fifty Algonquians and seizing women, children, and plunder. The Mohawk assault changed everything. It cut off the Algonquians from their ammunition sources to the north and west, shattered their security in the upper valley, and drove them into "continual motion, some toward Narragansett, others toward Wachusett." Driven from their fishing places and cornfields, and their crops ruined, they faced imminent starvation.[28] Hundreds fled northward. New York dispatched messengers promising to spare any Indians who surrendered to its forces.[29]

Algonquian resistance was suddenly crumbling with shocking rapidity. In June, the Christian Pennacook sachem Wannalancet brought one hundred Indians to Major Richard Waldron at Dover, in present-day New Hampshire. Wannalancet had attempted "to keep out of the way till the storm was over," he admitted, but now he entrusted himself to the English. To prove his good faith, he brought in the warriors who had captured the Kembal family.[30] Connecticut troops continued scouring Narragansett country that month, taking seventy-five Indians.[31] Connecticut authorized Major Talcott to march wherever he and his advisors thought best and "destroy the enemy as God shall deliver them into their hands."[32] Captain Henchman found his own success, marching his "weary and hungry" Massachusetts soldiers east to Marlborough and taking eighty-four Indians on the way. Captives reported that most Indians would accept any terms offered. Philip and Quinnapin set out for their homelands, according to Shoshanim, "much afraid because of our offer to join with the English." Prisoners claimed that Philip was resigned to defeat but remained resolved "to do what mischief he could do to the English."[33]

⚜

IN PLYMOUTH, HOWEVER, THE war was far from over. Wampanoags had been returning home to fish and plant since late March. In May their warriors unleashed a string of raids to seize cattle and destroy Plymouth's towns. On May 8, three hundred warriors descended on Bridgewater, though a powerful thunderstorm prevented them from burning more than thirteen houses and a few barns and killing some cattle. On May 11 and 13 they burned twenty-five structures on the outskirts of Plymouth town and destroyed what was left of Middleborough.[34] On May 16 they killed a man and burned a house, barn, and sawmill near Hingham. Later that month they hit Taunton, killing four men (fathers of a collective thirty-two children) and capturing two boys. Two hundred Indians were reported at nearby Titicut, "very busy killing cattle and horses."[35]

Plymouth proved powerless against the onslaught, having failed to muster an army since Pierce's company was destroyed. It was Captain Brattle's Massachusetts cavalry who attacked a group of Indians fishing near Rehoboth on May 24. They killed about a dozen, "took several arms with ammunition, kettles and other things, with two horses, [and] burned great stores of their fish." One English soldier was killed.[36] On June 10 Massachusetts warned that a "great number" of Wampanoags was gathering at Mount Hope. Only then did Plymouth organized a force of 150 English and 50 allied Wampanoags under Major William Bradford, who had recovered from the wound he suffered in December.[37]

There was some attempt at negotiation, but it came about by accident. As Plymouth's Captain Benjamin Church described it, he was on his way to Rhode Island to raise volunteers when, from his canoe, he encountered Sakonnets fishing along Sakonnet Point. One, known as "Honest George," informed him that their sachem Awashonks was nearby, that she "was not fond of maintaining a war with the English, and that she had left Philip and did not intend to return to him anymore." They arranged for Church to meet her two days hence. Church portrayed himself the hero, alleging that Rhode Island authorities told him he was crazy "to throw away his life" by going to the rendezvous. (His wife apparently agreed.) Nevertheless, he set out, carrying "a bottle of rum and a small roll of tobacco."

As he came ashore at the rendezvous, Awashonks and her son Peter "gave him their hands and expressed themselves glad to see him." They walked to some tall grass and sat down. Suddenly, more than a dozen warriors armed with guns, spears, and hatchets rose around them, their "hair trimmed and faces painted" for war. As Church recounted the story, he challenged Awashonks: "It is customary when people meet to treat of peace to lay aside their arms and not to appear in such hostile form as your people do." This provoked "a considerable noise and murmur," but Awashonks told her men to stand down. The tension was palpable.

Church offered rum and tobacco, but Awashonks made him drink the rum first to ensure that it was not poisoned. She asked why he had not returned to her the previous June, as promised. When he mentioned the attack on his men at Pocasset Neck, her warriors erupted. One moved toward Church wielding a club, but others restrained him. An interpreter explained that the man's brother had died in that fight. Church retorted that it was his brother's fault for starting it. Finally, a leading warrior steered the discussion back to the task at hand.

They sat down again. Church promised that if they submitted to Plymouth, they would receive the same benefits as the Pequots had. After discussing this for a while, the Sakonnet leaders assented, on the condition that Plymouth promise not to kill them or sell them as slaves. The Sakonnet commander bowed, according to Church, and offered his warriors to "help you to [take] Philip's head before Indian corn be ripe." Church sent Peter, Honest George, and another Sakonnet to confirm the treaty in Plymouth.[38]

They appeared before the council on June 28. Claiming to represent about thirty men, plus women and children, they requested "liberty to sit down in quietness on their lands at Sakonnet." The council questioned them sharply. Why should Plymouth grant their request, "since you have broken your engagements with us by joining with the sachem Philip at Mount Hope and other Indians, our profound enemies?" They had robbed many colonists of their lives, homes, and property, and "you are never able to make satisfaction for the wrong, nor make good the damage you have done us by your perfidious dealings."

Such words must have dismayed the Sakonnets, for it was on this charge that many of their kin had been sold into slavery. But Peter insisted they had not fought the English. "When the English army went out, we were afraid and desired to go over to Rhode Island," he explained, "but the young men there kept such a strict watch that we could not get over in safety. Then we were forced to hide ourselves in swamps, and the English army came and burnt our houses. And we, understanding that the Narragansetts were friends to the English, we went to them."

"Did the Indians burn the English houses before the army came?" the council asked.

"Yea, they burned their forsaken houses," Peter meekly admitted, so the Sakonnets had "no cause to be angry with the English."

"Did the English do you any wrong at any time, or speak high or threatening words to you that scared you? Speak freely, without fear."

"The English never did us any hurt or wrong to this day," Peter replied. "If they had, we would speak of it." Honest George then explained that when the war began, most Sakonnets "sat still and minded their work at home," but some did "go to Philip and fight with him." Others, who had gone to the Narragansetts, died defending Pessicus's fort.

The council declared that the Sakonnets would have to prove their fidelity. "We cannot make satisfaction for the wrong done," the third Sakonnet consented, "but if our women and children can be secured, we will do any service we can by fighting against the enemy." The council stipulated that Sakonnets who had fought the English had to be surrendered, and Peter must remain as a hostage, but the rest would be protected. The Sakonnet representatives then formally submitted to Plymouth. About ninety Sakonnets surrendered to Major Bradford's army at Pocasset on June 29–30 and were temporarily relocated to Sandwich. It was another blow to Philip's cause.[39]

THE SUDDEN COLLAPSE OF Algonquian power astonished colonists. For the first time since the war began, Massachusetts proclaimed a day of thanksgiving. This frustrated Increase Mather, who wanted another fast day, but even he acknowledged that the tide of the war was turning. He credited it to the fact that churches were finally renewing their covenants. (Thomas Walley was skeptical, noting that his church's renewal service was poorly attended.)[40]

By one estimate, between May 9 and June 29, five hundred Indians were captured and twenty colonists returned from captivity. William Hubbard encountered the Rowlandsons on the Boston-Charlestown road on June 28 and informed them their son Joseph had been ransomed at Dover. The following night, they learned that their daughter Mary had turned up in Providence accompanied by an Indian woman. That most captives were well cared for revealed much about the Indians' humanity, but Puritans gave the credit to God. As Rowlandson saw it, God had rescued them from captivity, just as he promised Israel in Deuteronomy.[41]

Even now, Narragansett leaders continued seeking a treaty. In late June, Potuck, counselor to the female Narragansett sachem Quaiapin, arrived in Providence. He claimed Daniel Gookin and John Eliot had sent for him and requested assistance getting to Boston. Although Potuck had participated in the attack on Providence in March, Roger Williams and other local leaders took him to Newport, promising safe conduct and a return to his people, many of whom waited for him at Warwick Point. Potuck's arrival in Newport created a sensation. According to magistrate William Harris, "some of the inhabitants girt on their swords and said he should not go out from the island alive." They claimed he "killed more English souls" by his counsel "than any had done with weapons." Harris was baffled that Providence promised Potuck safe conduct, believing Massachusetts would never honor such a promise and that Potuck's inevitable execution would provoke Narragansett retaliation. Nevertheless, the council sent Potuck to Boston.[42]

Meanwhile, Major Talcott marched into the region with three hundred Connecticut troopers and at least a hundred Mohegans and Pequots. They captured four Indians on July 1, and early the next morning they discovered Quaiapin's camp at Nipsachuck, below the eastern slope of a hill and protected on three sides by a "great spruce swamp." Talcott ordered an immediate attack. The Mohegans and Pequots, eager to engage the hated Narragansetts, rushed down the hill. Troopers galloped on each flank, passing around the hillsides and hitting the camp from opposite directions.

There was a "lamentable outcry" as warriors dashed for weapons and women grabbed children. Dozens were cut down, but others fled into the swamp, working their way to a small island two hundred yards in. Soldiers dismounted and plunged after them. Others rode to the far side. For three hours they slaughtered Indians—including old men and women, girls and boys—wherever they found them. Talcott reported that Quaiapin, "that old piece of venom," was slain, as was "our old friend Wuttawawaikessuk," the sachem Pessicus's envoy to Connecticut. So was Stonewall John. Of the 126 Narragansetts killed, 92 were women and children. The 45 who survived owed their lives to Mohegans or Pequots. Not a single Connecticut soldier was killed. It was not a battle; it was a massacre.[43]

The following day, Talcott learned that Potuck's band was waiting at Warwick Point "to make peace with some of Rhode Island." As Harris predicted, Talcott cared little for Providence's promises, let alone ongoing peace talks. He marched there on July 3 and attacked, slaughtering eighteen men and twenty-two women and children and taking twenty-seven prisoners. Colonists claimed they could hear the shooting from Providence. In just two days Talcott had shattered what remained of Narragansett power. Only one member of his army, an Indian, was killed.[44]

The Mohegans requested permission to torture a captured Narragansett who boasted of having killed nineteen colonists and a Mohegan. Connecticut officers watched with fascination as Mohegans formed a circle around the prisoner. Taking a knife, a warrior "cut one of his fingers round in the joint at the trunk of his hand" and "broke it off." Others followed suit, "blood sometimes spirting out in streams a yard from his hand," until only the stub of his hand remained. Colonial soldiers wept, but they did nothing to stop the "barbarous and unheard of cruelty."

The Narragansett victim suppressed "any sign of anguish," earning the admiration of his torturers, for whom such rituals were designed to bring cathartic release. When they asked how he liked the war, he said he "liked it very well and found it as sweet as Englishmen did their sugar." They made him "dance round the circle and sing," even as they cut the fingers from his other hand, then moved on to his toes: first one foot, then the other. They broke his legs, leaving him bleeding on the ground, yet he remained silent. Finally, they battered his head "till they had knocked out his brains."

Puritans had mixed feelings about the ordeal. Ipswich minister William Hubbard described the dead man as a "cruel monster" who deserved everything he got. Ignoring English complicity, Hubbard urged Christians to thank God for enlightening them so they would not commit such cruelty and predicted that one day God would do the same for Indians. But Connecticut's soldiers had dispensed plenty of their own cruelty, believing themselves agents of God's wrath against those who rejected his gospel and treacherously assaulted his people. Harris admired their ruthlessness, which he considered key to winning the war. "Connecticut men take very many and kill all," he wrote, "save some boys and girls," for they were hardened and "provoked by the barbarous inhumanity they have heard of and seen." Indians tried, whenever possible, to surrender to other colonies, who spared all "except known notorious murderers."[45]

Connecticut commended James Fitch, Talcott's chaplain, for service "accommodating to the design [of the war]," but when it dispatched Talcott to fight more of God's battles on July 15, the council suggested that he spare women and children when possible. Still, Deputy Governor Treat argued that Connecticut's claim to Narragansett country would be strongest if the Narragansetts were utterly crushed. "I cannot joy in the sparing of so many [of] our Indian enemies, lest their preservation should prove a reservation for further future scourge," he worried.[46]

No one had expected the war to take such a dramatic turn. Less than two months earlier, the colonies had been reeling from a seemingly endless string of disasters, Indians boasted of driving them to the sea, and negotiations appeared to be the only path to peace. But the battle at Turner's Falls, the Mohawk offensive, and Talcott's ruthless Narragansett campaign had reversed their fortunes. The colonies no longer needed to negotiate. Confident in the justice of their cause and that God was with them again, they could resume their war of conquest.

22

Algonquian Defeat

June 1676 to October 1676

As HUNDREDS OF Algonquians fell into their hands that summer of 1676, colonial authorities pursued what they considered a Christian balance between justice and mercy. They sought retribution for what they deemed treacherous rebellion and security for their godly society, with the ultimate goal of restoring prosperity and uncontested colonial dominion to New England. Some Indians were pressed into servitude or settlement under English dominion. Others were sentenced to foreign slavery or death. The war was not over. Philip, Weetamoo, Quinnapin, and hundreds of warriors remained at large in Wampanoag country. But as Plymouth's rejuvenated forces took the offensive, it was only a matter of time.

The Boston trial of Captain Tom Wuttasacomponom, the praying Indian ruler, set the tone for those that followed. Many colonists clamored for his execution, but James Quanapohit, the former spy and one of the praying Indians who had brought Captain Tom in, testified on his behalf. He described how Tom wept when the Nipmucs captured him at Hassanamesit, how he resisted recruitment, and how he fell ill. Captives confirmed that Tom had fled the Nipmucs. But at a preliminary hearing on June 14, soldiers accused him of participating in the attack on Sudbury. Captain Tom denied it, claiming he was sick at the time. The only offense he would admit was that "a devil put it into his head to be willing to go with [the Nipmucs from Hassanamesit]," out of fear that "the rage of the English" would land his people on Deer Island, or worse. "Everything looketh with a sad face," John Eliot admitted after visiting Wuttasacomponom the following day. "God frowneth."[1]

Massachusetts's praying Indian company requested pardons for Captain Tom and others who "have not done any wrong or injury unto the English" and were taken by the enemy "against their wills." The company had proven its devotion to "the English cause, which we judge is our own cause, and also God's cause, to oppose the wicked Indians, enemies to God and all goodness," the petitioners argued. The council had avowed its readiness "to do anything for us that was fit for us to ask and you to grant." Here was such an opportunity. Showing mercy would encourage other Indians to surrender. At the very least, the court should protect women and children.[2]

At the formal trial, on June 19, Edmund Rice of Marlborough reported seeing Captain Tom 110 yards away at Sudbury. "I saw the said Captain Tom there walking with a long staff, limping as he went." Abraham Gale claimed to have seen Wuttasacomponom among warriors beaten back from the Sudbury causeway, wearing the very same coat he was now, from about eighty yards distance. Both had known Tom "well" for years. Captain Edward Cowell's testimony seemed to conflict with Gale's, however, for he claimed to have heard Tom when his men were attacked three miles from Sudbury, recognizing "a grumbling sign or noise that he made." John Partridge added that when Indians attacked Medfield, "I did hear the very real voice of Captain Tom, such a voice as I have heard when once he came with his Natick soldiers to Medfield and commanded them, and that I have heard him pronounce at Natick."[3]

The court declared Wuttasacomponom guilty. He had failed to present "anything that might alleviate his withdrawing from the government of the English and joining with the enemy," it explained to the praying Indian company. The evidence was strong, and justice demanded his death. The court was willing to spare "the lives and liberty of those that have been our enemies on their coming in and submission of themselves," but not if they were "taken among our enemies." In other words, Captain Tom had not turned himself in; he had been captured. The judgment must have put a damper on a ceremony held the following day, in which Massachusetts awarded the Indian company a medal. Engraved on it was an Indian holding a bow and arrow, similar to the one on the colony seal asking the English to "come over and help us." In this case, the inscription praised the Indians for their help against "the heathen Natives of this land, they giving us peace and mercy at their hands."

Eliot visited Wuttasacomponom that day, urging him "to confess if it were true whereof he is accused." Captain Tom maintained his innocence, and Eliot believed him. Captain Henchman and Daniel Gookin appealed the verdict, but the council held firm. The following day was a fast day at North Church, so Eliot visited Captain Tom again before going to hear Increase Mather preach "sad prophesies to sick, sick New England." Despite his despair, Eliot sensed "a mighty presence and assistance of the spirit of grace" in the service. Afterward he confronted Massachusetts governor John Leverett. He begged "that Captain Tom might have liberty to prove that he was sick at the time when the fight was at Sudbury and that he was not there." But Leverett simply opined on "how bad a man Tom was." Eliot retorted "that at the great day he should find that Christ was of another mind." But Eliot was powerless to stop the execution.

The marshal led the prisoners to the gallows on June 22. Eliot walked with Wuttasacomponom. The praying Indian climbed the ladder, and a rope was placed around his neck. "I did never lift up hand against the English, nor was I at Sudbury," he proclaimed. "Only I was willing to go away with the enemies that surprised us." Then the ladder was knocked away, his body dropped, and the rope tightened. Eliot stared as the Christian Indian "lifted up his hands to heaven prayer-wise and so held them, till strength failed, and then, by degrees, they sunk down." Word spread that he had died "penitent, praying to God, not like the manner of the heathen."[4]

The day after the trial, the government issued a proclamation giving Indians two weeks to surrender in exchange for favorable terms. Eliot's former assistant James Printer, Captain Tom's son Nehemiah, and a dozen women and children surrendered just before the amnesty expired. Colonists accused James of treachery, claiming he "had done much mischief and stayed out as long as he could." William Hubbard later condemned him as a "notorious apostate" and "false villain," and Increase Mather agreed.[5] But James and Nehemiah promised to prove their loyalty by bringing in enemy heads, and James secured permission to recover praying Indians hiding around Natick and Magunkog, who "desired to come in and submit but were hindered."[6]

Wannalancet, the Christian Pennacook sachem, brought six sachems to Dover. Most came from north of the Merrimack River, but they also included Samuel Numphow, Wamesit's teacher, whose father had died from sickness. They signed a treaty with Major Richard Waldron on July 3.[7]

Three days later, the sachems Shoshanim of Nashaway and Muttaump of Quaboag wrote Governor Leverett, Eliot, Natick's ruler Waban, and other "chief men [of] our brethren praying to God" seeking favor for their captured wives. They still desired the "covenant of peace" they had negotiated with Massachusetts in May. "We have been destroyed by your soldiers, but still we remember it now, to sit still. Do you consider it again," they begged. "We do earnestly entreat you that it may be so by Jesus Christ. Oh, let it be so!" In a follow-up letter, Shoshanim described his futile effort to retrieve English captives and claimed he had protected Massachusetts's envoys from Philip. Praying sachems from Magunkog also wrote Eliot, Gookin, and Waban, claiming they had opposed Philip and that if Massachusetts had "sent word to kill Philip, we should have done it."[8]

Shoshanim's appeal to the gospel he had long opposed failed to impress the council. Two months earlier, a colonist charged, Shoshanim had boasted he would not accept peace until the English begged for it. Yet now the sachems invoked "that sacred name, which they had blasphemed, and in the blood of whose servants they had embalmed their hands." "Thus doth the Lord Jesus make them to bow before him and to lick the dust," the colonist boasted. The council informed the sachems that Indians who were treacherous or "barbarously bloody must not expect to have their lives spared," though "others that have been drawn into the war, and acting only as soldiers" would be spared if they surrendered. When two sachems came from Mount Wachusett "with renewed desires of peace," the council declared that it would not negotiate until all the captives were returned. Soon after, Shoshanim sent an enemy scalp, declaring his intent "to surrender himself to the mercy of the English."[9] Meanwhile, captives trickled in, including a seventeen-year-old carrying her little sister on her back, and a half-starved boy from Andover brought by the Indian woman who had cared for him.[10]

Massachusetts could afford to take a hard line now, because everything was going its way. James Printer reported that more Indians had died from starvation or sickness over the prior year than were killed by soldiers.[11] Guided by Indian allies, soldiers pursued hungry and exhausted Algonquians into the forests and swamps that once protected them. Indians betrayed their own people in exchange for their lives, leading Rhode Islander William Harris to exult that they were "afraid of the sight of each other, seeing their former friends are suddenly become their deadly enemies."[12]

Sagamore John of the praying town of Pakachoog surrendered, claiming he had been "forced" to join the attack on Brookfield "for fear of his own life." He was lying, but to prove his sincerity, on July 27 he delivered 180 men, women, and children, including two prisoners "bound with cords": the notorious praying Indian Matoonas and his son. As Matoonas's sachem, John volunteered to execute him himself. Matoonas was led to Boston Common, tied to a tree, and shot by John's men. They mounted his head beside that of his other son, executed before the war. "Thus did the Lord . . . retaliate upon him the innocent blood which he had shed," Mather exulted. Sagamore John's people were settled at Cambridge under the oversight of Captain Thomas Prentice, who, along with Gookin, had negotiated to purchase Quinsigamond from John before the war. The purchase was finalized on August 20. Soon after, John fled the region.[13]

Other Indians tried to escape to New York. A half-starved band led by old Pomham, the Shawomet sachem, was intercepted by colonial forces near Mendon on July 25. Pomham fought stubbornly even after he was wounded, pulling a soldier down and swinging his hatchet at him before another soldier killed him. Fifty of his people were killed or captured. Indians who eluded colonial forces and crossed the Connecticut River faced the dreaded Mohawks, who had already killed or captured some 140 warriors. The Agawam sachem Cospechy reached New York with some people, spurring Connecticut to demand that New York apprehend them for they had "most perfidiously broken their written covenant with the English . . . and done great spoil upon them by fire and sword."[14]

"Terror is fallen upon very many, who come in daily with submission, and the rest withdraw into places remote . . . flying from justice in small numbers," wrote a colonist. They blamed "Philip and other ill counselors as the causes of their misfortunes."[15] By one estimate, more than fourteen hundred Indians were captured between May 9 and July 26. Everywhere except Plymouth and far to the north, in Maine, the Algonquian war effort had collapsed.[16]

⟨≈⟩

THE WAR HAD COME full circle, with Philip back in Wampanoag country, where it all began. Increase Mather recognized that Philip remained dangerous: "Who knoweth how cruelly a dying beast may bite before his expiration?" Plymouth followed Connecticut and Massachusetts by offering life and liberty to Indians who surrendered. About two hundred did so, some of whom helped bring in dozens more. Several were executed. A warrior who "killed his enemy in the field in a soldier-like way" might receive amnesty, the government explained, but those who murdered women and children would not. The colony assigned captives to various locations "to work for their livings." Children could be indentured to English families until age twenty-five, "especially their parents consenting thereunto."[17]

But Philip still had to be defeated, and Plymouth's Major William Bradford struggled to make that happen. "I have taken such a weighty work upon me, and I see my weakness in it more and more, that unless the Lord uphold and support me under it, I shall dishonor his holy name and damage the colonies," he wrote. He trusted God and depended heavily on his Wampanoag allies, who had already taken some twenty of their kin. But when a captured Pocasset reported three hundred Wampanoags, Narragansetts, and "upland Indians" at Wepoiset, Bradford refused to go after them, even though his men could see their campfires in the gathering darkness as they sailed by. That same day, thirty Indians raided Swansea. They shot a young man named Hezekiah Willet, cut off his head and stripped his body, and carried off his African slave, Jethro. Enemy Pokanokets who knew Willet were "sorry for his death" and prepared him for burial by combing his hair and decorating it with wampum.[18]

On July 6 Jethro escaped and reported that the enemy numbered one thousand and was preparing to attack Taunton. Colonial forces repulsed the attack five days later. Jethro agreed to guide them to Philip's camp, but Bradford moved cautiously, fearing that Philip "was of great strength, and we too weak." By the time they arrived, on July 12, Philip was gone, though they captured about thirty Indians. A prisoner promised to lead them to Philip the next day, but again they arrived too late. They followed Indian tracks "many miles," killing fifteen or sixteen stragglers, "most old persons that were not so able to follow." Along the way, they found the "grievously mangled" body of a Massachusetts soldier who had been tortured and killed.

On July 14, they followed tracks into a "dismal swamp" and discovered some three hundred Indians. They killed or captured seventy-six, but Philip escaped to Pocasset Neck on a raft. "We have pursued him so close that do we almost despair," a soldier explained to his wife. "We have followed him very close from swamp to swamp, so that he is enforced to fly with a very small quantity of men." It was hard work, but "I hope with the blessing of God we shall accomplish our desire." On one occasion, they found a camp with kettles still "boiling over the fire," belts and baskets of wampum, and Indian dead unburied. "I look upon these as smiles and tokens of . . . [God's] returning again to us, if we can be a humble people and our sins prevent not," Bradford wrote. "I am persuaded and do verily believe that by the many prayers of his [people], and their sighs and groans, he hears in heaven and will grant, for our mediator's sake, the return of his gracious presence."[19]

"We daily long to hear from our army," Plymouth minister Thomas Walley wrote to John Cotton Jr. "Oh that God would pardon their sins and ours and make us all humble, that good may come unto us. A frame of heart suitable to God's dealings with us would give assurance of deliverance, but we are, I fear, far from it, which causeth many sad thoughts of heart." Cotton was more hopeful, attributing recent successes to the churches' covenant renewal ceremonies. But Walley pointed out that "the greatest success, if not the only success," had come where allied Indians served. It "is a humbling providence of God that we have so much need of them and cannot do our work without them," he wrote. "It should teach us to be wise in our carriage towards them."[20]

Captain Benjamin Church, who had recently persuaded the Sakonnets to sign a treaty with Plymouth, visited the Sakonnet camp at Buzzard's Bay to recruit warriors. He recalled finding many "Indians of all ages and sexes, some on horseback running races, some at football, some catching eels and flatfish in the water, some clamming." Awashonks, their female sachem, hosted him at a feast the likes of which he had never seen: "a curious young bass in one dish, eels and flatfish in a second, and shellfish in a third." Afterward they held a powwow. Their commander danced around the bonfire, swinging his spear and hatchet as if fighting the flames. After naming a "particular tribe of Indians, he would draw out and fight a new firebrand, and at his finishing his fight with each particular firebrand, would bow to him and thank him." He thus identified each of the "nations and tribes" they were to fight. Other warriors followed, committing themselves to service with the English.

The eighteen Sakonnets who joined Church's company of twenty-two Plymouth soldiers captured many Indians, including other Sakonnets, over the next few days. Plymouth authorized Church to promise life and liberty to those who joined his company, excluding "murderous rogues or such as have been principal actors in those villainies." His best success came when his soldiers surprised a group of women gathering hurtleberries on the edge of a "great cedar swamp." They killed or captured sixty-six, while the Sakonnets, operating separately, killed three and captured sixty-three.[21]

Word of Church's exploits spread. "I am heartily glad of the good successes of any that are instruments of God," Major Bradford wrote graciously. "The Lord yet continue it, and give him more and more." But Bradford defended his more cautious approach. "I have done my duty and neglected no opportunity to face upon the enemy, and I am verily persuaded that if we should [have] adventured without . . . [Massachusetts] forces, we had either been worsted or also lost many men." Better to be considered "slow . . . yea, even a coward, than to adventure the loss of any of my soldiers." He admitted that many officers "would have managed it better than myself," and some chafed at the bit, but "I shall not put myself out of breath to get before Ben Church. I shall be cautious. . . . I cannot outgo my nature."[22]

On Sunday, July 30, Plymouth governor Josiah Winslow learned of a large body of Indians approaching the Taunton River. He called Captain Church out of the morning service, and within hours Church was on the road with fifty men. Twenty-one soldiers from Bridgewater got there first, just as the Indians were crossing the river over a large fallen tree, and opened fire, killing as many as ten. Much to their surprise, many warriors threw down their weapons in surrender. They took seventeen prisoners—including Philip's sister—seven guns, and "twenty pounds of bullets and lead." Only later did they learn that Philip had been on the tree, having allegedly cut his hair in disguise.[23]

Church arrived the following day. Years later he claimed he was about to shoot an Indian sitting on a stump across the river when an allied Indian shouted that the man was friendly. Startled, the man turned around. Recognizing Philip, Church pulled the trigger, but Philip "threw himself off the stump, leaped down a bank on the side of the river, and made his escape." Crossing in pursuit, colonial forces picked up twenty-three Indians, including Philip's wife, Wootonakanuske, and nine-year-old son. The Sakonnets took another thirteen prisoners and killed several of Quinnapin's Narragansetts.

Church followed the Wampanoag tracks, capturing people too exhausted, sick, or hungry to keep up with the main body. His Wampanoag scouts overtook Philip's party shortly before sundown, and Church prepared to attack at dawn. He told his prisoners he could not spare any men to guard them, but that if they attempted escape "he would immediately kill them all."

The following morning, August 3, as the first glimmers of light penetrated the forest, Philip's scouts spotted Church's men. They took off for their camp, "yelling and howling" and making "the most hideous noise they could invent." By the time Church's men arrived, all they found were "kettles boiling and meat roasting upon their wooden spits."

The Wampanoags fled into a small swamp, so Church ordered his men to encircle it. They arrived at the far side just in time to intercept Philip's warriors, who stopped, unsure what to do. When one of Church's Wampanoags shouted that their lives would be spared if they surrendered, men, women, and children began doing so. Demoralized warriors allowed soldiers to take their guns, loaded and cocked, from their hands. But a few held out, engaging in a sharp skirmish, and for the third time in less than a week, Philip got away. Frustrated, Church marched for Bridgewater. He had taken 173 Indians in two days, losing only one English soldier, but he was exhausted, "his health impaired by excessive heats and colds and wading through rivers," sleepless nights, and the strain of command.

The Wampanoags were a shadow of their former selves. They could not protect their women and children, let alone feed them, and many decided that they would rather take their chances with the English than continue the fight. At least then they could fill their empty bellies. Church claimed that prisoners in Bridgewater "laughed as loud as the soldiers" while eating their first full meal in a long time. "You have now made Philip ready to die," they said, "for you have made him as poor and miserable as he used to make the English." William Hubbard later relished that Philip experienced "the captivity of his children, loss of his friends, slaughter of his subjects, [and] bereavement of all family relations." Increase Mather agreed. "It must needs be bitter as death to him to lose his wife and only son," he gloated, "and almost all his subjects and country too."[24]

The great sachems fell one after another. On August 5, after an Indian helped men from Taunton capture twenty-six Indians, they found a woman's "stark naked" body on the shore in Mattapoisett. It was Weetamoo, the Pocasset sachem, and Mattapoisett was her childhood home. Colonists speculated that she had drowned trying to cross the Taunton River, though some historians suspect that she was actually murdered. "God himself by his own hand brought this enemy to destruction," Mather claimed, "so that she was drowned just before the English found her." Seeing her head mounted on a pole in Taunton, Indian prisoners fell into what colonists considered a "most horrid and diabolical lamentation." Weetamoo's husband, Quinnapin, was wounded and captured by Rhode Islanders on his way to Narragansett country. Potuck, the Narragansett counselor whom Rhode Island sent to Boston with a safe conduct from Providence, was shot on Boston Common on August 10.[25]

CAPTAIN CHURCH RECALLED that he had just arrived at the house where his wife was staying on Aquidneck Island when Major Peleg Sanford and Captain Roger Goulding came galloping down the road. Reining in their horses, they asked "what he would give to hear some news of Philip." An Indian at Trip's Ferry claimed to have just left Philip. The Indian was bitter because Philip had killed his brother for advising Philip to make peace. He offered to guide the English to Philip's camp at Mount Hope. Sanford and Goulding volunteered to serve as aides. Church mounted his horse, dug in his spurs, and galloped toward the ferry. They crossed the river that night.[26]

It was now Saturday, August 12. To prevent Philip from escaping again, Church divided his company. One contingent, under Goulding, would crawl through the woods "on their bellies" toward Philip's camp. They would attack at dawn, driving the Pokanoket and his warriors into a swamp on the far side, where Church and the rest of the company would be waiting. Church organized this second contingent in pairs, each consisting of a colonist and an Indian, "at such distance as none might pass undiscovered between them." But the swamp was too large, and his men struggled to cover the area. "Sir," Church said, grasping Sanford's hand, "I have so placed them that 'tis scarce possible Philip should escape them."

Goulding and his men lay nervously in the dark after reaching Philip's camp. To their alarm, a warrior got up from his shelter and walked a few steps to relieve himself. When he had finished, he turned and looked toward Goulding. The captain panicked. He fired his gun, shattering the quiet of the early morning twilight. Church was confiding his fears to Sanford when the bullet "whistled over their heads." Nervous soldiers followed Goulding's cue and unleashed a volley. Startled, Philip threw his ammunition pouch and powder horn over his head, grabbed his gun, and dashed into the swamp wearing only "his small breeches and stockings." Unknowingly, he headed straight for Church's men. A colonist pulled the trigger first, but his gun misfired. His companion, a Pocasset named Alderman who once counseled Weetamoo, then fired two bullets from a double-barreled flintlock. One pierced Philip's heart. Another tore through his chest two inches higher. Philip "fell upon his face in the mud and water, with his gun under him."[27]

Soldiers cheered, "Huzzah! Huzzah! Huzzah!" Wampanoags grabbed Philip's legs and dragged him from the muck. Despising the sachem as a "doleful, great, naked, dirty beast" who had "caused many an Englishman's body to lie unburied and rot above ground," Church decided "not one of his bones should be buried." He ordered a Wampanoag to behead and quarter Philip, the fate of a traitor. Perhaps the Wampanoag was nervous about dishonoring a great sachem, but according to Church, he said that as "big as he was, he would now chop his ass for him." Church rewarded Alderman with Philip's dismembered hand, "to show to such gentlemen as would bestow gratuities upon him."[28]

John Cotton Jr. recalled that Philip's head was brought to Plymouth "in great triumph" shortly after a thanksgiving service, "so that in the day of our praises our eyes saw the salvation of God."[29] When the news reached Boston, the Massachusetts council exulted in the death of "that monster that hath caused us so much mischief" (though its encouragement was dampened by news that Indians had slaughtered a hundred colonists in Maine).[30] William Hubbard considered it fitting that Philip was killed by one of his own people. "Thus did divine vengeance retaliate upon this notorious traitor, that had against his league and covenant risen up against the government of Plymouth."[31] Increase Mather was delighted that, like King Agag of the Amalekites, Philip was "hewed in pieces before the Lord, cut into four quarters, and is now hanged up as a monument of revenging justice." It motivated him to finish his history of the war. True, some enemies remained at large, and violence in Maine was intensifying. But "dead Indians up and down" the country demonstrated what "a sad catastrophe will attend those that shall magnify themselves against the people of the Lord of Hosts." God had "wasted the heathen by sending the destroying angel amongst them," that his name "might not be profaned among the heathen."[32]

CAPTAIN CHURCH'S COMPANY captured many Indians over the following weeks, including Annawon, one of Philip's commanders. William Hubbard claimed Annawon confessed that "he could not but see the justice of the great God upon himself." The Nemasket sachem Tuspaquin, Philip's brother-in-law, surrendered after his wife and child were captured. Church claimed that he had promised Tuspaquin his life. Plymouth executed both men.[33]

Few Indians remained in Massachusetts except hundreds of captives "scattered up and down, to the great dissatisfaction of many English."[34] Most had fled, having held "a general meeting and agreed not to fight the English any longer," a captive claimed. They believed "God's hand is against them, the sickness destroying many of them, many more being very feeble and unable for service."[35] "We find only some skulking Indians in these parts, which now and then kill our cattle and horses in the woods," Massachusetts magistrate John Pynchon reported from Springfield. Nevertheless, colonial forces continued seizing Indians and destroying their provisions. Scouts discovered between fifty and sixty warriors and a hundred women and children heading west near Westfield, so Connecticut's Major John Talcott set out in pursuit with 120 men.[36] He attacked them on the west bank of the Housatonic River during the night of August 16, killing forty and capturing fifteen, while losing one Mohegan.[37]

Pessicus, the senior Narragansett sachem, and many other Indians had gone to Paquayag beyond the Hudson, though Pessicus was "very sick and as like to die as live." Pynchon protested that they included "our [Agawam] Indians, who most treacherously ruined this town, and some of them that we know murdered our people without any provocation." He feared their withdrawal was temporary and there would be no peace unless New York delivered their leaders to Massachusetts. Connecticut urged New York to "extirpate" the Indians at Paquayag "for the interest of God and the king and the good people of these parts."[38]

At least seventy warriors surrendered to Uncas's Mohegans, according to Norwich minister James Fitch, and "many aged men and women and children, and they are daily coming, and I hear of many more coming." Some were Wabquissets, Uncas's former tributaries, but Connecticut informed Uncas that because it was an English war the captives belonged to them. It allowed him to keep some, and many were settled near Norwich, where they were required to attend Fitch's teaching. Others were assigned to the Pequots or Ninigret's Narragansetts or to work for colonists. Those who left their assigned places could "be punished with death or transportation out of the country."

Connecticut ordered Captain George Denison to prevent "Indians from settling anywhere in the Narragansett country, so far as the line or limits of our charter do extend." Charging that Rhode Islanders had "lived dishonorably both to God, our king and nation" and that the war had reduced the region to "a *vacuum domicilium*," it claimed Narragansett country by right of conquest. Indians or colonists with "right or possession" had to submit their claims, and Connecticut would adjudicate them "as may best advantage religion and the safety of the inhabitants."[39]

Rhode Island, which rejected Connecticut's aggression, ruled that captives not condemned as "notorious persons" could be held as servants for nine years. It tried Quinnapin, the Narragansett sachem, on August 24. Quinnapin acknowledged his role as Canonchet's second-in-command and was charged with supporting the Narragansett attack on Pettaquamscut. He and three others were executed.[40] In Providence, captives were disposed of by a committee that included Roger Williams. It sold them to various buyers over the coming months, dividing the proceeds among the inhabitants. When an Indian known as Chuff struggled into town, with wounds that "were corrupted and stank," the authorities unanimously ordered him "shot to death, to the great satisfaction of the town."[41]

WHILE PRAYING INDIANS pursued the enemy, their families remained under English supervision. On August 7, with permission from praying town superintendent Daniel Gookin, six Indian women and children went to gather hurtleberries near Concord, escorted by an Indian soldier named John Stoolemester. One was Captain Andrew Pittimee's wife. Another, Pittimee's sister, was married to Thomas Speen and brought three children with her, including a nursing infant. While they were working, a dozen Massachusetts troopers confronted Stoolemester, confiscated his gun, and threatened to kill him, though they released him after he begged for his life. They stayed to smoke and trade with the women, bread and cheese for hurtleberries, before riding off. But four soldiers returned: Daniel Goble and his nephew Stephen Goble, from Concord; Daniel Hoar, whose father, John Hoar, had supervised the praying Indians at Concord; and Nathaniel Wilder, a refugee from Lancaster. They brought the women and children to an obscure spot, removed the women's coats, and killed them all.

Pittimee reported his family missing. Two days later, a search party found the bodies, "some shot through, others their brains beat out with hatchets." The soldiers were arrested, but recent history suggested that no jury would convict them. How could English soldiers be executed for killing Indians in time of war? "A sad thing," Increase Mather lamented in his diary. "It may be it will occasion the Indians to seek to revenge their blood." And "if justice be not done upon the murderers, God will take vengeance."[42]

The trial began on September 4. The accused soldiers, probably assisted by John Hoar, a lawyer, argued that Massachusetts law authorized them to kill Indians unescorted by colonists and that they had no idea who the women were, nor that they had permission to be there. As expected, most of their comrades confirmed their story, but this time one, Steven Mattuck, had the courage to tell the truth. He admitted that "some mention was made of Major Gookin giving those squaws liberty to gather huckleberries in that place" and of who they were.

It was Mattuck's testimony that made this trial different. The court declared all four men guilty of murder. Wilder himself had not killed anyone, but "if being present and seeing the fact done and consenting [to] it be murder," the court explained, "then we find him guilty." It sentenced the men to death. Many colonists were furious. One declared that "there was no fear of those being hanged, for there were three or four hundred men that would guard them from the gallows." Time would tell.[43]

Meanwhile, hundreds of Algonquians made their way to Dover in hopes of preserving their lives and liberty under the terms of the Pennacook sachem Wannalancet's July treaty. On August 28, Massachusetts ordered Gookin to dispatch Christian Indian messengers to proclaim that Indians who yielded English captives and surrendered would "have their lives given them and [be] freed from foreign slavery."[44] Shoshanim, the Nashaway sachem who had been trying to negotiate such terms for months, arrived at Dover saying he "heard there might be peace obtained." Major Waldron replied that it was "too late" and that he would send Shoshanim to Boston. He claimed Shoshanim "willingly submitted himself to their mercy."

So many Indians were gathering near Dover that anxious colonists implored the General Court to "secure or destroy" them. The court ordered Waldron to send them all to Boston. A prosperous trader, landowner, and longtime deputy, Waldron did not hesitate to rely on treachery. He instructed the Indians to assemble in a field so their men could be enlisted for service. He offered them food and drink. While they were eating, soldiers surrounded them, "80 fighting men and 20 old men, 250 women and children, 350 in all." Waldron recruited ten men, separating out "their families and some old men and theirs with Wannalancet's relations." The rest, including Wamesits and other Pennacooks covered by the July treaty, he shipped to Boston. Local leaders, fearing retaliation, protested Waldron's actions.[45]

Soon after, the Indian teacher Peter Jethro brought in his father, Old Jethro, and Monoco of Nashaway, believing that Waldron had promised them life and liberty. He also brought Muttaump, the sachem of Quaboag, and forty other Indians. When Waldron sent them to Boston, Gookin accused Waldron of treachery, but Waldron denied it. "I promised neither Peter Jethro nor any other of that company life or liberty, it not being in my power to do it," he claimed. "All that I promised was . . . that if he would use his endeavor and be instrumental for the bringing in [of] Monoco, etc., I would acquaint the governor with what service he had done and improve my interest in his behalf."[46]

Since Massachusetts claimed sovereignty over all Indians within its bounds, it considered enemy Indians rebels, and the penalty for rebellion under Massachusetts law was death. So the General Court suggested that Indians who had killed colonists be executed. The council decided particular cases, however, and it proved more lenient. In practice, only leaders and those accused of notorious violence were executed. Other warriors and their families were shipped abroad or, if they had surrendered under amnesty, sold locally. Many considered this policy merciful, but the enslavement of so many noncombatants was unusual. It reflected the influence of increasingly pervasive racist beliefs that Indians were destined to be a servile underclass. Gookin was deeply skeptical of the process. All it took was one accusation for a person to be condemned, yet colonists found it "very difficult, unless upon long knowledge, to distinguish Indians from one another."[47]

One of the most notable trials was of William Wannukhow and his sons, praying Indians brought in by James Printer. Thomas Eames accused the Wannukhows of killing his wife and several children. They denied involvement until magistrate Thomas Danforth promised Joseph Wannukhow that if he spoke truthfully, Danforth "would speak to the governor to spare his life." Joseph then admitted their presence during the attack but insisted they did not kill anyone and actually protected Eames's surviving children. His father and brother confirmed this, and the other witnesses were dead or in captivity. Nevertheless, the court sentenced them to death. They appealed, reminding the court that it promised "life and liberty unto such of your enemies as did come in and submit themselves to your mercy." They implored the magistrates, "We know that your honors are men of truth, fearing God, and will faithfully perform your promises, especially when it concerns so great a matter as the lives of men." True, they had followed Captain Tom to the Nipmucs. "But we had no arms and did not hurt the English, as many others have done that upon their submission to your mercy are pardoned."[48] The court rejected the appeal.

About fifty Indians were executed in Boston that summer. Eight sent by Major Waldron were shot to death on September 13. Eight days later, William Wannukhow and his sons were marched to the gallows alongside the English soldier Stephen Goble. "The weather was cloudy and rawly cold, though little or no rain," Samuel Sewall wrote in his diary. "Two impudent women" were among the spectators, and one "laughed on the gallows," but despite a report that hundreds of men would prevent Goble's hanging, the executions were carried out smoothly. "A sad thing," Increase Mather wrote, "that English and Indians should be executed together." Shoshanim and Monoco of Nashaway, Muttaump of Quaboag, and Old Jethro were led to Boston Common, halters around their necks, on September 26. The soldier Daniel Goble, being ill, was "drawn [to the gallows] in a car upon bedclothes." A "mad" English woman stole the rope intended for Goble's neck, so the executioner reused the rope that killed Shoshanim.[49]

Soldiers Daniel Hoar and Nathaniel Wilder petitioned for mercy two weeks later, claiming they had not personally killed any women or children. They confessed "following the multitude in many of the sins" of the war but insisted that they were upstanding citizens. Exhibiting the mercy it had refused to the Wannukhows, the court remitted their death sentence, ordering them to pay £10 each to the victims' families. For Pittimee and Speen, whose wives had been murdered, it was a bitter pill.[50]

The majority of the captives sent by Waldron from Dover were sold into slavery. That included Wamesits and other Pennacooks whose only crime was fleeing vigilante violence. Samuel Numphow was narrowly acquitted for lack of evidence. A woman named Mary Namesit and her baby were sold even though Waldron had recruited her husband. They spent two months in jail before Gookin got them out, and even then the council showed more concern that their purchasers be compensated than for the victims. A few other Indians were also redeemed.[51]

About 190 Indians, two-thirds of them women, girls, or infants, were sold at public auctions in August and September, with the proceeds, just under £400, helping pay for the war. In Plymouth, 169 people were sold late in the war. Some were purchased by local colonists, but at least 180 were shipped abroad on the *Seaflower*. Its captain, Thomas Smith, carried certificates from Plymouth and Massachusetts declaring that the captives had been "sentenced and condemned to perpetual servitude," being "duly convicted of being actors and abettors" of Philip in his "treacherous rebellion against the Crown." They had not only violated their "solemn league and covenant" "without any just cause or provocation," but had committed "notorious, barbarous, and execrable murders, villanies, and outrages." They could legally be sold in the lands of any Christian government.[52]

Indian soldiers like Punkapoag minister William Ahawton petitioned on behalf of family members. They saved some, but many more were never heard from again. Seven years after the war, enslaved Algonquians in Tangier managed to get a message to Eliot crying for help. He urged Robert Boyle of the New England Company to intervene on their behalf, but whatever efforts were made proved futile. A rare exception was Joseph Petavit, the Nipmuc minister who with his brother Sampson had saved Captain Wheeler's company from the Nipmucs before being taken from Hassanamesit with Captain Tom. Sampson had been "slain in fight" by praying Indians. Joseph was shipped to Jamaica, but Eliot managed to bring him back. Yet Joseph was still forced into local servitude on charges of having been "active against the English." A committee that included Gookin assigned many Indian children to serve in English households, where they were to be educated and taught Christianity, until they turned twenty-four. Gookin took in a few children, as did John Cotton Jr.[53]

Plymouth asked ministers for advice about what to do with Philip's young son. Cotton and a colleague submitted a brief report. They acknowledged Deuteronomy's stipulation that children should not be executed for their parents' sins but argued that it did not apply to this case: "Children of notorious traitors, rebels, and murderers, especially of such as have been the principal leaders and actors in such horrid villainies, and that against a whole country, yea, the whole interest of God, may be involved in the guilt of their parents, and may, *salva republica* [for the good of the state], be adjudged to death." They found several scriptural precedents: Saul's sons in 2 Samuel, Achan's in Joshua, and Haman's in Esther. Increase Mather supported Cotton's conclusion.

James Keith, Bridgewater's pastor, disagreed, arguing that such cases were unusual. He invoked 2 Chronicles 25:4, in which a king was praised for sparing the children of his father's assassins. "I long to hear what becomes of Philip's wife and his son," he wrote Cotton. "I hope God will direct those . . . to a good issue. Let us join our prayers at the throne of grace, with all our might, that the Lord would so dispose of all public motions and affairs that his Jerusalem in the wilderness may be the habitation of justice and the mountain of holiness."[54] But Plymouth sold the boy into slavery, and neither he nor his mother was ever heard from again.[55]

While fighting continued in Maine, the war was essentially over. The "heathen" had attempted "the utter extirpation and ruin of the interest of our Lord Jesus," Massachusetts declared in its thanksgiving proclamation, but "there now scarce remains a name or family of them in their former habitations." Nearly every Indian in the colony was dead, captured, or hiding in the wilderness.[56]

Epilogue

"TEARS OF WATER, yea of blood if we were able, are not enough to bewail the desolations that fire, blood, rapine, and cruelty hath made in New England," wrote colonist John Hall. About eight hundred colonists were dead, including perhaps 10 percent of military-age males, making it, per capita, one of the bloodiest wars in American history. Roughly half of colonial towns had been destroyed or severely damaged, producing thousands of homeless refugees, who became dependent on other colonists for charity. By one estimate, eight thousand cattle had been killed, and economic damages totaled at least £100,000. It would take the colonies decades to recover.

But the war was far more devastating for New England's first people. The number of Indian dead was probably at least three thousand. Thousands more fled the region, and at least five hundred were sold abroad. Dozens of towns were destroyed, never to be re-established. It has been estimated that the war reduced New England's Algonquian population from eleven thousand to fewer than five thousand. Nearly a third of those who remained were forced into servitude. Many others were confined to reserved lands, gradually reduced to dependency as wage-laborers or servants, and subjected to discriminatory laws. The emerging racial order would leave them exploited, marginalized, and impoverished for generations.[1]

This was not what Puritans had envisioned when they first came to America. They had imagined a benevolent spiritual conquest, in which Indians were liberated from Satan's tyranny and incorporated into the kingdom of Christ. Now they viewed the war as Christ's conquest, with Indians suffering Christ's just judgment. The ministers who wrote the war's first histories, Increase Mather and William Hubbard, described it as one of the "wars of the Lord," a phrase they took from the Old Testament's description of Israel's wars. Hubbard even claimed that of all wars since biblical times, it was the only one that "may truly be said to deserve that title."[2]

While a few Puritans questioned the justice of the war, Mather vigorously defended it. Had Massachusetts refused to help Plymouth as colonists were slaughtered, "the Lord would have been displeased" and "all the world would justly have condemned us," he argued. And it was "very manifest to impartial judges" that Plymouth was "innocent as to any wrongs that have been done to the heathen." It protected Philip from injury, even preserving his land for him when he would have sold it, and it gave him the most precious possible gift, the gospel. Yet Philip's Pokanokets responded with bloodshed. "Will not our God judge them?" Mather asked. "Yea, he hath, and will do so." Mather did not compare the war to Israel's conquest of Canaan, but he did compare it to Israel's wars against the Ammonites, Moabites, and Edomites, who attacked the Israelites on their way to Canaan. Like those nations, he explained, the Indians treacherously "fought to dispossess us of the land which the Lord our God hath given to us."[3]

In 1677 Mather published *A Relation of the Troubles Which Have Happened in New England By Reason of the Indians There*, focusing on events leading up to King Philip's War. Colonists did not always treat Indians justly, he admitted, but the culprits were those who came to America for "trade and worldly interests," not those who sought "the conversion of the heathen unto Christ." And Christ's kingdom prospered despite such injustice, for while in 1600 "there was not so much as one Christian in this land, there are now above fourscore English and six Indian churches."[4]

Mather also published a book purporting to show how faithfully God had answered his people's prayers. "How often have we prayed that the Lord would . . . frustrate the counsels of the heathen that sought our ruin?" How often had they prayed that he would send his "destroying angel" or cause Indians "to destroy one another?" They had prayed that God would avenge "the cruelty, treachery, and above all the blasphemy of these heathen," and God had done so.

God had fought for them. As a "stout Indian captain" admitted before his execution, the English would not have defeated the Indians had not—and now he began "striking upon his breast"—"Englishman's God maketh us afraid here." "O thou most high, thou has rebuked the heathen, thou hast put out their name for ever and ever!" Mather exalted. "Where are the six Narragansett sachems, with all their captains and counsellors? Where are the Nipmuc sachems, with all their captains and counsellors? Where is Philip and [Weetamoo] squaw-sachem of Pocasset with all their captains and counselors? [May] God do so to all the implacable enemies of Christ and of his people in New England!" Mather did not want his audience to be complacent. He reminded them that God would continue judging them if they did not repent. But, he warned, "let the world beware of doing any wrong to a praying people. . . . And woe to that man, whoever he be, upon whom the prayers of New England shall fall."[5]

MATHER'S HISTORY ATTRIBUTED every victory or defeat to the colonists' state of repentance. The book was welcomed by most ministers and helped Mather become New England's most prominent clergyman. But Hubbard's history was more reliable and successful. Though Hubbard also attributed every event to God's providential control, his narrative was more detailed and nuanced, less critical of the English, and did not attribute every twist and turn to their spiritual state.[6] While Mather lamented the colonies' failure to evangelize more Indians and their injustice toward praying Indians, Hubbard fed the rising tide of white supremacy by describing Indians as invariably treacherous and unlikely to become Christian.

He shared the colonists' view that Philip had "long experience of the gentleness and kindness of the English" but rebelled because of his "evil and malicious mind."[7] He viewed other Indians the same way. Time and again, colonists trusted them, only to be violently betrayed. Some argued that "the ruder sort of the English, by their imprudent and irregular actings, had driven them into this rebellion," but Hubbard disagreed. The Indians "naturally delight in bloody and deceitful actions," he maintained, seizing "any opportunity that might serve for a pretense to be put up on their barbarous practices."[8]

He told story after story to prove that treachery was one of the Natives' "natural vices." They owed their victories to "perfidious subtlety and falsehood, or to the advantage of season, place, and number, [rather] than any valor or courage." They betrayed their own kin to save their lives, proving "what little trust there is to be put in their words, promises, or engagements." "Subtlety, malice, and revenge seems to be as inseparable from them as if it were part of their essence." Like all pagans, they would never deal honestly unless motivated by fear or self-interest.[9]

Hubbard viewed the war as part of the ancient conflict between the Devil and God's people. The attempt to evangelize Philip's Wampanoags "hath given the first occasion of the quarrel, as usually it hath done in the world." The Devil instigated war to prevent their conversion, leading to their "utter destruction and extirpation from off the face of the earth," which would be the fate of all who rejected Christ. Yet this merely cleared a path for Christ's kingdom, for it "may be gathered, as we hope, that God is making way to settle a better people in their rooms and in their stead." It would "no doubt appear a work very beautiful in its season."[10]

Hubbard did not relegate all Indians to paganism. The fidelity of many Christian Indians, whose salvation was "worth far more pains and cost than ever yet was laid out upon that work," proved the Puritan mission had not failed. It was no small thing that in a land that had been in darkness for "all ages past . . . the light of the gospel should take so much place as to cause any number of those vassals of Satan, where he so long hath had his throne, professedly to own the name of the Lord Jesus Christ." What this meant for other Indians, he could not say. Perhaps God wanted the gospel preached to them only "to leave them without excuse."

Either way, colonial victory was essential, for civility must precede conversion, and civility required colonization. When Jesus "went forth conquering and to conquer, it was amongst the civil and not amongst the barbarous and savage nations of the world," Hubbard claimed. The "gentle means of courtesy, familiarity, and such like civil behavior" had not accomplished this, but war might. "Who knows what tendency the present troubles may have to such an end? For though a great number that are implacable and embittered against us in their spirits may be for the sake of our religion found hardened to their own destruction, yet a remnant may be reserved and afterward called forth, by the power of the gospel, to give glory to the God of the earth." Either way, Christ's kingdom would conquer.[11]

A FEW YEARS AFTER the war, at the encouragement of Massachusetts's leading ministers, Mary Rowlandson did what was unheard of for a woman. She wrote a book: *The Sovereignty and Goodness of God, Together with the Faithfulness of His Promises Displayed; Being a Narrative of the Captivity and Restoration of Mrs. Mary Rowlandson.* It was one of America's first bestsellers and became the model for a genre of American literature: the captivity narrative.[12]

Its primary theme was God's goodness to his undeserving people. "I can remember the time when I used to sleep quietly without workings in my thoughts, whole nights together, but now it is other ways with me," she wrote. "When all are fast about me, and no eye is open but his who ever waketh, my thoughts are upon things past, upon the awful dispensation of the Lord towards us: upon his wonderful power and might, in carrying of us through so many difficulties, in returning us in safety, and suffering none to hurt us." A second theme was Indian treachery. She conceded that Quinnapin, Philip, and others had treated her kindly, but she took every opportunity to portray praying Indians as false. One day, after the war had ended, she wrote, she saw an Indian who had once threatened to run her through strolling Boston's streets. For her, as for many colonists, no Indian could be trusted.[13]

Sudbury's minister, Edmund Brown, put it bluntly: "According to my most critical observation taken of many Indians and at several times, I assert that, as to the generality of those called praying Indians, I have found them to be . . . very false, whatever they pretend." They were treacherous thieves and "cutthroats," and "some of those few I judged honest have in these times turned renegades, been active assistants of our common enemy, and some imbrued their hands in English blood." True, some were faithful, but mainly because they wanted to be on the winning side. Brown argued that Indians who killed colonists during the war should be executed. Those who surrendered under amnesty should be sold abroad. The rest should be disarmed and confined to reservations, subject to the wartime law "whereby any Englishman traveling the woods and lighting upon such vagrant Indians out of their limits, may either take him or kill him." True, this did "not well consist with our declared intention to seek the conversion of the Indians," but that enterprise had failed anyway. "Their aversion from the gospel, their deriding, yea blaspheming the blessed name of Christ and his ways, declare such unworthy of the grace of the gospel."[14]

Samuel Nowell, the former military chaplain, echoed the emerging consensus. The colonies "have as fair a title [to New England] as any ever had since Israel's title to Canaan," he preached. God allowed some Indians to remain, not as members of English society, but to be "thorns in our sides" as Canaanites were for Israel. Like Israel and Edom, they would always be rivals.[15]

⬥⬥⬥

DANIEL GOOKIN WAS one of the few who challenged this racist narrative. Just before the war, the praying town superintendent had written hopefully about establishing an English-Indian school, the seed of an integrated Christian society. Now, the very idea seemed absurd, but he could make sure the fidelity and suffering of praying Indians was not forgotten. In his *Historical Account of the Doings and Sufferings of the Christian Indians in New England*, he portrayed Christian Indians as Jesus's most faithful followers and "the first professors, confessors, if I may not say martyrs, of the Christian religion among the poor Indians in America." It would not be published for many years, probably because its portrayal of New England was so negative.[16]

According to John Eliot, Gookin could have said much more: "Here is enough to give wise men a taste of what hath passed. Leave the rest unto the day of judgment, when all the contrivances and actings of men shall be opened before the all-seeing eye of our glorious judge."[17] Eliot regretted his own failure to record the terrible story of a war that nearly destroyed his life's work. "I cannot, I may not relate" such tragic happenings, he had written at the time, "but now on second thought I blame myself for it. Lord pardon all my many omissions."[18]

Most of Massachusetts's praying towns were never resettled. Massachusetts ordered the remaining praying Indians to be settled at Natick, Punkapoag, Wamesit, and Hassanamesit. There, supervised by government-appointed officials, they rebuilt their communities, heavily dependent on English charity for food, clothing, and other supplies. Many labored for colonists cutting wood, spinning, or building fences. Their children were apprenticed as servants. They continued to suffer occasional violence from colonists or Mohawks, not to mention the loss of land. And some, including Wannalancet, the Pennacook sachem, left New England to live among their northern kin. Gookin estimated the remaining population at 567, half the prewar total.[19]

Eliot believed the Devil had used the war "to defile, debase, and bring into contempt the whole work of praying to God," resulting in "a great apostasy" among Indians, especially the younger generation. Many Indian veterans became addicted to alcohol and would "spend all their wages and pawn any[thing] they had" for it. Drunkenness provoked quarreling, fighting, and other ills. He comforted himself that "through grace some stood and do stand, and the [mission] work is on foot to this day, praised be the Lord."[20]

Eliot and Gookin were attending an Indian service when old Waban, Natick's longtime ruler, stood to give voice to his people's suffering. "Since the war begun between the English and wicked Indians, we expected to be all cut off, not only by the enemy Indians, whom we know hated us, but also by many English, who were much exasperated and very angry with us," Waban admitted. "Then God stirred up the governor and magistrates to send us to the island, which was grievous to us, for we were forced to leave all our substance behind us, and we expected nothing else at the island but famine and nakedness." Thankfully, God stirred "up the hearts of many godly persons in England who never saw us, yet showed us kindness and much love and gave us some corn and clothing." God finally moved the council to recruit Indian men, "for it was always in our hearts to endeavor to do all we could to demonstrate our fidelity to God and to the English" "against theirs and our enemies." Yet even after the war colonists accused them of helping Indians run away from their masters. No matter what they did, colonists charged them with treachery. While the magistrates and many good colonists exhibited "more charity toward them," most colonists refused to accept them as equals in the body of Christ.

Gookin did not deny it. All he could do was observe that suffering was part of the Christian life. "Christ in the gospel teacheth all his disciples to take up the cross daily." Jesus was "most innocent, and always did good, yet some said of him, he had a devil" or that he opposed the government. He suffered patiently, and Christian Indians had to do the same. Gookin did not need to state the obvious implication: their English oppressors occupied the role of Jesus's enemies. "Waban, you know all Indians are not good," he said. "So tis with Englishmen . . . and this we must expect while we are in this world."[21]

At first it seemed as though nearly all Indians had left Massachusetts. Indians who returned clashed with colonial squatters, so in 1681 Massachusetts appointed a committee to negotiate the purchase of all Nipmuc land. Eliot and Gookin assisted its work, while praying Indians, including Waban and the veteran James Quanapohit, sold vast tracts to provide for their impoverished people. Over the next four decades, colonists acquired the entire region for negligible prices.[22]

Gookin died in 1687. Eliot continued his trips to Natick well into his eighties. "There is a cloud, a dark cloud, upon the work of the gospel among the poor Indians," he lamented shortly before his death. "[May] the Lord revive and prosper that work and grant it may live when I am dead."[23]

INCREASE MATHER BELIEVED that unlike Massachusetts, the people of Connecticut had "acquitted themselves like men and like Christians" toward local Indians, so God made those Indians "to be as a wall," protecting Connecticut from serious destruction. The colony ordered its captives distributed among colonists for terms of servitude, but Norwich minister James Fitch accused Uncas, the Mohegan sachem, of using "vile means" to prevent their "orderly settlement" and of poisoning their minds against Christianity. Some hoped Uncas had accepted Christianity, but Fitch complained that despite "the destruction which hath come upon multitudes of the heathen for their contempt of the offers of the gospel," Uncas stubbornly rejected it. Fitch suggested that the Mohegans and Pequots be offered the gospel once more, and "if yet they reject the things of their peace, their blood be upon their own heads."[24]

Ninigret, the great Narragansett sachem, died in 1676, but his Eastern Niantic community became a rallying point for other Narragansetts.[25] Connecticut claimed Narragansett country by right of conquest, arguing that the war left the land "void and therefore free for others to settle." Rhode Island strenuously resisted, observing that the Narragansetts had always been peaceable "till by the United Colonies they were forced to war, or [to] such submission as it seems they could not submit to." The dispute dragged on for many years before it was decided in favor of Rhode Island.[26]

The lands of the Narragansetts, Pokanokets, Pocassets, and other Algonquians who supported Philip were turned over to soldiers and other colonists for settlement. Many of the lands' previous inhabitants now labored as servants in colonial households. Others lived alongside colonial neighbors or moved to surviving Algonquian towns. Among Indians who had supported the colonies, many such towns remained, especially on Cape Cod, Martha's Vineyard, and Nantucket, and in Connecticut.

Across New England, over the following decades, Indians suffered increasing discrimination, exploitation, and poverty. They also suffered disproportionately from disease and war. As their populations declined, poverty forced them to sell more and more land. The use of debt, the courts, alcohol, trickery, trespassing, and fraud to manipulate sales became more common. Even the Mohegans, once so important to Connecticut's security, gradually lost nearly all their land. Many Algonquian towns—including Natick, Wamesit, and Punkapoag—ceased to exist. Their surviving inhabitants moved to key centers such as Mashpee, a protected reserve that preserved substantial autonomy, or Martha's Vineyard. They often intermarried with African Americans, also considered by white New Englanders to belong to an inferior caste.

Nevertheless, praying Algonquians maintained key elements of their identity and culture while adapting selectively to colonization. Christianity helped unite their communities around common practices and beliefs, even as it took on unique Algonquian forms. Many Narragansetts, Mohegans, and Pequots who had long resisted Christianity accepted it in the 1700s, during what might be called the long Indian Great Awakening. In each community, congregations emerged as central institutions.

Native reservations at Mashpee and Gay Head, on Martha's Vineyard, continue to flourish today. By far the largest Indian reservation is the Pequot Mashantucket reservation in Connecticut, home to the fabulous Pequot Museum. The Mohegans finally secured a much smaller reservation at Shantok at the end of the twentieth century. Rhode Island tried to erase the Narragansett tribe's identity, but the Narragansetts eventually won federal recognition and possess a small reservation with an old Narragansett church in Charlestown, Rhode Island. All that formally remains of John Eliot's praying towns are the tiny reservations at Hassanamesit (or Hassanamisco) and Chabanakongkomun (or Chaubunagungamaug) in Worcester County, Massachusetts. Other Indian communities, recognized or not, exist throughout New England.[27]

COLONIAL SUPREMACY MAY have been inevitable when English Puritans started migrating to New England. After all, the same story played itself out in one form or another in every part of North and South America, regardless of who the colonizers were. What made New England's story unique was how carefully the Puritans tried to live out their version of the Christian faith. They believed Christ was using them to spread his kingdom to America, liberating its people from sin and Satan. And while they hoped Christ's conquest would not require violent conflict, they knew it might and were prepared for it. They were all too confident about this and all too cavalier toward Algonquian culture and lives. By and large, they believed their methods were necessary and just and that they ultimately benefited those Native people who, by God's grace, accepted Christianity. The deplorable consequences of those efforts have been the story of this book.

Many Indians rejected Christianity and still do. But for others, Christianity became the key ingredient that held their communities together and enabled them to preserve their culture. They lamented, and still lament, the injustices and tragedies that devastated their people and the way Christianity was used to justify it. Yet they were thankful for the gospel and the hope it provided, not to mention the material goods Europeans brought. Many practiced Christianity in ways that preserved their communities and culture, embracing the core tenets of the faith Puritans proclaimed while rejecting assumptions of English cultural superiority or white supremacy.

The resilience of these communities, despite everything that has happened to them, is nothing short of remarkable.

Notes

Introduction

1. "Relation or Journall of the beginning and proceedings of the English Plantation settled at Plimoth in New-England," in *Chronicles of the Pilgrim Fathers of the Colony of Plymouth 1602–1625*, ed. Alexander Young (New York: De Capo Press, 1971), 118–120, 122–124.
2. "Relation or Journall," 125–128, 132–134, 140–141; William Bradford, *Of Plymouth Plantation 1620–1647*, ed. Samuel Eliot Morison (New York: Knopf, 1994), 66.
3. "Relation or Journall," 139–143.
4. "Relation or Journall," 143–146.
5. Roger Williams, *Key into the Language of America*, in *CWRW* 1:81.
6. "Relation or Journall," 149–150, 155–159; *OPP*, 69–70.
7. Alden T. Vaughan, *Roots of American Racism: Essays on the Colonial Experience* (New York: Oxford University Press, 1995), 3–33; Alden T. Vaughan and Virginia Mason Vaughan, "England's 'Others' in the Old and New Worlds," in *The World of John Winthrop: Essays on England and New England, 1588–1649*, ed. Francis J. Bremer (Boston: Massachusetts Historical Society, 2005), 22–74; Karen Ordahl Kupperman, *Settling with the Indians: The Meeting of English and Indian Cultures in America, 1580–1640* (Totowa, NJ: Rowman and Littlefield, 1980).
8. Laura M. Stevens, *The Poor Indians: British Missionaries, Native Americans, and Colonial Sensibility* (Philadelphia: University of Pennsylvania Press, 2004).

Chapter 1

1. Michael P. Winship, *Godly Republicanism: Puritans, Pilgrims, and a City on a Hill* (Cambridge, MA: Harvard University Press, 2012), 68–70; David D. Hall, *The Puritans: A Transatlantic History* (Princeton, NJ: Princeton University Press, 2019).
2. For this section, see John G. Turner, *They Knew They Were Pilgrims: Plymouth Colony and the Contest for American Liberty* (New Haven, CT: Yale University Press, 2020); Nathaniel Philbrick, *Mayflower: Voyage, Community War* (New York: Penguin, 2007).
3. *OPP*, 8.
4. *OPP*, 23–27; Nathaniel Morton, *New England's Memorial* (Boston: Congregational Board of Publications, 1855), 11–12; Edward Winslow, *Hypocrisie Unmasked* (Providence, RI: Club for Colonial Reprints, 1916), 89–90.
5. *OPP*, 47.
6. "Relation or Journall of the beginning and proceedings of the English Plantation settled at Plimoth in New-England," in *Chronicles of the Pilgrim Fathers of the Colony of Plymouth 1602–1625*, ed. Alexander Young (New York: De Capo Press, 1971), 121.
7. Kathleen J. Bragdon, *Native People of Southern New England, 1500–1650* (Norman: University of Oklahoma Press, 1996), 4.
8. Edward Winslow, "Good Newes from New England," in *Chronicles of the Pilgrim Fathers of the Colony of Plymouth 1602–1625*, ed. Alexander Young (New York: De Capo Press, 1971), 360–362; Bragdon, *Native People*, 142–143. For the following section, see David J. Silverman, *This Land Is Their Land: The Wampanoag Indians, Plymouth Colony, and the Troubled History of Thanksgiving* (New York: Bloomsbury, 2019), 45–120; Neal Salisbury, *Manitou and Providence: Indians, Europeans, and the Making of New England* (New York: Oxford University Press, 1982), 26–30, 62–66, 87–108; Alden T. Vaughan, *New England Frontier: Puritans and Indians 1620–1675* (Boston: Little, Brown, 1965), 3–23.
9. Silverman, *This Land*, 56.
10. John Smith, *Travels and Works of Captain John Smith*, ed. A. G. Bradley (Edinburgh: J. Grant, 1910), 2:933.
11. Silverman, *This Land*, 84.

12. Thomas Morton, *New English Canaan* (Amsterdam, 1637), 23.
13. Winslow, "Good Newes," 356–359.
14. "Relation or Journall," 167–169, 193, 196; *OPP*, 72, 83–84; Silverman, *This Land*, 142–143.
15. *OPP*, 77; "Relation or Journall," 161–162, 174, 178.
16. "Relation or Journall," 180–186; Silverman, *This Land*, 145.
17. "Relation or Journall," 186–194.
18. "Relation or Journall," 193, 196; Silverman, *This Land*, 151–152; Yasuhide Kawashima, *Puritan Justice and the Indian: White Man's Law in Massachusetts 1630–1763* (Middletown, CT: Wesleyan University Press, 1986), 227–228.
19. *OPP*, 81, 85.
20. Silverman, *This Land*, 124–125.
21. Turner, *They Knew They Were Pilgrims*, 73, 79; "Relation or Journall," 203, 205; Winslow, December 11, 1621, in *Chronicles of the Pilgrim Fathers of the Colony of Plymouth 1602–1625*, ed. Alexander Young (New York: De Capo Press, 1971), 233–234.
22. "Relation or Journall," 202–208; *OPP*, 87.
23. Winslow, "Good Newes," 367.
24. "Relation or Journall," 208–211.
25. "Relation or Journall," 214–220.
26. "Relation or Journall," 220–223; *OPP*, 88–89; Salisbury, *Manitou*, 120; Morton, *New England's Memorial*, 46.
27. "Relation or Journall," 224–229; *OPP*, 89.
28. Winslow, December 11, 1621, 230–238; *OPP*, 90.
29. "Cushman's Discourse," in *Chronicles of the Pilgrim Fathers of the Colony of Plymouth 1602–1625*, ed. Alexander Young (New York: De Capo Press, 1971), 268; Philbrick, *Mayflower*, 123–124.
30. "Cushman's Discourse," 256–260.
31. Cushman, "The Lawfulness of Removing," in *Chronicles of the Pilgrim Fathers of the Colony of Plymouth 1602–1625*, ed. Alexander Young (New York: De Capo Press, 1971), 241–248.
32. *OPP*, 96–97; Winslow, "Good Newes," 272, 280–284; Paul A. Robinson, "Miantonomi," in Robert S. Grumet, *Northeastern Indian Lives 1632–1816* (Amherst: University of Massachusetts Press, 1996), 19.
33. Winslow, "Good Newes," 285–292, 295; *OPP*, 98–99, 111, 114.
34. Turner, *They Knew They Were Pilgrims*, 91–94; Winslow, "Good Newes," 296–298, 327–330.
35. Winslow, "Good Newes," 313–323, 362–363.
36. Winslow, "Good Newes," 323–326.
37. Winslow, "Good Newes," 330–334; Richard Frothingham Jr., ed., *Phineas Pratt's Narrative* (Boston: T. R. Marvin & Son, 1858), 8–13.
38. Winslow, "Good Newes," 336–344.
39. Winslow, "Good Newes," 344–345; Silverman, *This Land*, 201–202.
40. Winslow, "Good Newes," 274, 355, 372.
41. Robinson to Plymouth, December 19, 1623, in Young, *Chronicles of the Pilgrim Fathers*, 474–475.

Chapter 2

1. Michael P. Winship, *Hot Protestants: A History of Puritanism in England and America* (New Haven, CT: Yale University Press, 2018), 68–70; John White, *The Planters Plea* (London, 1630), 66–77; Francis J. Bremer, *John Winthrop: America's Forgotten Founding Father* (Oxford: Oxford University Press, 2003), 151–153.
2. Lawrence Shaw Mayo, *John Endecott: A Biography* (Cambridge, MA: Harvard University Press, 1936), 6–20, quote on 20.
3. Winship, *Hot Protestants*, 74–77, quote on 71; Hall, *The Puritans*, 205–214.
4. Mayo, *John Endecott*, 23; Cradock to Endecott, February 16, 1629, in *MR* 1:384–385.
5. New England Company to Endecott, April 17, 1629, in *MR* 1:392–394.
6. Francis Higginson, *New England's Plantation* (Salem, MA: Essex Book and Print Club, 1908), 36; Alexander Young, ed., *Chronicles of the First Planters of the Colony of Massachusetts Bay* (Boston: Charles C. Little and James Brown, 1846), 201–202.
7. Nathaniel Morton, *New England's Memorial* (Boston: Congregational Board of Publications, 1855), 97–101.

8. Higginson, *New England's Plantation*, 106–107; William Cronon, *Changes in the Land: Indians, Colonists, and the Ecology of New England* (New York: Hill and Wang, 1983), 39–51; Kathleen J. Bragdon, *Native People of Southern New England, 1500–1650* (Norman: University of Oklahoma Press, 1996), 43, 118, 123; Dennis A. Connole, *The Indians of the Nipmuck Country in Southern New England, 1630–1750: An Historical Geography* (Jefferson, NC: McFarland, 2001), 17–19.

9. "Charlestown Records," in *Chronicles of the Pilgrim Fathers of the Colony of Plymouth 1602–1625*, ed. Alexander Young (New York: De Capo Press, 1971), 377–378.

10. *MR* 1:17; Yasuhide Kawashima, *Puritan Justice and the Indian: White Man's Law in Massachusetts 1630–1763* (Middletown, CT: Wesleyan University Press, 1986), 46.

11. Bremer, *John Winthrop*, 159–160; Massachusetts Bay Company to Endecott, October 16, 1629, in *MR* 1:408–409.

12. Bremer, *John Winthrop*, 79, 109, 129–130, 154–155.

13. Winthrop, "General Observations," in *WP* 2:111–114, and "Reasons to Be Considered," in *WP* 2:138–141.

14. White, *Planters Plea*, 1–6.

15. White, *Planters Plea*, 6, 10–16, 79.

16. White, *Planters Plea*, 27, 36.

17. White, *Planters Plea*, 39.

18. Virginia DeJohn Anderson, *New England's Generation: The Great Migration and the Formation of Society and Culture in the Seventeenth Century* (New York: Cambridge University Press, 1991), 47–66; Bremer, *John Winthrop*, 162–167.

19. White, *Planters Plea*, 65.

20. Bremer, *John Winthrop*, 169–170, 188; Winthrop to wife, March 28, 1630, in *WP* 2:225.

21. Larzer Ziff, *The Career of John Cotton: Puritanism and the American Experience* (Princeton, NJ: Princeton University Press, 1962), 36–70.

22. John Cotton, *God's Promise to His Plantation* (London, 1630), 3.

23. Cotton, *God's Promise*, 6, 17–18.

24. Cotton, *God's Promise*, 4–5; Alfred A. Cave, "Canaanites in a Promised Land: The American Indian and the Providential Theory of Empire," *American Indian Quarterly* 12, no. 4 (Autumn 1988): 277–297.

25. Cotton, *God's Promise*, 19; Stevens, *The Poor Indians*, 34–61.

26. Theodore Dwight Bozeman, *To Live Ancient Lives: The Primitivist Dimension in Puritanism* (Chapel Hill: University of North Carolina Press, 1988).

27. John Winthrop, "A Model of Christian Charity," in *Puritan Political Ideas 1558–1794*, ed. Edmund S. Morgan (Indianapolis, IN: Hackett, 2003), 76–78.

28. Winthrop, "A Model," 90–91.

29. Winthrop, "A Model," 92–93.

30. *WJ* 1:49–52, 58; Winthrop to wife, July 16 and September 9, 1630, in *WP* 2:302, 312–313; Bremer, *John Winthrop*, 191–196; David D. Hall, *A Reforming People: Puritanism and the Transformation of Public Life in New England* (New York: Knopf, 2011), 25–26; "Charlestown Records," 384–385.

31. *WJ* 1:57.

32. Ola Elizabeth Winslow, *Master Roger Williams: A Biography* (New York: Macmillan, 1957), 28; John M. Barry, *Roger Williams and the Creation of the American Soul: Church, State, and the Birth of Liberty* (New York: Penguin, 2012); Williams to Sadleir, 1652, in *CRW* 1:358; Roger Williams, *The Bloody Tenent Yet More Bloody*, in *CWRW* 4:65.

33. Williams to Cotton Jr., 1671, in *CRW* 2:630.

34. Winslow, *Master Roger Williams*, 99–101, 104; *OPP*, 257.

35. Williams to Winthrop, 1632, in *CRW* 1:8.

36. Winslow, *Master Roger Williams*, 103–105; Williams to Commissioners, in *CRW* 2:750–751.

37. *WJ* 1:59–60, 62; Dudley to Bridget, March 12–28, 1631, in *Letters from New England: The Massachusetts Bay Colony, 1629–1638*, ed. Everett Emerson (Amherst: University of Massachusetts Press, 1976), 68–69; *MR* 1:87; David Stewart Smith, "The Pennacook Indians and the New England Frontier, circa 1604–1733" (PhD dissertation, Union Institute, Cincinnati, 1998), 95–101.

38. *WJ* 1:61, 65; *OPP*, 257–258.

39. *WJ* 1:55–56, 63–64, 67–68, 90; *MR* 1:75–76, 83, 92, 96, 99–102; Dudley to Bridget, 74–82; William Wood, *New England's Prospect*, ed. Alden T. Vaughan (Amherst: University of Massachusetts Press, 1977), 88–90; Alden T. Vaughan, *New England Frontier: Puritans*

and Indians 1620–1675 (Boston: Little, Brown, 1965), 98–101; Virginia DeJohn Anderson, *Creatures of Empire: How Domestic Animals Transformed Early America* (Oxford: Oxford University Press, 2004); Virginia DeJohn Anderson, "Chickwallop and the Beast: Indian Responses to European Animals in Early New England," in *Reinterpreting New England Indians and the Colonial Experience*, ed. Colin G. Calloway and Neal Salisbury (Boston: Colonial Society of Massachusetts, 2003).

40. Howes to Winthrop Jr., March 26, 1632, in *WP* 3:73–74.
41. *New England's First Fruits*, in *ET*, 59.
42. *WJ* 1:83–84.
43. *WJ* 1:60, 63, 66–69, 76, 78–79, 82, 89–92; Wood, *New England's Prospect*, 79–80; Vaughan, *New England Frontier*, 101; *MR* 1:90.
44. Vaughan, *New England Frontier*, 97.
45. Winship, *Hot Protestants*, 87; George H. Williams, Norman Pettit, Winifred Herget, and Sargent Bush Jr., *Thomas Hooker: Writings in England and Holland, 1626–1633* (Cambridge, MA: Harvard University Press, 1975), 24–35.
46. See Hall, *Reforming People*; David D. Hall, *The Faithful Shepherd: A History of the New England Ministry in the Seventeenth Century* (Chapel Hill: University of North Carolina Press, 1972).
47. Williams, *Bloody Tenent of Persecution*, in *CWRW* 3:254.
48. John Cotton, *An Abstract of the Laws of New England* (London, 1641); Isabel Calder, "John Cotton's 'Moses His Judicials,'" *Publications of the Colonial Society of Massachusetts* 28 (1935): 86–94.
49. Cotton to Fiennes, March 1636, in *The Correspondence of John Cotton*, ed. Sargent Bush Jr. (Chapel Hill: University of North Carolina Press, 2001), 246–247.
50. Cotton Mather, *Magnalia Christi Americana*, 7 vols. (Hartford, CT: Silas Andrus & Son, 1853), 1:325.

Chapter 3

1. Alfred A. Cave, *The Pequot War* (Amherst: University of Massachusetts Press, 1996), 49–58; John W. De Forest, *History of the Indians of Connecticut from the Earliest Known Period to 1850* (Hartford, CT: Wm. Jas. Hamersley, 1851), 71–72; William Cronon, *Changes in the Land: Indians, Colonists, and the Ecology of New England* (New York: Hill and Wang, 1983), 95; E. B. O'Callaghan, *History of New Netherland* (New York: D. Appleton, 1846), 157; Laurence M. Hauptman, "The Pequot War and Its Legacies," 71–72, William A. Starna, "The Pequots in the Early Seventeenth Century," 33–34, 46, and Lynn Ceci, "Native Wampum as a Peripheral Resource in the Seventeenth-Century World-System," 58–60, in *The Pequots in Southern New England: The Fall and Rise of an American Indian Nation*, ed. Laurence M. Hauptman and James D. Wherry (Norman: University of Oklahoma Press, 1990); William Wood, *New England's Prospect*, ed. Alden T. Vaughan (Amherst: University of Massachusetts Press, 1977, 81; *OPP*, 203–204.
2. Cave, *The Pequot War*, 82–84; *WJ* 1:103, 107–110, 138, 144; *OPP*, 258–260, 270.
3. Brenda J. Baker, "Pilgrim's Progress and Praying Indians: The Biocultural Consequences of Contact in Southern New England," in *In the Wake of Contact: Biological Responses to Conquest*, ed. Clark Spencer Larsen and George R. Milner (New York: Wiley-Liss, 1994), 36; Starna, "The Pequots in the Early Seventeenth Century," 46.
4. *OPP*, 270–271.
5. J. Franklin Jameson, ed., *Johnson's Wonder-Working Providence 1628–1651* (New York: Charles Scribner's Sons, 1910), 80.
6. *WJ* 1:111, 114–115, 118; "New England's First Fruits," 59.
7. "The Early Records of Charlestown," in *Chronicles of the First Planters of the Colony of Massachusetts Bay, from 1623 to 1636*, ed. Alexander Young (Boston: Charles C. Little and James Brown, 1846), 386–387.
8. Winthrop to Rich, May 22, 1634, in *WP* 3:167.
9. Jameson, *Wonder-Working Providence*, 79–80.
10. Neal Salisbury, *Manitou and Providence: Indians, Europeans, and the Making of New England* (New York: Oxford University Press, 1982), 199–202; Yasuhide Kawashima, *Puritan Justice and the Indian: White Man's Law in Massachusetts 1630–1763* (Middletown, CT: Wesleyan University Press, 1986), 59; Dennis A. Connole, *The Indians of the Nipmuck Country in Southern New England, 1630–1750: An Historical Geography* (Jefferson, NC: McFarland, 2001), 141; Peter A. Thomas, *In the Maelstrom of Change: The Indian Trade and Cultural*

Process in the Middle Connecticut River Valley, 1635–1665 (New York: Garland, 1990), 201, 318; Cronon, *Changes*, 59–81; Kathleen J. Bragdon, *Native People of Southern New England, 1500–1650* (Norman: University of Oklahoma Press, 1996), 131–137.

11. Williams, *Bloody Tenent, CWRW* 4:461–462; *WJ* 1:116–117; Chester E. Eisinger, "The Puritans' Justification for Taking the Land," *Essex Institute Historical Collections* 84 (1948): 131–143.

12. *OPP*, 257; John M. Barry, *Roger Williams and the Creation of the American Soul: Church, State, and the Birth of Liberty* (New York: Penguin, 2012), 161–162.

13. Winthrop to Endecott, January 3, 1634, in *WP* 3:146–149; *WJ* 1:116–119; Francis J. Bremer, *John Winthrop: America's Forgotten Founding Father* (Oxford: Oxford University Press, 2003), 231–234.

14. *WJ* 1:118; *OPP*, 269–270.

15. *OPP*, 268–269.

16. "Captain Roger Clap's Memoirs," in *Chronicles of the Pilgrim Fathers of the Colony of Plymouth 1602–1625*, ed. Alexander Young (New York: De Capo Press, 1971), 363; *MR* 1:108; *WJ* 1:108.

17. Wood, *New England's Prospect*, 80.

18. *WJ* 1:118.

19. A fathom was about six feet of strung wampum, containing around 240–360 beads.

20. *WJ* 1:138–140; *OPP*, 291.

21. *OPP*, 291–292; Winthrop Jr. Commission, July 5, 1636, in *WP* 3:285.

22. *WJ* 1:124, 128, 132–134; Cave, *The Pequot War*, 86; Charles M. Andrews, *The Colonial Period of American History* (New Haven, CT: Yale University Press, 1936), 2:70.

23. *MR* 1:146, 148; *WJ* 1:151.

24. *OPP*, 280–285; *WJ* 1:157, 174–175; Cave, *The Pequot War*, 87–88; Andrews, *The Colonial Period*, 2:71–73.

25. Winslow to Winthrop Jr., June 22, 1636, in *WP* 3:274.

26. *OPP*, 290; *WJ* 1:159–160, 165.

27. Charles J. Hoadly, *The Warwick Patent* (Hartford, CT: Hartford Press, 1902); Cave, *The Pequot War*, 89–90.

28. Walter W. Woodward, *Prospero's America: John Winthrop, Jr., Alchemy and the Creation of New England Culture, 1606–1676* (Chapel Hill: University of North Carolina Press, 2010), 14–50.

29. Saybrook Company Agreement, in *WP* 3:198–199.

30. Lion Gardener, "Relation of the Pequot War," in *History of the Pequot War: The Contemporary Accounts of Mason, Underhill, Vincent and Gardener*, ed. Charles Orr (Cleveland, OH: Helman-Taylor, 1897), 122; Cave, *The Pequot War*, 91–92.

31. Cave, *The Pequot War*, 93, 96–98; *MR* 1:170–171; Andrews, *The Colonial Period*, 2:77–78; *WJ* 1:180–181; De Forest, *History of the Indians*, 83–84; Winthrop to Winthrop Jr., June 10, 1636, in *WP* 3:268–269; Francis Jennings, *The Invasion of America: Indians, Colonialism, and the Cant of Conquest* (Chapel Hill: University of North Carolina Press, 1975), 198.

32. *WJ* 1:142; Williams, *Bloody Tenent*, in *CWRW* 4:461–462; "Master John Cotton's Answer to Master Roger Williams," in *CWRW* 2:44–47.

33. Kawashima, *Puritan Justice*, 46–47; Ruth Barnes Moynihan, "The Patent and the Indians: The Problem of Jurisdiction in Seventeenth-Century New England," *American Indian Culture and Research Journal* 2, no. 1 (1977):10–13; Allan Greer, *Property and Dispossession: Natives, Empires and Land in Early Modern North America* (Cambridge: Cambridge University Press, 2018), 192–222; Jeremy Dupertuis Bangs, *Indian Deeds: Land Transactions in Plymouth Colony, 1620–1691* (Boston: New England Historic Genelogical Society, 2002), 15, 18.

34. *WJ* 1:149, 154–155, 157, 162–163, 168; *MR* 1:160–161; Winslow, *Williams*, 121–123; Barry, *Roger Williams*, 205–209; Williams to Mason and Prence, 1670, in *CRW* 2:610–611.

35. Roger Williams, *Mr. Cotton's Letter Lately Printed, Examined and Answered*, in *CWRW* 1:315.

36. Williams to Commissioners, 1677, in *CRW* 2:752; Barry, *Roger Williams*, 219.

37. Williams Testimony, 1661, in *CWRW* 6:316–317.

38. Williams to Mason and Prence, 1670, in *CRW* 2:611.

39. Barry, *Roger Williams*, 215, 220, 223–228.

Chapter 4

1. Michael Leroy Oberg, *Uncas: First of the Mohegans* (Ithaca, NY: Cornell University Press, 2003), 47–49; Laurie Weinstein-Farson, "Land Politics and Power: The Mohegan Indians in the Seventeenth and Eighteenth Centuries," *Man in the Northeast* 42 (1991): 10–15.

2. Brewster to Winthrop Jr., June 18, 1636, in *WP* 3:270–272.

3. *WJ* 1:161–162; Cave, *The Pequot War*, 90–91.

4. Vane to Winthrop Jr., July 1, 1636, in *WP* 3:282–283; Winthrop Jr. Commission, July 4, 1636, in *WP* 3:284–285.

5. Lion Gardener, "Relation of the Pequot War," in *History of the Pequot War: The Contemporary Accounts of Mason, Underhill, Vincent and Gardener*, ed. Charles Orr (Cleveland, OH: Helman-Taylor, 1897), 123–124.

6. *WJ* 1:183–184.

7. *WJ* 1:184–185; Julie A. Fisher and David J. Silverman, *Ninigret: Sachem of the Niantics and Narragansetts: Diplomacy, War, and the Balance of Power in Seventeenth-Century New England and Indian Country* (Ithaca, NY: Cornell University Press, 2014), 18–19.

8. Franklin Jameson, ed., *Johnson's Wonder-Working Providence 1628–1651* (New York: Charles Scribner's Sons, 1910), 162–164; *WJ* 1:186–187.

9. John Cotton, *An Abstract of the Laws of New England* (London, 1641); Isabel Calder, "John Cotton's 'Moses His Judicials,'" *Publications of the Colonial Society of Massachusetts* 28 (1935): 86–94, 14–15.

10. Francis J. Bremer, *John Winthrop: America's Forgotten Founding Father* (Oxford: Oxford University Press, 2003), 312–314; Margaret Ellen Newell, *Brethren by Nature: New England Indians, Colonists, and the Origins of American Slavery* (Ithaca, NY: Cornell University Press, 2015), 29–30; Steven T. Katz, "The Pequot War Reconsidered," *NEQ* 64, no. 2 (June 1991): 206–224; Ronald Dale Karr, "Why Should You Be So Furious? The Violence of the Pequot War," *Journal of American History* 85, no. 3 (December 1998): 876–909; *WJ* 1:186, 189.

11. Cave, *The Pequot War*, 109–110; Louis Effingham De Forest and Anne Lawrence De Forest, *Captain John Underhill, Gentleman, Soldier of Fortune* (New York: De Forest, 1934), 5–7 John Underhill, "Newes from America," in *History of the Pequot War: The Contemporary Accounts of Mason, Underhill, Vincent and Gardener*, ed. Charles Orr (Cleveland, OH: Helman-Taylor, 1897), 51.

12. Underhill, "Newes," 51–55; *WJ* 1:187–190; Kathleen J. Bragdon, *Native People of Southern New England, 1500–1650* (Norman: University of Oklahoma Press, 1996), 184–199.

13. Gardener, "Relation of the Pequot War," 126–127.

14. Williams to Winthrop, 1636, in *CRW* 1:54–55.

15. Underhill, "Newes," 55–58; *WJ* 1:188.

16. Underhill, "Newes," 58–60; Gardener, "Relation of the Pequot War," 127; *WJ* 1:188–189, 191–192.

17. *WJ* 1:189–190; Andrew Lipman, "'A Meanes to Knitt Them Together': The Exchange of Body Parts in the Pequot War," *WMQ* 65, no. 1 (January 2008): 17–18.

18. Gardener, "Relation of the Pequot War," 128–129; *WJ* 1:192; Cave, *The Pequot War*, 206–207.

19. *OPP*, 294–295; Williams to Mason and Prence, 1670, in *CRW* 2:611–612.

20. *WJ* 1:190–194.

21. Williams to Winthrop, May 27, 1638, in *CRW* 1:157–158; Paul Alden Robinson, "The Struggle Within: The Indian Debate in Seventeenth Century Narragansett Country" (PhD dissertation, State University of New York at Binghamton, 1990), 120–121; Francis Jennings, *The Invasion of America: Indians, Colonialism, and the Cant of Conquest* (Chapel Hill: University of North Carolina Press, 1975), 214.

22. *WJ* 1:194.

23. Gardiner to Winthrop Jr., November 6–7, 1636, in *WP* 3:319–321.

24. Gardener, "Relation of the Pequot War," 129–130.

25. Gardener, "Relation of the Pequot War," 131–133.

26. Bremer, *John Winthrop*, 283. For this section, see David D. Hall, *The Antinomian Controversy 1636–1638: A Documentary History* (Middletown, CT: Wesleyan University Press, 1968), 3–8.

27. Bremer, *John Winthrop*, 286–287; Michael P. Winship, *Making Heretics: Militant Protestantism and Free Grace in Massachusetts, 1636–1641* (Princeton, NJ: Princeton University Press, 2002), 112–113.

28. *WJ* 1:212; Underhill, "Newes," 60–61; Jameson, *Wonder-Working Providence*, 164.

29. *MR* 1:192–193.

30. Jameson, *Wonder-Working Providence*, 164.

Chapter 5

1. *CR* 1:19–20; *WJ* 1:265–266.
2. John Underhill, "Newes from America," in *History of the Pequot War: The Contemporary Accounts of Mason, Underhill, Vincent and Gardener*, ed. Charles Orr (Cleveland, OH: Helman-Taylor, 1897), 62–63, 71; John Mason, "Brief History of the Pequot War," in *History of the Pequot War: The Contemporary Accounts of Mason, Underhill, Vincent and Gardener*, ed. Charles Orr (Cleveland, OH: Helman-Taylor, 1897), 18–19; Philip Vincent, "A True Relation of the Late Battle Fought in New England," in *History of the Pequot War: The Contemporary Accounts of Mason, Underhill, Vincent and Gardener*, ed. Charles Orr (Cleveland, OH: Helman-Taylor, 1897), 100; *WJ* 1:213; Lion Gardener, "Relation of the Pequot War," in *History of the Pequot War: The Contemporary Accounts of Mason, Underhill, Vincent and Gardener*, ed. Charles Orr (Cleveland, OH: Helman-Taylor, 1897), 133.
3. Vincent, "A True Relation," 101.
4. *CR* 1:19–20; *WJ* 1:265–266.
5. *CR* 1:9.
6. Underhill, "Newes," 66.
7. Gardener, "Relation of the Pequot War," 134–135.
8. Underhill, "Newes," 66–67.
9. *WJ* 1:194.
10. Higginson to Winthrop, May, 1637, in *WP* 3:404–407, 1637.
11. Hooker to Winthrop, May, 1637, in *WP* 3:407–408, 1637.
12. Jameson, *Wonder-Working Providence*, 166–167; Mason, "Brief History of the Pequot War," 45.
13. Mason, "Brief History of the Pequot War," 20.
14. Underhill, "Newes," 67–69; Mason, "Brief History of the Pequot War," 20; Vincent, "A True Relation," 101; Gardener, "Relation of the Pequot War," 136.
15. Gardener, "Relation of the Pequot War," 135–136.
16. Underhill, "Newes," 69–77; Winthrop to Bradford, July 28, 1637, in *WP* 3:457; Gardener, "Relation of the Pequot War," 133–134.
17. Mason, "Brief History of the Pequot War," 20–22.
18. Ludlow to Pynchon, 1637, in *MHSC* Series 2, 8:235–236.
19. Williams to Massachusetts, May 1, 1637, in *CRW* 1:72–74, 78–79; Connole, *Nipmuck Country*, 7–9.
20. *WJ* 1:213–214.
21. Hall, *Antinomian Controversy*, 8–9, 253–254; *WJ* 1:215–216, 218.
22. Mason, "Brief History of the Pequot War," 23–25; Vincent, "A True Relation," 101–102; Patrick to Winthrop, May 23, in *WP* 3:421; Underhill, "Newes," 83; Carl Bridenbaugh, *Fat Mutton and Liberty of Conscience: Society in Rhode Island, 1636–1690* (Providence, RI: Brown University Press, 1974), 12–13.
23. Mason, "Brief History of the Pequot War," 25–26.
24. Mason, "Brief History of the Pequot War," 26–27; Vincent, "A True Relation," 102; Underhill, "Newes," 77–78.
25. Vincent, "A True Relation," 105–106.
26. Mason, "Brief History of the Pequot War," 27–28; Underhill, "Newes," 78. Underhill claims Mason attacked on the west side.
27. Vincent, "A True Relation," 106.
28. Underhill, "Newes," 78–81; Mason, "Brief History of the Pequot War," 28–30; Vincent, "A True Relation," 103–104; *OPP*, 296.
29. Mason, "Brief History of the Pequot War," 30–31; Underhill, "Newes," 81.
30. Underhill, "Newes," 81–82; Mason, "Brief History of the Pequot War," 31–33.
31. Mason, "Brief History of the Pequot War," 31–35; Underhill, "Newes," 83–84.
32. Williams to Winthrop, June 2 and 21, 1637, in *CRW* 1:82–84, 86; *WJ* 1:220–221.
33. Underhill, "Newes," 84–85; Vincent, "A True Relation," 106; Mason, "Brief History of the Pequot War," 35–36.
34. Williams to Winthrop, July 10, 1637, in *CRW* 1:96.
35. *CR* 1:10.
36. Winslow to Winthrop, June 5, 1637, in *WP* 3:428.

37. Humfrey to Winthrop, June 7, 1637, in *WP* 3:429.
38. Gardener, "Relation of the Pequot War," 137–138.
39. Williams to Winthrop, June 21 and 30 and August 20, 1637, in *CRW* 1:86–88, 113–114; *WJ* 1:225.
40. Stoughton to Winthrop, June 28, 1637, in *WP* 3:435.
41. Williams to Winthrop, June 30, 1637, August 20, and September 9, in *CRW* 1:88–89, 113–114, 118.
42. Stoughton to Winthrop, July 6, 1637, in *WP* 3:441–444.
43. Williams to Winthrop, July 10 and 15, 1637, in *CRW* 1:93, 101.
44. Underhill, "Newes," 85–86; Mason, "Brief History of the Pequot War," 36–37; Williams to Winthrop, July 3, 1637, in *CRW* 1:88; Cave, *Pequot War*, 159.
45. Mason, "Brief History of the Pequot War," 37–39; Davenport to "Peter," July 17, 1637, in *WP* 452–454; *WJ* 1:226–227; Winthrop to Bradford, July 28, 1637, in *WP* 3:456–457; "Indian Testimony," *MHSC* Series 5, 9:121; Kevin McBride, David Naumec, Ashley Bissonnette, and Noah Fellman, *Battle of Pequot (Munnacommock) Swamp, July 13–14, 1637: Site Identification and Documentation Project* (Washington, DC: U.S. Department of the Interior, 2019).
46. *WJ* 1:228–229; Winthrop to Bradford, July 28, 1637, in *WP* 3:457; Michael L. Fickes, "'They Could Not Endure That Yoke': The Captivity of Pequot Women and Children after the War of 1637," *NEQ* 73, no. 1 (March 2000):70.
47. Davenport to Peter, July 17, 1637, in *WP* 3:454.
48. *WJ* 1:228, 231; Winthrop to Bradford, July 28, 1637, in *WP* 3:457–458; Andrew Lipman, "'A Meanes to Knitt Them Together': The Exchange of Body Parts in the Pequot War," *WMQ* 65, no. 1 (January 2008): 20–22.
49. *WJ* 1:229–230; Neal Salisbury, "Toward the Covenant Chain: Iroquois and Southern New England Algonquians, 1637–1684," in *The Iroquois and Their Neighbors in Indian North America, 1600–1800*, ed. Daniel K. Richter and James H. Merrell (Syracuse, NY: Syracuse University Press, 1987), 62.
50. Mason, "Brief History of the Pequot War," 39–40.
51. *WJ* 1:238.
52. Steven T. Katz, "The Pequot War Reconsidered," *NEQ* 64, no. 2 (June 1991): 206–224; 213; Ronald Dale Karr, "Why Should You Be So Furious? The Violence of the Pequot War," *Journal of American History* 85, no. 3 (December 1998): 876–909; 882–883, 888–893, 907–909; James Drake, "Restraining Atrocity: The Conduct of King Philip's War," *NEQ* 70, no. 1 (March 1997): 36.
53. Underhill, "Newes," 81.
54. Mason, "Brief History of the Pequot War," 35.
55. *OPP*, 296.
56. Vincent, "A True Relation," 98, 109–110.
57. 2 Kings 14:5–6; Williams to Winthrop, July 15, 1637, in *CRW* 1:102; John Corrigan, "Amalek and the Rhetoric of Extermination," in *The First Prejudice: Religious Tolerance and Intolerance in Early America*, ed. Chris Beneke and Christopher S. Grenda (Philadelphia: University of Pennsylvania Press, 2011), 53–72.

Chapter 6

1. Margaret Ellen Newell, *Brethren by Nature: New England Indians, Colonists, and the Origins of American Slavery* (Ithaca, NY: Cornell University Press, 2015), 34, 56–57; Michael L. Fickes, "'They Could Not Endure That Yoke': The Captivity of Pequot Women and Children after the War of 1637," *NEQ* 73, no. 1 (March 2000): 61–68; Peter to Winthrop, 1637, in *WP* 3:450; Williams to Winthrop, June 30 and November 10, 1637, in *CRW* 1:88, 132; John Mason, "Brief History of the Pequot War," in *History of the Pequot War: The Contemporary Accounts of Mason, Underhill, Vincent and Gardener*, ed. Charles Orr (Cleveland, OH: Helman-Taylor, 1897), 39; *WJ* 1:226.
2. Williams to Winthrop, June 30, July 31, 1637, and February 28, 1638, in *CRW* 1:88–89, 108–109, 145–146.
3. Massachusetts Body of Liberties (1641), in S. Whitmore, *A Bibliographical Sketch of the Laws of Massachusetts Colony from 1630 to 1686* (Boston: Rockwell and Churchill, 1890), 53.
4. Williams to Winthrop, July 10, 15, 1637, in *CRW* 1:97, 101; Paul Alden Robinson, "The Struggle Within: The Indian Debate in Seventeenth Century Narragansett Country" (PhD dissertation, State University of New York at Binghamton, 1990), 122

5. Williams to Winthrop, August 20, 1637, in *CRW* 1:112–114; Roger Williams, *A Key into the Language of America*, in *CRWR* 1:145.
6. Robinson, "The Struggle Within," 121–122; *WJ* 1:226; Williams to Winthrop, September 9 and October 26, 1637, in *CRW* 1:117–120, 125–127; John J. Sainsbury, "Miantonomo's Death and New England Politics, 1630–1645," *Rhode Island History* 30, no. 4 (1971): 115.
7. *WJ* 1:238.
8. Williams to Winthrop, January 10, February 28, May 27, 1638, in *CRW* 1:140, 145–146, 157; *WJ*, 1:289–290; Hooker to Winthrop, December, 1638, in *WP* 4:78–79.
9. Williams to Winthrop, April 16, 1638, in *CRW* 1:150.
10. *WJ* 1:271.
11. Williams to Winthrop, June 7 and 14, July 23, 1638, in *CRW* 1:161–164, 168–169.
12. Ludlow to Winthrop, July 3, 1638, in *WP* 4:43–45; John A. Strong, "Wyandanch: Sachem of the Montauks," in *Northeastern Indian Lives 1632–1816*, ed. Robert S. Grumet (Amherst: University of Massachusetts Press, 1996), 52–53.
13. *OPP*, 299–300; Williams to Winthrop, August 1 and 14, 1638, in *CRW* 1:170–172, 176; *WJ* 1:273–274; *PR* 1:96–97; Glenn W. LaFantasie, "Murder of an Indian, 1638," *Rhode Island History* 38, no. 3 (August 1979): 67–77.
14. Williams to Winthrop, April 16, 1638, in *CRW* 1:150, 182–184; Williams, *Key*, in *CWRW* 1:261.
15. Alden T. Vaughan, *New England Frontier: Puritans and Indians 1620–1675* (Boston: Little, Brown, 1965), 150–151, 340–341; Mason, "Brief History of the Pequot War," 40.
16. Steven T. Katz, "The Pequot War Reconsidered," *NEQ* 64, no. 2 (June 1991): 206–224; 213; Ronald Dale Karr, "Why Should You Be So Furious? The Violence of the Pequot War," *Journal of American History* 85, no. 3 (December 1998): 220.
17. Williams to Winthrop, May 9, 1639, in *CRW* 1:196–197.
18. Julie A. Fisher and David J. Silverman, *Ninigret: Sachem of the Niantics and Narragansetts: Diplomacy, War, and the Balance of Power in Seventeenth-Century New England and Indian Country* (Ithaca, NY: Cornell University Press, 2014), 46; *CR* 1:32; Mason, "Brief History of the Pequot War," 40–44.
19. Williams to Winthrop, July 21, 1640, in *CRW* 1:203.
20. Bradford to Winthrop, June 29, 1640, in *WP* 4:258–259.
21. *WJ* 2:6.
22. Williams to Winthrop, August 7, 1640, in *CRW* 1:206.
23. Bradford to Winthrop, August 16, 1640, in *WP* 4:275.
24. Williams to Winthrop, July 21, 1640, in *CRW* 1:203.
25. *WJ* 2:6–7; Williams to Mason and Prence, 1670, in *CRW* 2:610.
26. *WJ* 2:18–19.
27. *WJ* 2:14–15.
28. Michael Leroy Oberg, *Uncas: First of the Mohegans* (Ithaca, NY: Cornell University Press, 2003), 89–90; Henry A. Baker, *History of Montville, Connecticut, formerly the North Parish of New London, from 1640–1896* (Hartford, CT: Lockwood and Brainard, 1896), 11–12; Wendy B. St. Jean, "Inventing Guardianship: The Mohegan Indians and Their 'Protectors,'" *NEQ* 72, no. 3 (September 1999): 368.
29. Anonymous, *MHSC* Series 3, 3:161–164; *WJ* 2:74.
30. Lion Gardener, "Relation of the Pequot War," in *History of the Pequot War: The Contemporary Accounts of Mason, Underhill, Vincent and Gardener*, ed. Charles Orr (Cleveland, OH: Helman-Taylor, 1897), 140–143; John A. Strong, "The Imposition of Colonial Jurisdiction over the Montauk Indians of Long Island," *Ethnohistory* 41, no. 4 (Autumn 1994): 563.
31. "Journal of New Netherland," in *NYCD* 1:183.
32. *WJ* 2:74–75; *CR* 1:73–74; Gardener, "Relation, of the Pequot War," 143; *MR* 2:27.
33. *WJ* 2:75–76; *MR* 2:23–24.
34. *WJ* 2:77–80; *PR* 2:46–47.
35. Gardener, "Relation, of the Pequot War," 139–140, 143; Michael Leroy Oberg, "'We Are All the Sachems from East to West': A New Look at Miantonomi's Campaign of Resistance," *NEQ* 77, no. 3 (September 2004): 479–480.
36. *WJ* 2:100–104.
37. *WJ* 2:240–241, 297, 309; Williams, 1658, in *CRW* 2:485; Williams to Winthrop, March 8, 1641, in *CRW* 1:215; Barry, *Williams*, 252–269; Bremer, *Winthrop*, 340–341.
38. *MR* 2:26–27; *WJ* 2:81.

39. John M. Barry, *Roger Williams and the Creation of the American Soul: Church, State, and the Birth of Liberty* (New York: Penguin, 2012), 272–273.
40. *WJ* 2:122–123; Dennis A. Connole, *The Indians of the Nipmuck Country in Southern New England, 1630–1750: An Historical Geography* (Jefferson, NC: McFarland, 2001), 61, 63; Sainsbury, "Miantonomo's Death," 123.
41. *ACUC* 1:10–11, 52; *WJ* 2:123; Neal Salisbury, *Manitou and Providence: Indians, Europeans, and the Making of New England* (New York: Oxford University Press, 1982), 230; *CRW* 2:453–454n6.
42. Winthrop to Saltonstall, July 21, 1643, in *WP* 4:410; Robinson, "The Struggle Within," 106.
43. *WJ* 2:124–126; *MR* 2:40.
44. *WJ* 2:131–135; *ACUC* 1:11; Haynes to Winthrop, January 17, 1644, in *WP* 4:506–507; Edward Winslow, *Hypocrisie Unmasked* (Providence, RI: Club for Colonial Reprints, 1916), 72–73; Fisher and Silverman, *Ninigret*, 62.
45. Russell Shorto, *The Island at the Center of the World: The Epic Story of Dutch Manhattan and the Forgotten Colony That Shaped America* (New York: Doubleday, 2004), 124; Michael Leroy Oberg, *Dominion and Civility: English Imperialism and Native America, 1585–1685* (Ithaca, NY: Cornell University Press, 1999), 139–140.
46. *WJ* 2:134–138; *ACUC* 1:10–12; Oberg, "Miantonomi's Campaign," 491–494.
47. *ACUC* 1:12, 14–15.
48. *WJ* 2:136.
49. Samuel Gorton, *Simplicity's Defence against Seven-Headed Policy* (Providence, RI: Marshall, Brown, 1835), 169; Haynes to Winthrop, January 17, 1644, in *WP* 4:506–507.
50. *WJ* 2:139–141, 145–150.
51. *WJ* 2:143.
52. *WJ* 2:161; Winslow to Winthrop, January 7, 1644, in *WP* 4:427–428; Mason to Winthrop, December 1, 1643, in *WP* 4:418–420; *WP* 4:431–435, 441–444, 507; Louis Effingham De Forest and Anne Lawrence De Forest, *Captain John Underhill, Gentleman, Soldier of Fortune* (New York: De Forest, 1934), 25–62.
53. *WJ* 2:157.

Chapter 7

1. Jenny Hale Pulsipher, "'Our Sages Are Sageles': A Letter on Massachusetts Indian Policy after King Philip's War," *WMQ* 58, no. 2 (April 2001): 436.
2. Richard W. Cogley, *John Eliot's Mission to the Indians before King Philip's War* (Cambridge, MA: Harvard University Press, 1999), 9–22, quote on 21.
3. Francis J. Bremer, *John Winthrop: America's Forgotten Founding Father* (Oxford: Oxford University Press, 2003), 310–312, 324, 334, 337; John Frederick Martin, *Profits in the Wilderness: Entrepreneurship and the Founding of New England Towns in the Seventeenth Century* (Chapel Hill: University of North Carolina Press, 1991); Robert C. Black III, *The Younger John Winthrop* (New York: Columbia University Press, 1966), 162.
4. *WJ* 2:99; *New England's First Fruits*, in *ET*, 58–59; "Winslow's Relation," 349–350; William Kellaway, *The New England Company 1649–1776: Missionary Society to the American Indians* (New York: Barnes & Noble, 1962), 4–11; Cogley, *Eliot's Mission*, 67–68.
5. *New England's First Fruits*, in *ETI*, 61–62; *WJ* 2:69.
6. *First Fruits*, 63–65; *WJ* 1:260; Eliot to Baxter, October 7, 1657, in F. J. Powicke, "Some Unpublished Correspondence of the Rev. Richard Baxter and the Rev. John Eliot," *Bulletin of the John Rylands Library* 15, no. 1 (1931): 157–158.
7. *First Fruits*, 74; Kristina Bross, *Dry Bones and Indian Sermons: Praying Indians in Colonial America* (Ithaca, NY: Cornell University Press, 2004), 3–8, 14.
8. Williams to Winthrop, February 28, 1638, in *CRW* 1:146.
9. Williams, *Key*, in *CWRW* 1:81, 86–88, 96–98; J. Patrick Cesarini, "The Ambivalent Uses of Roger Williams's *A Key into the Language of America*," *EAL* 38, no. 3 (September 2007): 372–374.
10. Roger Williams, *Christenings Make Not Christians*, in *CWRW* 7:35–36, 39–41; Williams, *Key*, in *CWRW* 1:83, 141; Richard W. Cogley, *John Eliot's Mission to the Indians before King Philip's War* (Cambridge, MA: Harvard University Press, 1999), 12–18, 21.
11. Henry Whitfield, ed., *The Light appearing more and more towards the perfect Day*, in *ET* 177–179; David J. Silverman, *Faith and Boundaries: Colonists, Christianity, and Community among*

the Wampanoag Indians of Martha's Vineyard, 1600–1871 (New York: Cambridge University Press, 2005), 17–24.

12. Edward Winslow, ed., "The Glorious Progress of the Gospel amongst the Indians of New England," in *ET* 148–150; Silverman, *Faith and Boundaries*, 24–25.

13. *MR* 2:55–56, 73; *WJ* 2:160, 169, 223; Cogley, *Eliot's Mission*, 30–39. Connole , 51–52, 66–69, 142–143; David Jaffee, *People of the Wachusett: Greater New England in History and Memory, 1630–1860* (Ithaca, NY: Cornell University Press, 1999), 34–42.

14. *WJ* 2:156–157.

15. *MR* 3:6–7.

16. *MR* 2:84, 134; Cogley, *Eliot's Mission*, 21–22.

17. John Eliot, *The Indian Grammar Begun* (Cambridge, MA, 1666), 66; Winslow, "The Glorious Progress," 160; Ola Winslow, *John Eliot: "Apostle to the Indians"* (Boston: Houghton Mifflin, 1968).

18. Thomas Shepard, *The Clear Sun-shine of the Gospel breaking forth upon the Indians in New-England*, in *ET* 124; Cogley, *Eliot's Mission*, 40; *WJ* 2:319; *The Day-Breaking, if not the Sun-Rising of the Gospell with the Indians in New England*, in *ET* 83–84.

19. *Day-Breaking, ET* 83–87; Shepard, *Clear Sun-shine*, 118, 136; Williams, *Key*, in *CWRW* 1:214.

20. *MR* 2:166, 176–179; Cotton, *Letters from New England*, 164; Cogley, *Eliot's Mission*, 42–43.

21. *Day-Breaking*, 87–88.

22. *Day-Breaking*, 88–89.

23. *Day-Breaking*, 91–94.

24. *Day-Breaking*, 95–100, quote on 96; Cogley, *Eliot's Mission*, 52–54.

25. George Madison Bodge, *Soldiers in King Philip's War* (Baltimore: Genealogical, 1976), 119–120.

26. Shepard, *Clear Sun-shine*, 114–116; Cogley, *Eliot's Mission*, 58.

27. Shepard, *Clear Sun-shine*, 116–117, 120–123, 125, 129, 131–132; *WJ* 2:318–320; Robert James Naeher, "Dialogue in the Wilderness: John Eliot and the Indian Exploration of Puritanism as a Source of Meaning, Comfort, and Ethnic Survival," *NEQ* 62, no. 3 (September 1989): 355–359.

28. *MR* 2:188–189; 3:105–106; Shepard, *Clear Sun-shine*, 123, 132; Cogley, *Eliot's Mission*, 59–60.

29. Shepard, *Clear Sun-shine*, 126–128; Cogley, *Eliot's Mission*, 54.

30. *Day-Breaking*, 95, 97, 99–100.

31. Shepard, *Clear Sun-shine*, 130–131; Winslow, "The Glorious Progress," 154.

32. Winslow, "The Glorious Progress," 151–152, 156, 159.

33. Shepard, *Clear Sun-shine*, 135; Winslow, "The Glorious Progress," 153; Daniel Gookin, *Historical Collections of the Indians in New England* (Boston: Apollo Press, 1792), 46; William Wood, *New England's Prospect*, ed. Alden T. Vaughan (Amherst: University of Massachusetts Press, 1977), 13, 100–101.

34. Shepard, *Clear Sun-shine*, 118–119.

35. Winslow, "The Glorious Progress, 152–154; Stewart-Smith, *Penacook Indians*, 144–145; Bross, *Dry Bones*, 62–63.

36. Winslow, "The Glorious Progress," 152; Shepard, *Clear Sun-shine*, 136–137.

37. Shepard, *Clear Sun-shine*, 133, 136, 138–139.

Chapter 8

1. Samuel Gorton, *Simplicity's Defence against Seven-Headed Policy* (Providence, RI: Marshall, Brown, 1835), 153–157; *WJ* 2:160.

2. *RICR* 1:134–137.

3. *RICR* 1:136–138.

4. *WJ* 2:168–169.

5. Brown to Winthrop, June 26, 1644, in *WP* 4:464–465; *MR* 2:72; *WJ* 2:172–173, 176.

6. *ACUC* 1:28–30; *A Declaration of Former Passages and Proceedings betwixt the English and the Narragansetts* (Boston, 1645), 4.

7. J. Patrick Cesarini, "The Ambivalent Uses of Roger Williams's *A Key into the Language of America*," *EAL* 38, no. 3 (September 2007): 472–474; Field, "Key for the Gate," 375–379; Barry, *Roger Williams*, 301–305; *RICR* 1:143–146.

8. "Charter of Narragansett to Massachusetts," in *NEHGR* 11:41–43; Walter W. Woodward, *Prospero's America: John Winthrop, Jr., Alchemy and the Creation of New England Culture, 1606–1676* (Chapel Hill: University of North Carolina Press, 2010), 53–56, 76–91.

9. Shawn Wiemann, "Lasting Marks: The Legacy of Robin Cassacinamon and the Survival of the Mashantucket Pequot Nation" (PhD dissertation, University of New Mexico, 2011), 123–138; William R. Carlton, "Overland to Connecticut in 1645: A Travel Diary of John Winthrop, Jr.," *NEQ* 13, no. 3 (September 1940): 504–505.

10. Winthrop Memorandum, in *WP* 5:17–18; *Declaration of Former Passages*, 4–5; Peters to Winthrop, May 1645, in *WP* 5:19; Frances Manwaring Caulkins, *History of Norwich, Connecticut: From Its Possession by the Indians, to the Year 1866* (Hartford, CT: Case, Lockwood, 1866), 40–44; *CR* 2:74.

11. Peters to Winthrop, May 1645, in *WP* 5:19; Gardener, "Relation," 143–144.

12. Williams to Winthrop, June 25, 1645, in *CRW* 1:224–225.

13. *ACUC* 1:32–33.

14. *Declaration of Former Passages*, 5–6.

15. Downing to Winthrop, August 1645, in *WP* 5:38.

16. *Declaration of Former Passages*, 7.

17. *ACUC* 1:33–35; Edward Winslow, *Hypocrisie Unmasked* (Providence, RI: Club for Colonial Reprints, 1916), 84–86.

18. *ACUC* 1:38–40; Paul Alden Robinson, "The Struggle Within: The Indian Debate in Seventeenth Century Narragansett Country" (PhD dissertation, State University of New York at Binghamton, 1990), 159.

19. *ACUC* 1:41–48, 88; Gorton, *Simplicity's Defense*, 171; Robinson, *Struggle Within*, 169–170.

20. Pynchon to Winthrop, September 15, 1645, in *WP* 5:45; *ACUC* 1:86.

21. Williams, *Christenings*, in *CWRW* 7:31–32.

22. Kevin A. McBride, "The Legacy of Robin Cassacinamon: Mashantucket Pequot Leadership in the Historic Period," in *Northeastern Indian Lives, 1632–1816*, ed. Robert S. Grumet and Anthony F. C. Wallace (Amherst: University of Massachusetts Press, 1996), 81; Julie A. Fisher and David J. Silverman, *Ninigret: Sachem of the Niantics and Narragansetts: Diplomacy, War, and the Balance of Power in Seventeenth-Century New England and Indian Country* (Ithaca, NY: Cornell University Press, 2014), 64; *ACUC* 1:99; New London Petition, 1646, in *WP* 5:111–112; Michael Leroy Oberg, *Uncas: First of the Mohegans* (Ithaca, NY: Cornell University Press, 2003), 117–118.

23. Winthrop to Uncas, June 20, 1646, in *WP* 5:82–83; Peter to Winthrop Jr., June 29, 1646, in *WP* 5:85–86.

24. Winthrop to Peter, September 3, 1646, in *WP* 5:100–101.

25. *ACUC* 1:66–69, 72–74, 81; *WJ* 2:348–349; New London Petition, 1646, in *WP* 5:111–112; Oberg, *Uncas*, 117–118.

26. *ACUC* 1:101; Dennis A. Connole, *The Indians of the Nipmuck Country in Southern New England, 1630–1750: An Historical Geography* (Jefferson, NC: McFarland, 2001), 58–61.

27. *ACUC* 1:74–76; Eaton to Winthrop, August 6, 1646, in *WP* 5:95; *WJ* 2:272.

28. *ACUC* 1:70–71, 82.

29. Uncas and Cassasinamon Agreement, February 24, 1647, in *WP* 5:131; Winthrop to Winthrop Jr., May 14, 1647, in *WP* 5:161; Williams to Winthrop Jr., May 28, 1647, in *CRW* 1:234.

30. *ACUC* 1:97–102.

31. Williams to Whipple, August 24, 1669, in *CRW* 2:595.

32. *ACUC* 1:86–87; *WJ* 2:324; Fisher and Silverman, *Ninigret*, 68.

33. Winthrop Jr. to Hopkins, February 10, 1647, in *WP* 5:127–128.

34. *ACUC* 1:87–89.

35. *ACUC* 1:106.

36. Williams to Winthrop Jr., August 20, 1647, in *CRW* 1:235.

37. *WJ* 2:343; Connole, *Nipmuck Country*, 71.

38. Pynchon to Winthrop, July 5, 1648, in J. J. H. Temple, *History of North Brookfield, Massachusetts* (North Brookfield, MA, 1887), 36–37; *WJ* 2:344.

39. *WJ* 2:348–349; Williams to Winthrop Jr., September 11, 1648, in *CRW* 1:241–242; Richard I. Melvoin, *New England Outpost: War and Society in Colonial Deerfield* (New York: W. W. Norton, 1989), 33–34; Peter A. Thomas, *In the Maelstrom of Change: The Indian Trade and Cultural Process in the Middle Connecticut River Valley, 1635–1665* (New York: Garland, 1990), 200; Deborah L. Madsen, "Colonial Legacies: The Pynchons of Springfield and the Hawthornes of Salem," in *Early America Re-explored: New Readings in Colonial, Early National, and Antebellum Culture*, ed. Klaus H. Schmidt and Fritz Fleischmann (New York: Peter Lang, 2000), 54–56.

40. Pynchon to Winthrop, July 5, 1648, in Temple, *History of North Brookfield*, 36–38.

41. Dudley to Winthrop, July 9, 1648, in Temple, *History of North Brookfield*, 38–39; *WJ* 2:344.
42. *ACUC* 1:116; Commissioners to Winthrop Jr., September 13, 1648, in *WP* 5:252.
43. Williams to Winthrop, September 11, 1648, in *CRW* 1:241–242.
44. Mason to Winthrop Jr., September 4 and 9, 1648, in *WP* 5:249–251; *WJ* 2:348–350; *ACUC* 1:116; Commissioners to Winthrop Jr., September 13, 1648, in *WP* 5:252; Williams to Winthrop Jr., September 23, 1648, in *CRW* 1:248.
45. Williams to Winthrop Jr., October 10, 1648, in *CRW* 1:251; *WJ* 2:350; *ACUC* 1:117–118; Mason to Winthrop Jr., September 17, 1648, in *WP* 5:253.
46. Winthrop Jr. to Mason, September 19, Haynes to Winthrop Jr., September 20, Hopkins to Winthrop Jr., November 1, Mason to Winthrop Jr., September 17, 1648, all in *WP* 5:253, 255–256, 276–277.
47. Williams to Winthrop Jr., October 10, 1648, in *CRW* 1:252; *CRW* 1:244–248.
48. *ACUC* 1:111–112; Hopkins to Mason, November 21, 1648, in *WP* 5:281–282.
49. Mason to Winthrop Jr., 1648, in *WP* 5:263.
50. New London Protest, in *WP* 5:124 (incorrectly dated); Woodward, *Prospero's America*, 130.
51. Williams to Winthrop Jr., 1649 and January 29, 1649, in *CRW* 1:269, 271; Winthrop to Winthrop Jr., February 3, 1649, in *WP* 5:311.
52. Adam Winthrop to Winthrop Jr., March 14, 1649, in *WP* 5:319.
53. Wilson to Winthrop Jr., March 26, 1649, in *WP* 5:325.
54. Hopkins to Winthrop, March 20, 1649, in *WP* 5:321–322; *ACUC* 2:417–418; Wiemann, *Lasting Marks*, 171, 184–189.
55. *ACUC* 2:416–417; Williams to Winthrop, 1649, in *CRW* 1:277–278; Williams to Elizabeth Winthrop, 1649, in *WP* 5:326.
56. Williams to Winthrop Jr., June 13, 1649, in *CRW* 1:290.
57. *ACUC* 2:417–418, 1:143–145; Williams to Winthrop, March 20, 1650, in *CRW* 1:311–312.
58. Winthrop to Commissioners, July 1649, in *WP* 5:354.
59. *ACUC* 1:145–146.
60. Winthrop to Haynes, August 28, 1649, in *WP* 5:360–361, and February 16, 1650, in *WP* 6:20; Williams to Winthrop and Mason, August 26, to Field, September 13, and to Winthrop, October 25, 1649, all in *CRW* 1:292–294, 299.
61. *ACUC* 1:168–169. Massachusetts officials, including Endecott, protested this action. *ACUC* 2:419–420; John Frederick Martin, *Profits in the Wilderness: Entrepreneurship and the Founding of New England Towns in the Seventeenth Century* (Chapel Hill: University of North Carolina Press, 1991), 62.
62. Williams to Winthrop, October 9, 1650, in *CRW* 1:322–323.
63. Winthrop to Atherton (date incorrect), in *WP* 6:77–78.
64. Williams to Winthrop, October 9, 17 and 23, 1650, in *CRW* 1:322–323, 325–327.
65. Williams to Massachusetts, in *CRW* 1:353.
66. Winthrop to Williams, November 10, 1650, in *CRW* 1:328.

Chapter 9

1. Henry Whitfield, ed., *The Light appearing more and more towards the perfect Day*, in *ET* 190, 195.
2. Whitfield, *The Light appearing*, 186–189, 191; Edward Winslow, ed., "The Glorious Progress of the Gospel amongst the Indians of New England," in *ET* 153.
3. John Eliot, "A Late and Further Manifestation of the Progress of the Gospel amongst the Indians in New England," in *ET* 303.
4. John Eliot and Thomas Mayhew Jr., "Tears of Repentance," in *ET* 268.
5. Whitfield, *The Light appearing*, 186–187, 191.
6. William Kellaway, *The New England Company 1649–1776: Missionary Society to the American Indians* (New York: Barnes & Noble, 1962), 10–13; John G. Turner, *They Knew They Were Pilgrims: Plymouth Colony and the Contest for American Liberty* (New Haven, CT: Yale University Press, 2020), 209; Whitfield, *The Light appearing*, 186, 198; Richard W. Cogley, *John Eliot's Mission to the Indians before King Philip's War* (Cambridge, MA: Harvard University Press, 1999), 76–83.
7. *WJ* 2:311; Winslow, "Glorious Progress," 144–147; Whitfield, *The Light appearing*, 185–186; Kristina Bross, *Dry Bones and Indian Sermons: Praying Indians in Colonial America* (Ithaca, NY: Cornell University Press, 2004), 12–13; Karen Ordahl Kupperman, *Settling with*

the Indians: The Meeting of English and Indian Cultures in America, 1580–1640 (Totowa, NJ: Rowman and Littlefield, 1980), 110; Cogley, *Eliot's Mission*, 83–90, 96–97, 103.

8. Kellaway, *New England Company*, 10–16, 36, 62–63; *RICR* 1:367–369; *ACUC* 1:163–164.

9. Whitfield, *The Light appearing*, 191–192, 195; Bross, *Dry Bones*, 31–34; Stephen Carl Arch, "The Edifying History of Edward Johnson's Wonder-Working Providence," *EAL* 28 (1993): 42–55; Cogley, *Eliot's Mission*, 90–97; Revelation 11:15.

10. Whitfield, *The Light appearing*, 190–191, 197–198; Henry Whitfield, "Strength out of Weakness," in *ET* 221.

11. Whitfield, *The Light appearing*, 200–201; Thomas Shepard, *The Clear Sun-shine of the Gospel breaking forth upon the Indians in New-England*, in *ET* 134.

12. Whitfield *The Light appearing*, 201–202; Eliot, "A Late and Further Manifestation," 303–304; Cogley, *Eliot's Mission*, 56–57, 105; Dane Morrison, *A Praying People: Massachusett Acculturation and the Failure of the Puritan Mission, 1600–1690* (New York: Peter Lang, 1995), 76–79, 125–128; Jean M. O'Brien, *Dispossession by Degrees: Indian Land and Identity in Natick, Massachusetts, 1650–1790* (Cambridge: Cambridge University Press, 1997), 33–36; *ERTD* 4:258–259, 263–264.

13. Whitfield, *The Light appearing*, 196–197, 202–203.

14. Whitfield, *The Light appearing*, 203–205.

15. Whitfield, "Strength," 222–224; Eliot, "A Late and Further Manifestation," 303–304; Cogley, *Eliot's Mission*, 105; Weld, *New England Company*, 64–65.

16. Whitfield, "Strength," 231–232, 243; Kellaway, *New England Company*, 64–65.

17. Daniel Gookin, *Historical Collections of the Indians in New England* (Boston: Apollo Press, 1792), 41; Connole, *Nipmuck Country*, 107; O'Brien, *Dispossession*, 52–58; Bross, *Dry Bones*, 152; Naeher, "Indian Exploration of Puritanism," 364–365; Richard W. Cogley, "Idealism vs Materialism in the Study of Puritan Missions to the Indians," *Method & Theory in the Study of Religion* 3, no. 2 (1991): 173.

18. Whitfield, "Strength," 226–229; Cogley, "Idealism vs Materialism," 171.

19. John Eliot, *The Christian Commonwealth* (London, 1659), i, vi, x, 8–9.

20. *ACUC* 1:203–204.

21. Whitfield, "Strength," 229–233, 242–243.

22. *MR* 3:246.

23. Eliot to Winslow, October 20, 1651, in *NEHGR* 36:292.

24. Whitfield, *The Light appearing*, 180–184; Whitfield, "Strength," 239–241; Cogley, *Eliot's Mission*, 172–176; David J. Silverman, *Faith and Boundaries: Colonists, Christianity, and Community among the Wampanoag Indians of Martha's Vineyard, 1600–1871* (New York: Cambridge University Press, 2005).

25. Cogley, *Eliot's Mission*, 154, 182, 184–185; *ACUC* 1:196; Whitfield, "Strength," 226, 234–236, 243, 246; Endecott to Winthrop, August 15, 1651, in *WP* 6:134–135.

26. Whitfield, "Strength," 225–226; John Eliot, "A further Account of the progress of the Gospel Amongst the Indians in New England," in *ET* 378; Williams to Winthrop Jr., 1649, in *CRW* 1:281.

27. Eliot to Corporation, December 8, 1652, in *NEHGR* 36:294–296; Eliot, July 19, 1652, and August 29, 1654, in *John Eliot and the Indians: 1652–1657*, ed. Wilberforce Eames (New York: Adams & Greaves, 1916), 9, 21; Eliot and Mayhew, "Tears," 285.

28. Williams to Massachusetts, October 5, 1654, in *CRW* 2:409.

29. Eliot and Mayhew, "Tears," 268–272; Daniel K. Richter, *Facing East from Indian Country: A Native History of Early America* (Cambridge, MA: Harvard University Press, 2003), 111–119; Joshua David Bellin, "'A Little I Shall Say': Translation and Interculturalism in the John Eliot Tracts," in *Reinterpreting New England Indians and the Colonial Experience*, ed. Colin G. Calloway and Neal Dominion (Boston: Colonial Society of Massachusetts, 2003), 52–83.

30. Eliot and Mayhew, "Tears," 272–274.

31. Eliot and Mayhew, "Tears," 276–282; 1 Corinthians 11:14.

32. Eliot and Mayhew, "Tears," 265.

33. Naeher, "Indian Exploration of Puritanism," 352–354; Richter, *Facing East*, 126–129; Linford D. Fisher, "Native Americans, Conversion, and Christian Practice in Colonial New England, 1640–1730," *Harvard Theological Review* 102, no. 1 (2009): 112; Eliot and Mayhew, "Tears," 288–289.

34. Eliot and Mayhew, "Tears," 259–260; Bross, *Dry Bones*, 17–20; Karen Ordahl Kupperman, "Errand to the Indies: Puritan Colonization from Providence Island through the Western Design," *WMQ* 45, no. 1 (January 1988): 94.

35. *MR* 3:281–282.

36. Cogley, *Eliot's Mission*, 146–147; *MR* 3:301.

37. *ACUC* 2:106; Eliot, "Further Manifestation," 304–305; Cogley, *Eliot's Mission*, 140–141; Gookin, *Collections*, 44; John Eliot, "A Brief Narrative of the Progress of the Gospel amongst the Indians in New England, in the year 1670," in *ET* 403.
38. *MR* 3:348; Connole, *The Indians of Nipmuck Country*, 104.
39. Cogley, *Eliot's Mission*, 142–145; Gookin, *Collections*, 45, 48; *MR* 4(1):317, 363.
40. *ACUC* 2:123–124.
41. *MR* 3:365–366; Neal Salisbury, "Contextualizing Mary Rowlandson: Native Americans, Lancaster and the Politics of Captivity," in *Early America Re-explored*, 114.
42. Eliot, "A Late and Further Manifestation," 305–308.
43. Eliot, "A Late and Further Manifestation," 311–312, 315, 317–319.
44. *ACUC* 2:118, 431; Kellaway, *New England Company*, 32–34, 39–40, 61–73, 92–94; Cogley, *Eliot's Mission*, 223.
45. *ACUC* 2:105–107, 128, 134, 176; John Eliot, "A Further Accompt of the Progresse of the Gospel amongst the Indians in New England," in *ET* 331; Cogley, *Eliot's Mission*, 117–124, 178–186, 219–223; Connole, *Nipmuck Country*, 100; Kellaway, *New England Company*, 92–141; Bross, *Dry Bones*, 53; Gookin, *Collections*, 32–36.
46. Frank Kelleter, "Puritan Missionaries and the Colonization of the New World: A Reading of John Eliot's *Indian Dialogues* (1671)," in *Early America Re-explored*, 90–92; Fisher, "Native Americans," 112; *ACUC* 2:242.
47. Cogley, *Eliot's Mission*, 172–177, 194–195; Eliot to Lloyd, October 8, 1657, in *Some correspondence between the governors and treasurers of the New England company in London and the commissioners of the United Colonies . . .*, ed. John W. Ford (London: Spottiswoode, 1896), 1; Eliot, "Further Accompt," 332.
48. Eliot to Baxter, October 7, 1657, *Bulletin of the John Rylands Library* 15, no. 1 (1931): 158; Gookin, *Collections*, 26.
49. "Extracts of Letters to Rev. Thomas Prince," *CHSC* 3 (1895): 275–276; Cogley, *Eliot's Mission*, 183; *ERTD* 4:260.
50. *ACUC* 2:168, 182; Martin, 62–63; Eliot to Atherton, June 4, 1657, in *MHSC* Series 1, 2:9; *MR* 4(1):334; Yasuhide Kawashima, *Puritan Justice and the Indian: White Man's Law in Massachusetts 1630–1763* (Middletown, CT: Wesleyan University Press, 1986), 28–29.
51. Eliot, "Further Accompt," 333, 336–340; Eliot, "Further Account," 387; Laura M. Stevens, *The Poor Indians: British Missionaries, Native Americans, and Colonial Sensibility* (Philadelphia: University of Pennsylvania Press, 2004), 20.
52. Eliot, "Further Account," 360–361, 376–377; Cogley, *Eliot's Mission*, 108, 133–135.
53. Eliot, "Further Account," 364–366; Eliot and Mayhew, "Tears," 292–293; Cogley, *Eliot's Mission*, 180.
54. Eliot, "Further Account," 371, 385–386; Bross, *Dry Bones*, 77–83.
55. Eliot, "Further Account," 373–375, 387, 389–390, 393–395.
56. Cogley, *Eliot's Mission*, 136, 194.
57. O'Brien, *Dispossession*, 34–42; Morrison, *Praying People*, 128–149; *ERTD* 4:252–255, 279–286.
58. Eliot to Thorowgood, in *ET* 425.
59. *ERTD* 4:258–260.
60. *ERTD* 4:246–249.
61. *ERTD* 4:250–252; Cogley, *Eliot's Mission*, 109; O'Brien, *Dispossession*, 37–38.
62. *MR* 4(2):49; O'Brien, *Dispossession*, 39.

Chapter 10

1. Harry M. Ward, *The United Colonies of New England 1643–90* (New York: Vantage, 1961), 168; Charles T. Gehring, ed., *Correspondence 1647–1653*, New Netherland Documents Series (Syracuse, NY: Syracuse University Press, 2000), 11:183–184, 188.
2. Walter W. Woodward, *Prospero's America: John Winthrop, Jr., Alchemy and the Creation of New England Culture, 1606–1676* (Chapel Hill: University of North Carolina Press, 2010), 182–199.
3. *ACUC* 2:8–12, 64; Minor to Winthrop, April 2, 1653, in *WP* 6:275–276.
4. *ACUC* 2:12, 23–25, 426; Katherine Grandjean, *American Passage: The Communications Frontier in Early New England* (Cambridge, MA: Harvard University Press, 2015), 96.
5. John Eliot, "A Late and Further Manifestation of the Progress of the Gospel amongst the Indians in New England," in *ET* 305; John Eliot, "A further Account of the progress of the Gospel Amongst the Indians in New England," *ET* 362–363, 378–379.
6. *ACUC* 2:4–6.
7. *ACUC* 2:6–9.

8. *ACUC* 2:10-11, 27-28; Newe-come to Winthrop, December 1, 1652, in *WP* 6:234.

9. *ACUC* 2:12-13, 22-25.

10. *ACUC* 2:25-26.

11. *ACUC* 2:428-429.

12. *ACUC* 2:27-52; Mason to Winthrop, 1653, in *WP* 6:258; Stanton to Winthrop, 1653, in *WP* 6:289-290; Ward, *United Colonies*, 179-180; Grandjean, *American Passage*, 106-107; Effingham, *Underhill*, 64-69.

13. *ACUC* 2:52-57; *MR* 3:311-316.

14. *ACUC* 2:74-76.

15. *ACUC* 2:58.

16. Stone to Blinman, June 12, 1653, in *WP* 6:298-299.

17. Throckmorton to Winthrop, August 15, 1653, in *WP* 6:309-310; Julie A. Fisher and David J. Silverman, *Ninigret: Sachem of the Niantics and Narragansetts: Diplomacy, War, and the Balance of Power in Seventeenth-Century New England and Indian Country* (Ithaca, NY: Cornell University Press, 2014), 79-80; *ACUC* 1:18-19, 2:88, 97-98; Winthrop to Ninigret, in *WP* 6:339; Williams to Massachusetts, October 5, 1654, in *CRW* 2:412; John A. Strong, "The Imposition of Colonial Jurisdiction over the Montauk Indians of Long Island," *Ethnohistory* 41, no. 4 (Autumn 1994): 563."

18. *ACUC* 2:94-99, 101-104, 111.

19. James to Winthrop, April 4, 1654, in *WP* 6:372.

20. Williams to Massachusetts, October 5, 1654, in *CRW* 2:412-413.

21. *ACUC* 2:114-115, 429-430.

22. *ACUC* 2:125-126, 129-133, 144-145.

23. *ACUC* 2:434-437.

24. Williams to Massachusetts, October 5, 1654, in *CRW* 2:408-413.

25. Williams to Winthrop, October 9, 1654, in *CRW* 2:416-417.

26. *ACUC* 2:145-148; *WP* 6:458-470.

27. Michael Leroy Oberg, *Uncas: First of the Mohegans* (Ithaca, NY: Cornell University Press, 2003), 139; *ACUC* 2:142-143, 168, 284-285.

28. *ACUC* 2:148-150.

29. *CR* 1:304-305; Oberg, *Uncas*, 141-143.

30. *ACUC* 2:158-159, 169-172.

31. *CR* 1:307.

32. *MR* 3:436-437.

33. Mason to Winthrop, June 1657, in *MHSC* Series 4, 7:421-422; Oberg, *Uncas*, 144-145; Fisher and Silverman, *Ninigret*, 83; Frances Manwaring Caulkins, *History of New London, Connecticut, From the First Survey of the Coast in 1612, to 1860* (New London, CT: H. D. Utley, 1895), 127; Caulkins, *History of Norwich*, 45; *RICR* 1:362-363; *CR* 1:301-302.

34. *ACUC* 2:178-179, 190-193, 196.

35. Woodward, *Prospero's America*, 153-154; Robert C. Black III, *The Younger John Winthrop* (New York: Columbia University Press, 1966), 173-178; *CR* 1:301.

36. William Cronon, *Changes in the Land: Indians, Colonists, and the Ecology of New England* (New York: Hill and Wang, 1983), 99; Virginia DeJohn Anderson, *Creatures of Empire: How Domestic Animals Transformed Early America* (Oxford: Oxford University Press, 2004), 144; Neal Salisbury, "Indians and Colonists in Southern New England after the Pequot War: An Uneasy Balance," in *The Pequots in Southern New England: The Fall and Rise of an American Indian Nation*, ed. Laurence M. Hauptman and James D. Wherry (Norman: University of Oklahoma Press, 1990), 83; Stephen Innes, "The Pynchons and the People of Early Springfield," in *Early Settlement in the Connecticut Valley: A Coloquium at Historic Deerfield*, ed. John W. Ifkovic and Martin Kaufman (Deerfield, MA : Historic Deerfield, 1984), 26; Richard I. Melvoin, *New England Outpost: War and Society in Colonial Deerfield* (New York: W. W. Norton, 1989), 83-85.

37. Pynchon to Winthrop, February 16 and May 22, 1658, in *PP* 60:22-23, 25; Peter A. Thomas, *In the Maelstrom of Change: The Indian Trade and Cultural Process in the Middle Connecticut River Valley, 1635-1665* (New York: Garland, 1990), 294; Peter A. Thomas, "Bridging the Cultural Gap: Indian/White Relations," in *Early Settlement in the Connecticut Valley: A Coloquium at Historic Deerfield*, ed. John W. Ifkovic and Martin Kaufman (Deerfield, MA : Historic Deerfield, 1984), 12-14.

38. *ACUC* 2:211.

39. *ACUC* 2:199-200; Samuel G. Drake, *The Book of the Indians*, 8th ed. (Boston: Antiquarian Bookstore, 1841), 80-81.

40. Denison and Stanton, March 15, 1659, in Massachusetts Archives 30:77; Oberg, *Uncas*, 149.
41. *ACUC* 2:211; *CR* 1:318.
42. Welles to Endecott, March 27, 1659, in *MHSC* Series 5, 8:54–55; *ACUC* 2:227.
43. Mason to Connecticut, August 22, 1659, in *MHSC* Series 4, 7:423–424; *ACUC* 2:213–215, 221–227, 236–237.
44. *CR* 1:576–577; *ACUC* 2:247.
45. Winslow to Winthrop, July 17, 1660, in *MHSC* Series 5, 1:387–389.
46. *ACUC* 2:247–249.
47. James N. Arnold, ed., *The Records of the Proprietors of the Narragansett* (Providence, RI: Narragansett Historical, 1894), 14–15.
48. Salisbury, "Indians and Colonists," 90; Cronon, *Changes*, 102–103; Paul Alden Robinson, "The Struggle Within: The Indian Debate in Seventeenth Century Narragansett Country" (PhD dissertation, State University of New York at Binghamton, 1990), 192–196; Thomas, *Maelstrom of Change*, 202, 324; Anderson, *Creatures of Empire*, 150–152; John Frederick Martin, *Profits in the Wilderness: Entrepreneurship and the Founding of New England Towns in the Seventeenth Century* (Chapel Hill: University of North Carolina Press, 1991), 45, 78; Allan Greer, *Property and Dispossession: Natives, Empires and Land in Early Modern North America* (Cambridge: Cambridge University Press, 2018), 225.
49. Fisher and Silverman, *Ninigret*, 89, 92; Martin, *Profits*, 58–79; Sydney V. James, *The Colonial Metamorphoses in Rhode Island: A Study of Institutions in Change* (Hanover, NH: University Press of New England, 2000), 88–96.
50. *MR* 4(1):353, 357; *ACUC* 2:266.
51. Fisher and Silverman, *Ninigret*, 89; Martin, *Profits*, 59–69; *RICR* 1:464; Atherton to Winthrop Jr., August 30, 1659, in WFP, MHS; Richardson to Winthrop, July 9, 1659, "Scuttup's Confirmatory Deed," Rhode Island to United Colonies, August 23, 1659, and confirmation of Coginaquend deeds, all in *MHSC* Series 5, 9:7–12, 22–23; Williams to Mason and Prence, June 22, 1670, in *CRW* 2:614.
52. Atherton to Winthrop, October 13, 1660, in WFP, MHS; Richard S. Dunn, "John Winthrop, Jr., and the Narragansett Country," *WMQ* 13, no. 1 (January 1956): 72–73; Arnold, *Records of the Proprietors*, 10–15; Fisher and Silverman, *Ninigret*, 96; Martin, *Profits*, 67; Howard M. Chapin, *Sachems of the Narragansetts* (Providence: Rhode Island Historical Society, 1931), 72; Williams to Providence, August 25, 1658, in *CRW* 2:484–494.
53. "Cartwright's Answer to the Massachusetts Narrative of Transactions with the Royal Commissioners," in *Clarendon Papers* (New York: New York Historical Society, 1870), 90. https://catalog.hathitrust.org/Record/010524246; Arnold, *Records of the Proprietors*, 19–21; Dunn, "John Winthrop," 73; Lisa Brooks, *Our Beloved Kin: A New History of King Philip's War* (New Haven, CT: Yale University Press, 2019), 45; Bradstreet to Connecticut and Hutchinson to Winthrop, September 24, 1661, in *MHSC* Series 5, 9:31–32; Black, *Younger John Winthrop*, 210.
54. *CR* 1:359; Oberg, *Uncas*, 154–155; Wendy B. St. Jean, "Inventing Guardianship: The Mohegan Indians and Their 'Protectors,'" *NEQ* 72, no. 3 (September 1999): 365–377.
55. Brooks, *Our Beloved Kin*, 27–30, 35, 40–44; Eugene Aubrey Stratton, *Plymouth Colony: Its History and People, 1620–1691* (Salt Lake City: Ancestry, 1986), 78–79, 101–102, 176–177; Martin, *Profits*, 80.
56. *PR* 3:192, 4:24; Brooks, *Our Beloved Kin*, 42, 54–55; Jeremy Dupertuis Bangs, *Indian Deeds: Land Transactions in Plymouth Colony, 1620–1691* (Boston: New England Historic Genelogical Society, 2002), 66.
57. H. Temple, *History of North Brookfield, Massachusetts* (North Brookfield, MA, 1887), 43, 46; *PR* 3:192; Eliot to Endecott, March 28, 1661, in *MHSP* 3:312–313.
58. *MR* 4(2), 23.
59. *ACUC* 2:268–269; Dennis A. Connole, *The Indians of the Nipmuck Country in Southern New England, 1630–1750: An Historical Geography* (Jefferson, NC: McFarland, 2001), 78.
60. *PR* 4:8, 16–17; Brooks, *Our Beloved Kin*, 45–50; Martin, *Profits*, 80; David J. Silverman, *This Land Is Their Land: The Wampanoag Indians, Plymouth Colony, and the Troubled History of Thanksgiving* (New York: Bloomsbury, 2019), 257–258.
61. Cotton to Mather, in *MHSC*, Series 4, 8:233–234; William Hubbard, *The History of the Indian Wars in New England: from the first settlement to the termination of the war with King Philip in 1677*, ed. Samuel G. Drake (Roxbury, MA: W. E. Woodward, 1865), 1:49–51; Silverman, *This Land*, 258–260.
62. *PR* 4:25–26.

Chapter 11

1. Francis J. Bremer, *The Puritan Experiment: New England Society from Bradford to Edwards*, revised ed. (Hanover, NH: University Press of New England, 1995), 141–146; Jenny Hale Pulsipher, *Subjects unto the Same King: Indians, English, and the Contest for Authority in Colonial New England* (Philadelphia: University of Pennsylvania Press, 2015), 45; William Kellaway, *The New England Company 1649–1776: Missionary Society to the American Indians* (New York: Barnes & Noble, 1962), 36.

2. *MR* 4(1):450–452, 454, 4(2):5–6.

3. *MR* 4(2):58, 74, 164–166; Michael P. Winship, *Hot Protestants: A History of Puritanism in England and America* (New Haven, CT: Yale University Press, 2018), 191–192.

4. Adrian Chastain Weimer, *Martyr's Mirror: Persecution and Holiness in Early New England* (New York: Oxford University Press, 2011), 98–117.

5. Richard S. Dunn, "John Winthrop, Jr., and the Narragansett Country," *WMQ* 13, no. 1 (January 1956): 74–75.

6. *CR* 1:582–583; Benjamin Trumbull, *History of Connecticut*, 2 vols. (New Haven, CT: Maltby, Goldsmith, 1818), 1:511–512.

7. Denison to Winthrop, in *MHSC*, Series 5, 9:27–29.

8. Winthrop to Corporation, in *MHSC*, Series 5, 9:45–47.

9. *ACUC* 2:255–257; Boyle to Winthrop, April 21, 1664, in *MHSP* 5:376.

10. Robert C. Black III, *The Younger John Winthrop* (New York: Columbia University Press, 1966), 212–218, 221–225, 228, 232–233; *Calendar of State Papers Colonial, America and West Indies: Volume 5, 1661–1668*, ed. W. Noel Sainsbury et al. (London, 1880), 71–73 (item 223); Richard W. Cogley, *John Eliot's Mission to the Indians before King Philip's War* (Cambridge, MA: Harvard University Press, 1999), 208–209; Kellaway, *New England Company*; *CR* 2:3–11.

11. *ACUC* 2:274–275, 286–287.

12. *ACUC* 2:266–267; *RICR* 1:454.

13. *ACUC* 2:287–288; Atherton Petition, in *MHSP* 10:391; Lisa Brooks, *Our Beloved Kin: A New History of King Philip's War* (New Haven, CT: Yale University Press, 2019), 57; *MHSC*, Series 5, 9:34–36.

14. Hutchinson to Winthrop, September 22, 1662, in *MHSC*, Series 5, 9:38–39; Dunn, "John Winthrop," 74.

15. Black, *Younger John Winthrop*, 226–231; Winthrop to Hutchinson, September 2, 1662, in *MHSC*, Series 5, 9:33–34.

16. Clarke-Winthrop Agreement, April 7, 1663, in *MHSC*, Series 5, 8:82–83.

17. Black, *Younger John Winthrop*, 239–241, 256; Narragansett Inhabitants to Connecticut, July 3, 1663, *CHSC* 21:144–145; *CR* 1:407.

18. Scott to Hutchinson, April 29, and King to Colonies, June 21, 1663, in *MHSC*, Series 5, 9:53–55.

19. *RICR* 2:1–21; Dunn, "John Winthrop," 81–82; Brooks, *Our Beloved Kin*, 61–62.

20. *ACUC* 2:298–299, 308–309; Dunn, "John Winthrop," 75–79. Black, *Younger John Winthrop*, 208–209, 234–236, 247–254; *CR* 1:386–390, 411, 433–434, 2:36; *MHSC*, Series 5, 8:77–81; Southertown Propositions, in *MHSC*, Series 5, 9:58–59.

21. *ACUC* 2:307; Arnold to Winthrop, March 10, 1664, in *RICR* 2:29–30, 34–36, 42–49; Connecticut Commission, April 2, 1664, in *MHSC*, Series 5, 9:59–62; Williams to Winthrop, May 28, 1664, in *CRW* 2:527–528; Black, *Younger John Winthrop*, 257–258.

22. *MR* 4(2):158–162; Black, *Younger John Winthrop*, 199–200, 269–282, 286; Pulsipher, *Subjects*, 50–52; Commissioners to Winthrop, February 4 and March 9, 1665, in *MHSC*, Series 5, 9:62–63, 66.

23. Scuttup Statement, December 28, 1664, in *MHSC*, Series 5, 9:70–71.

24. Carr Report, in *Calendar of State Papers Colonial, America and West Indies: Volume 5, 1661–1668*, ed. W. Noel Sainsbury et al. (London, 1880) (item 1103); John Hull, "Memoir and Diaries," in *Puritan Personal Writings: Diaries*, ed. Sacvan Bercovitch (New York: AMS, 1983), 216.

25. "Cartwright's Answer," in Clarendon Papers, 90–91.

26. *RICR* 2:60; Pulsipher, *Subjects*, 55–56.

27. Williams to Massachusetts, May 12, 1656, in *CRW* 2:450–451; Joshua Micah Marshall, "'A Melancholy People': Anglo-Indian Relations in Early Warwick, Rhode Island, 1642–1675," *NEQ* 68, no. 3 (September 1995): 402–428; Daniel Gookin, *Historical Collections of the Indians in New England* (Boston: Apollo Press, 1792), 68–70.

28. Carr Report, in *Calendar of State Papers*, 5 (item 1103); *CRW* 2:552; *RICR* 2:132, 135; Paul Alden Robinson, "The Struggle Within: The Indian Debate in Seventeenth Century Narragansett Country" (PhD dissertation, State University of New York at Binghamton, 1990), 202–203.
29. *MR* 4(2):130–131, 167, 274–275; Pulsipher, *Subjects*, 50–67.
30. *MR* 4(2):229–231, 233–234.
31. *MR* 4(2):274–275; *RICR* 2:94–95; Massachusetts to Narragansetts, September 5, 1668, in *NNRC*, https://nativenortheastportal.com/annotated-transcription/digcoll3644, accessed August 12, 2022; Pulsipher, *Subjects*, 58, 64–69, 81–82.
32. *RICR* 2:132–135, 138; Robinson, "Struggle Within," 201.
33. Williams to Carr, March 1, 1666, in *CRW* 2:550–551.
34. Julie A. Fisher and David J. Silverman, *Ninigret: Sachem of the Niantics and Narragansetts: Diplomacy, War, and the Balance of Power in Seventeenth-Century New England and Indian Country* (Ithaca, NY: Cornell University Press, 2014), 104; Michael Leroy Oberg, *Uncas: First of the Mohegans* (Ithaca, NY: Cornell University Press, 2003), 161; Stanton to Mason, July 8, 1669, in *NNRC*, http://nativenortheastportal.com/annotated-transcription/digcoll1018184-0, accessed August 12, 2022.
35. Mason to Winthrop, March 18, 1669, and Cassacinamon Petition, May 5, 1669, both in Winthrop Family Transcripts, MHS.
36. *CR* 2:548–549; Long Island to Mason, June 30, 1669, in *NNRC*, http://nativenortheastportal.com/annotated-transcription/digcoll2993, accessed August 12, 2022.
37. Fisher and Silverman, *Ninigret*, 108–109; Noyes to Winthrop, March 25, 1667, in *MHSC*, Series 3, 10:67–69; *CR* 2:34, 549; Stanton to Mason, in *NNRC*, http://nativenortheastportal.com/annotated-transcription/digcoll1018184-0, accessed August 12, 2022; Gallup and Stanton Deposition, July 1669, in *NNRC*, http://nativenortheastportal.com/annotated-transcription/digcoll2110, accessed August 12, 2022); Osborn Relation, July 20, 1669, in *NNRC*, https://nativenortheastportal.com/annotated-transcription/digcoll2996, accessed August 12, 2022.
38. *CR* 2:550; Jason W. Warren, *Connecticut Unscathed: Victory in the Great Narragansett War, 1675–1676* (Norman: University of Oklahoma Press, 2014), 106.
39. Lovelace to Rhode Island, July 5, 1669, in *NYCD* 14:624; *RICR* 2:264–276.
40. *RICR* 2:273–274, 277–279, 285–286; Strong, "Colonial Jurisdiction," 576–580.
41. *RICR* 2:477–478; *MHSC*, Series 5, 9:74–76.
42. Newell, *Brethren*, 118.

Chapter 12

1. Daniel Gookin, *Historical Collections of the Indians in New England* (Boston: Apollo Press, 1792), 24.
2. Richard I. Melvoin, *New England Outpost: War and Society in Colonial Deerfield* (New York: W. W. Norton, 1989), 43–48; Peter A. Thomas, *In the Maelstrom of Change: The Indian Trade and Cultural Process in the Middle Connecticut River Valley, 1635–1665* (New York: Garland, 1990), 242–259; Neal Salisbury, "Toward the Covenant Chain: Iroquois and Southern New England Algonquians, 1637–1684," in *The Iroquois and Their Neighbors in Indian North America, 1600–1800*, ed. Daniel K. Richter and James H. Merrell (Syracuse, NY: Syracuse University Press, 1987), 66–67; Winthrop to Williams, February 6, 1665, in *CRW* 2:531.
3. Gookin, *Collections*, 24–26.
4. Commissioners to Boyle, September 13, 1665, in *Some correspondence between the governors and treasurers of the New England company in London and the commissioners of the United Colonies…*, ed. John W. Ford (London: Spottiswoode, 1896), 13; Richard W. Cogley, *John Eliot's Mission to the Indians before King Philip's War* (Cambridge, MA: Harvard University Press, 1999), 149–150.
5. *MR* 4(2):329–330.
6. Leslie Stephen and Sidney Lee, eds., *Dictionary of National Biography* (New York: Macmillan, 1908), 8:152–153; John Frederick Martin, *Profits in the Wilderness: Entrepreneurship and the Founding of New England Towns in the Seventeenth Century* (Chapel Hill: University of North Carolina Press, 1991), 23–25; Louise A. Breen, *Daniel Gookin, the Praying Indians, and King Philip's War: A Short History in Documents* (New York: Routledge, 2019), 7–8; Frederick William Gookin, *Daniel Gookin 1612–1687* (Chicago, 1912).

7. Gookin, *Collections*, 22, 47; Eliot to Boyle, September 6, 1669, in *Some correspondence between the governors and treasurers of the New England company in London and the commissioners of the United Colonies . . .*, ed. John W. Ford (London: Spottiswoode, 1896), 29–30; Cogley, *Eliot's Mission*, 147; Dennis A. Connole, *The Indians of the Nipmuck Country in Southern New England, 1630–1750: An Historical Geography* (Jefferson, NC: McFarland, 2001), 53–54; Lisa Brooks, *Our Beloved Kin: A New History of King Philip's War* (New Haven, CT: Yale University Press, 2019), 43.

8. John Eliot, "A Brief Narrative of the Progress of the Gospel amongst the Indians in New England, in the year 1670," in *ET* 403, 405; Gookin, *Collections*, 23, 26–27, 47; Cogley, *Eliot's Mission*, 31, 35, 110, 141–142, 238; Reuben Gold Thwaites, ed., *The Jesuit Relations and Allied Documents: Travels and Explorations of the Jesuit Missionaries in New France 1610–1791* (Cleveland, OH: Burrows Bros., 1896–1901), 53:137–145; John Cotton, "The Missionary Journal of John Cotton, Jr., 1666–1678," ed. Len Travers, in *MHSP*, Series 3, 109:91; Eliot to Boyle, September 6, 1669, in *Some correspondence between the governors and treasurers of the New England company in London and the commissioners of the United Colonies . . .*, ed. John W. Ford (London: Spottiswoode, 1896), 30.

9. Quantisset petition, in MA 30:138a; Eliot to Massachusetts, September 3, 1667, in MA 30:138; *MR* 4(2):357–358; Cogley, *Eliot's Mission*, 155; Gookin, *Collections*, 50.

10. *MR* 4(2):357–359; Quaiapin to Massachusetts, October 7, 1667, in MA 30:140; Connole, *Nipmuck Country*, 80.

11. Williams to Massachusetts, May 7, 1668, in *CRW* 2:576–577.

12. *MR* 4(2):386; Nipmuc submission, in MA 30:146; Eliot, August 22, 1673, in *MHSC* Series 4, 1:128; Gookin, *Collections*, 53; Cogley, *Eliot's Mission*, 155–156; Brooks, *Our Beloved Kin*, 171–173.

13. Eliot, "Brief Narrative," 401–402; Gookin, *Collections*, 33–34, 43; Eliot to commissioners, September 4, 1671, in *MHSP* 17:248–249; Connole, *Nipmuck Country*, 114–115.

14. John Eliot, "Indian Dialogues," in *John Eliot's Indian Dialogues: A Study in Cultural Interaction*, ed. Henry W. Bowden and James P. Ronda (Westport, CT: Greenwood, 1980), 71–72, 75; Eliot to Baxter, June 27, 1671, in F. J. Powicke, "Some Unpublished Correspondence of the Rev. Richard Baxter and the Rev. John Eliot," *Bulletin of the John Rylands Library* 15, no. 2 (1931): 462.

15. Eliot, "Indian Dialogues," 86, 88–89, 98, 102–103, 119.

16. Gookin, *Collections*, 37–39; Richard W. Cogley, "Idealism vs Materialism in the Study of Puritan Missions to the Indians," *Method & Theory in the Study of Religion* 3, no. 2 (1991): 172.

17. Gookin, *Collections*, 38–39.

18. Connole, *Nipmuck Country*, 114–120.

19. Eliot to Boyle, September 6, 1669, in *Some correspondence between the governors and treasurers of the New England company in London and the commissioners of the United Colonies . . .*, ed. John W. Ford (London: Spottiswoode, 1896), 29; Eliot, "Brief Narrative," in *ET* 405–406; Cogley, *Eliot's Mission*, 156.

20. Gookin, *Collections*, 48–49; Eliot, "Brief Narrative," in *ET* 405; Cogley, *Eliot's Mission*, 145.

21. Eliot to commissioners, September 4, 1671, and Eliot to Ashurst, December 1, 1671, both in *MHSP* 17:248–250; Eliot, "Brief Narrative," in *ET* 403–404; Cogley, *Eliot's Mission*, 142–143.

22. Gookin, *Collections*, 49–50, 52–53; Cogley, *Eliot's Mission*, 157.

23. Connole, *Nipmuck Country*, 149.

24. Shawn Wiemann, "Lasting Marks: The Legacy of Robin Cassacinamon and the Survival of the Mashantucket Pequot Nation" (PhD dissertation, University of New Mexico, 2011), 223–225, 235.

25. Michael Leroy Oberg, *Uncas: First of the Mohegans* (Ithaca, NY: Cornell University Press, 2003), 168.

26. John T. Fitch, *Puritan in the Wilderness: A Biography of the Reverend James Fitch, 1622–1702* (Camden, ME: Picton, 1993), 61–106.

27. *CR* 2:157–158.

28. Oberg, *Uncas*, 155–157.

29. Eliot to commissioners, September 4, 1671, in *MHSP* 17:248.

30. Fitch, *Puritan*, 124–125.

31. *ACUC* 2:354.

32. Daniel Coit Gilman, *Historical Discourse, Delivered in Norwich, Connecticut, September 7, 1859* (Boston: Geo. C. Rand and Avery, 1859), 12–13.

33. Gookin, *Collections*, 46–47; Colin G. Calloway, "Wannalancet and Kancagamus: Indian Strategy and Leadership on the New Hampshire Frontier," *Historical New Hampshire* 43, no. 4 (Winter 1988): 270.

34. Gookin, *Collections*, 53–54; *MR* 3:365–366; Neal Salisbury, "Contextualizing Mary Rowlandson: Native Americans, Lancaster and the Politics of Captivity," in *Early America Re-explored*, 119–120; Brooks, *Our Beloved Kin*, 73, 110; Connole, *Nipmuck Country*, 49–50, 55; Jafee, *Wachusett*, 35, 54–59.

35. Gookin, *Collections*, 49–50; Cogley, *Eliot's Mission*, 156; J. H. Temple, *History of Framingham, Massachusetts, Early Known as Danforth's Farms, 1640–1880* (Framingham, MA, 1887), 58–59.

36. Gookin, *Collections*, 50–53; William Hubbard, *The History of the Indian Wars in New England: from the first settlement to the termination of the war with King Philip in 1677*, ed. Samuel G. Drake (Roxbury, MA: W. E. Woodward, 1865), 1:260; "A True Account of the Most Considerable Occurrences that have Happened in the Warre between the English and Indians in New-England," in *The Old Indian Chronicle*, ed. Samuel G. Drake (Boston: Samuel A. Drake, 1867), 279–280; Connole, *Nipmuck Country*, 149–155.

37. Gookin, *Collections*, 54; Cogley, *Eliot's Mission*, 158–160; *MR* 4(2):109–110.

38. Gookin, *Collections*, 68–69.

39. Gookin, *Collections*, 43–45, 48.

40. Eliot, August 22, 1673, in *MHSC* Series 4, 1:124–126; Jean M. O'Brien, *Dispossession by Degrees: Indian Land and Identity in Natick, Massachusetts, 1650–1790* (Cambridge: Cambridge University Press, 1997), 42–51.

41. Gookin, *Collections*, 29, 42, 54–56; Linford D. Fisher, "Native Americans, Conversion, and Christian Practice in Colonial New England, 1640–1730," *Harvard Theological Review* 102, no. 1 (2009): 11–114.

42. Eliot, August 22, 1673, in *MHSC* Series 4, 1:127–128; Jenny Hale Pulsipher, *Swindler Sachem: The American Indian Who Sold His Birthright, Dropped Out of Harvard, and Conned the King of England* (New Haven, CT: Yale University Press, 2018), 112; Eliot to Baxter, October 7, 1657, *Bulletin of the John Rylands Library* 15, no. 1 (1931): 158; Chauncy to Boyle, October 2, 1664, in *Some correspondence between the governors and treasurers of the New England company in London and the commissioners of the United Colonies . . .*, ed. John W. Ford (London: Spottiswoode, 1896), 10.

43. Jenny Hale Pulsipher, "Massacre at Hurtleberry Hill: Christian Indians and English Authority in Metacom's War," *WMQ* 53, no. 3 (July 1996): 461–462; Yasuhide Kawashima, *Puritan Justice and the Indian: White Man's Law in Massachusetts 1630–1763* (Middletown, CT: Wesleyan University Press, 1986).

44. Gookin, *Collections*, 79–82.

45. Gookin, *Collections*, 45; Cogley, *Eliot's Mission*, 143–144; *MR* 4(1):317, 363, 4(2):82–83.

46. Gookin, *Collections*, 83–84.

47. Harry S. Stout, *The New England Soul: Preaching and Religious Culture in Colonial New England* (Oxford: Oxford University Press, 1986), 77–78.

48. Eleazer Mather, *A Serious Exhortation to the Present and Succeeding Generation in New England* (Boston, 1678), 8–9.

49. Theodore Dwight Bozeman, *To Live Ancient Lives: The Primitivist Dimension in Puritanism* (Chapel Hill: University of North Carolina Press, 1988), 287–343.

50. W. Stoughton, *New England's True Interest; Not to Lie* (Cambridge, MA, 1670), 17.

51. Samuel Willard, *Useful Instructions for a professing People in Times of great Security and Degeneracy* (Cambridge, MA, 1673), 52.

52. Mather, *Serious Exhortation*, 20.

53. Hall, *Faithful Shepherd*, 234–237; Samuel Danforth, *A Brief Recognition of New-England's Errand into the Wilderness* (Cambridge, MA, 1671), 10–11, 18.

54. Urian Oakes, *New England Pleaded with, And pressed to consider the things which concern her Peace at least in this her Day* (Cambridge, MA, 1673), 21–22, 62.

55. Michael G. Hall, *The Last American Puritan: The Life of Increase Mather 1639–1723* (Middletown, CT: Wesleyan University Press, 1988), 29–47.

56. Increase Mather, *The Day of Trouble Is Near* (Cambridge, MA, 1674), 11, 21–22, 24, 26, 28, 30–31.

Chapter 13

1. John Frederick Martin, *Profits in the Wilderness: Entrepreneurship and the Founding of New England Towns in the Seventeenth Century* (Chapel Hill: University of North Carolina Press, 1991), 79; Jeremy Dupertuis Bangs, *Indian Deeds: Land Transactions in Plymouth Colony, 1620–1691* (Boston: New England Historic Genelogical Society, 2002), 29–30, 103, 162–163; David J. Silverman, *This Land Is Their Land: The Wampanoag Indians, Plymouth Colony, and the Troubled History of Thanksgiving* (New York: Bloomsbury, 2019), 263–266, 268–269; Allan Greer, *Property and Dispossession: Natives, Empires and Land in Early Modern North America* (Cambridge: Cambridge University Press, 2018), 234, 260–263; Yasuhide Kawashima, *Puritan Justice and the Indian: White Man's Law in Massachusetts 1630–1763* (Middletown, CT: Wesleyan University Press, 1986), 60–70; *MHSC*, Series 1, 2:40; Virginia DeJohn Anderson, *Creatures of Empire: How Domestic Animals Transformed Early America* (Oxford: Oxford University Press, 2004), 145, 177, 189, 193, 195, 215–217, 223–225; William Cronon, *Changes in the Land: Indians, Colonists, and the Ecology of New England* (New York: Hill and Wang, 1983), 131–132; Virginia DeJohn Anderson, "King Philip's Herds: Indians, Colonists, and the Problem of Livestock in Early New England," *WMQ* 51, no. 4 (October 1994): 601–624.

2. Silverman, *This Land*, 250, 269–270; Margaret Ellen Newell, *Brethren by Nature: New England Indians, Colonists, and the Origins of American Slavery* (Ithaca, NY: Cornell University Press, 2015), 113–114, 123–125, 134; Eugene Aubrey Stratton, *Plymouth Colony: Its History and People, 1620–1691* (Salt Lake City: Ancestry, 1986), 107–109.

3. David J. Silverman, "The Church in New England Indian Community Life: A View from the Islands and Cape Cod," in *Reinterpreting New England Indians*, 272–273; David J. Silverman, *Faith and Boundaries: Colonists, Christianity, and Community among the Wampanoag Indians of Martha's Vineyard, 1600–1871* (New York: Cambridge University Press, 2005), 43–48; Roger H. King, *Cape Cod and Plymouth Colony in the Seventeenth Century* (Lanham, MD: University Press of America, 1993), 228–230; *PR* 4:80; Silverman, *This Land*, 325–326.

4. J. Patrick Cesarini, "John Eliot's 'A Brief History of the Mashepog Indians,' 1666," *WMQ* 65, no. 1 (January 2008): 101–104, 114, 123–126, 128–129.

5. John G. Turner, *They Knew They Were Pilgrims: Plymouth Colony and the Contest for American Liberty* (New Haven, CT: Yale University Press, 2020), 253–255; John Cotton, "The Missionary Journal of John Cotton, Jr., 1666–1678," ed. Len Travers, in *MHSP*, Series 3, 109: 52–58.

6. Silverman, *This Land*, 247–248; Silverman, *Faith and Boundaries*, 74; Cotton, "Journal," 71, 81; Silverman, "The Church in the Indian Community Life," 270.

7. Eliot to commissioners, August 25, 1664, in *NEHGR* 9:131–132; Nathaniel Saltonstall, "A Continuation of the State of New England, 1676," in *Narratives of the Indian Wars 1675–1699*, ed. Charles H. Lincoln (New York: Charles Scribner's Sons, 1913), 55; Richard W. Cogley, *John Eliot's Mission to the Indians before King Philip's War* (Cambridge, MA: Harvard University Press, 1999), 196–197; Lisa Brooks, *Our Beloved Kin: A New History of King Philip's War* (New Haven, CT: Yale University Press, 2019), 61–64; Jill Lepore, *The Name of War: King Philip's War and the Origins of American Identity* (New York: Vintage, 1998), 28–47.

8. *RICR* 2:192–195, 198–199.

9. *PR* 4:164–166.

10. Turner, *They Knew They Were Pilgrims*, 245–247.

11. John Eliot, "A Brief Narrative of the Progress of the Gospel amongst the Indians in New England, in the year 1670," in *ET* 400–401.

12. Cotton "Journal," 52–58; Cotton to Commissioners, September 7, 1671, in *CJCJ* 85; Turner, *They Knew They Were Pilgrims*, 252–253. https://www.colonialsociety.org/node/1855.

13. Eliot, "Brief Narrative," 403; Ann Marie Plane, "'The Examination of Sarah Ahhaton': The Politics of 'Adultery' in an Indian Town of Seventeenth-Century Massachusetts," In *Algonquians of New England: Past and Present*, ed. Peter Benes (Boston: Boston University Press, 1993), 14–25; "Examination of Sarah Ahaton," Yale Indian Papers, https://findit.library.yale.edu/yipp/catalog/digcoll:3641, accessed August 12, 2022.

14. John Eliot, "Indian Dialogues," in *John Eliot's Indian Dialogues: A Study in Cultural Interaction*, ed. Henry W. Bowden and James P. Ronda (Westport, CT: Greenwood, 1980), 120–122.

15. Eliot, "Indian Dialogues," 124–129.

16. Eliot, "Indian Dialogues," 143–149.

17. Cole Deposition, in *MHSC* Series 1, 6:211.

18. Bellingham to Prence, March 24, 1671 (with Winslow note), and Hinckley and Bacon to Prence, April 6, 1671, both in WFP-II, MHS; *RICR* 2:370.

19. Gookin to Prence, April 12, and Prence to Gookin, April 26, 1671, both in *MHSC* Series 1, 6:198–201; Hinckley and Bacon to Prence, April 6.

20. William Hubbard, *The History of the Indian Wars in New England: From the first settlement to the termination of the war with King Philip in 1677*, ed. Samuel G. Drake (Roxbury, MA: W. E. Woodward, 1865),1:54–55.

21. Turner, *They Knew They Were Pilgrims*, 258–259; Silverman, *This Land*, 280–282; Prence to Bellingham, May 5, 1671, in WFP-II, MHS.

22. *PR* 5:63–64, 66–67.

23. Eliot to Baxter, June 27, 1671, 462; F. J. Powicke, "Some Unpublished Correspondence of the Rev. Richard Baxter and the Rev. John Eliot," *Bulletin of the John Rylands Library* 15, no. 2 (1931).

24. Eliot to Prence, June 16, 1671; Convers Francis, *Life of John Eliot, the Apostle to the Indians* (New York: Harper & Brothers, 1840), 267–268; Cogley, *Eliot's Mission*, 157, 311, n57.

25. *PR* 5:70–71.

26. Silverman, "The Church in New England Indian Community Life," 268–269; Silverman, *Faith and Boundaries*, 85–87.

27. *PR* 5:64, 74–75; *MHSC*, Series 1, 5:193–197; Brooks, *Our Beloved Kin*, 118–119.

28. *PR* 5:76–77; Prence to Rhode Island, August 23, 1671, in WFP-II, MHS.

29. Natick to mediators, in *MHSC*, Series 1, 6:201–203. The instructions specify the "Missogkonnog" Indians, apparently associated with Philip.

30. Walker to Prence, September 1, 1671, in *MHSC*, Series 1, 6:197–198.

31. Thomas Hutchinson, *The History of the Colony of Massachusett's Bay* (London: M. Richardson, 1765), 281; *PR* 5:77; Paul J. Lindholdt, ed., *John Josselyn, Colonial Traveler: A Critical Edition of Two Voyages to New-England* (Hanover, NH: University Press of New England, 1988), 101; Bellingham to Prence, September 5, 1671, in John Davis Papers, MHS; Rawson to Prence, September 8–9, 1671, in WFP-II, MHS.

32. *PR* 5:78–79.

33. Kristina, *Dry Bones and Indian Sermons: Praying Indians in Colonial America* (Ithaca, NY: Cornell University Press, 2004), 117–118, 138.

34. Prence to Awashonks, October 20, 1671, in *MHSC* Series 1, 5:197.

35. Silverman, *This Land*, 264–265, 286–289; Bangs, *Indian Deeds*, 98, 108–109, 141, 162–164; *PR* 5:138.

36. *PR* 7:191; Brooks, *Our Beloved Kin*, 117–121; Turner, *They Knew They Were Pilgrims*, 265–268; Bangs, *Indian Deeds*, 452; Cotton, "Journal," 94.

37. Easton to Winslow, May 26, 1675, https://ourbelovedkin.com/awikhigan/easton-letter-weetam oodocqr3jpg, accessed August 15, 2022; Brooks, *Our Beloved Kin*, 115, 124–126.

38. Daniel Gookin, *Historical Collections of the Indians in New England* (Boston: Apollo Press, 1792), 56–67, quote on 60; Cotton, "Journal," 92–96.

39. Increase Mather, *A Relation of the Troubles which have happened in New-England, By reason of the Indians there: From the Year 1614 to the Year 1675* (Boston, 1677), 74; *A Report of the Record Commissioners, Containing the Roxbury Land and Church Records*, 2nd ed. (Boston: Rockwell and Churchill, 1884), 192–193; Hubbard, *Wars*, 1:60–61; Increase Mather, *Diary by Increase Mather, March 1675–December, 1676*, ed. Samuel A. Green (Cambridge: Cambridge University Press, 1900), 42; Brooks, *Our Beloved Kin*, 122, Lepore, *War*, 265, fn80.

40. John Easton, "A Relation of the Indyan Warr," in *A Narrative of the Causes which led to Philip's Indian War . . .*, ed. Franklin B. Hough (Albany, NY: J. Munsell, 1858), 3–4; Silverman, *This Land*, 480.

41. *PR* 10:362.

42. Mather, *Relation*, 74.

43. Hubbard, *Wars*, 1:61–62.

44. Mather, *Relation*, 74–75; Yasuhide Kawashima, *Igniting King Philip's War: The John Sassamon Murder Trial* (Lawrence: University of Kansas Press, 2001), 99–100.

45. Easton, "Relation," 1–3.

46. *PR* 10:362–363.

47. Hubbard, *Wars*, 1:63; Easton, "Relation," 4.

48. *PR* 5:159; Kawashima, *Igniting King Philip's War*, 104–105; Brooks, *Our Beloved Kin*, 122–123; Turner, *They Knew They Were Pilgrims*, 274; Silverman, *This Land*, 270–271, 299–300; Bangs, *Indian Deeds*, 476–477.

49. Brooks, *Our Beloved Kin*, 123; Bangs, *Indian Deeds*, 481–484.
50. Increase Mather, "A Brief History of the Warr with the Indians in New-England," in *So Dreadfull a Judgment: Puritan Responses to King Philip's War 1676–1677*, ed. Richard Slotkin and James K. Folsom (Hanover, NH: University Press of New England, 1978), 87.
51. Daniel Gookin, *An Historical Account of the Doings and Sufferings of the Christian Indians in New England, in the Years 1675, 1676, 1677* (New York: Arno Press, 1972), 440–441. Citations from Gookin's *Account* have been edited based on a transcription generously provided by Adrian Chastain Weimer.
52. *PR* 10:363; Nathaniel Saltonstall, "The Present State of New-England with Respect to the Indian War," in *Narratives of the Indian Wars 1675–1699*, ed. Charles H. Lincoln (New York: Charles Scribner's Sons, 1913), 27.
53. *PR* 5:167–168; Kawashima, *Igniting King Philip's War*, 105–106.
54. Easton, "Relation," 4.
55. Turner, *They Knew They Were Pilgrims*, 274.
56. *PR* 5:167; Cotton, "Journal," 97.
57. *PR* 10:363.
58. Williams to Winthrop, June 13, 1675, in *CRW* 2:691.
59. Easton, "Relation," 4.
60. Brown to Winslow, June 11, 1675, in WFP-II, MHS.
61. Winslow to Weetamoo, June 15, 1675, in WFP-II, MHS.
62. *PR* 10:363–364.
63. Gorton Jr. to Winslow, in *MHSC* Series 1, 6:94.
64. Benjamin Church, "Entertaining Passages relating to Philip's War," in *So Dreadfull a Judgment: Puritan Responses to King Philip's War 1676–1677*, ed. Richard Slotkin and James K. Folsom (Hanover, NH: University Press of New England, 1978), 397–400; *PR* 10:363.
65. Easton, "Relation," 6–11.
66. Easton, "Relation," 10–15.
67. *A Brief and True Narration of the Late Wars Risen in New-England* (London, 1675), 4.
68. Daniel R. Mandell, *King Philip's War: Colonial Expansion, Native Resistance, and the End of Indian Sovereignty* (Baltimore: Johns Hopkins University Press, 2010), 48–49.
69. Saltonstall, "Present State," 27; *Brief and True Narration*, 4; *ACUC* 2:364; George Madison Bodge, *Soldiers in King Philip's War* (Baltimore: Genealogical, 1976), 87–88; Winslow to Leverett, June 21, 1675, in MA 67:202; Turner, *They Knew They Were Pilgrims*, 277.

Chapter 14

1. David J. Silverman, *This Land Is Their Land: The Wampanoag Indians, Plymouth Colony, and the Troubled History of Thanksgiving* (New York: Bloomsbury, 2019), 272–275.
2. Williams to Winthrop, June 13 and 25, 1675, in *CRW* 2:691–695; Helen Schatvet Ulmann, ed., *Colony of Connecticut Minutes of the Court of Assistants 1669–1711* (Boston: New England Historic Genealogical Society, 2009), 42–43.
3. J. H. Temple, *History of North Brookfield, Massachusetts* (North Brookfield, MA, 1887), 75–76; Sachem testimonies, in MA 30:169–170.
4. Plymouth Proclamation, June 22, 1675, in *The Correspondence of John Cotton Junior*, ed. Sheila McIntyre and Len Travers (Boston: Colonial Society of Massachusetts, 2009), 108.
5. William Hubbard, *The History of the Indian Wars in New England: From the first settlement to the termination of the war with King Philip in 1677*, ed. Samuel G. Drake (Roxbury, MA: W. E. Woodward, 1865), 1:186–187.
6. John Easton, "A Relation of the Indyan Warr," in *A Narrative of the Causes which led to Philip's Indian War...*, ed. Franklin B. Hough (Albany, NY: J. Munsell, 1858), 16–17, 24.
7. Hubbard, *The History of the Indian Wars*, 1:187–188; Newman to Cotton, April 19, 1676, in *CJCJ*, 150.
8. Mather, "History," 88; Hubbard, *The History of the Indian Wars*, 1:64–66; Easton, "A Relation of the Indian War," 17; Cudworth to Winslow, June 27, 1675, Boston Athenaeum; *A Brief and True Narration of the Late Wars Risen in New-England* (London, 1675), 5; Thomas to Winslow, June 25, 1675, in *MHSC* Series 1, 6:86–87.
9. Nathaniel Saltonstall, "The Present State of New-England with Respect to the Indian War," in *Narratives of the Indian Wars 1675–1699*, ed. Charles H. Lincoln (New York: Charles Scribner's Sons, 1913), 28–29.

10. Mather, "History," 88.
11. *ACUC* 2:463; Leverett to Winslow, June 23, 1675, Boston Athenaeum.
12. George Madison Bodge, *Soldiers in King Philip's War* (Baltimore: Genealogical, 1976), 46–47.
13. Denison's Commission and Instructions, June 26 and 28, 1675, *NEHGR* 23:321–323.
14. Increase Mather, *Diary by Increase Mather, March 1675–December, 1676,* ed. Samuel A. Green (Cambridge: Cambridge University Press, 1900), 13.
15. Bodge, *Soldiers,* 59–63; Douglas E. Leach, "Benjamin Batten and the London Gazette Report on King Philip's War," *NEQ* 36, no. 4 (December 1963): 508; Wait Winthrop to Winthrop, July 4, 1675, in *MHSC* Series 5, 8:402.
16. Williams to Winthrop, June 27, 1675, in *CRW* 2:698–699.
17. Williams to Wait Winthrop, July 7, 1675, in *CRW* 2:702.
18. Stanton to Connecticut, June 30, 1675, in WFP, MHS; New London, June 29, in *A Narrative of the Causes which led to Philip's Indian War . . .,* ed. Franklin B. Hough (Albany, NY: J. Munsell, 1858), 42–43; Wetherell to Winthrop, June 30, 1675, in *MHSC* Series 3, 10:119.
19. Cudworth to Winslow, June 27, 1675, Boston Athenaeum.
20. Winslow to Freeman, June 28, 1675, in WFP-II, MHS; Winslow to Leverett, June 28, Davis Papers, MHS.
21. Benjamin Church, "Entertaining Passages relating to Philip's War," in *So Dreadfull a Judgment: Puritan Responses to King Philip's War 1676–1677,* ed. Richard Slotkin and James K. Folsom (Hanover, NH: University Press of New England, 1978), 402; Hubbard, *The History of the Indian* Wars, 1:69; Douglas Edward Leach, *Flintlock and Tomahawk: New England in King Philip's War* (New York: Macmillan, 1958), 51–52; Massachusetts to Pynchon, July 10, 1675, in WP, MHS.
22. Hubbard, *The History of the Indian Wars,* 1:70–72; Church, "Entertaining Passages," 403–404; Massachusetts to Pynchon, July 10, 1675, in WP, MHS; Leach, *Flintlock,* 40; Bodge, *Soldiers,* 87–89; Increase Mather, "A Brief History of the Warr with the Indians in New-England," in *So Dreadfull a Judgment: Puritan Responses to King Philip's War 1676–1677,* ed. Richard Slotkin and James K. Folsom (Hanover, NH: University Press of New England, 1978), 89; Leach, "Batten," 513.
23. Massachusetts to Pynchon, July 10, 1675, in WP, MHS; Daniel Gookin, *An Historical Account of the Doings and Sufferings of the Christian Indians in New England, in the Years 1675, 1676, 1677* (New York: Arno Press, 1972), 434, 441–443; Leach, "Batten," 514–515; *MR* 5:44–45; Patrick M. Malone, *The Skulking Way of War: Technology and Tactics among the New England Indians* (Lanham, MD: Madison Books, 1991), 52–55, 61, 99.
24. Freeman to Winslow, July 3, 1675, in *MHSC* Series 1, 6:91; Eric B. Schultz and Michael J. Tougias, *King Philip's War: The History and Legacy of America's Forgotten Conflict* (Woodstock, NY: Countryman, 1999), 92.
25. Hubbard, *The History of the Indian* Wars, 1:72–73; "James Quanapohit's Relation," in J. H. Temple, *History of North Brookfield, Massachusetts* (North Brookfield, MA, 1887), 112; *Brief and True Narration,* 5.
26. Church, "Entertaining Passages," 404–409; Hubbard, *The History of the Indian* Wars, 1:79–83; Winslow to Cudworth, July 6, 1675, and Cudworth to Winslow, July 9, 1675, both in WFP-II, MHS; Winslow to Leverett, July 6, 1675, Davis Papers, MHS; Schultz and Tougias, *King Philip's War,* 238–241.
27. Easton, "Relation," 18–20; Lisa Brooks, *Our Beloved Kin: A New History of King Philip's War* (New Haven, CT: Yale University Press, 2019), 158–159.
28. Pynchon to Winthrop, July 2, 1675, in *PP* 1:137.
29. Massachusetts to Connecticut, July 5 and 10, 1675, in CA-War-I, 5, 7; Fitch to Allyn, July, 1675, in *CR* 2:336–337; Leach, *Flintlock,* 56; Gookin, *Account,* 445; Mason to Winthrop, July 14, 1675, *CHSC* 21:213–214; Saltonstall, "Present State," 32; Shawn Wiemann, "Lasting Marks: The Legacy of Robin Cassacinamon and the Survival of the Mashantucket Pequot Nation" (PhD dissertation, University of New Mexico, 2011), 207–250, 286–287; *CR* 2:574–576.
30. Williams to Wait Winthrop, July 7, 1675, in *CRW* 2:701; Williams to Whipple, 1669, in *CRW* 2:599.
31. Sanders to Fitz-John Winthrop, July 3, 1675, in *MHSC* Series 5, 1:426–427.
32. Wait Winthrop to Winthrop, July 8, 1675, *CHSC* 21:210–211.
33. *MHSC,* Series 5, 8:168; Robert C. Black III, *The Younger John Winthrop* (New York: Columbia University Press, 1966), 297–298, 327, 329, 339.
34. Winthrop to Wait (misidentified), July 9, 1675, in *MHSC* Series 5, 8:170–171.

35. Winthrop to Wait, July 8, 1675, in WFP, MHS.
36. Wait to Winthrop, July 9, 1675, in *A Letter Written by Capt. Wait Winthrop from Mr. Smiths in Narragansett to Govr. John Winthrop of the Colony of Connecticut* (Society of Colonial Wars, 1919), in WFP, MHS 19; Wait to Winthrop, July 8, 1675, *CHSC* 21:209–210; Saunders to Wait Winthrop, July 7, 1675, in WFP, MHS.
37. Wait to Winthrop, July 9, 1675, in WFP, MHS, 19–23.
38. Franklin B. Hough, ed. *A Narrative of the Causes which led to Philip's Indian War . . .*, (Albany, NY: J. Munsell, 1858), 62–63; Gold Order, July 14, 1675, *CHSC* 21:212–213.
39. Winthrop to Savage and Winthrop to Wait (misidentified), July 12, 1675, in *MHSC* Series 5, 8:171–174.
40. Hubbard, *The History of the Indian Wars*, 1:75–79.
41. Tomson to Winslow, July 10, 1675, Davis Papers, MHS; Schultz and Tougias, *King Philip's War*, 111–115.
42. Winslow to Leverett, July 18, 1675, in WFP-II, MHS.
43. Saltonstall, "Present State," 30–31; *Brief and True Narrative*, 5.
44. Mather, "History," 90.
45. Hubbard, *The History of the Indian Wars*, 2:41.
46. Church, "Entertaining Passages," 410–411; Hubbard, *The History of the Indian* Wars, 1:83; Winslow to Leverett, July 11, 1675, and Leverett to Winslow, July 17, 1675, both in WFP-II, MHS.
47. Gookin, *Account*, 443, 460–461.
48. Massachusetts to Pynchon, July 10, 1675, in WP, MHS.
49. Curtis Report, July 16, 1675, in Levi Badger Chase, *The Bay Path and along the Way* (Norwood, MA: Plimpton, 1919), 136–140; Leach, *Flintlock*, 85.
50. Curtis Report, July 16, 1675, 140–143.
51. *Brief and True Narration*, 5; Saltonstall, "Present State," 30; Mather, "History," 90–91.
52. Bradford to Cotton, July 21, 1675, *CJCJ* 109.
53. Cudworth to Winslow, July 20, 1675, in *MHSC*, Series 1, 6:84; Bradford to Cotton, July 21, 1675, *CJCJ* 109.
54. Winslow to Leverett and Winslow to Cudworth, July 18, 1675, in WFP-II, MHS.
55. Hubbard, *The History of the Indian Wars*, 1:84–87; Bradford to Cotton, July 21, 1675, *CJCJ* 109; Gookin, *Account*, 444; Cudworth to Winslow, July 20, 1675, in *MHSC*, Series 1, 6:84–85.
56. Leach, *Flintlock*, 69; Hubbard, *The History of the Indian Wars*, 1:86; Henchman to Leverett, July 31, 1675, in George Madison Bodge, *Soldiers in King Philip's War* (Baltimore: Genealogical, 1976), 49–50.
57. Winslow to Leverett, July 28, 1675, in MA 67:229; Winslow to Winthrop, July 29, 1675, in *MHSC* Series 5, 1:429–430; Winslow to Leverett, July 6, 1675, Davis Papers, MHS.
58. Walley to Cotton, July 25 and August 2, 1675, *CJCJ* 111–113; Jeremiah 9:12.
59. Eliot to Winthrop, July 24, 1675, in *MHSC* Series 5, 1:424–426.
60. Curtis Report, July 24, 1675, 151–153; Daniel Gookin, *Historical Collections of the Indians in New England* (Boston: Apollo Press, 1792), 49–50.
61. Hutchinson's Commission, July 27, 1675, in George Madison Bodge, *Soldiers in King Philip's War* (Baltimore: Genealogical, 1976)106; Brooks, *Our Beloved Kin*, 181.
62. Thomas Wheeler, "A Thankful Remembrance of God's Mercy to Several Persons at Quabaug or Brookfield," in *So Dreadfull a Judgment: Puritan Responses to King Philip's War 1676–1677*, ed. Richard Slotkin and James K. Folsom (Hanover, NH: University Press of New England, 1978), 243–244; Bodge, *Soldiers*, 107; Gookin, *Account*, 448; *Brief and True Narration*, 6; Saltonstall, "Present State," 35.
63. Thomas to Winslow, August 11, 1675, in Richard LeBaron Bowen, *Early Rehoboth: Documented Historical Studies of Families and Events in This Plymouth Colony Township*, 4 vols. (Rehoboth, MA: Rumford, 1948), 3:92. https://archive.org/details/earlyrehobothdoc03bowe.
64. Henchman to Leverett, July 31, 1675, in George Madison Bodge, *Soldiers in King Philip's War* (Baltimore: Genealogical, 1976), 49–50.
65. Newman to Henchman and Hunt to Henchman, July 30, 1675, in Richard LeBaron Bowen, *Early Rehoboth: Documented Historical Studies of Families and Events in This Plymouth Colony Township*, 4 vols. (Rehoboth, MA: Rumford, 1948), 3:89–91.
66. Newman to Thomas, July 30, 1675, in Richard LeBaron Bowen, *Early Rehoboth: Documented Historical Studies of Families and Events in This Plymouth Colony Township*, 4 vols. (Rehoboth, MA: Rumford, 1948), 3:91.

67. Henchman to Leverett, July 31, 1675, in Bodge, *Soldiers*, 49–50; Fitz-John to Winthrop, July 26, 1675, *CHSC* 21:217–218; Fitz-John Winthrop, July 28, 1675, in *MHSC* Series 6, 3:447–448; Gookin, *Account*, 445; Saltonstall, "Present State," 32.

68. Thomas Report, in Richard LeBaron Bowen, *Early Rehoboth: Documented Historical Studies of Families and Events in This Plymouth Colony Township*, 4 vols. (Rehoboth, MA: Rumford, 1948), 3:94–99; Gookin, *Account*, 445–446; Hubbard, *The History of the Indian* Wars, 1:89–90; Henchman to Governor, July 31, 1675, in Bodge, *Soldiers*, 49–50; Church, "Entertaining Passages," 412.

69. Wheeler, "A Thankful Remembrance," 244–246; Gookin, *Account*, 447–448; Brooks, *Our Beloved Kin*, 185.

70. Wheeler, "A Thankful Remembrance," 246, 249–250; Louis E. Roy, *Quaboag Plantation alias Brookefield: A Seventeenth Century Massachusetts Town* (West Brookfield, MA: Heffernan, 1965), 73, 157–159; Schultz and Tougias, *King Philip's War*, 155–157; Temple, *History of North Brookfield*, 90; Pynchon to Winthrop, August 7, 1675, in *PP* 1:142.

71. Wheeler, "A Thankful Remembrance," 240–241, 246–250.

72. Pynchon to Connecticut, August 4 and 6, 1675, in *PP* 1:138–139; *CR* 2:345–346.

73. Wheeler, "A Thankful Remembrance," 248, 250–254; Hubbard, *The History of the Indian* Wars, 1:100–102; Gookin, *Account*, 449.

74. Thomas Hutchinson, *The History of the Colony of Massachusetts Bay*, 2nd ed., 3 vols. (London, 1765) 1:293–294. The original says August 5, but that was a Thursday.

Chapter 15

1. Thomas to Winslow, August 11, 1675, in Richard LeBaron Bowen, *Early Rehoboth: Documented Historical Studies of Families and Events in This Plymouth Colony Township*, 4 vols. (Rehoboth, MA: Rumford, 1948), 3:92, https://archive.org/details/earlyrehobothdoc03bowe; Thomas Report, in Richard LeBaron Bowen, *Early Rehoboth: Documented Historical Studies of Families and Events in This Plymouth Colony Township*, 4 vols. (Rehoboth, MA: Rumford, 1948), 3:99, https://archive.org/details/earlyrehobothdoc03bowe.

2. Increase Mather, *Diary by Increase Mather, March 1675–December, 1676*, ed. Samuel A. Green (Cambridge: Cambridge University Press, 1900), 15; Nathaniel Saltonstall, "The Present State of New-England with Respect to the Indian War," in *Narratives of the Indian Wars 1675–1699*, ed. Charles H. Lincoln (New York: Charles Scribner's Sons, 1913), 38; Increase Mather, "A Brief History of the Warr with the Indians in New-England," in *So Dreadfull a Judgment: Puritan Responses to King Philip's War 1676–1677*, ed. Richard Slotkin and James K. Folsom (Hanover, NH: University Press of New England, 1978), 91–92.

3. Thomas Wheeler, "A Thankful Remembrance of God's Mercy to Several Persons at Quabaug or Brookfield," in *So Dreadfull a Judgment: Puritan Responses to King Philip's War 1676–1677*, ed. Richard Slotkin and James K. Folsom (Hanover, NH: University Press of New England, 1978), 255.

4. William Hubbard, *The History of the Indian Wars in New England: From the first settlement to the termination of the war with King Philip in 1677*, ed. Samuel G. Drake (Roxbury, MA: W. E. Woodward, 1865), 1:104.

5. Saltonstall, "Present State," 26.

6. *A Brief and True Narration of the Late Wars Risen in New-England* (London, 1675), 3.

7. Saltonstall, "Present State," 28; J. H. Temple, *History of North Brookfield, Massachusetts* (North Brookfield, MA, 1887), 101.

8. Saltonstall, "Present State," 26.

9. Dennis A. Connole, *The Indians of the Nipmuck Country in Southern New England, 1630–1750: An Historical Geography* (Jefferson, NC: McFarland, 2001), 23–25; Gaffee, *Wachusett*, 64–65; James Drake, "Symbol of a Failed Strategy: The Sassamon Trial, Political Culture, and the Outbreak of King Philip's War," *American Indian Culture and Research Journal* 19, no. 2 (1995): 111–141; Neal Salisbury, "Indians and Colonists in Southern New England after the Pequot War: An Uneasy Balance," in *The Pequots in Southern New England: The Fall and Rise of an American Indian Nation*, ed. Laurence M. Hauptman and James D. Wherry (Norman: University of Oklahoma Press, 1990), 82, 89; Ruth Barnes Moynihan, "The Patent and the Indians: The Problem of Jurisdiction in Seventeenth-Century New England," *American Indian Culture and Research Journal* 2, no. 1 (1977): 15; Richard W. Cogley, *John Eliot's Mission*

to the Indians before King Philip's War (Cambridge, MA: Harvard University Press, 1999), 196–197; Lisa Brooks, *Our Beloved Kin: A New History of King Philip's War* (New Haven, CT: Yale University Press, 2019), 163–165.

10. Pynchon to Winthrop, August 19, 1675, in *PP* 1:146–147; Peter A. Thomas, *In the Maelstrom of Change: The Indian Trade and Cultural Process in the Middle Connecticut River Valley, 1635–1665* (New York: Garland, 1990), 308.

11. *CR* 2:348–350; Pynchon to Winthrop, August 12, 1675, in *PP* 1:145.

12. Leete to Winthrop, August 16, 1675, in *MHSC* Series 4, 7:576.

13. Hubbard, *The History of the Indian Wars*, 1:106–108; Mosely to Leverett, August 16, 1675, in George Madison Bodge, *Soldiers in King Philip's War* (Baltimore: Genealogical, 1976), 66–67; Pynchon to Allyn, August 22, 1675, in *PP* 1:148; Cotton to Walley, September 23, 1675, *CJCJ* 116; Brooks, *Our Beloved Kin*, 196; Stoddard, YIP, https://findit.library.yale.edu/yipp/catalog/digcoll:3866, accessed August 15, 2022.

14. Stoddard, YIP; Mather, "History," 94–95; Pynchon to Allyn, August 25, 1675, in *PP* 1:149; *CR* 2:353–354.

15. Hubbard, *The History of the Indian Wars*, 1:109–110; Stoddard to Winthrop, August 25, 1675, *CHSC* 21:223; Connecticut to Fitz-John Winthrop and Mason, September 5, 1675, in *MHSC* Series 6, 3:449; Mather, "History," 93, 95–96; Brooks, *Our Beloved Kin*, 194; Lisa Brooks, "Ktsi Amiskw, the Great Beaver," https://ourbelovedkin.com/awikhigan/ktsi-amiskw, accessed August 15, 2022; Fitch to Winthrop, August 30, 1675, in WFP, MHS.

16. Stoddard to Winthrop, August 25, 1675, *CHSC* 21:223.

17. Stoddard, YIP.

18. Allyn to Winthrop, September 10, 1675, in WP, MHS.

19. Pynchon to Allyn, August 25, 1675, in *PP* 1:149.

20. Thomas, *Maelstrom*; Peter A. Thomas, "Bridging the Cultural Gap: Indian/White Relations," in *Early Settlement in the Connecticut Valley: A Coloquium at Historic Deerfield*, ed. John W. Ifkovic and Martin Kaufman (Deerfield, MA : Historic Deerfield, 1984), 14–17; Richard I. Melvoin, *New England Outpost: War and Society in Colonial Deerfield* (New York: W. W. Norton, 1989), 49–58.

21. *CR* 2:351–353, 355–356.

22. Petition (incorrect date), in MA 67:220.

23. Henchman to Leverett, July 31, 1675, in George Madison Church, *Soldiers in King Philip's War* (Baltimore: Genealogical, 1976), 49–50; Benjamin Church, "Entertaining Passages relating to Philip's War," in *So Dreadfull a Judgment: Puritan Responses to King Philip's War 1676–1677*, ed. Richard Slotkin and James K. Folsom (Hanover, NH: University Press of New England, 1978), 411–412; Winslow to Leverett, July 28, 1675, in MA 67:229; *PR* 5:173–174; John Easton, "A Relation of the Indyan Warr," in *A Narrative of the Causes which led to Philip's Indian War . . .*, ed. Franklin B. Hough (Albany, NY: J. Munsell, 1858), 21.

24. Saltonstall, "Present State," 30.

25. Eliot Petition, August 13, 1675, *ACUC* 2:451–453, quoting Revelation 11:15.

26. Council, September 22, 1675, in MA 30:177a; John G. Turner, *They Knew They Were Pilgrims: Plymouth Colony and the Contest for American Liberty* (New Haven, CT: Yale University Press, 2020), 253–255; John Cotton, "The Missionary Journal of John Cotton, Jr., 1666–1678," ed. Len Travers, in *MHSP*, Series 3, 284; Saltonstall, "Present State," 30.

27. *CR* 2:354–356, 358–362; Jason W. Warren, *Connecticut Unscathed: Victory in the Great Narragansett War, 1675–1676* (Norman: University of Oklahoma Press, 2014), 78–82, 90.

28. Hubbard, *The History of the Indian Wars*, 1:110–111; Mather, "History," 96; Connecticut to Fitz-John Winthrop and Mason, September 5, 1675, in *MHSC* Series 6, 3:448; *CR* 2:363; Bodge, *Soldiers*, 127; Michael J. Puglisi, *Puritans Besieged: The Legacies of King Philip's War in the Massachusetts Bay Colony* (Lanham, MD: University Press of America, 1991), 102.

29. Mayhew to Winthrop, September 10, 1675, in *MHSC* Series 4, 7:43.

30. Hubbard, *The History of the Indian Wars*, 1:111–112.

31. Pynchon to Leverett, September 8, 1675, in *PP* 1:152–153; Massachusetts to Pynchon, September 15, 1675, in MA 67:255.

32. Mather, "History" 97.

33. Denison to Waldron, August 17, 1675, *NEHGR*, 23:324.

34. Daniel Gookin, *Historical Collections of the Indians in New England* (Boston: Apollo Press, 1792), 47; Daniel Gookin, *An Historical Account of the Doings and Sufferings of the Christian Indians in New England, in the Years 1675, 1676, 1677* (New York: Arno Press, 1972), 462–464.

35. Gookin, *Account*, 436–437.
36. Anthony and James to Massachusetts, July 19, 1675, in MA 67:220.
37. Saltonstall, "Present State," 39; Gookin, *Account*, 456–457; Brooks, *Our Beloved Kin*, 192.
38. Gookin, *Account*, 436, 449–451, 456, 460–461; Mather, "History," 92; Bodge, *Soldiers*, 352; Samuel A. Green, *Groton during the Indian Wars* (Cambridge: Cambridge University Press, 1883), 18.
39. Gookin, *Account*, 455–457, 461; *RCAMB* 1:53–54.
40. Saltonstall, "Present State," 40.
41. Gookin, *Account*, 467.
42. Mosely to Leverett, October 5, 1675, in Bodge, *Soldiers*, 68.
43. Saltonstall, "Present State," 39–40; Gookin, *Account*, 466.
44. Gookin, *Account*, 453–454, 460, 462; Saltonstall, "Present State," 41.
45. John G. Metcalf, *Annals of the Town of Mendon from 1659 to 1880* (Providence, RI: E. L. Freeman, 1880), 65–66.
46. Gookin, *Account*, 467; Upham to Council, October 1, 1675, in Bodge, *Soldiers*, 287; John Frederick Martin, *Profits in the Wilderness: Entrepreneurship and the Founding of New England Towns in the Seventeenth Century* (Chapel Hill: University of North Carolina Press, 1991), 25–27.
47. Gookin, *Account*, 457–461; Brooks, *Our Beloved Kin*, 197.
48. *RCAMB* 1:53–54.
49. Saltonstall, "Present State," 27–28.
50. Gookin, *Account*, 454, 459, 462; Jenny Hale Pulsipher, *Subjects unto the Same King: Indians, English, and the Contest for Authority in Colonial New England* (Philadelphia: University of Pennsylvania Press, 2015), 152–153; *Brief and True Narration*, 6.
51. *ACUC* 2:364–365.
52. *PR* 5:202; Smith to Winthrop, August 5, 1675, in Richard LeBaron Bowen, *Early Rehoboth: Documented Historical Studies of Families and Events in This Plymouth Colony Township*, 4 vols. (Rehoboth, MA: Rumford, 1948), 3:92. https://archive.org/details/earlyre hobothdoc03bowe 3:101.
53. Connecticut to Smith, August 8, 1675, in Charles Hoadly, ed., *Hoadly Memorial Early Letters and Documents Relating to Connecticut 1643–1709* (Hartford: Connecticut Historical Society, 1932), 18.
54. Fitch to Winthrop, August 30, 1675, in WFP, MHS; Smith to Winthrop, September 3, 1675, in Daniel Berkeley Updike, *Richard Smith: First English Settler of the Narragansett Country, Rhode Island* (Boston: Merrymount, 1937), 110–111.
55. Gookin, *Account*, 465–466; Saltonstall, "Present State," 43.
56. Gorton to Winthrop, September 11, 1675, in *MHSC* Series 4, 7:628–631.
57. Smith to Winthrop, September 3 and 12, 1675, in Updike, *Smith*, 110–112.
58. Leete to Winthrop, September 21 and 23, 1675, in *MHSC* Series 4, 7:577–580.
59. Stanton to Winthrop, September 22, 1675, in WFP, MHS; Brooks, *Our Beloved Kin*, 205–207.
60. Saltonstall, "Present State," 44–45; Smith Depositions, September 29, 1675, in MA 30:177; *CR* 2:371.
61. Mather, *Diary*, 43.
62. Mather, "History," 97–99; Cotton to Walley, September 23, 1675, *CJCJ* 116; *CR* 2:368; Hubbard, *The History of the Indian Wars*, 1:112–119; Allyn to Fitz-John Winthrop, September 20, 1675, in *MHSC* Series 6, 3:450–451; Bodge, *Soldiers*, 133–137, 140; Sylvester Judd, *History of Hadley* (Springfield, MA: H. R. Hunting, 1905), 141.
63. Daniel R. Mandell, *King Philip's War: Colonial Expansion, Native Resistance, and the End of Indian Sovereignty* (Baltimore: Johns Hopkins University Press, 2010), 77–81.
64. Mather, "History," 102–103.
65. *New-England's Present Sufferings under Their Cruel Neighboring Indians* (London, 1675), 3–5, 7–8; Quaker Testimony, August 24, 1675, in WP, MHS.

Chapter 16

1. Massachusetts to Pynchon, September 15 and 24, 1675, in MA 67:255, 263–264.
2. George Madison Bodge, *Soldiers in King Philip's War* (Baltimore: Genealogical, 1976), 143; Douglas Edward Leach, *Flintlock and Tomahawk: New England in King Philip's War* (New York: Macmillan, 1958), 185–187; Jenny Hale Pulsipher, *Subjects unto the Same King: Indians, English, and the Contest for Authority in Colonial New England* (Philadelphia: University of Pennsylvania Press, 2015), 160–168.

3. Commissioners' Orders, September 24, 1675, in *NEHGR* 23:23–24.
4. *CR* 2:369, 372; Mason to Fitz-John Winthrop, September 6, 1675, in WP, MHS; Pynchon to Massachusetts, September 30, 1675, in *PP* 1:154–156; Nathaniel Saltonstall, "The Present State of New-England with Respect to the Indian War," in *Narratives of the Indian Wars 1675–1699*, ed. Charles H. Lincoln (New York: Charles Scribner's Sons, 1913), 47; Mosely to Leverett, October 5, 1675, in George Madison Bodge, *Soldiers in King Philip's War* (Baltimore: Genealogical, 1976), 68; Michael Leroy Oberg, *Uncas: First of the Mohegans* (Ithaca, NY: Cornell University Press, 2003), 179.
5. Pynchon to Massachusetts, October 8, 1675, in *PP* 1:157–158; Leach, *Flintlock*, 89; William Hubbard, *The History of the Indian Wars in New England: From the first settlement to the termination of the war with King Philip in 1677*, ed. Samuel G. Drake (Roxbury, MA: W. E. Woodward, 1865), 1:120–123; Appleton to Leverett, October 12, 1675, in Isaac Appleton Jewett, *Memorial of Samuel Appleton of Ipswich, Massachusetts* (Cambridge, MA: Rolles and Hougthon, 1850), 99–100; Pynchon to Russell, October 5, 1675, in *PP* 1:156; Russell to Massachusetts, October 6, 1675, in MA 67:288.
6. Pynchon to Joseph Pynchon, October 20, 1675, in *PP* 1:164–165; Pynchon to Massachusetts, October 8, 1675, and Pynchon to Leverett, October 8 and 12, 1675, both in *PP* 1:157–163.
7. Increase Mather, "A Brief History of the Warr with the Indians in New-England," in *So Dreadfull a Judgment: Puritan Responses to King Philip's War 1676–1677*, ed. Richard Slotkin and James K. Folsom (Hanover, NH: University Press of New England, 1978), 104; Increase Mather, *Diary by Increase Mather, March 1675–December, 1676*, ed. Samuel A. Green (Cambridge: Cambridge University Press, 1900), 18.
8. Hubbard, *The History of the Indian Wars*, 1:123.
9. Leverett to Russell, October 9, 1675, in *NEHGR* 48:319–321.
10. Massachusetts to Pynchon, October 4, 1675, in George Madison Bodge, *Soldiers in King Philip's War* (Baltimore: Genealogical, 1976), 146–147.
11. Leverett to Pynchon, October 9, 1675, in *NEHGR* 48:319.
12. Saltonstall, "Present State," 47–49.
13. *MR* 5:46.
14. Daniel Gookin, *An Historical Account of the Doings and Sufferings of the Christian Indians in New England, in the Years 1675, 1676, 1677* (New York: Arno Press, 1972), 451–452, 467–471.
15. Michael G. Hall, *The Last American Puritan: The Life of Increase Mather 1639–1723* (Middletown, CT: Wesleyan University Press, 1988).
16. Mather, *Diary*, 18.
17. Mather, "History," 105; Mather, *Diary*, 44; Hall, *Last American Puritan*, 107.
18. Gookin, *Account*, 462–465, 471–472; *MR* 5:57–58; Massachusetts to Henchman, September 30, 1675, and Safe Conduct, in MA 30:178–179; Numphow's Report, October 12, 1675, in MA 30:182; Lisa Brooks, *Our Beloved Kin: A New History of King Philip's War* (New Haven, CT: Yale University Press, 2019), 209–211; Richard W. Cogley, *John Eliot's Mission to the Indians before King Philip's War* (Cambridge, MA: Harvard University Press, 1999), 147.
19. Gookin, *Account*, 472–474; *MR* 5:56–57; *RCAMB* 1:53–54; Bodge, *Soldiers*, 267.
20. *MR* 5:64.
21. Gookin, *Account*, 471–472, 474–475; *MR* 5:58, 68; Denison, October 28, 1675, in *NEHGR* 23:327; Brooks, *Our Beloved Kin*, 218; Michael Leroy Oberg, *Dominion and Civility: English Imperialism and Native America, 1585–1685* (Ithaca, NY: Cornell University Press, 1999), 82.
22. Williams to Leverett, October 11, 1675, in *CRW* 2:704–706.
23. Paine, October, and Smith, October 8, 1675, in *Further Letters on King Philip's War* (Providence, RI: Freeman, 1923), 12–16; Margaret Ellen Newell, *Brethren by Nature: New England Indians, Colonists, and the Origins of American Slavery* (Ithaca, NY: Cornell University Press, 2015), 183–185.
24. Pray to Oliver, October 20, 1675, in *MHSC* Series 5, 1:105–110.
25. *ACUC* 2:360–361.
26. Smith to Winthrop, October 27, 1675, in *Smith*, 112–113; *CR* 2:379.
27. Gookin, *Account*, 475–477; "James Quanapohit's Relation," in J. H. Temple, *History of North Brookfield, Massachusetts* (North Brookfield, MA, 1887), 113–114; Massachusetts to Smith, November 6, 1675, in MA 68:46b.
28. Hubbard, *The History of the Indian Wars*, 1:128–129; Gookin, *Account*, 477–480; Sill Instructions, November 2, 1675, in George Madison Bodge, *Soldiers in King Philip's War* (Baltimore: Genealogical, 1976), 267–268; *MR* 5:51; Henchman to Massachusetts, November

3 and 5, 1675, in John G. Metcalf, *Annals of the Town of Mendon from 1659 to 1880* (Providence, RI: E. L. Freeman, 1880), 71–72.

29. Henchman, November 10, 1675, in *NEHGR* 25:10–11; Hubbard, *The History of the Indian Wars*, 1:129–131.

30. Gookin, *Account*, 480–482.

31. Appleton to Leverett, October 12, 1675, in Jewett, *Appleton*, 102; Bodge, *Soldiers*, 142.

32. Jewett, *Appleton*, 98–105, 109–110; Connecticut to commissioners, October 7, 1675, *CHSC* 21:227–228.

33. Jewett, *Appleton*, 106, 113–117; *CR* 2:265–268; Mosely to Leverett, October 16, 1675, in George Madison Bodge, *Soldiers in King Philip's War* (Baltimore: Genealogical, 1976), 69; Appleton to Leverett, October 17, 1675, in Jewett, *Appleton*, 108.

34. Saltonstall, "Present State," 48–49; Hubbard, *The History of the Indian Wars*, 1:123–125, 133; Mather, "History," 105–106; Warner Examination, February 25, 1675, in *A Narrative of the Causes which led to Philip's Indian War . . .*, ed. Franklin B. Hough (Albany, NY: J. Munsell, 1858), 143–144; Schultz and Michael J. Tougias, *King Philip's War: The History and Legacy of America's Forgotten Conflict* (Woodstock, NY: Countryman, 1999), 180.

35. Jewett, *Appleton*, 121–148; *MR* 5:66–67; *CR* 2:381; Hubbard, *The History of the Indian Wars*, 1:126–128, 131–134; Leach, *Flintlock*, 99.

36. Mather, *Diary*, 19, 44; *MR* 5:59–64.

37. Saltonstall, "Present State," 49; Nathaniel Saltonstall, "A Continuation of the State of New England, 1676," in *Narratives of the Indian Wars 1675–1699*, ed. Charles H. Lincoln (New York: Charles Scribner's Sons, 1913), 54.

38. "A Farther Brief and True Narrative of the late Wars risen in New-England," in *The Old Indian Chronicle*, ed. Samuel G. Drake (Boston: Samuel A. Drake, 1867), 317–318.

39. Gookin to Smith, November, 1675, in MA 30:188.

40. Gookin, *Account*, 482–485; Eliot to Boyle, December 17, 1675, in *MHSP* 17:252; Walley to Cotton, November 18, 1675, *CJCJ* 119.

41. Council, December 9, 1675, in MA 30:190; Gookin, *Account*, 484–485; Chelmsford Petition, December 13, 1675, in MA 30:186.

42. Gookin, *Account*, 529–531; Pulsipher, *Subjects*, 142–143; Council, November 12, 1675, in MA 30:185a.

43. Council, November 26 and 30 and December 16, 1675, in MA 30:185b–c, 187.

44. Gookin, *Account*, 485–486; Eliot to Boyle, December 17, 1675, in *MHSP* 17:251–252; *RICR* 193.

Chapter 17

1. William Hubbard, *The History of the Indian Wars in New England: From the first settlement to the termination of the war with King Philip in 1677*, ed. Samuel G. Drake (Roxbury, MA: W. E. Woodward, 1865), 1:92.

2. Gookin to Smith, November, 1675, in MA 30:188; Nathaniel Saltonstall, "A Continuation of the State of New England, 1676," in *Narratives of the Indian Wars 1675–1699*, ed. Charles H. Lincoln (New York: Charles Scribner's Sons, 1913), 55; David J. Silverman, *This Land Is Their Land: The Wampanoag Indians, Plymouth Colony, and the Troubled History of Thanksgiving* (New York: Bloomsbury, 2019), 315.

3. Commissioners' Draft, in *MHSC* Series 5, 9:99.

4. Douglas Edwards Leach, "A New View of the Declaration of War against the Narragansetts, 1675," *Rhode Island History* 15, no. 2 (April 1956): 33–41.

5. *ACUC* 2:357, 456–457; *MR* 5:69; Allyn to Fitz-John Winthrop, November 23, 1675, in WFP, MHS.

6. Winslow's Commission, November, 1675, in *MHSC* Series 3, 1:66–68.

7. *ACUC* 2:457–458.

8. Arthur J. Worrall, "Persecution, Politics, and War: Roger Williams, Quakers, and King Philip's War," *Quaker History* 66, no. 2 (Autumn 1977): 73–86.

9. John Easton, "A Relation of the Indyan Warr," in *A Narrative of the Causes which led to Philip's Indian War . . .*, ed. Franklin B. Hough (Albany, NY: J. Munsell, 1858), 23, 26–27, 29–30; Clarke, November 19, 1675, in *Some Further Papers Relating to King Philip's War* (Providence: Society of Colonial Wars in the State of Rhode Island, 1931), 11.

10. Williams to Winthrop, December 18, 1675, *CRW* 2:708–709.

11. Easton, "Relation," 26–27; Douglas Edward Leach, *Flintlock and Tomahawk: New England in King Philip's War* (New York: Macmillan, 1958), 120.

12. Leach, *Flintlock*, 119–122; *ACUC* 2:358–359.

13. Increase Mather, "A Brief History of the Warr with the Indians in New-England," in *So Dreadfull a Judgment: Puritan Responses to King Philip's War 1676–1677*, ed. Richard Slotkin and James K. Folsom (Hanover, NH: University Press of New England, 1978), 107.

14. Walley to Cotton, November 18, 1675, *CJCJ* 119.

15. Bishop to Mather, 1676, in *MHSC*, Series 2, 5:300.

16. Saltonstall, "Continuation," 62–64; Leverett to Williamson, December 18, 1675, in *NNRC*, https://nativenortheastportal.com/node/16590, accessed August 16, 2022; Leach, *Flintlock*, 123.

17. Hubbard, *Wars*, 1:138–139; Newman to Cotton, December 16, 1675, *CJCJ* 120; *PR* 5:182–183; *MHSP* Series 2, 1:230; Nathaniel Saltonstall, "The Present State of New-England with Respect to the Indian War," in *Narratives of the Indian Wars 1675–1699*, ed. Charles H. Lincoln (New York: Charles Scribner's Sons, 1913), 48.

18. Oliver, January 26, 1676, in George Madison Bodge, *Soldiers in King Philip's War* (Baltimore: Genealogical, 1976), 174; Dudley to Leverett, December 15, 1675, in George Madison Bodge, *Soldiers in King Philip's War* (Baltimore: Genealogical, 1976), 192; Benjamin Church, "Entertaining Passages relating to Philip's War," in *So Dreadfull a Judgment: Puritan Responses to King Philip's War 1676–1677*, ed. Richard Slotkin and James K. Folsom (Hanover, NH: University Press of New England, 1978), 412–413; Newman to Cotton, December 16, 1675, *CJCJ*, 120; Easton, "Relation," 27–28.

19. Dudley to Leverett, December 15, 1675, in Bodge, *Soldiers*, 192; Winthrop to Treat, December 18, 1675, in *MHSC* Series 5, 8:174–175; Easton, "Relation," 27; Saltonstall, "A Continuation," 57, 61; Oliver, January 26, 1676, in Bodge, *Soldiers*, 174; Hubbard, *Wars*, 1:139–143; Newman to Cotton, December 16, 1675, *CJCJ* 121; Leach, *Flintlock*, 127; Lisa Brooks, *Our Beloved Kin: A New History of King Philip's War* (New Haven, CT: Yale University Press, 2019) 240; Dudley to Leverett, December 21, 1675, in Bodge, *Soldiers*, 193; Church, "Entertaining Passages," 415.

20. Oliver, January 26, in Bodge, *Soldiers*, 174; Hubbard, *Wars*, 1:143–146; Benjamin Thompson, "New England's Crisis," *So Dreadfull a Judgment: Puritan Responses to King Philip's War 1676–1677*, ed. Richard Slotkin and James K. Folsom (Hanover, NH: University Press of New England, 1978), 223; Dudley to Leverett, December 21, 1675, 193; Bodge, *Soldiers*, 289; Saltonstall, "A Continuation," 58.

21. Hubbard, *Wars*, 1:146–148; *CR* 3:5–6n.

22. Dudley to Leverett, December 21, 1675, 193; Shove to Cotton, December 31, 1675, *CJCJ* 123.

23. Church, "Entertaining Passages," 413–415.

24. *CR* 3:5–6n.

25. Church, "Entertaining Passages," 415–416.

26. Dudley to Leverett, December 21, 1675, 193–194; Mather, "History," 108; Saltonstall, "A Continuation," 59, 61; Oliver, January 26, 1676, in Bodge, *Soldiers*, 174; Hubbard, *Wars*, 1:147–149; *CR* 3:5–6n; Bull Petition, in George Madison Bodge, *Soldiers in King Philip's War* (Baltimore: Genealogical, 1976), 484.

27. *A Letter Written by Dr. Simon Cooper of Newport on the Island of Rhode Island to the Governor and Council of the Connecticut Colony* (Providence, RI: Standard, 1916), 21.

28. Shove to Cotton, December 31, 1675, *CJCJ* 123; Mather, "History," 108; Bull Petition, 484; Bodge, *Soldiers*, 465.

29. Oliver, January 26, in Bodge, *Soldiers*, 174; Dudley to Leverett, December 21, 1675, 193–194; Hubbard, *Wars*, 1:150–152; Newman to Cotton, January 10, 1676, *CJCJ* 127; Mather, "History," 108; Saltonstall, "A Continuation," 59, 65; "James Quanapohit's Relation," in J. H. Temple, *History of North Brookfield, Massachusetts* (North Brookfield, MA, 1887), 116–117; Williams to Leverett, January 14, 1676, *CRW* 2:712; Eric B. Schultz and Michael J. Tougias, *King Philip's War: The History and Legacy of America's Forgotten Conflict* (Woodstock, NY: Countryman, 1999), 262–265.

30. Mather, "History," 108–109; Increase Mather, *Diary by Increase Mather, March 1675–December, 1676*, ed. Samuel A. Green (Cambridge: Cambridge University Press, 1900), 45.

31. Shove to Cotton, December 31, 1675, *CJCJ* 123.

32. Cotton to Mather, January 3, 1676, *CJCJ* 125.

33. "A Farther Brief and True Narrative of the late Wars risen in New-England," in *The Old Indian Chronicle*, ed. Samuel G. Drake (Boston: Samuel A. Drake, 1867), 316.
34. Easton, "Relation," 27–31.
35. New Haven and Fairfield to Connecticut, January 10, 1676, *CHSC* 21:230.
36. Wait Winthrop, *Some Meditations Concerning Our Honorable Gentlemen and Fellow-Soldiers, in Pursuit of those Barbarous Natives in the Narragansett Country* (New London, 1721).
37. Commissioners to Connecticut, December 25, 1675, *CHSC* 21:229–230; *PR* 5:184.
38. Hubbard, *Wars*, 1:154, 157–159; *CR* 2:391–395, 398; Saltonstall, "A Continuation," 65–66; *ACUC* 2:412; Shove to Cotton, December 31, 1675, *CJCJ* 123.
39. *A Copy of a Letter Written to the Soldiers that were at Narragansett in the Army* (Boston, 1707).
40. Leete to Winthrop, January 5, 1676, in *MHSC*, Series 4, 7:583.
41. Hubbard, *Wars*, 1:161.
42. Saltonstall, "A Continuation," 65–66; Leach, *Flintlock*, 136–137; Hubbard, *Wars*, 1:157–162; Williams to Leverett, January 14, 1676, *CRW* 2:712–713.
43. Easton, "Relation," 29–31; commissioners to Winslow, January 11, 1676, in WFP, MHS.
44. *CR* 2:396; Palmer to Winslow, January 16, 1676, in *MHSC* Series 1, 6:89–90.
45. Williams to Leverett, January 14, 1676, *CRW* 2:711–714; Oliver, January 26, 1676, 1, in Bodge, *Soldiers*, 75; Hubbard, *Wars*, 1:162; *CR* 2:401.
46. Gookin, *Account*, 486.
47. "James Quanapohit's Relation," 112–114; Quanapohit testimony, in J. H. Temple, *History of Framingham, Massachusetts, Early Known as Danforth's Farms, 1640–1880* (Framingham, MA, 1887), 59–60.
48. "James Quanapohit's Relation," 114–117; Quanapaug's Information, in *MHSC* Series 1, 6:206–208; Brooks, *Our Beloved Kin*, 248.
49. "James Quanapohit's Relation," 114–118; Gookin, *Account*, 487–489; *CR* 2:397–398; "Squaw Interview," 1676, in MA 30:202a.
50. Mather, *Diary*, 45.
51. Hubbard, *Wars*, 1:164–165; *CR* 2:402; Nathaniel Saltonstall, "A New and Further Narrative of the State of New-England," in *Narratives of the Indian Wars 1675–1699*, ed. Charles H. Lincoln (New York: Charles Scribner's Sons, 1913), 79; Franklin B. Hough, ed., *A Narrative of the Causes which led to Philip's Indian War . . .* (Albany, NY: J. Munsell, 1858), 177.
52. Saltonstall, "Continuation," 66; Douglas Edward Leach, *A Rhode Islander Reports on King Philip's War: The Second William Harris Letter of August, 1676* (Providence: Rhode Island Historical Society, 1963), 1–3, 16–17; Worrall, "Persecution, Politics, and War," 75; *CRW* 2:506–513, 556–570, 597, 639.
53. Palmes to Connecticut, January 26, 1676, in *CR* 2:402–403; Brooks, *Our Beloved Kin*, 245; Williams to Commissioners, 1678, *CRW* 2:764; Bodge, *Soldiers*, 204.
54. Stanton, February 9, in *Narrative of the Causes*, 140–141; Saltonstall, "Continuation," 67–68; Hubbard, *Wars*, 1:165; Church, "Entertaining Passages," 417; Leach, *Flintlock*, 141–142; "A True Account of the Most Considerable Occurrences that have Happened in the Warre between the English and the Indians in New-England," in *The Old Indian Chronicle*, ed. Samuel G. Drake (Boston: Samuel A. Drake, 1867), 250; Mary Rowlandson, "The Sovereignty & Goodness of God," in *So Dreadfull a Judgment: Puritan Responses to King Philip's War 1676–1677*, ed. Richard Slotkin and James K. Folsom (Hanover, NH: University Press of New England, 1978), 318.
55. Cotton to Walley, February 4, 1676, *CJCJ* 134.
56. Walley to Cotton, February 16, 1676, *CJCJ* 136.
57. Mather, "History," 109–110.
58. Mather, *Diary*, 23–25, 45.
59. J. H. Temple, *History of Framingham, Massachusetts, Early Known as Danforth's Farms, 1640–1880* (Framingham, MA, 1887), 72–78; Richard W. Cogley, *John Eliot's Mission to the Indians before King Philip's War* (Cambridge, MA: Harvard University Press, 1999), 126; Gookin, *Collections*, 44; Hinckley to wife, February 10, 1676, in *MHSC* Series 4, 5:1; John Eliot, "A Brief Narrative of the Progress of the Gospel amongst the Indians in New England, in the year 1670," in *ET* 403.
60. Gookin, *Account*, 491–492; Wamesit Petition, in MA 30:191; Groton to Massachusetts, February 6, 1676, Samuel A. Green, *Groton during the Indian Wars* (Cambridge: Cambridge University Press, 1883), 23.

Chapter 18

1. Daniel Gookin, *An Historical Account of the Doings and Sufferings of the Christian Indians in New England, in the Years 1675, 1676, 1677* (New York: Arno Press, 1972), 489–490; Dennis A. Connole, *The Indians of the Nipmuck Country in Southern New England, 1630–1750: An Historical Geography* (Jefferson, NC: McFarland, 2001), 142–143, 180; Lisa Brooks, *Our Beloved Kin: A New History of King Philip's War* (New Haven, CT: Yale University Press, 2019), 247.

2. Mary Rowlandson, "The Sovereignty & Goodness of God," in *So Dreadfull a Judgment: Puritan Responses to King Philip's War 1676–1677*, ed. Richard Slotkin and James K. Folsom (Hanover, NH: University Press of New England, 1978), 323–325; William Hubbard, *The History of the Indian Wars in New England: From the first settlement to the termination of the war with King Philip in 1677*, ed. Samuel G. Drake (Roxbury, MA: W. E. Woodward, 1865), 1:165–166.

3. Gookin, *Account*, 490.

4. Douglas Edward Leach, *Flintlock and Tomahawk: New England in King Philip's War* (New York: Macmillan, 1958), 158–159; Rowlandson, "Sovereignty," 325; Hinckley to wife, February 10, 1676, in *MHSC* Series 4, 5:1; George Madison Bodge, *Soldiers in King Philip's War* (Baltimore: Genealogical, 1976), 353.

5. Salisbury, "Contextualizing Mary Rowlandson," 108–109, 115, 123; Massachusetts to Connecticut, March 11, 1676, in CA-War-I, 45b–c.

6. Rowlandson, "Sovereignty," 325–329; "James Quanapohit's Relation," 116; Brooks, *Our Beloved Kin*, 70, 257.

7. Rowlandson, "Sovereignty," 329–330.

8. Walley to Cotton, February 16, 1676, *CJCJ* 136; Belknap extracts from Mather diary, in *MHSP* 3:319; Increase Mather, "A Brief History of the Warr with the Indians in New-England," in *So Dreadfull a Judgment: Puritan Responses to King Philip's War 1676–1677*, ed. Richard Slotkin and James K. Folsom (Hanover, NH: University Press of New England, 1978), 109; "News from New England," in *The Old Indian Chronicle*, ed. Samuel G. Drake (Boston: Samuel A. Drake, 1867), 304.

9. Page Deposition, February 15, 1676, in MA 68:136; Gookin, *Account*, 491, 494; Shepard Deposition, February 15, 1676, in MA 68:136b.

10. Hubbard, *Wars*, 1:169–171; Gookin, *Account*, 493–494; Rowlandson, "Sovereignty," 329; Newman to Cotton, March 14, 1676, *CJCJ* 138–140; Wilson to Massachusetts, February 14, 1676, and Medfield to Massachusetts, February 21, 1676, in William S. Tilden, *History of the Town of Medfield, Massachusetts* (Boston: Geo. H. Ellis, 1887), 81–82, 87.

11. Rowlandson, "Sovereignty," 330–331.

12. Petition, February 22, 1676, in MA 68:140–141.

13. Gookin, *Account*, 497–500; Mather, "History," 111.

14. Gookin, *Account*, 495–497; Hubbard, *Wars*, 1:223; Jenny Hale Pulsipher, *Subjects unto the Same King: Indians, English, and the Contest for Authority in Colonial New England* (Philadelphia: University of Pennsylvania Press, 2015), 143–144.

15. *MR* 5:72.

16. Notes, February 28, 1676, in MA 30:193–193a.

17. Deposition March 14, 1676, in MA 30:192; Council, in MA 30:193b; Scott Petition, in MA 30:196; *RCAMB* 1:60–61.

18. Council, February 29, 1676, in MA 30:194a; MA 30:197, 200a.

19. Council, March 8 and 20, 1676, in MA 30:195, 198a; Mayes Petition, March 29, 1676, in MA 30:199.

20. Council, March 14, 1676, in MA 30:197.

21. Dorchester Petition, March 23, 1676, in MA 30:198b.

22. Wharton to Winsley, February 10, 1676, CSP, colonial series 9:350–351 (item 816).

23. Cobbet to Mather, 1677, *NEHGR* 7:214–215.

24. "A Short Account of the General Concerns of New York," in *Documents Relative to the Colonial History of the State of New York*, ed. E. B. O'Callaghan, Berthold Fernow, John Romeyn Brodhead, and Edmund Bailey O'Callaghan (Albany, NY, 1856–1857) 3:255; Franklin B. Hough, ed., *A Narrative of the Causes which led to Philip's Indian War . . .* (Albany, NY: J. Munsell, 1858), 145–149; Brooks, *Our Beloved Kin*, 271–274; Michael Leroy Oberg, *Dominion and Civility: English Imperialism and Native America, 1585–1685* (Ithaca, NY: Cornell University Press, 1999), 160–166; *CR* 2:407.

25. *CR* 2:407–409, 417–422; Winthrop to Stanton, February 12, 1676, in *MHSC* Series 5, 8:175–176; Allyn to Winthrop, February 18, 1676, in *MHSP* Series 1, 13:234; Winthrop to Leete, February 29, 1676, in *MHSC* Series 5, 8:176–177.

26. *PR* 5:177–178, 183; David J. Silverman, *This Land Is Their Land: The Wampanoag Indians, Plymouth Colony, and the Troubled History of Thanksgiving* (New York: Bloomsbury, 2019), 326–328.

27. Mather, "History," 111; *PR* 5:185, 187.

28. Massachusetts to Connecticut, March 11, 1676, in CA-War-I, 45b–c; Gookin, *Account*, 500.

29. Kattenanit Petition, February 14, 1676, in Neal Salisbury, *The Sovereignty and Goodness of God: With Related Documents*, 2nd ed. (Boston: Bedford/St. Martin's, 2017), 131.

30. Gookin, *Account*, 491, 501–502.

31. Gookin, *Account*, 502–505; Brooks, *Our Beloved Kin*, 289–290; Fairbanks Petition, in MA 30:200.

32. Rowlandson, "Sovereignty," 330–334, 336, 358; Quanapohit testimony, in J. H. Temple, *History of Framingham, Massachusetts, Early Known as Danforth's Farms, 1640–1880* (Framingham, MA, 1887), 59–60.

33. Hubbard, *Wars*, 1:204–205; Mather, "History," 111–112; Rowlandson, "Sovereignty," 334–337; Nathaniel Saltonstall, "A New and Further Narrative of the State of New-England," in *Narratives of the Indian Wars 1675–1699*, ed. Charles H. Lincoln (New York: Charles Scribner's Sons, 1913), 81, 89; Bodge, *Soldiers*, 98; Brooks, *Our Beloved Kin*, 265–269.

34. Hubbard, *Wars*, 1:205; "True Account," in *The Old Indian Chronicle*, ed. Samuel G. Drake (Boston: Samuel A. Drake, 1867), 253; Gookin, *Account*, 505; Savage to Massachusetts, March 16, 1676, in *MHSC* Series 3, 1:68–70; Russell to Massachusetts, March 16, 1676, in MA 68:163–164; Saltonstall, "A New and Further Narrative," 81.

35. Hubbard, *Wars*, 1:195–196; Newman to Cotton, March 14, 1676, *CJCJ* 140; Samuel A. Green, *Groton during the Indian Wars* (Cambridge: Cambridge University Press, 1883), 21; Michael J. Puglisi, *Puritans Besieged: The Legacies of King Philip's War in the Massachusetts Bay Colony* (Lanham, MD: University Press of America, 1991), 110.

36. Hubbard, *Wars*, 1:193–194, 196–200; Saltonstall, "A New and Further Narrative," 83; Mather, "History," 112–113.

37. Saltonstall, "A New and Further Narrative," 78.

38. Hubbard, *Wars*, 1:220–222.

39. Massachusetts to Savage, March 14, 1676, in MA 68:160; Denison, March 27, 1676, in Bodge, *Soldiers*, 214; Willard to Massachusetts, March 29, 1676, in Bodge, *Soldiers*; Green, *Groton*, 39–43.

40. Hubbard, *Wars*, 1:179; Saltonstall, "A New and Further Narrative," 81–82; Leach, *Flintlock*, 166; Mather, "History," 113.

41. *RICR* 2:533–535.

42. *CR* 2:418, 422.

43. Hubbard, *Wars*, 1:178–179; Saltonstall, "A New and Further Narrative," 84; *PR* 5:204–206; Leach, *Flintlock*, 166; Increase Mather, *Diary by Increase Mather, March 1675–December, 1676*, ed. Samuel A. Green (Cambridge: Cambridge University Press, 1900), 45; Mather, "History," 112.

44. *CR* 2:423.

45. Hubbard, *Wars*, 1:205–207; Saltonstall, "A New and Further Narrative," 85–86; Mather, "History," 113–114; Savage to Massachusetts, March 28, 1676, in MA 68:189.

46. Brocklebank to Massachusetts, March 28, 1676, in Bodge, *Soldiers*, 213; Massachusetts to Savage, April 1, 1676, in Bodge, *Soldiers*, 99; *CR* 2:433; Hubbard, *Wars*, 1:208–209, 247; Mather, "History," 113–115.

47. *PR* 5:187; Rowlandson, "Sovereignty," 338; Saltonstall, "A New and Further Narrative," 84–85; Hubbard, *Wars*, 1:173–177; Douglas Edward Leach, *A Rhode Islander Reports on King Philip's War: The Second William Harris Letter of August, 1676* (Providence: Rhode Island Historical Society, Rehoboth 1963), 40–43; Newman to Cotton, March 27, 1676, in Richard LeBaron Bowen, *Early: Documented Historical Studies of Families and Events in This Plymouth Colony Township*, 4 vols. (Rehoboth, MA: Rumford, 1948), 3:14, and April 17, *CJCJ* 149; Massachusetts to Savage, April 1, 1676, in Bodge, *Soldiers*, 99; Lawrence K. LaCroix, "Captain Pierce's Fight: An Investigation into a King Philip's War Battle and Its Remembrance and Memorialization" (MA thesis, University of Massachusetts, 2011).

48. Winslow to Massachusetts, March 27, 1676, in MA 68:177; *PR* 5:192–193.

49. Newman to Cotton, April 19, 1676, *CJCJ* 149; Kingsley to minister, May, 1676, in *Rehoboth*, 3:20–22; *CR* 2:433.

50. Newman to Cotton, April 19, 1676, *CJCJ* 148–150; Williams, April 1, 1676, *CRW* 2:721–724; Hubbard, *Wars*, 1:181; Saltonstall, "A New and Further Narrative," 86–87; Leach, *A Rhode*

Islander, 44–47; Harris to Williamson, August 12, 1676, in *RIHSC* 10:171; Eric B. Schultz and Michael J. Tougias, *King Philip's War: The History and Legacy of America's Forgotten Conflict* (Woodstock, NY: Countryman, 1999), 282.

51. Council, March 31, 1676, in MA 10:233.
52. Hinckley to Leverett, 1676, Davis Papers, MHS.

Chapter 19

1. Harris to Williamson, August 12, 1676, in *RIHSC* 10:163, 172–175; Douglas Edward Leach, *A Rhode Islander Reports on King Philip's War: The Second William Harris Letter of August, 1676* (Providence: Rhode Island Historical Society, 1963), 18–19, 34–37, 58–61.
2. CR 2:411–412, 427–429; William Hubbard, *The History of the Indian Wars in New England: From the first settlement to the termination of the war with King Philip in 1677*, ed. Samuel G. Drake (Roxbury, MA: W. E. Woodward, 1865), 2:55–59; Leach, *A Rhode Islander*, 48–49; Kevin McBride, Doug Currie, David Naumec, Ashley Bissonnette, Noah Fellman, Laurie Pasteryak Lamarre, Heather Manwaring, and Meagan Lankowsky, "The 1676 Battle of Nipsachuck: Identification and Evaluation" (2013), 19–20, 42.
3. Nathaniel Saltonstall, "A New and Further Narrative of the State of New-England," in *Narratives of the Indian Wars 1675–1699*, ed. Charles H. Lincoln (New York: Charles Scribner's Sons, 1913), 91; Hubbard, *Wars*, 1:182–183, 2:59–60; Leach, *A Rhode Islander*, 50–51, 58–59; CR 2:432; Harris to Williamson, August 12, 1676, in *RIHSC* 10:172; Increase Mather, "A Brief History of the Warr with the Indians in New-England," in *So Dreadfull a Judgment: Puritan Responses to King Philip's War 1676–1677*, ed. Richard Slotkin and James K. Folsom (Hanover, NH: University Press of New England, 1978), 115.
4. CR 2:432; Saltonstall, "A Further Narrative," 89–90; Increase Mather, *Diary by Increase Mather, March 1675–December, 1676*, ed. Samuel A. Green (Cambridge: Cambridge University Press, 1900), 27–28.
5. Benjamin Thompson, *A Funeral Tribute to the Honorable Dust of that most Charitable Christian, Unbiased Politician, and Unimitable Pyrotechnist, John Winthrop Esq* (Boston, 1676).
6. RICR 193; Hubbard, *A General History of New England, from the Discovery to 1680*, in *MHSC* Series 2, 6:642; *Records of the Suffolk County Court 1671–1680: Part II, PCSM*, vol. 30 (Cambridge: Cambridge University Press, 1933), 695, https://www.colonialsociety.org/node/274.
7. Massachusetts to Secretary of State, April 5, 1676, in *Documentary History of the State of Maine* (Portland, ME: Bailey and Noyes, 1869–1916), series 2, 6:110.
8. Massachusetts to Savage, April 1, 1676, in George Madison Bodge, *Soldiers in King Philip's War* (Baltimore: Genealogical, 1976), 98–99.
9. Daniel Gookin, *An Historical Account of the Doings and Sufferings of the Christian Indians in New England, in the Years 1675, 1676, 1677* (New York: Arno Press, 1972), 506, 509; George Madison Bodge, *Soldiers in King Philip's War* (Baltimore: Genealogical, 1976), 101; Savage council, in MA 68:235.
10. Hubbard, *Wars*, 1:189–190, 194–195, 201, 209–210, 221–222, 228; Mary Rowlandson, "The Sovereignty & Goodness of God," in *So Dreadfull a Judgment: Puritan Responses to King Philip's War 1676–1677*, ed. Richard Slotkin and James K. Folsom (Hanover, NH: University Press of New England, 1978), 343; Mather, "History," 115–116; CR 2:433; Cotton to Walley, April 17, 1676, *CJCJ* 147; Keith to Hinckley, April 17, 1676, in *MHSC* Series 4, 5:6–8; Edward Leach, *Flintlock and Tomahawk: New England in King Philip's War* (New York: Macmillan, 1958), 168–169; Rawson to Winslow, April 21, 1676, in Bodge, *Soldiers*, 226; Plymouth to Massachusetts, April 26, 1676, in MA 68:234; Saltonstall, "A New and Further Narrative," 94–95.
11. Gookin, *Account*, 506–507, 509–510; Council, April 14, 1676, in MA 30:201; Hunting Orders, in MA 68:211–211a.
12. *PR* 5:193–194.
13. Cotton to Newman, April 17, 1676, *CJCJ* 146.
14. Walley to Cotton, April 17, 1676, *CJCJ* 144–145.
15. Cooper to Hinckley, April 14, 1676, in *MHSC* Series 4, 5:2–4; *PR* 5:185.
16. Williams to Hinckley, April 16, 1676, in *MHSC* Series 4, 5:5–6.
17. Keith to Hinckley, April 17, 1676, in *MHSC* Series 4, 5:6–8.
18. Newman to Cotton, April 19, 1676, *CJCJ* 148–150.
19. Plymouth to Massachusetts, April 26, 1676, in MA 68:234.
20. Rowlandson, "Sovereignty," 338–339, 347–348.

21. Rowlandson, "Sovereignty," 340–346, 351; Lisa Brooks, *Our Beloved Kin: A New History of King Philip's War* (New Haven, CT: Yale University Press, 2019), 263–265, 279; Salisbury, "Contextualizing Mary Rowlandson," 127–128.

22. Rowlandson, "Sovereignty," 359.

23. Massachusetts to Connecticut, March 11, 1676, in CA-War-I, 45b–c; Gookin, *Account*, 507–508; Increase Mather, *Diary by Increase Mather, March 1675–December, 1676*, ed. Samuel A. Green (Cambridge: Cambridge University Press, 1900), 25; Massachusetts to sachems, March 31, 1676, and sachems to Massachusetts, in Henry S. Nourse, ed., *The Early Records of Lancaster, Massachusetts 1643–1725* (Lancaster, MA: W. J. Coulter, 1884), 110–111; Hubbard, *Wars*, 1:248; Salisbury, "Contextualizing Mary Rowlandson," 130–131.

24. Rowlandson, "Sovereignty," 347–352; Sachems to Massachusetts, in Nourse, *Lancaster*, 111–112.

25. Rowlandson, "Sovereignty," 352–353; Kristina Bross, *Dry Bones and Indian Sermons: Praying Indians in Colonial America* (Ithaca, NY: Cornell University Press, 2004), 12–13; Karen Ordahl Kupperman, *Settling with the Indians: The Meeting of English and Indian Cultures in America, 1580–1640* (Totowa NJ: Rowman and Littlefield, 1980), 147–148, 168–169, 179.

26. Sudbury Petition, October 11, 1676, in Bodge, *Soldiers*, 223–224.

27. Cowell Deposition, June 19, 1676, in Bodge, *Soldiers*, 225–226; Hubbard, *Wars*, 1:210, 212; Leach, *Flintlock*, 173–174.

28. Hubbard, *Wars*, 1:211; Gookin, *Account*, 510–511; Saltonstall, "A Further Narrative," 92–93.

29. Sudbury Petition, October 11, 1676, in Bodge, *Soldiers*, 224; Warren and Peirce Petition, 1679, in Bodge, *Soldiers*, 227; Gookin, *Account*, 510.

30. Saltonstall, "A Further Narrative," 93–94; Hubbard, *Wars*, 1:211–212; "True Account," in *The Old Indian Chronicle*, ed. Samuel G. Drake (Boston: Samuel A. Drake, 1867), 255–256.

31. Gookin, *Account*, 510–512; "True Account," 255; Brooks, *Our Beloved Kin*, 287; Warren and Peirce Petition, in Bodge, *Soldiers*, 227; Hubbard, *Wars*, 1:213.

32. Jacob to Massachusetts, April 22 and 24, 1676, in Bodge, *Soldiers*, 215–216.

33. Gookin, *Account*, 510; Sudbury Petition, in Bodge, *Soldiers*, 224;

34. Saltonstall, "A Further Narrative," 94.

35. Rowlandson, "Sovereignty," 354–356, 362; *MR* 5:82–83.

36. Rowlandson, "Sovereignty," 356–358; Pauline Turner Strong, *Captive Selves, Captivating Others: The Politics and Poetics of Colonial American Captivity Narratives* (Boulder, CO: Westview, 1999), 100.

37. Rowlandson, "Sovereignty," 360; *MR* 5:82–83; Russell to Connecticut, May 15, 1676, in CA-War-I, 71; Hoar to Massachusetts, 1682, in *English Origins of New England Families, NEHGR* Series 2, 2:363.

38. Rowlandson, "Sovereignty," 361–362; Hubbard, *Wars*, 1:216, 223–224; Mather, "History," 117–118.

39. *CR* 2:423–425, 435.

40. Hubbard, *Wars*, 1:183; Mather, "History," 116–117; Connecticut to Massachusetts, April 27, 1676, in MA 68:235a.

41. Bodge, *Soldiers*, 232–237.

42. Turner, April 25, 1676, in Bodge, *Soldiers*, 238.

43. Marshall, April 27, 1676, in MA 68:202.

44. Pessicus's Messenger, *CHSC* 21:241–242.

45. Hadley to Connecticut, April 29, 1676, in CA-War-I, 67a; Hadley to Massachusetts, April 29, 1676, in Bodge, *Soldiers*, 242.

46. Connecticut to Pessicus, May 1, 1676, in *CR* 2:439–440; Connecticut to Hadley, May 1, 1676, in CA-War-I, 67b.

Chapter 20

1. R. Hutchinson, *The Warr in New-England Visibly Ended* (London, 1677), 1.

2. Edward Perry, "A Warning to New England," in *A Memorable Account of the Christian Experiences and Living Testimonies of That Faithful Servant of Christ Edward Perry* (Philadelphia, 1726), 63–64, 68–69, 72, 76.

3. William Hubbard, *The Happiness of a People in the Wisdom of Their Rulers* (Boston, 1676), 25, 31, 41.

4. Hubbard, *Happiness*, 31, 46–48.
5. Hubbard, *Happiness*, 49–54, 60.
6. Hubbard, *Happiness*, 54–59.
7. Hubbard, *Happiness*, 61–63.
8. Anne Kusener Nelsen, "King Philip's War and the Hubbard-Mather Rivalry," *WMQ* 27, no. 4 (October 1970): 621–624; Dennis R. Perry, "'Novelties and Stile Which All Out-Do': William Hubbard's Historiography Reconsidered," *EAL* 29, no. 2 (1994): 169–170.
9. *MR* 277–78; *RICR* 193.
10. Increase Mather, *Diary by Increase Mather, March 1675–December, 1676*, ed. Samuel A. Green (Cambridge: Cambridge University Press, 1900), 29.
11. Increase Mather, "A Brief History of the Warr with the Indians in New-England," in *So Dreadfull a Judgment: Puritan Responses to King Philip's War 1676–1677*, ed. Richard Slotkin and James K. Folsom (Hanover, NH: University Press of New England, 1978), 121–122.
12. Bishop to Mather, July 8, 1676, in *MHSC* Series 4, 8:299–300.
13. Increase Mather, "An Earnest Exhortation to the Inhabitants of New-England," in *So Dreadfull a Judgment: Puritan Responses to King Philip's War 1676–1677*, ed. Richard Slotkin and James K. Folsom (Hanover, NH: University Press of New England, 1978), 170–174.
14. Mather, "Exhortation," 174–181, 196.
15. Mather, "Exhortation," 186–190.
16. Mather, "Exhortation," 191–195, 198–199.
17. *CR* 2:280–283, 383, 389; Connecticut ministers, *CHSC* 21:234–239; James Fitch, *An Explanation of the Solemn Advice, Recommended by the Council in Connecticut colony* (Boston, 1683), 67–72.
18. Mather, "History," 146–147.
19. Kingsley, May, 1676, in Richard LeBaron Bowen, *Early Rehoboth: Documented Historical Studies of Families and Events in This Plymouth Colony Township*, 4 vols. (Rehoboth, MA: Rumford, 1948), 3:20–23.
20. Walker, "Captain Peirce and his Courageous Company," in Richard LeBaron Bowen, *Early Rehoboth: Documented Historical Studies of Families and Events in This Plymouth Colony Township*, 4 vols. (Rehoboth, MA: Rumford, 1948), 3:34–38.
21. Walker, "The Stratagem of the Indians," in Richard LeBaron Bowen, *Early Rehoboth: Documented Historical Studies of Families and Events in This Plymouth Colony Township*, 4 vols. (Rehoboth, MA: Rumford, 1948), 3:39.
22. Walker, "The First Smile of God in This Land," in Richard LeBaron Bowen, *Early Rehoboth: Documented Historical Studies of Families and Events in This Plymouth Colony Township*, 4 vols. (Rehoboth, MA: Rumford, 1948), 3:40–41, 45–46.
23. Thompson, "Crisis," 216–217; Jane Donahue Eberwein, "'Harvardine quil': Benjamin Thompson's Poems on King Philip's War," *EAL* 28, no. 1 (1993): 8–12.
24. Benjamin Thompson, "New England's Crisis," in *So Dreadfull a Judgment: Puritan Responses to King Philip's War 1676–1677*, ed. Richard Slotkin and James K. Folsom (Hanover, NH: University Press of New England, 1978), 219–221.
25. Thompson, "Crisis," 224–227, 229–230.
26. Eberwein, "'Harvardine quil,'" 13.

Chapter 21

1. *MR* 5:96–97; William Hubbard, *The History of the Indian Wars in New England: From the first settlement to the termination of the war with King Philip in 1677*, ed. Samuel G. Drake (Roxbury, MA: W. E. Woodward, 1865), 1:225; Increase Mather, "A Brief History of the Warr with the Indians in New-England," in *So Dreadfull a Judgment: Puritan Responses to King Philip's War 1676–1677*, ed. Richard Slotkin and James K. Foldom (Hanover, NH: University Press of New England, 1978, 118.
2. Increase Mather, *Diary by Increase Mather, March 1675–December, 1676*, ed. Samuel A. Green (Cambridge: Cambridge University Press, 1900), 46.
3. Daniel Gookin, *An Historical Account of the Doings and Sufferings of the Christian Indians in New England, in the Years 1675, 1676, 1677* (New York: Arno Press, 1972), 506, 509; George Madison Bodge, *Soldiers in King Philip's War* (Baltimore: Genealogical, 1976), 101; Savage council, in MA 68:235, 516–517; *MR* 5:84; William Kellaway, *The New England Company 1649–1776: Missionary Society to the American Indians* (New York: Barnes & Noble, 1962), 117.

4. Gookin, *Account*, 517–518; General Court, May 10, in MA 30:201b; *MR* 5:85–87, 94–96; *RICR* 193.
5. Russell to Connecticut, May 15, 1676, in CA-War-I, 71.
6. *MR* 5:82–83; Dennis A. Connole, *The Indians of the Nipmuck Country in Southern New England, 1630–1750: An Historical Geography* (Jefferson, NC: McFarland, 2001), 203.
7. Hubbard, *Wars*, 1:217–218; Mather, "History," 118.
8. *MR* 5:93–94.
9. Henry S. Nourse, ed., *The Early Records of Lancaster, Massachusetts 1643–1725* (Lancaster, MA: W. J. Coulter, 1884), 113–114; "True Account," in *The Old Indian Chronicle*, ed. Samuel G. Drake (Boston: Samuel A. Drake, 1867), 272; Lisa Brooks, *Our Beloved Kin: A New History of King Philip's War* (New Haven, CT: Yale University Press, 2019), 305.
10. *CR* 2:285–286,
11. Russell to Connecticut, May 15, 1676, in CA-War-I, 71.
12. Nathaniel Saltonstall, "A New and Further Narrative of the State of New-England," in *Narratives of the Indian Wars 1675–1699*, ed. Charles H. Lincoln (New York: Charles Scribner's Sons, 1913), 95–96; Russell to Connecticut, May 22, 1676, in Sylvester Judd, *History of Hadley* (Springfield, MA: H. R. Hunting, 1905, 165–166; Mather, "History," 119–120; "True Account," 260–261; Hubbard, *Wars*, 1:229–233; David J. Silverman, *Thundersticks: Firearms and the Violent Transformation of Native America* (Cambridge, MA: Belknap, 2016), 116.
13. George Sheldon, *A History of Deerfield, Massachusetts* (Greenfield, MA: E. A. Hall, 1895), 162–166. Hubbard, *Wars*, 1:232–234; "True Account," 261–262; Saltonstall, "A New and Further Narrative," 96; Mather, "History," 119–120.
14. Mather, "History," 120; George Madison Bodge, *Soldiers in King Philip's War* (Baltimore: Genealogical, 1976), 247; Russell to Connecticut, May 22, 1676, in Judd, *History of Hadley*, 165–166.
15. Sheldon, *Deerfield*, 166–168.
16. "True Account," 272; Brooks, *Our Beloved Kin*, 305–306.
17. Russell to Connecticut, May 22, 1676, in Judd, *Hadley*, 166; J. H. Temple, *History of North Brookfield, Massachusetts* (North Brookfield, MA, 1887), 125; *CR* 2:278–279, 442–444; Connecticut to Massachusetts, May 20, 1676, in YIP.
18. *CR* 2:449; *MR* 5:92, 96–97.
19. Newbury to Allyn, May 26, 1676, in Sheldon, *Deerfield*, 171.
20. Newbury to Connecticut, May 30, 1676, in *CR* 2:450; Hubbard, *Wars*, 1:234–235; Mather, "History," 121.
21. *CR* 2:441, 444; Nowwaquanv to Connecticut, October 7, 1676, *CHSC* 21:252–253.
22. *CR* 2:450–451; "True Account," 266.
23. Ephraim Report, June 10, 1676, in MA 30:202–203; *CR* 2:447–448, 466; Talcott to Connecticut, June 8, 1676, in Temple, *North Brookfield*, 125–126; "True Account," 264; Massachusetts to Winslow, June 10, 1676, in MA 69:16b.
24. "True Account," 263; Hubbard, *Wars*, 1:235–236; Mather, "History," 122; Cotton to Walley, June 10, 1676, *CJCJ* 152; Massachusetts to Connecticut, July 7, 1676, in *CR* 2:465; Brooks, *Our Beloved Kin*, 309; Bodge, *Soldiers*, 57.
25. "True Account," 264; Quanapohit's testimony, in J. H. Temple, *History of Framingham, Massachusetts, Early Known as Danforth's Farms, 1640–1880* (Framingham, MA, 1887), 59–60; Henchman to Massachusetts, June 11, 1676, in Lemuel Shattuck, *A History of the Town of Concord* (Boston: Russell, Odiorne, 1835), 62.
26. Mather, "History," 123–124; Hubbard, *Wars*, 1:244–246.
27. Mather, "History," 120, 124, 126–127; Hubbard, *Wars*, 1:236–239; *CR* 2:455–456; Douglas Edward Leach, *A Rhode Islander Reports on King Philip's War: The Second William Harris Letter of August, 1676* (Providence: Rhode Island Historical Society, 1963), 80–81.
28. Harris to Williamson, August 12, 1676, in *RIHSC* 10:177–178; Henchman to Massachusetts, June 30, 1676, in Bodge, *Soldiers*, 57; *CR* 2:455.
29. Franklin B. Hough, ed., *A Narrative of the Causes which led to Philip's Indian War . . .* (Albany, NY: J. Munsell, 1858), 165–168.
30. Council, June 15, 1676, in MA 30:204; "True Account," 264–266; Cobbet, *NEHGR* 7:217.
31. Hubbard, *Wars*, 1:243–244; Mather, "History," 123.
32. *CR* 2:455.
33. Henchman to Massachusetts, June 30, 1676, in Bodge, *Soldiers*, 57–58; "True Account," 262, 272.

34. Hubbard, *Wars*, 1:184, 189–192, 220; Mather, "History," 119.
35. Winslow to Hinckley and Freeman, May 23, 1676, in *MHSC* Series 4, 5:8–10.
36. Hubbard, *Wars*, 1:226; Mather, "History," 121; *MR* 5:97.
37. Massachusetts to Winslow, June 10, 1676, in MA 69:16b; *PR* 5:197–199.
38. Benjamin Church, "Entertaining Passages relating to Philip's War," in *So Dreadfull a Judgment: Puritan Responses to King Philip's War 1676–1677*, ed. Richard Slotkin and James K. Folsom (Hanover, NH: University Press of New England, 1978), 421–428; Hubbard, *Wars*, 1:268–270.
39. *PR* 5:201–203.
40. Cotton to Walley, June 10, 1676, and Walley to Cotton, June 26, 1676, *CJCJ* 152–153; Mather, *Diary*, 31; *RICR* 193–194; Mather, "History," 127–130.
41. Cobbet, *NEHGR* 7:218; Mary Rowlandson, "The Sovereignty & Goodness of God," in *So Dreadfull a Judgment: Puritan Responses to King Philip's War 1676–1677*, ed. Richard Slotkin and James K. Folsom (Hanover, NH: University Press of New England, 1978), 362–364.
42. Harris to Williamson, August 12, 1676, in *RIHSC* 10:175–176; Leach, *A Rhode Islander*, 70–73; *RICR* 2:548.
43. *CR* 2:458–459; Hubbard, *Wars*, 1:251–253; Saltonstall, "A New and Further Narrative," 96; Kevin McBride, Doug Currie, David Naumec, Ashley Bissonnette, Noah Fellman, Laurie Pasteryak Lamarre, Heather Manwaring, and Meagan Lankowsky, "The 1676 Battle of Nipsachuck: Identification and Evaluation" (2013), 125–129.
44. *CR* 2:459; Bradford to Cotton, July 5, 1676, *CJCJ* 154.
45. Hubbard, *Wars*, 2:62–65; Leach, *A Rhode Islander*, 76–77; Jill Lepore, *The Name of War: King Philip's War and the Origins of American Identity* (New York: Vintage, 1998), 13.
46. *CR* 2:460, 463; Fitch to Allyn, July 14, 1676, Connecticut to Talcott, July 15, 1676, and Treat to Connecticut, July 16, 1676, *CHSC* 21:246–250.

Chapter 22

1. *RICR* 194; Quanapohit's testimony, in J. H. Temple, *History of Framingham, Massachusetts, Early Known as Danforth's Farms, 1640–1880* (Framingham, MA, 1887), 59–60; Lisa Brooks, *Our Beloved Kin: A New History of King Philip's War* (New Haven, CT: Yale University Press, 2019), 310–311.
2. Daniel Gookin, *An Historical Account of the Doings and Sufferings of the Christian Indians in New England, in the Years 1675, 1676, 1677* (New York: Arno Press, 1972), 527–528.
3. Depositions, in MA 30:204b–205a and George Madison Bodge, *Soldiers in King Philip's War* (Baltimore: Genealogical, 1976), 225–226.
4. *RICR* 194–195; Gookin, *Account*, 528–529; "True Account," in *The Old Indian Chronicle*, ed. Samuel G. Drake (Boston: Samuel A. Drake, 1867), 267; "Sewall," in *MHSC* Series 5, 5:14; Brooks, *Our Beloved Kin*, 312; Brooks, *Peace Medal*, https://americanindian.si.edu/static/exhibitions/infinityofnations/woodlands/239269.html, accessed August 17, 2022.
5. William Hubbard, *The History of the Indian Wars in New England: From the first settlement to the termination of the war with King Philip in 1677*, ed. Samuel G. Drake (Roxbury, MA: W. E. Woodward, 1865), 1:249; Increase Mather, "A Brief History of the Warr with the Indians in New-England," in *So Dreadfull a Judgment: Puritan Responses to King Philip's War 1676–1677*, ed. Richard Slotkin and James K. Foldom (Hanover, NH: University Press of New England, 1978), 130; Harris to Williamson, August 12, 1676, in *RIHSC* 10:178; "True Account," 269.
6. Brooks, *Our Beloved Kin*, 313; Massachusetts to Gookin, July 3, 1676, in MA 30:207.
7. Treaty, July 3, 1676, in Bodge, *Soldiers*, 304.
8. "True Account," 270–273; J. H. Temple, *History of Framingham, Massachusetts, Early Known as Danforth's Farms, 1640–1880* (Framingham, MA, 1887), 56–57.
9. "True Account," 270, 274, 276–277.
10. Cobbet, *NEHGR* 7:218.
11. Mather, "History," 130.
12. Douglas Edward Leach, *A Rhode Islander Reports on King Philip's War: The Second William Harris Letter of August, 1676* (Providence: Rhode Island Historical Society, 1963), 74–75.
13. Hubbard, *Wars*, 1:260–261, 286–287; Gookin, *Account*, 513; "True Account," 278–280; Mather, "History," 135; Dennis A. Connole, *The Indians of the Nipmuck Country in Southern New England, 1630–1750: An Historical Geography* (Jefferson, NC: McFarland, 2001), 153, 209;

Leach, *Rhode Islander*, 80–83; William Lincoln, *History of Worcester, Massachusetts* (Worcester, MA: Charles Hersey, 1862), 17.

14. Hubbard, *Wars*, 1:255, 259; Mather, "History," 131–135; "True Account," 277–278; Leach, *A Rhode Islander*, 74–75; *CR* 2:461–462, 466–467.

15. R. Hutchinson, *The Warr in New-England Visibly Ended* (London, 1677), 1–2.

16. Cobbet, *NEHGR* 7:218.

17. Mather, "History," 131–133; *PR* 5:204–207, 209–210.

18. Benjamin Church, "Entertaining Passages relating to Philip's War," in *So Dreadfull a Judgment: Puritan Responses to King Philip's War 1676–1677*, ed. Richard Slotkin and James K. Folsom (Hanover, NH: University Press of New England, 1978), 428–430; Hubbard, *Wars*, 1:240–241, 251; Mather, "History," 128–130; "Letter of Major William Bradford, Eldest Son of Governor William Bradford of Plymouth Colony, Pocasset, June 30, 1676," *Old Northwest Genealogical Quarterly* 8 (1905): 226–227; "True Account," 269; "Diary of Samuel Sewall, 1674–1729," vol. 1, in *MHSC* Series 5, 5:14.

19. Hubbard, *Wars*, 1:253–257; "Sewall," in *MHSC* Series 5, 5:14–15; Cotton to Walley, July 19, 1676, *CJCJ* 162–163; Edward Leach, *Flintlock and Tomahawk: New England in King Philip's War* (New York: Macmillan, 1958), 215; Bradford to Cotton, July 18, 1676, *CJCJ* 159–160; Collymer to wife, July 16, 1676, in Benjamin Church, *The History of King Philip's War*, ed. Henry Martyn Dexter (Boston: John Kimball Wiggin, 1865), 105.

20. Walley to Cotton, July 18, 1676, and Cotton to Walley, July 19, 1676, *CJCJ* 158, 161–163; *Plymouth Church Records 1620–1859: Part I*, PCSM, vol. 22 (Cambridge: Cambridge University Press, 1920), 148–152.

21. Church, "Entertaining Passages," 430–442; Hubbard, *Wars*, 1:257–258.

22. Bradford to Cotton, July 24, 1676, *CJCJ* 164–165.

23. Hubbard, *Wars*, 1:261–262; Church, "Entertaining Passages," 442–443; Mather, "History," 135–136; Willis account, in *MHSC* Series 2, 7:157–158; Leach, *Rhode Islander*, 84–85.

24. Church, "Entertaining Passages," 443–447; Hubbard, *Wars*, 1:262–263; Mather, "History," 136.

25. Hubbard, *Wars*, 1:263–265; Mather, "History," 137–138; Brooks, *Our Beloved Kin*, 324–326; Cassandra Hradil and Maggie King, "Lockety Fight: Unraveling Centuries of Silence," https://ourbelovedkin.com/awikhigan/lockety-fight?path=pocasset, accessed August 17, 2022; Harris, *Rhode Islander*, 84–85.

26. Church, "Entertaining Passages," 448–449; Hubbard, *Wars*, 1:265–266.

27. Church, "Entertaining Passages," 449–451; Mather, "History," 139; Hubbard, *Wars*, 1:271–272; Brooks, *Our Beloved Kin*, 323.

28. Church, "Entertaining Passages," 451–452; *CR* 2:470–471.

29. *Plymouth Church Records*, 152–153.

30. Rawson to Winslow, August 20, 1676, in WFP-II, MHS.

31. Hubbard, *Wars*, 1:272.

32. Mather, "History," 139–143; Increase Mather, *Diary by Increase Mather, March 1675–December, 1676*, ed. Samuel A. Green (Cambridge: Cambridge University Press, 1900), 34.

33. Church, "Entertaining Passages," 452–462; Hubbard, *Wars*, 1:273–278; Leach, *Flintlock*, 238.

34. Council, August 7, 1676, in MA 30:209.

35. Hunting to Marlborough, August 10, 1676, in MA 69:41a.

36. Pynchon to Leverett, August 15, 1676, in *PP* 1:167–168.

37. Hubbard, *Wars*, 1:279–280; Trumbull, *History of Connecticut*, 1:348–349; *CR* 2:469.

38. *CR* 2:468–469, 471–472; Pynchon to Leverett, August 15 and 26, 1676, in *PP* 1:167–171. Other reports had Pessicus killed by the Mohawks. Hubbard, *Wars*, 2:131; "Sewall," in *MHSC* Series 5, 5:23.

39. *CR* 2:472–475, 477.

40. Court-martial, August, in Franklin B. Hough, ed., *A Narrative of the Causes which led to Philip's Indian War* ... (Albany, NY: J. Munsell, 1858), 173–190; *RICR* 2:549–550, 586.

41. *The Early Records of the Town of Providence*, 21 vols. (Providence, RI: Snow & Farnham, 1899), 15:151–161; Margaret Ellen Newell, *Brethren by Nature: New England Indians, Colonists, and the Origins of American Slavery* (Ithaca, NY: Cornell University Press, 2015), 151, 170–171.

42. Gookin, *Account*, 513–515; Jenny Hale Pulsipher, "Massacre at Hurtleberry Hill: Christian Indians and English Authority in Metacom's War," *WMQ* 53, no. 3 (July 1996): 459–460; Mather, *Diary*, 46.

43. Gookin, *Account*, 514; *RCAMB* 1:71–73; Pulsipher, "Massacre," 463–464; Interview, September 4, 1676, in MA 30:214a; Woodcock Deposition, September 12, 1676, in MA 30:221a.

44. Massachusetts to Gookin, August 28, 1676, in MA 30:214.
45. Jenny Hale Pulsipher, *Subjects unto the Same King: Indians, English, and the Contest for Authority in Colonial New England* (Philadelphia: University of Pennsylvania Press, 2015), 225–226; Gookin, *Account*, 492; Waldron to Leverett, September 2, 1676, in Lisa Brooks, "Richard Waldron's Letter: The Capture of Shoshanim," https://ourbelovedkin.com/awikhi gan/richard-waldrons-letter-the-capture-of-shoshanim, accessed August 17, 2022; Hubbard, *Wars*, 1:280–281, 2:130–133; Waldron to Leverett, September 10, 1676, in George Madison Bodge, *Soldiers in King Philip's War* (Baltimore: Genealogical, 1976), 307; Waldron to Leverett, September 6, 1676, and Shapleigh and Daniel to Leverett, September 6, 1676, in Lisa Brooks, Allyson LaForge and Lauren Tuiskula, "Captivity at Cocheco," https://ourbelovedkin.com /awikhigan/cocheco?path=wabanaki-coast, accessed August 17, 2022; Bodge, *Soldiers*, 293–295.
46. Mather, *Diary*, 46–47. "Sewall," in *MHSC* Series 5, 5:23; Waldron to Leverett, September 10, 1676, in Bodge, *Soldiers*, 307; Waldron to Gookin, November 2, 1676, in Bodge, *Soldiers*, 309.
47. *MR* 5:114–115; Gookin, *Account*, 492; Jill Lepore, *The Name of War: King Philip's War and the Origins of American Identity* (New York: Vintage, 1998), 156; Brooks, *Our Beloved Kin*, 337; Drake, "Restraining Atrocity."
48. Temple, *Framingham*, 74, 76–78; Brooks, *Our Beloved Kin*, 318.
49. Mather, *Diary*, 46–47. "Sewall," in *MHSC* Series 5, 5:22–23; Hubbard, *Wars*, 1:200–201; David J. Silverman, *This Land Is Their Land: The Wampanoag Indians, Plymouth Colony, and the Troubled History of Thanksgiving* (New York: Bloomsbury, 2019), 347.
50. Pulsipher, *Subjects*, 157–158; *MR* 5:117.
51. Gookin, *Account*, 491–492; Depositions, in MA 30:219–219a; Gookin, November 20, 1676, and Council, November 23, 1676, both in MA 30:228–228a; Brooks, *Our Beloved Kin*, 338; Bodge, *Soldiers*, 309; Lepore, *War*, 156–157.
52. Newell, *Brethren*, 168–169; Lepore, *War*, 154, 162–163; *ACUC* 2:401; Bodge, *Soldiers*, 479–480.
53. Petitions, in MA 30:176, 30:207a, 30:191a, 30:229; Gookin, *Account*, 449; Newell, *Brethren*, 179–180; Eliot to Boyle, 1683, in *MHSC* Series 1, 3:183; "Indian Children," *NEHGR* 8:270–273; Brooks, *Our Beloved Kin*, 337; Turner, *Pilgrims*, 306.
54. Cotton and Arnold to commissioners, September 7, 1676, Mather to Cotton, October 20, 1676, Keith to Cotton, October 30, 1676, all in *MHSC*, Series 4, 8:689–690.
55. Cotton to Mather, March 19–20, 1677, *CJCJ* 188; Lepore, *War*, 153.
56. *MR* 5:130.

Epilogue

1. Hall to Symonds, June 22, 1676, in John Hall Letters, American Antiquarian Society; Kyle F. Zelner, *A Rabble in Arms: Massachusetts Towns and Militiamen during King Philip's War* (New York: New York University Press, 2009), 201; Anderson, "King Philip's Herds," 622–623; Jill Lepore, *The Name of War: King Philip's War and the Origins of American Identity* (New York: Vintage, 1998), xii, 177; Jenny Hale Pulsipher, "Massacre at Hurtleberry Hill: Christian Indians and English Authority in Metacom's War," *WMQ* 53, no. 3 (July 1996): 459; Paul Alden Robinson, "The Struggle Within: The Indian Debate in Seventeenth Century Narragansett Country" (PhD dissertation, State University of New York at Binghamton, 1990), 252; David J. Silverman, *This Land Is Their Land: The Wampanoag Indians, Plymouth Colony, and the Troubled History of Thanksgiving* (New York: Bloomsbury, 2019), 334, 348; Margaret Ellen Newell, *Brethren by Nature: New England Indians, Colonists, and the Origins of American Slavery* (Ithaca, NY: Cornell University Press, 2015), 158–213.
2. Increase Mather, "A Brief History of the Warr with the Indians in New-England," in *So Dreadfull a Judgment: Puritan Responses to King Philip's War 1676–1677*, ed. Richard Slotkin and James K. Foldom (Hanover, NH: University Press of New England, 1978), 81; William Hubbard, *The History of the Indian Wars in New England: From the first settlement to the termination of the war with King Philip in 1677*, ed. Samuel G. Drake (Roxbury, MA: W. E. Woodward, 1865),1:12.
3. Mather, "History," 145, 152.
4. Increase Mather, *A Relation of the Troubles which have happened in New-England, By reason of the Indians there: From the Year 1614 to the Year 1675* (Boston, 1677), 75–76
5. Increase Mather, *An Historical Discourse concerning the Prevalency of Prayer* (Boston, 1677), 4–7, 10, 19.

6. Anne Kusener Nelsen, "King Philip's War and the Hubbard-Mather Rivalry," *WMQ* 27, no. 4 (October 1970): 626-629.

7. Hubbard, *Wars*, 1:277; Kristina Bross, *Dry Bones and Indian Sermons: Praying Indians in Colonial America* (Ithaca, NY: Cornell University Press, 2004), 164-165; Kelleter, "Puritan Missionaries," 97.

8. Hubbard, *Wars*, 2:93-95.

9. Hubbard, *Wars*, 2:206-207, 261.

10. Hubbard, *Wars*, 1:279, 2:262, 269-270.

11. Hubbard, *Wars*, 2:271-277.

12. Lepore, *War*, 125; Salisbury, "Contextualizing Mary Rowlandson," 134-135, 141.

13. Mary Rowlandson, "The Sovereignty & Goodness of God," in *So Dreadfull a Judgment: Puritan Responses to King Philip's War 1676-1677*, ed. Richard Slotkin and James K. Folsom (Hanover, NH: University Press of New England, 1978), 341, 353.

14. Jenny Hale Pulsipher, "'Our Sages Are Sageles': A Letter on Massachusetts Indian Policy after King Philip's War," *WMQ* 58, no. 2 (April 2001): 442-448.

15. Samuel Nowell, "Abraham in Arms," in *So Dreadfull a Judgment: Puritan Responses to King Philip's War 1676-1677*, ed. Richard Slotkin and James K. Foldom (Hanover, NH: University Press of New England, 1978), 276, 287.

16. Gookin, *Account*, 522-523; J. Patrick Cesarini, "'What Has Become of Your Praying to God?': Daniel Gookin's Troubled History of King Philip's War," *EAL* 44, no. 3 (2009): 506.

17. Daniel Gookin, *An Historical Account of the Doings and Sufferings of the Christian Indians in New England, in the Years 1675, 1676, 1677* (New York: Arno Press, 1972), 431.

18. *RICR* 193.

19. Gookin, *Account*, 518-521, 532-533; General Court, 1677, *NEHGR* 8:273; Pulsipher, "Our Sages Are Sageles," 437; Lisa Brooks, *Our Beloved Kin: A New History of King Philip's War* (New Haven, CT: Yale University Press, 2019), 339.

20. *RICR* 193, 195-196.

21. Gookin, *Account*, 522-523.

22. Hubbard, *Wars*, 1:287; Dennis A. Connole, *The Indians of the Nipmuck Country in Southern New England, 1630-1750: An Historical Geography* (Jefferson, NC: McFarland, 2001), 140-141, 230-253; Jean M. O'Brien, *Dispossession by Degrees: Indian Land and Identity in Natick, Massachusetts, 1650-1790* (Cambridge: Cambridge University Press, 1997); Pulsipher, "Massacre," 486; Yasuhide Kawashima, *Puritan Justice and the Indian: White Man's Law in Massachusetts 1630-1763* (Middletown, CT: Wesleyan University Press, 1986), 232-233, 237.

23. Linford D. Fisher, "Native Americans, Conversion, and Christian Practice in Colonial New England, 1640-1730," *Harvard Theological Review* 102, no. 1 (2009): 11-114, 104; Dane Morrison, *A Praying People: Massachusett Acculturation and the Failure of the Puritan Mission, 1600-1690* (New York: Peter Lang, 1995), 160.

24. Mather, "History," 141-143; Hubbard, *Wars*, 1:288; Fitch Suggestions, *CHSC* 21:257-259; *CR* 2:297-298, 435, 479-482;

25. Julie A. Fisher and David J. Silverman, *Ninigret: Sachem of the Niantics and Narragansetts: Diplomacy, War, and the Balance of Power in Seventeenth-Century New England and Indian Country* (Ithaca, NY: Cornell University Press, 2014), 134.

26. Rhode Island to Connecticut, 1676, in *RICR* 2:556-558.

27. Jean M. O'Brien, *Dispossession by Degrees: Indian Land and Identity in Natick, Massachusetts, 1650-1790* (Cambridge: Cambridge University Press, 1997), 381-385; Linford D. Fisher, *The Indian Great Awakening: Religion and the Shaping of Native Cultures in Early America* (Oxford: Oxford University Press, 2012); William S. Simmons, *The Narragansett* (New York: Chelsea House, 1989); David J. Silverman, *This Land Is Their Land: The Wampanoag Indians, Plymouth Colony, and the Troubled History of Thanksgiving* (New York: Bloomsbury, 2019), 355-427; David J. Silverman, *Faith and Boundaries: Colonists, Christianity, and Community among the Wampanoag Indians of Martha's Vineyard, 1600-1871* (New York: Cambridge University Press, 2005); Daniel R. Mandell, *Behind the Frontier: Indians in Eighteenth-Century Eastern Massachusetts* (Lincoln: University of Nebraska Press, 2000); Daniel R. Mandell, *Tribe, Race, History: Native Americans in Southern New England, 1780-1880* (Baltimore: Johns Hopkins University Press, 2008).

Index